TO THE STUDENT: The following learning support is available through your college bookstore:

Study Guide by Casady/Lehman for *Business Communications, Tenth Edition* by Himstreet/ Baty/Lehman

One-on-One Instructional Software by Casady/Lehman for *Business Communications, Tenth Edition* by Himstreet/ Baty/Lehman

The *Study Guide* and the *One-on-One Instructional Software* will help you with course material by acting as a tutorial, review, and study aid. If these items are not in stock, ask the bookstore manager to order copies for you.

BUSINESS COMMUNICATIONS

Wadsworth Series in Business Education

Carbone, *Modern Business English: A Systems Approach*

Clark/Clark, *HOW 6: A Handbook for Office Workers,* Sixth Edition

Clark/Clark, *Universal Transcription*

Guffey, *Business English,* Fourth Edition

Guffey, *Essentials of Business Communication,* Second Edition

Himstreet/Baty/Lehman, *Business Communications,* Tenth Edition

Kupsh/Rhodes, *Automated Office Systems*

Lundgren/Lundgren, *Records Management in the Computer Age*

Penrose/Rasberry/Myers, *Advanced Business Communication,* Second Edition

Rittman/Gonzalez, *Effective Business Communication*

Ruch/Crawford, *Business Reports: Written and Oral*

Tedesco, *Telecommunications for Business*

Wells, *Communications in Business,* Fifth Edition

TENTH EDITION

BUSINESS COMMUNICATIONS

William C. Himstreet
Professor Emeritus, University of Southern California

Wayne Murlin Baty
Professor Emeritus, Arizona State University

Carol M. Lehman
Associate Professor, Mississippi State University

Wadsworth Publishing Company
Belmont, California
A Division of Wadsworth, Inc.

Developmental Editor: Maureen Brooks
Production Editor: Eve Mendelsohn Lehmann
Manufacturing Coordinator: Marcia M. Locke
Interior Designer: Glenna Collett
Art Designer: Thompson-Steele Book Production
Interior Artist: Interactive Composition Corporation
Cartoonist: George Ulrich
Cover Designer: DFL Publications
Cover Artist: David Bishop
Compositor: Interactive Composition Corporation
Cover Printer: Henry N. Sawyer Co., Inc.
Text Printer and Binder: R.R. Donnelley & Sons

2 3 4 5 6 7 8 9 10—97 96 95 94 93

Printed in the United States of America.

Library of Congress Cataloging in Publication Data
Himstreet, William C.
    Business communications—10th ed. / William C. Himstreet, Wayne Murlin Baty,
Carol M. Lehman.
      p.   cm.
    Includes bibliographical references and index.
    ISBN 0-534-92897-8
    1. Commercial correspondence. 2. Business report writing. 3. Business
communication. I. Baty, Wayne Murlin. II. Lehman, Carol M. III. Title.
HF5721.H5 1992
658.4'5--dc20

92-26389
CIP

PREFACE

The first edition of *Business Communications* was published over thirty years ago. Many of the concepts presented in the first edition still hold true today; however, the environment in which we communicate has changed significantly.

Technology, globalization of our economy, and legal and ethical concerns all affect the way we communicate in the business setting of the 1990s. To remain in step with the times, the tenth edition of *Business Communications* is revised to address these concerns as well as others.

Another very significant change in this tenth edition is the addition of a third member of our author team. Dr. Carol M. Lehman, Associate Professor of Management and Information Systems in the College of Business and Industry at Mississippi State University, brings to the text added depth in communication technology, much insight into the ethical aspects of business communication, and a personal writing ability and team compatibility that have multiplied the strength of our team. She has authored numerous other books, is contributing significantly to the professionalism in business communication, and conducts on-going research to accompany her outstanding classroom teaching.

32 YEARS AND 10 EDITIONS OF TIMELESS HALLMARKS

- ◆ **Sentence-by-sentence analyses** provide the rationale for idea sequences and word choices of writing samples. Students see specific applications of the principles and how to develop effective business communication skills.
- ◆ **Before-and-after examples of writing** illuminate and explain both the common errors and the most effective methods to use in business communication.
- ◆ **Marginal questions and notes,** pioneered by Himstreet and Baty in the third edition, act as quick self-checks and aid students in reviewing material by highlighting text content.
- ◆ **Strong emphasis in thinking and outlining before beginning to write** helps students achieve clarity and tact and simplify their writing.
- ◆ **Grammar and mechanics review** in Appendix B provides a reference, clear examples, and self-correcting pre-tests and post-tests to help students see where grammar review is needed. Plus, basic style in writing is covered in Chapters 7 and 8.
- ◆ **"Check Your Writing" Checklists** provide a quick way for students to evaluate their documents.
- ◆ **A spectrum of end-of-chapter writing assignments** gives students practice writing about familiar situations as well as more sophisticated business exercises.
- ◆ **Thorough discussions of the job search, the resume, and employment letters** vividly show students how they can apply the principles to get the right job—and succeed!

ADDITIONS TO THE TENTH EDITION

Reviews from users of the ninth edition of *Business Communications* and frequent discussions with our peers in education led to many of the changes in this tenth edition.

1. **NEW** student foreword, "Effective Communication Skills: Key Ingredient in Career Success," helps students understand the link between career success and effective oral and written communication. Examples from current business magazines and personal anecdotes of several communication mentors are designed to motivate students to approach the course with added incentive.

2. **NEW** chapter, "Ethical and Legal Guidelines" (Chapter 6) builds awareness of ethical issues facing students now and on the job. Using a framework for analyzing ethical issues, students develop skill in finding solutions to ethical dilemmas that do not compromise their own personal values. Specific guidelines help students learn to filter their messages to ensure that they are using effective communication ethically. Numerous examples from students' daily life, the business world, and case problems give students ample opportunity to analyze complex issues where right and wrong may not be clear.

3. **REORGANIZATION** of chapters as a result of consistent feedback from reviewers and ninth edition users emphasizes that students should first build a theoretical foundation before encountering the writing applications portion of the text. Therefore, all theoretical content and discussion of factors affecting business communication appear in the first eight chapters. Specifically, Part I remains unchanged with three chapters related to communication foundations and oral communication. Part II, "Analyzing Critical Factors Influencing Communication Effectiveness," now contains Chapter 4, "Cross-Cultural Communication at Home and Internationally" (formerly Chapter 18), and Chapter 5, "Electronic Communication Technology" (formerly Chapter 17), and Chapter 6, "Ethical and Legal Guidelines." Part III, which consists of the two chapters on using words and style effectively, completes the students' theoretical foundation and leads them to the ten writing chapters that follow. If you prefer to have your students begin writing earlier, you can easily adapt the sequence and content of this flexible text to meet your students' specific needs.

4. Three employment chapters are combined into two. Chapter 13 now logically combines writing effective resumes and application letters. The content is updated to include new examples of resumes and letters formatted using desktop publishing capabilities for students seeking traditional business positions. Students are provided a checklist for enhancing employment credentials using advanced technology. Chapter 14 includes interviewing successfully and writing all other employment communications. The interviewing section now

includes practical suggestions for ensuring a successful performance appraisal interview from the interviewer's and interviewee's perspectives.

5. Complete integration of international, technological, ethical, legal, and interpersonal implications reinforces the importance of these factors in all phases of communication—oral and written (see examples of new writing activities that follow). Colorful two-tier icons are positioned in the margin of end-of-chapter material to help you select applications and cases that require students to address these implications.

6. **COMMUNICATION MENTORS** provide relevant advice. Your students will have a priceless opportunity to "look over the shoulders" of a panel of 13 communication mentors—all corporate or governmental leaders representing various disciplines and various levels of management. As your students study a particular principle, one or more of the communication mentors discuss how a communication principle actually works in today's dynamic business environment, share related strategies for communicating effectively, or simply provide concrete advice for developing the needed skill; see Figure 1.

♦ Carefully integrated within the text, these comments reinforce crucial communication principles as well as bring convincing realism to the material. In addition, we believe that these communication mentors may serve as a catalyst for opening students' eyes to the relevance of this course in their professional development.

♦ The picture and brief profile on each mentor in the new student foreword ("Effective Communication Skills: Key Ingredient in Career Success") acquaints your students with the communication

---

COMMUNICATION MENTOR

Being faced with questions of ethics during your career is a very real possibility. Now is the time to prepare yourself. Decide now what your values are, what you believe in, what honesty and integrity and fairness really mean to you. Write it all down on a sheet of paper; keep the paper in a safe place. Making these judgments now will prepare you to handle a difficult situation if it occurs later on, because you'll already know what kind of person you are, and you'll know what you should do.

H. Devon Graham, Jr.
Southwest Regional Managing Partner
Arthur Andersen & Co.

FIGURE 1 Communication Mentor

mentor panel. An icon of a briefcase alerts students that they are learning from the real-life experiences of corporate executives.

7. **NEW** chapter-opening objectives guide the student through the learning experiences required in the chapter.

8. Important terms are printed in italics for easy recognition, and definitions are stated precisely in easy-to-understand terms.

9. **NEW** full-document format adds realism to the letters, memos, resumes, and reports and reinforces students' understanding of standard business formats. As shown in Figure 2, these visually appealing documents, complete with real-life letterheads, provide welcome breaks in the regular text discussion.

A critical part of this text since the first edition, SENTENCE-BY-SENTENCE ANALYSIS of poorly and well-written messages helps students see why they should avoid certain techniques or incorporate others into their own writing. A General Writing Guidelines section (Chapter 9) and Check Your Writing checklists summarize major writing principles.

Icon clearly distinguishes poor example.

Commentary directs students' attention to an international address format and appropriate salutation. Other topics reinforced this way include document formats and layout enhancements using advanced technology.

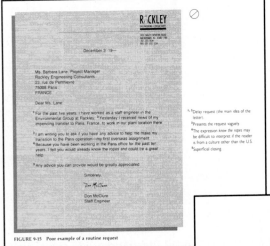

FIGURE 9-15   Poor example of a routine request

Letter content provides incidental learning and demonstrates effective writing techniques. This letter exposes students to viable strategies for preparing for an international assignment.

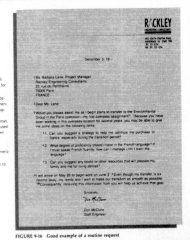

FIGURE 9-16   Good example of a routine request

FIGURE 2   Fully formatted letters with commentary

10. Completely **NEW PHOTOS** and more appealing illustrations, as shown in Figure 3, in addition to more realistic business-world examples provide students a clear picture of the specific communication theory and concepts being discussed.

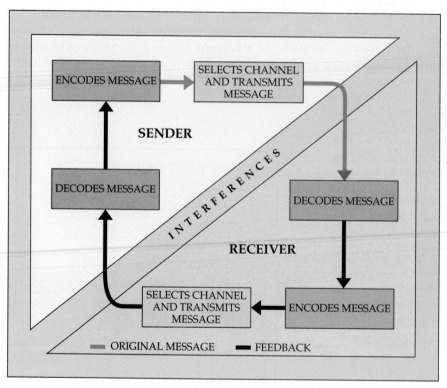

FIGURE 3   Colorful illustrations add visual appeal and clarity

11. Completely **REVISED END-OF-CHAPTER ACTIVITIES** provide students with new, challenging problems to solve. Activities now

   ◆ Portray business situations relevant in various business disciplines. A distinctive two-tier icon positioned beside the end-of-chapter writing activities (Chapters 9–18) helps you select exercises, applications, and cases relevant to your students' interests/needs.
   ◆ Require students to consider international, ethical, legal, interpersonal, and technological implications inherent in the problem.
   ◆ Include a broad range of difficulty to meet the needs of various levels of student needs—a request made by countless reviewers and ninth edition users. The level of each activity is clearly indicated in

the *Instructor's Edition*. The four levels include

1. Analyzing the strengths and weaknesses of a poorly written document and revising the document incorporating the critique; see Figure 4.

---

5. Analyze the letter on page 346. Pinpoint its strengths and weaknesses and then revise the letter.

Requires students to analyze a poorly written letter and incorporate their critique. A complete, poorly written letter accompanies this exercise.

FIGURE 4   Level 1 activity

2. Composing a document based on the information provided in the case problem; see Figure 5. Students may provide fictitious details if necessary.

1. **Customized Drinking Cups Are Wrong Size.**   Athletic concessions at Spinner College placed an order for 50,000 twenty-ounce plastic cups at 15 cents each from Custom Plastics Products. Each cup was to be imprinted with the college's mascot and this year's basketball slogan, "Soaring to New Heights." When the concessions manager was inspecting the order, he immediately noticed that the vendor had sent 16-ounce cups and not the 20-ounce cups that were ordered. Because concession items must be priced in 50-cent intervals to expedite service time, the regular drink price of $1.50 cannot be adjusted to reflect the reduced quantity. After serious consideration, the manager decided that selling the 16-ounce drink for the same price would be inadvisable. Basketball season starts in only two weeks; therefore, the manager must act quickly.

Required: As the concessions manager, write the vendor explaining the error in the shipment and asking that the order be filled correctly and quickly. Address the letter to Custom Plastics Products, 1200 Ridgewood Road, Springfield, MO 65808-1200.

Includes all information students need to solve the writing problem. Challenging new cases require students to solve realistic business problems occurring in disciplines ranging from marketing to information systems and others.

Icon denotes *management* as the major content area.

FIGURE 5   Level 2 activity

3. Conducting limited library research to locate relevant information needed to solve the problem; see Figure 6.

6. **Earning a Finder's Fee for Exceptional British Stamps.**   A client who wishes to start for his son a collection of high-quality European stamps has asked you, a dealer in European stamps, to locate them. You have located a solid page of 100 stamps issued 10 years ago to commemorate British statesman Winston Churchill. This page is intact; no rows have been removed. Your own investigation has authenticated the dyes and inks on the stamps; you have also inspected the glue on the back and found no flaws. In short, the stamps are in mint condition. The owner paid 50 British pounds for the entire sheet and wishes to sell it for 200 pounds. You feel that the stamps are a very good buy for a beginning collector.

Required:
1. Locate the currency exchange rate so that you can give your client the price in U.S. dollars. Add 10 percent to the price for a finder's fee.
2. Write a sales letter to Glenn Marshall, 1103 Commerce Street, Denton, TX 76205-2955.

Requires limited library research. In this case, students must locate the currency exchange rate to convert British pounds to dollars.

Icon denotes *marketing* as the major content area and *international* as a special implication students must address.

FIGURE 6   Level 3 activity

4. Conducting extensive research and/or analyzing a complex issue—whatever is needed to make an informed decision; see
Figure 7. Students must gear their language to write the appro-

Requires students to
- Analyze an ethical dilemma using the framework presented in Chapter 6. Critical-thinking questions help students organize their thoughts.
- Convey the decision to the appropriate audience(s) from the options provided.
- Justify the decision in a memo to the supervisor.
- Respond to an e-mail message reinforcing the discussion of electronic communication in Chapter 4.

Icon denotes *finance* as the major content area and *ethics* as a special implication students must address.

Case 1. Analyzing an Ethical Situation: A Sound Decision or a Clever Way Out? In an effort to secure a large investment account, Harrelson Inc. has decided to host a weekend boating expedition for a select group of prospective clients.

Today you received the following electronic message from your supervisor.

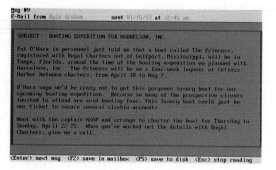

When you reached the captain, he explained that the owner does not usually allow unscheduled charters. After you convinced him of the importance of chartering *The Princess* for this expedition, the captain offered to let you charter the boat for $1,000 a day (normal rate is $2,000). He assured you he would submit the money to the owner and explain the situation when he returned to the home port.

Required:
1. Decide whether it is ethical to accept the captain's offer. Consider these points:
   a. What are the relevant facts?
   b. What are the ethical issues raised by the decision to charter the boat under these circumstances?
   c. Who (which stakeholders) will be affected by this decision?
   d. What are the costs and benefits imposed by each alternative on each person listed in step (c)?
   e. What are the firm's obligations to each person listed in step (c)?
   f. What should you as the firm's representative do?
2. Based on your decision, complete *one* of the following:
   a. Write to the captain accepting the offer to charter the boat, confirming the $1,000 rate, and providing details about the dates. Decide whether any other information should be included to ensure that the captain fulfills his side of this verbal contract. Address the letter to Bryan Martinez, 234 Sandy Beach Road, Tampa, FL 33602-2098.
   b. Having decided to refuse the captain's offer, write a persuasive letter to the owner requesting a special charter. Based on your ethical analysis, decide whether to mention the captain's offer. Address the letter to Andrew Robinelli, Royal Charters, 4029 Beach Drive, Gulfport, MS 39507-0234.
   c. Do any other options exist? If so, write the letter or memo to the appropriate person.
3. Awaiting a reply from the owner or the captain (depending on the decision made in step 2), write a persuasive memo to your supervisor (Kyle Graham) informing him of your action and including your analysis of this ethical situation.

FIGURE 7 **Level 4 activity**

priate documents to the intended audience(s) from the options given (e.g., supervisor and client/customer). You can easily locate these problems in a separate section, Cases for Analysis.

Introducing New *One-on-One Instructional Software*

One-on-One Instructional Software, available with the tenth edition, helps your students learn effective communication principles. Students complete carefully designed questions and applications and receive clear, specific feedback so that they can identify problem areas and direct their study in positive directions. While *One-on-One's* on-line instruction helps students improve their writing, it also reduces the amount of time you spend tutoring students individually.

Students complete two types of reinforcement exercises:

1. *Study Guide.* Students complete the 15 true-false and 15 multiple-choice questions for each chapter designed to help them master key principles. As shown in Figure 8, the feedback provided for each incorrect response clearly explains why the student's response is wrong and directs him or her to a page in the textbook for further study. Building this solid theoretical foundation will prepare your students for the practical applications (writing problems) in the text and will lead to improved scores on objective tests.

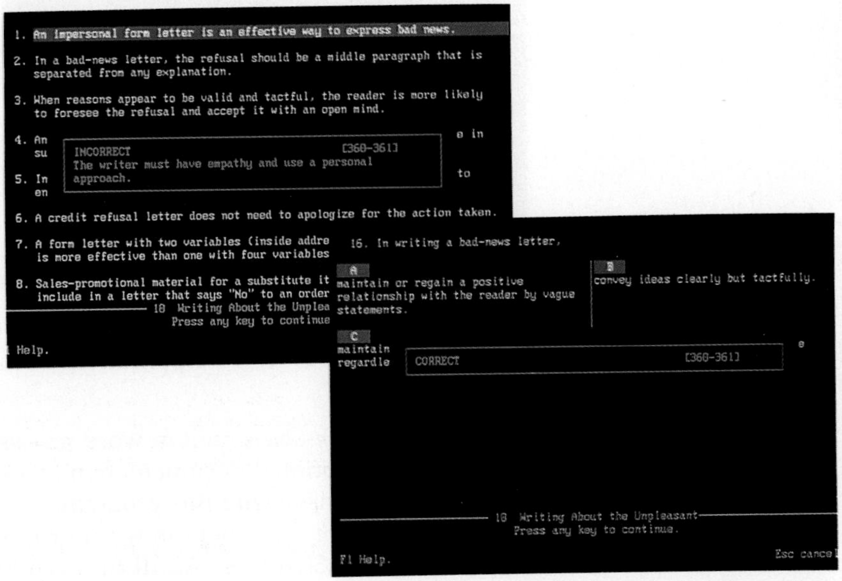

FIGURE 8   Sample feedback screens from the Study Guide section of *One-on-One*

2. *Practical applications (for Chapters 9–18).* Students must solve two business-writing problems for each chapter. First, they critique portions of texts (paragraphs within an entire letter or sections of letters that are difficult to write) and revise the text accordingly. With a simple keystroke, students compare their critique and revisions with a succinct list of strengths and weaknesses and suggested revisions. Before tackling the second application, students answer several critical-thinking questions that require them to analyze the situation and organize their thoughts. Comparing their document with the suggested solution prepares students to write a similar document for evaluation. The sample screens in Figure 9 illustrate the two practical applications that develop skill in writing bad-news messages (Chapter 10).

FIGURE 9 **Sample screens from the Practical Applications section of** *One-on-One*

To accommodate the computer needs of various groups, we have developed two options for completing the Practical Applications. Students can

1. Edit and compose documents using *One-on-One*'s built-in word processor. An on-line help facility and detailed printed documentation (packaged with the disk) will help students revise using this program.
2. Edit and compose documents using *One-on-One*'s built-in word processor and then convert the documents to ASCII files. ASCII files can be easily loaded into business-level software and integrated with spreadsheet or graphics files or enhanced with desktop publishing capabili-

ties. To facilitate this conversion, a convert-to-ASCII command appears in a pull-down menu, and easy-to-follow procedures are also included in the documentation.

If you do not have computer capabilities, you and your students can reap these same benefits from the printed *Study Guide*. The *Study Guide* has been completely revised to contain the teaching and learning tools included with the *One-on-One Instructional Software*. Students simply turn to the correct section of the *Study Guide* to confirm correct answers and to seek explanations for incorrect answers. In addition, as in previous editions, the *Study Guide* contains a comprehensive review of major grammar principles with exercises and answers. This edition also contains a review of the 132 most frequently misspelled words in business. Twelve words are introduced in the first eleven chapters; proofreading exercises review the entire list.

INSTRUCTIONAL RESOURCES

In addition to the *One-on-One Instructional Software*, a complete package of other instructional resources complements the textbook and offers materials and activities for classroom use. The instructional resources were designed to simplify and strengthen the study of business communication. We believe their use can make both in-class and out-of-class time more effective. The faster the turnaround time between submitting homework and receiving feedback, the better the learning.

Instructor's Edition

For the first time, the *Instructor's Manual* appears both in the front of the special *Instructor's Edition* and in the *Test Bank and Resource Guide*. You can choose either to carry the separate *Test Bank and Resource Guide* or to simply use the *Instructor's Edition*, which has two colored ribbons to mark the chapter of the text you plan to discuss and the corresponding page in the *Instructor's Manual* at the front of the book. The following resources are included in the *Instructor's Manual*:

◆ Teaching suggestions.
◆ Solutions to end-of-chapter review questions.
◆ Solutions to writing exercises, applications, and cases for analysis.
◆ Current reading lists for each chapter. A rich resource of real-world communication strategies, this list allows you to lead your students to outstanding articles that reinforce and supplement the text. To capture students' interest, selections were taken from business magazines and practitioner journals rather than academic-type journals.

Test Bank and Resource Guide

COMPLETELY REVISED, the *Test Bank and Resource Guide* contains approximately 1,000 all-new test questions. All questions have been evaluated for clarity and accuracy, and many have been field tested. Specifically, the following changes will aid you in selecting the right questions to meet the needs of your particular class:

◆ Choose from 20 true-false and 30 multiple-choice questions for each chapter and Appendix A ("Document Format and Layout Guide").
◆ Locate the correct answer and the page number on which the answer appears printed conveniently at the left margin.
◆ Readily select an appropriate balance of factually oriented and application questions. Simply refer to the marginal notation, **fact** or **appl,** for the classification of each question. Approximately 75 percent of the questions are factual; and 25 percent, application.

The *Test Bank and Resource Guide* also includes the complete *Instructor's Manual,* grammar exercises and solutions, and transparency masters. Grammar exercises offer extended in-class coverage. The transparency masters include solutions to exercises and cases, formatted for clear, easy projection.

Computerized Test Generator

Available free to adopters, the *Computerized Test Bank Generator* allows you to edit, add, or delete test-bank questions to produce a customized test. The *Computerized Test Bank Generator* is available for both IBM compatible or Macintosh systems.

Color Acetate Transparencies

In addition to the transparency masters, a package of approximately 100 fully developed one-, two-, and four-color overhead transparencies is available on adoption. The package is keyed to the text and includes:

◆ Many of the figures in the text.
◆ Key communication concepts.
◆ Activities designed to reinforce concepts presented in the text.
◆ Solutions to selected end-of-chapter writing exercises, applications, and cases.

Study Guide

A supplementary book for student use, the *Study Guide* is designed to reinforce learning. It includes these sections:

◆ Study Guide and Practical Applications included with the *One-on-One Instructional Software.* Students simply turn to the correct section of the

Study Guide to compare their answers with suggested solutions. Page references direct students to appropriate pages in the text for further study.

♦ Comprehensive review of major grammatical principles with exercises and answers.

♦ Exercises to help students master the 132 frequently misspelled words in business writing. Twelve words are introduced in the first eleven chapters; proofreading exercises review the entire list.

Videotapes with Teaching/Learning Materials

To enliven your classroom and to increase your students' skills, you can use the six videotapes available with the tenth edition. Students "go inside" real companies and meet real business executives to learn effective communication strategies. Each video ends with "Business Tips," a focused review of the major principles the executives explained. And most importantly, the content of the videos has been carefully prepared to correspond with the major concepts presented in each of the six parts of *Business Communications*.

Teaching/learning materials are available to help you integrate these videotapes in your classroom. A full-page discussion of each tape appears in the appropriate place within the text. Each of these "Video Connections"

♦ Previews the major points discussed in the film.

♦ Includes five discussion questions that you can assign for homework or use to promote class discussion.

♦ Includes an application requiring students to apply key principles (students must write letters and memos for video applications in Parts IV–VI after writing has been introduced).

To facilitate learning, the *Instructor's Edition* contains

♦ An outline of the major points presented in the videotape.

♦ Suggested answers to the discussion questions and applications.

♦ Five challenging multiple-choice questions that can be easily added to an objective test prepared for a unit of study.

A colorful icon helps students easily locate each "Video Connection" preview/exercise page in the textbook. To remind you that a videotape is available for a particular topic, the icon marks each video at the appropriate location in the Contents. Each of the six segments is stored on a separate cassette for your convenience. The segments include

| Part I
Chapter 3 | Public Speaking | Salsbury Communications, Inc.
Ventura County, California |
| Part II
Chapter 4 | Cross-Cultural
Communication
at Home | Pacific Bell Directory
Orange County, California |

Part III Chapter 7	Using Words Effectively	Sales Development Associates, Inc. St. Louis, Missouri
Part IV Chapter 11	Writing to Persuade	Tracy-Locke/Pharr Public Relations, Dallas, Texas
Part V Chapter 14	Communicating About Work and Jobs	Venture Stores, Inc. St. Louis, Missouri
Part VI Chapter 15	Research Methods and the Report Process	Sygnis, Inc. Little Rock, Arkansas

ACKNOWLEDGMENTS

The authors express their sincere appreciation to all persons who have contributed to this textbook. These include:

◆ The many faculty members with whom we have worked and the many professional educators who have reviewed, critiqued, and made significant contributions to each edition, and particularly to this one. These truly professional educators include:

Vanessa Dean Arnold
University of Mississippi

Mona Casady
Southwest Missouri State University

John Cole
University of Akron

Linda Devernoe
*State University of New York
at Cobleskill*

R. Neil Dortch
University of Wisconsin–Whitewater

Debbie DuFrene
Stephen F. Austin State University

Earl Dvorak
Indiana University at Bloomington

Georgia Hale
Arkansas State University

Margaret Hebert
University of Houston–Downtown

Rovena Hillsman
*California State University–
Sacramento*

Donna Luse
Northeast Louisiana University

Linda Munilla
Georgia Southern University

Judy Nixon
*University of Tennessee
at Chattanooga*

Rita Noel
Western Carolina University

Ruth Richardson
University of North Alabama

Joan Roderick
Southwest Texas State University

James Scott
Utah State University

Camille Bacon Smith
Temple University

Ted Stoddard
Brigham Young University

Carol Strickland
William Carey College

Rose Ann Swartz
Ferris State University

Dona Vasa
University of Nebraska–Lincoln

◆ Those individuals who prepared ancillary materials that coordinate with the content of the text. These individuals are Debbie DuFrene (video instructional material), Jeré Littlejohn (*Test Bank*), Mona Casady (*One-on-One Instructional Software* and *Study Guide*), and Adam Crosley (video production).

◆ Students in Dr. Lehman's classes, who completed many of the new exercises and suggested desirable changes.

◆ Mark Lehman, who generously contributed his wealth of experience to aid in developing challenging business-world problems similar to those encountered in today's business environment.

◆ Lee Wilkins for her creative contributions to portions of the text; Julie Liddell, Belinda Boykin, and Zelma Fulgham, graduate students, who tirelessly researched current communication topics, assisted in generating ideas, and keyed manuscript.

We also thank our spouses, Maxine Himstreet, Maxine Baty, Mark Lehman, and Dr. Lehman's young sons, Matthew and Stephen, for their constant support throughout such a lengthy and demanding project. We also appreciate the help provided by the various members of the publisher's staff that made this edition possible.

William C. Himstreet   *Wayne Murlin Baty*   *Carol M. Lehman*

BRIEF CONTENTS

Effective Communication Skills: Key Ingredient
in Career Success   *xxxiii*

PART I   COMMUNICATION FOUNDATIONS AND ORAL COMMUNICATION   1

1 Organizational Setting for Business Communication   3
2 Interpersonal Communication and Listening   23
3 Public Speaking and Oral Reporting   57

PART II   ANALYZING CRITICAL FACTORS INFLUENCING COMMUNICATION EFFECTIVENESS   85

4 Cross-Cultural Communication at Home and Internationally   87
5 Electronic Communication Technology   117
6 Ethical and Legal Guidelines   155

PART III   USING WORDS AND STYLE EFFECTIVELY   191

7 Using Words Effectively   193
8 Using the Techniques of Style   237

PART IV   COMMUNICATING THROUGH LETTERS AND MEMORANDUMS   289

9 Writing About the Routine and the Pleasant   291
10 Writing About the Unpleasant   359

11 Writing to Persuade   *407*
12 Writing Special Letters   *473*

PART V   COMMUNICATING ABOUT WORK AND JOBS   515

13 Preparing Resumes and Application Letters   *517*
14 Job Interviews, Employment Messages,
and Performance Appraisals   *585*

PART VI   COMMUNICATING THROUGH REPORTS   637

15 The Report Process and Research Methods   *639*
16 Managing Data and Using Graphics   *673*
17 Organizing and Writing Short Reports
and Proposals   *705*
18 Writing a Formal Report   *749*

APPENDIX A   Document Format and
Layout Guide   *A-1*
APPENDIX B   Grammar Review and
Exercises   *B-1*
APPENDIX C   Grading Symbols   *C-1*

INDEX   *I-1*

CONTENTS

Effective Communication Skills: Key Ingredient in Career Success *xxxiii*

Applicants Are Screened for Communication Skills *xxxv*

The Value of Good Communication Skills *xxxvi*

How Can You Develop Effective Communication Skills? *xxxvii*

References *xxxix*

Communication Mentors *xl*

PART I   COMMUNICATION FOUNDATIONS AND ORAL COMMUNICATION   1

1   Organizational Setting for Business Communication   3

Purposes of Communication 6

Four Levels of Communication 6

Communicating in Groups 7
    Purposes of Groups 7
    Factors in Group Communication 8
    Communication Mentor 9

Characteristics of Formal Organizations 10
    Goal Orientation 10
    Specialization of Individuals and Units 11
    Interdependence of Units and Individuals 11
    Formalized Hierarchy 11

Organizational Structure and Communication 12

External and Internal Systems 14
    Systems in Action 14
    The Grapevine as an Internal System 15
    Communication Mentor 17

Communication Flow in Organizations 17
    Downward Communication 17
    Upward Communication 19
    Horizontal or Lateral Communication 20
    Communication Mentor 20

Summary 21

Review Questions 21

Exercises 22

2   Interpersonal Communication and Listening   23

The Human Communication Process 25
    The Sender Encodes the Message 26
    The Sender Selects an Appropriate Channel and Transmits the Message 27
    The Receiver Decodes the Message 28
    The Receiver Encodes a Message to Clarify Any Misunderstandings 29
    Interferences Hinder the Process 30

Some Behavioral Factors in Communication   31
   Theory of Human Communication   31
   Human Needs   33
   Management Styles   34
   One-to-One Communication   35
   Johari Window   36
Word and Nonword Messages   37
   Intrapersonal Communication and
     Decoding   38
   Messages Without Words   38
   Communication Mentor   40
   Communication Mentor   41
Listening as an Interpersonal Skill   42
Bad Listening Habits and Practices   43
Listening for Positive Results   45
   Communication Mentor   46
   Intensive Listening   46
   Casual Listening   47
   Listening for Feelings with Empathy   47
   Listening for Information   50
   Listening for Problem Solving   51
Suggestions for Effective Listening   52
Summary   53
Review Questions   54
Exercises   54

**3   Public Speaking and Oral
    Reporting   57**
Controlling Speech Qualities   58
   Phonation   58
   Communication Mentors   59
   Articulation   60
   Pronunciation   61
Knowing Your Audience   61
   Communication Mentor   62
Selecting a Topic   62
   Communication Mentor   63
Planning Your Speech   64
   Planning Your Strategy   64
   Outlining Your Speech   65
Delivering Your Speech   68
Using Style in Speeches   69
Making an Oral Report   70
   Planning Your Presentation   71
   Using Visual Aids   73
   Communication Mentor   76
   Keeping Within Time Limits   80
Summary   81
References   81
Review Questions   82
Exercises   83
Video Connection   84

**PART II   ANALYZING CRITICAL FACTORS INFLUENCING
COMMUNICATION EFFECTIVENESS   85**

**4   Cross-Cultural Communication at
    Home and Internationally   87**
Intercultural Communication Opportunities   88
   International Business Activities at Home
     and Abroad   89
   Communication Mentor   91
   The Foreign Firm's American Employee   92
   Multiculturalism and Demographic Trends
     in the United States   93
   The American Firm's Minority
     Employee   95
Nature of Culture   95
   Elements of Culture   96
   Manifestations of Culture   97

Barriers to Cross-Cultural Communication   98
   Stereotypes   99
   Time as Language   100
   Space as Language   101
   Body Language   101
   Translation Problems   102
   Communication Mentor   103
Guides to Good Cross-Cultural
   Communication   103
   General Principles   103
   Written Communication   104
   Oral Communication   106
   Communication Mentor   109
Summary   110

References *110*
Review Questions *111*
Exercises *112*
Video Connection *116*

**5   Electronic Communication
      Technology   117**
Manipulating Data *119*
      Word Processing *119*
      Spreadsheets *124*
      Databases *125*
Presenting Data *128*
      Printing *128*
      Desktop Publishing *130*
      Communication Mentor 133
      Graphics Programs *133*
Sharing Data *135*
      Electronic Mail *135*
      Communication Mentor 139
      Teleconferencing *141*
Putting It All Together: The Executive
   Workstation *142*
Computers and Barriers to Communication *144*
      Barriers Caused by Systems *144*
      Barriers to Manipulating Data *144*
      Ineffective Presentations *147*
      Barriers to Electronic Communication *148*
Summary *149*
Review Questions *150*
Exercises *152*

6   Ethical and Legal Guidelines   155
The Foundation for Ethical Behavior *157*
      Communication Mentor 158
      Communication Mentor 162
Causes of Unethical Behavior in the
   Workplace *162*
      Excessive Emphasis on Profits *162*
      Misplaced Corporate Loyalty *163*
      Obsession with Personal
         Advancement *163*
      Expectation of Not Getting Caught *164*
      Unethical Tone Set by Top
         Management *164*
      Communication Mentor 165
      Uncertainty About Whether an Action Is
         Wrong *165*
      Unwillingness to Take an Ethical
         Stand *166*
      Communication Mentor 166
Framework for Analyzing Ethical Dilemmas *167*
      Legal Considerations *167*
      Company and Professional Codes of
         Conduct *170*
      Ethical Principles and Theories *173*
      Communication Mentor 175
      Communication Mentor 178
Communicating Decisions Ethically and
   Responsibly *178*
Summary *184*
References *185*
Review Questions *186*
Exercises *186*
Cases for Analysis *188*

PART III USING WORDS AND STYLE EFFECTIVELY   191

7   Using Words Effectively   193
      Communication Mentors 194
Self-Check *196*
Word Choice *197*
      Preciseness *197*
      Simplicity and Formality *197*
      Communication Mentor 198
      Communication Mentor 200

Parallelism *200*
Tone *201*
Bias-Free Language *207*
Word Categories *211*
      Words That Label *212*
      Words That Replace *213*
      Communication Mentor 215
      Words That Show Action *220*

Words That Describe *224*
Words That Join *228*
Words That Show Relationships *229*
Summary *230*
References *233*
Review Questions *233*
Exercises *235*
Video Connection *236*

**8 Using the Techniques of
      Style   237**
Analyzing Writing Style *239*
Self-Check *241*
Phrases *242*
    Certainties *242*
    Clichés *243*
    Communication Mentor 247
    Conciseness *249*
    Surprise, Doubt, and Judgment *252*
Sentences *253*
    Structure *253*
    Misplaced Elements *255*
    Dangling Modifiers *256*

Expletives *258*
Platitudes *259*
Active and Passive Voices *259*
Subjunctive Mood *260*
Emphasis *261*
Punctuation *265*
Paragraphs *267*
    Topic Sentence *267*
    Coherence *268*
    Readability *268*
    Communication Mentor 269
    Variety *271*
    Emphasis *272*
Compositions *273*
    Unity *273*
    Sequence *273*
    Transition *274*
    Emphasis *275*
Editing and Rewriting *275*
    Content, Organization, and Style *277*
    Grammar *277*
    Format and Layout *277*
    Communication Mentor 278
Summary *281*
References *283*
Review Questions *283*
Exercises *285*

**PART IV COMMUNICATING THROUGH LETTERS
               AND MEMORANDUMS   289**

**9 Writing About the Routine and the
      Pleasant   291**
Empathy *292*
    Cultivating a "You" Attitude *295*
    Communication Mentor 295
    Using Your Knowledge of the Receiver *296*
    Communication Mentor 299
Organization *299*
    Why Organization Is Essential *300*
    How to Organize Letters and
        Memorandums *301*

Business Letters *303*
    Communication Mentor 303
    Routine Claims *305*
    Routine Letters About Credit *311*
    Routine Letters About Orders *315*
    Letters About Routine Requests *321*
Memorandums *328*
    Communication Mentor 331
    Good News Memorandums *332*
    Routine Memorandums *334*
Summary *339*

References *339*
Check Your Writing *340*
Review Questions *341*
General Writing Guidelines *342*
Exercises *344*
Applications *344*
Cases for Analysis *356*

**10 Writing About the
      Unpleasant 359**
Communication Mentor *361*
Empathy *361*
      Sequence of Ideas *361*
      Style *364*
      Communication Mentor *365*
Saying "No" to an Adjustment Request *366*
Saying "No" to a Credit Request *369*
Saying "No" to an Order for Merchandise *372*
Saying "No" to a Request for a Favor *379*
Initiating Communication About the
      Unpleasant *381*
Special Problems in Writing About the
      Unpleasant *385*
      First Paragraph *386*
      Communication Mentor *386*
      Bad-News Sentence *388*
      Last Paragraph *389*
Summary *391*
Check Your Writing *393*
Review Questions *394*
Exercises *394*
Applications *395*
Cases for Analysis *404*

11 Writing to Persuade 407
Sales Letters *408*
      Plan Before You Write *409*
      First Paragraph: An Attention Getter *412*
      Communication Mentor *415*
      Introducing the Product *416*
      Convince the Readers with Evidence *419*

      Last Paragraph: Motivating the Reader to
            Action *424*
      Writing a Complete Sales Letter *427*
      Printing and Mailing *427*
Requests and Collection Letters *431*
      A Persuasive Request for Action *431*
      Communication Mentor *441*
      The Collection Series *446*
Summary *452*
Reference *453*
Check Your Writing *454*
Review Questions *457*
      Sales Letters *457*
      Persuasive Requests and Collection
            Letters *457*
Exercises *458*
Applications *459*
Cases for Analysis *468*
Video Connection *472*

12 Writing Special Letters 473
Communication Mentor *474*
Congratulations *475*
      Writing Congratulations *475*
      Replying to Congratulations *476*
Condolences *477*
Invitations *478*
      Writing Invitations *478*
      Replying to Invitations *479*
Thank Yous *481*
News Releases *482*
Seasonal Messages *484*
Welcomes and Farewells *484*
Evaluations *486*
      Positive Qualities *486*
      Negative Qualities *489*
      Communication Mentor *495*
Regrets *495*
Summary *500*
Check Your Writing *503*
Review Questions *504*
Exercises *504*
Applications *505*
Cases for Analysis *511*

PART V   COMMUNICATING ABOUT WORK AND JOBS   515

13 Preparing Resumes and Application Letters   517
Setting Goals and Planning   518
Getting Essential Information   520
   Self-Analysis   520
   Career Analysis   520
   Job Analysis   523
   Interview with a Career Person   524
   Company/Job Profile   525
Planning Your Resume   530
   Identification   532
   Job and/or Career Objective   533
   Summary of Achievements   533
   Qualifications   535
   Personal Information   538
   References   539
Constructing a Resume   541
   Selecting the Organizational Plan   541
   Communication Mentor   542
   Enhancing the Layout   545
Examples of Resumes   547
Finding Prospective Employers   549
   Career Services Centers   552
   Employers' Offices   555
   Employment Agencies and Contractors   555
   Help-Wanted Ads   555
   Libraries   555
   Professional Organizations   556
Application Letters   557
   Communication Mentor   559
   Content   559
   Organization   564
   Style   564
   Mechanics   568
   Examples of Application Letters   569
Summary   573
References   574
Check Your Writing   575
Review Questions   577
Exercises   577
Applications   580
Cases for Analysis   581

14 Job Interviews, Employment Messages, and Performance Appraisals   585
Types of Interviews   586
   Employment Interviews   587
   Informational Interviews   587
   Sales or Persuasive Interviews   587
   Communication Mentor   588
Types of Employment Interviews   588
   Structured and Computer-Assisted Interviews   588
   Unstructured Interviews   589
   Stress Interviews   589
Job Interviewer's Role   590
   Preparing for the Interview   590
   Meeting Face to Face—The Interchange   590
   Evaluating the Interview   592
   Some Interview Guidelines   592
   Interviewer Prohibitions   593
Job Interviewee's Role   595
   Preparing for the Interview   595
   Communication Mentor   597
   Communication Mentor   598
   Meeting Face to Face—The Interchange   598
   Communication Mentor   604
   Communication Mentor   607
   Communication Mentor 608
   Practicing for Interviews   608
Preparing Other Employment Messages   609
   Follow-Up Letters   609
   Thank-You Letters   610
   Communication Mentor   611
   Application Forms   611
   Job-Acceptance Letters   614
   Job-Refusal Letters   615
   Resignation Letters   615
   Recommendation Letters   618
Performance Appraisals   624
   Guidelines for Employees   625
   Communication Mentor   626
   Guidelines for Supervisors   627

Communication Mentor 629
Summary 629
References 630
Review Questions 631

Applications 632
Cases for Analysis 633
Video Connection 636

PART VI COMMUNICATING THROUGH REPORTS 637

15 The Report Process and Research Methods 639
Knowing the Characteristics of Reports 640
    What Is a Report? 641
    Proposals as Special Reports 644
    Basis for a Report: A Problem 645
    Communication Mentor 645
Recognizing and Defining a Problem 646
    Using Hypotheses and Statements
        of Purpose 646
    Communication Mentor 646
    Limiting the Problem 648
    Defining Terms Clearly 648
Selecting a Method of Solution 649
    Library Research 649
    Normative Survey Research 655
    Observational Research 658
    Experimental Research 659
Collecting Data Through Surveys 659
    Questionnaires 660
    Communication Mentor 661
    Rating Scales 663
Arriving at an Answer 665
    Organizing the Data 667
    Collecting the Appropriate Data 667
Interpreting Data 667
    Communication Mentor 668
Summary 669
References 669
Review Questions 669
Exercises 670
Video Connection 672

16 Managing Data and Using Graphics 673
Managing Quantitative Data 674

    Common Language 675
    Measures of Central Tendency 676
    Communication Mentor 677
Using Graphics 679
    Communication Mentor 680
    Tables 681
    Communication Mentor 682
    Bar Charts 684
    Line Charts 687
    Pie Charts 690
    Pictograms 691
    Maps 692
    Flowcharts 692
    Other Graphics 695
Introducing Tables and Graphs in the Text 695
Summary 699
Review Questions 699
Exercises 700

17 Organizing and Writing Short Reports and Proposals 705
Parts of a Report 706
    Preliminary Parts 709
    Communication Mentor 711
    Report Text 712
    Addenda 713
Organizing Report Findings 714
Form Reports 718
    Communication Mentor 719
Characteristics of Short Reports 722
Proposals 726
    Parts of a Proposal 728
    Communication Mentor 731
    Sample Short Proposal 734
Summary 734
Review Questions 737

Applications   *738*
Cases for Analysis   *747*

18   Writing a Formal Report   *749*
Procedures for Writing   *750*
   Communication Mentor   751
Techniques of Conviction and Style   *752*
Documenting Reports   *754*
   Communication Mentor   755

Preparing Citations   *756*
Preparing a Bibliography   *763*
Using Headings Effectively   *769*
The Complete Report   *770*
Summary   *772*
References   *772*
Check Your Writing   *773*
Review Questions   *776*
Applications   *777*
Case for Analysis   *790*

APPENDICES

**A   Document Format and
   Layout Guide   *A-1***
Appearance   *A-1*
   Proofreaders' Marks   *A-1*
   Paper   *A-1*
   Placement of Text on the Page   *A-3*
   Justification   *A-4*
   Spacing   *A-5*
   Word Division   *A-6*
Punctuation Styles and Letter Formats   *A-7*
   Mixed and Open Punctuation   *A-7*
   Letter Formats   *A-7*
Standard Letter Parts   *A-11*
   Heading   *A-11*
   Inside Address   *A-11*
   Salutation   *A-14*
   Body   *A-14*
   Complimentary Close   *A-14*
   Signature Block   *A-14*
   Reference Initials   *A-15*
Special Letter Parts   *A-15*
   Mailing Notation   *A-15*
   Attention Line   *A-15*
   Reference Line   *A-16*
   Subject Line   *A-16*
   Second-Page Heading   *A-16*
   Company Name in Signature Block   *A-17*
   Enclosure Notation   *A-18*
   Copy Notation   *A-18*

   Postscript   *A-19*
Memorandum Formats   *A-20*
   Formal   *A-22*
   Simplified   *A-22*
Envelopes   *A-22*

**B   Grammar Review and
   Exercises   *B-1***
Self-Check   *B-1*
Words Frequently Misused   *B-3*
Nouns   *B-17*
Pronouns   *B-18*
Verbs   *B-22*
Adjectives and Adverbs   *B-26*
Sentence Structure   *B-28*
Abbreviations   *B-30*
Capital Letters   *B-31*
Numbers   *B-33*
Punctuation   *B-35*
Spelling   *B-46*
Self-Check   *B-48*
Review Quiz   *B-59*

C   Grading Symbols   *C-1*

Index   *I-1*

CREDITS

Preface Opener, Foreword Opener, and all Part Openers were photographed by John Curtis (Wadsworth).

Chapter One: Opener, Roy Morsch (The Stock Market); p. 8, Jeff Smith (The Image Bank); p. 16, Jim Pickerell.

Chapter Two: Opener, John Cleare (Mountain Camera); p. 24, Kim Steele (The Image Bank); p. 27, Walter Bibikow (The Image Bank); p. 29, Al Cook (Stock Boston); p. 48, Jim Pickerell (Stock Boston).

Chapter Three: Opener, Bob Daemmrich (Stock Boston); p. 69, Ed Bock (The Stock Market); p. 71, Charles Gupton (Stock Boston); p. 75, Matthew Borkoski (Stock Boston); p. 77, © 1991 Aldus Corporation. All rights reserved.

Chapter Four: Opener, John Curtis (Wadsworth); p. 89, Courtesy of Polaroid, Inc.; p. 90, Superstock; p. 98, Derek Berwin (The Image Bank); p. 108, Courtesy of International Business Machines, Inc.

Chapter Five: Opener, Lou Jones; p. 129 left, Courtesy of Epson, Inc.; p. 129 middle, Courtesy of International Business Machines, Inc.; p. 129 right, Courtesy of Hewlett Packard; p. 134, *Lotus* (8/91, p. 50); p. 138, Walter Bibikow (The Image Bank); p. 140 top, Courtesy of International Business Machines, Inc.; p. 140 bottom, Peter Garfield (The Stock Market); p. 142, Jim Pickerell; p. 149, Peter Garfield (The Stock Market).

Chapter Six: Opener, John Coletti (Stock Boston); p. 157, Pamela Price (Picture Group); p. 158, James Perella (Ingersoll-Rand); p. 163, David Dempster (Wadsworth); p. 172, Institute of Management Accountants; p. 174, Jeffrey MacMillan (*U.S. News & World Report*).

Chapter Seven: Opener, Comstock; p. 195, Billy E. Barnes (Stock Boston); p. 204, Sobel/Klonsky (The Image Bank); p. 211, Bob Daemmrich (Stock Boston); p. 225 left, Peter Menzel (Stock Boston); p. 225 right, John Curtis (Wadsworth).

Chapter Eight: Opener, John Curtis (Wadsworth); p. 238, Janeart Ltd. (The Image Bank); p. 240, Reference Software International; p. 243, King Features Syndicate, Inc.; p. 250, David Dempster (Wadsworth) p. 262, Carlos Alejandro.

Chapter Nine: Opener, John Curtis (Wadsworth); p. 293, Touchstone (Shooting Star); p. 300, Henley & Savage (Tony Stone Worldwide); p. 306, King Features Syndicate, Inc.; p. 320, New England Business Service, Inc.; p. 330, Jim Brown (The Stock Market).

Chapter Ten: Opener, Ed Bock (The Stock Market); p. 362, United Features Syndicate, Inc.; p. 375, RB Studio (The Stock Market); p. 379, Dorothy Littell (Stock Boston); p. 385, Chris Hackett (The Image Bank).

Chapter Eleven: Opener, John Curtis (Wadsworth); p. 409, Washnik Studio (The Stock Market); p. 411, Gary Gladstone (The Image Bank); p. 441, Gabe Palmer (The Stock Market); p. 446, Wide World Photos.

Chapter Twelve: Opener, John Curtis (Wadsworth); p. 475, Frank Herholdt (Tony Stone Worldwide); p. 487, King Features Syndicate, Inc.; p. 489, TriStar (Shooting Star); p. 495, Michael Justice (Picture Group).

Chapter Thirteen: Opener, John Curtis (Wadsworth); p. 526, John Curtis (Wadsworth); p. 531, Bruce Barthel (The Stock Market); p. 532, Wheeler Group, Inc. 1985; p. 539, United Features Syndicate, Inc.; p. 556, Jim Pickerell; p. 558, John Curtis (Wadsworth).

Chapter Fourteen: Opener, John Curtis (Wadsworth); p. 599, Jim Pickerell; P. 600, *Delta Pi Epsilon Journal* (292 (2), Spring, 1987, p. 47–55); p. 603, Reprinted by permission: Tribune Media Services; p. 618, John Curtis (Wadsworth); p. 625, KPMG Peat Martwick.

Chapter Fifteen: Opener, Chris Sorensen (British Airways); p. 647, Chris Jones (The Stock Market); p. 649, Universal Press Syndicate; p. 656, John Coletti (Stock Boston); p. 668, Courtesy of Coca-Cola USA.

Chapter Sixteen: Opener, Brett Froomer (The Image Bank); p. 676, Courtesy of New York Stock Exchange; p. 679, Motion Picture & Television Photo Archive, Disney; p. 697, Courtesy of First Interstate Bancorp, 1990 Annual Report, p. 7. Illustration by C. Przewodek. Photography by Chuck Nacke (Black Star) and Linda Enger.

Chapter Seventeen: Opener, Michael Krasowitz (FPG International); p. 715, Richard Palsey (Stock Boston), p. 719, FPG International; p. 729, Department of Defense Photo by MSGT Ken Hammond USAF; p. 731, King Features Syndicate, Inc.

Chapter Eighteen: Opener, John Curtis (Wadsworth); p. 751, Courtesy of Bracken Books; p. 755, Laima Druskis (Stock Boston).

Appendices: p. A8, Southwestern Publishing Co.; p. B46, Reprinted with permission from March 1992 issue of *The Secretary*. Copyrighted 1992 Professional Secretaries International.

EFFECTIVE COMMUNICATION SKILLS: KEY INGREDIENT IN CAREER SUCCESS

What is success? Is it graduating at the top of your class? Getting elected to an office? Being on a winning sports team? Inventing a new product? Getting a promotion?

Success means different things to different people. In the most general sense, success usually means achieving the goals you have set for yourself. For most people, this entails having meaningful work, financial security, a family and home, and the ability to work for and contribute to the causes of your choice.

What goals you set, how you set them, and how you define your personal vision of success is up to you. Achieving success is then largely dependent on your own hard work and your commitment to developing the skills necessary to reaching the goals you set for yourself.

As a business student, your vision of success likely includes a career that will be filled with many challenges and responsibilities. Whether you aspire to be a manager, accountant, economist, financial analyst, computer programmer, market researcher, or any other professional, your ability to communicate effectively is essential. Good speaking and writing skills often are the only qualities that can bring your ability to the attention of others and put you first in line for a deserved promotion or challenging assignment.

Business leaders today adamantly support the relevance of communication skills to career success. *The Wall Street Journal,* other newspapers, and business and general magazines often contain personal accounts of a professional's progress toward career success and the skills responsible for achieving that success. Not surprisingly, communication skills are a common thread throughout many of these personal anecdotes, as the following statements indicate:

> *Thomas G. Martin, Director of Corporate Development, Community Coffee Company, Inc.:* Neglecting the development of effective oral and written communication skills is a sure way to ensure a dead-end career. Unfortunately, effective communication skills do not come naturally but must be studied, developed, and practiced *daily.*

> *Hugh B. Jacks, President, BellSouth Services:* Learning to communicate well should be a top priority for anyone aspiring to lead or advance in a career. Strong technical skills are needed, but technical ability alone will not result in career advancement. Those who develop only technical skills always will work *for* people who have both technical and leadership abilities, and communication is the key ingredient in leadership.

> *Dennis R. Beresford, Chairman, Financial Accounting Standards Board:* In accounting and all other professions, we must have the appropriate technical skills. But if we cannot communicate what we know, the value of the technical skills is lessened. For example, knowing how to compute corporate income taxes is a valuable skill. Being able to tell others how to do it magnifies the value of that technical skill. Others can capitalize on your knowledge only if you can communicate it.

> *Cynthia Pharr, President and CEO, Tracy-Locke/Pharr Public Relations:* More than ever, sharp communication skills are essential to success. Ronald Reagan was called "the great communicator" and considered

the "media president" because of his powerful ability to persuade via the media. Similar skills are required of today's business executives. Recent estimates are that chief executive officers of America's largest companies spend over 70 percent of their time on external affairs—communicating the messages of their companies. Businesspeople aspiring to top management slots should be increasingly eager to improve their ability to communicate, especially their public speaking skills.

Communication in today's business environment is becoming increasingly important because of the rapidly changing technology of the computer age and the highly competitive global economy. Businesses of all sizes—not just large corporations—are using computers to handle the large volume of information that must be processed quickly. Managers are turning to executive workstations (microcomputers) to increase their productivity and save time. Their primary applications include word processing, spreadsheet, data management, graphics, and telecommunications. Business graduates who can communicate effectively using electronic communication technology will compete more favorably for available positions. Beginning businesspeople possessing these skills are more likely to earn respect, admiration, and positive performance appraisals from their supervisors.

APPLICANTS ARE SCREENED FOR COMMUNICATION SKILLS

Because the ability to communicate effectively plays an important part in a businessperson's success on the job, many employers have begun to view the ability to write and speak effectively as an important factor in selecting employees. Therefore, employers and professional certifying groups are screening applicants for skills in oral and written communication. For example,

◆ BellSouth Services requires applicants to complete an extensive questionnaire that includes essay questions. In addition, applicants are given a test similar to the ACT college entrance exam that includes a section on word usage.
◆ A small manufacturing firm requires applicants for all positions, including line workers, to write instructions for completing a typical task.
◆ Interviewers ask for specific evidence of applicants' communication and interpersonal skills. In other words, applicants are not asked, "Can you communicate well," but rather, "Give me a specific incident when you communicated effectively or worked well with others." This question is often followed with, "Good; now give me another example. . . ."

◆ The American Institute of Certified Public Accountants (AICPA) issued a statement presenting its view of comunication skills (Roy and Mac-Neil, 1967, pp. 218–219):

> To [CPAs] the ability to express [themselves] well is more than the hallmark of educated [persons]; it is a professional necessity. Inability to express [their] findings in understandable, explicit, unambiguous, intelligible English can be self-defeating, potentially misleading, and possibly disastrous to clients, creditors, and investors. . . . We feel justified, therefore . . . in being unequivocal about this requirement of the common body of knowledge for beginning CPAs: *candidates who cannot write the English language at least as well as a minimum-threshold should be denied admission to the profession, if need be on this account alone.*

The state boards of accountancy are standing behind this powerful statement. One important commitment to high communication standards is the recent change in the grading of the CPA exam. Accounting experts now evaluate technical content *and* assess communication competence. In addition, accounting departments are revising their curricula to include greater emphasis on communication and interpersonal skills—two of the three categories of skills needed for success in public accounting.

THE VALUE OF GOOD COMMUNICATION SKILLS

Having good communication skills can give a job candidate an edge over other prospects. Once hired, developing these abilities can lead to promotions and advancements. However, people who have poor oral and written communication skills cannot expect to get the best jobs, nor can they expect to earn promotions if they do not make the effort to improve these vital skills. In some cases, employees have lost their jobs due to their inadequate communication skills. A high percentage of accounting firms reported poor writing skills as a major reason for terminating entry-level accountants (Cherry and Wilson, 1987). And this list goes on and on.

How can poor communication skills alone merit such serious consequences? Xerox's response is concise but quite clear: "People who can't communicate aren't much use in a corporate environment." Exxon executives advise, "The world's best idea isn't any good if the originator can't explain it or work with others to make it a reality." Communication skills are also at the top of Kodak's list: "If someone has a good idea but can't sell it, how will that idea ever be any good to the company? Ideas must be sold to be used" ("Making It in the Corporate World," 1990, p. 9).

These executives and many more agree that employees with inadequate communication skills contribute very little to a company. Furthermore, employees' ineffective messages can cause costly mistakes and damage a company's reputation. For example, suppose a supervisor's unclear instructions caused employees to redo several tasks, which in turn delayed production three weeks. The production delay could cause customers to lose faith in the company and possibly to cancel their orders.

Production backups and lost customers aren't the only fallout from this supervisor's inadequate communication. The frustrated employees are likely to have negative feelings toward the supervisor. Low morale often leads to reduced productivity. In addition to costly mistakes, unnecessary delays, and a frustrated work force, the company must also bear the cost of selecting and training both the employees who are subsequently fired for poor writing skills and their replacements.

The message is becoming clear to more and more companies today. Companies facing today's intense competition *cannot afford* the costs of ineffective communication. In addition to screening employees for communication skills, some companies are providing writing and speaking instruction for their employees at all levels—including presidents and chief executive officers. These companies realize the value of good communication. They see that time and money are wasted and goodwill is damaged when communication is ineffective. Employees who possess good oral and written communication skills are valuable to their employers. They continue to practice and develop their skills and are rewarded for their efforts with recognition and advancement.

HOW CAN YOU DEVELOP EFFECTIVE COMMUNICATION SKILLS?

Completing this business communication course is an excellent way for you to begin acquiring the communication skills needed in today's highly competitive, automated business environment. The textbook is carefully designed to help you communicate effectively. You can

1. Read and study up-to-date discussions to master basic principles of communication (written and oral).
2. Study the numerous examples of poorly written and well-written examples and then incorporate effective writing techniques in your own writing.
3. Complete the cases and exercises to gain necessary practice in applying the principles of good writing when communicating sound business decisions.

While learning important communication principles, you also will have a priceless opportunity to "look over the shoulders" of several successful business leaders. These individuals have willingly agreed to serve as your "communication mentors" as you study this textbook. After you have studied a particular principle, one or more of your mentors will discuss how a communication principle actually works in today's dynamic business environment, share related strategies for communicating effectively, or simply provide concrete advice for developing the needed skill.

Your communication mentors represent various disciplines including accounting, finance, communications, government, public relations, and many others. When you see the icon of a briefcase, you will know you are "looking over the shoulder" of one of your mentors and learning from the real-life experiences of a business executive who is successful in his or her field.

To help you become acquainted with your communication mentors, we've included a brief introduction at the end of this section. Take a moment to connect the mentors' names with their pictures, the companies or organizations they represent, and their basic responsibilities. The better you know your mentors, the more closely you can relate to them as they contribute their valuable skills to your professional development.

Like many of the technical skills you have acquired, developing effective communication skills rests on your ability to reason logically and to make sound decisions. However, three specific commitments are necessary for you to develop effective communication skills:

1. Attempt to see things from your audience's perspective rather than from your own. That is, have empathy for your audience. Being empathic isn't as simple as it seems, particularly when dealing with today's cross-cultural work force. Erase the mind-set, "I know what *I* want to say and how *I* want to say it." Instead, ask, "How would my audience react to this message? How can I word this message so that my audience can easily understand it?"

2. Revise your documents until you cannot see any additional ways to improve them. Resist the temptation to think of your first draft as your last draft. Instead, look for ways to improve and be willing to incorporate valid suggestions once you have completed a draft. Remember that skilled speech writers might rewrite a script 15 or 20 times. Writers in public relations firms revise brochures and advertising copy until perhaps only a comma in the final draft is recognizable from the first draft. Your diligent revising will yield outstanding dividends. Specifically, the audience (your supervisor, your employees, or a client/customer, for example) is more likely to understand and accept your message. The dividend of diligent revising in this course is the increased probability that you will receive a favorable grade.

3. Be willing to allow others to make suggestions for improving your writing. Most of us consider our writing very personal. That is, we are reluctant to share what we have written with others and are easily offended if others suggest changes. This syndrome, called writer's pride

of ownership, can needlessly prevent us from seeking assistance from experienced writers—a proven method of improving communication skills. On the job, you will share your writing with the recipient (your supervisor, your employees, or a client/customer). Because a great deal of what is written in business today is written collaboratively, you will be required to subject your writing to review by others. To prepare for this workplace requirement, use this class to become more comfortable with allowing others to read and critique your writing. You have nothing to lose but much to gain: exposure to successful techniques used by more seasoned writers and the chance to improve your writing skills.

To capitalize on the technical skills in your career field, you must begin developing effective communication skills. Once you are competent in your field *and* effective in communicating that knowledge to others, you can reap the rewards sure to come your way: increased ability to secure a job, to keep a job, and to earn deserved promotions to positions of higher visibility and responsibility.

REFERENCES

Cherry, A. A., & Wilson, L. A. (1987). *A study of the writing skills of accounting majors in California.* Unpublished study.

Making it in the corporate world. (1990, March). *Tomorrow's Business Leader*, pp. 8–10.

Roy, R. H., & MacNeill, J. H. (1967). *Horizons for a profession: The common body of knowledge for certified public accountants.* New York: American Institute of Certified Public Accountants.

COMMUNICATION MENTORS

DENNIS R. BERESFORD   *Chairman, Financial Accounting Standards Board*

As chairman of the Financial Accounting Standards Board (FASB) since January 1987, I conduct meetings and public hearings of the FASB and act as its spokesperson before many groups, including government agencies and congressional committees. The FASB is the private-sector body that establishes standards for financial reporting by businesses and not-for-profit organizations.

MIKE ESPY   *U.S. House of Representatives*

As a member of the U.S. Congress, I took an oath to defend the U.S. Constitution, to bear allegiance to our country, and to discharge the duties of my office faithfully. My most important duty is to represent the views of Mississippi's Second Congressional District as we draft and pass legislation for the general welfare of the entire country. My committee assignments include serving on the House Budget Committee and the House Agriculture Committee and chairing the Lower Delta Mississippi Caucus and several task forces.

H. DEVON GRAHAM, JR.   *Southwest Regional Managing Partner, Arthur Andersen & Co.*

I oversee the audit, tax, and business advisory practices for Arthur Andersen's offices in Houston, New Orleans, San Antonio, Oklahoma City, Tulsa, and Denver. In this capacity, I am responsible for the quality and development of our practice in this region. The main components of this responsibility include recruiting and training talented professionals, meeting and exceeding our clients' expectations of service, and aggressively expanding our practice in the areas of our competence.

JERE W. HESS, JR. *Director, Personnel & Public Relations, Peavey Electronics*

I am responsible for all employee-related activities for a worldwide work force of almost 2,000. These functions include selection, training, compensation, organizational development, environmental protection, safety, industrial hygiene, security, employee welfare, and employee communications.

My public relations activities include representing the company at local, state, regional, national, and international events and interacting constantly with the media. In addition, I assist the president in strategic planning.

JAMES F. HURLEY *Senior Vice President, CalFed Inc.*

As head of the Investor Relations and Corporation Communications Division, I am responsible for investor relations, financial public relations, and general media communications of CalFed, a consumer-based financial services corporation. CalFed is the parent of California Federal Bank, the nation's fifth largest savings institutuion.

HUGH B. JACKS *President, BellSouth Services*

Serving as president of BellSouth Services involves performing selected lead staff functions and providing central services for the BellSouth companies throughout a nine-state region. Specific areas of responsibility include information systems, human resources, benefits administration, security, training, treasury and comptroller functions, property management, and other support services. I also serve on the board of directors of several organizations.

BEVERLY R. KUEHN *Branch Manager, CTX Mortgage Company, a division of Centex Corporation*

As branch manager, my chief responsibility includes managing the operations of a branch office of CTX Mortgage Company, a mortgage lender specializing in loans for new and existing residential housing. Maintaining an open, honest flow of communication with the loan applicant while originating and processing the loan expedites the loan process. I am also responsible for keeping the corporate office abreast of operations and providing up-to-date information and support to the home builders. Commitment to communicate effectively with these three groups increases our number of satisfied customers, builders, and corporate executives and leads to a more favorable bottom line.

DAVID MARTIN *President, Sygnis, Inc.*

Business and political research are an integral part of my professional career. As president of Sygnis, I have coordinated market research and polling for a broad variety of corporations, special interest groups, and news organizations. My experience also includes political candidate and issue research ranging from state legislative districts and counties to congressional, gubernatorial, and senatorial campaigns. Sygnis is owned by ALLTEL Corporation, the nation's fifth largest independent telephone company.

LYNN MARTIN *U.S. Secretary of Labor*

As a member of President Bush's cabinet and his chief adviser on labor and employment and training policies, my responsibilities include

◆ Directing the wide-range work of the Department of Labor, which was created by Congress in 1913 to ". . . foster, promote and develop the welfare of the wage earners of the United States. . . ."
◆ Improving wage earners' working conditions and advancing their opportunities for profitable employment.
◆ Overseeing and providing leadership in the administration and enforcement of laws and programs that affect the lives of working Americans.

THOMAS G. MARTIN   *Director of Corporate Development, Community Coffee Company, Inc.*

As director of corporate development, my key role is executing strategic acquisitions. Specifically, my duties include identifying and evaluating acquisition possibilities, negotiating a satisfactory contract, and organizing transition activities for the company. Performing these duties requires me to communicate with consultants, leaders of numerous companies, legal and accounting professionals, the board of directors, and employees at all levels.

TERENCE E. MCSWEENEY   *Director of Communications, PGA of America*

I direct the communications effort of the Professional Golfers' Association of America, the world's largest working sports organization. My responsibilities include (1) supervising public relations efforts to promote the association; (2) coordinating media relations programs to assist the nation's media in their coverage of the PGA; and (3) overseeing internal and external communications vehicles such as books, programs, magazines, news releases, and speeches. I am also responsible for developing an effective corporate identification program.

CARROLL M. PERKINS   *General Manager, Salt River Project*

I am responsible for carrying out all policies set by the board of directors of the Salt River Project (SRP). The SRP is the nation's oldest and most successful multi-purpose reclamation project. With annual revenues in excess of $1.1 billion, it supplies water and electricity for more than a half million users in the Phoenix area.

CYNTHIA PHARR   *President & CEO, Tracy-Locke/Pharr Public Relations*

In my role as president and chief executive officer of a full-service public relations firm, I develop communication strategies for our clients, manage a firm composed of professional communicators, lead new business development activities, and provide senior-level counsel to executives.

COMMUNICATION FOUNDATIONS AND ORAL COMMUNICATION

CHAPTER 1 Organizational Setting for Business
          Communication
CHAPTER 2 Interpersonal Communication and Listening
CHAPTER 3 Public Speaking and Oral Reporting

ORGANIZATIONAL SETTING FOR BUSINESS COMMUNICATION

OBJECTIVES

When you have completed
Chapter 1, you should be
able to

- Understand the vocabu-
  lary used in discussing
  communication and its
  role in organizations.

- Recognize and identify
  elements operating in interpersonal and group
  communication.

WHEN BROWNSVILLE RESIDENTS THINK OF THE HOME CENTER, a full-service home building store, their initial images are of the modern, two-story store on the corner of Washington and Webster streets, endless rows of different size nails and tools for every job imaginable, appealing displays of the newest doors and lighting fixtures, lumber stacked to the ceiling in large sheds filled with the scent of freshly cut pine, and the familiar sight of forest green Home Center trucks weaving throughout the community. Obviously this image of The Home Center focuses on physical character-istics without regard for the people—managers, sales and stock clerks, ac-counting and payroll clerks, and janitors who contribute significantly to the success or failure of the company.

The ability of people to work cooperatively to accomplish tasks and to gain satisfaction from their work depends on people's ability to com-municate information that motivates, instructs, and controls performance. The pressing need to communicate effectively applies to people at every level of the company. No one in the company is exempt

◆ From the president who is responsible for communicating company goals and philosophy.
◆ To managers who explain work assignments and evaluate performance objectively so employees are motivated to perform outstanding work.
◆ To employees who are willing to share ideas and suggestions for doing work more efficiently or for improving the quality of life in the com-pany.

The following on-the-job scenes illustrate how inadequate communi-cation skills might affect the success of The Home Center:

> The Home Center has decided to expand its product line to include decorative windows available from a reputable supplier beginning April 1. Marketing has developed an advertising cam-paign promoting the new line to major contractors in the area and assuring April delivery dates. When frustrated sales clerks begin reporting their inability to fill orders for decorative windows, an embarrassed purchasing manager is left to explain the problem: purchasing had not bothered to tell marketing that the supplier has postponed delivery by three weeks; therefore, marketing should have been instructed to postpone the advertising cam-paign to coincide with the new delivery date.

> After the president's severe reprimand about the sharp rise in inventory cost, the purchasing manager bluntly instructs the

buyers to "take advantage of every quantity discount available." Noting that the manager is angry and clearly unwilling to provide further explanation, the confused buyers decide to do as they were told. Unfortunately, the manager's first indication that his explanation was insufficient came when he received a message from an irate warehouse manager who demanded to know *where* he was supposed to store 500 lawn mowers—at least a three-year supply based on prior years' demand.

Conversations all over the company—in the company break room, across the sales counters, in the lumber sheds, and at the copy and fax machines—all seem to lead to the same subject. Employees are discontented over the company's unwillingness to listen to employees' concerns about work schedules. For instance, almost all employees are objecting to not knowing until Thursday whether they are scheduled to work the weekend. As if planning for weekend babysitters and canceling personal plans aren't bad enough, the company is refusing to allow employees to adjust their schedules to accommodate personal needs. Just last week, Mary, an only child, had to call in sick so that she could take her elderly mother to an out-of-town heart specialist. What *else* was she to do? Just recently, the human resources manager commented that absenteeism is getting out of hand, and anyone can see that employee morale is at an all-time low.

Effective communication could have prevented each of these costly mistakes. Imagine the positive results if

◆ The purchasing and advertising managers had coordinated their efforts to expand the new product line.
◆ The purchasing manager had controlled his anger and focused first on providing clear, thorough information about controlling inventory costs, second had made the buyers feel secure enough to clarify the confusing instructions, and third had provided valuable feedback about their work.
◆ Management had not ignored the frequent, consistent information coming to them through the grapevine—an informal, yet accurate indication of employees' major concerns.

Had you been involved in any of these situations, would you have possessed the communication skills needed to prevent the problem? Regardless of your career or your level within an organization, your ability to communicate will affect the success of the organization and your advancement within that organization. Studying this textbook is an excellent way to begin refining oral and written communication skills so that you are prepared for the many communication challenges awaiting you.

PURPOSES OF COMMUNICATION

Communicating is a pervasive process.

We could choose any one of the many definitions of communication for our study of communication in business. The most suitable, in our opinion, is that communication is a process by which information is exchanged between or among individuals through a common system of symbols, signs, and behavior. As a process, communicating has synonyms such as expressing feelings, conversing, speaking, corresponding, writing, listening, and exchanging.

People communicate to satisfy needs in both their work and nonwork lives. People want to be heard, appreciated, and wanted. They also want to accomplish tasks and achieve goals. Obviously, then, a major purpose of communication is to help people feel good about themselves and about their friends, groups, and organizations.

Communication informs, persuades, and entertains through verbal and nonverbal messages. Verbal means "through the use of words," either written or oral. To be precise, speakers and writers should avoid using "verbal" when they mean "oral." In this book, *oral* and *spoken* will identify speech communication; *written* will identify writing tasks.

Can a person send verbal and nonverbal signals simultaneously?

Nonverbal means "without the use of words." People constantly send nonverbal messages through body motions, appearance, aromas, clothing, uniforms, facial expressions, jewelry, automobiles, and a variety of other symbols, signs, and behaviors.

FOUR LEVELS OF COMMUNICATION

As we have said, the primary function of communication is to convey meaning or information through words, symbols, signs, or actions. People form messages by combining pieces or bits of information. This communicative process takes place on four levels:

1. *Intrapersonal communication* occurs when an individual processes information based on his or her own experiences. It is, in a sense, communication within one person. Communication may be impaired when the sender has significantly different experiences from the recipient because the recipient may be unable to process the information on an intrapersonal level.

2. *Interpersonal communication* takes place primarily when two people are involved in the process. As mentioned, they have two goals: (1) They want to accomplish whatever task confronts them, and (2) they want

to feel better about themselves as a result of the exchange. These two goals are commonly referred as task goals and maintenance goals, respectively, and they exist side by side in varying degrees in most of our daily activities.

3. *Group communication* occurs among more than two people: a committee, a club, or all the students enrolled in a class. Groups are formed usually because the combined efforts of a number of people result in greater output than the individual efforts of the same number of people. In other words, groups can do more for the individuals than the individuals can do for themselves.

4. *Organizational communication* arises when groups discover that they are unable to accomplish their goals without some kind of organization. Thus organizations as we know them are really combinations of groups formed in such a way that large tasks may be accomplished.

Despite the differences in size and complexity, each of these levels of communication continues to have task and maintenance goals. The idea of maintenance goals can be expanded, or divided, into two distinct goals: (1) a self-maintenance goal that describes the individual's need to maintain his or her personal worth or psychological well-being and (2) a group maintenance goal that describes the group's need to maintain its *esprit de corps*—the nontask relationships they have established by interacting with one another as a team.

The study of organizational communication is a subject on which entire books have been written, but a brief review of communication in the organization will help us understand the role of management in the organizational communication process.

COMMUNICATING IN GROUPS

Most of your oral communication in business will occur in one-to-one relationships, which are discussed in Chapter 2. You will probably also make oral reports and speeches. Your second most frequent oral communication activity will likely occur when you participate in groups, primarily groups within the organizational work environment. Group and committee work have become crucial in most organizations. Group meetings can be productive when members understand something about groups and how they operate.

Purposes of Groups

Groups form for synergistic effects; that is, through pooling their efforts, group members can achieve more collectively than they could individually. At the same time, the social nature of groups contributes to the self-maintenance goals of members. Communication in small groups leads to group decisions that are generally superior to individual decisions.

What is the motivation for forming groups?

How is an organization different from a group?

What is the difference between a task goal and a maintenance goal?

What is meant by synergy?

Small groups or "think-tanks" are an excellent communication environment. Working in a small group motivates, helps stimulate creative thinking, and develops positive office rapport.

The group process can motivate members, improve thinking, and assist attitude development and change. The emphasis that groups place on task and maintenance activity is based on several factors in group communication.

Factors in Group Communication

As you consider the following factors in group communication, try to visualize their relationship to some groups to which you have belonged in school, church, athletics, and social activities.

Leadership. The ability of a group leader to work toward task goals while, at the same time, contributing to the development of group and individual maintenance goals is often critical to group success.

Could maintenance goals be served during task activities?

Longevity. Groups formed for short-term tasks, such as to arrange a dinner and program, will spend more time on the task than on maintenance. However, groups formed for long-term assignments, such as an audit of a major corporation by a team from a public accounting firm, may devote much effort to maintenance goals.

Size. The smaller the group, the more its members have the opportunity to communicate with each other; conversely, large groups often inhibit communication because the opportunity to speak and interact is limited. When broad input is desired, large groups may be good. When expert opinion is the goal, smaller groups may be more effective. Interestingly, large groups generally divide into smaller groups for maintenance purposes, even when the large group is task oriented. Although much research has been conducted in the area of group size, no optimal number of members has been identified. Groups of five to seven members are thought to be best for decision-making and problem-solving tasks. An odd number of members is preferred because deciding votes are possible and tie votes are infrequent.

Perception and Self-Concept. People who are invited to join groups have perceptions of how the group should operate and what it should achieve. In addition, each member has a self-concept that dictates fairly well how he or she will behave. Comics try to be humorous, those known to be aggressive will attempt to be confrontational and forceful, and those who like to be known as moderates will behave in moderate ways by settling arguments rather than initiating them. When expectations and satisfaction of self-concepts fall short, groups will probably be ineffective.

Status. Some group members will appear to be better qualified than others. Consider a group in which the chief executive of the organization is a member: When the chief executive speaks, members agree; when members speak, they tend to direct their remarks to the one with high status—the chief executive. People are inclined to communicate with peers as their equals, but they tend to speak upward to superiors and downward to subordinates. In general, groups require balance in status and expertise rather than homogeneity.

> Some congressional committees have over 50 members to ensure that various special interests groups and geographic regions are represented.

> What is the preferred pronunciation of "status"?

COMMUNICATION MENTOR

Any corporate team or group of employees is no different from a symphony orchestra. To function effectively, each individual in the group must work in harmony to achieve the group's goals. All members of the symphony must have the opportunity to contribute to the end product. The maestro—the stroker—must ensure that each member of the team receives equal recognition within the group. Fairhandedness is always the general rule. Soloists need not apply.

Terence E. McSweeney
Director of Communications
PGA of America

Group Norms.   A norm is a standard or average behavior. All groups possess norms. A teacher's behavior helps establish classroom norms. If a teacher is generally late for class, students will begin to arrive late. If the teacher permits talking during lectures, the norm will be for students to talk. People conform to norms because conformity is easy and nonconformity is difficult and uncomfortable. Conformity leads to acceptance by other group members and creates communication opportunities.

The performance of groups depends on several factors, but none is more important than leadership. The leader can establish norms, determine who can speak and when, encourage everyone to contribute, and provide the motivation for effective group activity.

CHARACTERISTICS OF FORMAL ORGANIZATIONS

What elements distinguish a formal organization from a group? Both are made up of individuals, and both have goals. Some groups may exceed the size of some organizations in terms of the number of members. Essentially, formal, large organizations are characterized not by a single factor but by a combination of

What are the four critically related characteristics of formal organizations?

1. Goal orientation.
2. Specialization of individuals and units.
3. Interdependence of units and individuals.
4. Formalized hierarchy.

Goal Orientation

Organizations can accomplish some things individuals and groups cannot do by or for themselves. For example, the task goals of individuals and groups may generate such complicated and sizable endeavors that more complex entities are necessary to accomplish them.

Consider the example of a small retail lumber store that expands beyond the owner's personal ability to cope with it. In this case, the store concentrates on providing building supplies to local contractors. When the owner's son graduates from college, he joins the company with visions of expanding the family business. Soon, hand tools, paint, landscape supplies, and a variety of other items fill the shelves. Business is good, and more space is needed. As a result, they lease a larger building in a more desirable location. They need more employees to handle the expanded business. It isn't too long before the store is handling prefabricated doors and windows, lighting fixtures, carpeting, housewares, sporting equipment, and the great variety of products available in many modern home center stores.

Specialization of Individuals and Units

The new home center calls for more employees and for some skills not available within the family. Developing advertising campaigns, creating point-of-sale displays, purchasing merchandise for resale, maintaining inventories, keeping accounting and personnel records, and exercising control over a variety of activities are tasks that require specialization.

To exercise the necessary control over the wide range of activities, management also has organized its employees into functional units called departments: operations, human resources, and finance. Within these departments, further specialization of labor occurs. Purchasing, for example, has specialists in lumber, carpeting, hardware, and so on. As the complexity of the undertaking increases, greater specialization is required. This specialization leads to the next characteristic of the large organization.

Interdependence of Units and Individuals

The large organization is now composed of smaller units, and these units are composed of individuals. Because of specialization in the large, formal organization, each of the smaller units (or departments) is dependent on the other units to some extent. Efforts on the part of the sales staff are very much dependent on a steady and uninterrupted flow of merchandise provided by the inventory-control department. Regular reports from these units to finance provide the basis for an efficient record-keeping system that can, in turn, provide information to assist management in planning and decision making.

Within each of these departments, specialization of people leads to interdependence of individuals. Thus, interdependence exists among both departments and individuals. All, however, are organized so that the goals of the organization can be achieved. In the everyday work of the organization, the task goals of the total organization exist side by side with the group-maintenance goals of the departmental units and the self-maintenance goals of the individuals involved. The interdependence of units and individuals applies equally to both task goals and maintenance goals.

Does *interdependence* mean "mutual dependence"?

Formalized Hierarchy

To achieve its goals, the organization needs to direct and coordinate the interdependence of units and individuals toward a desired end. Formal organizational structure results from efforts to achieve coordination. As shown in Figure 1-1, the original lumber store has grown into a sizable home center with a formalized hierarchy.

The formalized hierarchy ensures that communication occurs effectively as an element in coordination. Coordination, in turn, results from effective communication and well-organized programs or systems.

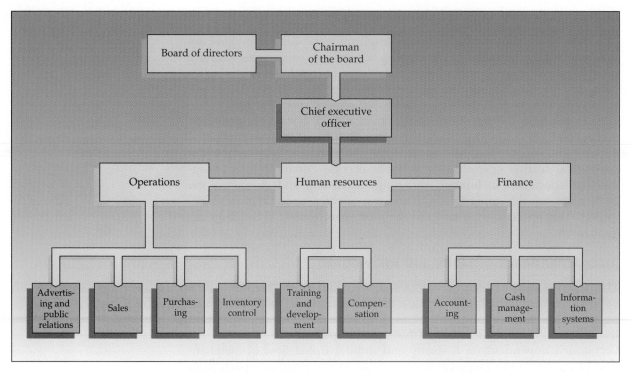

FIGURE 1–1   Organizational chart: The Home Center

These four characteristics are acquired as the organization develops, and they probably are acquired in the order listed. As goals expand beyond the capacity of the current organization, additional specialization is necessary to achieve them. As specialization increases, interdependence also increases. And as interdependence of individuals and units increases, the need for formalized structure or hierarchy to ensure communication and hence coordination becomes greater.

ORGANIZATIONAL STRUCTURE AND COMMUNICATION

Are most organizational charts pyramid shaped?

Almost any knowledgeable person can sketch an organizational chart similar to the one for The Home Center, but not everyone can describe what the chart represents. Traditionally, organizational charts have been used to describe the authority structure of the organization. People in higher positions in the chart appear to have greater authority than those at lower levels. If used to describe communication in the organization, however, the chart may be entirely inadequate. May people talk only to those immediately above or below them, that is, only to those employees whose positions on the chart are connected to theirs by an uninterrupted line? Is each department on the chart autonomous and shielded from relationships with other departments? If units and individuals depend on one another, the chart does not define the communication structure.

Nor does the chart necessarily define the role structure—the relative importance of each department or individual participating in the organization. The chairman of the board occupies the highest spot on the chart, but the actual role may have little to do with the success or failure of the organization. Someone in the lowest level on the chart—in finance, for example—may play a role of considerably greater importance than the position's status on the chart would indicate.

Does position on the organizational chart indicate one's impact on an organization?

Organizational charts help define the scope of the organization and assist people in getting a total view. Because people generally occupy roles and perform functions in all those spaces in the organizational chart, the pictured structure could seldom be considered a final answer. At the same time, the organizational structure is much easier to talk about when everyone uses the same graphic presentation.

The organizational structure does affect the behavior of individuals and units within it. Most organizations are pyramid shaped. The higher a person is on the pyramid, the greater are the apparent authority and rewards. Most people probably strive for a higher position on the pyramid; this striving may determine relationships with peers, subordinates, and superiors. Competition has become a characteristic of the American way of life. People and organizations compete for a greater share of scarce resources, for a limited number of positions at the top of organizations, and for esteem in their professions. Such competition is a healthy sign of the human desire to succeed; and in terms of economic behavior, competition is fundamental to the private-enterprise system. At the same time, when excessive competition replaces the cooperation necessary for success, communication may be diminished, if not eliminated.

Might competition for promotion be a likely barrier to effective communication?

Just as we want to look good in the eyes of our peers, superiors, and subordinates, units within organizations want to look good to one another. This attitude may cause behavior to take the competitive form of "I win, you lose" instead of a cooperative spirit characterized by "I win, you win." As a result, excessive competition may have a negative influence on the performance of the organization; everybody loses.

At the same time, the organization may change behavior when effective communication takes place. Most conflict among people and groups results from a lack of understanding. When one unit is uninformed about the importance or function of another, needless conflicts may occur as groups attempt to better themselves at the expense of others. Interestingly enough, a group engaged in competition tends to solidify and become cohesive with great internal group morale. As a conse-

Within the groups that make up an organization, what is usually the basis for conflicts?

quence, the competitive spirit of the group may intensify and lead to further deterioration of communication with other groups. It's easy to visualize what such activity may do to cooperative efforts in the total organization. Therefore, although competition is appropriate and desirable in many situations, management must take steps through open communication to reduce competition and to increase cooperation. Cooperation is more likely when the competitors have an understanding of others' importance and functions. This statement is as true of cooperation among individuals as it is of cooperation among groups within organizations.

Organizational structures are designed by management as a means of controlling the behavior of members and units. Some of the previous comments have pointed to problems introduced by rigid organizational structures, but other problems occur when individual- or group-maintenance goals mix with the task goals of the organization.

EXTERNAL AND INTERNAL SYSTEMS

Two systems of organizational communication simultaneously influence human behavior. The *external* system is typified by the formal organizational chart, which is created by management to control individual and group behavior and to achieve the organization's goals. Essentially, the external system is dictated by the technical, political, and economic environment of the organization. Within this external system, people are required to behave in certain ways simply to get the work done. Because it is dictated by environmental forces existing outside the needs of the individuals in the organization, the system is called *external*.

External systems are imposed on people.

The *internal* system develops as people interact within the formal, external system and certain behavior patterns emerge—patterns that accommodate social and psychological needs. To distinguish between the two systems, return to The Home Center and its organizational chart. The owner works full time in the purchasing department, which is subordinate to and apparently has a reporting relationship to the operations department. Quite likely, however, the people in the operations department don't give the owner a bad time. Their behavior in the external system is minimal and just enough to get the work done. In the internal system, however, their behavior is adapted, depending on their personal perceptions of the owner.

Internal systems are developed among people.

Systems in Action

As another example, if the work hours for office staff are 8:00 a.m. to 5:00 p.m., that is part of the external system. But if one office employee begins at 4:50 to clear the desk, put on outdoor clothing, and get ready to run for the door promptly at 5:00, this behavior may spread to all others in the office and become a part of the internal system. The external system, then, requires certain behaviors to get the work done, nothing more. The internal system develops from emergent behaviors and assists in achieving maintenance goals. These two systems operate concurrently but in varying degrees in all organizations, and management must recognize and work with both.

When participants rely almost entirely on the formalized external system as a guide to behavior, the system might be identified as a *bureaucracy*. Procedures manuals, job descriptions, organizational charts, and other written materials dictate the required behavior. Communication channels are followed strictly, and red tape is abundant. Procedures are generally followed exactly; terms such as *rules* and *policy* serve as sufficient reasons for actions. But even the most formal organizations cannot function long without an internal system emerging. As people operate within the external system, they must interact on a person-to-person basis and create an environment conducive to satisfying their personal emotions, prejudices, likes, and dislikes.

In the college classroom, for example, the student behavior required to satisfy the external system is to attend class, take notes, read the text, and pass examinations. On the first day of class, this behavior probably is typical of almost all students, particularly if they did not know one another prior to attending the class. As the class progresses, however, the internal system emerges and overlaps the external system. Students become acquainted, sit next to people they particularly like, talk informally, and may even plan ways to beat the external system. Cutting class and borrowing notes are examples. Soon, these behaviors become norms for class behavior. Students who do not engage in the internal system may be viewed with disdain by the others. Obviously, the informality of the internal system is good for people because it helps satisfy maintenance goals. At the same time, it affects communications.

The Grapevine as an Internal System

The grapevine, often called the rumor mill, is perhaps the best known informal communication system. It is actually a component of the internal system. As people talk casually during coffee breaks and lunch periods, the focus usually shifts from topic to topic. And one of the topics most certainly would be work—job, company, supervisor, fellow employees. Even though the external system calls for very definite communication channels, the grapevine tends to develop and operate within the organization.

As a communication channel, the grapevine is reputed to be speedy but inaccurate. In the absence of alarms, the grapevine may be the most effective way to let occupants know that the building is on fire. It certainly beats sending a written memorandum!

How can an employee's taking small amounts of inventory home for personal use affect the external system?

Why call this information system "the grapevine"?

Businesspeople often speak informally about on-the-job issues. This communications network is referred to as "the grapevine"—a valuable source of accurate information as well as rumor.

The grapevine often is thought of as a channel for inaccurate communication. In reality, it is no more or less accurate than other channels. Even formal communication may become inaccurate as it passes from level to level in the organizational hierarchy. The inaccuracy of the grapevine has more to do with the message input than with the output. For example, the grapevine is noted as a carrier of rumor, primarily because it carries informal messages. If the input is rumor, and nothing more, the output obviously will be inaccurate. But the output may be an accurate description of the original rumor.

For the college student, the grapevine carries much valuable information. Even though the names of the good teachers may not be published, students learn those names through the grapevine. How best to prepare for certain examinations, teacher attitudes on attendance and homework, and even future faculty personnel changes are messages that travel over the grapevine. In the business office, news about promotions, personnel changes, company policy changes, and annual salary adjustments often are communicated by the grapevine long before being disseminated by formal channels.

A misconception about the grapevine is that the message passes from person to person until it finally reaches a person who can't pass it

Do you ever participate in the grapevine?

COMMUNICATION MENTOR

Instead of condemning or resisting the informal communication network that exists among employees, managers must learn to *use* it. For example, after two major force reductions at the Salt River Project, a rumor spread that a third layoff was imminent. Effective in spreading false information, the company grapevine was also useful in counteracting the rumor.

Carroll M. Perkins
General Manager
Salt River Project

on—the end of the line. Actually, the grapevine works through a variety of channels. Typically, one person tells two or three others, who each tell two or three others, who each tell two or three others, and so on. Thus, the message may spread to a huge number of people in a very short time. Additionally, the grapevine has no single, consistent source. Messages may originate anywhere and follow various routes. More will be said about sources and routes later in this chapter.

Management must recognize that an informal, internal system will emerge from even the most carefully designed formal, external system. To ignore this fact is to attempt to manage blindfolded. Yet some managers do try to work exclusively with the external system. Achieving organizational goals must be extremely difficult for them. As long as people interact, the organization will have both systems.

COMMUNICATION FLOW IN ORGANIZATIONS

The flow of communication within the organization may be upward, downward, or horizontal, as shown in Figure 1-2. Because these three terms are used frequently in communication literature, they deserve some clarification. Although the concept of flow seems simple, direction has meaning for those participating in the communication process.

Downward Communication

Downward communication flows from superior to subordinate, from policy makers to operating personnel, or from top to bottom on the organizational chart. As messages move downward through successive levels of the organization, they seem to get larger. A simple policy statement from

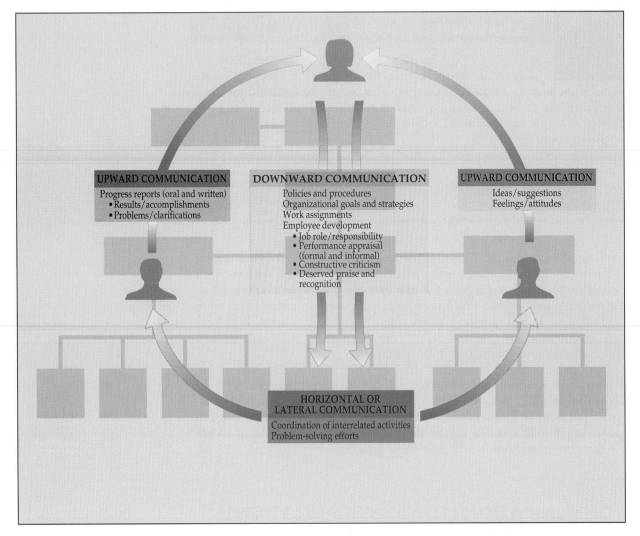

UPWARD COMMUNICATION
Progress reports (oral and written)
• Results/accomplishments
• Problems/clarifications

DOWNWARD COMMUNICATION
Policies and procedures
Organizational goals and strategies
Work assignments
Employee development
• Job role/responsibility
• Performance appraisal
(formal and informal)
• Constructive criticism
• Deserved praise and
recognition

UPWARD COMMUNICATION
Ideas/suggestions
Feelings/attitudes

**HORIZONTAL OR
LATERAL COMMUNICATION**
Coordination of interrelated activities
Problem-solving efforts

FIGURE 1–2   Flow of communication within an organization

Is a college class an example of downward communication?

the top of the organization may grow into a formal plan for operation at lower levels.

Teaching people how to do their specific tasks is an element of downward communication. Another element is orientation to a company's rules, practices, procedures, history, and goals. Employees learn about the quality of their job performance through downward communication.

Downward communication normally involves both written and oral methods and makes use of the following guidelines:

1. People high in the organization usually have greater knowledge of the organization and its goals than do people at lower levels.
2. Both oral and written messages tend to become larger as they move downward through the organization. This expansion results from attempts to prevent distortion and is more noticeable in written messages.
3. Oral messages are subject to greater changes in meaning than are written messages.

The receiver's reaction to a message is called *feedback*, which is a technical term in communication theory. When a supervisor sends a message to a lower-level employee who then asks a question or nods assent, the question and the nod are signs of feedback. Feedback is considered in detail in Chapter 2. Feedback may flow both downward and upward in organizational communication.

> **Why do messages seem to get longer as they move downward?**

Upward Communication

Communication upward, although necessary and valuable, does contain risks. Upward communication generally is feedback to downward communication. When management requests information from lower organizational levels, the resulting information becomes feedback to that request. Employees talk to superiors about themselves, their fellow employees, their work and methods of doing it, and their perceptions of the organization. These comments are feedback to the downward flow transmitted in both oral and written form by group meetings, procedures or operations manuals, company news releases, and the grapevine.

Accurate upward communication keeps management informed about the feelings of subordinates, helps management identify both difficult and potentially promotable employees, and paves the way for even more effective downward communication. At the same time, upward communication is often misleading because employees generally will tell management what they believe management wants to hear rather than what it should be told. Employees reporting upward are aware that their communications carry the risk of putting them on the spot. They might commit themselves to something they cannot handle, or they might communicate incorrectly.

> **How is feedback from subordinates helpful to managers?**

These factors, then, are important to consider when upward communication flow is involved:

1. Upward communication is primarily feedback to requests and actions of superiors.
2. Subordinates often tell the superior what they think the superior wants to hear even though their messages might contradict their true observations and perceptions.
3. Upward communication is based on trust in the supervisor.
4. Upward communication frequently involves risk to an employee.

Horizontal or Lateral Communication

Horizontal or lateral communication describes exchanges between organizational units on the same hierarchical level. These exchanges reveal one of the major shortcomings of organizational charts. Charts don't leave much room for horizontal communication when they picture authority relationships by placing one box higher than another and define role functions by placing titles in those boxes. Yet horizontal communication is the primary means of achieving coordination in an organization. In The Home Center, for instance, the chart implies that people in operations can't communicate directly with people in human resources or finance without going through the chief executive officer. Obviously, that would be a rather difficult way to operate a complex organization.

In fact, horizontal communication exists as part of the internal system even though it is not defined by the formal chart. Workers at the same level tend to talk with one another about their work, their superiors, and their working conditions. They also talk with one another about various personal, nonwork problems. Thus, horizontal communication can contribute to self-maintenance goals as well as to task goals.

Management must recognize that informal, horizontal communication takes place in any system or organization where people are available

What benefit results from lateral communication?

COMMUNICATION MENTOR

Traditionally, most communication within American businesses has been downward communication. Until recent years, the majority of companies in this country followed a militaristic model with decisions made by the general and carried out by the privates.

Many people have become uncomfortable with this model because it tends to breed mediocrity and low employee morale. When information does not flow upward, employees justly feel that they are not being listened to or heard, and many good ideas never reach the top. When information does not flow sideways, various departments work in isolation, and the benefits of synergy are lost.

Any company that wants to remain competitive and successful in today's business environment must develop and use channels of communication that flow in all directions.

Hugh B. Jacks
President
BellSouth Services

to one another. The informal communication and behavior that is not task oriented develop alongside formal task communication and behavior, contributing to morale, to improvements in ways to accomplish tasks, and to clarification of upward and downward communication. Formalized horizontal communication serves a coordinating function in the organization. Units coordinate their activities to accomplish task goals just as adjacent workers in a production line coordinate their activities.

Coordination is the most important goal of lateral communication.

SUMMARY

Groups and organizations exist because people working together can accomplish more and make better decisions than can the same people working individually. In other words, the total is greater than the sum of the parts.

As tasks increase in size and complexity, specialization is required and interdependence of people and units is critical. These elements are organized to achieve goals, and the resulting entity is an organization. Communication helps control and coordinate the work of the organization through a formal, external system and an informal, internal system. The external system exists to accomplish tasks, and the internal system serves a personal-maintenance purpose that results in people feeling better about themselves and others. Because these systems operate simultaneously, a modified system emerges that combines qualities of both.

Communication flows upward, downward, and horizontally or laterally. These flows often defy the ability of management to describe them graphically. To cope with communication problems in organizations, management should (1) attempt to balance the external and internal systems, (2) use the systems for effective task accomplishment and maintenance purposes, and (3) indicate by example their concern for effective communication.

Organizations are strengthened when people have a knowledge of and skill in interpersonal communication, which we discuss in Chapter 2.

"Effective communicators" tend to succeed.

REVIEW QUESTIONS

1. What are the two forms of verbal communication?
2. What is the difference between interpersonal and intrapersonal communication?
3. What are the two major goals of both interpersonal and group communication?
4. Synergy results from group work. What is synergy?
5. How does the longevity of a group task affect its attention to maintenance efforts?

6. Why is an odd number of group members frequently desirable?
7. Why do people conform to norms?
8. Four factors combine to characterize large, formal organizations. What are they?
9. How might an organizational chart fail to indicate the relative importance of positions or individuals on the chart?
10. How might the pyramid shape of an organization chart affect individual and group performance?
11. What is a possible cause of most conflict between or among groups?
12. What is the system of organizational communication called when it relies on rules, procedures, and formalities?
13. What is the system of organizational communication called when it is characterized by maintenance activities?
14. Does the grapevine lend itself to easy tracking? Why?
15. Why do downward messages tend to become larger as they travel through successive organizational levels?
16. Is organizational control achieved through lateral communication or through upward-downward communication?
17. What technical term describes the receiver's reaction to a message?
18. How might upward communication create a risk for an employee?

EXERCISES

1. Draw an organizational chart to depict the external system of communication within an organization with which you are familiar. Using the terminology presented in the chapter, briefly explain your answer.
2. Using the same organization you selected in Exercise 1, distinguish between the external and internal systems of organizational communication. Provide several examples to illustrate the two distinct systems. What was management's response to the internal system you are describing? Based on your reading of the chapter, what suggestions can you offer for improving the organizational communication structure of this organization?
3. In groups assigned by your instructor, complete the following activity: (a) Select one group member to develop a short message (instructor may provide one). The first member whispers this message to the second member, the second member to the third member, and so on. Finally, the first member repeats the original message. (b) As a group, compile a list of similarities between this familiar game of "gossip" and the grapevine, a distinct part of the informal, internal system. Based on your group discussion, offer a few suggestions to managers for dealing with the grapevine.
4. Be prepared to describe the communication in a group with which you are familiar.

INTERPERSONAL COMMUNICATION AND LISTENING

OBJECTIVES

When you have completed Chapter 2, you should be able to

♦ Develop effective methods of improving interpersonal communications and human relations.

♦ Explain how behavioral sciences and management theories help management understand better the role of communication, particularly in the workplace.

♦ Develop effective listening skills.

ROCK CLIMBING IS A STRENUOUS AND OFTEN DANGEROUS SPORT. The professional rock climber knows the value of physical preparation, which includes strengthening exercises for every major muscle group. In addition, she or he must possess the proper equipment: ropes or cable, harnesses, gloves, clamps, spikes, clothing suitable to the activity and climate, and other necessary tools. Finally, the climber knows that research is sometimes integral; it helps to know something about the terrain and any additional obstacles that may occur. The true sportsperson will not be threatened by a wall of stone that appears impossible to scale. Instead, she or he will be driven to accept the challenge, anticipating the physical and emotional rush upon reaching the summit after pushing the body to its limits. With each expedition, the climber visualizes the thrill of getting past the barrier of rock to see the expanse of sky and the panorama of earth below.

In some ways, communication can be similar to rock climbing. Developing good communication skills takes practice and the desire for challenge. Frequently, proper communication requires some research and extra effort. Many barriers to effective communication exist and must be overcome. But the successful manager tackles the obstacles head-on, looking forward to taking down communication barriers and reaping the rewards good communication skills bring.

What percentage of a manager's time is spent communicating?

Studies have shown that managers spend approximately 60 to 80 percent of their time involved in some form of communication including

Managers spend up to 80 percent of their time communicating. This communication can take the form of meetings, working in small groups, writing reports, and speaking with employees and clients. Because communication is such a vital part of day-to-day business, developing excellent communication skills is imperative for your career success.

- Attending meetings and writing reports related to strategic plans and company policy.
- Presenting information to large and small groups.
- Explaining work assignments.
- Evaluating and counseling employees.

Effective communicators realize that communication is not an automatic process. That is, the message is not interpreted correctly just because the manager transmitted it. Rather than thinking, "*Anybody* could understand these instructions; they're crystal clear," the prudent manager anticipates possible breakdowns in the communication process—the unlimited ways the message can be misunderstood. This mind-set motivates the manager to design the initial message effectively and to be prepared to intervene at the appropriate time to ensure that the message received is as close as possible to the message sent.

What is the goal of the effective communicator?

Understanding the communication process model is an excellent way to begin improving your communication skills. Then, an abundance of practice will allow you to refine those skills, which are used so frequently during a usual workday and which are so critical to career success.

How can you improve your communication skills?

THE HUMAN COMMUNICATION PROCESS

A major advance in communication theory came with Claude Shannon's 1949 publication of his mathematical theory of communication. He and other information theorists at the Bell Telephone Laboratories were concerned with the process of transferring signals accurately from sender to receiver. Their concern was not with words or word meanings but with coded material sent from one machine to another—from a satellite to earth or from one computer to another, for example.

At about the same time, behavioral scientists were putting together a theory of human communication from accumulated research. This general theory has much in common with the work of the information theorists. Even though one was concerned with machine-to-machine communication and the other with people-to-people communication, both groups were writing and talking about a similar process. Consider the simplified form of the communication process model presented in Figure 2-1. The stages of the model are as follows:

1. The sender encodes a message.
2. The sender selects an appropriate channel and transmits the message.
3. The receiver decodes the message.
4. The receiver encodes a message (feedback) to clarify any part of the message not understood. Feedback involves (a) the receiver encoding a message, (b) the receiver selecting a channel and transmitting the mes-

What are the stages of the communication process model?

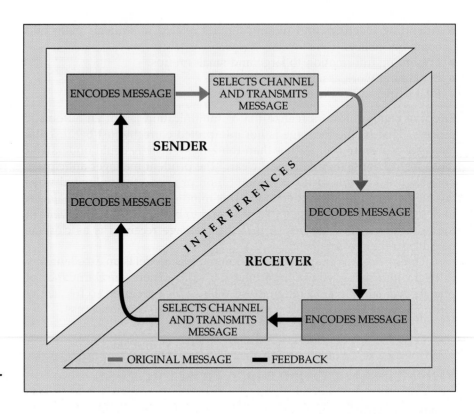

FIGURE 2-1   The communication process model

sage, and (c) the sender decoding the message. The sender and receiver continue to reverse roles until the message is understood.

5. The sender and receiver remove or minimize interferences that hinder the communication process.

The Sender Encodes the Message

The message originates with the sender who transmits it to the receiver. The sender carefully designs a message by selecting (1) words that clearly convey the message and (2) nonverbal signals (gestures, stance, tone of voice, and so on) that reinforce the verbal message. The process of selecting and organizing the message is referred to as *encoding*. The sender's primary objective is to encode the message in such a way that the message received is as close as possible to the message sent. Knowledge of the receiver's educational level, experience, viewpoints, and other information aid the sender in encoding the message. If information about the receiver is unavailable, the sender can put himself or herself in the receiver's position to gain fairly accurate insight for encoding the message.

Selecting the verbal and nonverbal message is called encoding.

Knowledge about the receiver aids the sender in encoding the message. What type of information could be helpful?

Managers must never assume that their messages are interpreted the same way by every employee. Instead, executives should anticipate possible breakdowns in communication and try to overcome these gaps. This manager is explaining an assignment to an employee in a face-to-face situation, allowing for feedback and nonverbal cues.

Chapters 7 and 8 provide guidance in using words effectively; nonverbal communication is covered in greater detail later in this chapter.

Obvious breakdowns in the communication process at the encoding stage occur if the sender uses

- Words not present in the receiver's vocabulary.
- Ambiguous, nonspecific ideas that distort the message.
- Nonverbal signals that contradict the verbal message.
- Expressions such as "uh" or grammatical errors, mannerisms (excessive hand movements, jingling keys), or dress that distracts the receiver.

Can you think of other breakdowns in the encoding process?

Of course, this list is only a beginning of possible problems at the encoding stage.

The Sender Selects an Appropriate Channel and Transmits the Message

To increase the likelihood that the receiver will understand the message, the sender carefully selects an appropriate channel for transmitting the message. Three typical communication channels are

1. *One way, not face to face.* Written documents such as letters, memos, reports, and press releases prepared traditionally or sent electronically (electronic mail, facsimile, voice-mail).
2. *Two way, face to face.* Informal conversations, interviews, oral reports, speeches, and teleconferences.
3. *Two way, not face to face.* Telephone conversations and intercom announcements.

What are the three typical communication channels?

Selecting an inappropriate channel can cause the message to be misunderstood and can adversely affect human relations with the receiver. For example, for a very complex subject, a sender might begin with a

Describe other situations when each of the three communication channels would be appropriate.

written document and follow up with a face-to-face discussion after the receiver has had an opportunity to study the document. Written documents are required when legal matters are involved and written records must be retained. A face-to-face meeting is a more appropriate channel for sending sensitive, unpleasant messages. For example, consider a supervisor calling an employee into a private office to discuss the employee's continual violation of safety regulations. A face-to-face meeting provides two distinct benefits: (1) The manager can solicit immediate feedback from the receiver to clarify misunderstandings and inaccuracies in the message. (2) In addition to hearing what the receiver is saying (the verbal message), the manager can "read" equally important nonverbal cues (tone of voice, body movements, and so on). The manager may feel comfortable with what the receiver is saying, but the nonverbal message may indicate that the receiver is overamplifying the problem or is underestimating the importance of the warning. The manager's discerning choice of a channel—meeting with the employee face to face rather than calling or writing a disciplinary memo—marks this manager as sensitive and empathetic, qualities that foster trust and open communication.

The Receiver Decodes the Message

Why is a decoded message sometimes different from an encoded one?

The receiver is the destination of the message. The receiver's task is to interpret the sender's message, both verbal and nonverbal, with as little distortion as possible. The process of interpreting the message is referred to as *decoding*. Because words and nonverbal signals have different meanings to different people, countless problems can occur at this point in the communication process. Obvious breakdowns in communication occur at this stage if

Provide specific examples of breakdowns in decoding that you have experienced.

◆ The sender inadequately encodes the original message. For example, the sender may use words not present in the receiver's vocabulary; use ambiguous, nonspecific ideas that distort the message; or use nonverbal signals that distract the receiver or contradict the verbal message.

◆ The receiver is intimidated by the position or authority of the sender. This tension may prevent the receiver from concentrating on the message effectively enough to understand it clearly. Furthermore, an intimidated receiver may be afraid to ask for clarifications because of the perceived fear that questions might be associated with incompetence.

◆ The receiver is unwilling to attempt to understand the message because the topic is perceived to be too difficult to understand. Regardless of the clarity of a message explaining procedures for operating a computer software program, a receiver terrified of computers may be incapable of decoding the message correctly.

◆ The receiver is unreceptive to new and different ideas; that is, stereotypical visions and prejudices prevent the receiver from viewing the message with an open mind.

Executives must choose the appropriate channel for sending messages. This industrial hygienist has chosen to communicate face-to-face to be certain that the chef understands this important message.

The infinite number of breakdowns possible at each stage of the communication process makes us marvel that mutually satisfying communication ever occurs. The complexity of the communication process amplifies the importance of the next stage in the communication process—feedback to clarify misunderstandings.

Communication, a seemingly simple task, is a complex process.

The Receiver Encodes a Message to Clarify Any Misunderstandings

When the receiver responds to the sender's message, the response is called *feedback*. The feedback may prompt the sender to modify or adjust the original message to make it clearer to the receiver. Feedback may be verbal or nonverbal. A remark such as "Could you clarify . . ." or a perplexed facial expression provides clear feedback to the sender that the receiver does not yet understand the message. Conversely, a confident "Yes, I understand," and an upward nod of the head are likely to signal understanding or encouragement.

Can you provide other examples of verbal and nonverbal feedback?

Interferences Hinder the Process

Senders and receivers must learn to deal with the numerous factors that interfere with the communication process. These factors are referred to as *interferences* or *barriers* to effective communication. The previous examples have illustrated some of the interferences that may occur at various stages of the communication process. For example:

◆ Differences in educational level, experience, and culture and other characteristics of the sender and the receiver increase the complexity of encoding and decoding a message.

◆ Physical interferences occurring in the channel include loud talking near an area where a supervisor is explaining a work assignment, distracting and annoying static on a telephone line, or an overly warm room used for a lengthy staff meeting. Many companies schedule officer retreats at hotels or remote lodges to eliminate physical and mental interferences such as constant interruptions and other distractions present in workday surroundings. These retreats allow employees to disconnect themselves from routine responsibilities enough to participate effectively in strategic planning sessions, leadership development, cultural awareness workshops, and other executive meetings.

◆ A supervisor too rushed or too insecure to allow subordinates to ask questions or offer suggestions (feedback) creates a formidable barrier to effective communication. This supervisor loses time and money from errors made because unclear messages are not clarified and generates negative feelings because employees perceive their opinions to be unwelcome.

Let's consider another example to illustrate the stages in the communication process. While reading the following scenario, notice that the sender and receiver function in dual roles. That is, they both serve as sender and receiver, giving and receiving feedback (encoding and decoding messages) until the original receiver understands the message.

Can you add to this list of interferences to effective communication? What suggestions can you offer for removing or minimizing each interference you listed?

What are the consequences of refusing to permit feedback when communicating with others?

An irate audit partner barges into a senior accountant's work area (located in the center of a large, open office) wildly waving a file in his hand. Not seeming to notice that several others were standing nearby and without giving a greeting, the partner rudely throws a report on the desk. He says, "Just look at this report, Jill! Haven't you read any accounting pronouncements during the last two years?"

Startled at first, Jill takes just a few seconds to gain her composure and then replies, "Obviously, Jack, you have a major concern with the Blackwell report. Could you tell me exactly what the difficulty is?"

A little calmer now, Jack answers, "I've read through this report several times, and I just don't understand. Why doesn't the report contain a disclosure of market risks as required by SFAS No. 105?"

With a quiet sigh, Jill answers, "The industry specialists in our New York office assured me that a market risk disclosure is unnecessary in this case. I included their explanation with complete documentation in a memo placed in the Blackwell audit file."

Nodding his head, the partner says, "Fine; that particular disclosure was my only concern. Prepare the report for my signature, and let's try to get it to the client by tomorrow at the latest. Good work, Jill."

The communication process model will help identify the problems that the partner and accountant dealt with to finally reach an understanding, as shown in Figure 2-2.

SOME BEHAVIORAL FACTORS IN COMMUNICATION

As long as humans are involved in communication, the process will not be perfect. Human frailties such as prejudice, ego involvement, subjectivity, and varying reactions to the environment contribute to problems of communicating. Additionally, differences between senders and receivers in vocabularies, educational and occupational backgrounds, age, appearance, cultural elements, and other factors create barriers to effective communication.

When the industrial revolution of the nineteenth century led to large-scale industries, giant companies, and labor unions, management had to be concerned about better ways to cope with these significant changes. Management theorists looked to the behavioral sciences for patterns of human social activities and guides to human behavior to provide a framework for management in the industrial age. These same patterns have proved fruitful to managers in our sophisticated high-technology environment. As we go from a manufacturing to a service and technological base, the classical foundations are modified to cope with change.

Theory of Human Communication

Behavioral scientists working in the fields of sociology and psychology have strongly influenced business management by stressing interpersonal communication problems in the business environment. Various contributions to a theory of human communication emphasize that difficulties lie

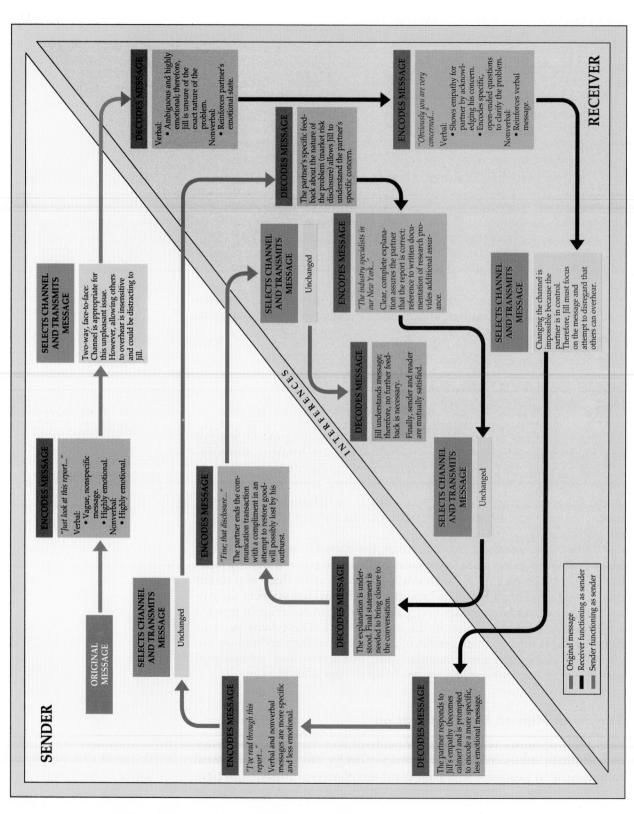

FIGURE 2-2 The communication process model in action

not so much with what we say or write but with what goes on in our minds and in the minds of those with whom we are communicating. Thus, the tasks in communication can be viewed as bridging the gap between one mind and another primarily by the use of words. Specifically, the theory of human communication stresses the importance of such factors as social situation, role, status, rules, and instructions in understanding social action and personal intent.

A *social situation* is established when people enter into a communication exchange and their behavior is organized around a common task. Participants assume individual *roles* that arise from their parts in the activity. They also have *status,* which is their position based on the "organizational chart" or other prescribed functions. Role is an informal part; status is a formal position. College seniors assume authoritative roles; freshmen play submissive roles. The administrative assistant to an executive, because of position in the executive office, may play a role considerably more authoritative and powerful than the position in the organizational structure might suggest.

Are role and status always equal for a person?

Within the business world, of course, such symbols (status symbols) as job titles, uniforms, office decor, and support staff help us identify status. Actions, time with the firm, work habits, and proximity to authority lead to roles higher than status. Good communicators can differentiate role and status.

All games are played by *rules*. In business, the unwritten rules come from the internal system and maintenance activity. Written rules are formal company policies and procedures. The rules help determine who may talk with whom, what or what not to say, how long a session may last, and how to present a message. As people live and work, they learn the rules of the game, as they must, to create places for themselves. *Instructions* assist receivers in understanding message meaning and intent. Nonverbal signs such as facial expressions, body movement, perspiration, and posture give clues about the sender's feelings and intentions.

Does your campus have any unwritten rules?

Human Needs

Psychologist Abraham Maslow developed the concept of hierarchy of needs through which people progress, as shown in Figure 2-3. In our society, most people have reasonably satisfied their lower-level physiological needs and security and safety needs. Beyond these two basic need levels, people progress to satisfy the three upper levels: social, ego, and self-actualizing needs.

As people satisfy needs at one level, they move on to the next. The levels that have been satisfied still are present, but their importance diminishes.

Effective communicators are able to identify and appeal to need levels in various individuals or groups. Advertising is designed to appeal to need levels. Luxury-car ads appeal to ego needs, breath freshener ads ap-

When a need level is satisfied, does it go away?

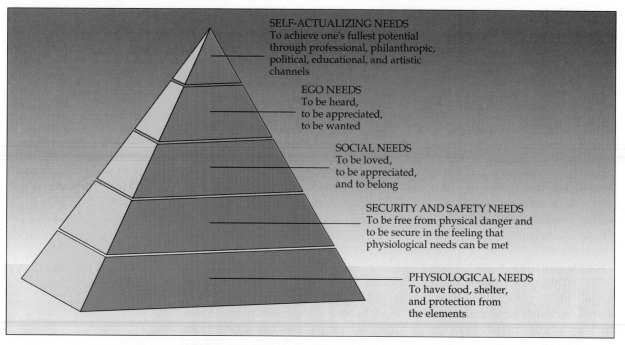

FIGURE 2-3   Maslow's hierarchy of needs

peal to social needs, and fire alarm ads appeal to security and safety needs. In business, efforts to help people satisfy needs are essential. A satisfied worker is generally more productive than a dissatisfied one.

Management Styles

Douglas McGregor, a management theorist, attempted to distinguish between the older, traditional view that workers are concerned only about satisfying lower-level needs and the modern view that production can be enhanced by assisting workers in satisfying higher-level needs.

Theory Y is people oriented.
Under the older view, management exercised strong control, emphasized the job to the exclusion of concern for the individual, and sought to motivate solely through external incentives—a job and a paycheck. McGregor labeled this management style Theory X. Under the modern style, Theory Y, management strives to balance control and individual freedom. By treating the individual as a mature person, management lessens the need for external motivation: treated as adults, people will act as adults. Combining Maslow's and McGregor's ideas leads to the conclusion that "the right job for the person" is a better philosophy than "the right person for the job."

Recent efforts to develop greater job satisfaction have involved workers in "team" and "quality circle" programs. Rather than relying on single-task, production-line approaches, the "team," as used in some automobile and other heavy-manufacturing industries, builds the product from beginning to end. Each team member is capable of performing most of the production jobs.

"Quality circles" are voluntary groups of workers who meet with supervisors or management periodically to identify production problems and propose solutions. The external motivation characteristic of McGregor's Theory X is replaced by intrinsic motivation provided by involvement, cooperation, and opportunities to be heard and appreciated.

One-to-One Communication

Several years ago, transactional analysis was developed and often practiced as a means of analyzing behavior patterns in interpersonal relationships. One of the most important contributions of transactional analysis is the concept of *stroking*.

Research indicates that babies left unattended or ignored for extended periods can develop physical as well as psychological problems. Babies require coddling, patting, and loving; in transactional analysis terms, these actions are called stroking. Adults also require stroking for mental health—but of a different sort. Saying "Good morning" to another person is a stroke. The reply, "Same to you," is another stroke. Although this exchange may seem incidental and unimportant, imagine the reactions if the two were friends and no exchange took place.

Stroking applies human relations principles.

Getting a pat on the back from the supervisor, receiving a congratulatory phone call or letter, and taking the time to listen to another person are examples of everyday stroking. By paying attention to the importance of strokes, managers can greatly improve communication and people's feelings about their work.

People engage in communication with others in the hope that the outcome may lead to mutual trust, mutual pleasure, and psychological well-being. The communication transaction is a means of sharing information about things, ideas, tasks, and selves.

When two strangers first meet, their knowledge about each other might be nil. Assume, for example, that two employees meet at the vending machine in the company break room. After an introduction—"Hello, I'm John Robbins"; "Hello, I'm Susan Smith"—they know something about each other, if only the other's name and gender. They probably also gain an impression about the other person through appearance and dress. At this point, they know only superficial things about each other.

As the transaction continues, the two learn more and more about each other. Susan soon learns that John is the recently hired human resources manager. She says, "Yes, I'd heard that you were joining the company. Welcome aboard. I'm a data-entry operator in inventory control." John continues, "I'm glad to know you, Susan. If you have a couple of minutes, could you tell how you feel about the current flexible scheduling? Do you have any suggestions for making it work better?" As a result of this exchange, Robbins learns a little more about Smith—her knowledge and commitment to the company—as well as valuable information about a company procedure. Susan has learned that management cares about her opinion of a work-related issue. This casual interaction becomes a definite stroke that is likely to enhance Susan's feelings about her work.

As the relationship between John and Susan develops, they continue to learn more about each other. Their behavior leads to trust, and this trust leads to freer conversation.

Johari Window

The nature of sharing is that people learn not only about others but also about themselves. The Johari Window, shown in Figure 2-4 (named for its creators, *Jo*seph and *Harri*ngton), illustrates this concept. The upper left-

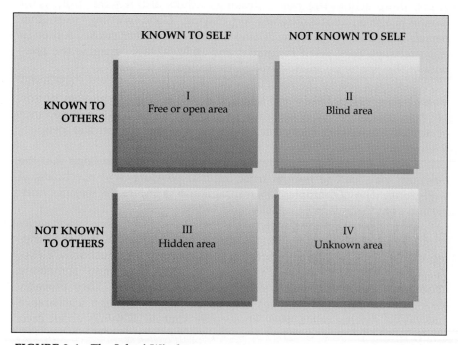

FIGURE 2-4 The Johari Window

hand area, labeled "I," or "free area," represents what we know about ourselves and what others know about us. Area II, the blind area, designates those things others know about us but that we don't know about ourselves; for example, you are the only person who can't see yourself as you really are. Things we know about ourselves but that others don't know about us occupy the hidden or secret area, III. Area IV includes the unknown: things we don't know about ourselves and others don't know about us.

Each of these areas may vary in size according to the degree that we can learn about ourselves from others and to the degree that we are willing to disclose things about ourselves to others. Only through reciprocal sharing can people learn about themselves and about others. In communication practice, such sharing occurs only when people develop *trust* in each other. Trust is something that must be earned. We are usually willing to tell people about our school records, our jobs, and other things that aren't truly personal. But we share personal thoughts, ambitions, and inner feelings only with selected others—those whom we have learned to trust. Trust is a quality we develop from experience with others. Through performance, we earn the trust of others. The relationships existing between supervisor and employee, doctor and patient, and lawyer and client are those of trust, but only in specific areas. In more intimate relationships—wife and husband, brother and sister, parent and child—deeper, personal feelings are entrusted to each other. When a confidant demonstrates that he or she can be trusted, trust is reinforced and leads to an expansion of the open area of the Johari Window. In business, the supervisor-employee relationship is often strengthened to the point where nonwork elements can be discussed freely.

The idea that trust and openness lead to better communication between two people also applies to groups. People engaged in organizational development (OD) are concerned with building large organizations by building effective small groups. They believe effectiveness in small groups evolves mostly from a high level of mutual trust among group members. The aim of OD is to open emotional as well as task-oriented communication. To accomplish this aim, groups often become involved in encounter sessions designed to enlarge the open areas of the Johari Window.

Everyone has hidden area items. What are yours?

Good friends listen; listeners become good friends.

WORD AND NONWORD MESSAGES

Although most concern in communication study is given to verbal messages, nonword messages and meanings other than those expressed in words are all around and bombard us regularly.

Intrapersonal Communication and Decoding

In the discussion of human communication theory, we mentioned the need to be sensitive to nonverbal elements of communication. Nonverbal communication includes any communication occurring without the use of words. Gestures, body motions, clothing, grooming, uniforms, aromas, facial expressions, and hundreds of other factors bring messages to people from all angles at any time. What we do with this bombardment of messages depends very much on our past experiences and our perceptions of ourselves and of the world around us. Probably no two people are identical in these respects.

Intrapersonal communication is perhaps the purest and most basic form of communication. The role we play in communicating with others depends on how we communicate with ourselves. We process incoming messages—received by our eyes, ears, skin, nose, or tasting organs—by selecting, evaluating, and interpreting them in terms of previous experiences. Additionally, we generate messages internally, either physically or psychologically. We process those messages in the same way we process messages arising from external stimuli.

As you study communication, consider how you perceive yourself in various situations. Do you see yourself the same way in all situations? Or do you perceive yourself a little differently in your various roles as student, friend, citizen, employee, brother or sister, son or daughter, or parent? Self-concepts are composed of all the things we know about ourselves either consciously or subconsciously. We each have a physical perception of ourselves—how we look to others; how we walk, smell, sound; and how we perform in physical activities.

We also have perceptions about ourselves as social creatures. We have ideas about how we appeal to others, how we interact socially, how we handle emotions, and how we communicate in large or small groups. And certainly we have perceptions about our intellectual selves: how we study, how we fare in terms of grades, and how deeply we become interested in intellectual things.

The simple schematic of the communication process presented earlier in this chapter becomes inadequate when we complicate the process by introducing the concept that each human will process incoming messages in different ways depending on previous experiences and self-perceptions.

Messages Without Words

A *metacommunication* is a message that, although *not* expressed in words, accompanies a message that *is* expressed in words. For example, "Don't be late for work" gives that admonition (communication); yet the sentence may imply (but not express in words) such additional ideas as "You are frequently late, and I'm warning you," or "I doubt your dependabil-

---

How do you react when a police car follows yours?

How do others perceive you? Is that your own perception?

ity" (metacommunications). "Your solution is perfect" may also convey a metacommunication such as "You are efficient," or "I certainly like your work." Whether we are speaking or writing, we can be confident that those who receive our messages will be sensitive to the messages expressed in words and to the accompanying messages that are present but not expressed in words.

A *kinesic* communication is an idea expressed through nonverbal behavior. Messages can be conveyed through winks, smiles, frowns, sighs, attire, grooming, and all sorts of body movements. The science of kinesics seeks to gain knowledge about the impact of body movements on communication. Some examples of kinesic messages follow:

Action	*Possible Kinesic Message*
A wink or light chuckle follows a statement.	"Don't believe what I just said."
A manager is habitually late for staff meetings.	"My time is more important than yours. You can wait for me."
A supervisor lightly links his arm around an employee's shoulders at the end of a formal disciplinary conference.	"Everything is fine; I'm here to help you solve this problem." Alternatively, the action may be considered paternalistic—a parent comforting a child after necessary discipline.
An employee smokes in areas other than those designated for smoking.	"I don't have to obey company rules that infringe on my personal rights. A little smoke won't hurt anyone."
A job applicant submits a resume containing numerous spelling and grammatical errors.	"My spelling and grammar skills are deficient." An alternative meaning is "For you I didn't care to do my very best."
The supervisor looks up but then returns her attention to her current project when an employee arrives for a performance appraisal interview.	"The performance appraisal interview is not an important process. You are interrupting more important work."
A group leader sits at a position other than at the head of the table.	"I want to demonstrate my equality with other members."

Kinesic communications and metacommunications have characteristics that all communicators should take into account:

1. *Unworded messages cannot be avoided.* Both written and spoken words convey ideas in addition to the ideas contained in the words used. All

Would a refusal to answer a question be classfied as a kinesic communication?

COMMUNICATION MENTOR

Whether you are the sender or receiver, one skill will help you more than any other. Unfortunately, this skill only comes from experience. We're talking about developing an "ear" for nuance. Most of us say as much indirectly—through inflection, pauses, accelerations, and volume changes—as we do directly.

Learning from these subtle suggestions is not analytical detective work though; it's making the extra effort to mentally lean into what the other person is saying or asking and truly participating in the feeling being expressed. That means blocking out your own agenda for the time being. You will learn more from this skill than you will ever learn from so-called "body language."

James F. Hurley
Senior Vice President
CalFed Inc.

---

actions—and even the lack of action—have meaning to those who observe them.

2. *Unworded messages may have different meanings for different people.* If a committee member smiles after making a statement, one member may conclude that the speaker was trying to be funny; another may conclude that the speaker was pleased about having made such a great contribution; another may see the smile but have no reaction to it.

3. *Unworded messages may be intentional or unintentional.* "You are right about that" may be intended to mean "I agree with you" or "You are right on *this* issue, but you have been wrong on all others discussed." The sender may or may not intend to convey the latter and may or may not be aware of doing so.

What unworded messages might accompany "Drive carefully"?

4. *Unworded messages may get more attention than worded messages.* If a supervisor rhythmically taps a pen while making a statement, the words may not register in the mind of the employee. An error in basic grammar may get much more attention than does the idea that is being transmitted.

5. *Unworded messages provide clues about the sender's background and motives.* For example, excessive use of big words may suggest that a person reads widely or has an above-average education; it may also suggest a need for social recognition or insecurity about social background.

6. *Unworded messages are influenced by the circumstances surrounding the communication.* Assume that two men (Ward and Sam) are friends who work for the same firm. When they are together on the job, Ward

sometimes puts his hand on Sam's shoulder. To Sam, the act may mean nothing more than "We are close friends." But Ward becomes a member of a committee that subsequently denies a promotion for Sam. Afterward, the same act could mean "we are still friends"; but it could also arouse resentment. Because of the circumstances, the same act could now mean something like "Watch the hand that pats; it can also stab."

7. *Unworded messages can actually contradict the accompanying worded message.* "We appreciate your writing to us when you have a problem" may be taken to mean the opposite when nothing has been done to solve the problem or to explain the lack of action. When actions and words appear to be in conflict, receivers place more confidence in the message communicated by action. And keep in mind that when police discover that a suspect's words and actions are incongruent, their suspicion about the suspect becomes stronger.

8. *Unworded messages may be beneficial or harmful.* Words or actions can be accompanied by unworded messages that help or hurt the sender's purpose. Metacommunications and kinesic communications can convey something like "I am efficient in my business and considerate of others," or they can convey the opposite. They cannot be eliminated, but they can be made to work for communicators instead of against them.

Although no one can give a set of rules for interpreting unworded messages, awareness of their presence and impact will improve chances of choosing correct words and encoding messages effectively.

COMMUNICATION MENTOR

Frequently the unintended misuse of a word, the inflection of a word, or a gesture can lead to misinterpretation. This can happen to even the most effective communicators. Eliciting feedback from an individual or an audience will ensure that the words you intend to communicate are being heard.

Trying to read between the lines is something akin to chasing a shadow: you know it is there, but you'll never be able to grasp it. Accept what people say on the surface. If you are unsure of their message, ask them to repeat it in different words so that you can be sure of their intent.

Terence E. McSweeney
Director of Communications
PGA of America

LISTENING AS AN INTERPERSONAL SKILL

Want to get a job? Want to keep a job? Want to get promoted? If so, become a good listener! Good listening habits pay off in several ways:

Listening is an example of stroking.

1. Good listeners are liked by others because they satisfy the basic human needs of being heard and being wanted.
2. Job performance is improved when downward oral messages are received and understood.
3. Accurate feedback from subordinates provides evidence of job performance.
4. Both superiors and subordinates may acquire greater job security from fewer mistakes or ignored messages.
5. People who listen well are able to separate fact from fiction, to cope effectively with false persuasion, and to avoid having others use them for personal gain. In other words, good listeners don't "get taken" very often.
6. Listening opens doors for ideas and thus encourages creativity.
7. Effective listeners are constantly learning—gaining knowledge and skills that lead to increased job performance, advancement, and increased job satisfaction.
8. Job satisfaction increases when people know what is going on, when they are heard, and when they participate in the mutual trust that develops from good communication.

As a skill, listening depends on our abilities to receive and decode both worded and unworded messages. The best-devised messages and sophisticated communication systems will not work unless people on the receiving end of oral messages actually listen. Senders of oral messages must assume their receivers can and will listen, just as senders of written messages must assume their receivers can and will read.

Can you detect when another is not listening?

Most managers spend a major part of their day listening and speaking with subordinates, superiors, customers, and a variety of business or industry colleagues and associates. In business, government, and education, listening is a part of face-to-face communication. It constitutes an interpersonal skill as critical as the skill of speaking.

Keep in mind, however, that the need for listening occurs in two types of situations: (1) face-to-face situations of an interview nature and (2) formal situations in which an audience listens to a speaker. One is intimate, the other impersonal.

In interview situations, for example, while I am speaking, you supposedly are listening. As the listener, you interpret my message and plan what you will say next. I watch you for some form of feedback and, if necessary, adjust my message. This interaction typifies the classic communication process pictured in Figure 2-1.

In the formal, speech–listening situation, the speaker intends to provide the audience with information in such a way that listeners will accept the message and perhaps act in a way the speaker intended. Speech listening differs from face-to-face interview listening primarily in the limited opportunity for the speech maker and the audience to provide and respond to feedback. Formal speakers obtain broad but limited feedback from audiences, which may enable speakers to adapt their messages to the feedback. At the same time, the audience receives little speaker feedback short of interrupting the speech for clarification.

We engage in formal listening to varying degrees when listening to a speech, sermon, or lecture. We engage in interview-type listening when we are in face-to-face, two-person situations or in small group discussion. For many people, face-to-face meetings consume most of their working time.

What kinds of feedback occur during speeches?

BAD LISTENING HABITS AND PRACTICES

Physicians can't cure people of ailments unless their diagnoses reveal the nature of the ailment. In the same way, you can't improve your listening unless you understand some of the nonphysical ailments of your own listening. One way to begin is to examine a few common listener ailments, to identify those that may affect your own listening, and to work on cures for them. Most of us have developed bad listening habits in one or more of the following areas.

Do any of the following habits apply to you?

◆ *Faking attention.* Have you ever had an instructor call on you to respond to a question in class only to find you weren't listening? Have you ever had a parent, friend, or fellow worker ask you a question and find you weren't listening? Have you ever left a classroom lecture and later realized that you had no idea what went on? Have you ever been introduced to someone only to find that thirty seconds later you missed the name?

If you had to answer "yes" to any of these questions, join the huge club of "fakers of attention." This club is rather large because almost all people belong. Isn't it wonderful that we can look directly at a person, nod, smile, and pretend to be listening? We even fake giving feedback.

◆ *Welcoming disruptions.* Listening properly requires both physical and emotional effort. As a result, we welcome disruptions of almost any sort when we are engaged in somewhat difficult listening. The next time someone enters your classroom or meeting room during a lecture, notice how almost everyone in the room turns away from the speaker and the topic to observe the latecomer. Yielding to such disruptions begins early in life. Perhaps it is a form of curiosity.

Watch for this event to happen soon.

◆ *Overlistening.* Overlistening occurs when listeners attempt to record in writing or in memory so many details that they miss the speaker's major points. Overlisteners "can't see the forest for the trees." Typical of this type of bad listening habit is the old story about the college freshmen who, on the first day of class when the professor begins with, "Good morning," put it in their notes.

◆ *Stereotyping.* Most people use their prejudices and perceptions of others as a basis for developing stereotypes. As a result, we make spontaneous judgments about others based on their appearances, mannerisms, dress, speech delivery, and whatever other criteria play a role in our judgments. If a speaker doesn't come up to our standards in any of these areas, we simply turn off our listening and assume the speaker can't have much to say.

◆ *Dismissing subjects as uninteresting.* People tend to use "uninteresting" as a rationale for not listening. Unfortunately, the decision is usually made before the topic is ever introduced. A good way to lose a teacher's respect is to ask, "Are we going to have anything important in class today?" if you have to (or want to) miss that day's class. Lord Chesterton once said we have no such thing as an uninteresting subject, only disinterested listeners.

◆ *Failing to observe nonverbal aids.* Good listening requires use of eyes as well as ears. To listen effectively you must observe the speaker. Facial expressions and body motions always accompany speech and contribute much to messages. Unless you watch the speaker, you may miss the meaning.

In addition to recognizing bad listening habits and the variety of barriers to effective listening, you should also recognize that listening isn't easy. Many bad listening habits develop simply because the speed of spoken messages is far slower than our ability to receive and process them. Normal speaking speeds are between 100 and 150 words a minute. The human ear can actually distinguish words in speech in excess of 500 words a minute, and many people read at speeds well beyond 500 words a minute. Finally, our minds process thoughts at thousands of words a minute.

Because we can't speak fast enough to challenge human listening equipment, listeners have the primary responsibility for making oral communication effective. We do seem to listen to gifted speakers, but they are rare. In our everyday activities, good listening requires considerable mental and emotional effort. Note the barriers that create communication problems between speakers and listeners, as shown in Figure 2-5.

Study carefully the barriers listed in Figure 2-5, and compile a list of other barriers that affect your ability to communicate with friends, teachers, coworkers, supervisors, and others. By being aware of these interferences, you can make concentrated efforts to remove these interferences whenever possible.

Can you think of any occupational stereotypes?

Why is watching the speaker important?

Most people run out of breath at 200 to 250 words a minute.

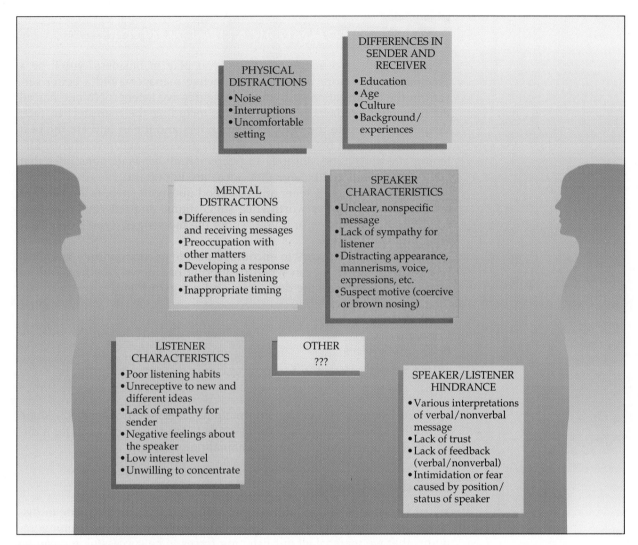

FIGURE 2-5 Communication barriers

LISTENING FOR POSITIVE RESULTS

Listening involves much more than hearing or receiving. Once received, the message must be interpreted. Interpretation is a mental, not a physical, process. A final step is for the receiver to determine what action should be taken. The message might be stored for later use, as is done with educationally learned material; or it might be dismissed, as is often done with insignificant messages.

Casual chitchat usually goes unstored.

COMMUNICATION MENTOR

No matter what role you play in business, you'll be a more valuable and effective manager—and a better servant to the organization— if you're an aggressive listener. No one has all the answers in today's business world, including the manager. In fact, the people closest to the work usually understand it best and are the best sources of ideas on how to improve work processes and procedures. Listening attentively and sincerely to people on all levels demonstrates that you respect them and believe their ideas are important.

If you're a good listener and ask good questions, people are likely to tell you the truth, offer worthwhile suggestions, and tell you what they need. If you don't listen or if you "shoot the messenger," you'll only hear what you want to hear.

One of the best ways to encourage people to communicate openly is to give them strokes, even when they bring bad news. The best way to give strokes is to keep the door open and not get upset.

Hugh B. Jacks
President
BellSouth Services

We listen to (1) receive information, (2) solve problems, (3) share with others, and (4) persuade or dissuade. Each reason may call for a different style of listening or for a combination of styles.

Intensive Listening

When we listen to obtain information, solve problems, or persuade or dissuade (as in arguments), we listen intensively. Intensive listening requires that we marshal all our listening forces to be successful and can be achieved by following some of these suggestions:

1. Try to become involved in the material by making written or mental notes.
2. Attempt to predict or anticipate the speaker's future points.
3. Watch speakers for any nonverbal clues that will help you understand the speaker's point of view and emotional state.
4. Provide listener feedback either orally or through nonverbal nods, facial expressions, or body movements to encourage further speaker comments and behavior adjustment.
5. Try to avoid yielding to your stereotypes, personal judgments, and distractions.

Involvement improves listening.

Casual Listening

Listening for pleasure, recreation, amusement, and relaxation is casual listening. Some people have the radio on all day long; it provides background music and talk during daily routines and work periods, just as the car radio provides "companionship" for most commuters. Casual listening provides relaxing "breaks" from more serious tasks and supports our emotional health.

An interesting concept about all listening, but particularly true of casual listening, is that people are selective listeners. We listen to what we want. In a crowded room in which everyone seems to be talking, you can block out all the noise and engage in the conversation you are having with someone. Casual listening doesn't require much emotional or physical effort, which is one of the reasons people engage in small talk.

Listening for Feelings with Empathy

Empathy occurs when a person attempts to share another's feelings or emotions. Counselors attempt to use empathetic listening in dealing with their clients. Good friends often provide empathetic listening for each other. Empathy is a valuable trait developed by people who are skilled in interpersonal relations. The interesting thing about empathetic listening is that it more often than not results in reciprocal listening. When we take the time to listen to another, the courtesy is generally returned. Empathy leads to sharing.

Empathetic listening is strong stroking.

Many people in positions of authority have developed excellent listening skills that apply to gaining information and to problem solving. However, just as many people have failed to develop good listening practices that work effectively in listening for feelings. For example, a meeting between a supervisor and an employee might go something like this:

> "Linda, I really need to talk to you about something important."
>
> "That so, Maria? Well, take a seat and let me hear about it," the supervisor says in a friendly tone as she continues to stare in a perplexed way at a stack of papers on her desk.
>
> As Maria takes a seat, Linda continues, "Maria, you think you have a problem, eh? How would you like to have the ones I'm faced with now? First, I'm right in the middle of union negotiations for the new three-year contract, I've had several problems with our supervisory crew in the Midland plant, and somebody has botched up our inventory procedure so we're running short and will have to back-order with several customers."
>
> Finally Linda asks hastily, "Well, what's your problem, Maria?"

Intimidated by her supervisor's preoccupation with her own problems and her abrupt manner, Maria decides today is not an appropriate time to get any assistance. To end the conversation without looking foolish, she quickly decides to ask a few questions about a routine procedure.

Before Maria has a chance to speak, however, the supervisor suddenly signals the end of the discussion by saying, "Maria, I have another appointment now. If you'd like, we can continue our discussion later. I want to be of help, and my door is always open to you." She returns her attention to her work before Maria moves from her chair.

Maria leaves completely frustrated, her problem still on her mind and unresolved.

Because of the supervisor's poor listening habits, Maria probably feels worse after the meeting than she did before. The supervisor learned nothing from the exchange. What if Maria's problem were company related? Good listening might have resulted in information helpful to solving the supervisor's own problems.

Empathy and listening skills are major components of communication. For good interpersonal communication, try to understand the speaker's point of view, listen without interrupting, show interest in the speaker's comments, and provide feedback.

What specific effective listening techniques did the supervisor violate? First, the supervisor was too preoccupied with her own problems to take the time to listen for Maria's message—not to mention her feelings. Talking too much and giving strong nonverbal signals that she was not interested in what Maria had to say destroyed Maria's desire to talk. Despite the rough beginning, a gentle, empathetic, open-ended question might have encouraged Maria to share her information. Instead, the abrupt, emotion-laden question ("Well, what's your problem?") resembled a drilling question-and-answer session. (Remember, Maria did not use the word "problem" in her initial approach.)

Total empathy can never be achieved simply because no two people are exactly alike, and one can never really become the other person. The more similar our experiences, however, the better our opportunity to put ourselves in the other person's shoes. If two people have been skydiving, for example, one can appreciate how the other felt the first time. Listening with empathy involves some genuine tact along with other good listening habits. Remember that listening for feelings normally takes place in a one-to-one situation. Close friends who trust each other tend to engage in self-disclosure easily. Empathetic listening is enhanced when the participants exhibit trust and friendship. Here are some suggestions:

Why can't perfect empathy be achieved?

1. *Get in step with the speaker.* Try to understand the speaker's background, prejudices, and points of view. Listen for emotionally charged words and watch for body language as clues to the speaker's underlying feelings.
2. *Do not interrupt the speaker.* Try to understand the speaker's full meaning, and wait patiently for an indication that you should enter the conversation. In addition, minimize environmental and mental distractions that serve as barriers to effective listening. For example, a supervisor's closing the office door to reduce distracting noise and refusing to accept phone calls during a performance appraisal interview enable the speaker and listener to concentrate more fully on the message.
3. *Let the speaker know you are interested in listening and are an active partner in the exchange of information.* Show genuine interest by remaining physically and mentally involved; for example, avoid daydreaming, yawning, frequently breaking eye contact, looking at your watch or papers on your desk, whispering to a person nearby, and allowing numerous interruptions (phone calls or others breaking in to ask questions). Praise the speaker for his or her willingness to share information. As a result, you can realistically expect to receive additional information from this individual. Supervisors who show genuine interest will find that they receive valuable feedback from employees. In addition, the open, trusting work environment increases employee morale and productivity.

How can you let a speaker know you are listening and are involved?

4. *Encourage the speaker to continue by providing appropriate, supportive feedback.* Develop your own encouraging signs such as a nod of the head, a throat-clearing sound, a smile, and even an encouraging grunt.

5. *Take advantage of your opportunity to speak to evaluate your understanding of the message and the speaker's feelings.* One way to check your level of understanding is to make reflective statements—an important part of active listening. You simply restate in your own words what you think the other person has said. This paraphrasing will reinforce what you have heard and allow the speaker to correct any misunderstanding. For example, when Neil says, "I really dislike the new production supervisor," an empathetic coworker might summarize or reflect Neil's message by saying, "You think he isn't a nice person?" Then Neil might say, "Oh, I don't dislike him as a person; but a supervisor, he's not. He's quite good at giving out instructions; the problem is he never stops long enough to find out whether I understand anything he's said. Then he's furious when the job isn't done correctly the first time."

   The reflective statement confirms that the listener has understood the message correctly. The statement also elicits a response that helps reveal the true source of the problem: frustration that the supervisor's communication style does not allow for feedback.

6. *Use probing prompts to encourage the speaker to discuss a particular aspect of the message more thoroughly.* These prompts (statements or questions) help speakers define their problems more concretely and specifically. In the previous example of the disgruntled employee, the coworker might say, "I realize that you aren't getting along with the new production supervisor, but I'm not entirely sure what he does that makes you so irritated." Like the reflective statement used previously, this probing prompt summarizes Neil's message, but it also encourages him to explore his feelings and to identify the true source of the problem—inadequate feedback.

Frequently you may have to combine listening intensively and listening for feelings. Performance appraisal interviews, disciplinary conferences, and other sensitive discussions between supervisors and employees require listening intensively for accurate understanding of the message and listening empathetically for feelings, preconceived points of view, and background. The interviewing process also may combine the two types of listening. Job interviewers must try to determine how someone's personality, as well as skill and knowledge, will affect job performance.

Listening for Information

Listening for information should be restricted to the search for data or material. In the classroom, for example, the instructor usually has a strategy for guiding the class to desired goals. The instructor will probably

---

Reflective statements summarize or "reflect" the speaker's message. Why are they an important part of effective listening?

Provide another example of an effective probing prompt.

Effective listening habits build goodwill.

stress several major points and use supporting evidence to prove or to reinforce them. When engaged in this type of listening, you could become so engrossed with recording every detail that you take copious notes without using an outline. The end result is a set of detailed notes without any organization.

Understand the outlining process. When you take notes, use a logical system such as the roman-numeral outline that uses I-A-1-a schemes to carry an outline to four levels (one major item with three degrees of subitems). If you find yourself with a lot of information beyond I-A levels, you are probably making notes of detailed information that is not essential to your success in the course.

In the process of listening for information, watch the speaker. Most speakers have developed a set of mannerisms composed of gestures and vocal inflections to indicate the degree of importance or seriousness they attach to portions of their presentation. Above all else, listening for information requires that listeners be able to separate fact from fiction, comedy from seriousness, and truth from untruth.

> **Listen for principles and methods—not minor details.**

Listening for Problem Solving

Unlike listening for information, problem-solving listening involves greater use of your analytical ability to proceed through problem-solving steps. You should have an understanding of the problem, recognize whatever limitations are involved, and know the implications of possible solutions. Watching some talented top executives in situations calling for problem-solving listening reveals some interesting methods and approaches to this kind of listening.

Many "great minds" are doodlers.

1. A pen or pencil often becomes an ally in the analytical process. Jot down items that should be introduced as feedback to the speaker.
2. Doodling can help you assemble your ideas for drawing a meaningful solution to the problem.
3. Listen with the speaker, but try to think ahead at times, as well. Thinking ahead can help you develop a sense of the speaker's logic.
4. Become a good summarizer. When your turn comes to respond, trace the development of the discussion and then take off from there with your own analysis.
5. Don't be hesitant about "tailgating" on the ideas of others. Creative ideas are generated in an open discussion related to problem solving.

Creativity results from good listening habits applied in a free-wheeling discussion. Most of our ideas emanate from external stimuli rather than silent introspection. When we listen effectively, we increase our capacity to create.

SUGGESTIONS FOR EFFECTIVE LISTENING

From the communication process, we know that the availability of feedback and the opportunity to observe the nonverbal signs that accompany worded messages are the critical factors in effective communication. Face-to-face, interpersonal communication is the most effective level of communication because both factors are present. A telephone conversation, providing for instant feedback but no nonverbal signs, is the second level of effectiveness. The least effective level, the written message, provides for neither instant feedback nor nonverbal signs. Because it is the least effective level and is used so widely and so frequently, written communication receives major attention in the study of business communication.

The two critical factors in face-to-face communication are feedback and nonverbal signs.

Because of the availability of both feedback and nonverbal signs, you can enhance the effectiveness of your face-to-face listening by following these suggestions:

1. *Watch the speaker.* Gestures, facial expressions, and eye movements can add much to the words used and the meaning intended. If the speaker can't look you in the eye, the sincerity of the remarks may be questioned. Of course, the opposite is probably true: firm eye contact may indicate added sincerity or firmness.
2. *Provide feedback.* You can acknowledge understanding, agreement, disagreement, and a variety of other feedback responses through facial

expressions, sounds, and gestures. This feedback allows the speaker to provide whatever restatement or added information may be necessary or continue with the discussion.

3. *Take the time to listen.* Because people in a face-to-face communication are serving as senders and receivers simultaneously, they may become so preoccupied with thoughts about what to say that they fail to listen.

4. *Use your knowledge of speakers to advantage.* In most jobs, face-to-face oral communication occurs between people who already know each other. Through experience, you will begin to recognize others' speaking and organizing traits. Some people simply seem to run on and on with details before making their point. Ask them what they had for dinner, and in reply you'll probably be given recipes for each item and a description of the dining room's decor. With this type of speaker, you'll learn to anticipate the major point but not pay much attention to the details. Other speakers give conclusions first and perhaps omit support for them. In this case, you'll learn to ask feedback questions to obtain further information.

Use feedback to get the meaning.

SUMMARY

People engaged in communication encode and decode messages while simultaneously serving as both senders and receivers. In the communication process, feedback helps people resolve possible misunderstandings and thus improve communication effectiveness. Feedback and the opportunity to observe nonverbal signs are always present in face-to-face communication, the most effective communication level.

From the behavioral sciences and the work of several pioneering management theorists, we know that people

1. Want to be heard, appreciated, and wanted.
2. Like to be treated as adults and to know that their ideas and suggestions have been considered.
3. Require "stroking" for their personal well-being.
4. Process messages based on their own experiences and not necessarily the way others might anticipate.

Listening, the most used communication skill, is crucial in interpersonal communication. Additionally, the quality of listening affects organizational communication, helps determine success in education and in careers, and provides evidence of listener empathy. Perhaps the most important suggestion for developing good listening habits is to *take the time to listen.* Good listening methods will then become habit, and you will find them of great value in job interviews, which we discuss in Chapter 14.

REVIEW QUESTIONS

1. What percentage of a manager's time is spent communicating? Give examples of the types of communications managers complete.
2. Explain the five stages in the communication process.
3. Explain the following terms and their relationship to the communication process: (a) sender, (b) encode, (c) channel, (d) receiver, (e) decode, (f) feedback, and (g) interferences or barriers.
4. Distinguish between the two primary components of a message.
5. What are the three channels typically used to transmit messages? Provide several examples of each channel.
6. What types of differences between sender and receiver create barriers to communication?
7. How does *role* differ from *status*?
8. Is a security officer's uniform a status symbol? What quality or qualities does it add to the officer's messages?
9. What is the relationship between written and unwritten rules in business communication and between the external and internal systems in organizations?
10. School clubs, groups, and societies help people satisfy which of Maslow's need levels?
11. What is meant by "stroking"?
12. What are three reasons people engage in one-to-one communication?
13. The willingness of a person to self-disclose depends on what factor in a relationship?
14. When a manager says to the sales staff, "Let's try to make budget this year," what are some of the possible metacommunications?
15. What are some payoffs of effective listening on the job?
16. What is a primary cause of bad listening habits?
17. What is meant by "people listen selectively"?
18. Good listening for feelings depends on what listener trait?
19. How does "overlistening" occur?
20. Why is face-to-face communication more effective than telephone communication? Than written communication?

EXERCISES

1. In groups of three, develop a list of 12 to 15 annoying habits of yours or of others that create barriers to effective communication. Be prepared to present the list to the class.
2. In groups assigned by your instructor, use the chart on page 55 to develop a list of possible interferences (barriers) that may occur at each stage of the communication process. You may refer to the list of annoying habits generated in Exercise 1.
3. Refer to the conversation (communication transaction) between the supervisor and employee in the cartoon on page 51. Analyze the effectiveness of this conversation using the communication process

Stage of Communication Process	Interference	Suggestion for Improvement
Encoding	_____	_____
Channel	_____	_____
Decoding	_____	_____
Feedback	_____	_____

model; use Figure 2-1 as a guide. Identify problems (interferences or barriers) occurring at each stage of the communication process and provide suggestions for improvement. Be prepared to discuss your analysis with the class or in small groups assigned by your instructor.

4. Recall a recent conversation that you have had with a friend, teacher, coworker, supervisor, or some other person. Write a brief scenario including the dialogue and a description of the nonverbal messages transmitted between the sender and receiver. Analyze the effectiveness of this conversation using the communication process model; use Figure 2-1 as a guide. Identify problems (interferences or barriers) occurring at each stage of the communication process and provide suggestions for improvement. Be prepared to discuss your analysis with the class or in small groups assigned by your instructor.

5. List the strokes you receive and give in the next 24 hours. What was the apparent motive of each? How did the receiver react? Did the closeness of the relationship (relative, friend, stranger) affect the way the stroke was received? Did the exchange affect the relationship? Explain.

6. Discuss how a supervisor's understanding of the Johari Window could increase the effectiveness of performance appraisal interviews, disciplinary actions, and other difficult discussions with employees.

7. Compile a list of situations during the next two days that illustrate the influence of metacommunication on the understanding of a message. Use the eight characteristics of unworded messages to describe specifically the overall effect of the metacommunication on the communication process.

8. Prepare a record of your listening, speaking, reading, and writing activities and time spent in each during the hours of 8 a.m. to 5 p.m. for the next two days. You should attempt to record the time spent doing each activity for each one-hour time block in such a way that you obtain a total time for each activity. Be prepared to share your distribution with the class.

9. Prepare a list of situations (both personal and business related) that would require you to listen intensively while also listening for feelings with empathy.

10. Critique your own listening skills. You may find it helpful to ask a friend to help you be objective in your assessment; ask your instruc-

tor to provide a listening profile to guide your thinking. Prepare a three-column list. Label the first column *Listening Strength;* the second column *Listening Weakness;* and the third column *Strategy for Improvement.* In groups assigned by your instructor, discuss your ideas and plans for improving your listening skills.

11. Discuss a situation that you have faced that provides evidence of bad listening habits. Consider your experiences in school, employment, organizations, and interpersonal relationships. Based on the information gained from reading this chapter, give specific suggestions that would have improved the exchange.

12. In groups assigned by your instructor, select one of the business-related situations identified in Exercise 11. (a) Role-play the communication exchange in a way that violates several of the effective listening techniques presented in the chapter. Repeat the role-playing activity and correct the bad listening habits. (b) At your instructor's direction, present the ineffective listening version of the activity to the class. Ask the class to identify the bad listening habits and suggest ways for correcting them. If time permits, repeat the skit incorporating the class's suggestions.

13. Read an article from a current magazine or journal about one of the concepts presented in this book or select a topic assigned by your instructor. Give a short (two- or three-minute) oral presentation. Instruct the class to listen attentively but not to take notes. If your instructor directs, incorporate one or more of the distractions discussed in the chapter. Prepare three to five questions to ask the class about the material (either multiple choice, true-false, or short answer).

14. In groups of two assigned by your instructor, complete the following: (a) Write a 50- to 75-word response to one of the following statements or one provided by your instructor:
    a. Whatever your career field, communication skills are a key ingredient in your career success (specify a career).
    b. In an increasingly competitive global economy, the need for developing effective cross-cultural communication skills is imperative.
    c. Rapidly changing technology has revolutionized the way a business communicates.
    d. What would business be like if legality were a company's only ethical benchmark or criterion?
    e. Business is less (or more) ethical today than it was a decade ago.
    (b) Assign one group member to serve as reader and one group member to serve as respondent. The reader will read the short essay prepared in Step a. The respondent will complete the following: (i) summarize the message in 15 seconds, (ii) summarize the message in one sentence, (iii) summarize the message in one word used in the message, and (iv) summarize the message in one word *not* used in the message. (c) Reverse roles and repeat Step b.

PUBLIC SPEAKING AND ORAL REPORTING

OBJECTIVES

When you have completed Chapter 3, you should be able to

- Follow a program to improve or refine the qualities of your speech.

- Analyze the audience for your oral presentations.

- Plan and organize public speeches and oral reports.

- Deliver speeches with increasing confidence.

JENNIFER WALKS TOWARD THE CONFERENCE ROOM where she will give her first presentation. She has written notes for her speech and prepared appropriate visual aids. She has practiced her speech in front of her mirror. The night before, she organized her notes and visual materials, planned what she would wear, and visualized how successful her presentation would be. But when Jennifer steps into the room and sees the people seated in front of her, she feels her heart beating faster and her palms getting sweaty. However, she is not overwhelmed; she knows that she is in control of the presentation and that her physical reactions are normal. She smiles, takes a deep breath, and begins to speak, knowing that this aspect of her job will become easier with experience and practice.

<hr>

Do these comments apply to anyone you know?

Throughout your career, you too will be judged by the effectiveness with which you communicate orally in your daily activities. You might make a presentation to your peers in committee work, to subordinates as part of a training or information program, or to superiors at a board of directors or shareholders meeting. In each case, your reputation is on the line. When you are effective, you gain status and earn respect. You find managing others easier, and you become promotable to increasingly higher levels. You may even take on a more attractive personal appearance as a by-product of your speaking ability.

CONTROLLING SPEECH QUALITIES

Knowledge about and skill in three important qualities of speech—phonation, articulation, and pronunciation—are necessary to the development of effective speaking habits. Let's briefly look at each.

Phonation

Phonation involves both the production and the variation of the speaker's vocal tone. We project our voices and convey feelings—even thoughts—by varying our vocal tones. Such elements as pitch (how high or low the tones are), intensity (how loud the tones are), and duration (how long the tones are held) are factors in phonation. These factors permit us to recognize other people's voices over the telephone. Anyone who studies oral communication should also remember that changes in phonation occur with changes in emotional moods.

<hr>

Identify someone with a good voice.

In general, good voices have medium or low pitch, are easily heard but not too loud, carry smooth sounds, and are flexible in conveying emotional moods. Weak or poor voices generally have a very high or monotonous pitch, are too soft or too loud for comfortable listening, are jerky and distracting, or may lack flexibility.

COMMUNICATION MENTORS

Effective public speaking skills . . .

A comfortable command of public speaking is one of the most empowering skills any businessperson can have. Whether they are physicians, engineers, politicians, or salespeople, the best speakers will always have a better chance of rising to a leadership position. All management hopefuls should begin training early and often for public speaking—through high school and college debate, speech classes, as toastmasters, in organizations—in fact, at any podium available to them.

Cynthia Pharr
President & CEO
Tracy-Locke/Pharr Public Relations

"Absolute power" comes from being able to speak in public whether you are addressing a few or hundreds. If you master this art, you will be sought after no matter what type of career you choose.

Jere W. Hess, Jr.
Director, Personnel & Public Relations
Peavey Electronics

Never be afraid to ask for help if you're preparing for an important presentation. Ask someone to help you rehearse; get feedback and pay attention to it. If you feel you need extra help, get professional assistance. The time and money you spend can make a real difference in all of your presentations.

H. Devon Graham, Jr.
Southwest Regional Managing Partner
Arthur Andersen & Co.

Practicing the following exercises can be helpful to anyone trying to achieve good voice qualities:

1. *Breathe properly and relax.* Nervousness affects normal breathing patterns and is reflected in vocal tone and pitch. The better prepared you are, the better your phonation will be. Although relaxing may seem difficult to practice before a speech, a few deep breaths, just as swimmers take before diving, can help.

2. *Listen to yourself.* A tape recording of your voice reveals much about pitch, intensity, and duration. Most people are amazed to find their voices are not quite what they had expected. "I never dreamed I

sounded that bad" is a common reaction. Nasal twangs usually result from a failure to speak from the diaphragm, which involves taking in and letting out air through the larynx, where the vocal cords operate. High pitch may occur from the same cause, or it may be a product of speaking too fast.

3. *Develop flexibility.* The good speaking voice is somewhat musical, with words and sounds similar to notes in a musical scale. Read each of the following sentences aloud and emphasize the underscored word in each. Even though the sentences are identical, emphasizing different words changes the meaning.

<u>I</u> am happy you are here.	Maybe I'm the only happy one.
I <u>am</u> happy you are here.	I really *am*.
I am <u>happy</u> you are here.	Happy best expresses my feeling.
I am happy <u>you</u> are here.	Yes, *you* especially.
I am happy you <u>are</u> here.	You may not be happy, but I am.
I am happy you are <u>here</u>.	Here and not somewhere else.

Articulation

Good articulation means clear speech.

An articulate speaker produces smooth, fluent, and pleasant speech. *Articulation* is the way in which a speaker produces and joins sounds. Faulty articulation is usually caused by (1) organic disorders of the teeth, mouth, tongue, lips, and other speaking equipment; (2) lack of education; or (3) personal carelessness. *Snoo* for *What's new* is an example of carelessness. *Dis, wid,* and *dem* for *this, with,* and *them* may result from a lack of knowledge and education. Various forms of lisping may result from organic disorders. These examples should not be confused with *dialect,* which people informally call "an accent." A dialect is a variation in pronunciation, usually of vowels, from one part of the country to another. Actually, everyone speaks a dialect; and speech experts can often identify, even pinpoint, the section of the country from where a speaker comes. In the United States, people often describe dialects as New England, New York, Southern, Texan, Ozark, Midwestern, Mountain, and Western. Within each of these, minor dialects may arise regionally or from immigrant influence. The simple fact is that when people interact, they influence each other even down to speech sounds. Many prominent speakers may have developed a rather universal dialect that seems to be effective no matter who the audience is.

To improve your articulation, most authorities suggest that you become aware of common errors. Make your tongue, lips, and teeth do the jobs they should to produce proper sounds. Next, understand the speech sounds. Vowels, for example, are always sounded with the mouth open and the tongue clear of the palate. Consonants are responsible primarily for the distinctness of speech and are formed by an interference with or stoppage of outgoing breath.

Pronunciation

The dictionary provides the best source to review pronunciation. People may articulate perfectly but still mispronounce words. Perhaps the best rule is to pronounce words in the most natural way. The dictionary often gives two pronunciations for a word. The first one is the desired pronunciation and the second an acceptable variation. For example, to adopt a pronunciation commonly used in England such as *shedule* for *schedule* or *a-gane* for *again* could be considered affected speech. In other cases, the dictionary allows some leeway. The first choice for pronouncing *data* is to pronounce the first *a* long, as in *date;* but common usage is fast making pronunciation of the short *a* sound, as in *cat,* acceptable. Good speakers use proper pronunciation and refer to the dictionary frequently in both pronunciation and vocabulary development.

When your voice qualities combine to make your messages pleasingly receptive, your primary concerns revolve around knowing your audience and developing appropriate messages.

> Learn the vowel sound symbols used in dictionaries.

KNOWING YOUR AUDIENCE

Because all audiences are not the same, speakers must be able to identify characteristics common to each audience. A research scientist should not deliver a speech to a lay audience in highly technical terms. A speech about acid rain to a farm group should address the farmers' problems, for example, and not focus on scientific causes of acid rain. People listen to speeches about things of interest to them. "What's in it for me?" is the question most listeners ask. Here are some important facts you can obtain about most audiences: ages, sexes, occupations, educational levels, attitudes, values, broad and specific interests, and needs, if any.

Your analysis of most of these factors enables you to direct your speech specifically to your audience. In addition to these factors, you should also consider certain things about the occasion and location. Patriotic speeches to a group of military veterans will differ from speeches to a group of new recruits, just as Fourth of July speeches will differ from Memorial Day speeches. Seek answers to the following questions when you discuss your speaking engagement with someone representing the group or audience:

> What other facts might be helpful to know about your audience?

> Is retirement planning a good topic for an audience of 25-year-olds?

1. How many will be in the audience?
2. Will I be the only speaker? If not, where does my presentation fit in the program? What time of day?
3. How much time will I be permitted? Minimum? Maximum?
4. What are the seating arrangements? How far will the audience be from the rostrum? Will a microphone be available?
5. Is the audience required to attend?

COMMUNICATION MENTOR

Accepting an invitation to speak is a wonderful opportunity and a major responsibility. Above all, make sure your speech is truly yours—that it reflects your sincere beliefs and your individual style—no matter who writes the first draft. Always edit and practice until you are comfortable with the individual words and the overall message. Members of the audience deserve to hear a speaker who is prepared, sincere, interested, and interesting.

They also deserve to hear a speech that was written with them in mind, so know your audience's interests and concerns. At the end of the speech, each listener should be able to answer the question: "Why is this message important to me?"

Public speaking is nerve-racking for most people, so start practicing now. Run for an office on campus; volunteer to introduce someone at a large gathering; or seek out any other worthwhile situation in which you'll be forced to stand before a crowd and speak.

Hugh B. Jacks
President
BellSouth Services

Answers to these questions reveal whether the speaking environment will be intimate or remote, whether the audience is likely to be receptive and alert or nonreceptive and tired, and whether you will have to develop additional motivational or persuasive devices.

Well-known speakers are generally well prepared.

As a general observation, audiences *do* want to be in tune with a speaker. A well-prepared speaker can establish audience rapport easily. Your speaking goal is to have the audience react favorably to you and to your message. Keep in mind that your success will be judged by only one group: the audience. From planning your speech to practicing its delivery, focus your preparation on the audience.

SELECTING A TOPIC

Good public speaking usually doesn't come naturally. Good speakers spend far more time preparing than giving their speeches. A major criterion for speech success is: *Select a topic that is of interest to you!* If you can't show interest, how can you expect your audience to do so? If you have taken a public speaking class, you will know that it isn't always easy to select a topic of interest not only to you but also to your audience. These suggestions might help:

1. In addition to topics of personal interest, try to narrow the selection further by concentrating on topics about which you can display enthusiasm.
2. Because speaking about yourself is easy, talk about your work, your hobbies, your special educational pursuits, your politics, or your views on current problems about which you are especially knowledgeable.
3. For young groups, use inspirational or motivational messages. Analyze mature audiences using the criteria discussed under "Knowing Your Audience."
4. Attempt to select topics about which you know more than the audience and that tend to complement the interests of the audience.

In making your topic selection, remember that your speech must have an objective:

1. What reaction or action do you want from your audience?
2. What idea do you want them to accept?
3. What would you like them to learn?

Whatever you select as a topic, you should keep in mind your objective. Any speech you might give will ultimately aim to achieve one or more of these objectives: to persuade, entertain, instruct, or inform. When you attempt to integrate more than two of these objectives in one speech, your job becomes very complicated.

Speaking is better when you use specific personal incidents.

COMMUNICATION MENTOR

As a member of Congress, I present at least 85 speeches a year. The audiences vary greatly from lawyers, environmentalists, physicians, and manufacturers to farmers, hunters, school children, and the general public. With the abundance and complexities of public policy issues, I attempt to inform the different groups about the topics that most interest and affect them. I attempt to strip each issue of its bureaucratic vagueness and present it using clear and concise language. A democracy works best as the general public better understands the issues.

The Honorable Mike Espy
U.S. House of Representatives

PLANNING YOUR SPEECH

The process of planning your speech evolves from your speech objective or objectives. The traditional purposes of speeches are

Hint: Don't take yourself too seriously.

1. *To entertain.* After-dinner speeches are generally designed to entertain. Although these speeches may have a secondary objective of informing or persuading through their messages, the content and delivery are developed with entertainment in mind.
2. *To inform.* When your major objective is to have the audience understand a body of information, concentrate on the logical presentation of content.
3. *To persuade.* Political speeches fall in the persuasive category because they attempt to influence or change the attitudes or actions of an audience.

Entertaining and informative speeches use the following expository types of organization:

These organizational types are easy to prepare and easy to follow.

1. *Narrative—telling a story.* Autobiographical stories and tales of adventure are examples of narration.
2. *Descriptive—describing a situation.* Speeches about how certain companies or industries handle problems of personnel, competition, new-product development, and similar topics are common at trade and industry association meetings.
3. *Explanatory—using a logical sequence.* Explanation is the basis for many talks *within* organizations. The talks are designed to explain existing or new policies and procedures to staff members.

Persuasive speeches succeed only when audiences react as the speaker intended. To obtain desired reactions, speakers must convince listeners of the benefits the desired action holds for them. Appeals to reason or to emotions such as pride, fear, love, economy, safety, health, and quality motivate human action.

Although persuasive speeches may also use narration, description, and explanation, speakers seldom achieve their expository speech objectives by relying on the appeals of persuasion. Too much persuasion may lead the audience to distrust the factual material in expository speeches. The distinction between expository and persuasive speeches is helpful in planning and outlining your speech.

Planning Your Strategy

With an understanding of the purpose of your speech—why you are giving it, what you hope to achieve—and a conception of the size, interest, and background of the audience, you should arrive at the best type of speech organization to use.

Make a few written notes about your purpose and about the makeup of the audience, keeping in mind the time of day and the probable attitudes and mental alertness of the audience. These notes should assist you in selecting content for your speech.

Outlining Your Speech

Assume you are a successful business executive and are well known as the chairperson of the local "Just Say No" campaign. You have been invited to speak at a major session of an all-day conference of the Key Clubs from colleges in your community. Key Clubs are service clubs similar to Kiwanis Clubs, and members are generally above average academically and oriented to community service. You speak at 10 a.m, and you will have 30 minutes to present your message. About 300 students—both men and women—will be your audience.

For once, you won't have to worry about raising money for the campaign. Your audience analysis indicates that this age group could benefit from a talk about the long-range effects of drug use and addiction. In turn, these community-oriented students could spread your message among youth throughout the area.

Your analysis indicates that a simple message about the widespread use of drugs—a topic suitable for adult groups—isn't what is needed. You want the audience to react in two ways: (1) say "no" to drugs and (2) carry the message to their peers and younger people. How can you convince this audience that they will benefit by taking active roles in the fight against drugs? You should appeal primarily to their already deep sense of service. Your supporting appeal should be developed around their own health and welfare. Yours must be a motivational speech.

To build the foundation for an emotional appeal, you may draw from several examples, methods, and techniques first to ensure audience understanding and then to reinforce it. For example,

1. *Use statistical support.* Are statistics or other quantitative measures available to lend authority and believability to your points? Surely you can find material on numbers of addicts, ages, dollars spent on drugs, and the cost to society in lost work time and hospital treatment.

   Items 1, 2, and 3 may be read as part of the speech.

2. *Use anecdotes.* Anecdotes are stories having a relationship to the speech topic or a moral ending. Stories about prominent citizens or role-model athletes who support your program or who perhaps have had careers ruined by drugs have strong emotional appeal.

3. *Use quotes from prominent people.* Comments made by other authorities are always helpful. In the case of drug problems, the surgeon general, the local chief of police, a hospital administrator, a sports hero, and a border patrol administrator represent sources of quotations.

4. *Use jokes.* You know young people like humor, but you rule jokes out of this speech. You simply can't find any that are closely related to

   Be careful with jokes.

your topic, and you know this relationship must exist for any joke in any speech to be effective.

5. *Use visual displays.* Slides, flip charts, and hand-held objects are effective in many speaking situations. Try to think of visual displays that will complement your oral presentation.

In a typical talk of 30 to 45 minutes, you can plan on two things. First, time permits development of only a few major points. Second, your audience can absorb only a few major points regardless of the length of the speech. Thus, you might outline a presentation as follows:

Experienced speakers use simple outlines.

I.   Introduction
    A. Purpose
    B. Justification of or importance of the topic
II. Major point 1 with support
    A. Anecdotes
    B. Statistics
    C. Quotes of authorities
III. Major point 2 with support
    A. Anecdotes
    B. Statistics
    C. Quotes of authorities
IV. Major point 3 with support
    A. Anecdotes
    B. Statistics
    C. Quotes of authorities
V.   Summary and conclusion

Note how anecdotes, statistics, *and* quotations are used to support each major point. Making every statement in a talk into a major point—something to be remembered—is impossible, unless the talk lasts only two or three minutes. Consider a speaker who is seeking contributions to a highway safety campaign in the school system. The major purpose of the talk is to persuade people to give to the program. To develop this point, however, the speaker will probably build the talk around two or three major points:

Highway safety must be improved.

Young people are the most susceptible to effective safety education.

Highway safety is everyone's business.

Statistics, stories, and quotes to support these points are plentiful. Accidents, injuries, and fatalities occur daily and records are maintained. Stories abound about the cost of accidents, increasing insurance rates, and the effects of alcohol and drugs on drivers. With this strong evidence, the speaker might spend only a couple of minutes encouraging people to contribute.

Your speech on how to say "no" to drugs will draw on the same type of support for major points. Here are some ideas for your major points:

Case studies and incidents strengthen points.

Drugs are harmful to health.

Expensive drug habits lead to crime.

People who say "no" take pride in themselves.

Drug use is detrimental to employee performance and lowers corporate productivity.

Children of addicts are also addicted.

Community service is a good citizen's commitment.

Helping others rewards you with good feelings.

Once you have selected your major points, locate your supporting material. You may also reverse the process when you have a supply of major points from which to choose. In that case, use those for which you have a supply of supporting material. The best sources for supporting material will come from your everyday reading and listening. The broader your reading, the greater will be your supply of material.

News and business publications such as *Time, Business Week,* and *The Wall Street Journal* are outstanding sources of information to support your points.

Although stories, statistics, quotations, and the like may seem trivial, they are critical to effective speaking. They retain listener interest, provide proof and evidence supporting major points, and often provide the humor and enlightenment that turn an otherwise dreary topic into a stimulating message. They are among the professional speaker's most important inventory items. How does a speaker accumulate these items? Most obtain them from personal reading. When they come across something that seems worth remembering, they write it down.

Like any other kind of story, a speech has a beginning, a body, and an ending. Your content really constitutes the body of the speech, but the beginning and ending are very important. What you say at the beginning sets the stage for your entire performance and initiates your rapport with the audience. The speech on highway safety might well have begun with "Just last year 15 young people from our community were killed in the prime of their lives by automobile crashes that could have been avoided."

Such an opening certainly would get attention. So too would an opening such as this for your speech to young people on drugs: "I live in a quiet, middle-class, comfortable neighborhood. That is until just a few months ago when four young people from three different families were killed in an automobile accident following a party at which drugs were used." What people hear first in a speech has much to do with how they accept your message.

You also must end the talk effectively. Work hard to develop a closing that will impress your audience and leave them with the major points of your speech. The impact is even greater if the ending can relate to your opening. "So my friends, make your community drug free so you and your friends can grow up to enjoy the benefits of health, education, family, and freedom" would close the "no" to drugs speech strongly. In fact, you wouldn't have to say "Thank you." Simply stand back and accept the applause.

Applause is a speaker's reward.

DELIVERING YOUR SPEECH

All speeches fall into one of the following categories of delivery style:

Scary?

1. *The impromptu speech.* Impromptu speaking may be frightening to most people because the speaker is called on without prior notice. In some cases, speakers can anticipate the request and formulate thoughts. In any case, impromptu speaking should be direct and frank. Someone not properly informed can simply say, "Thank you," for being called on and explain why the opportunity is being declined.

2. *The extemporaneous speech.* Extemporaneous speeches are planned, prepared, and rehearsed but not written in detail. Professionals use extemporaneous style. Simple cues written on small index cards may provide enough material for the speaker to talk meaningfully for long periods. Familiarity with the material makes this style effective. Teachers use it because material may be adapted to different class situations, just as public speakers may adapt their material to different audiences.

3. *The memorized speech.* Memorization has the greatest limitations of the speech styles. Speakers are almost totally unable to react to feedback, and—as everyone who attended elementary school knows—the speaker who forgets a point and develops a mental block may lose the entire speech. Memorized speeches tend to sound monotonous, restrict natural body gestures and motions, and lack conviction. For short religious or fraternal rites, however, the memorized presentation is often impressive.

This situation never happened to you, did it?

4. *The written-and-read speech.* For complex material and technical conference presentations, written-and-read speeches ensure content coverage. Additionally, this style protects speakers against being misquoted and also fits into exact time constraints, as in television or radio presentations. Written-and-read speeches often prevent speaker-audience rapport, particularly when speakers keep their eyes and heads buried in their manuscripts. If you use this method, write in large letters, avoid using difficult words that might cause you to stumble, and highlight in color items that need particular emphasis.

Watch political speeches.

Electronic devices now make it possible to project manuscripts on transparent screens on each side of the speaker's podium. Thus, the speaker may read the manuscript but appear to be speaking extemporaneously.

USING STYLE IN SPEECHES

Although all the following suggestions are appropriate for formal public speaking, most also apply to other speaking styles and situations:

1. Expect a few "butterflies" before you speak. A touch of nervousness probably means you'll be a success.
2. Once you are standing, try to select a few friendly faces in the audience. Speak to them because it is easier to speak to a few than to the audience as a whole. A sea of nondescript faces is a difficult audience. When you make eye contact with a few, as shown in Figure 3-1, you'll appear to be speaking to each person in the audience.
3. Use gestures naturally. Body motions really can't be practiced. But try to be conscious of overusing your hands and arms. Remember the snide observation that "Some people wouldn't be able to speak at all if they couldn't use their hands."
4. At least until you gain some confidence and experience, use a lectern to hold your notes and to steady a shaky hand. Keep in mind, though, that weaning yourself from the lectern will eliminate a physical barrier between you and the audience. Without the lectern, you'll speak more naturally.
5. Use jokes or humor appropriately. If you can't tell a joke well, don't use one or *you* may be the joke! Humor must be related to your speech content. Good speakers tell jokes primarily about themselves. Refrain from any humor that may reflect negatively on race, color, religion, the opposite sex, age, and nationality. Poor-taste humor can destroy an otherwise good speech.
6. Watch your audience. They'll tell you how you're doing and whether

A little nervousness is to be expected when one gives an oral presentation. Advance preparation in the form of making notes, practicing, and developing a confident, positive attitude, however, will reduce jitters and lead to a successful speech.

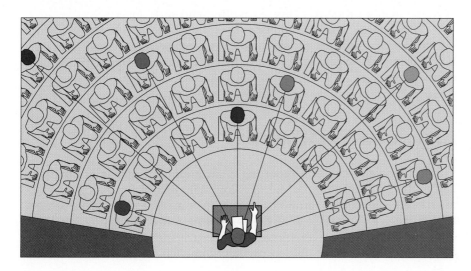

FIGURE 3–1 Selecting listeners for eye contact

you should shorten your speech. Be attentive to negative feedback in the form of talking, coughing, moving chairs, and other signs of discomfort.

7. Work particularly hard on your closing remarks. A good closing serves to leave the audience in a good mood and may help overcome some possible mistakes made during the speech.

8. Dress carefully and tastefully. Appropriate clothing and good grooming affect audiences positively.

9. Appear confident and appear to enjoy making the speech.

10. Avoid annoying speech habits. Clearing your throat or uttering a soft cough constantly will shift audience attention from the speech to the speaker. Additionally, avoid the following words and phrases:

Correct your error immediately rather than leave it as is.

You know	After each statement
Well,	Before each statement
Like I said	
Myself	For "me" or "I"
Between you and I	"Between you and me" is correct.
What I hear you saying is	
Near miss	It was a miss; use "near hit."
Basically	Before many statements that aren't basic
Bare naked, visually eyeball, overcrowded, senseless murder, and visual view	And other such idiomatic redundancies

Public speaking is both an art and a skill. Careful planning and practice are essential for building skill in speaking. If you feel more confident when reading from a manuscript, do so. A poor extemporaneous speech is worse than a properly delivered written-and-read speech.

Why prepare your own introduction?

Your status lends credibility to your speeches. If the audience doesn't know much about you, insist on a proper, impressive introduction. Professional speakers prepare their own introductions. You should do the same.

MAKING AN ORAL REPORT

Within organizations, oral reporting is an important means of obtaining and exchanging information for decision making and for policy development. Oral reporting is an efficient way to communicate because several people receive the message at the same time rather than individually at different times. It also constitutes an effective means of communicating because the audience is able to provide immediate feedback for clarifica-

Oral reports are a common and often informal form of business communication. This manager has prepared a short, informative oral presentation supported by visual aids, and he has anticipated questions that his colleagues will ask about his findings.

tion. As a result, oral reporting can significantly reduce message distortion and misunderstanding.

You may be surprised at how soon you will be called on to make an oral report after you join an organization. This method of communication is used far more frequently than you might imagine. Because you make oral reports primarily to peers and superiors, you should take advantage of this opportunity and be sure you present yourself in a favorable way.

Good oral reporters get promoted.

Planning Your Presentation

Oral reports differ from stand-up, public speeches in several ways:

1. Much more is usually known about the audience for an oral report, and the speaker is probably known by most members of the audience. The oral report is normally given *within* the organization.
2. Because the audience is smaller, the setting for the oral report is more intimate than the setting for a formal speech.
3. The audience is more likely to ask questions during oral presentations.
4. The time allotted for an oral report tends to be short. Thus, you must plan your presentation carefully so it covers the topic fully yet concisely.
5. The primary purpose of an oral report is to inform, not to entertain.

Oral reports should be expository; that is, narrative, descriptive, or explanatory. Do not use appeals to emotion. Even a salesperson should not use emotional appeals when addressing a group of company officers about ways to solve problems and benefit the organization. Persuasion is an outcome of logical topic development. A broad outline for an oral report should include

Support your ideas with factual information rather than emotional appeals.

   I. Purpose of the report as an introduction.
  II. Discussion, including
     A. Method of research and background material.
     B. Presentation of findings.
 III. Conclusions and implications as an ending.

Many types of reports can be planned around this outline: reviews of economic conditions; summaries of new methods, practices, or policies; periodic reports of progress; studies of personnel; analyses of financial problems; and reports of research.

Unlike a written report, your oral report does not have chapter headings and subheadings to guide the reader. Thus, you should plan to use topic sentences to indicate when you change from one part of the report to another. Statements such as "Next, I will describe the two major problems that our proposal must address" are helpful. You can also make a longer-than-normal pause between the end of one section and the beginning of the next. You may even indicate a change from topic to topic by changing your body position noticeably.

You can list major topics on a posterboard or flip chart and can simply point to each one as you begin to talk about it. By using techniques that indicate a topic change, you will help your audience follow your presentation. If they make an effort, most will have a mental outline of your presentation.

As a general observation, the audience will have a built-in interest in an oral report. This interest gives the speaker an advantage over the public speech in which the speaker must build audience interest as the talk develops. Now we'll look at some features of the oral report; many of these features distinguish reporting from public speaking.

Introduction. In both oral reports and speeches, the speaker should thank the one who made the introduction. "Thank you, Mr. President" after the introduction for an oral report and "Thank you for your kind introduction, Ms. Garcia" for a speech are adequate. Then you follow with your own introduction to your presentation. The public speaker uses the opening as an effort to capture the attention of the audience. Startling statements, jokes related to the topic, famous quotations, and anecdotal stories are familiar speech openings.

For the oral report, you might use one of those speech openings if you believe it appropriate; but because your purpose is to report, not to entertain, you should seek to stay with your subject. An opening statement such as "When we were granted the approval to open a new branch office in Watson, we assigned a team to select the best possible inner-city location" introduces the subject immediately and sets the stage for the rest of the report. If you want to organize your report in a direct sequence, you might begin with "I want to inform you about why and how we selected the corner of Main and First in Watson as the location for our newest branch office."

Body. You will recall from the discussion of speech organization that major points are supported by anecdotes, statistics, and quotes. As you prepare your oral report, however, you will have to support your major points with factual information. The design of your paragraphs will become readily apparent to your listeners if you begin with a topic sentence and follow with the supporting material. For example, "Three possible sites for the branch were available—Main and First, the Roseburg Mall, and the City National Bank building at Main and Twelfth. As this chart shows, pedestrian foot traffic is . . ."uses the topic sentence and follows with an introduction to the factual data to be presented.

Summary. In a public speech, the ending is often an urgent plea for the members of the audience to take some action or to look on the subject from a new point of view. In the oral report, the terminal or summary section is like that of the written report. State your conclusion and support it with the highlights from your supporting evidence: "In summary, we selected the Main and First location because it had. . . ."

> Effective oral reports have an introduction, a body, and a concluding summary.

Using Visual Aids

Visual aids are important to oral reports because they reinforce the spoken word. Through the use of visuals, a speaker hits the listener (receiver) with double impact—through the eyes and the ears. An ancient Chinese proverb says, "Tell me, I'll forget. Show me, I may remember. But involve me and I'll understand." Graphics also provide the audience with a means of resolving possible communication problems with the speaker by providing answers in advance of questions. Visuals should never overwhelm the speaker. They should be used to emphasize points, not to substitute for the speech.

One study has shown that the use of visuals has a dramatic impact on the presentation. Specifically, when computer-generated overhead transparencies or slides were used to present an idea, the presenter was perceived to be 43 percent more persuasive than in meetings where visuals were not used. The study also concluded that the use of visuals could reduce the length of a typical meeting by 28 percent (Antonoff, 1990).

Skilled speakers generally develop a set of visual aids before they determine exactly what they will say about each one. Typical visuals include the following:

◆ *Text*. Helps audience visualize major ideas and follow the flow of the presentation more easily, for example, the outline of the presentation or a list of major considerations in a feasibility study.
◆ *Graphics, pictures, or models*. Illustrate complex information or major points so they can be understood more easily than if they were presented orally, for example, a pie chart depicting sales trends or a picture or replica of the new product line.

Many speakers will go to a great deal of effort to prepare a good visual—and then not use it effectively! Inexperienced speakers often ignore the visual altogether or fall into the habit of simply nodding their heads toward the visual. Neither of these techniques is adequate for involving the audience with the visual. In fact, if the material is complex, the speaker is likely to lose the audience completely.

To enhance the impact of your presentations, follow these guidelines for preparing and using visual aids:

Why are you advised to limit the number of visuals used in a single presentation?

1. *Limit the number of visual aids used in a single presentation*. Too many visuals can overwhelm, bore, and tire the audience. While the audience values being able to "see" your points, they also welcome the variety provided by listening and the break from concentrating on visuals, especially if they are being displayed in a darkened room. Take a thorough look at the entire presentation and prepare visuals needed to (a) direct the reader's attention to major points and (b) clarify or illustrate complex information.

Keep visuals simple and easy to read.

2. *Include only one major idea on each visual*. This rule requires you to keep the visual simple and allows you to make the print large enough for the audience to see. Too much detail may lead the audience to concentrate on unimportant items and makes letters and figures too small to be read from a distance. Keep the text lines short so the eye can follow them easily. Shortening the text lines has the added benefit of opening up the page with more white space, thus giving the eye a break and making the visual look more appealing.

An effective visual provides at-a-glance comprehension.

3. *Keep the design simple and clean*. Resist the temptation to clutter the page with too many colors, fonts (type styles), and graphics. "Less is more" is a cardinal rule when preparing an effective visual. Computer technology has raised the standards for presentation materials; however, inexperienced designers are likely to use the power of the technology to make visuals overly complex and difficult to understand. For example, squeezing too many ideas or too much data into a text chart or a graph and using every available font, color, texture, clip-art (predrawn art available on disk, scanned art, or company logos), cartoon, or decorative border defeats the purpose of a visual. Your goal is to provide the audience with at-a-glance comprehension. After spending time experimenting with numerous features available on presentation soft-

Effective visual aids make an oral report more comprehensible and persuasive. When choosing graphics to support your report, make sure they illustrate only your major points, that they are simple and easily understood, and that they do not command all the attention.

ware (few companies provide training in graphic design), experienced users usually learn that the most effective visuals are simple and clean, not colorfully chaotic.

4. *Be sure that the visual is large enough to be seen by everyone in the audience.* For text charts, enlarge the print or select a font size that is large enough for the audience to read. Using the larger print may reduce the number of words that will fit on the visual. If necessary, create a separate visual for the idea you were forced to omit. Because your visuals are meant to summarize rather than duplicate your script, limiting the amount of text is acceptable.

5. *Proofread the visual carefully following the same systematic proofreading procedures used for printed letters and reports.* Misspellings in handouts or displays can be very embarrassing and can adversely affect your credibility. Many presentation software programs have built-in spellcheckers to help ensure complete accuracy. When preparing visuals that are customized for a prospective client, double-check to be certain that names of people, companies, and products are spelled correctly.

Misspellings in visuals are inexcusable.

6. *Paraphrase the visual rather than read it line for line.* To increase the quality of your delivery, develop a workable method of recording what you plan to say about each graphic. For example, record your statements on a small index card for each visual. As you proceed from one visual to another, simply move to the next card. Sometimes you may write notes lightly in pencil directly on the back of posters or the borders framing transparencies. You can then refer to these notes without the audience's seeing them. If you are using the computer and the appropriate software to display your visual aids, you can input your notes directly on the screen containing the visual. When you display the vis-

Small notes placed on visuals provide discreet prompts as you discuss the visual.

ual, the audience sees only the visual while you conveniently (and discreetly) refer to the notes on the computer monitor.

7. *During the presentation, step to one side of the visual so the audience can see it.* Use a pointer if necessary. Direct your remarks to the audience, not the graphic; in other words, maintain eye contact with the audience.

Figure 3-2 illustrates the various types of visuals that can be used to enhance an oral report. Let's examine some of the visual devices available to speakers. (Graphics are discussed in more detail in Chapter 16.) The most common are (1) handouts; (2) chalkboards and whiteboards; (3) flip charts and posters; (4) projected visuals; (5) videotapes, audiotapes, filmstrips, and films; and (6) models and physical objects.

Handouts.   Printed handouts are the dominant type of presentation materials used; about 47 percent of presenters surveyed in a study of 900 participants used handouts (Antonoff, 1990). Even though you can fit more information on a printed page than on other visuals, avoid doing so. Keep handouts simple. Summarize major points, but do not provide the audience with your entire presentation. If possible, distribute the handout when it is needed rather than at the beginning of the presentation. Otherwise, the audience may read the handout while you are explaining background information needed to understand the idea presented in the handout.

 COMMUNICATION MENTOR

Here are a few tips on graphic presentation:

1. Bring your audience to some interim conclusion before proceeding to your next chart or slide.
2. If you know members of your audience, try to think of how they will be listening (for broad concepts, biases, fine points, conclusions), and cater to those areas in your text and graphics.
3. Don't go too wild with colors, whether you're using the nearly limitless palette of a computer software program or simply marker pens. If your colors are too "hot," they will be distracting to your content or, worse yet, will trivialize it in the eyes of your audience. Check the colors on television commercials that vitalize words and images.
4. Make sure everyone can see and hear you.

James F. Hurley
Senior Vice President
CalFed Inc.

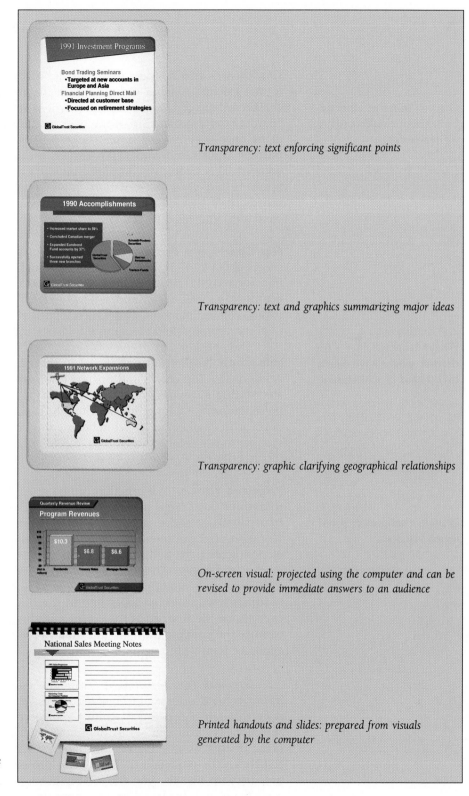

Transparency: text enforcing significant points

Transparency: text and graphics summarizing major ideas

Transparency: graphic clarifying geographical relationships

On-screen visual: projected using the computer and can be revised to provide immediate answers to an audience

Printed handouts and slides: prepared from visuals generated by the computer

FIGURE 3–2 Visual aids enhance the effectiveness of oral reports

Chalkboards and Whiteboards.   Chalkboards are useful for preparing in-formal visuals to small groups. Some major problems presented by the chalkboard or whiteboard are the slickness and lack of cleanliness of some boards, poor penmanship of the user, and the failure of the user to erase items once they have been considered. If you plan to use this method, practice beforehand and make certain the equipment is satisfactory. If your visual is sizable or complex, you will find it helpful to place it on the board before your presentation. Many portable chalkboards or white-boards have two sides, thus permitting you to keep your material from view until you need it.

Can you think of other ad-vantages of chalkboards or whiteboards?

Flip Charts and Posters.   Flip charts consist of a pad of paper with sheets about 2′ × 3′, fastened at the top and mounted on an easel with a tray for colored pens. Posters are prepared on single sheets of poster-board of various sizes and colors and displayed on an easel. Poster paints, colored markers, and various types of press-on letters can be used to prepare professional-looking flip charts and posters.

The speaker can prepare a series of visuals before the presentation and simply "flip" from one visual to the next as the speech progresses. Additionally, flip charts and posters often are used to record ideas gener-ated during a discussion or to display material (such as an outline of the presentation) for a long time. Although they serve many of the same pur-poses as a chalkboard or whiteboard, flip charts and posters permit the speaker to use color to advantage and to prepare material in advance, fac-tors not always available with a chalkboard or whiteboard.

What advantage does a flip chart or poster have over a chalkboard or whiteboard?

Projected Visuals.   Visuals that can be projected on a large screen are ef-fective for both large and small audiences. Examples include overhead transparencies, slides, and computer-generated visuals. During your pre-sentation, you can refer to specific parts of the visual by pointing to them on the screen. In addition, you can move from one visual to another quickly and easily. An advantage of projected visuals is their adaptability to overlay presentations. For example, a speaker can display only the headings and projected sales line in the first visual. The second visual, overlaid on the first, adds the actual sales line. This technique is effective because the speaker wants to talk about projected sales before getting the audience involved in actual sales and the reasons for the discrepancies.

Provide examples of pro-jected visuals.

Overhead transparencies. Transparencies can be made of anything from freehand drawings to printed pages by simply running the original copy through a copying machine capable of copying onto clear acetate. Additionally, you can write on transparencies with specially designed pens; in this way, a blank transparency serves the same purpose as a chalkboard or whiteboard. If you use presentation graphics software to prepare your visuals, you can simply generate an overhead transparency from the visual displayed on the computer screen.

Slides. Presentations built around 35-millimeter slides usually involve several visuals in a planned sequence and are displayed with a carousel or other slide projector. A major disadvantage is that the room usually is darkened. However, for presentations involving ordinary photography (depicting persons, places, and things), the slide method is the most appropriate. For example, colorful photographs of Hawaii's beautiful sandy beaches and scenes of happy tourists enjoying the entertainment and experiencing the Polynesian culture are effective means to attract tourists to Hawaii.

Another way to produce slides is to use presentation graphics software programs. These programs allow you to generate slides from the visuals displayed on the computer screen. Computer-generated visuals, projected with a computer and an overhead projection panel (connected to an ordinary overhead projector), provide the same sophistication as 35-millimeter slides. A major advantage is that you save the expense and effort required to prepare photographic slides.

Computer presentations. Increasing numbers of speakers are preparing highly professional presentation materials using computers and presentation graphics software. To illustrate the process of preparing computer-generated visuals, consider the steps for preparing a series of text visuals for a presentation: (1) Input your ideas into a built-in outliner that will help you organize your thoughts; (2) select features for displaying the text (font, type size, color, texture, border, clip-art, captions, and others); (3) view and edit each visual, indicating the exact sequence of each visual and the special effects (graphics, sound, and motion) between visuals if they are to be projected using the computer; and (4) generate printed handouts, slides, overhead transparencies, or a slide show for an on-screen presentation. Many programs provide templates (prepared designs) that suggest features and even colors that work well together. You simply select the template, and your information (text or graphics) is automatically formatted. After viewing the results, you can revise the format if you wish. These templates help the novice presenter resist the temptation to create overwhelmingly complex visuals simply because the technology is available.

An automated on-screen presentation that runs unattended is quite effective for a booth in a trade show where you must attract the attention of passersby. Another effective use of automated on-screen presentations is a customized presentation for a potential client/customer or employees working in remote locations. The clients or employees can run the presentation on their own personal computers privately at their convenience and are able to repeat the presentation as many times as necessary (the software used to create the presentation is not needed to run it).

On the other hand, using an automated on-screen presentation may overwhelm a smaller, face-to-face audience. This captive audience may be distracted by the special effects used to move from one idea to another. In

Provide another example of an oral report that would require a photographic slide.

Describe the procedure required to prepare a computer-generated visual.

List two situations where an automated on-screen presentation is effective.

addition, the fully automated on-screen presentation limits the human interaction important in typical meetings or presentations.

Automation eliminates one of the major advantages of projecting visuals directly from the computer screen—the capability of adapting the visual to accommodate the audience. Suppose you displayed a visual depicting a market share projection, and the company's comptroller questioned your assumptions and suggested another scenario. Rather than saying, "I'll get back to you," or attempting to describe the changes orally, you can easily access the spreadsheet software to revise the file used to create the visual. The visual is automatically revised, and you can respond to the comptroller's "what if" question with full graphic support. This capability contributes to a more powerful, persuasive presentation and pinpoints the need for the most effective communication technology available. Competitive managers are taking advantage of computer-based capabilities to enhance their communication skills.

Videotapes, Audiotapes, Filmstrips, and Films.   Videotapes, audiotapes, filmstrips, and films can be used to illustrate major points. For example, a videotape showing mock interviews would be an effective aid in illustrating effective interviewing strategies in a human resources management training seminar. In today's visual age, an audience relates well to the color and elaborate production provided by these visuals. Many speakers, however, allow a videotape or film to become the entire presentation. This practice violates a central principle in using visuals: The visual is intended to supplement your speech and is *not* a substitute for it.

Because more and more companies are recognizing the value of employee training and development, public relations agencies report that the production of training videos is becoming a larger part of their total work. These highly professional training videos carry expensive price tags; a conservative estimate is $1,500 per minute. Videotapes, like computer presentations, can be conveniently mailed to potential customers/clients and employees in remote locations.

Models and Physical Objects.   A sample of a product or a replica to exact scale allows the audience to visualize and become involved with the idea being presented. For example, an airline manager involved in a training seminar wanted to convince the airline to replace foil food containers with fiber containers. He brought some pastry packed in one of the fiber containers to the seminar. As the participants bit into the sweet, moist pastry, they became "instant believers" (Rockey, 1977).

Keeping Within Time Limits

If your presentation is part of a busy program, be prepared to complete it within the allotted time. In many organizations, speakers have one or more rehearsals before making reports to groups such as a board of directors. These rehearsals, or dry runs, are made before other executives, and

Explain how projecting visuals from a computer improves the quality of feedback.

are critiqued, timed, revised, and rehearsed again. In some organizations, sessions are videotaped so participants can see how they come across.

Questions often disrupt carefully laid plans. At the same time, questions provide feedback, clarify points, and ensure understanding. More often than not, people ask questions that will be answered in a later part of the presentation. In these cases, you should say something like, "I believe the next slide will clarify that point. If not, we will come back to it." If the question can be answered quickly, the speaker should do so while indicating that it will also be covered later in the presentation. If necessary, the speaker might also indicate that questions will be answered following a certain portion of the presentation. In any case, rehearsal should include a session on questions that might be raised. Then, the talk can be altered to anticipate the questions.

Look to the meeting chairperson for additional time, if necessary.

The importance of oral reports cannot be overstressed. College students often wonder why they should practice oral reports; yet many find they must make such presentations early in their careers. Their futures may hinge on the effectiveness of their performance.

SUMMARY

Oral communication plays an important role in the day-to-day conduct of business. Conversations and phone calls represent informal communication. Speeches, talks, and oral reports make particular demands on people as formal communication.

Public speaking differs from oral reporting primarily in the nature of the audiences. The audience for an oral report is generally smaller, better known to the speaker, and more likely to create a less formal, more intimate speaking environment. An oral report audience probably demands more logical development of ideas and rejects emotional persuasion.

Oral report and public speaking methods and techniques are similar, but they do differ in some respects. Although vocal qualities must be controlled in any speaking situation, public speakers must also be concerned about the physical setting, the need for eye contact with a larger audience, and perhaps wide variations in audience interest. The oral reporter makes greater use of visual aids and often must adjust to audience interruptions. Skill in speaking before groups is a valuable quality that can be developed through training and practice.

REFERENCES

Antonoff, M. (1990). Presentations that persuade. *Personal Computing, 14*(7), 60–65, 67–68.

Rockey, E. H. (1977). *Communicating in organizations*. Cambridge, MA: Winthrop Publishers.

REVIEW QUESTIONS

1. Who is the best speaker currently on the national political scene? What qualities make this speaker effective?
2. How do articulation and pronunciation differ?
3. What are some of the things a speaker should attempt to learn beforehand about the audience? What is the best source for this information?
4. Would you attempt to use jokes in speeches if the speech might be aided by a joke or two? What suggestions would you give to a prospective speaker about the use of jokes?
5. How does the scheduled time of a speech play a part in speech preparation?
6. Can you list two topics on which you believe you are qualified to give a five- or ten-minute talk?
7. What does narration mean? How does a narrative speech differ from a descriptive one?
8. What are the traditional purposes of speeches?
9. How might too much persuasion on the part of the speaker affect the audience when the purpose of the speech is to inform or to entertain?
10. What items, materials, or methods might a speaker use to assist or to reinforce audience understanding?
11. Why are the opening and closing portions of a speech so important?
12. Why is memorization a hazardous speech style?
13. What speaking style is most used by professional speakers?
14. In general, how does oral reporting differ from public speaking?
15. How is persuasion developed in oral reporting?
16. Why is oral reporting an effective and efficient way to communicate?
17. What is the key element in the opening of an oral report?
18. How might the ending of an oral report differ from the ending of a public speech?
19. Discuss three guidelines for preparing and using visual aids.
20. What are the chief advantages of chalkboards and whiteboards?
21. List at least three guidelines for preparing visuals that provide "at-a-glance" comprehension.
22. What advantages does a flip chart or poster have over a chalkboard or whiteboard?
23. Discuss the advantages gained from using projected visuals—overhead transparencies, slides, or computer-generated visuals—to enhance your speech or oral report.
24. Describe at least two situations in which an automated on-screen presentation would be (a) an effective choice of visual aids and (b) an ineffective choice of visual aids.
25. Describe at least two situations in which a model or physical object could be used to supplement your speech or oral report.

EXERCISES

1. Evaluate the speaking skill of a well-known TV newscaster or commentator. What are the strengths? Weaknesses? Offer suggestions for improving the person's oral communication skills. Pay special attention to speech qualities, audience eye contact, rapport, and organization.

2. Critique your own speaking skills. You may find it helpful to ask a friend to help you be objective in your assessment. Prepare a three-column list. Label the first column *Speaking Strength;* the second *Speaking Weakness;* and the third *Strategy for Improvement.* In groups assigned by your instructor, discuss your improvement plan in an effort to gain additional ideas for enhancing your speaking skills.

3. In groups of four assigned by your instructor, select four topics related to effective business communication or some other business-related topic. A group leader may randomly assign a topic to each member or allow the members to select a topic. You may select the following questions or use them as a guide for developing similar ones:
   a. Whatever your career field, communication skills are a key ingredient in your career success (specify a career).
   b. In an increasingly competitive global economy, the need for developing effective cross-cultural communication skills is imperative.
   c. Rapidly changing technology has revolutionized the way a business communicates.
   d. What would business be like if legality were a company's only ethical benchmark or criterion?
   e. Business is less (or more) ethical today than it was a decade ago.
   Following a brief preparation time, each member will give a one- to two-minute oral report to the group. After all oral reports are given, the group will briefly discuss the strengths and weaknesses of each report and attempt to provide each member with a few specific suggestions for improvement.

4. Read an article from a current magazine or journal about one of the concepts presented in this chapter or in another chapter in the textbook, or select a topic assigned by your instructor. Give a short (two-to-three-minute) oral presentation.

5. Prepare a two- to three-minute report on a business topic of your choice or other topic as assigned.

6. As a part of a team of four, present a mock annual shareholders' meeting before the class. You should work from an annual report of a major company. One person should be the chief executive officer, one the chief operating officer, one the financial officer, and one the chief marketing officer. Each will speak for two to three minutes. The CEO should preside and introduce each of the others appropriately before each speaks. Your report should include a review of the year's activities, plans for the next year, and information about the firm's role in the community.

Salsbury Communications, Inc.

Fear of public speaking is reported to be the number one fear of American adults, rated even ahead of death and loss of spouse. This enormous fear results primarily from the typical lack of experience in public-speaking situations. Practice is the most effective antidote for fear, and the speaker who can overcome the fear of public speaking certainly possesses a marketable skill.

The accomplished speaker gives careful attention to the nonverbal dimensions, articulation of words, topic selection, and content structuring. When the verbal and nonverbal channels match, the speaker stands a much greater chance of having the audience believe the message.

Discussion Questions

1. What five characteristics does Greg Salsbury mention as nonverbal dimensions of oral communication? Why are they considered nonverbal?

2. What does Salsbury say is the best way to overcome nervousness in public speaking? How much of this technique is desirable?

3. What is the most critical part of an oral presentation? Why?

4. What role does humor play in public speaking?

5. Salsbury uses the 1984 presidential race between Reagan and Mondale as an example of the importance of having "everything in sync." Explain the concept, referring to the two candidates for examples.

Application

You have been asked to give a brief oral presentation to a group of high school students at a career day on why students should consider a career in your chosen field.

1. Prepare a three-point outline for the talk that includes an introduction, body, and summary.

2. Be prepared to make your presentation to the class (maximum length of three minutes).

ANALYZING CRITICAL FACTORS INFLUENCING COMMUNICATION EFFECTIVENESS

CHAPTER 4   Cross-Cultural Communication at Home and
Internationally
CHAPTER 5   Electronic Communication Technology
CHAPTER 6   Ethical and Legal Guidelines

CROSS-CULTURAL COMMUNICATION AT HOME AND INTERNATIONALLY

OBJECTIVES

When you have completed Chapter 4, you should be able to

- Communicate more effectively across cultures.

- Relate to the problems of cross-cultural communication.

- Work with employers or employees with greater appreciation for cultural differences.

FOR MOST AMERICANS, McDonald's is part of the local geography. Its golden arches beckon the hungry of all ages to come in for a quick meal of basic American cuisine—a hamburger, french fries, and a soda. This fast-food mecca is common in virtually every corner of the United States. When the franchise opened its first restaurant in Moscow, it met with confusion, excitement, and crowds.

Managers from the Canadian subsidiary of McDonald's, Inc. trained Russian workers in cooking and in Ray Kroc's "QSC & V" management formula, which emphasizes "quality, service, cleanliness, and value." The Russians were amazed at the fast-food workers' practice of smiling and being courteous to the customers. Trainees had to be schooled in eating a Big Mac, a new experience for most Muscovites. The fast-food container is thrown away without a second thought by Americans; but when Mc-Donald's in Moscow first opened, customers took home the plastic utensils and foam containers as souvenirs. Many Americans go to McDonald's because the food is inexpensive and quick. For Muscovites, a 45-minute wait in line is "quick," and the trip is a major social event; a McDonald's meal costs the average person a half-day's pay. You may have difficulty imagining that something so common in contemporary American culture is such a novelty and extravagance for people from other cultures. Successful cross-cultural communications require that you be aware of cultural differences, never make assumptions, and always be courteous and willing to adapt (Moore, 1990).

Whatever your career field—marketing, accounting, finance, business information systems, or education—you must exchange information and ideas with employers, employees, customers, clients, suppliers, government officials, and many others. As you read in Chapter 2, communicating with people of similar backgrounds is not a simple, automatic process. Communicating with people from other cultures poses even greater challenges. Expanding opportunities to work in multinational companies and an increasingly diverse work force demand that you develop tools for improving your performance in a multicultural environment. Whether you find yourself working for a multinational company or a domestic company with a culturally diverse work force, your ability to communicate effectively with people from other cultures will affect the degree of success you have in getting your job done.

INTERCULTURAL COMMUNICATION OPPORTUNITIES

The fact that awareness of other cultures is of growing importance to businesspeople is clear simply from watching the news or reading the newspaper. Stories about the balance of trade, competition from foreign

American managers in the 1990s must be aware of cultural diversity in the work force. In addition, you are likely to have to communicate with businesspeople from other cultures.

businesses, increased investment opportunities in Europe, the possible loss of jobs, and the growing number of immigrants looking for work abound. Sweeping changes taking place throughout the world promise to expand international business. For example, the unification of East and West Germany, the economic reform and restructuring of the former USSR, and the restructuring of the European Economic Community will significantly alter the international marketplace. For companies with the *desire* and the *skill* to conduct business with these new foreign markets, the future provides challenging opportunities. Your keen awareness of intercultural differences will enable you to deal effectively with the special challenges you may encounter when working for a multinational company or a culturally diverse work force.

International Business Activities at Home and Abroad

During the past four decades, U.S. firms have established plants in Europe, Central and South America, and Asia. At many U.S. corporations, such as Dow Chemical, Gillette, and IBM, more than 40 percent of total sales have come from foreign operations in a recent year. U.S. companies such as Motorola are opening subsidiaries in Japan. Not only has the Tokyo market helped Motorola capture about one third of the world's market of cellular phones, it has helped boost Motorola's ability to prosper in other markets. A memo from Motorola's top management read, "Japan is a marketplace where excellence in implementation, on-time delivery, full customer support, timely introduction of products, and competitive pricing can be nothing less than consistently perfect. . . . After competing in Japan, the rest of the world is a cakewalk" (Impoco, 1991).

Can you name other foreign companies with plants in the United States?

Over the past decade, foreign investment in the United States has increased at a steady rate. It is possible that you may work for one of these companies; and if so, you must be prepared to adjust to the intercultural differences in top management.

More recently, Asians (primarily Japanese) and Europeans have built plants in the United States. Operating three auto-assembly facilities and an engine plant in the United States, Honda boasts that two-thirds of the 855,000 Hondas sold in America are made in America with 75 percent domestic content—meaning that three-fourths of the price tag is based on American labor, components, and other costs (Magnusson, Treece, & Symonds, 1991).

What is the level of foreign investment today?

In 1990 foreign investment was over $403 billion a year, about 96 percent of the value of U.S. investment abroad (Hoffman, 1992). Japan is a major source of the growth of foreign ownership of U.S. businesses. Japanese success in world markets has produced a high standard of living that can be sustained only by selling worldwide. Thus, Japanese companies are expanding to the United States with increasing frequency and are employing more and more Americans. Four of the largest foreign employers in the U.S. are Japanese; they are Honda, Bridgestone/Firestone, Sony, and Toyota Motor (Hoerr, Spiro, Armstrong, & Treece, 1990). Both foreign-company and domestic workers must learn to adapt and adjust to the intercultural differences.

Did you know that a Japanese-owned company now owns the rights to Michael Jackson's music?

Additionally, periods of a weakened dollar on international markets have encouraged foreigners to buy pieces of the United States. For example, by purchasing CBS Records, Inc. and Columbia Pictures Entertainment, Inc. Sony, the Japanese electronics giant, now provides movies and sound tracks for its customers to play on Sony VCRs and CD players. Mitsubishi Estate Co. purchased approximately 60 percent of the Rockefeller Center, an American landmark, and most of Verbatim from Eastman Kodak. In addition, the bright green BP stations constantly remind us of the familiar orange and white American-owned Gulf stations recently bought out by British Petroleum.

The standardization of Europe's diverse national markets in the 12-nation European Economic Community (EEC) will open up a vast, single market—areas long dominated by national monopolies and multiple standards and regulations. For example, Europe's six different technical standards for production of mobile telephones kept manufacturing runs low—not enticing for volume-minded producers. However, switching to a single standard as part of the EEC standardization will open the "floodgates" for foreign investors including the Japanese (Toy, Levine, Maremont, & Miller, 1991). Japan is standing in the front of the line ready to diffuse its total quality management and just-in-time production techniques into European markets. American companies, many competing with the Japanese at home, are positioning themselves to reap the benifits of rich European markets. "Whoever wins Europe will win the war," a statement made by a European marketing vice-president, accurately describes the intense competition ahead among Japan, the United States, and Europe (Toy et al., 1991).

How is the EEC affecting foreign investment?

As a result, you will have to confront problems created by cultural differences. The reason is that business communications happen in the context of a society. How messages are decoded and encoded is not just a function of the experiences, beliefs, and assumptions of the person sending or receiving those messages. Equally vital is how those attributes of the individual are shaped by the society in which he or she lives.

Each of us learns patterns of behavior from our society. These patterns affect how we perceive the world, what we value, and how we act. They can create barriers to communication if we encounter a person whose behavior follows different patterns. In the past, the potential communication problems arising from such situations were not so great

COMMUNICATION MENTOR

Many people today are involved in "international" business dealings in their careers. You will almost certainly be a part of a global network, in some form or another, during the course of your career. Good communications skills—straight talking, careful listening—are even more vital when dealing with people from other cultures.

H. Devon Graham, Jr.
Southwest Regional Managing Partner
Arthur Andersen & Co.

because cross-cultural contacts were fewer. In an era of global economies, mutual economic interdependence, multinational corporations, and multiculturalism, these contacts are frequent—and often awkward. Understanding how culture can erect barriers to communication and knowing ways to break down those barriers are keys to success in this modern world.

The Foreign Firm's American Employee

The strain that arises during this process of adaptation is the result of the clash between two distinct cultures. It may be particularly acute in the case of Japanese-American employees of a Japanese firm; with the physical attributes of a Japanese worker or manager, they may be mistakenly assumed to be part of the Japanese culture. But the culture that shaped their values and behavior was different.

Douglas Kitani is Japanese-American, born and raised in the Pacific Northwest and college educated. As a U.S. export representative for Mitsui and Company, a Tokyo-based firm, he often deals with Japanese citizens. He is frequently confusing to them. "They're not used to someone being so independent, who cooks for himself, lives on his own," the 26-year-old said. "They wonder why I don't live with my parents to save money."

Another Japanese-American employee of a U.S.-based Japanese firm feels the strain in a different way. "You're supposed to act like an insider, but you don't get the perks," he said. "They expect too much without giving rewards." On the other hand, some Japanese firms that have been in the United States for many years, such as banks, provided executive opportunity for educated Japanese-Americans.

Other firms are experiencing a similar problem found at one stage or another in most multinational corporations. The question is how to treat nationals with managerial ability. Mitsubishi International Corporation (MIC) does more than half its trading volume in the United States; and it made good sense to hire Americans, who now fill approximately 80 percent of the work force of the American subsidiary.

Managers at foreign subsidiaries—especially Japanese—have found that salaries are low primarily because foreign companies do not offer stock options, a large part of U.S. executives' pay packages. Many Japanese believe that most Americans are unable to lead simply because they do not adopt Japanese leadership styles or will "jump ship" as soon as a better offer comes along. Therefore, they are not placed in the same category as Japanese managers who commit their entire careers to the company. Promotions are more difficult to achieve in Japanese subsidiaries than in U.S. firms or European subsidiaries because the top three management layers are typically Japanese. In addition, U.S. executives

What challenges are facing U.S. managers in foreign companies?

Can you locate a recent account of the culture shock felt by a U.S. manager working in a foreign company?

are often channeled into high-profile public relations roles rather than manufacturing or production decision-making functions. One American working in a Japanese trading company pinpointed this major cultural barricade: "The most difficult part of working for the Japanese is that you will always be working *with* the organization. You will never be *of* the organization because you are not Japanese" (Hoerr et al., 1990).

Cultural differences do play a role in how we observe others. Whatever the cause of the problem, MIC recognized its existence and has begun to initiate promising American managers into the idiosyncrasies of the company. A number of Americans have been promoted into upper-level positions and serve as members of the board of directors. A few Americans are spending two-year stints with Mitsubishi in Japan, working side-by-side with key contacts in the company and building effective personal networks. In addition, the firm sponsors week-long retreats during which Americans and Japanese work together on simulated business projects in an effort to foster closer relationships.

Multiculturalism and Demographic Trends in the United States

The United States traditionally has accepted individuals from other lands. The flow of immigrants was reduced for many decades, however. At the same time, descendants of the latest immigrants were intermarrying, breaking down the barriers between subcultures, and creating a sense that the dominant culture was more dominant than in truth it was.

As the "melting pot," the United States developed a reputation for melding disparate groups into one common culture that bridged cultural gaps. Such blending did take place to an extent; as they lived their new lives in the new land, immigrants did adopt key elements of the dominant culture. To perceive this blending as the major aspect of the new nationals' experience, however, may be misleading.

What have you learned from your ancestry?

Rather than being a melting pot, the United States created an environment in which people of varying cultures could live. People with common heritage generally collected together, formed their own neighborhoods and worked intently at retaining their original culture, while still sharing in the common culture to an extent.

In the 1970s, with the influx of large numbers of immigrants from Southeast Asia and Latin America, Americans began to confront the fact that the melting pot was an unfortunate metaphor for the immigrant experience. The new immigrants, as in the past, gathered together when possible. They tried, as much as possible, to retain their traditional customs and language, looking for some familiarity in their new world. Consequently, *mosaic* seems to be a more accurate term than *melting pot* to reflect the changing demographics (Solomon, 1990). As in a mosaic, small distinct groups are combined to form the pattern or design of the U.S. population and work force.

The rise in new immigrants is not the only recent demographic trend that affects business. The maturing of the "baby-boom" generation, a relatively low birthrate, and increasing life spans have led to a higher average age in the population. The flood of females entering the job market has substantially changed the American work force. The increase in the number of white female, African-American, and Hispanic-American workers is illustrated in Figure 4-1. The makeup of the work force, traditionally dominated by white males, is changing; and workers must learn to adapt to this diversity.

With each percentage change in the composition of the work force, some aspect of cross-cultural communication becomes increasingly important. Whether you are a male or a female, a member of a racial minority, a native or an immigrant, or a member of any other demographic group, your ability to reach out to members of other groups will have much to do with the success of cross-cultural communication throughout the world.

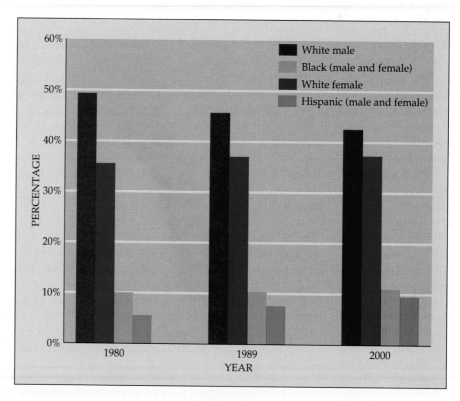

FIGURE 4-1   The changing demographics of the U.S. work force
Source: **Bureau of labor statistics, 1991; 2000 amounts projected.**

The American Firm's Minority Employee

Changing demographics have forced American-owned companies to face ethnic diversity. The following situation posed to a diverse group of workers shows the challenges presented by a diverse work force:

> On a sea voyage, you are traveling with your wife, your child, and your mother. The ship develops problems and starts to sink. Of your family, you are the only one who can swim and you can only save one other individual. Which one would you save?

More than 60 percent of the U.S. men responding said they would save the child, 40 percent would save the wife, and none would have saved the mother. In the Eastern and Asian countries, 100 percent said they would save the mother. Their rationale was you can always remarry and have more children, but you cannot have another mother (McCaffrey & Hafner, 1985). The answers reflected the global span of their backgrounds. We view everything through the prisms of our own experience, causing obvious problems in communicating with people from different backgrounds and experience bases.

Many American companies are addressing the issues raised by multiculturalism. Because more than half its employees were foreign born, Esprit de Corp, a women's clothier, added English classes to its training program. At times, limited knowledge of English creates problems. Slang and hurried instructions can make minority workers' lives miserable. Cultural customs can interfere as well. For example, a Korean administrative assistant nodded her head as her supervisor gave instructions about a computer spreadsheet program. Her nod indicated only that she had been listening. When she failed to do as instructed, she was crestfallen. She had not *understood* what had been said. When miscommunication occurs, both sides are frustrated and often angry. Increasing numbers of companies are providing diversity-training seminars to help workers understand and appreciate the cultures of coworkers. A successful program at Ethicon, Inc., a subsidiary of Johnson & Johnson, required men and women to reverse roles so that they could better understand the communication patterns and backgrounds of the opposite sex (Ehrlich, 1990).

Several generations will undoubtedly be required to learn to deal effectively with the ethnic minority work force. As these changes evolve, subtle changes will probably occur in the dominant culture as well. Such changes have occurred throughout America's history as people of different backgrounds have joined and contributed to our culture.

What elements of the dominant American culture have been adopted from an immigrant group's subculture?

THE NATURE OF CULTURE

As technology continues to make our world more compact, business is becoming international, whether at home or abroad. The *culture* of a people is the product of their living experiences within their own society. It

Can you describe your own culture?

could be described as "the way of life" of a people and includes a vast array of behaviors and beliefs.

Elements of Culture

Culture reaches into all aspects of our lives, touching the most basic dimensions of human interaction. Although the forms or content of these elements varies from place to place, each culture is built on a foundation of the following elements:

Are the norms of students the same as the norms of businesspeople?

- ◆ *Values.* Values are the culture's underlying assessment of what is good or bad, acceptable or unacceptable. They concern issues such as time, work, change, spirituality, and materialism.
- ◆ *Norms.* Values find their expression in norms, the guidelines for action within the culture. Norms can be unwritten customs, such as the proper way to introduce one person to another, or the accepted kind of dress for a date. Norms may also be codified as laws.
- ◆ *Symbols.* Each culture has certain objects, gestures, sounds, or images that contain special meaning for that culture. The American flag symbolizes our nation's independence and strength; a red-white-and-blue package tries to associate itself with those meanings. Advertising, which in some respects is the use of cultural symbols, requires sensitivity to the specific meanings of the symbols employed.

What kinds of things are part of cultural knowledge?

- ◆ *Language.* How people communicate in speaking and writing as well as nonverbally is shaped by culture. Language is the medium through which culture is passed from one generation to the next. It also reflects cultural values and norms. Spanish, for instance, has two second-person pronouns, one formal (*usted*) and the other more informal (*tu*). The formal "you" is a sign of respect used when addressing a superior or a new acquaintance, whereas the informal "you" is reserved for family and friends. English does not have this fine distinction. A U.S. businessperson, unfamiliar with the distinction in Spanish, could unintentionally offend a Spanish-speaking client by using the incorrect form.
- ◆ *Knowledge.* The last element of culture is the body of facts and information that a people accumulate over time. A cliché of American movies set in Europe during World War II shows a German spy disguised to be an American soldier. He is discovered by his failure to know a fact about baseball. This episode reveals a truth about culture: the members of a culture share a common pool of knowledge that influences how they view the world.

Culture has three key characteristics. First, it is learned by people over time. They are not born knowing their culture but acquire it through interactions with others. The family; schools; social institutions such as churches, clubs, and businesses; and the media all play a part in teaching each member of a society the expectations and norms of behavior.

Second, the various components of culture are interrelated. In the United States, for instance, the high value placed on material goods is related to the use of economic well-being as a measure of success and happiness. These values provide support for the approval placed on independence of mind and action, which in turn is connected to the existence of a relatively fluid class structure. The list of connections could go on, but these examples alone make it clear that each of these components of American culture is connected to others.

Third, the main characteristic of culture is that it is shared. In other words, the various aspects of culture are common to many individuals. No country has one unified culture, however. Human societies are so large and diverse that many different cultures can exist within them; these are called *subcultures*. Although each subculture differs from others, they often share some traits that derive from the main or dominant culture.

Manifestions of Culture

Each society exhibits its culture in many ways. Certainly customs, the accepted way of interacting with others, are expressions of the culture. The American practice of shaking hands reflects the value that is placed on the individual. Indians greet each other with a slight bow to honor the divine spark that they believe resides in each person.

Institutions also manifest culture. The structures and roles of churches, schools, social organizations, businesses, and governments all reflect the way the people of that culture see the world. These institutions, in turn, develop cultures of their own that influence the people within the institution.

Ways of thinking are another way that culture shows itself. Americans have a culturally supported belief in progress. They interpret developments in light of this belief, always looking for evidence that progress has occurred or will eventually take place. Faith in progress combines with faith in rationalism to produce an optimistic, problem-solving approach to difficulties. After all, if things tend toward progress, a difficulty must be temporary. It's simply a matter of using your head to find the solution.

Finally, culture is manifested in language. Culture enables us to acquire a language that we may use in common with others of the same culture. Language is an outgrowth of culture and not the reason for culture. English is the language of Australia, Jamaica, and South Africa, as well as Great Britain, Canada, and the United States; but all of these cultures are very different—in fact, even their forms of English differ.

What other language is used differently in different countries?

In sum, culture provides us with the standards for behavior and gives us a feeling of identification and belonging; we feel a part of something larger than ourselves. Problems occur between people of different cultures primarily because people tend to assume that their own cultural norms are the right way to do things. They wrongly believe that the specific patterns of behavior desired in their own cultures are universally valued.

BARRIERS TO CROSS-CULTURAL COMMUNICATION

Because cultures give different definitions to such basics of interaction as values and norms, people raised in two different cultures may clash. Let's explore some of the main areas in which those clashes take place:

◆ Stereotypes
◆ Time as language
◆ Space as language
◆ Body language
◆ Translation problems

Treat each person that you meet as an individual. When you judge a person by how you feel about his or her race, class, or ethnic background, you stereotype that person, which can lead to many problems, including communication difficulties.

Stereotypes

One group often forms a mental picture of the main characteristics of another group, creating preformed ideas of what people in this group are like. These pictures, called *stereotypes*, color the way members of the first group interact with members of the second. When they observe a behavior that conforms to that stereotype, the validity of the preconceived notion is reinforced. They view the other person as a representative of a class of people rather than as an individual.

Are stereotypes fair?

All cultures have stereotypes about the other cultures they have encountered. These stereotypes can get in the way of communication when people interact on the basis of the imagined representative and not the real individual. One way of exploring the force of stereotypes is to review those held about Americans.

The American stereotype does exist although it may undergo drastic change as our previously unchallenged world dominance in international trade fades. The abundance of natural resources, our industrial strength, and our consumer economy have made us appear affluent and wasteful in the eyes of some foreigners. "Visiting foreigners are often astonished to see cars less than ten years old heaped in junkyards. These cars would probably still be on the road in most countries, because other cultures seem more inclined to foster an awareness of the need for conserving resources and preserving material goods" (Phatak, 1992).

We attempt to control nature; many other cultures worship it as part of their religions. We also seem to seek status through the acquisition of material things—automobiles, imported shoes, designer jeans—whereas many other cultures can get along with mass transportation, ordinary footwear, and any pair of pants. The irony of this material orientation is clear from the following anonymous piece:

Much of the world also likes our shoes and jeans.

Only in America

He drove his German car made of Swedish steel and interior of Argentine leather to a gasoline station, where he filled up with Arab oil shipped in a Liberian tanker and bought two French tires, composed of rubber from Sri Lanka.

At home he dropped his Moroccan briefcase, hung up his Scottish tweed wool coat, removed his Italian shoes and Egyptian cotton shirt, then donned a Hong Kong robe and matching slippers from Taiwan.

More comfortable now, he poured a cup of hot Brazilian coffee into an English coffee mug, set a Mexican placemat on an Irish linen tablecloth atop a Danish table varnished with linseed oil from India. Then he filled his Austrian pipe with Turkish tobacco, lit it, and picked up a Japanese ballpoint pen with which he wrote a letter to his congressman demanding to know why the United States has an unfavorable balance of trade.

Americans are also looked upon by many others as strong individualists, aggressive, "macho" in the case of men. These traits have been fostered and reinforced by the movies we export and by our taking on the role of an international police force.

Additional elements in the American stereotype are our attitudes toward formality, time, and change. We generally act informally, perhaps in keeping with our reputation of rugged individualism. Many other cultures place a high value on formality, rituals, and social rules. They also place the family, group, and organization before individuals. To Americans, "time is money." In certain other cultures, time is the cheapest commodity and an inexhaustible resource. It represents the person's life span on earth, which is only part of eternity. Americans look on change as inevitable but also attempt to initiate and control it. In many other cultures, change is seen as inevitable; but no attempt is made to initiate it.

If much of the world looks at us according to these stereotypes, how do we look at the rest of the world? Rather than attempting to describe stereotypes we have of other peoples, let it be said that we all do some stereotyping, both individually and collectively. We have our good guys, bad guys, and so-so guys. If we have no personal experience on which to draw, we use popular news sources to develop secondhand judgments.

Stereotyping is a pervasive activity. It also is a barrier to communication in international relations—political, economic, and social. The problems of being seller or buyer, employee or employer, superior or subordinate, or based at home or in a foreign location are all affected by a person's culture and the stereotypes the person learns from his or her culture.

Time as Language

In our own hemisphere, Latin Americans have a different attitude toward time than do North Americans or Europeans. Anyone who has visited Mexico and arranged taxi service to arrive at a certain time can attest to the two time frames of Mexico—clock time and "Mexican" time.

This observation is not made to denigrate Mexicans. It simply explains the different values the two cultures place on time. Americans, like some northern Europeans who are also concerned about punctuality, make appointments, keep them, and complete them without wasting time.

In some cultures—such as Latin America—the language of time says that important things take longer than unimportant ones. An interesting thing about cultures that pay little attention to appointment keeping is that once the appointment begins, the host will probably spend more than the agreed-on time and show more hospitality and generosity than Americans generally expect. The next visitor may be kept waiting interminably, but that visitor will also receive the same cordial, considerate treatment.

Can you list your need preferences in order of importance to you?

What is stereotyping? How does it develop?

How do you value time?

The language of time is based on cultural factors often not understood by others. In the Middle East and in many countries of Asia, life on earth is only a tiny portion of a person's total time, including life after death. In that perspective, what difference does an hour or so make?

Space as Language

Space operates as a language just as time does. In America, large offices are frequently reserved for executives as status symbols. In many parts of the world, large offices are for clerical workers and smaller ones for executives. Not much space is required for thinking and planning, so large areas are reserved as working spaces.

In all cultures, the distance between people functions in communication as "personal space" or "personal territory." In the United States, for example, for intimate conversations with close friends and relatives, we are willing to stay within about a foot and a half of each other; for casual conversations, up to two or three feet; for job interviews and personal business, four to twelve feet; and for public occasions, more than twelve feet. The next time you are on an elevator in a public building notice how uncomfortable most people appear. They usually stare either at the floor or at the ceiling because their personal territory has been invaded and they must stand shoulder to shoulder with strangers.

But in many foreign cultures, close personal contact is accepted. Men customarily kiss each other on the cheek when they are introduced or when they meet. To the American "macho," this is normally an embarrassing situation; to the foreigner, it is no more personal than shaking hands. As a rule, we tend to move away when someone enters our personal territory. By observing the behavior of others, we can gain some idea of their concept of personal territory, which can assist us in our own attempts to communicate.

Watch for examples of personal space.

Body Language

The familiar North American symbol for "okay" or "everything is all right" is made by forming a circle with the thumb and forefinger. In other cultures the same gesture may mean zero, as in France; money, as in Japan; or a vulgarity, as in Brazil. The familiar symbol of "V" for victory formed by the index and middle fingers is an insulting sign in much of Europe, particularly in the United Kingdom, unless the palm faces the receiver of the message.

We nod our heads up and down to indicate agreement or "yes." In other parts of the world, the nod indicates only that the person heard what was said. In Bulgaria and some other Eastern European countries, the up-and-down head motion means "no" and the side-to-side motion "yes"—just the opposite of our meanings. Other cultures indicate "no" by a jerk of the head or a back-and-forth waving of a finger, as we sometimes do when saying "no-no" to a child.

You can have your appointment or interview cut short in most Arabian countries if you sit in such a way that the sole of your shoe is visible—an insulting symbol. The solution is to sit with feet flat on the floor.

The "business lunch" is an American tradition; much business is transacted on the golf course, on tennis courts, and at social functions as well. However, in most parts of the world, dining and recreation are social functions and not the place or time to conduct business. So, "when in Rome. . . ."

Translation Problems

Words in one language do not always have an equivalent meaning in other languages, and the concepts the words describe are often different as well. A study of how Japanese and North American business students understood the concept of profit concluded this way: "It is important for the American to understand that his definition of *profit* as solely corporate gain—involving as it will the maximization of short-term gains—conflicts with the Japanese definition, which necessarily involves a long-term view of things" (Sullivan & Kameda, 1982). When the meaning of a word is not agreed on in advance, later misunderstanding is a strong possibility.

In a humorous and helpful book about marketing overseas, David A. Ricks (1983) highlights the problems of translating with several examples of U.S. advertising and product labels that resulted in different meanings when translated. General Motors promoted its cars in Belgium with "Body by Fisher," a phrase familiar to Americans; but in Flemish, the translation was "Corpse by Fisher." "Come alive with Pepsi" became "Come out of the grave . . ." in German and "Bring your ancestors back from the dead" in parts of Asia. Some products didn't succeed: Pet milk failed in France because *pet* means, among other things, to break wind. In Mexican slang, *fresca* means lesbian. A U.S. product failed in Sweden because its name translated to enema, which the product was not.

Even within English-speaking countries, words can vary greatly in meaning. A U.S. manager, who recently transferred to the United Kingdom operations of a major U.S. corporation, was somewhat disarmed by the mixed reactions (perplexed and amused) he received when he used the familiar expression "Get back to me at your leisure." Later a fellow worker explained the cross-cultural blunder: the word *leisure* as well as water closet is commonly used to refer to the restroom. In addition, the familiar reference to James Bond, Agent 007 (double 0 - 7), is typical of references to double numbers and letters in the United Kingdom. For example, in the United States, the phone number "555-6733" is most often stated number by number, "5 5 5 - 6 7 3 3," and "Dunwoody," a street name, is spelled aloud letter by letter. In contrast, in the United King-

List other business blunders you have read about.

COMMUNICATION MENTOR

While riding from the airport with our plant manager on my second trip to the U.K., I referred to the "overpass" we had just gone under. "Oh, you mean the flyover?" he questioned. Even though the plant manager and I were speaking the same language, we quickly learned that words in our cultures have totally different meanings. Being sensitive to the differences in word meanings is vitally important when communicating with people from different cultures.

Jere W. Hess, Jr.
Director, Personnel & Public Relations
Peavy Electronics

dom, you would commonly hear "triple 5 - 6 7 double 3 ." Likewise, Dunwoody Drive is spelled "D u n w - double-o - d y ."

Translators can be helpful, but keep in mind that a translator is working with a second language and must listen to one language, mentally cast the words into another language, then speak them. This process is difficult and opens the possibility that the translator will fall victim to one or more of the cultural barriers.

GUIDES TO GOOD CROSS-CULTURAL COMMUNICATION

With so many barriers to communication, is it possible for people of one culture to understand those of another? The very existence of international business argues for the affirmative; if understanding were not possible, no agreements could be reached between firms from different countries. Nevertheless, pitfalls clearly exist. Anyone who enters the business world today must be aware of these potential trouble spots and of ways of avoiding them.

General Principles

A good guideline for someone about to engage in business with a person from another country is to learn about that person's culture. Many sources of useful information are available. Experienced businesspeople have written books recounting some of the subtle but important ways that people in other countries communicate. Simple networking can generate the names of other businesspeople who have made contact with another culture; a phone conversation or a lunch may provide pointers on what to do and what not to do. Large corporations with frequent and extensive dealings in other lands often establish workshops in which employees receive briefing and training before accepting overseas assignments. Learning the language is an invaluable way of becoming more familiar with another culture.

Another basic guide to communicating is to have patience—with yourself and the other person. Conversing with someone from another country, when one of you is likely to be unfamiliar with the language being used, can be difficult and time consuming. It is not the same as the free-and-easy way you have of talking with a colleague. By being patient with mistakes, making sure that all questions are answered, and not hurrying, you are more likely to make the outcome of the conversation positive.

The third basic rule of communicating is to get help when you need it. If you aren't sure what is being said—or why something is being said in a certain way—ask for clarification. If you feel uneasy about going into a conversation with someone from another culture, try to bring along someone you trust who understands that culture. That way, you have a resource if you need help.

Written Communication

When writing for intercultural audiences, keep in mind some of these suggestions:

1. Write naturally but avoid abbreviations, slang, acronyms, technical jargon, sports and military analogies, and other devices that may cause confusion to those unfamiliar with American usage. Those speaking English as a second language learn English from a textbook; therefore, they may have difficulty understanding directions to complete a project "ASAP" (as soon as possible) or to convert to "WYSIWYG" (what you see is what you get) software. They may be mystified when you reject bid proposals that are "out of the ball park" or "way off target," recruit job applicants who are "sharp as brass tacks," or refer to the supervisor as "the top gun."

2. Avoid words that trigger emotional responses such as anger, fear, or suspicion. Such words are often referred to as "red flag" words because they elicit the same response as a red flag waved in front of a raging bull. "Hot buttons," the term used in a popular training film, *Communicating Across Culture* (1987), conveys a similar connotation. Regardless of the term used, words such as "gal," "boy," and

Two excellent sources are *Managing a Diverse Work Force* **by Fernandez and** *Going International* **by Copeland and Griggs.**

Provide an example for each of the devices listed.

List several words you would label "red flag."

"handicapped" are a sure way to shut a reader's mind to your message, making understanding practically impossible and destroying any chance of trust and cooperation.

3. Use simple terms but attempt to be specific as well. Some of our simplest words—for example, the word "fast," which has several meanings—might be interpreted within the context of each situation in which they are used. Likewise, avoid use of strong adjectives such as "fantastic" and "terrific" because they may be misinterpreted as overly dramatic or insincere.

4. Follow the same techniques for increasing readability you would use in writing to someone fluent in English: (a) write short, simple sentences containing only one idea, and (b) construct short paragraphs that focus on developing one major idea.

5. Use the message-planning principles you will learn in this course. In addition, learn the subtle differences in the ways different cultures organize messages, especially those presenting bad news. For example, Germans tend to be more direct with bad news, but other cultures avoid negative messages or camouflage them so expertly that the reader might not even be able to recognize them.

6. Use graphics, visual aids, and forms whenever possible because they simplify the message.

7. Use figures for numbers. This system is almost universal. Keep in mind, however, that most people in the world use the metric system. Be aware of differences in the way numbers are written. For example, 2,400.00 in the United States is written as 2400,00 in other countries.

8. Write out the name of the month in international correspondence to avoid misunderstandings. When using a number to represent the month, many countries state the date before the month; for example, 10.2 1992 for February 10. Readers from the United States might easily interpret this message to mean October 2, 1992, because in the United States we state the month first (2/10/92).

9. Become familiar with the traditional format of letters in the country of the person to whom you are writing and attempt to adapt your format as much as possible. Note the following differences:

    a. The formality of the salutation and complimentary close. The Germans, who prefer a formal salutation such as "Very Honored Mr. Professor Jones," might be offended by your choice of an informal "Dear Jim," a salutation you believed was appropriate because you had met and done prior business with Professor Jones.

    b. The position of various letter parts such as the letter address and the writer's name and title. For example, in German letters the company name follows the complimentary close and the signature block is omitted, leaving the reader responsible for deciphering the writer's signature (Varner, 1987).

Oral Communication

In face-to-face communication, attempt to be natural while at the same time being aware of cross-cultural issues. Rely on these suggestions when communicating orally with an intercultural audience:

1. Avoid any actions—even subtle ones—that could be perceived to mean you believe your culture does things better than another. Instead, remind yourself constantly that the lifelong programming that guides a person's values and identity *differs* from culture to culture. One simple example clarifies this point. Although in the United States, we might believe that senior citizens would probably be happier retiring to the temperate climate in Arizona, other cultures might view this practice as scandalous: "Look how they treat older people in this country—its awful" (McCaffrey & Hafner, 1985). Rather than chiding Asians for their formalities and meaningless fillers, open-minded U.S. managers understand that Asians value developing long-term relationships highly.

    Other cross-cultural insensitivities that reduce a manager's effectiveness include refusing to exchange (or learning to exchange correctly) bilingual business cards with the Japanese, failing to learn that "yes" really means "no" in some cultures, and presuming that all workers in a U.S. foreign subsidiary speak passable English. Cross-culturally naive managers, who continue to insist that culture does not affect international business, will make many cross-cultural mistakes. Unfortunately, this poor performance, in turn, will make it difficult for the company to capitalize on international business opportunities: in-company people will be reluctant to accept overseas assignments and the company's reputation in the foreign country will be damaged (McCaffrey & Hafner, 1985).

2. Attempt to minimize your stereotype of a culture. Instead focus on the other person as an individual. Empathize with the audience; that is, view the situation from the audience's viewpoint rather than your own.

3. Try to understand some of the cultural elements that distinguish you from others in the communication process. To "see ourselves as others see us"—the gift Robert Burns asked for—is excellent advice for communicating with any audience and especially one from a different culture (Marcus, 1991). Strive to see yourself as the audience sees you and not as you see yourself.

4. As with writing, avoid slang, jargon, figurative expressions, "red flag" words, and other devices peculiar to American usage.

5. Enunciate words carefully and speak somewhat more slowly when communicating with those who speak English as a second language. However, avoid the temptation to speak in a very loud voice to get your point across.

Based on your experience interacting with someone from another culture, list several customs that are different from your own. Do you appreciate that their culture differs from your own or do you insist that your customs are better (more practical and sensible) than the customs of the cultures?

Describe yourself as you believe others see you.

6. Do not hesitate to provide feedback or ask whether the other person has understood. Avoid asking "Is that clear?" or "Do you understand?" Both of these direct statements might elicit a "yes" answer if the person thinks saying "no" may be interpreted as incompetence or if the person's culture advocates saying "yes" to save face. Consider the following subtle, yet effective, techniques of verifying understanding.

    a. Observe the other person carefully throughout the conversation for signs of misunderstanding. You might ask, for example, if you or the listener might restate the idea in another way; rephrasing the message is far superior to repeating the same words more loudly.

    b. Conclude meetings or telephone calls with a clear understanding of what has been agreed on and what actions are necessary. Immediately following the oral meeting (telephone or face to face), send a letter or facsimile outlining these points.

7. Resist the temptation to interrupt the speaker before the message is complete. Your interruption would be considered rude in any culture. Moreover, the speaker may be intimidated by attention focused on his or her English skills. Of course, the obvious negative effect is that you may misinterpret the message if you do not hear the speaker's entire message.

8. Become familiar with appropriate conventions for greetings and introductions in various cultures. For example, should you use the traditional American handshake or some other symbol of greeting? Is using the person's first name acceptable? Can you introduce yourself, or must you have someone else who knows the other person introduce you? Are business cards critical, and what rules should you follow when presenting a business card? Gaining competence in greetings and introductions will enable you to make a positive initial impression and thus to concentrate on the purpose of your meeting rather than agonize over an awkward, embarrassing slip in protocol. Your audience will appreciate your willingness to learn and value their customs.

9. When you have advance notice about a meeting, do some research about the participants' country or countries. A 1988 study by the National Geographic Society found that Americans—youths and adults—were unable to locate countries on a world map. Americans ranked below both Asians and Europeans in this simple task. Nothing would be more embarrassing and offensive than to reveal total ignorance about others. In other words, lack of preparation is not *smart* for business. In an article about negotiating with the Japanese, Flannigan (1990) chided Americans for depending on the other side for advice. "A Japanese company would never negotiate with Americans without having at least one member of its team who speaks proficient English.

Ask questions but do not interrupt needlessly.

What is the appropriate protocol for greetings and introductions in the United States?

How familiar are you with geography and current and past events in other countries?

Before speaking with persons from different cultures, you need to prepare by studying those cultures. In addition, when speaking across cultural and language gaps, remember to be courteous, speak clearly, and avoid using slang or regionalisms.

Expect to face a negotiator who has read Hemingway and can tell you Babe Ruth's batting average. Conversely, if you go to the table with people who can't speak Japanese or find Yamaguchi-ken on a map and have never heard of Isao Harimoto or Natsume Sosecki—you may get taken to the cleaners. It's the oldest rule in the book: know your opponent."

10. Expect to spend extra time communicating with people from other cultures, especially people who are not time conscious and who believe that personal relationships are the basis of business dealings. Be patient with what you may consider time-consuming formalities and courtesies and lengthy decision-making styles when you would rather get right down to business or move on to the next point. Be patient and attentive during long periods of silence; in many cultures people are inclined to stay silent unless they have something significant to say or if they are considering (not necessarily rejecting) an initial offer. In fact, some Japanese have asked how Americans can think and talk at the same time. Understanding this pattern of conversation can prevent you from making unnecessary concessions such as selling the store before the other side even has a chance to reply. Understanding can help you feel more comfortable during these seemingly endless moments of silence and less compelled to fill the gaps.

11. Become familiar with the subtle differences in nonverbal communication and adapt your own practices to avoid creating barriers to effective communication. Nonverbal areas to investigate include gestures,

posture, body language, eye contact, dress, emotional expression, and time (relative importance, length of work day, holidays). Some nonverbal behavior of other countries is well known by now. For instance,

◆ The Japanese greet with a respectful bow rather than the traditional handshake.

◆ Maintaining eye contact, the hallmark of a person to be trusted for North Americans, is often considered impolite by the Japanese, who believe that keeping the eyes lowered is a sign of respect. Some cultures and ethnic groups, including Asian females and African-Americans, listen without direct eye contact, which is often frustrating to North Americans who inaccurately perceive that the listener is uninterested and not listening.

◆ The time-conscious North American can expect to be kept waiting for an appointment in Central America, the Middle East, and other countries where the North American sentiment "time is money" is not accepted.

◆ North Americans, who often slap each other on the back or put an arm around the other as a sign of friendship, receive disapproval from the Japanese, who avoid physical contact. For example,

> Can you list other differences in nonverbal behavior patterns that could affect your ability to communicate effectively with a person from a different culture or ethnic group?

COMMUNICATION MENTOR

Because of the global nature of our economy, fluency in a second language is a vocational skill—one that increases your marketability in the workplace. The Salt River Project recruits employees who can conduct conversations in Spanish and translate written materials from Spanish to English or English to Spanish. However, many of our applicants place little emphasis on their knowledge of a second language.

So that you can compete for the many jobs that involve communicating with people of different cultures, reserve some of your elective hours for taking a series of foreign language courses (enough to gain some degree of fluency) or a refresher course in the foreign language you studied in high school. Then, above all, when preparing your resume, be certain to *exploit* your ability to communicate in other languages—especially if you know the job sought requires such skills.

Carroll M. Perkins
General Manager
Salt River Project

Japanese shopkeepers place change on a plastic plate to avoid physical contact with customers (Flannigan, 1990).

Being aware of differences in nonverbal behavior minimizes unnecessary embarrassment as well as confusion that can be detrimental to achieving the goal desired.

SUMMARY

Language, values, attitudes, and other cultural traits change very slowly. Therefore, communicating interculturally calls for recognition of the cultural elements that cause people to view things differently and thus create barriers to communication.

A relatively new factor in intercultural communication in business and industry has been created by foreign-owned businesses establishing American plants and hiring American workers to work for foreign managers. Older patterns dealt with international trade and American-owned firms' employing ethnic minority workers. Communication may be difficult under all three conditions.

Instead of attempting to forget about or ignore cultural factors, workers and employers can improve communication by recognizing them and by considering people as individuals rather than as members of stereotypical groups. Suggestions for improving written and oral communication include many of the same practices recommended for communication within a culture. An important difference, however, is to avoid the use of terms peculiar to a language or terms open to several interpretations.

The business school graduate of today will almost certainly work for a multinational firm or have to interact with one. For many people, the growing area of international business will require them to work overseas as their careers progress; their success or failure will very likely depend on skill in communicating in an intercultural environment.

REFERENCES

Copeland L., & Griggs, L. (1985). *Going international: How to make friends and deal effectively in the global marketplace.* New York: Random House.

Ehrlich, E. (1990, August 6). Anger, shouting, and sometimes tears. *Business Week,* p. 55.

Fernandez, J. P. (1991). *Managing a diverse workforce.* Lexington, MA: D. C. Heath.

Flannigan, T. (1990). Successful negotiating with the Japanese. *Small Business Reports, 15*(6), 47–52.

Hoerr, J., Spiro, L. N., Armstrong, L., & Treece, J. B. (1990, December 17). Cultural shock at home: Working for a foreign boss. *Business Week*, pp. 80–81, 84.

Hoffman, M. S. (Ed.). (1992). *The world almanac and book of facts*. New York: Pharos Book.

Impoco, J. (1991, June 24). Fighting Japan on its home turf. *U.S. News & World Report*, pp. 50–52.

McCaffrey, J. A., & Hafner, C. R. (1985, October). When two cultures collide: Doing business overseas. *Training Development Journal*, pp. 26–31.

Magnusson, P., Treece, J. B., & Symonds, W. C. (1991, November 18). Honda, is it an American car? *Business Week*, pp. 105–107, 109, 112.

Marcus, B. W. (1991). Cross-cultural concerns. *New Accountant*, 6(6), 21, 42.

Moore, T. (1990, February). For the Leninists, it's Mac in the U.S.S.R. *U.S. News & World Report*, pp. 10–11.

Phatak, A. V. (1992). *International dimensions of management* (3rd ed.). Boston: PWS-KENT.

Ricks, D. A. (1983). *Big business blunders*. Homewood, IL: Dow Jones–Irwin.

Solomon, J. (1990, September 12). Learning to accept cultural diversity. *The Wall Street Journal*, p. B1.

Sullivan, J. H., & Kameda, N. (1982). The concept of profit and Japanese-American business communication problems. *Journal of Business Communication*, 19(1), 33–39.

Toy, S., Levine, J. B., Maremont, M., & Miller, K. L. (1991, June 3). The battle for Europe. *Business Week*, pp. 44–50, 52.

U.S. Bureau of the Census. (1991). *Statistical abstract of the United States: 1991* (111th ed.). Washington, DC: Author.

Valuing diversity part III: Communicating across cultures. (1987). [Film]. San Francisco: Copeland Griggs Productions, Inc.

Varner, I. I. (1987). Internationalizing business communication courses. *Bulletin of the Association for Business Communication*, 50(4), 11.

REVIEW QUESTIONS

1. Provide evidence to support the statement that chances are great that you will be involved in international business activities or have to communicate across cultural gaps.
2. How does a culture benefit a people?
3. What recent world events have affected the level of international investment?
4. What factors have caused and are causing the decline in the dominance of the white male in leadership roles in the United States?
5. What challenges are facing U.S. managers in foreign companies? Provide an example of the culture shock felt by a U.S. manager working in a foreign company.
6. What dangers are inherent in the stereotyping of a people?
7. What effect might religion have on "the language of time"?

8. The United States seems to have problems dealing with relatively small countries such as Vietnam, Iran, and Nicaragua. Suggest some cultural differences that lead to such problems.

9. What is meant by "We view everything through the prism of our own experience"?

10. How do slang expressions and idioms endanger cross-cultural communication?

11. Stereotyping is considered both bad and good. What are some helpful or good aspects of stereotypes? What precautions can you take to minimize your stereotyping as you prepare to communicate with someone from another culture?

12. How can you elicit accurate feedback in cross-cultural communication?

13. Discuss three guidelines for writing to an intercultural audience, telling why they are important.

14. Discuss three guidelines for communicating orally to an intercultural audience, telling why they are important.

EXERCISES

1. To what extent does growing diversity affect you in your current affiliations? Consider your classes, part-time employment, organizations, and other activities. With what cultures are you in contact?

2. XYZ Corporation has not yet sought global markets for its products. Its president believes that international sales involve too many complexities and, therefore, would not be profitable. As a new manager, you must convince the president to reconsider the company's position on international sales. Using specific incidents from current newspapers and magazines, show how other businesses are profitably expanding their markets through international trade. Be prepared to share your ideas with the class.

3. Assess your adaptability to other cultures. You may find it helpful to ask a friend to help you be objective in your assessment. Ask your instructor to provide an assessment sheet to guide your thinking. Prepare a three-column list and label the first column *Strength,* the second column *Weakness,* and the third column *Strategy for Improvement.* In groups assigned by your instructor, discuss your improvement plan in an effort to gain additional insight for enhancing your intercultural communication skills.

4. Interview an international student, professor, or businessperson in your area. Your purpose is to learn about this person's culture and customs, communication practices in his or her country, and general advice for adapting to other cultures. Encourage the interviewee to

share specific problems he or she faces and ways of addressing those problems. Summarize your findings in a short report, and be prepared to share it with the class.

5. Interview a businessperson returning from an assignment in another country or one who has experience working in a foreign-owned company in the United States. Ask this person to evaluate his or her preparation for the assignment and to discuss specific problems in communicating and how those problems were addressed. Summarize your findings in a short report, and be prepared to share it with the class.

6. Read an article in a newspaper, journal, or magazine about intercultural communication. Write a brief summary of the article, and be prepared to share it with the class.

7. In groups of three, discuss each of the following critical incidents. Identify how you think the different cultures will interact.

a. A U.S. engineer working with a subsidiary in Asia begins a general meeting of his professional staff by praising one manager for his outstanding work on a report.

b. A U.S. manager sees two Arab-American employees arguing and decides to stay out of it.

c. While his American supervisor waits, a Latino manager starts a budget-planning meeting by chatting casually and taking care of other "formalities."

d. After carefully presenting the benefits of his company's product, a sales representative from the United States presses an Indonesian buyer for a sales decision and eventually asks directly whether the buyer wishes to place an order.

e. A human resources manager becomes irate when an Asian woman does not look at him directly during a performance appraisal interview—or some other face-to-face discussion.

f. Two managers have applied for an overseas assignment in Asia. One is a highly aggressive marketing expert with proven managerial experience; the other is a good team worker with a high degree of interpersonal skill. Which one would you choose and why?

g. As negotiations with Malaysian business executives become quite lengthy, a group of U.S. businesspersons become less formal, repeatedly crossing their legs in such a way that the soles of their shoes are visible.

h. A U.S. executive, committed to preparing reports with the most up-to-date information possible, required that all periodic reports be submitted approximately two days before the composite report was to be submitted to the president. Now that she has been transferred to the Mexico operation, she plans to follow this same practice.

   i. Discouraged about the slow pace of negotiations with the Japanese, a U.S. manager suggested that the senior-level people from each side meet alone to attempt to work out the differences.

   j. Eager to finalize negotiations with a group of United Kingdom (U.K.) business executives, a U.S. manager agreed to play golf the following day with a number of the U.K. executives with whom he had been negotiating. Eager to finalize some of the details of the deal, the U.S. manager diplomatically introduces one of the points of discussion between holes.

   k. A female executive is being considered for transfer to a Middle Eastern country to negotiate the location of a new plant.

   l. Arriving at the first meeting with a Japanese executive, a U.S. manager hurriedly pulls his business card from his pocket. Disregarding the fact that the card had bent slightly as he pulled it from his pocket, he hands the card to the Japanese executive with his name and title facing himself. Politely he accepts a business card from the Japanese executive. Holding the card with one hand, the U.S. manager quickly skims the name and title on the card while moving to place his briefcase on the table, signaling his desire that the meeting begin.

8. Recall a recent conversation that you have had with a person from another culture or another region within the United States—a friend, teacher, coworker, supervisor, or some other person. Write a brief scenario including the dialogue and a description of the nonverbal messages transmitted. Analyze the effectiveness of this conversation using the communication process model; use Figure 2-2 as a guide. Identify problems (interferences or barriers) occurring at each stage of the communication process and provide suggestions for improvement. Considering the barriers you have identified and the information gained from reading this chapter, give specific suggestions for improving this communication exchange. Be prepared to discuss your analysis with the class or in small groups assigned by your instructor.

9. In groups assigned by your instructor, select one of the critical incidents described in Exercise 7 or the situation identified in Exercise 8.

   a. Role-play the communication exchange violating intercultural communication principles. Repeat the role-playing exercise correcting the communication errors.

   b. At your instructor's direction, present the ineffective intercultural exchange to the class. Ask the class to identify the problems and suggest ways for correcting them. If time permits, repeat the skit incorporating the class's suggestions.

10. Prepare a checklist of factors to guide a businessperson in researching the culture of a foreign country. To begin your checklist, consider the broad ideas discussed in this chapter (values, symbols, language, and nonverbal communication); but include specific factors within each

broad category. For example, the broad idea of nonverbal communication might include factors such as gestures, time, space, handshake or other greeting, touching, and others.

11. Select a foreign country or an ethnic culture in the United States that you know little about. Using the checklist prepared in Exercise 10, perform one or more of the following tasks:

    a. Develop a cultural profile of the country or culture you selected. Briefly provide guidelines about each factor included in your checklist.

    b. Write a report designed to provide managers with specific guidelines for integrating successfully into this culture without suffering from culture shock.

    c. Develop your information (or selected portions) into a training program for managers preparing to do business with this culture. Prepare appropriate visual aids and handouts to support your ideas. Present the training program to your class if directed by your instructor.

12. Technology has increased the amount and speed of global communication. Increased globalization has affected various disciplines in unique ways. Identify one area (issue) in your own discipline that has been significantly influenced by globalization. Prepare a short report explaining the issue and its effect on the discipline.

Pacific Bell Directory

The United States is a nation of cultural diversity. Each wave of immigration, whether prompted by religious, political, or economic reasons, has added new facets to our distinct culture. The term *eclectic* has been used to describe this diversity; it refers to that which is made up of components from various sources and implies that the result is the sum of many perspectives.

As businesses attempt to serve the diverse needs of an eclectic community, recognizing and respecting cultural differences becomes increasingly important. The management of Pacific Bell Directory discusses this vital concept in terms of the unique characteristics of the Southern California marketplace. Yet, each business operates in its own cross-cultural environment. While the particular cultural components may vary, the same communication challenges exist.

Discussion Questions

1. Stephanie Dollschnieder refers to an important ingredient in successful cross-cultural communication as "cutting each other slack." What does she mean? Give examples of how this strategy can be accomplished.
2. What part do respect and trust play in cross-cultural communication? How are they related concepts?
3. To what extent is courtesy a universal concept?
4. How does the "salad bowl" concept of culture differ from the traditional "melting pot" idea?
5. Jan Birkelbach talks about the wide array of behavior within cultural groups and cautions against generalizing that all members of a specific group fit a certain stereotype. Give examples of several such cultural stereotypes.

Application

You must make a short presentation to your company's sales staff concerning the cultural diversity of your community and the importance of effective cross-cultural communication.

1. Find out what cultural groups are present in your community and in what proportions. (Your chamber of commerce or city offices may be of help.)
2. Interview one or more persons from each of the major cultural groups in your community. Indentify what is unique about their language, nonverbal communication, perception of time, customs, family life, etc.
3. Prepare an outline for your talk, emphasizing the importance of cross-cultural communication and including several suggestions for improving cross-cultural communication in your community.

ELECTRONIC COMMUNICATION TECHNOLOGY

OBJECTIVES

When you have completed Chapter 5, you should be able to

♦ Identify the benefits of using word-processing, spreadsheet, and database programs to manipulate data.

♦ Recognize how printers and desktop publishing and presentation graphics software are useful to enhance the overall impact of a document.

♦ Recognize how e-mail, facsimile, teleconferencing, and other technologies facilitate sharing data effectively.

♦ Identify barriers that could prevent you from using electronic tools effectively.

THE SPRINTER WARMS UP BEFORE THE RACE. He stretches, breathes deeply, and concentrates on winning. At the command to line up, he walks to his starting block, crouches into place, and waits to hear the gunshot signaling the beginning of the fifty-yard dash. But when he hears the loud bang, he remains frozen at the starting point, watching the other sprinters race toward the finish.

This scenario is literally a nightmare for professional runners. They train, work hard, practice, diet, lift weights, sacrifice personal time to work toward their goals, and try not to let anything interfere with their achievement of those goals. In some ways, business managers face the same situation. They have studied, completed internships, and made many sacrifices to get closer to their ultimate goals. Unless they can use electronic tools to access, assemble, and communicate information in a timely manner, however, they may end up like the sprinter—stuck in the blocks, left behind at the start.

Can a computer do all the work of communicating?

Electronic tools have not eliminated the need for basic communications skills. If anything, these electronic tools, like all new tools and techniques, create new obstacles or barriers to communication that must be overcome. These tools, however, also create opportunities, which range from the kinds of communications that are possible to the quality of the messages themselves. Electronic tools for communication can help people

1. Communicate quickly and efficiently with others over long distances.
2. Locate information for messages.
3. Communicate in a timely way.
4. Shape their messages to be clearer and more effective.

In one chapter, we cannot explain all aspects of electronic tools in detail. However, we can describe those features that facilitate communication. We also can outline some of the problems that can arise in messages created with these electronic tools and describe some techniques to avoid these pitfalls.

Three broad types of electronic technology that expedite the quick and accurate flow of communication exist. These are not the only kinds of electronic tools available. Some programs have been developed to handle an organization's accounting functions. Others are used to design new products on screen rather than with pencil and paper. Many programs offer specialized tools aimed at specific needs of businesspeople. You will study the following three broad categories because they are common to the tasks faced by most managers, whatever their industry or special concerns:

1. *Tools for manipulating data.* This group includes what may be the three main uses of computers: word processing, used to write letters, memos, and reports; spreadsheets, used to organize and analyze numbers; and databases, used to store and access large amounts of data.

2. *Tools for presenting data.* This category includes programs that run printers, desktop publishing programs, and applications that create graphs.
3. *Tools for sharing data.* This growing category provides the capability of sharing data quickly and efficiently, often from one computer to another. These tools include electronic- and voice-mail systems, facsimile machines, transmitting and computing from remote locations, cellular phones, and teleconferencing systems.

MANIPULATING DATA

Businesses run on words, numbers, and data. The three main categories of electronic applications—word-processing programs, spreadsheets, and databases—facilitate the varied and efficient manipulation of these three kinds of information.

Word Processing

Many different word-processing systems are available, but each performs similar functions. *Word processing* allows you to

1. Enter text by keyboarding the copy, similar to the way you enter text on a typewriter.
2. Make changes to the text.
3. Save the document for future use.
4. Print the document.

In a sense, a word-processing system is an advanced typewriter that permits creating, editing, and printing text.

If a computer is capable of performing only word processing and no other electronic functions, it is called a *dedicated* word processor. Alternatively, the machine could be a general-purpose computer that can run all of the applications discussed here and, for this particular function, can use any one of a number of popular word-processing programs such as *WordPerfect*, *Microsoft Word*, and *Wordstar*. The general-purpose computer can be a small personal computer (or PC) or a large mainframe computer. It may have the capability of being used by one or by many individuals.

Using word-processing software to create business communications has many benefits. Some features of these programs permit the easy formatting of text with **boldfacing**, underlining, or *italicizing* for emphasis. Others allow rapid movement within a document to review or revise the text. Reports and longer documents become less tedious to produce because of features that facilitate writing and editing:

1. *Insert and delete.* The insert feature allows you to enter new copy—from one character to several paragraphs—anywhere in the document. The

Word processing enables you to revise your document easily.

Will word processing eliminate the need to write well?

delete feature allows you to remove text, from a single character to many pages.

2. *Block.* The block feature allows you to identify any portion of the document as a block, which can then be deleted, moved to another location, or copied from one position to another. If after keyboarding a long report, you decide that a paragraph makes more sense in another location, you can create a block and use the move feature. You can use the block and copy features to repeat a complicated table in more than one part of a report.

3. *Search and replace.* The search-and-replace feature is helpful when you have consistently misspelled a word throughout a document or decide to change a word throughout a report. The power of this feature is immediately apparent if you have ever manually searched a long document for a particular word and then input the change each time, hoping you had located every occurrence of the word. For example, with just a few keystrokes, you can use the search-and-replace feature to change "multicultural" to "cross-cultural" every time it appears in your 50-page report. In addition to the time saved, an important benefit is the increased confidence in the accuracy of your work.

Revisions that significantly enhance the quality of the memorandum in Figure 5-1 can be made efficiently using word-processing features (insert and delete, block, and search-and-replace features). Because revisions are simple, writers using word-processing software are much more likely to revise a document than writers using traditional methods.

4. *Spellcheck, thesaurus, and writing-analysis software.* Other beneficial features are stored references such as dictionaries and thesauruses. Writing-analysis software aids in producing an effective message.

With spellcheck, you can automatically check the spelling of every word in a document against the program's dictionary. The words misspelled or not included in the dictionary are highlighted. You simply select the correct spelling from a list provided by the computer or input the correct spelling if it does not appear in the list. Some programs allow you to add words to the dictionary.

The thesaurus feature automatically generates a list of synonyms and antonyms for any word you wish. You may choose one from the list to substitute for the original. This feature can help you find words with very precise meanings and add freshness and variety to your writing.

Writing-analysis software used in conjunction with word-processing software helps writers improve their writing style and locate grammatical errors. After the writer composes a document using word-processing software, the writing-analysis software checks the document against the grammar and style principles stored in the program and generates a list of suggestions for improving the document. Popular writing-analysis programs include *Grammatik* and *RightWriter*.

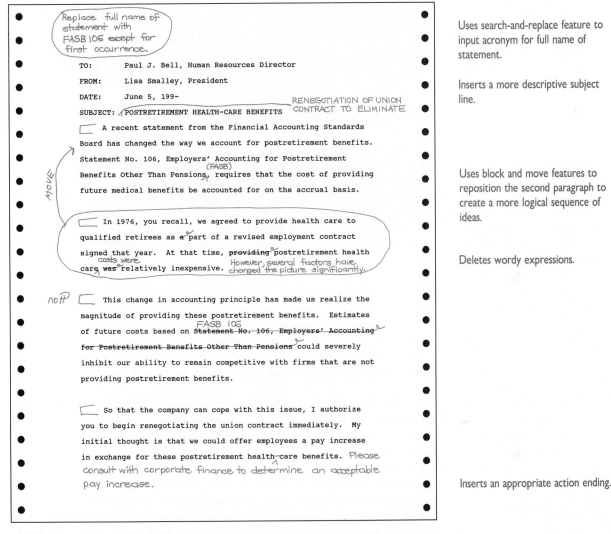

FIGURE 5-1 Word-processing features (insert and delete block, and search and replace) simplify revisions of documents.

5. *Redlining and document comment.* The redline feature and document comment features are beneficial when several people contribute to one document, a common practice in business today. Traditionally, one author uses a red pen to edit drafts before passing them on to another author. Today, authors often share disks and use redlining to mark text that has been added, deleted, or edited. The redline marks are removed from the file when each author has approved the changes.

    Asked to approve the memorandum in Figure 5-2, the production manager changes the delivery date and authorizes a discount for a par-

```
TO:      Greg Martin, Sales Representative
FROM:    Kenneth Moore, Production Scheduler
DATE:    June 15, 19--
SUBJECT: DELIVERY DATE FOR GRANT CORPORATION ORDER

I'm excited about the negotiations you have under way with Grant Corporation.
Understanding that delivery is a critical issue in securing the order, I have
researched every possibility for completing the order as quickly as possible.

Based on current commitments and initial production estimates for the Grant
order, I believe we can provide the order by September 30 if we schedule 20
percent overtime October 15.  Because we receive many rush of orders during
July, you must close this contract quickly to assure this delivery date.
Thus, we'll stand by the September 30 October 15 delivery date until June 30.

We recognize that Grant Corporation prefers full shipment of its orders.
However, to eliminate the need to rent temporary warehouse space to store
completed merchandise, you are authorized to offer Grant Corporation a
2 percent discount for a half-order shipped before October 1.

Excessive overtime is a sensitive issue with our work force.  Thus,
overtime must be reserved for emergencies.  Extend the delivery date to at
least October 15 on the Grant order.  Also, do your best to convince Grant
to accept the discount for the half-order shipment.
S:\GRANT.ORD                                    Doc 1 Pg 1 Ln 1" Pos 1"
```

FIGURE 5-2
Redlining and a document comment alert co-author of proposed changes and provide needed feedback.

tial order. The proposed additions are displayed in ▣, and proposed deletions appear in ▣. On a printed copy of this document, the additions appear in bold; and a line goes through the words to be deleted. The exact appearance may vary depending on the setup of your system.

Document comments allow writers to insert reminders and notes to themselves and coauthors. These comments can be displayed for easy reference or hidden to eliminate distractions. The production manager's explanation for the delayed delivery date appears in the comment box in Figure 5-2.

6. *Automatic contents page, index, and document references.* Most of the sophisticated word-processing programs include a feature that generates a contents page, index, and document references automatically. This feature saves time in the initial creation of these pages and in their updating if pagination changes during editing. You will learn more about this time-saving feature when you study the report-writing chapters.

7. *Mail merge.* This feature facilitates large-scale mailings. The text of the letter is basically the same for all recipients, but the letter is personalized by adding variables—information that is different for each recipient. For example, the variables shown in parentheses in the standard text in Figure 5-3 are the client's name, address, salutation, and conference attended. The personalized letter is prepared by combining the standard text with a list of variables for each letter. Special codes instruct the software to insert the variables in the appropriate location in

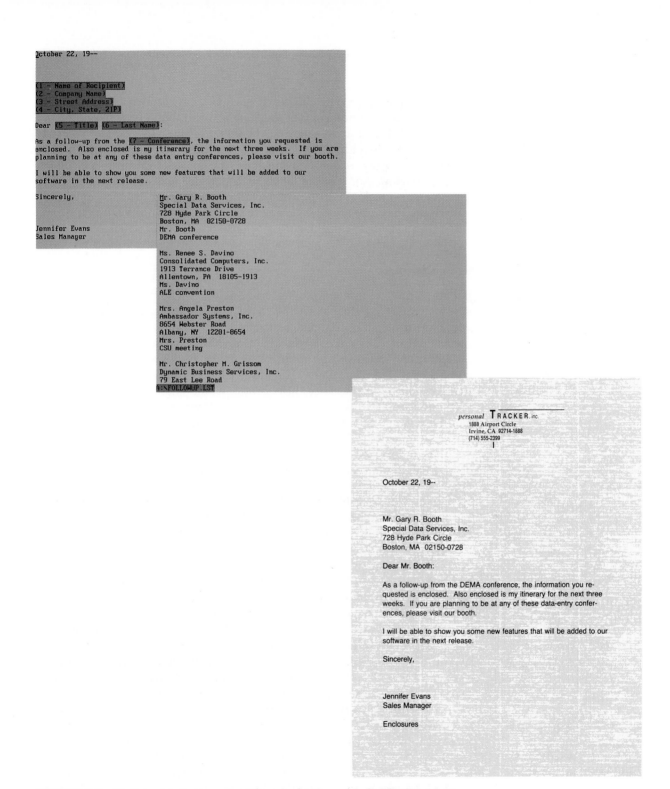

FIGURE 5-3 Mail-merge feature simplifies production of individualized letters and mass mailings.

the standard text. With this feature, each client receives an original letter instead of a photocopy of the standard text with his or her name individually typed in—a laborious task that creates a less than favorable impression. In addition, you can use the sort feature to arrange the addresses in numeric order according to ZIP code. Printing the letters and envelopes or mailing labels in this order will eliminate the time-consuming task of sorting mass mailings according to U.S. Postal Service regulations.

Spreadsheets

For preparing reports containing any analysis of numbers, an electronic spreadsheet is invaluable. An *electronic spreadsheet* is a forecasting and decision-making tool that can be thought of as replacement for, and enhancement of, a calculator. As with a calculator, you can add, subtract, multiply, and divide using a spreadsheet; in addition, you can manipulate and analyze data easily. The spreadsheet's forecasting ability allows the user to ask, for instance, how profits would change if costs and sales were reduced by 10 percent or increased by 5 percent. The ability to calculate these variable forecasts—called "what-if" questions—quickly is one of the main benefits of spreadsheets.

To understand how such a program works, think of a spreadsheet as an arrangement of columns and rows, as shown in Figure 5-4. The area where columns and rows intersect is a *cell*. The letter at the top of the column and the number to the left of the row are used to identify the cell; the location is called the *cell address*. For example, in Figure 5-4 cell address C12 contains the amount 346.

A cell can contain a label (text), a number, or a formula. For example, cell A15 contains the word *Partner*, cell G14 contains the number 160, and cell I14 contains the formula "+G14*H14," which calculates manager revenue for 1993. (Note that an asterisk (*) is used instead of × to indicate multiplication.) Once a value is entered in H14 (average billing rate), the corresponding value of cell I14 (revenue) is automatically recomputed. By supplying a new number in cell I14, the spreadsheet recalculates the values in three other cells and displays new results: K14 (percent change in manager revenue), I17 (total revenue), and K17 (percent change in total revenue). Such formulas are the key to "what if" analysis.

The spreadsheet can transform a vast amount of numerical data into information that can be used for decision making. By condensing data into organized tables, the spreadsheet greatly assists the manager in using the data. Once it has been created, a spreadsheet can be inserted into a document with word-processing software. To depict complex data more clearly, the manager can also quickly construct a graphic using the prepared spreadsheet, as shown in Figure 5-5. The manager inserts the

Describe two specific business applications for a spreadsheet. What benefits would they provide the business?

```
 orksheet  ange  opy  ove  ile  rint  raph  ata  iew  ystem  uit   ↑↓
I14: (C0) +G14*H14
    A    B    C     D       E    F    G      H        I    J    K    L  ↑
1                      Dixon, Garrett & Associates
2                       Projection of 1993 Revenue
3                           January 15, 1993
4
5           !---------------------------!---------------------------!-----------!
6           !       1992 Actual         !       1993 Projected       !           !
7           !---------------------------!---------------------------!           !
8           !        Average            !        Average            ! Percent   !
9           ! Hours Billing  Revenue    ! Hours Billing  Revenue    !Change in  !
10   Level  !(000s) Rate/Hr. ($000s)    !(000s) Rate/Hr. ($000s)    ! Revenue   !
11          !------ -------- -------     !------ -------- -------    !-----------!
12 Staff    !  346    $55    $19,030  !   280    $60    $16,800  !   -11.7%!
13 Senior   !  268    $80    $21,440  !   245    $90    $22,050  !     2.8%!
14 Manager  !  142   $140    $19,880  !   160   $150    $24,000  !    20.7%!
15 Partner  !   66   $220    $14,520  !    90   $240    $21,600  !    48.8%!
16          !---------------------------!---------------------------!-----------!
17   Totals !  822    $91    $74,870  !   775   $109    $84,450  !    12.8%!
18          !===========================!===========================!=========!
19
20
DIXON.WK1   [1]                                                        READY
```

FIGURE 5-4 Spreadsheet simplifies computing of projected change in composition of billable hours.

stacked-bar chart in a memo to the managing partner to reinforce her explanation of the change in the composition of billable hours. Using the same spreadsheet, she can easily generate a visual aid (transparency, slide, or printed handout) to support an oral report. Incorporating a spreadsheet or graphic generated from a spreadsheet into a document can be invaluable for communicating complex information efficiently. Popular spreadsheet programs include *Lotus 1-2-3, Microsoft Excel,* and *Quattro Pro.*

Databases

Lists are important in business. All businesses have a number of lists that must constantly be created, updated, and maintained. The information in them is often vital to the production of certain reports. Because the best report is useless if it isn't timely, the information in the lists must be easy to retrieve and accurate.

Database software allows the creation of useful lists. It organizes the data, permits them to be updated, and allows them to be retrieved in a variety of report formats. The reports in turn can be used for decision making or other purposes. Well-known database programs include *dBase, R:base,* and *Paradox.*

Data are stored in a hierarchical structure, progressing from the smallest unit (field) to the largest (database). Just as the words *city, county, state,* and *nation* describe progressively broader units of territory, the words *field, record, file,* and *database* describe progressively broader units of information. Think of a college's database of students. Each stu-

TO: Ron Tindel, Managing Partner
FROM: Christine Freeland, Human Resources Manager *C.F.*
DATE: January 15, 1992
SUBJECT: PROJECTION OF 1993 REVENUE

The projected revenue for 1993 has been calculated as shown in the
graph. To review the spreadsheet containing these calculations, you may
access DIXON.WK3.

The following factors were considered in preparing these projections:
(1) The business downturn has developed into a prolonged recession,
thus reducing our clients' willingness to entertain consulting engagements.
(2) Our typical staff turnover is declining primarily because of reductions
in hirings at competing companies. (3) Increased client expectations are
demanding the use of staff with extensive business experience.

The amount of work is expected to be about the same as in 1992. Fewer
professional hours will be required because more experienced accountants
will perform more of the work. Staff hours will decline as we hire fewer
college graduates. Increased billing rates and a different mix of hours
among the levels will result in a 12.8 percent increase in total revenues.

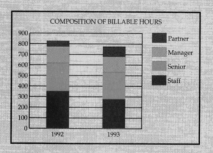

Please inform me of any changes you wish to incorporate in this projection.
With your approval, I will prepare a final projection of 1993 revenue.

**FIGURE 5-5   Stacked bar graph clarifies complex relationship and reinforces
manager's major point.**

dent's name, address, phone number, total credits, and so on, make up the fields of his or her record. The records for each student in a class make up the file for the entire class. The files of all classes of all teachers make up the database for the school.

Think of a database as a large electronic file cabinet where all data, such as names and subjects, are cross-referenced. Because data are cross-referenced, needed information can be located quickly and easily. Suppose you had a business with 10,000 customers and wanted the names of all those who purchased $5,000 to $10,000 worth of products during January and February. With a database, you can compile the list far more quickly and accurately than you could manually.

Is this electronic file cabinet more convenient than a metal one?

In addition to the ability to organize large amounts of data, databases offer two other advantages:

1. *Data integrity.* Some assurance exists that the data will be accurate and complete.
2. *Data security.* The data are secure because access to a database is controlled through several built-in data security features.

Data integrity is possible because, unless the machine fails, data stored in a database will not be lost or misplaced, as a file folder might be. Because updating is relatively easy, the database is more likely to be current. In fact, some updating can be automatic. For example, a system can be established that automatically checks a customer's address against the existing database of customers when an invoice is issued. If the search reveals that the address differs from that in the database, the program will automatically change the stored address to the new one.

Data security exists because users must enter an identification code or a password to gain access to the database, thus protecting it from unauthorized personnel. In addition, a system can be devised that permits only certain authorized workers to change information in the database, even though a broader range of workers can access the data.

Security problems exist for all computer systems.

Types of Databases. Databases are classified as internal or external. *Internal databases* contain intracompany information such as financial, sales, or production data. An internal database for a wholesaler, for example, might contain all possible retailers in different geographic locations. From these data, a list of retailers in the Midwest could be compiled and printed in a few minutes.

External databases are libraries of information that can be accessed using a modem to obtain more broadly applicable information. The Dow-Jones Retrieval Service, for example, may be accessed for up-to-the-minute stock and bond information. Databases can provide important business information quickly and relatively inexpensively. Some external databases charge a membership fee; others charge for each call.

Other databases allow users to access major newspapers.

Database Searches. To use the information in a database, you must conduct a database search, which requires knowing the search procedures and how to construct a search strategy.

Database searching, once a complicated task performed only by research librarians, has become more "user-friendly"; that is, the process is easier to learn and use. For some database systems, you may need 30 to 45 minutes to master retrieval techniques; some of the more complicated systems may require a few hours.

In the past, obtaining information from a database required complex questions worded in difficult-to-learn languages. Now, users can more easily communicate with a database by using English-like query languages such as Structured Query Language (SQL). Commands such as *Select Names from Marketing Students Where Major Equals "Marketing"* might be used to retrieve the names of all students with a major in marketing. Modern database technology also can use artificial intelligence (AI) software that enables the user to communicate with the database in even simpler English. For example, the command previously stated in query language might be as simple as *What Students Have a Major in Marketing?* As you can see, database query languages are becoming more accessible, enabling almost everyone to communicate with databases.

PRESENTING DATA

Being able to access and manipulate data is not enough; the course of daily business often requires that these data be communicated to others. Various kinds of computer software, along with some specialized hardware, make very effective tools for creating convincing presentations.

Printing

The printed page remains one of the main vehicles for business communication. The quality of appearance of a printed document depends not only on the software but on the printer as well. To help you distinguish between these printers, we will consider the four factors that affect your decision of which printer to purchase: (1) print quality, (2) speed, (3) graphics capability, and (4) price. The two most prominent types of printers are dot matrix and laser.

Dot Matrix. *Dot matrix* is the least expensive printing alternative. These printers have a mechanism called a *printhead* with a number of points called *pins* that strike the ribbon in various combinations to create characters (patterns of dots) on the paper. The closer together the dots are, and the greater the number of dots in the same space, the better the quality of the printed character.

Margin notes:

What does "user-friendly" mean?

Doesn't this seem easy?

The number of dots in a given area is called the *resolution.*

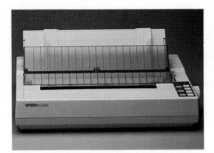

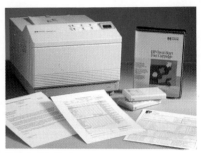

9-pin dot-matrix printer   *24-pin dot-matrix printer*   *Laser printer*

Dot-matrix printers generally come with at least two printing modes that produce different print qualities. The draft mode is the most efficient but yields the poorest quality. In this mode, the dots forming each character are clearly visible; and the output is not appropriate for external correspondence. The draft mode is suitable for preparing internal correspondence; routine business documents; and drafts of proposals, reports, and letters/memos at high speeds.

The near-letter-quality mode produces higher resolution output. Printing each character twice reduces the visible space between dots. Unfortunately, the print speed is significantly reduced in this mode. Although more-expensive dot-matrix printers produce characters with exceptional quality, the print quality remains inadequate for external business correspondence.

Dot-matrix printers also can be used to print certain graphic images, a capability that makes them versatile. Dot-matrix printers are currently available in 9-pin and 24-pin models. The 24-pin model produces better character quality and is more expensive. Sample text produced by a 9-pin printer in draft and near-letter-quality modes is shown in Figure 5-6; 24-pin printouts appear in Figure 5-7.

Laser. *Laser* printers produce characters of the highest quality available for printers that are commonly used in business. These printers use lasers and a process similar to photocopying to produce a page of characters at a time. Because the characters can be shaped in the form of the letters traditionally supplied by professional typesetters for publishing, these printers are considered near-typeset quality. Laser printers also possess the capability of handling sophisticated graphic images. Note the quality of the bar charts shown in Figure 5-9 on page 134, a report produced using desktop publishing capabilities and a laser printer.

Print speed is a significant advantage of laser printing. Manufacturers advertise laser printers with print speeds of 4 to 17 pages per minute. The disadvantage of laser printers is the cost: approximately three times as much as dot-matrix printers.

List several reasons that would convince a business to buy a laser printer.

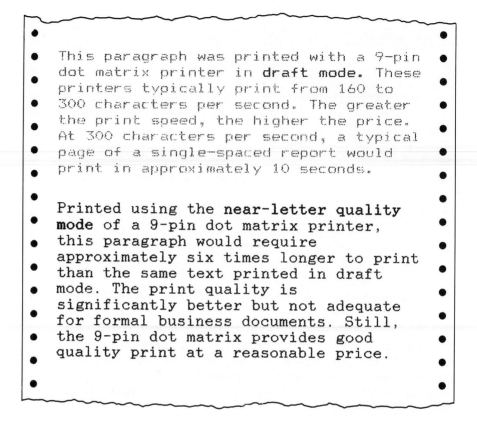

This paragraph was printed with a 9-pin
dot matrix printer in **draft mode.** These
printers typically print from 160 to
300 characters per second. The greater
the print speed, the higher the price.
At 300 characters per second, a typical
page of a single-spaced report would
print in approximately 10 seconds.

Printed using the **near-letter quality
mode** of a 9-pin dot matrix printer,
this paragraph would require
approximately six times longer to print
than the same text printed in draft
mode. The print quality is
significantly better but not adequate
for formal business documents. Still,
the 9-pin dot matrix provides good
quality print at a reasonable price.

FIGURE 5-6 Examples of draft and near-letter-quality text produced on a 9-pin dot-matrix printer

Laser printers offer a number of typefaces that can be enlarged (scaled) within a wide range, from tiny letters to letters larger than a standard sheet of paper. The typeface can be varied to emphasize specific information. Some of these variations include *italic,* **boldface,** shadow, and outline. Sample text produced by a laser printer is shown in Figure 5-8.

Special models of both dot-matrix and laser printers are capable of printing in color. Color can be used to emphasize specific information and to increase the visual appeal of the message.

Desktop Publishing

Until recently, most communications intended for use within an organization were prepared using typewriters or, more recently, word processors connected to letter-quality printers. Even reports, however formal, generally had a typewriter-quality look. Some materials, primarily important publications such as prospectuses and annual reports, were prepared using the standard methods of publishing, including high-quality typesetting that produces clear, sharp letters such as the type you are reading in this book.

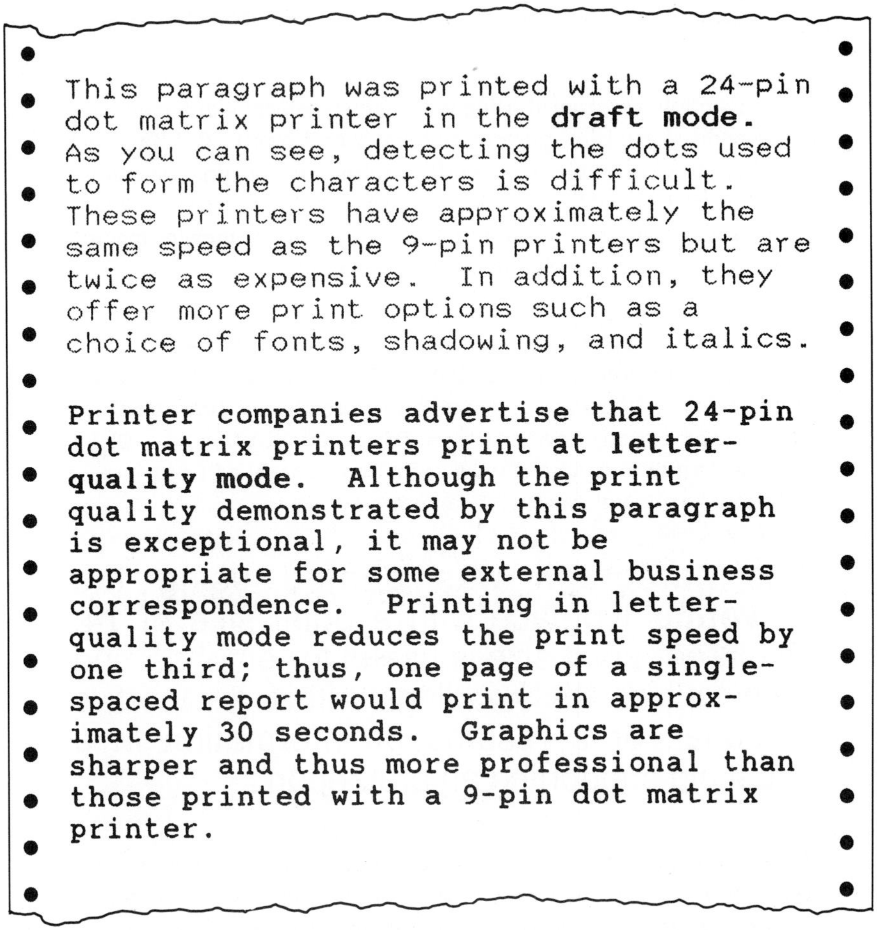

This paragraph was printed with a 24-pin dot matrix printer in the **draft mode.** As you can see, detecting the dots used to form the characters is difficult. These printers have approximately the same speed as the 9-pin printers but are twice as expensive. In addition, they offer more print options such as a choice of fonts, shadowing, and italics.

Printer companies advertise that 24-pin dot matrix printers print at letter-quality mode. Although the print quality demonstrated by this paragraph is exceptional, it may not be appropriate for some external business correspondence. Printing in letter-quality mode reduces the print speed by one third; thus, one page of a single-spaced report would print in approximately 30 seconds. Graphics are sharper and thus more professional than those printed with a 9-pin dot matrix printer.

FIGURE 5-7 Examples of draft and near-letter-quality text produced on a 24-pin dot-matrix printer

The growing capabilities of personal computers have changed these practices. Now one person or a work group within an organization can use sophisticated page-layout software to drive a personal computer and a laser printer to create near-typeset-quality documents at lower cost than was possible in the past. This phenomenon, called *desktop publishing*, helps managers and other workers surpass simple word processing by using typography, design elements, and even graphic images to create communications that are persuasive and professional looking.

In the typical flow of desktop publishing, a document (or a number of documents) is created, edited, and proofread in a word-processing program. It is then brought into a page-layout, or desktop publishing, program such as *Ventura Publisher* or *PageMaker*, where the text can be styled with different typefaces, sizes, and other enhancements, such as rules, boxes, and other graphic devices.

Graphic images can range from a pie chart showing the distribution

This paragraph was printed using the **Times** typeface with a point size of 10 (approximately 12 pitch or elite typewriter print). **Boldface** and *italics* are used to emphasize specific information. Unlike typewriter print, this proportional face varies the spacing between words to give a professional, typeset appearance and to eliminate uneven spacing between words in copy with justified right margins.

For contrast, this paragraph was printed using 12-pitch typewriter print. Note that the **Times** typeface, illustrated in the previous paragraph, has serifs (curves at the top and bottom). This ornate serif type style can be used effectively to display the text of a report.

This paragraph was printed using the **Helvetica** typeface with a point size of 14. The larger point size is useful for emphasizing such text as the headings within a report, a proposal, or a resume or information in a visual aid supporting an oral report.

Because the **Helvetica** typeface, illustrated in this paragraph and the previous paragraph, does not have serifs (curves at the top and bottom of the letter), it is simple and easy to read. A sans serifs (without serifs) typeface is effective for displaying text enlarged for emphasis, complex data, or visuals to be read from a distance.

FIGURE 5-8 Laser printers produce typeset-quality text at high speed.

of total sales among six regions to the picture of a new building to supplement a newsletter article announcing the opening of a new division. The text and graphics are combined electronically to make a complete presentation. When printed on a laser printer, the result can be a convincing report or newsletter.

Graphics are available from several sources:

Which of these sources of graphics are available to you?

1. Electronic spreadsheet and presentation graphics software are used to generate graphics.

COMMUNICATION MENTOR

Due to continually improving technology, one can only imagine how broadly desktop publishing will be used in businesses of the future. Students should find desktop publishing "know-how" to be an increasingly important and marketable skill.

Cynthia Pharr
President & CEO
Tracy-Locke/Pharr Public Relations

2. Limited clipart (predrawn graphics stored on disk) comes with top-of-the line word-processing software, and additional disks can be purchased separately.
3. Drawing software such as *Adobe Illustrator* and *CorelDRAW* allows desktop publishers to draw their own images (flowcharts, pictograms, scaled drawings of products, and so on).
4. Scanners convert printed images (graphics, photos, signatures, letterheads, and text) to electronic files that can be integrated into a document.

By using desktop publishing, you can create a company or corporate image at a fraction of the cost once required. This software can be used to create business cards, letterheads, forms, in-house newsletters, direct-mail advertising, catalogs, manuals, sales reports, and countless other publications. Some of these documents can be created through the use of top-of-the-line word-processing programs. See Figure 5-9 for an example.

Graphics Programs

Pie charts, bar graphs, and line graphs can be generated by graphics software to help people grasp a point more readily than they can interpret a narrative or even a table. Look at the increasing use of graphics in newspapers and television news reports; the communications professionals who create these messages are aware of the direct impact that pictures can have on the reader or viewer.

As more and more information circulates, graphics take on even greater importance. Decision makers, who don't have the time to wade through pages of written text searching for key information, are among the primary beneficiaries of graphic presentations. A manager may win the day by supporting her case for expansion with a line graph showing the resulting increase in profits. A salesperson might close a deal by

What is easier to understand, the weather map or the meteorologist's description?

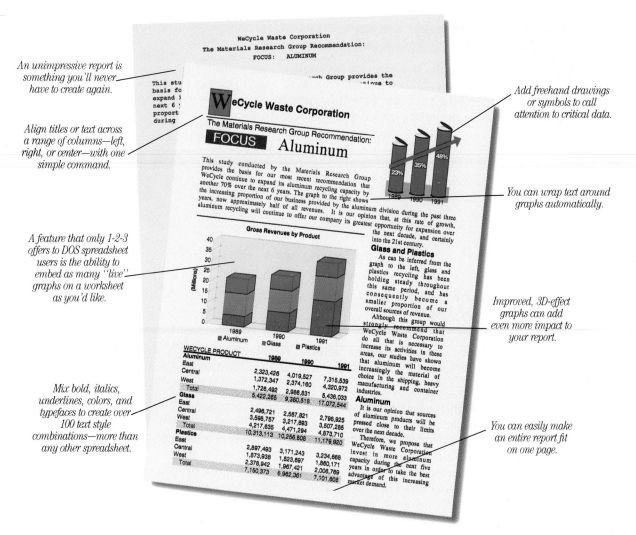

FIGURE 5-9   **Desktop publishing creates highly professional business documents.**

backing up his proposal with five bar graphs illustrating the superiority of his product over the competition's.

The use of graphics in presentations has grown greatly in recent years because of the development of increasingly capable programs for generating graphs on personal computers. Such packages as *Harvard Graphics, Freelance Plus,* and *Microsoft Chart* create standard graph types that work as shells within which data are placed to produce a polished, professional-looking image. The images can be produced quickly and efficiently, as well. The graph shown in Figure 5-10 was created in less than two minutes with the use of *Adobe Illustrator*.

Once generated, graphs can be printed separately in black and white or given more elaborate treatment. Most graphing programs allow the user to create color images that can be either printed on paper using special color printers or turned into slides or transparencies to form part of an oral presentation. Also they can be brought into a document being produced using desktop publishing software to serve as a graphic highlight to a report or story.

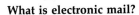

Convert a graphic to a transparency to support an oral report.

SHARING DATA

The rise of computers has added another kind of communications to the practice of business—electronic communications. We have already seen that a modem can link someone with a personal computer to a large database, allowing the computer user to access important and up-to-date information such as stock and bond prices. Computerized communications can also link individuals in other ways.

Electronic Mail

Offices use a number of traditional methods for sending a document, depending on the time constraints and the cost of the method. The U.S. Postal Service can be relied on for two- to four-day delivery or overnight service within the United States. Many private carriers provide overnight or second-day service. For messages that must be sent faster than those methods can manage, electronic mail is used.

Electronic mail is most commonly defined as person-to-person communication in which the transmission and receipt of the message takes

What is electronic mail?

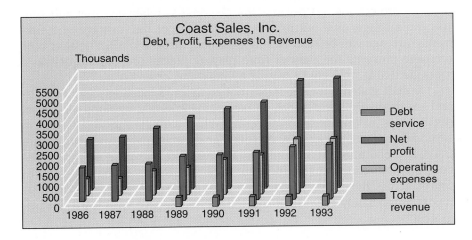

FIGURE 5-10 A computer graphic can be created, changed, and printed quickly and efficiently.

place through a computer. Electronic mail, or *e-mail*, as it is sometimes called, can be categorized as either internal or external.

Internal E-mail. Within a company, electronic mail can be used to distribute memos, reports, and documents without sending them through the mailroom. Suppose a sales manager completes a report and wants the division managers to review it before they all meet that afternoon. Before electronic mail, she would have had to get a messenger to hand deliver the document to the various recipients. Using the company's internal electronic-mail system, however, the manager can deliver the report to each of the others almost instantly.

Two basic systems handle the flow of information within a company: (1) microcomputers wired for networking and (2) multiuser systems. In a network, a number of individual personal computers are linked using wires or cables, a modem, and communications software. In a multiuser system, rather than using a separate computer with its own processor, each user has a keyboard and a monitor attached by cable to a large mainframe computer. In either system, communications software can enable one user to send messages to others almost instantly.

These systems help solve the problem of "telephone tag." Approximately 70 percent of business phone callers *do not* reach the person they called on the first try. The result is a game of tag, as the caller and the person called keep trying to reach the other unsuccessfully. With electronic mail, the caller simply keys in a message and sends it to an electronic mailbox. Receivers are notified that a message awaits them, and they respond to the caller as soon as the message is read.

For example, the electronic message in Figure 5-11 is the partner's response to the memo shown earlier in Figure 5-5. The partner sent his reactions to the human resources manager's projection electronically for three reasons: (1) The electronic message will reach the manager more quickly than a printed memo and thus will expedite the completion of the revenue projections. (2) Because the response is relatively brief and simple, the manager will not need a printed copy of the message; the electronic message can be read and immediately discarded. (3) The electronic message prevents the partner from playing "telephone tag" to deliver a message that is unlikely to require a verbal response.

E-mail systems that operate on a company's existing computer system are relatively inexpensive. In fact, some in-house systems send messages for as little as 5 to 7 cents each. When a single message is sent to several recipients, the savings are even greater compared with the cost of traditional communication methods. For example, suppose the vice president of production must inform six regional sales managers, located in offices across the country, that they must postpone sales of a particular model immediately because of complaints of defective workmanship. Ob-

---

What is telephone tag?

Can you think of another example when an e-mail is an appropriate message medium?

```
Transmit  Block  Lists  Insert  Handling  Draft  Save  Print  Quit
Send this message

        TO:  Christine Freeland, Personnel Manager
      FROM:  Ron Tindel, Managing Partner
        C:
   SUBJECT:  PROJECTION OF 1993 REVENUES
ATTACHMENTS:
                    NEW MESSAGE TEXT

The assumptions used to prepare the projection of 1993 revenues seem
reasonable with one exception. The recession will make it difficult to
collect a $240 billing rate for partners. Therefore, let's maintain the 1992
billing rate of $220 for partners.

Please have the revised revenue projections for 1993 ready for my review when
I return on January 21.

16-Jan-93  10:35 am
```

FIGURE 5-11 Instant feedback provided in electronic-mail message expedites the completion of an assignment.

viously, timely delivery is a critical factor because the purpose of the message is to prevent the shipment of any more orders. Mail service is too slow, and the telephone system is inconvenient because the regional offices are located within several time zones. In fact, the East Coast offices have already closed for the day. E-mail is the appropriate medium for this message. With only a few keystrokes, the vice president sends one electronic message that reaches all managers instantly at a low cost.

External E-mail.   With external electronic mail, the message is transmitted over telephone lines using a modem and communications software. The caller keys in a telephone number, connects with another user, and the two can "talk" from their keyboards, with the messages displayed on their monitors. As with internal communications, messages can be stored in the recipient's computer if he or she is not there when the call comes through. The benefit is that time is not lost when a caller does not connect with the recipient.

Another form of external communications involves connecting to a system of information exchange called an *electronic bulletin board*. A bulletin board is organized by individuals interested in a particular topic or area of study; by dialing the number of the bulletin board from their computers, individuals can, for instance, share tips for using software or learn how to solve a problem with a printer.

Voice mail is another recent development in electronic communications. With this method, you use your telephone to dial a voice-mail service and store an oral message; it is then delivered to the person you're calling. The audio quality of the message is similar to the actual voice. Since virtually everyone has a telephone, this service is not limited to owners of specialized equipment.

A flexible and inexpensive form of electronic mail is *facsimile transmission* or fax. A fax machine reads a document that has been inserted into the machine and transmits the document (text, pictures, and graphics) over telephone lines to another fax machine that receives the message and prepares a printed copy of the document.

Because increasing numbers of companies of all sizes are using fax machines, entrepreneurs are putting fax machines that take credit cards into airport lounges, hotel lobbies, and convention centers. To use them, you simply insert your credit card in the machine, dial the number you want to reach, and send your document.

The advantage of fax transmission is its speed. For example, a high-speed fax machine can transmit a page in about 20 seconds. Improved machines offer print quality comparable to that of a copy machine. In addition, fax machines are easy to operate. Because they can be pro-

---

What are the advantages of a fax machine?

A fax machine is a very useful tool for business communication. This manager is sending an architectural drawing to a client via fax for approval, thus avoiding a costly and possibly ineffective telephone call while saving time.

COMMUNICATION MENTOR

The facsimile machine is another tool that has increased my staff's effectiveness in disseminating information quickly and easily. Before the fax machine, getting news releases to the media involved either mailing, which meant at least a day's delay, or telephoning, a time-consuming process. With the fax machine, we get our news releases to the media in an instant.

The Honorable Mike Espy
U.S. House of Representatives

grammed, the cost of transmission can be cut by sending the message in evening hours to take advantage of lower phone rates. Sending fax transmission also facilitates communicating with people in different time zones.

Some individuals who work from their homes use electronic mail to transmit their work from their home to the office. The major advantages of *telecommuting*, as this concept is called, are the reduced time and expense of commuting and the increased flexibility of working hours. Rather than spending two to three hours a day commuting to work in an urban area, for example, employees use a modem, telephone lines, and a remote workstation to transmit their work to their supervisors electronically. Memos, reports, even whole books can be transmitted in this way.

News reporters can send their stories this way.

In addition, practitioners from various disciplines are using modems and telephone lines to transmit information quickly and cost effectively. For example:

◆ Accountants transmit income tax returns to the Internal Revenue Service.
◆ Private investors transmit investment transactions to stockbrokers.
◆ Sales representatives calling on customers in remote locations transmit orders to the home office to facilitate quick delivery (and foster good customer relations).

Can you provide another example of electronic communication?

◆ Professionals working away from their office (for example, in clients' offices or other remote sites) transmit information back to the office. For instance, an engineer transmits detailed production information so that personnel in the home office can begin analyzing the data. Auditors transmit financial information collected while working in clients' offices to expedite completion of the final audit report.

Transmitting information and computing from remote locations have become more prevalent because of the availability of *laptop* and *notebook*

A laptop computer allows you to work in any situation—on the street, on a plane, or in a hotel room. This manager is taking advantage of this technology by working on a report while waiting for his flight to arrive.

computers. Laptops, which are about the size of a large book, and even smaller notebook computers give professionals access to computing power regardless of where they are—hotel room, airplane, taxi, or client's office. These portable systems are battery operated and generally contain secondary storage (a floppy disk drive, a hard disk drive, or both), a screen, and a keyboard.

How do portable computer systems benefit users?

Managers use portable computers for two major reasons: (1) to make every minute of a busy schedule count and (2) to generate and communicate up-to-the-minute information without returning to their desktop computers. As technology improves, manufacturers are attempting to enhance the quality of the images displayed on the monitor and the quality of the printouts. Poor-quality images and printouts have been the major disadvantages of portable systems.

Cellular service (mobile phones) is a relatively new technology and a powerful communication tool, especially for managers who are on the

This executive is using a cellular telephone. By having this communication tool, she can make important calls when she is away from the office, maintain strong relationships with clients and colleagues, and make use of otherwise unproductive time spent in her car.

move (those who spend several hours commuting to and from work, travel from one meeting or work site to another, or work at sites with no access to a telephone) and must stay in immediate reach of the home office at all times. The increased productivity resulting from the more efficient use of time justifies the use of cellular service. Cellular phones also help managers stay in closer contact with coworkers and with current and prospective clients and customers. Quick, courteous responses build strong interpersonal relations, which in turn lead to increased employee commitment and an edge over competitors. As cellular service expands to reach remote areas as well as urban areas, cellular phones will soon become a standard business tool.

> **Efficient use of time and closer contact with coworkers, clients, and customers are convincing reasons to use a cellular phone.**

Teleconferencing

Electronic mail offers an alternative to written and oral messages, memos, letters, or reports. Teleconferencing is an alternative to face-to-face meetings that allows several people at different locations to communicate electronically. This system can eliminate or reduce the high costs of face-to-face meetings: travel, hotels, food, and time lost in transit.

The three main types of teleconferencing are audio teleconferencing, audiographic teleconferencing, and audiovideo teleconferencing. A fourth, educational teleconferencing, is usually a combination of the three main types.

Audio Teleconferencing.   Telephone companies have offered teleconferencing facilities for business use for many years. The telephone conference call, in which the phone company arranges for several people in different geographic locations to be on the same line at the same time, is an example of this type of teleconferencing. Today's electronic phones are capable of establishing the necessary connections from the console itself.

> **Psychologically, the distance factor still exists.**

Audiographic Teleconferencing.   In addition to the voice portion of the teleconference, graphics may be transmitted using facsimile devices. The audiographic teleconference might take place in a room specifically designed for the purpose, with hand-held microphones for each participant and machines for sending images of documents or still photos of conference participants.

Audiovideo Teleconferencing.   The audiovideo teleconference takes advantage of all media—audio, graphics, and video. A specially equipped room is necessary for an audiovideo teleconference: speakers provide the audio feedback, facsimile devices send graphics, and cameras transmit the video portion of the conference. Participants can engage in group discussions while observing one another's facial expressions and gestures. Major television news programs frequently use two-way video equipment

Another useful technological means for business communication is teleconferencing. By opting for the teleconference, businesspeople can conduct important meetings while saving the time and money that would be spent on travel.

to show both the interviewer and interviewee; audiovideo teleconferencing is a similar process.

Educational Teleconferencing.   Educational programs on television bring the class to the student rather than the student to the class. With closed-circuit television and feedback audio equipment, actual campus classes can be sent to remote classrooms or even to a business organization's educational facility. Students in remote classrooms can contact the actual classroom when they have questions or answers. The same system can be used with ill or disabled students in elementary and secondary schools. Although the possibilities of teleconferencing in education are almost boundless, the intellectual, social, and psychological growth that occurs when students attend school with one another argues against sole reliance on this technique.

PUTTING IT ALL TOGETHER: THE EXECUTIVE WORKSTATION

Executive workstations bring all the electronic tools previously described to one place. The *executive workstation* consists of a personal computer or a keyboard and monitor linked to a mainframe. In either case, the workstation has the ability to use a number of computerized tools.

Because of the diversity of the executive's duties, the workstation needs capabilities for word processing, spreadsheet analysis, and database management. With these programs, the workstation provides the executive with flexibility in writing and revising written material, analyzing data, interacting with databases, and preparing reports based on the accumulated information.

Some software programs, called *integrated programs,* include all three of these main applications in one common form. They share similar key combinations to initiate commands for manipulating data or formatting reports. By creating common structures for files, integrated programs facilitate the use of one kind of data in another—for example, the use of a spreadsheet in a report being prepared on the word processor.

Some executive workstations add other software programs to these core applications. Depending on the manager's area of responsibility, his or her workstation could be equipped with desktop publishing or graphics-generating programs. Providing these workstations with electronic communications programs is typical.

Executives can use their workstations not only to carry out these important functions but also to plan their days. Scheduling or calendar programs allow managers to query the computer about their schedules and plan conferences accordingly. In a shared system, such as a network or multiuser system, the computer system can scan the calendars of a number of people to determine the best meeting time for all individuals involved.

An added benefit of such programs is the fact that they can prevent time conflicts when assistants are making schedules for their supervisor. By making up-to-the-minute schedule information available to both executive and assistant, they prevent duplicate booking of time.

Another software tool that can aid the executive is the *personal information manager.* These programs facilitate scheduling and the organizing of random notes. They use very sophisticated methods of linking disparate bits of information through key words and phrases to allow the executive to thumb electronically through scores of notations in search of, for instance, all references to a particular client.

Although the executive workstation allows executives and assistants to work more efficiently by communicating through the computer, some executives are hindered by the fear of new technology. Many who start out feeling uneasy about their new machine, however, soon learn that the equipment can liberate them by performing boring and repetitive tasks quickly and by providing easy and rapid access to vital information.

To take advantage of these tools, an executive must be able to do the following tasks:

1. Type at a speed of 40 to 50 words per minute.
2. Create or revise text using a word processor.

List the various applications that a manager can perform at an executive workstation.

3. Analyze data from spreadsheets.
4. Access and retrieve database information.
5. Plan and schedule activities.
6. Use the electronic mail system to send and receive messages.

COMPUTERS AND BARRIERS TO COMMUNICATION

Like all communication tools, computers both help and hinder good communication. In some respects, the requirements or capabilities of the machine can lead the user astray when creating or interpreting a message. We will examine how this can occur in each of the areas previously studied.

Barriers Caused by Systems

Compatibility with existing systems must be analyzed before purchasing computer hardware or software.

The very nature of computers—the way they record, move, and manipulate data—can create barriers to communication. First, keep in mind that all computers do not work in exactly the same way. The engineering of the central processing unit channels the way programs work and data are recorded, but different computers are engineered differently. Some systems have certain important core structures in common, and data stored on one system can be retrieved on another. But with other systems, that is not the case. System incompatibility, then, is one barrier to communication between computers. Large companies often have a management information system (MIS) department that focuses on the organization's computer systems. The staff of that department, which has special expertise in the area, can advise you on whether you would be able to share data or make contact with another computer at another location.

A second systemic barrier to communication stems from the way people use computers. These machines follow a rigid logic. They are very structured, and the person using them must be very structured as well, or he or she will become lost in the rigor of the machines. Ignoring the proper sequence for leaving a program and turning off the machine, for instance, could result in the loss of some data. Forgetting to issue the commands to store a report on a disk loses the report.

Although computers must be commanded in a logical and structured way, you should not be afraid of the computer or afraid of making a mistake. You must be careful to perform tasks, when necessary, in a step-by-step fashion and not try to skip ahead.

Barriers in Manipulating Data

Word Processing. The rigidity of the computer's logic can cause problems when using a software program such as word processing. Because computers are able to perform so many tasks so rapidly, people form the mistaken notion that the machines are infallible and don't realize that a computer carries out instructions without hesitation and without judgment.

Overreliance on spellcheckers is a prevalent and costly mistake that damages the effectiveness and the credibility of the message. Documents must be proofread to avoid errors such as those in the following example, in which words were spelled correctly but used incorrectly. The sentences as they were input and checked for spelling read as follows:

He was <u>complemented</u> on his choice office furniture: desks, chairs, <u>filling</u> cabinets, and <u>son</u>. The <u>manager's</u> <u>hardly</u> approved.

Unfortunately, what was intended was the following message:

He was <u>complimented</u> on his choice <u>of</u> office furniture: desks, chairs, <u>filing</u> cabinets, and <u>so on</u>. The <u>managers</u> <u>heartily</u> approved.

To enhance your proofreading skills, carefully review the systematic proofreading procedures presented on pages 275–281 of Chapter 8.

Similarly, using software to analyze writing is ineffective if the writer accepts the software's critique without evaluating whether the suggestion is appropriate for the particular message being written. A writer should ask, "Does the technique suggested achieve my desired objectives?" For example, using active voice to achieve clear, vivid images is an effective writing principle; but it is not recommended when conveying bad news.

Using the automatic search-and-replace feature may also cause undesired results. Read the following paragraph:

Each person present at the demonstration was given a list of word-processing commands. The office manager later reprimanded the man who raised the question about the reliability of the software.

Suppose that the search and replace feature were used to replace the word *man* with *woman*. This seemingly innocent change causes the following incoherence:

Each person present at the demonstration was given a list of word-processing <u>comwomands</u>. The office <u>womanager</u> later <u>repriwomaned</u> the woman who raised the question about the reliability of the software.

The computer changed *every* instance in which the letters *man* appeared in sequence to the word *woman*. Computers do not exercise judgment;

they carry out commands. Users must be sure to construct their commands in such a way as to get the results they really want.

The mail-merge feature also can lead to barriers to communication. The most frequent complaint about this feature is that form letters are impersonal. Many people simply refuse to read such letters for that reason. Constructing a good standard letter that doesn't sound like a form letter can circumvent this problem. To make a form letter more personal,

1. Add more variables to the standard letter so you have more opportunity to tailor it to the individual.
2. Use personalized envelopes instead of mass-produced mailing labels.
3. Be sure to spell names correctly.
4. Produce a higher-quality document by using a better grade of paper and better-quality printers.

Spreadsheets.   The main barrier to good communication with a spreadsheet is the use of incorrect formulas for manipulating data. Whenever you create a template for a particular spreadsheet, be sure to check the validity of the formulas by running a sample test with some data.

Garbage in, garbage out!

Another barrier stems from the confidence that people develop in the results produced by a spreadsheet. Because the computer has such vast capabilities, users assume that a computer-generated report must be correct. However, the results are only as good as the data that are entered in the first place. Check for the following specific items:

1. Verify data entered into the spreadsheet against the source from which they came.
2. Evaluate results to be certain that they are reasonable. If the results seem questionable, begin by rechecking the accuracy of formulas and data input into the spreadsheet.
3. Check to ensure that the assumptions behind "what-if" projections are reasonable.
4. Critique the spreadsheet design carefully to be certain that it *reinforces* the accuracy of your data. Misspelled words, inconsistent formats (for example, some headings are centered and parallel headings appear flush left), and illogical or unattractive arrangement of data could create a serious question in the reader's mind: "Because these errors are present, *how* can I be confident that the data are correct?"

Today's highly sophisticated spreadsheet software may be intimidating to some novice users. As a result, these users may underutilize spreadsheets or avoid them altogether. As an important first step, reluctant users must resolve to overcome the forceful tendency to avoid topics that appear to be difficult. With an open mind, they can commit the time and energy needed to develop a marketable tool in today's information age: the ability to process information quickly and accurately. If necessary, they should seek adequate training by asking for help from coworkers who are experienced spreadsheet users, attending in-house computer training sessions, or enrolling in college computer-application classes.

Databases.   A problem may arise if databases are not properly designed. A database usually has a limit on the number of fields per record that can be used. When constructing a database, you need to decide which fields are necessary. Inexperienced database designers will try to create fields for all possible data about a customer or client rather than identify and omit unnecessary data. The result is a poorly designed database that is difficult and time-consuming to use.

Ineffective Presentations

Type, design, and graphics introduce new considerations that were once the concern of only graphic artists or typesetters. Desktop publishing puts a very useful tool in the hands of the untrained user; unfortunately, the results often show the lack of training. Having the tools to design does not make you a designer. Newcomers to desktop publishing, enchanted with the effects that can be created with type, rules, shadows, and boxes, clutter documents with too many type styles or with too many lines. The result is not an effective presentation but a jumble of words and graphic elements that confuse and alienate the reader.

> **How does too much variety get in the way of communicating?**

By following some simple principles of design, however, the budding desktop publisher can effectively use the tools at his or her disposal:

1. *Keep it simple.* The worst thing to do is everything. The more variety included on the page, the more difficulty the reader will have in following the message. Restricting the document to no more than two or three typefaces and just a few special effects is often the best approach. Other variations remain available for another publication.
2. *Keep it consistent.* Treat comparable elements in the same way. All the headlines in a newsletter with five stories should be in the same typeface and style. Save special treatments for material that is special.

> **Emphasis should be given to the main points in the communication.**

3. *Let form follow function.* The document should be styled in such a way that it looks like what it is. A purchase order need not be elegant; the menu of an expensive restaurant should look more dignified than the price list of a dry-cleaning service.

A similar problem may arise with graphics-generating programs: A person may be so eager to create eye-catching graphics that the actual relationships of data are distorted. The purpose of graphs is to emphasize, not obscure, points. Be careful to use graphics reasonably.

Barriers in Electronic Communication

Electronic mail (including voice mail) is a handy way to communicate quickly and conveniently with another worker or with a database. Problems can arise if the system is used inappropriately or if messages are too long or poorly organized. The following guidelines will help you use this tool effectively:

Give an example of a good voice-mail message.

1. Messages on electronic- or voice-mail systems should be related to business and not designed to give the recipient a good laugh. Resist the urge to "personalize" the message that identifies your voice mailbox and informs callers that you are unavailable. This message should be highly professional, giving the caller a clear indication of when you will return the call.

2. Do not flood the system with "junk mail." One of the key benefits of electronic mail is to allow workers to communicate more effectively than they are able to with traditional means. If the system is clogged with unnecessary messages, many of which the reader feels compelled to answer, productivity will be lost, not gained.

3. Be conscientious in checking and responding to your electronic messages; otherwise, you may miss important information needed to complete your assignments. By ignoring electronic messages from co-workers, you can erode any efforts made to create an open, honest work environment.

4. Decide whether the electronic- or voice-mail system is an appropriate channel for your message. These systems are designed for transmitting information typically sent through printed memos; they are *not* intended for formal communication such as performance appraisals or disciplinary action. As the sender, you are responsible for choosing the most effective channel for your message; technology simply increases your choices of channels. In other words, even though a message can be sent faster and more efficiently using electronic or voice mail, you still may elect to schedule a face-to-face meeting if the message is sensitive, highly emotional, or subject to misinterpretation.

5. Lengthy, detailed information is for printed memos, not electronic- or voice-mail messages. Requiring your reader or listener to remember or to write down a significant amount of information shows that you have no empathy for your audience struggling to take notes from the monitor or listening and relistening to your recorded message. Lengthy messages are likely to become distorted and thus cause costly delays and mistakes. When sending a voice-mail message, repeat important information to give listeners a second chance to hear it or to confirm what they heard the first time. For example, you will probably introduce yourself at the beginning of the message. If you leave a phone number at the end, repeat your name and state the phone number very slowly twice.

Innovations in computer and communciations technology are developing rapidly. Successful executives stay abreast of what new technologies are available and how they can improve their businesses, and they are not afraid to learn new skills. This executive is accessing data from a CD-ROM.

6. Organize your message carefully beforehand just as you would a traditionally prepared message. Present information in the order it is likely to be needed. For example, describe the nature and purpose of an upcoming meeting before giving the specifics (date, place, time); otherwise, the reader or listener may have to reread portions of an electronic memo or review an entire voice-mail message to extract the details. Busy managers will appreciate your using empathy (putting yourself in the reader's or listener's position) to determine a logical, efficient sequence of information.

SUMMARY

Some people mistakenly think of electronic tools for business communication as substitutes for basic communication skills. However, they are tools that augment and enhance the communication process.

The main categories of these tools are

1. Tools for manipulating words, numbers, and data, called word-processing, electronic spreadsheet, and database programs, respectively.

2. Tools for presenting information, including desktop publishing and graphics-generation programs.

3. Tools for communicating electronically from one computer to another.

These tools may be used individually or in combination. Executive workstations bring many tools together in one place.

As with all tools, computer programs must be used properly to enhance communication. Even spellchecking, an apparently straightforward use of computers, can result in errors if not used properly. Although the electronic tools described in this chapter can make communication easier or the presentation of a message more effective, they are no substitute for the basic communications skills the user must possess.

REVIEW QUESTIONS

1. What are the three categories of electronic communication? Briefly discuss how each category facilitates the quick and accurate flow of information.

2. Review the following word-processing features: insert; delete; block and move; block and copy; search and replace; redlining and document comment; spellcheck; thesaurus; writing-analysis software; automatic contents page, index, and document references; and mail merge. Which feature would you select for each example?

   a. Two lines of copy were omitted.

   b. Words were misspelled.

   c. One sentence needs to be removed.

   d. The product number was incorrect twelve times.

   e. Three paragraphs on the first page need to be moved to page 10.

   f. Because last-minute data were required to ensure accuracy and usefulness, a lengthy report was prepared with only two to three hours remaining to complete the preliminary and addenda parts (all parts except the report itself).

   g. Because of a backlog in production, 25 orders of Model XL-100 will be delayed for approximately three weeks. A letter must be sent informing customers of the delay.

   h. A complicated table on page 2 needs to be used again on page 14.

   i. Software developers prepared a description of a new software program and submitted it to the sales department on disk. After revising the description for inclusion in a consumer catalog, the advertising manager returned the disk to the software developers for revisions and approval.

   j. You cannot think of a word to use in place of "advent."

   k. You have earned low ratings on the "Written Communication

Skills" section of your past couple of performance appraisals. Your supervisor told you that simply "trying harder" was not sufficient; you must locate some means for identifying and overcoming your problems before your next review.

3. Discuss how word-processing features can aid in producing a document that is written collaboratively (composed by more than one writer or at least requiring the input and approval of another person). Provide an example of a business document that would logically involve collaborative writing.

4. Explain how word-processing software makes preparing form letters more efficient than traditional communication methods.

5. Discuss the procedures for making a form letter more personal.

6. Describe the major functions of an electronic spreadsheet. Explain how each of these functions increases the effectiveness of communication.

7. Provide an example of how the electronic spreadsheet or graphics generated from the spreadsheet can be used to reinforce or clarify the major points presented in a business document. Perhaps you can share a situation encountered in your part-time employment, student activities, or another class.

8. Why are databases important in business? Identify a number of different types of databases a company might have. Give an example of a database that would help you.

9. Briefly distinguish between the two major types of printers, keeping in mind the four factors that affect the decision to buy a printer.

10. Describe the general process of preparing a document using desktop publishing. How does this process affect communication?

11. Give an example of how desktop publishing or graphics-generating software can be a barrier to communication.

12. What are the four sources of graphics to be integrated into desktop published documents? Discuss any experience you have had working with any of these sources.

13. Is growth expected in the desktop publishing field? How will this activity affect employees entering business fields?

14. What contributions do graphics make to the effectiveness of a business document? What effect has technology had on the use of graphics? Explain.

15. Describe the advantages of electronic mail. Discuss your experience with electronic communication.

16. What is telecommuting and what are its major advantages? Provide an example from your experience or knowledge of a practitioner's use of modems and telephones to transmit information quickly and cost effectively.

17. Discuss how laptop and notebook computers facilitate communication.

18. Discuss the primary benefits of cellular phone service. What general factors determine whether an employee could profit from a cellular phone? List several job categories that you believe could profit from cellular phones.
19. Explain what is meant by "personal information management."
20. Briefly discuss the barriers caused by the following communication tools: (1) systems, (2) word processing, (3) spreadsheets, (4) databases, (5) desktop publishing and graphics-generating software, and (6) electronic communication.

EXERCISES

1. Management has asked you to suggest ways to improve office productivity. You conduct interviews with several employees. What are your solutions to the following problems?
   a. A memo takes two or three days to get from one department to another.
   b. Sales executives are very frustrated about the excessive time spent in air travel for regional product-information meetings.
   c. Telephone tag is a problem for many employees.
   d. Proposals with misspelled words often reach supervisors.
   e. Information is lost in crowded cabinets and cannot be retrieved in time to assist in decision making.
   f. Administrative assistants become upset when asked to make changes or revisions in documents because they have to spend hours retyping entire documents.
   g. Compiling reports is an extremely time-consuming task. For example, someone wants to know the names of all customers who purchased $2,000 or more worth of Brand X last year. An employee complains that pulling this information from the company files will take months. Furthermore, the information may not be accurate and may be unavailable for other states.
   h. Coworkers, contractors, and bank loan officers frequently need to reach the vice president of a land development company readily so that they can make or implement decisions. However, reaching the vice president is nearly impossible as he is often away from the home office visiting building sites, meeting with contractors, negotiating bank loans, or traveling between these various locations.
   i. A producer in a California film studio is irritated when filming is stopped to wait for a scriptwriter working in a remote location to rewrite and mail a portion of script. The producer's apprehension is legitimate because delays are the major cause of a film's exceeding budget, a common occurrence for this producer recently.

2. Perform an automatic search-and-replace procedure on any word in a one-page document using any word-processing program. Be prepared to discuss any problems that occur as a result of the automatic search-and-replace feature.

3. Keyboard the following memo and perform a spellcheck using any word-processing software. Proofread a printed copy of the memo. Use the standard proofreaders' marks shown in Appendix A to mark any corrections. Write a brief report summarizing your observations about this process.

September 2, 19--

Brian Davis, Vice President of Sales

INSTALLATION OF CELLULAR SERVICE BY JANUARY 1

At last the time is right for giving our sales staff cellular phones.

During last years budgeting process, we determined that cellular phones would not be cost effective until cellular service reached our Western sales region. Yesterday at the Chamber of Commerce meeting, the sales manager of Cellular North, Inc. announced that their service territory would be extend as of January 1. There expanded territory will include our Western region.

Let's procede immediately with the installation of cellular facilities. I am convinced that having our system full operable by January 1 will provide our sales staff a advantage over our competitors. You have the authority to acquire the necesssary equipment and to schedule training seminar to educate the sales representatives on the most affective use of this technology.

Despite the large capitol investment, I am very supportive of this investment. Cellular north has assured me that the increased productivity of our staff will permit us to recoup our investment with a couple of months. For that reason, I will be quite eager to reveiw you periodic progress reports.

Anthony DelCarlo
President

---

4. Keyboard a one-page document using any word-processing program or compose a brief message, depending on your instructor's guidelines. Use a writing-analysis program to generate a critique of the document. Outline the major writing improvements suggested by the computer. List any observations you can make about these suggestions. For example, do you believe the suggestions are valid, or should you overrule some of them? Explain.

5. Bring to class samples of documents produced on printers of varying quality. Discuss the effect the quality of print has on the message.

6. After consulting advertising and design books and periodicals, write a two-page report presenting principles of effective page layout and design.

7. Request and perform a library database search on one of the topics in this chapter or one that your instructor assigns. Researching back two years, locate an article on microfilm and print a copy. Hand in the list and the copy of the article.

8. Describe a communication obstacle you have encountered when using an electronic communication tool. If you do not have a personal experience, describe one that could happen. How did (would) you deal with the barrier? What insights did (might) you gain from this experience? What have you learned from reading this chapter that could have aided (could aid) you in overcoming this barrier?

9. Study carefully the following spreadsheet designed to compute payroll for Creative Images, Inc. Identify any errors and explain how each error could influence the effective transfer of this information.

```
 Worksheet  Range  Copy  Move  File  Print  Graph  Data  View  System  Quit   ↑↓
A1: [W17] 'Creative Images, Inc.
          A              B           C      D        E         F          G      ↑
1    Creative Images, Inc.
2    Payroll Summary
3
4
5                                          Hourly    Gross    With-       Net
6    Employee         Dept.       Hrs.     Wage      Pay      oldings     Pay
7
8    Day, Bart        Sales        45      13.5      641.25    243.60     397.65
9    Harden, Lisa     Delivery     40       8.5      340.00    125.00     215.00
10   Lambert, Matt    Maintanence  25       5.5      137.50     50.50      87.00
11   Dollar, Janice   Sales        48       5        260.00    198.80      61.20
12   Jones, Alan      Delivery     40       8.25     330.00    125.45     204.55
13   Kelly, Melanie   Sales        48      12.5      650.00    247.90     402.10
14   Patterson, Kim   Sales        40      15        600.00    228.00     372.00
15   Sanford, Jon     Sales        41      14        581.00    220.75     360.25
16
17                                                 3,539.75  1,219.25   2,099.75
18                                                 ==========================
19
20
PAYROLL.WK1  [1]                                                          READY
```

ETHICAL AND LEGAL GUIDELINES

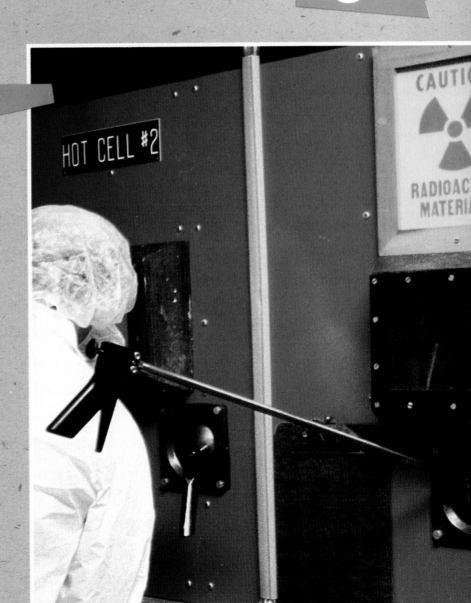

OBJECTIVES

When you have completed Chapter 6, you should be able to

- Define ethics and identify the process by which individuals develop the foundation for making ethical decisions.

- Identify the common causes for unethical behavior in the workplace.

- Use an ethical decision-making framework to facilitate identifying and effectively communicating solutions that conform to your personal values.

- Recognize the importance of taking moral responsibility for all communication (oral and written) transmitted and actions taken.

A YOUNG LAB TECHNICIAN at a large plutonium fuel plant became increasingly aware of her corporation's lax safety regulations. She began to look for areas of potential danger. Shortly thereafter, she was contaminated by radioactive material in the plant and had to submit to a painful scrub-down and a harrowing battery of physical tests. After her potentially deadly exposure to the material, she continued to investigate the plant's safety mechanisms, looking for possible trouble spots that could cause a great deal of damage to the workers and to the community.

When she discovered what appeared to be dangerous weaknesses in the way the highly concentrated and deadly plutonium was contained, she told the Atomic Energy Commission and *The New York Times.* She believed that by communicating the facts, she (and others) would force the company to enact more stringent safety measures. Instead, she received anonymous threats, which she believed were from company officials. However, she continued her attempts to spread the word about the danger the plant posed. While on her way to meet with a reporter from the *Times* and a member of her union, she was killed in a mysterious automobile accident.

Some people thought she should have kept the information to herself, that she should not have blown the whistle on her employer for actions she deemed dangerous. But Karen Silkwood held onto her beliefs and did what she believed was right; and partially because of the attention she generated from her claims against the plant, Kerr-McGee was forced to shut down its facility at Crescent, Oklahoma (Marshall, 1975).

Unethical behavior in the workplace is reported by the press almost daily.

Other examples of unethical conduct include Beechnut's selling infant apple juice without a trace of apple in the ingredients (Traub, 1988); Johnson & Johnson's using a rival's trade secret, for which it was ordered to pay a $116.3 million fine (Kelly, 1991); E. F. Hutton's committing 2,000 counts of mail and wire fraud (Gellerman, 1986); and the publishers of a best-selling photography book, *A Day in the Life of America,* using computers to alter the composition of the cover photograph (Ansberry, 1989). Savings and loan officers have used depositors' funds for speculative investments, and investment bankers have used inside information to gain an advantage over traders in the stock market. These are just a few of the numerous unethical business activities that are reported by the press almost daily. Indeed, one source estimates that between 1976 and 1986, roughly two-thirds of America's 500 largest corporations were involved in some form of unethical behavior (Gellerman, 1986).

Describe an unethical act you have witnessed in school or at work.

Matters of ethics are seldom clear-cut issues of right vs. wrong and often contain many ambiguous elements. In addition, the pressure appears to be felt most strongly by lower-level managers who are least experienced doing their jobs. Many of these managers are recent business school graduates.

The savings and loan scandal is an example of unethical conduct gone out of control. Officers used depositors' money for speculative investments to earn more money for themselves. When the scheme failed, depositors were told their hard-earned money was unavailable. Ethical issues are not separate from business decisions. As a manager, you must be aware of the pressure to make unethical choices and know how to make sound decisions instead.

Because the chances of your being faced with an ethical dilemma are likely, what can you do now to prepare for dealing with pressure to compromise personal values? First, remember that only if you have definite beliefs on a variety of issues and the courage to practice them will you be able to make sound ethical judgments. Second, learning to analyze ethical dilemmas (identify the consequences of your actions) will help you make decisions that conform to your own value system. Thus, unless you know what you stand for and how to analyze the ethical issue, you become a puppet, controlled by the motives of others, too weak to make a decision on your own. What will you do?

THE FOUNDATION FOR ETHICAL BEHAVIOR

Although ethics is a common point of discussion, many might find defining ethics quite challenging. Most people immediately associate ethics with standards and rules of conduct, morals, right and wrong, values, and honesty. Dr. Albert Schweitzer defined ethics as "the name we

With what do most people associate ethics? Define ethics.

give to our concern for good behavior. We feel an obligation to consider not only our own personal well-being, but also that of others and of human society as a whole" (Slayton, 1980, p. 5). In other words, ethics refers to the principles of right and wrong that guide us in making decisions that affect others.

Although the recorded accounts of ethical misconduct would seem to indicate that businesses are dishonest and unscrupulous, keep in mind that millions of business transactions are made daily on the basis of honesty and concern for the welfare of others. Why should a business make ethical decisions? What difference will it make? James E. Perrella, executive vice president of Ingersoll-Rand Company, has a powerful reply to these questions (Slayton, 1991, p. 7):

Why should a business make ethical decisions?

> Our question of today should be, what's the right thing to do, the right way to behave, the right way to conduct business? Don't just ask, is it legal?
>
> Have you ever considered what business would be like if we all did it? If every businessman and businesswoman followed the Golden Rule?
>
> My company would not have to file a lawsuit alleging that counterfeit bearings were sold to Boeing Company by a California-based bearing supplier. . . . Congress would not have to tighten curbs on insider trading. Companies would not have to require employees to sign codes of ethics or establish strict guidelines for purchasing agents to follow.
>
> Many people including many business leaders would argue that such an application of ethics to business would adversely affect bot-

COMMUNICATION MENTOR

Being faced with questions of ethics during your career is a very real possibility. Now is the time to prepare yourself. Decide now what your values are, what you believe in, what honesty and integrity and fairness really mean to you. Write it all down on a sheet of paper; keep the paper in a safe place. Making these judgments now will prepare you to handle a difficult situation if it occurs later on, because you'll already know what kind of person you are, and you'll know what you should do.

H. Devon Graham, Jr.
Southwest Regional Managing Partner
Arthur Andersen & Co.

tom-line performance. I say nay. . . . Good ethics, simply, is good business. Good ethics will attract investors. Good ethics will attract good employees. . . .

You can do what's right. Not because of conduct codes. Not because of rules or laws. But because you know what's right.

Just how do we know what's right? Obviously many of our basic morals and values are developed during our early, formative years, from birth through high school. The pervasive influence of parents, relatives, leaders/teachers/coaches in church and school, and other significant individuals have contributed to our sense of honesty and integrity and led us to cultivate other values that mold ethical decisions. For example, consider how the following actions might affect a young person's moral development:

How are our basic morals and values developed?

◆ Parents thoughtlessly violate laws, especially when they believe they will not be caught; for example, driving at speeds significantly above the speed limit, littering highways and other property, or "pirating" computer software.
◆ A parent returns a piece of merchandise that was accidentally broken and claims that it was damaged before it was purchased.
◆ Parents and others you respect routinely cheat on their income taxes by overstating the value of contributions or claiming vacation expenses as deductible business expenses.
◆ Parents routinely complete a child's homework to ensure that the child earns a high grade or perhaps just to minimize the amount of time spent completing homework each evening.
◆ Parents or older siblings neglect to tell a sales clerk of an error made in their favor, for example, if they received too much change, were charged the sale price for an item not on sale, or were not charged for an item.
◆ Teachers copy audiotapes, records, videotapes, or sheet music and rationalize that the action is all right because these copyrighted materials are being used for educational purposes.
◆ Community and religious leaders, coaches, parents, and others make derogatory remarks and off-color jokes about minorities, the handicapped, or other groups.

What other actions might affect a young person's moral development?

Each of these actions advocates self-interest with total disregard for the law or the welfare of other people. Continual exposure to this "me-for-me" interest communicates the belief that this behavior is acceptable; unfortunately, this value system is the one taken to the workplace.

Throughout our lives, we continue to re-evaluate and set new priorities and thus adjust our basic value system, for better or for worse. For example, whenever we make a difficult ethical decision, we reinforce our basic values of honesty and integrity and build our character. However,

Basic values may gradually erode if we make even small compromises in our ethical behavior.

making even small compromises in ethical behavior can lead to more serious unethical behavior and perhaps even to illegal actions.

Recent examples of celebrated figures who struggled with ethical dilemmas that eventually turned into legal problems illustrate a gradual erosion of ethical character. Pete Rose, baseball's greatest hitter, gradually acquired a gambling problem that earned him a jail sentence. Steroid use by Olympic sprinter Ben Johnson caused him to be stripped of his gold medal (Bates, 1990).

> Blatant illegalities don't happen overnight. Just like arsenic poisoning, unethical behavior comes in small daily doses. This attitude can grow from pushing to the front of the check-out line to shoplifting to drafting inflated and dishonest resumes to becoming a government contractor taking bribes under the table. (Bates, 1990, p. 19)

Why do individuals commit unethical acts?

Sometimes individuals commit unethical acts because they do not identify a particular situation as an ethical issue. The problem is that many ethical issues are unapparent or seemingly benign. Further inspection of the issue, however, reveals a discrete, but very real, compromise of personal values. In some instances, individuals are being pressured to act unethically by individuals such as employers, peers, parents, and coaches or leaders who may not have a malicious or calculating motive. Examine the following commonplace unethical behaviors:

◆ Copying from another student's test paper to achieve a certain grade point average (pressure to meet parents' expectations or to pass a course).

◆ Using test files to prepare for an exam (readily available; peers are using them).

◆ Not contributing your share to a group project.

Examine your own daily life. Can you provide other examples of temptations to be unethical?

◆ Plagiarizing on a term paper.

◆ Copying a computer software program so that you can complete class assignments on your own computer rather than endure the inconvenience of using a computer lab.

◆ Deciding not to report a student who you witnessed cheating on an exam.

◆ Listing false qualifications on a resume to increase your chances of securing a job, scholarship, or internship.

◆ Keeping money disbursed in error by an automatic teller at your local bank. Suppose you request $100 and, to your amazement, the machine disburses $1,000. Your receipt, however, states that only $100 has been withdrawn from your account—which means that the $900 would not be traceable to you (Miller, 1990).

Likewise, identifying ethical issues in typical workplace situations may be difficult, and coworkers and superiors may apply pressure for seemly logical reasons. To illustrate, examine each of the following workplace situations for a possible ethical dilemma:

◆ A law clerk is instructed to disassemble a client's accounting records to hinder the IRS from detecting the client's fraudulent tax reporting.

◆ A staff accountant of a CPA firm owns stock in a bank that has an outstanding loan with one of the CPA firm's audit clients.

◆ A salesperson who travels extensively feels cheated that personal telephone calls are not reimbursed travel expenses. Consequently, the salesperson overstates car mileage to cover the cost of the telephone calls.

◆ Clerks in the human resources department often divulge information obtained from personnel files while they talk with coworkers during lunch and coffee breaks. In particular, they have tried to keep the grapevine current on new participants in the company's employee assistance programs (drug and alcohol abuse), insurance claims for psychiatric care or other unusual medical expenses, changes in insurance beneficiaries, and performance appraisal ratings.

◆ To protect his job, a transportation manager decides not to question an international shipment of goods that he believes is prohibited by governmental trade sanctions (that is, shipping high technology or military equipment to specified countries).

◆ In designing a foreign manufacturing plant, a company plans to reduce the safety and environmental standards below those used in its U.S. plants. By satisfying only the foreign government's lower standards, the company will significantly reduce construction and operation costs.

◆ In a letter to an investor, an investment manager enthusiastically reports that the client's stock portfolio has experienced 24 percent growth. The letter omits the fact that the stock market as a whole has increased 32 percent in the same period.

◆ To increase the revenues generated from its service departments, a company intentionally increases the complexity of its product. As a result of these changes, repairs are more likely to be made by an authorized service department.

◆ Angry at her superior for an unfavorable performance appraisal she received, an employee leaks confidential information (for example, trade secrets such as a recipe or product design, marketing strategies, or product development plans) to an acquaintance who works for one of the company's competitors.

Have you experienced any pressure to perform unethical acts at your job?

Your fundamental morals and values provide the foundation for making ethical decisions; however, even minor concessions in day-to-day ethical decisions can gradually weaken this foundation. One way to safeguard your ability and willingness to act ethically and responsibly is to be keenly aware of common pressures to compromise your personal value system.

COMMUNICATION MENTOR

Succeeding will be much easier if you approach your business career knowing that very few short-term rewards exist for ethical behavior within the workplace. (Within the *worker*, yes, but not within the workplace.) The exact opposite is true for unethical behavior.

It probably goes without saying that your manager will not come to you and say, "I'm pleased to note that over the past six months you have consistently exceeded our expectations by not cheating on your expense accounts. You're looking good for a bonus!" Meanwhile, by "padding" expense accounts over the same six months, an unethical coworker may be defrauding the company of enough money to cover, let's say, a pair of good shoes and a great Italian dinner.

It will be frustrating and maddening when you experience this irony of ethics in one or more of its many forms. You will have to call time and again on the instinctive resource that says the long-term results of ethical behavior will *absolutely* be better than the short-term results of unethical behavior; that walking in a stolen pair of shoes with a bad taste in your mouth isn't worth it.

James F. Hurley
Senior Vice President
CalFed Inc.

CAUSES OF UNETHICAL BEHAVIOR IN THE WORKPLACE

What are the major causes of unethical behavior in the workplace?

Understanding the major causes of unethical behavior in the workplace will help you become sensitive to signals of escalating pressure to compromise your values. Research on unethical corporate behavior has identified several potential causes of unethical behavior. These causes include excessive emphasis on profits, misplaced corporate loyalty, obsession with personal ambition, expectation of not getting caught, unethical tone set by top management, uncertainty about whether the action is wrong, and unwillingness to take an ethical stand.

Excessive Emphasis on Profits

The first, and probably most important, cause of unethical behavior appears to be an excessive emphasis on corporate profits. In the Beechnut

Corporations are constantly working to earn higher profits than competing companies. Because of this fierce competition, employees may feel pressured to consider unethical plans to "help" their company. Employees must learn to recognize management's pressure to compromise ethical standards, and top management must create a corporate culture that does not reward employees for unethical actions.

apple juice case, corporate executives first bought the suspicious but inexpensive juice concentrate at a time when profits were down. Nestlé, their corporate parent, was demanding both improved profits and a positive cash flow. Given Beechnut's recent performance, these goals were somewhat unreasonable, at least in the short term. To keep their jobs, however, and to do what was best for the company, the Beechnut executives may have felt compelled to cut corners wherever possible.

A heavy emphasis on profits may send a message to many managers that the end justifies the means. In other words, if only the amount of earnings per share matters in assessing managerial performance, the message to managers is "do whatever is necessary to increase the bottom line." Thus, managers justify unethical acts because they are in the "best interest" of the company.

What would you do if your supervisor asked you to do something you believe is unethical?

Misplaced Corporate Loyalty

The response by Beechnut's executives to unrealistic profit goals may have revealed another factor that contributes to unethical acts: a misplaced sense of corporate loyalty. Hence, managers may actually believe that their actions, however questionable, are for the good of the company.

Obsession with Personal Advancement

Managers who wish to outperform their peers or are working for the next promotion may feel that they cannot afford to fail. They may do whatever it takes to achieve the objectives assigned to them. To ensure favorable measures of success, managers may attempt to minimize controllable expenses long enough to earn a promotion. For example, a manager may neglect preventive maintenance of equipment, reduce or postpone essential research and development, or bypass selected quality-control points. These actions may make the manager (and even the company) look good in the short run, but continued disregard for these critical factors is detrimental to the long-term well-being of a company.

Expectation of Not Getting Caught

Managers who believe that the end justifies the means often believe that the unethical activity will never be discovered. Unfortunately, a great deal of improper behavior escapes detection in the business world. Therefore, this cause of unethical behavior is a difficult one to correct.

What are other examples of unethical behavior that may go undetected?

Under intense pressure to meet production quotas, a production manager may cut corners on certain quality-control measures. For example, the manager may bypass inspecting bolts to ensure that they meet specifications (size and resistance) or may ship finished merchandise without completing the exact inspection agreed to in the sales contract (such as a requirement that *every* unit, not a random sample, be inspected).

Believing no one will ever find out, employees are tempted to falsify records such as expense accounts. They may overstate the cost of meals to compensate for unauthorized expenses (phone calls, entertainment, laundry service) or include expenses not actually incurred (meals paid for by others or nonexistent taxi fares). Similarly, sales representatives may overreport the number of sales contacts made during a certain period if they believe no control measure will reveal the true effort they expended. Employees who call in sick and spend the day conducting personal business or enjoying an extra-long weekend have little fear that management will discover this unethical activity.

Unethical Tone Set by Top Management

How does the ethical behavior of top management affect the ethical behavior of other employees in the company?

Another cause of unethical behavior relates to the corporate culture. If top managers are not perceived as highly ethical, lower-level managers may be less ethical as a result. Employees have little incentive to act ethically if their superiors do not set an example and encourage and reward ethical behavior. The following actions by top management clearly set the tone for unethical behavior:

◆ The sales manager emphatically requires sales representatives to promise delivery of orders on the date required by a potential customer—even if the representatives know the production schedule is backlogged and will not permit prompt delivery.

COMMUNICATION MENTOR

In many large companies, employees are notorious for abusing their sick-leave privileges such as calling in to report illness and then spending the day conducting personal business. Salt River Project provides some incentive for meeting higher ethical standards by paying employees for half of any sick leave accumulated over a base number of days. This policy also allows some sick leave to be used for taking care of sick relatives.

Carroll M. Perkins
General Manager
Salt River Project

◆ The vice president of finance requires the purchasing agent to buy all supplies and office equipment from a company owned by the vice president's brother, even though the purchasing agent can document that the supplies could be purchased for a lower price elsewhere.
◆ The staff development director routinely copies articles, complete software documentation manuals, training guides, and preview copies of training films for distribution at staff development seminars. Although several employees have brought this clear-cut infringement of copyright laws to the attention of the company president, no action has been taken.
◆ According to the grapevine, several managers have violated the company policy against copying company software for use on computers at home.

Uncertainty About Whether an Action Is Wrong

Many times managers are placed in situations in which the line between right and wrong is not clearly defined. When caught in this grey area, the perplexed manager asks, "How far is too far?" The following situations place managers in such a quandary:

Is an action always clearly right or wrong?

◆ A company bids for a job that requires expertise the company does not have but would acquire if the bid is ultimately received. For example, a computer systems company bids to install a sophisticated network system even though the company has no experience in installing networks. A construction company with no experience in building high-security correctional facilities bids to build a jail or state prison.

◆ A firm bills a client the amount quoted, but the actual time required to complete the project was significantly less than estimated or other savings reduced the actual cost.
◆ A consulting firm performs similar consulting jobs for competing companies and is, therefore, privy to confidential information.

Unwillingness to Take an Ethical Stand

Often employees know what is right or wrong but are not willing to take the risk of challenging a wrong action. Furthermore, employees may lack the confidence or the skill needed to confront others with sensitive ethical issues. They may remain silent and then justify the unwillingness to act. Consider the risk involved in speaking out on each of the following workplace situations:

◆ You report that you are being sexually harassed or that you are aware that another employee is being sexually harassed.

Why do you think some people are unwilling to take an ethical stand?

COMMUNICATION MENTOR

If you are ever, at any stage of a business career, unlucky enough to find yourself in a routinely unethical environment, you will discover quite rapidly that there is a seductive "quality" to it. Whether practiced on a company-wide or departmental scale, there will be a "team spirit" among the unethical group that subtly states: "Look at the impunity with which we ignore certain ethical standards and get such good results. Come on, our success can be yours."

This situation is, as the tire ad used to say, "where the rubber meets the road." If your personal ethical principles are extremely strong and uncompromised up to this point, you can be a holdout and, depending on the level of your job and degree of influence, try to become an agent of change. This is a courageous *and* perilous route, along which you will certainly need increased authority, responsibility and decision-making powers. If you are relatively inexperienced and your business ethics are largely untested, I promise you it will not be long before you feel the magnetic pull of your fellows. Before this situation happens and potentially ruins your chance for a solid career and a sense of personal contentment, the best solution is to run, not walk, to a job where ethical behavior prevails.

James F. Hurley
Senior Vice President
CalFed Inc.

♦ You inform management that the public relations director is violating copyright laws by scanning copyrighted designs and cartoons for use in in-house publications and in promotional material prepared for distribution outside the company.

♦ You report that coworkers are using the company long-distance telephone service for personal use or are reporting unauthorized expenses on expense reports.

FRAMEWORK FOR ANALYZING ETHICAL DILEMMAS

After you have determined that an ethical issue is part of a situation you are facing, the next step is to select the appropriate analytical tools to help you handle the situation. By analyzing ethical dilemmas from multiple perspectives, you may be able to find solutions that better conform to your own personal values. The flow chart shown in Figure 6-1 represents a framework for making an ethical decision and for supporting that decision in a written or oral message. The framework instructs you (the decision maker) to complete the following four-step process after you have identified a possible course of action:

1. Identify the legal implications of the alternative and determine whether the alternative adheres to contractual agreements and company policy. If yes . . .
2. Determine whether the alternative is consistent with any company or professional codes of ethics. If yes . . .
3. Use ethical principles and theories to assess whether the alternative judged to be legal (Step 1) and in compliance with codes of ethics (Step 2) is ethical. If yes . . .
4. Implement the alternative and communicate ethical decisions to appropriate individuals inside or outside the organization.

If the result of any of the first three steps is No, select another alternative. The following sections discuss each step in the process in detail.

Legal Considerations

The first step in making ethical decisions involves identifying possible legal implications. In other words, is the alternative legal? Does it comply with relevant contractual agreements or company policy? The law specifically outlines the "black" area—those alternatives that are clearly wrong. Obviously obeying the law is in the best interest of all concerned: you as an individual, your company, and society. In addition, contractual agreements between the organization and another group provide explicit guidance in selecting an ethically responsible alternative.

What action is taken (1) if the alternative is legal and complies with pertinent contractual agreements or (2) the alternative violates the law and contractual agreements?

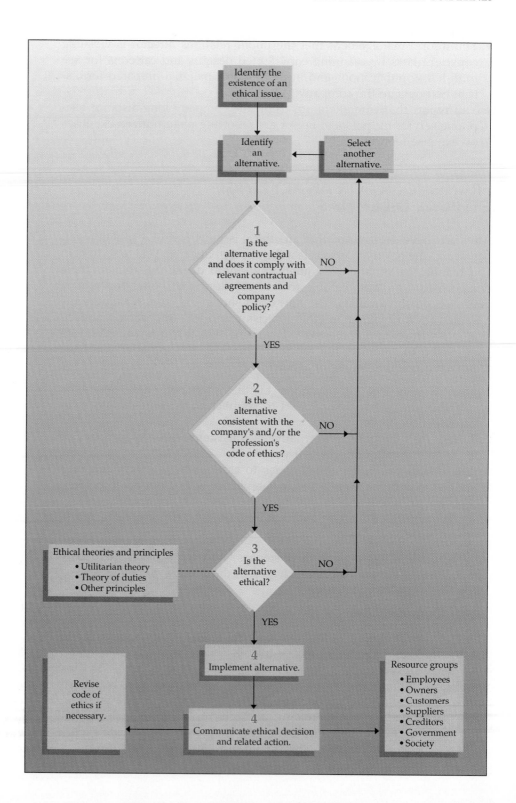

FIGURE 6-1 Framework for analyzing ethical issues

If the alternative is legal and complies with pertinent contractual agreements and company policy, you may advance to the next decision point in the framework. On the other hand, if the alternative is illegal or violates contractual agreements or company policy, you must select and evaluate another alternative.

For example, suppose you have discovered that products recently shipped contained component parts that had not been subjected to your company's standard quality inspection. You are confident that an ethical issue is involved. What are the legal implications of this action? To answer that question, suppose the uninspected component was

Type of Product	Legal Implications
A part for the engine of an air force fighter jet.	Federal laws may govern contracts between the Department of Defense and its contractors. Obey the law. Select another alternative.
The paint used in the production of a child's toy.	Product safety laws may govern the quality and content of this component. Obey the law. Select another alternative.
The paper used in the production of a textbook.	No laws have been violated; however, a breach of contract may be involved. Consult the contract and abide by it. Select another alternative if necessary.

An organization may exchange information or make financial transactions with a variety of resource groups, as shown in Figure 6-2. Consequently, when interacting with any of these resource groups, the employee must identify the legal implications affecting the appropriate resource group(s). For example, a variety of laws and contractual agreements apply to an organization's interaction with its employees. Laws have been enacted to protect employee rights related to equal opportunity, sexual harassment, workplace safety, benefits, privacy, performance appraisal, and employee recommendations. Likewise, laws and contracts affect interactions with owners, customers, suppliers, creditors, government, society, and others.

What are the major legal areas affecting interactions with customers? Owners? Suppliers? Creditors? Government? Society?

General legal guidelines for topics related to business communications (e.g, illegal interview questions and employee recommendations) are included in this textbook. However, this textbook is not intended to serve as a comprehensive legal reference.

Your employer will require you to become an expert in the laws that affect your particular area. When you encounter an unfamiliar area, you must investigate any possible legal implications. Suppose an advertising manager of an auto dealership decides to use film footage of a family arriving at a local festival in a make of mini-van sold by the dealer. To identify specific legal guidelines related to using a person's likeness, the man-

What level of legal expertise in your area of competence will your employer expect you to have?

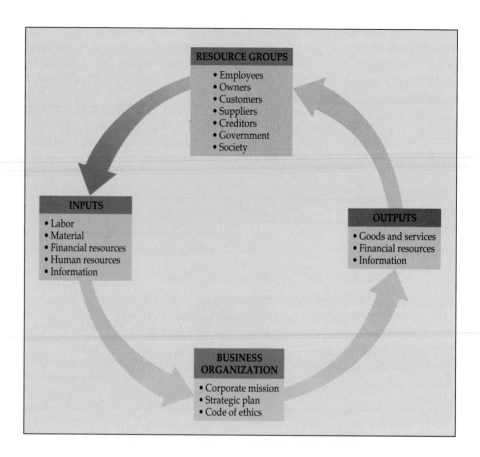

FIGURE 6-2 Interactions between a business organization and its resource groups

ager would carefully research this unfamiliar topic. The research provides the basis for the content of a letter to the family seeking their permission to use the footage in a television advertisement. In short, every message, whether written or spoken, should be carefully examined to ensure that it adheres to applicable laws and pertinent contractual agreements and company policy. This careful scrutiny applies to messages sent to resource groups inside or outside the organization. Your meticulous research will give you necessary evidence and confidence in your ability to defend your message if required.

Company and Professional Codes of Conduct

If the alternative is legal and complies with relevant contractual agreements and company policy, your next step is to consult your company's or profession's *code of ethics.* This written document summarizes the company's or profession's standards of ethical conduct. Some companies refer to this document as a *credo* or *standards of ethical conduct.*

Increasing numbers of companies and professional organizations have issued codes of ethics. However, in the formative years of many major companies, founders had to uphold their high ethical principles without the support of published codes of ethical conduct. For example:

◆ Bristol and Myers listened as a chemist talked with them about a quinine pill that could contain a third as much quinine as the genuine item but looked the same. Bristol said to Myers: "Make out a check to this man; he's through" (Oliverio, 1990, p. 19).

◆ John Queeny, Monsanto's founder, received the following advice when the company faced the strong possibility of bankruptcy: close down the plant, lay off all the workers, and reopen with new people at lower wages. "Since when," Queeny asked, "do we lie to our employees?" Engrained in Monsanto's culture today is Queeny's philosophy: "Doing the right thing is never open to question" (Mahoney, 1990, p. 24).

◆ Samuel Price (one of the founders of the public accounting firm that became Price Waterhouse) was pressured to undertake work on the guarantee of a fee to be charged only if the report was favorable. With no clearly stated principles to back him up, he explained, "Our charges must in no way be dependent upon the result of the examination and the only way to impress this upon them is simply to refuse to proceed until charges and outlays are provided for" (Oliverio, 1990, p. 19).

These founders firmly believed that ethical behavior was a definite way to ensure the success of their companies. They set the tone for ethical standards at the top and established practices that supported their views.

Carefully review the code of ethics to determine whether the alternative is contrary to the standards set forth in the code. In addition, the code of ethics may provide suggestions for resolving the issue. If the alternative violates the code of ethics, you must evaluate another alternative beginning with the first step in the framework, the legality of the alternative.

What action should you take if the alternative does not adhere to the standards of ethical conduct presented in your company's or profession's code of ethics?

The Standards of Ethical Conduct for Management Accountants is shown in Figure 6-3. It states clearly, "Management accountants shall not commit acts contrary to these standards nor shall they condone the commission of such acts by others within their organizations." Four major categories of responsibility include competence, confidentiality, integrity, and objectivity. The code outlines specific procedures for handling ethical conflicts that cannot be resolved by following established company policy.

More and more companies have issued codes of ethics.

To become aware of the ethical behavior advocated by your intended profession, locate its code of ethics. You may find the code printed in a professional or practitioner journal in your field. In addition, talking with professors or practitioners in your field and reading articles in professional journals will acquaint you with basic ethical views held by your profession.

What ethical conduct does your profession advocate?

Standards of Ethical Conduct for Management Accountants

Management accountants have an obligation to the organizations they serve, their profession, the public, and themselves to maintain the highest standards of ethical conduct. In recognition of this obligation, the Institute of Management Accountants, formerly the National Association of Accountants, has promulgated the following standards of ethical conduct for management accountants. Adherence to these standards is integral to achieving the *Objectives of Management Accounting*.[1] Management accountants shall not commit acts contrary to these standards nor shall they condone the commission of such acts by others within their organizations.

COMPETENCE
Management accountants have a responsibility to:

- Maintain an appropriate level of professional competence by ongoing development of their knowledge and skills.
- Perform their professional duties in accordance with relevant laws, regulations, and technical standards.
- Prepare complete and clear reports and recommendations after appropriate analyses of relevant and reliable information.

CONFIDENTIALITY
Management accountants have a responsibility to:

- Refrain from disclosing confidential information acquired in the course of their work except when authorized, unless legally obligated to do so.
- Inform subordinates as appropriate regarding the confidentiality of information acquired in the course of their work and monitor their activities to assure the maintenance of that confidentiality.
- Refrain from using or appearing to use confidential information acquired in the course of their work for unethical or illegal advantage either personally or through third parties.

INTEGRITY
Management accountants have a responsibility to:

- Avoid actual or apparent conflicts of interest and advise all appropriate parties of any potential conflict.
- Refrain from engaging in any activity that would prejudice their ability to carry out their duties ethically.
- Refuse any gift, favor, or hospitality that would influence or would appear to influence their actions.
- Refrain from either actively or passively subverting the attainment of the organization's legitimate and ethical objectives.
- Recognize and communicate professional limitations or other constraints that would preclude responsible judgment or successful performance of an activity.
- Communicate unfavorable as well as favorable information and professional judgments or opinions.

- Refrain from engaging in or supporting any activity that would discredit the profession.

OBJECTIVITY
Management accountants have a responsibility to:

- Communicate information fairly and objectively.
- Disclose fully all relevant information that could reasonably be expected to influence an intended user's understanding of the reports, comments, and recommendations presented.

RESOLUTION OF ETHICAL CONFLICT

In applying the standards of ethical conduct, management accountants may encounter problems in identifying unethical behavior or in resolving an ethical conflict. When faced with significant ethical issues, management accountants should follow the established policies of the organization bearing on the resolution of such conflict. If these policies do not resolve the ethical conflict, management accountants should consider the following course of action:

- Discuss such problems with the immediate superior except when it appears that the superior is involved, in which case the problem should be presented initially to the next higher managerial level. If satisfactory resolution cannot be achieved when the problem is initially presented, submit the issues to the next higher managerial level.

  If the immediate superior is the chief executive officer, or equivalent, the acceptable reviewing authority may be a group such as the audit committee, executive committee, board of directors, board of trustees, or owners. Contact with levels above the immediate superior should be initiated only with the superior's knowledge, assuming the superior is not involved.
- Clarify relevant concepts by confidential discussion with an objective advisor to obtain an understanding of possible courses of action.
- If the ethical conflict still exists after exhausting all levels of internal review, the management accountant may have no other recourse on significant matters than to resign from the organization and to submit an informative memorandum to an appropriate representative of the organization.

Except where legally prescribed, communication of such problems to authorities or individuals not employed or engaged by the organization is not considered appropriate.

[1] Institute of Management Accountants, formerly National Association of Accountants, *Statements on Management Accounting: Objectives of Management Accounting*, Statement No. 1B, June 17, 1982.

FIGURE 6-3   An example of a professional code of ethics

(From Statement on Management Accounting: Objectives of Management Accounting (Statement No. 1B), 1982, by The National Association of Accountants, New York. Reprinted by permission)

Today many companies are providing comprehensive ethics awareness programs designed to help employees understand and adhere to the company's ethical standards. These programs should help management identify breakdowns in the system and then develop solutions to correct these problems. In addition, the United States Sentencing Commission has issued new sentencing guidelines that are expected to become law. These guidelines impose tougher sentences for corporate white-collar crime and provide strong incentives for companies to establish meaningful compliance programs to deter and report criminal conduct by their employees (Slayton, 1991).

What benefits do ethics awareness programs provide?

Ethical Principles and Theories

At this point, assume your alternative has passed the first two tests; that is, it (1) is legal and complies with contractual agreements and company policy and (2) adheres to the company's or profession's code of ethics. Contrary to the views of many decision makers, your analysis is not yet complete. Recall the powerful statement by James Perrella, Ingersoll-Rand's corporate leader: "What's the right thing to do, the right way to behave, the right way to conduct business? Don't just ask, is it legal?" (Slayton, 1991, p. 7). Thus, the final—and extremely important—test your alternative must satisfy is the test of integrity. Is it ethical? If, after careful analysis, you judge the alternative to be ethical, you may implement it; otherwise, you must evaluate another alternative.

Why is your ethical analysis not complete after you have determined that an alternative is legal, contractual, and complies with existing codes of ethics? What is the next step in your analysis?

Numerous principles and ethical theories are available to help individuals and companies analyze ethical issues. A simple and ancient principle, the Golden Rule, "Do unto others as you would have them do unto you," is still an effective yardstick for measuring ethical conduct. Perrella referred to the improved quality of business if everyone followed the Golden Rule. The Quakers' uncomplicated approach also has merits: "In all your dealings, leave the other people at least as well off as you found them."

Somewhat more sophisticated but still straightforward are the six points in the Pagano Model for determining whether a proposed action is ethical (Mathison, 1988, p. 781). You must answer the following six questions honestly:

1. Is the proposed action legal—the core starting point?
2. What are the benefits and costs to the people involved?
3. Would you want this action to be a universal standard, appropriate for everyone?
4. Does the action pass the light-of-day test? That is, if your action appeared on television or others learned about it, would you be proud?
5. Does the action pass the Golden Rule test? That is, would you want the same to happen to you?

Even though a corporate decision may be legal, it could be unethical. Many food manufacturers have come under close scrutiny by watchdog groups for making products labeled "lite" or "low-fat" when in fact most of the calories in the food are derived from fat. For persons on low-fat diets, this misinformation could be a potential cause of illness or even death. Legality is not enough; an awareness of and concern for the consequences of your decisions are necessary as well.

6. Does the action pass the ventilation test? Ask the opinion of a wise friend with no investment in the outcome. Does this friend believe that the action is ethical?

Which principles or theories do you apply when evaluating an ethical decision?

Various theories and principles of ethical behavior have been proposed. You must evaluate them and choose the one (or several) that most closely parallels your own moral system. Two ethical theories that have received widespread acceptance in both the philosophical and the business communities are the utilitarian theory and the theory of duties. They can serve as analytical tools to help you analyze complex ethical situations and evaluate alternative actions.

The major premise of the utilitarian theory involves selecting the alternative that brings the greatest good to the greatest number.

Utilitarian Theory. Utilitarianism, probably the most widely studied theory of ethics, defines the moral worth of any action or practice solely by its consequences (Bentham, 1789/1948; Mill, 1863/1957; Sidgewick, 1874/1966). The major premise of this theory is that in all situations one ought to do that which provides the greatest balance of good over harm for everyone. Thus, an ethical decision maker must estimate the impact of each alternative action on all organizational stakeholders (the persons or groups who will be affected by the decision) and then select the one that optimizes the satisfaction of the greatest number of people.

For simplicity, the major stakeholders of any organization consist of five groups: owners, employees, customers, local communities, and society at large. Applying the utilitarian theory in an organization involves carefully elaborating the costs and benefits imposed by a particular decision or action on each of these five groups. The decision imposing the fewest costs and most benefits across all groups is the one that should be selected.

As an example, consider the decision that Weyerhaeuser Company might make about whether to continue to manufacture disposable diapers or to get out of the business. The production of disposable diapers has been labeled unethical by some people because of the undesirable effects of disposable diapers on the environment. Indeed, some groups are pushing for legislation that would either ban the use of disposable diapers or impose a usage tax on them. Analyzing this ethical situation using utilitarian theory requires you to assess the costs and benefits created by the production of these diapers for all key stakeholders. This analysis is shown in Figure 6-4.

This simplified utilitarian analysis shows why Weyerhaeuser's decision is such a difficult one. The major short-term benefits of diaper production for the company, its employees, and its customers all appear to be quite positive. However, in the long run, the costs of using this convenient product may be quite significant at the societal level. Whenever such tradeoffs exist, analyzing an issue using a second ethical theory, the theory of duties, is useful.

Why is this called the utilitarian theory?

What do you think Weyerhaeuser should do?

COMMUNICATION MENTORS

When faced with an ethical or legal decision, . . .

Simply remember to "do unto others as you would have them do unto you."

Jere W. Hess, Jr.
Director, Personnel & Public Relations
Peavey Electronics

Immediately stop the communication and consult an expert—your immediate supervisor, an attorney, or an outside consultant.

Thomas G. Martin
Director of Corporate Development
Community Coffee Company, Inc.

Stakeholder	Costs	Benefits
Owners		Disposable diaper business is currently highly lucrative.
Employees		Increased production allows employees to continue to be employed and to earn wages.
Customers		Because Weyerhaeuser's diapers are sold under private labels (e.g., Kroger or Revco diapers), they tend to be cheaper than the major brands, thereby saving the customer money.
		Babies benefit because disposable diapers keep them dryer longer than cloth diapers.
		Busy parents in today's fast-moving society benefit from the convenience.
Local communities	No impact different from costs imposed on society.	
Society	Bulky diapers require 100 years to degrade.	
	Disposable diapers create massive amounts of trash in valuable landfill space. The diaper industry argues that these products comprise only 2 percent of landfill space; others argue that even this small amount is too much because landfill space is at a premium.	

FIGURE 6-4　Analysis of disposable diaper production using the utilitarian theory

The Theory of Duties.　In simplest terms, a "duty" is an obligation to take specific steps (Freeman & Gilbert, 1988). One of the fundamental theories of duties is Ross's (1930) doctrine of *prima facie* duties. These *prima facie* (self-evident) duties include (1) not harming innocent people, (2) keeping promises, (3) showing gratitude, (4) acting in a just way, and

What are Ross's *prima facie* duties?

(5) providing reparations to those who have been harmed by one's actions. These duties are not ethical absolutes but are considered to be highly desirable moral tenets that should be honored whenever possible (Beauchamp & Bowie, 1979).

To use this theory as an ethical decision tool, you must again consider the organization's major stakeholders: owners, employees, customers, local communities, and society. Then determine which of Ross's five duties are relevant to the decision under consideration, and of these, which may be violated for any of the stakeholders.

Applying the theory of duties to the disposable diaper dilemma leads to new insights on the issue, as shown in Figure 6-5.

As these assessments show, applying ethical theories is not an easy task. The analytical process, however, enhances your critical thinking

Stakeholder	Obligation(s)
Owners	Keeps promise to earn profits, as diaper production earns more money than a comparable investment in another product.
Employees	Keeps promise to provide employment.
Customers	Keeps promise to provide demanded product at fair price.
Local communities	No duties different from those imposed on society.
Society	May not meet promise of protecting the environment. Manufacturers argue diapers are degradable; however, critics contend only under ideal conditions where sunshine and air can exert their effects.
	Harm caused by excess trash to innocent people living in future generations is unknown. Uncertain of the cost of cleaning up the environment and how quality of life will be affected.
	Could make reparations for harm by setting up recycling centers for its diapers, but at the expense of profits for its shareholders.

FIGURE 6-5 Analysis of disposable diaper production using the theory of duties

COMMUNICATION MENTOR

A *preventive defense* is as important in business ethics as it is in athletics; you want to be as good at avoiding unethical situations as you are at handling them when you have no choice. Here are a few preventive suggestions:

a. When you apply for a new job or a transfer to new responsibilities in the same company, ask in your interviews what ethical philosophies your supervisors believe in and how you will be involved in carrying these beliefs out. Don't go overboard on this, but leave a clear message that you believe in ethical behavior under all business and economic circumstances.

b. As you work your way up the ranks in a job, watch for signs ahead of you that the ethical "rules" are sometimes being pushed to their limits. If managers condone this behavior for long, they will be readily lured to the next level of behavior. Guess who they may turn to then?

c. Always have a plan for how you will react ethically in a crisis. A company is most prone to unethical behavior during a crisis, whether it is an economic plunge, a product emergency, a real or perceived "scandal," or a natural disaster. This is a time to be aggressive; make yourself part of the team dealing with the crisis and stress and re-emphasize the need to focus on the long-term effects that the company's decisions will have on its future. Keep a file handy on winners and losers in major crisis management cases and cite the results. You'll emerge from the crisis in a stronger role and, hopefully, so will your company.

James F. Hurley
Senior Vice President
CalFed Inc.

about the consequences of any action. Even if no right answer is possible, clear thinking will help you and any ethically conscious manager better understand the nature of the issue at hand.

COMMUNICATING DECISIONS ETHICALLY AND RESPONSIBLY

The in-depth analysis required by this ethical framework will help you critically examine relevant issues and identify an ethically acceptable alternative. The analysis also will provide you with the logical reasoning needed to write a convincing report to support your decision. Just as important as your analytical decision-making skills is your ability to communicate your ethical decision and related action to appropriate resource groups—the final step in the framework.

The effective communicator will reap unlimited benefits from communicating the ethical decision to a customer, owner, employee, or top management. These benefits include

What are the benefits of being able to communicate ethical decisions effectively?

◆ Increased likelihood that the message will yield the desired response from the reader.
◆ Courage to deal with ethical issues otherwise ignored because of insecurity in communicating about sensitive or unpleasant issues.
◆ Positive business relationships built on honest disclosure of information.
◆ Justified respect from superiors as an honest, sensitive, highly effective communicator worthy of challenging and rewarding opportunities.

What are other benefits of being an effective communicator?

This partial list of the benefits of effective communication emphasizes the power language can provide. The familiar directive "with power comes responsibility" applies especially to your use of communication skills. Because effective communication is such a powerful tool, you must accept responsibility for using it for *one and only one* purpose: to uphold your own personal values and your company's standards of ethical conduct.

Language is a powerful tool that must be used responsibly and ethically.

Before speaking or writing, use the following guidelines to help you filter your message to ensure that you are using effective communication skills responsibly and ethically:

1. Is the information stated as truthfully, honestly, and fairly as possible? Have you included all information relevant to the reader even if it is contrary to your argument? One of the workplace dilemmas discussed earlier illustrates the enticing error of omission. Is it ethical for the stock investor to withhold the overall stock market growth so that the client is unable to compare his or her stock growth to a standard? Likewise, suppose a company president decides to disclose the financial benefits of a plant closing. When writing the company's annual report to the stockholders, is it ethical for him to omit the downside of the plant closing—3,000 employees were laid off in a town where the plant was the primary employer? Gaining a reputation for sending messages that disclose complete and accurate information (regardless of whether it supports your views) builds a solid foundation for strong, long-lasting relationships.

2. Are the ideas expressed clearly and understandably? In other words, if a message is to be classified as honest, you must be reasonably confident that the reader can understand the message accurately. To accomplish this goal, select words that convey the exact meaning intended and that are within the reader's vocabulary. To illustrate this point, evaluate the following explanation a computer representative gave to a customer who was having difficulty transferring data between two microcomputer systems:

Ethical messages disclose complete information—both positive and negative.

Highly Technical Message Damages Goodwill

Your computer has high-density secondary storage devices that have antiquated the format utilized by older computers. The sectors on high-density disks have been condensed and thus cannot be recognized by earlier generation hardware. To facilitate the transfer of data between the two systems,

Improved Version Is Easy to Understand

Your new computer has high-density disk drives that allow your computer to store more data on a disk than many older computers. These older computers format disks in double-density format and, therefore, cannot read disks formatted in high-density format. However,

format the storage medium using the syntax prescribed in your documentation manual.

newer computers with high-density disk drives *can* read disks in the double-density format. To prepare a disk for use in either of your microcomputers, simply format the disk in double-density format. To do this, input the following DOS command at the C ⟩ prompt: format /4.

When using euphemisms (see Chapter 7 for a definition) be sure your motive is to cushion the blow of the negative information and not to ridicule the reader or prompt the reader to misconstrue the true message. For example, is it ethical for a politician to talk about *tax enhancements* rather than *tax increases* if the intent is to distort the voters' perceptions? Is it truthful for a military spokesperson to speak of *friendly casualties* to minimize and, in some cases, avoid the negative publicity inherent in reporting the number of soldiers killed accidentally by the military's own weapons? Chapters 7 and 8 provide techniques for using words and style effectively. Chapter 9 provides the foundation for learning to express a message from the reader's viewpoint.

3. Are unpleasant ideas stated tactfully and positively to preserve the reader's self-worth and to build future relationships? Becoming adept at communicating negative information will give you the confidence needed to handle sensitive situations in a positive, constructive manner rather than to ignore them until they get out of control. For example, a supervisor, uncertain how to approach an employee about low productivity, may (1) intimidate or antagonize the employee if the negative information is not carefully presented or (2) continually postpone the confrontation until the only recourse is to terminate the employee. Compare the poor and improved versions of the following memo:

Inability to convey negative information tactfully hinders a manager's effectiveness.

Negative Tone Damages Goodwill

TO: Josh Martin
FROM: Lee Sanford
DATE: January 5, 19—
SUBJECT: ACCOUNTS RECEIVABLE MUST BE CONTROLLED

Improved Message Builds a Strong Relationship

TO: Josh Martin
FROM: Lee Sanford
DATE: January 5, 19—
SUBJECT: STRATEGIES FOR EVALUATING COLLECTION PROCEDURES

Accounts receivable are out of control.

What has happened to the credit checks that are supposed to control such grotesque delinquency? The company has provided you with staff to perform these credit checks and to contact overdue accounts. Maybe it would be a good idea if you started using them.

Josh, this problem is unexcusable, and I expect to see improvement right away.

Accounts receivable continue to grow. Because this rising delinquency rate is approaching an alarming level, I believe we must evaluate our current procedures to identify a viable solution. Therefore, please begin a full-scale evaluation of the collection process immediately. Specifically, you might begin by

1. Scheduling a meeting with the sales staff to discuss our current credit limits and our methods of granting credit. Based on this input, make the necessary changes.

2. Evaluating the effectiveness of the procedures used to collect past-due accounts. For example, could you revise the collection letters so that they appeal more effectively to the needs of specific customers? Should we consider modifying the time intervals between collection notices?

As you evaluate the collection process, call me if you need additional input. I look forward to seeing the results of the plans you initiate.

Even though Josh is clearly responsible for the problem, the revised memo is more tactful and offers suggestions for solving the problem. The memo ends with a final offer of help rather than a threat.

Obviously, being able to say "no" without alienating everyone is a priceless tool when you must take a stand on a difficult ethical issue. Chapter 10 and portions of Chapter 12 will help you gain skill in conveying negative information while retaining the goodwill of the reader.

4. Does the message embellish or exaggerate the facts? Legal guidelines related to advertising provide clear guidance for misrepresentation of products or services; however, overzealous sales representatives or imaginative writers can use language skillfully to create less-than-accurate perceptions in the minds of the readers. Businesses have learned the hard way that overstating the capabilities of a product or service (promising more than can be delivered) is not good for business in the long run.

   Persuading the reader to take a particular action (buy a product or service, provide an adjustment on a nonroutine claim, or agree to grant a favor) are covered in Chapter 11. Developing skill in writing persuasively will be important throughout your profession. Using effective persuasion techniques to write a winning resume and application letter, the topic of Chapters 13, will be especially helpful as you begin your career. These techniques should *not* be used, however, if your motive is to exploit the reader.

5. Is your viewpoint supported with objective facts? Are facts accurately documented to allow the reader to judge the credibility of the source and to give credit where credit is due? Can opinions be clearly distinguished from facts?

   Do you have a conflict of interest that will prevent you from preparing an unbiased message? Suppose a company has determined it must close one of its plants because of excess capacity. The controller has been appointed to a committee to evaluate the plant sites and determine which should be closed. Questions such as these must be answered: Which plant is least efficient? Which plant closing will have the least negative impact on the community? Which plant is least desirably located? Which plant is least adaptable to future product changes?

   Before coming to corporate headquarters, the controller managed one of these plants and still knows many of the management team and workers at the plant. The executive must explain the exact nature of her bias to her superiors so they can determine whether she should be removed from the committee to protect the usefulness of the recommendation. Chapters 16–18 will guide you in learning to write objective, well-documented reports.

6. Are graphics carefully designed to avoid distorting facts and relationships? For example, is it ethical for a company to overstate an insignificant change in unit sales by using a graph with inappropriate scales (see the graph on the left at the top of the next page) or to use confusing graphic styles to *deliberately* hide negative information? Chapter 16 presents the principles of using graphics to enhance the readability of information.

Inaccurate Scale Creates Misconception

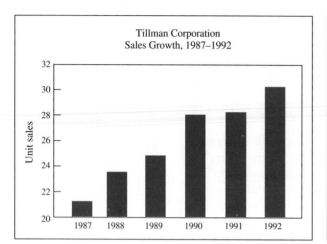

Scale Beginning at Zero Portrays Data Accurately

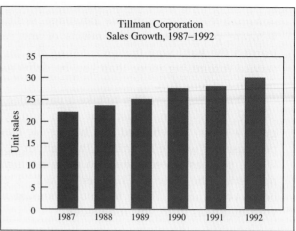

If you are committed to using effective writing principles to promote ethically acceptable actions, you are now ready to begin mastering the principles of effective business communication presented in the remaining chapters in this text.

SUMMARY

Many practicing managers report that they feel pressure to compromise their own moral values. Because this pressure is apparently so common, you must be prepared to cope with complex ethical dilemmas early in your career. Common causes of unethical behavior in the workplace include emphasis on profits, misplaced corporate loyalty, obsession with personal ambition, expectation of not getting caught, unethical tone set by top management, uncertainty about whether an action is wrong, and unwillingness to take an ethical stand.

Today, clearly stated codes of ethics and strict sentencing guidelines for corporate crime are resulting in corporate cultures that foster high moral responsibility. A framework for making an ethical decision and for supporting that decision in a written or oral message involves (1) considering the legal implications of the decision, (2) referring to company or professional codes of conduct for direction, (3) using ethical theories and principles to determine an ethical course of action, and (4) effectively communicating the ethical decision to appropriate individuals. Enhanced ability to analyze ethical dilemmas and to express ideas clearly and tactfully will increase your chances for success in the business world.

REFERENCES

Ansberry, C. (1989, January 26). Alterations of photos raise host of legal, ethical issues. *The Wall Street Journal*, p. 1B.

Bates, L. D. (1990). Making the right choices. *Tomorrow's Business Leader*, 22(2), 17–19.

Beauchamp, T. L., & Bowie, N. E. (Eds.). (1979). *Ethical theory and business*. Englewood Cliffs, NJ: Prentice-Hall.

Bentham, J. (1948). *An introduction to the principles of morals and legislation*. New York: Hafner. (Original work published 1789)

Freeman, R. E., & Gilbert, D. R. (1988). *Corporate strategy and the search for ethics*. Englewood Cliffs, NJ: Prentice-Hall.

Gellerman, S. W. (1986, July–August). Why "good" managers make bad ethical choices. *Harvard Business Review*, pp. 85–90.

Kelly, K. (1991, May 20). When a rival's trade secret crosses your desk. . . ." *Business Week*, p. 48.

Mahoney, R. J. (1990). Ethics: Doing the right thing at Monsanto. *Management Accounting*, 72(12), 24.

Marshall, E. (1975, January 18). Plutonium scandal: The Karen Silkwood case. *The New Republic*, pp. 8–9.

Mathison, D. L. (1988). Business ethics cases and decision models: A call for relevancy in the classroom. *Journal of Business Ethics*, 10(7), 781.

Mill, J. S. (1957). *Utilitarianism*. Indianapolis: Bobbs-Merrill. (Original work published 1863)

Miller, R. L. (1990). *Economic issues for consumers*. St. Paul: West Publishing.

Oliverio, M. E. (1990). Tone at the top among early entrepreneurs. *Management Accounting*, 72(2), 19.

Ross, W. D. (1930). *The right and the good*. Oxford, England: Hackett Publishing.

Sidgewick, H. (1966). *The methods of ethics*. New York: Dover. (Original work published 1874)

Slayton, M. (1980). *Common sense & everyday ethics*. Washington, DC: Ethics Resource Center.

Slayton, M. (1991, May–June). *Ethics Journal*. Washington, DC: Ethics Resource Center.

Traub, J. (1988, July 24). Into the mouths of babes. *New York Times Magazine*, p. 27 II.

Note: Selected portions of this chapter were extracted with permission from Spencer, B. A., & Lehman, C. M. (1990). Analyzing ethical issues: Essential ingredient in the business communication course. *Bulletin of the Association of Business Communication*, 53(3), 7–16.

REVIEW QUESTIONS

1. List several examples of unethical conduct by a business organization or its employees.
2. Why is it important for college students to gain skill in dealing with ethical issues?
3. Discuss the factors that contribute to a person's ability to make an ethical decision.
4. Is it acceptable to make small compromises in ethical conduct? Explain.
5. Provide personal and workplace examples of pressure placed on individuals to compromise ethical principles.
6. What are the most common causes of unethical behavior in the workplace?
7. What are the three decision points in the ethical framework?
8. What three factors must be considered before an alternative passes the legality decision point?
9. What are resource groups? How do they affect the analysis of an ethical issue?
10. What is a code of ethics? What purpose does it serve?
11. What are the advantages of comprehensive ethics awareness programs?
12. Discuss the new sentencing guidelines issued by the United States Sentencing Commission. What effect should these guidelines have on ethics in the workplace?
13. Briefly describe the major premises of (a) the utilitarian theory and (b) the theory of duties.
14. List several benefits gained from communicating effectively.
15. What are the six guidelines to ensure that your message is being communicated responsibly and ethically?

EXERCISES

1. Discuss the ethical principle(s) or systems that you think would be helpful to you in determining whether an issue is ethical. Do not limit your analysis to the principles and systems presented in the chapter.
2. Discuss an ethical issue that you have faced. Consider your experiences in school, employment, organizations, and so on. How did you deal with the issue? What insights have you gained from this experience? What have you learned from reading this chapter that could have aided you in handling this issue more effectively?
3. Discuss one of the ethical issues (personal or workplace) presented in this chapter. Use the framework presented in this chapter to analyze

the situation. Based on your analysis, what decision would you have made? Justify your answer.

4. Locate in a current newspaper or magazine an example of an illegal act by a business organization or its employee(s). Choose an incident as closely related as possible to your intended profession. Prepare a written summary of the article.

5. Locate in a current newspaper or magazine an example of an unethical (not illegal) behavior by a business organization or its employee(s). Choose an incident as closely related as possible to your intended profession.
   a. Prepare a written summary of the article.
   b. Use the framework presented in this chapter to analyze the case of unethical behavior. Based on your analysis, what decision would you have made? Justify your answer.

6. Locate the code of ethics of your intended profession. Outline the major responsibilities placed on its practitioners. What procedures are provided by the code of ethics to assist practitioners in resolving ethical issues?

7. Complete the following chart to identify possible interactions a business organization has with various resource groups.

Resource Group	Interaction	Legal Implications
Employees	Equal opportunity/ discrimination/sexual harassment	Civil Rights Act of 1964 and subsequent amendments; company policy
	Workplace safety	OSHA laws; labor contracts; company policy
	Benefits	Labor contracts; company policy
	Employee recommendations	Libel and slander laws, company policy
Owners	_____	_____
Customers	_____	_____
Suppliers	_____	_____
Creditors	_____	_____
Government	_____	_____
Society	_____	_____

CASES FOR ANALYSIS

Case 1.   Is Hiring the Homeless to Purchase Tickets Ethical?   You are a junior partner in a small ticket brokerage firm in Omaha, Nebraska. The purpose of your company is to purchase tickets to popular concerts and sporting events, which will be resold. Your typical market is upper-level executives and other professionals who do not have time to stand in long lines to purchase their own tickets.

The concert promoter allows each individual to purchase only four tickets to a particular event. In the past, you hired students to stand in line to purchase tickets. Even paying minimum wage, you found this practice to be far too expensive to maintain adequate profits.

You soon realized that some other, less-expensive method must be identified to secure the tickets. Several weeks ago you hired a homeless person to stand in line. While he was waiting in line, you gave him two meals (pizza for lunch and chicken for dinner). In return for the four tickets, you paid him $50. Quite pleased with this experiment, you hired more homeless people to purchase tickets. They seemed to like the food and the money, and your profits rose steadily.

You thought everything was going well until yesterday, when you received a phone call from one of the record stores where tickets are sold. The store manager was upset about two things. First, loyal customers were complaining that they have stood in line for hours, only to be told that all tickets had been sold. Second, she complained that these individuals camping out in front of her store may damage the store's image. One particularly irate customer voiced displeasure in having to wait in line with "shabby-looking people with unwashed hair."

Today the morning paper contained a very brash article questioning the ethics of your practice. With paper in hand and very disturbed, Carmen Morgan, the senior partner, rushes into your office. Having already read the article, you quickly say, "Honestly, this negative publicity came as a real surprise to me. I believed that we were not only serving our customers but were also helping the homeless—giving them two meals and money they otherwise would not have had."

Regaining her usual calm disposition, your partner asks you to analyze this practice more thoroughly, and you agree to provide a written report of your analysis. Starting your analysis, you ask yourself these questions: *Are you really helping the homeless, or are you taking advantage of their predicament? Are you hurting anyone? Should you continue to hire the homeless to buy tickets? If so, should you change your procedures somehow?*

Required:

1. Use the ethical framework presented in this chapter to analyze the case. Based on your analysis, what decision would you make? Consider the answers to the following critical-thinking questions:

a. What are the relevant facts?
b. What are the ethical issues raised by the decision to employ the homeless in this manner?
c. Who are the stakeholders affected by this decision?
d. What legal/contractual considerations must be addressed?
e. Does a code of ethics provide guidance for reaching a decision?
f. What are the costs and benefits imposed by each alternative upon each stakeholder?
g. What are the brokerage firm's obligations to each stakeholder?
h. What should the brokerage firm do?
2. Outline the major points in your recommendation to your partner.
3. Compose the memorandum to your partner if your instructor requires you to do so.

Case 2. Is Reducing Quality to Cut Costs Ethical? Curry-Nichols Industries, a major supplier of engine parts for a major airplane manufacturer, has developed a new production process. This process reduces the cost of production by 11 percent. The new product meets company, governmental, and customer safety standards; but the risk of failure is greater than using the present, more costly production method. Part failure, if it occurs, will cause the engine to shut down during flight.

MANAGEMENT	MIS	CONSUMER
Ethics	International	Legal

Required:
1. Use the framework presented in this chapter to analyze the situation. Based on your analysis, what decision would you make? Outline the major points of your answer to the company president.
2. As vice president of production, you adamantly opposed implementing the new production process. However, you have been instructed to initiate the more efficient process. Should your memo to the production supervisor include the issues involved in this ethical decision? Or should you provide only the details needed for the supervisor to implement the plan? Outline the major points of your answer to the production supervisor.
3. Compose the memorandum to the president and the memorandum to the production supervisor if your instructor requires them.

Case 3. Replacing Humans with Machines: Is an Ethical Issue Involved? Bradford Corporation currently employs five workers to produce Part W-132. The engineering department has identified a robotic machine that can produce the same quantity and quality of parts and would reduce annual production costs by $15,000. The five employees would be terminated if the machine were placed in service. Last year Bradford earned $9.6 million, or $3.00 per share (3.2 million shares). As vice president of production, you must submit a recommendation to the company president.

MANAGEMENT	MIS	CONSUMER
Ethics	International	Legal

Required:

1. Use the framework presented in this chapter to analyze the situation. Based on your analysis, what decision would you make?
2. Outline the major points of your answer to the company president.
3. Compose the memorandum to the president if your instructor requires you to do so.

Case 4.   Is the Proposed Action Ethical?   Select an ethical dilemma from the following descriptions of the "Cases for Analysis" at the ends of Chapters 9–12. Turn to the appropriate case and read the complete case problem.

◆ Chapter 9, Case 1. Is it ethical to accept a boat captain's offer to make an "unapproved charter" that is sure to secure the accounts of several sizable investment clients?
◆ Chapter 9. Case 3. Should prior products produced with less-than-adequate materials be recalled?
◆ Chapter 10, Case 3. What action is appropriate when an accountant has knowledge that a client has filed a fraudulent tax return?
◆ Chapter 11, Case 2. Is it ethical for a company to donate bottled water to military troops stationed overseas—or is it shrewd public relations?
◆ Chapter 12, Case 3. Is it ethical to overlook a vendor's error to your advantage?

Required:

1. Use the framework presented in this chapter to analyze the situation. Based on your analysis, what decision would you make?
2. Outline the major points of your answer to the intended audience.
3. Compose the letter or memorandum to the appropriate audiences if your instructor requires you to do so.

USING WORDS AND STYLE EFFECTIVELY

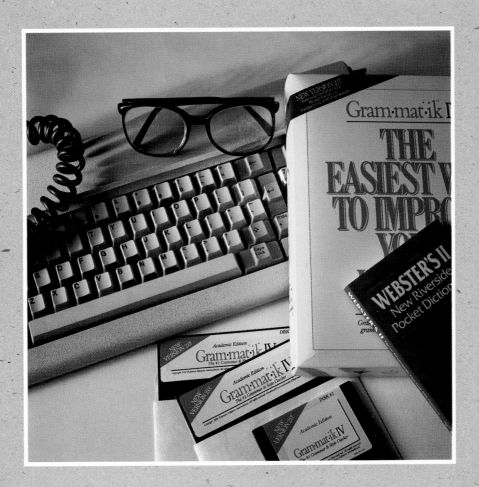

CHAPTER 7   Using Words Effectively
CHAPTER 8   Using the Techniques of Style

USING WORDS EFFECTIVELY

OBJECTIVES

When you have completed Chapter 7, you should be able to

- ◆ Choose words that will be understood.

- ◆ Choose words that promote positive business relationships.

- ◆ Choose words that meet high standards of grammatical correctness.

At THE WINTER OLYMPICS IN GRENOBLE, FRANCE, a twenty-four-year-old Frenchman stands on the Olympic platform and hears his national anthem being played as he accepts his rewards. For Jean-Claude Killy, this moment is the culmination of years of hard work, perseverance, and practice.

Born in 1943 in the French Alps, Jean-Claude Killy began skiing at the age of three. He fell in love with the sport and by his teens was one of the fastest skiers on the slopes. Even broken bones and serious illnesses such as tuberculosis and hepatitis could not diminish his desire to excel at his chosen sport.

At Grenoble, the world acknowledged Killy as its Olympian extraordinaire when he won gold medals in the slalom, the giant slalom, and the downhill events. He was only the second man in Olympic history to accomplish that feat. Today, Killy is still recognized as the world's premier skier. He was recently the chairperson of the 1992 Winter Olympics held in Albertville, France, near his home village of Val d'Isere. He has earned a lifetime of success through his love of his sport, dedication to his goals, and hard work (McRitz, 1969).

When athletes like Killy first envision their goals, they work hard to master the basics of their sports. In much the same way, managers and employers who strive for success must first master the basics of written and oral communication. Building good communication skills is like acquiring athletic skills: to succeed in either field, you must first establish a goal and possess the desire to achieve it. Then you must work hard, often

COMMUNICATION MENTORS

Obviously you should follow the conventional rules of grammar, spelling, and punctuation in preparing written materials. Mistakes in these areas automatically *sabotage* your communication efforts.

Hugh B. Jacks
President
BellSouth Services

Nothing diminishes credibility faster than misspellings, incorrect grammar, misuse of words or even typographical errors.

Terence E. McSweeney
Director of Communications
PGA of America

Although spelling, grammatical, and other errors in content may seem isolated and trivial to you, these mistakes can cause great damage to your credibility. The receivers of your messages that contain mistakes are much less likely to take you and your ideas seriously than they would if you had taken special care to proofread and convey the correct information.

repeating and practicing fundamental tasks over and over. You must persevere to overcome obstacles and not succumb to failure or mediocrity until you reach your goal and reap the rewards.

Executives are spending more and more time at the keyboard. Because their errors in spelling, word usage, punctuation, and sentence structure can damage their credibility, many are taking refresher courses. Some major corporations now offer grammar-review sessions for their executives because they realize that principles taught in a basic English course really are applicable in business. Peter Drucker, a world-renowned authority on management, categorizes English as a *vocational* course because its principles can be *applied* on the job.

How can errors in business documents affect credibility?

Because mistakes in word usage can confuse, distract, and mislead the reader, a brief review is in order. The principles selected for discussion represent the types of errors most frequently found in the writings of undergraduate and graduate students and business executives. If you already know these principles, a review will decrease the likelihood of forgetting to apply them. For those of you who don't know them, study them, so that you can learn to express your ideas more effectively.

The discussion of word usage is not all-inclusive. It is limited to the most important considerations in word choice and in correct usage of words in certain categories. As a preliminary check, complete the following self-check to see whether you already know the principles discussed in this chapter.

SELF-CHECK

Cover the answers in the right-hand column with a sheet of paper. Identify the error(s) in the words used in each sentence in the left column. Slide the cover sheet down and read the answer. Do your re- visions agree with the correct sentences? The numbers in parentheses following the correct sentences refer to the pages in the text where the principles that are covered in the sentence are discussed.

Example:

Only one of the sales representatives were invited.	Only one of the sales representatives <u>was</u> invited. (221)

1. Remove the circular file from the path of perambulation.	Remove the <u>wastebasket</u> from the <u>aisle</u>. (199)
2. You neglected to specify your desired delivery date.	Please <u>inform us of</u> your desired delivery date. (202 and 243)
3. If you recall, sales skyrocketed last month.	If you recall, sales increased <u>by 10 percent</u> last month. (197)
4. The *Communication Dispatch* is a very expensive magazine that will keep you updated on the latest communication technology.	<u>For $30 a year</u>, the *Communication Dispatch* will keep you updated on the latest communication technology. (197)
5. The public relations director appreciated you contributing to the monthly employee newsletter.	The public relations director appreciated <u>your</u> contributing to the monthly employee newsletter. (213)
6. The site selection committee presented their report to the board of directors.	The <u>site-selection</u> committee presented <u>its</u> report to the board of directors. (217)
7. You can use desktop publishing software to create interesting, appealing graphics.	<u>Managers</u> can use desktop publishing software to create interesting, appealing graphics. (Other nouns could be used for "managers.") (215)
8. Reallocation of the resources will be finalized at the end of the fiscal period.	The resources will be <u>reallocated</u> at the end of the fiscal period. (212)
9. The sales manager failed to consider the long term consequences of the decision.	The <u>long-term consequences of the decision were not considered</u>. (224)
10. Each foreman must submit a weekly report of his department's absenteeism record.	Each <u>supervisor</u> must submit a weekly report of <u>departmental absenteeism</u>. (209)

WORD CHOICE

If words are well chosen, a reader or listener will likely (1) understand the message clearly and (2) react favorably to the writer or speaker. In other words, the major concerns are *clarity* and positive *human relations*. Each of the following factors is an important consideration in word choice: preciseness, simplicity and formality, repetition, and parallelism.

Clarity and human relations are major concerns of communicators.

Preciseness

Normally, specific words serve business writers better than general words. Specific words are more vivid:

General	Specific
One of our delivery trucks is out of commission.	One of our delivery trucks has two flat tires.
Congratulations on your recent honor.	Congratulations on being named employee of the month.
Please submit the completed report as soon as possible.	Please submit the completed report by March 15.
Sales skyrocketed this month.	Sales increased 10 percent this month.

Sometimes, however, general words serve better than specific words:

General	Specific
Thank you for the explanation of your financial status.	Thank you for writing to me about your problems with creditors and the possibility of your going bankrupt.
Frank told me about what happened last week.	Frank told me about the tragedy in your family.

In getting along with others, general statements can be useful; they can keep negative ideas from getting more emphasis than they deserve. In addition, writers who don't have specific information or for some reason don't want to divulge it use general words. *For vivid business communication, use specific words.*

General words are sometimes preferred.

Simplicity and Formality

The degree of formality in writing is dictated by the nature of the message and the backgrounds of those who will read it. The writing in dissertations, theses, legal documents, and high-level government documents is expected to be formal. Business memorandums, letters, and reports are expected to be informal. Business writers prefer the informal words from the left column rather than the formal words from the right column:

Informal	*Formal*
end	terminate
get	procure
pay	remunerate
support	corroborate
use	utilize
explain	elucidate

Why not use big words to impress people?

Simple, informal words, compared with formal words, are readily understood, easier to spell, require less time in keyboarding and less space on a page, and are less likely to draw attention away from the idea being expressed. If a reader stops to question the writer's motive for using words similar to those in the right-hand column, the impact of the message may be seriously diminished. Likewise, the impact would be diminished if the reader stopped to question a writer's use of simple, informal words. That distraction is unlikely, however, if the message contains good ideas that are well organized and well supported. Under these conditions, simple words enable a reader to get the message clearly and quickly.

Using words that have more than two or three syllables when they are the most appropriate is acceptable. However, you should avoid regu-

COMMUNICATION MENTOR

Too many writers go to great lengths to "write right." In their attempts to sound learned, they muddy the message beyond comprehension. The best writing closely imitates speech. It is to the point. It uses familiar words and is interesting, and its sentences are short enough to follow. In other words, the message communicates.

Cynthia Pharr
President & CEO
Tracy-Locke/Pharr Public Relations

Use simple words to convey clear meaning.

lar use of a long, infrequently used word when a simpler, more common word has the same meaning. Professionals in some fields often use specialized terminology when communicating with colleagues in the same field. In this case, the audience is likely to understand the words, and using the language of the trade, or jargon, saves time. However, when communicating with people outside the field, professionals should select simple, common words to convey messages.

Having been encouraged to use simple words, you may question the value of building a vocabulary. People who have large vocabularies are more likely to find just the right word for expressing an idea, to understand what others have written, and to make a good score on college-entrance and certain employment tests. Moreover, some studies have found a high correlation between vocabulary and executive success. Although the research does not necessarily show that vocabulary was the *cause* of executives' movement up the promotional ladder, it does suggest that for some reason top executives have extensive vocabularies. Perhaps the personal qualities that resulted in an extensive vocabulary were the same qualities that resulted in promotion.

Students of business should build their vocabularies, but the purpose of business messages is not to advertise a knowledge of infrequently used words. It is to transmit a clear and tactful message. For the informal writing that is practiced in business, *use simple words instead of more complicated words that have the same meaning.*

Why build a good vocabulary?

COMMUNICATION MENTOR

Whether a student, lawyer, or member of Congress, developing an effective writing style is essential for success. To enhance my ability to communicate, I attempt to add new words to my vocabulary each day—to acquire additional building blocks needed to construct thoughts and ideas. With the right words, your thoughts can become clear messages.

The Honorable Mike Espy
U.S. House of Representatives

Parallelism

In the following pairs of sentences, the ideas are the same. Which is stated better and why?

We have three stated goals: to increase production, to expand our market, and recruiting skilled workers.

We have three stated goals: to increase production, to expand our market, and to recruit skilled workers.

Mark received a superior rating in completing required paperwork, interacting with coworkers and customers, and the way he conducted himself in staff meetings.

Mark received a superior rating in completing required paperwork, interacting with coworkers and customers, and presenting his ideas in staff meetings.

Re-examine the first sentence in each pair. Because one of the three elements is presented in a form different from the others, that element does not belong—it is not parallel. The variation in construction weakens the emphasis given to each phrase in the series. The inconsistency may also distract the reader's attention from the message.

In each pair, the second sentence is better. It presents similar phrases in a similar way grammatically:

We have three stated goals: ‖ to increase production,
                          ‖ to expand our market,
                    and ‖ to recruit skilled workers.

Mark received a superior rating in ‖ completing required paperwork,
                                     ‖ interacting with coworkers and
                                     ‖ customers,
                           and   ‖ presenting his ideas in staff meetings.

Can you identify the parallel elements in the following sentences?

They invested in stocks and bonds, and considered mutual funds.
She illustrated her lecture with graphs, charts, and slides, and presented a skit.

In both pairs, two independent clauses are the parallel elements. The subject "they" in the first pair and "she" in the second pair must be repeated so that each parallel item has the same sentence elements (subject, verb, and others). In the second sentence, "graphs," "charts," and "slides" are also parallel items—three nouns connected with *and*.

          ‖ They invested in stocks,
   and   ‖ they considered mutual funds.

          ‖ She illustrated her lecture with graphs, charts, and slides,
   and   ‖ she presented a skit.

When ideas appear together for a certain purpose, they should have commonality in grammar. If one of the ideas is presented in a different way grammatically, it appears to be out of place. Commonality in grammatical presentation is called *parallel construction*.

The principle of parallel construction applies not only to elements in a series that appear in a sentence but also to major units in an outline, to subunits that appear under a major unit, and to headings that appear on printed pages. If one major heading is a complete sentence, so should the others; if one subheading is a question, so should other subheadings under that division. *Present multiple units in the same way grammatically.*

> What is parallel construction and why is it important?

> What items within a resume would require careful attention to parallel construction?

Tone

Tone is the way a statement sounds. The tone of a message conveys the writer's or speaker's attitude toward the message and the receiver. Chances for achieving good human relations are diminished when the tone of a message is overly negative, condescending, too formal, demeaning, or overly euphemistic.

Positive or Negative Tone. In the following pairs of sentences, note the difference in tone between the first and second example:

Don't forget to submit your time and expense report by noon on Friday.

Remember to submit your time and expense report by noon on Friday.

We cannot ship your order until you send us full specifications.

You will receive your order as soon as you send us full specifications.

Our new electronic mail system will not be installed by the first of the year.

Our new electronic mail system will be installed by February 1.

You neglected to indicate the specifications for Part No. 332-3.

Please send the complete specifications for Part No. 332-3 so we can complete your order quickly.

The first sentence in each pair contains a negative word or phrase—"don't," "cannot," "will not," and "neglected." In each pair, both sentences are sufficiently clear; but the positive words in the second sentence make the message more diplomatic. The second sentence sounds more pleasing and does a better job of promoting human relations. For good human relations, rely mainly on *positive words—words that speak of what can be done instead of what cannot be done, of the pleasant instead of the unpleasant.*

Positive words are *normally* preferred, but sometimes negative words are more effective in achieving the dual goals of *clarity* and positive

---

But don't forget: negative words can be useful.

Use words with positive tone to promote human relations.

human relations. For example, addition of negative words can sharpen a contrast (and thus increase clarity):

Use an oil-based paint for this purpose; <u>do not use</u> latex.

Manuscripts are to be printed; handwritten material is <u>not</u> acceptable.

When pleasant, positive words have not brought desired results, negative words may be justified. For example, a supervisor may have used positive words to instruct an accounts payable clerk to verify that the unit price on the invoice matches the unit price on the purchase order. Discovering later that the clerk is not verifying the invoices correctly, the supervisor may use negative words such as *"No, that's the wrong way,"* demonstrate once more, and explain. If the clerk continues to complete the task incorrectly, the supervisor may feel justified in using even stronger negative words. The clerk may need the emotional jolt that negative words can provide. *When the purpose is to sharpen contrast or when positive words have not evoked the desired reaction, use negative words.*

Condescending Tone. Condescending words seem to connote that the communicator is temporarily coming down from a level of superiority to join the receiver on a level of inferiority. Note these examples:

> **Condescension is a reminder of inequality.**

As a retired editor of best sellers, I could assist you in editing your PTA newsletter.

With my Ph.D. and your GED, we should be able to work out a suitable set of by-laws for the new club.

Such reminders of inequality seriously hamper communication. *Avoid use of condescending words.*

Euphemistic Tone. A euphemism makes an idea seem better than it really is. For example, the idea of picking up neighborhood garbage does not sound especially inviting. Someone who does such work is often referred to as a *sanitation worker.* This term has a more pleasant connotation than *garbage collector.* Business writers prefer the euphemistic terms in the right column to the negative terms in the left column:

Negative Tone	*Euphemistic Tone*
died	passed away
fired	agreed to resign
aged or elderly	senior citizen
secretaries	office support staff

Euphemisms are words or phrases we use to make something seem better than it really is. In some cases, euphemisms are acceptable and simply an attempt to be positive and sensitive. However, euphemisms go wrong when they are seen as excessive or sarcastic. For example, this man would probably prefer to be called a janitor instead of his official title, "maintenance engineer."

bagger	courtesy clerk
soldiers killed by their own forces	friendly casualties
Complaint Department	Customer Service
Repair Department	Maintenance Department
Inspection Department	Quality Control

Some **euphemisms are acceptable.**

We generally recognize such expressions for what they are—distasteful ideas presented with a little sugar coating. Knowing that the sender was simply trying to be polite and positive, we are more likely to react favorably than unfavorably. Yet we should avoid euphemisms with excess sugar coating or those that appear to be deliberate sarcasm. For example, to refer to a janitor as a *maintenance engineer* is to risk conveying a negative metacommunication such as "We wish this janitor held a more respectable position, but we do the best we can by making it sound good." To the receiver (and to the janitor), just plain *janitor* would sound better. *Use euphemisms when the purpose is to present unpleasant thoughts politely and positively; avoid them when they will be taken as excessive or sarcastic.*

Flattering Tone. Compliments (words of deserved praise) normally elicit favorable reactions. They can increase a receiver's receptivity to subsequent statements. Yet even compliments can do more harm than good if paid at the wrong time, in the wrong setting, in the presence of the wrong people, or for a suspicious motive.

Insincere compliments are detrimental to good communication.

Flattery (words of *un*deserved praise) may be gracefully accepted, but the net result is almost always negative. Although flattery *can* be accepted as a sincere compliment, the recipient is more likely to interpret undeserved praise as an attempt to curry favor. Suspicion of motive makes effective communication less likely. *Give sincere compliments judiciously; avoid flattery.*

Skip the flattery.

Demeaning Tone. Read the following pairs of sentences. Which sentence seems more appropriate and why?

The pencil pushers (or bean counters) require that all requisitions be approved by the inventory manager.

The accountants require that all requisitions be approved by the inventory manager.

As it entered the plant gate, the bus carrying the scabs was struck by rocks.

As it entered the plant gate, the bus carrying the strikebreakers was struck by rocks.

Coach Roberts intends to concentrate on recruiting skilled players this season.

Coach Roberts intends to concentrate on recruiting quarterbacks, running backs, and receivers this season.

Be sure the turtles understand the importance of meeting next week's deadline.

Be sure the management trainees understand the importance of meeting next week's deadline.

In each of the preceding pairs, the first sentence can be taken as contempt for an occupation or a specific job. Like words that attack races or nationalities, words that ridicule occupations work against a writer's purpose. An expression that is designed to make an idea seem negative or disrespectful (sometimes called a *dysphemism*) is a demeaning expression. Many demeaning expressions are common across regions and perhaps even cultures. Some demeaning expressions belong to a particular company. For example, "turtles" in the last pair of sentences was coined in one firm to mock first-year employees for the slow pace at which they completed their work. Because such expressions divert attention from the real message to emotional problems that have little to do with the message, *avoid demeaning expressions.*

Connotative Tone.   Human relations can suffer when connotative words are inadvertently used instead of denotative words. The denotative meaning of a word is the literal meaning that most people assign to it. The connotative meaning is the literal meaning plus an extra message that reveals the speaker's or writer's qualitative judgment. Here is an example:

Denotative	*Connotative*
The support staff traveled to the workshop in Stephen's <u>car</u>.	The support staff traveled to the workshop in Stephen's <u>foreign job</u>.

The second message contains a denotative meaning and an additional message: The author of the sentence has a bias for or against foreign cars. The connotation may needlessly introduce thoughts about whether the purchase of foreign cars is wise. While thus occupied, the mind may not pay sufficient attention to the statements that follow "foreign job."

Denotative	*Connotative*
Have you read the latest <u>memo from the supervisor</u>?	Have you read the latest <u>commandment from above</u>?
Another <u>employee forum</u> has been scheduled for tomorrow.	Another <u>gripe session</u> has been scheduled for tomorrow.

Note the commonality between connotations and metacommunications. Both involve messages that are implied. In the preceding illustrations, the connotations seem to be more harmful than helpful. At times, however, connotations can be helpful:

Denotative	*Connotative but Positive*
<u>Research and Development</u> has developed yet another outstanding production process.	Our corporate <u>think tank</u> has developed yet another outstanding production process.
John's likable personality <u>is beneficial</u> when he negotiates labor contracts.	John's likable personality <u>has made him a miracle worker</u> when he negotiates labor contracts.

Compared with denotative words, connotative words invite a wider range of interpretation. Words that elicit a positive reaction from one person could elicit a negative reaction from another.

The appropriateness of connotations varies with the audience to which they are addressed and the context in which they appear. For example, "foreign job" might be received differently by a group of teenagers and a group of senior citizens. The expression is less appropriate in a research report than in a popular magazine.

Connotations are influenced by the passage of time. "May I pour you some more coffee?" may have a connotation of genuine desire to serve if asked during a meal. An hour later, the same words could connote, "Don't you think it's about time for you to leave?"

In business writing *rely mainly on denotative words or connotative words that will elicit a favorable reaction*. By considering the audience, the context, and the timing, you can usually avoid connotative words that elicit unfavorable reactions.

Bias-Free Language

Because sending a clear message is so important, a writer or a speaker cannot afford the risk of sending an insensitive message. In addition, managers in today's highly competitive, diverse work force cannot afford to alienate employees and customers. Therefore, select words carefully to eliminate any trace of insensitivity regarding gender, race or ethnic group, religion, age, or disability.

Gender Bias. Pay special attention to the pronouns "him" and "his" in the following sentences:

When your accountant completes year-end financial statements, ask <u>him</u> to send a copy to the loan officer.

The human resources manager must evaluate <u>his</u> employees' performance at least twice a year.

When the gender of a noun ("accountant" in the first sentence and "manager" in the second) has not been revealed, do not use a masculine pronoun. Although this usage was once standard and accepted, it can be considered offensive today. The reader's attention may be diverted from the message to the writer's stereotypical attitudes and insensitivity. *Avoid using the pronoun* he *when referring to a group of people that may include women.*

What hidden message could these sentences relay?

A teacher must complete in-service training to update <u>her</u> certification.

If a secretary is to advance in today's business environment, <u>she</u> must develop excellent computer skills.

The writers of these sentences are communicating an insensitive message between the lines that "only females serve in certain professions." *Avoid referring to males and females in stereotyped roles and occupations.*

Sensitive, unbiased writers make sure that their writing does not contain gender-biased language. Computer writing software is now capable of highlighting gender-biased references. Once it is identified, gender-biased language can be corrected in a variety of ways:

1. Avoid use of a pronoun completely.

> Not: When your auditor arrives, <u>he</u> is to go. . . .
> Instead: Upon arrival, <u>your auditor</u> is to go. . . .

2. Repeat the noun.

> Not: . . . the courtesy of your guide. Ask <u>him</u> to. . . .
> Instead: . . . the courtesy of your guide. Ask <u>the guide</u> to. . . .

How can you avoid gender-biased language?

3. Use a plural noun.

> Not: If a supervisor needs assistance, <u>he</u> can. . . .
> Instead: If supervisors need assistance, <u>they</u> can. . . .

(Because "they" can refer to men only, women only, or both, it avoids implying that supervisors can be men only.)

4. Use pronouns from both genders.

> Not: Just call the manager. <u>He</u> will in turn. . . .
> Instead: Just call the manager. <u>He</u> or <u>she</u> will in turn. . . .

Occasional use of "he or she" may not be particularly distracting, but repeated use can take attention away from the message.

Although the English language has a common-gender plural pronoun (*they*), it does not have such a pronoun in the singular (except for *it*, which is hardly appropriate for referring to people, and *one*, the use of which is seldom advisable). *Avoid using masculine pronouns that may be considered offensive.*

Can you identify possible gender bias in the following sentences?

The <u>fireman</u> worked tirelessly to free the child trapped in the well.

The <u>businessman</u> travels approximately four months a year.

Substituting "firefighters" for "fireman" and "executive" (or a specific job title such as "insurance agent") for "businessman" is a simple way to eliminate gender bias in these sentences. Many occupational titles have been changed to reflect genuine sensitivity to gender:

Can you add to these examples of alternatives to gender-biased terms?

Gender Biased	*Sensitive*
businessman	executive, manager, businessperson
career woman	professional
foreman	supervisor
stock boy	stock clerk
bag boy	courtesy clerk
working mother	working parent

Avoid designating an occupation by gender. For example, why include "lady" in "A lady doctor is opening a hematology clinic next month"? The doctor's profession, not her gender, is the point of the message. Similarly, avoid using the -*ess* ending to differentiate genders in an occupation:

Gender Biased	*Sensitive*
steward or stewardess	flight attendant
waiter or waitress	server
host or hostess	host
author or authoress	author
poet or poetess	poet

Could the expressions used in the following sentences be perceived as insensitive or biased?

Preparing the company's annual report is a <u>man-sized</u> task.

After reviewing each applicant's credentials, we concluded that Charles Morrow is the <u>best man</u> for the job.

This estimate of the <u>manpower</u> needed to install this information system is quite conservative.

In the first sentence, substituting "enormous" or "immense" for "man-sized" accurately describes the magnitude of the task without running the risk of offending the reader. Similarly, "best man" would be better as "best person," and "manpower" would be better as "number of workers." Avoid commonly used expressions in which "man" represents all humanity, such as "Man does not live by bread alone," and stereotypical characteristics, such as "manpower," "man and wife," "man-made goods," and "work of four strong men."

Race and Ethnic Group, Age, Religion, and Disability Bias. Changes in the demographics of the work force are requiring managers to design bias-free messages in terms of race and ethnic group, age, religion, and disability. In fact, companies are investing in diversity workshops designed to raise awareness of racial and gender bias and to seek ways to change. One participant summed up his experience this way: "These days I pay more attention to a person's competency than to whether that person fits a classical mold" (Ehrlich, 1990).

The guidelines for writing gender-sensitive messages also apply to writing messages sensitive to race and ethnic group, age, religion, and disability: *Avoid referring to these groups in stereotypical ways, and avoid emphasizing age, ethnic group, religion, or disability when these factors are not relevant.* Can you identify the insensitivities in the following examples?

Alfonso Perez, the <u>Spanish</u> clerk in the Quality Control Division, immediately identified the discrepancy in the raw materials.

Keith's <u>Irish</u> temper flared today when we learned of the new production quotas.

The <u>black</u> mayor of Aberdeen has announced his bid for re-election.

The <u>Jewish</u> account executive has designed a creative point-of-sale display for the Pearson campaign.

Bart Neilson, the <u>55-year-old</u> president of Garvy-Wheaton Bank, has resigned to accept a position with another company.

References to race or ethnic group in the first three sentences are irrelevant, just as gender is immaterial in the earlier example, "The lady doctor. . . ." Eliminating the president's age will not alter the meaning of the last sentence.

Does either of the following sentences communicate a hidden negative message?

<u>Blind</u> employees will receive company memorandums by voice mail.

The new elevator is for the exclusive use of the <u>handicapped</u> employees and should not be used by <u>normal</u> employees.

When communicating about people with disabilities, use the "people first" language supported by Tyler (1990): Refer to the person first and the disability second. The emphasis is appropriately focused on the person's ability rather than on the disability. Avoid words with negative or judgmental connotations such as *handicap, unfortunate, afflicted,* and

Today's work force is diverse, filled with the dynamism of people from many differing racial or ethnic groups, people of all ages and abilities, and people of both genders. Because of this great diversity, you must be very careful to use language that shows your sensitivity toward and recognition of these various groups.

victim. When describing people without disabilities, use the word *typical* rather than *normal;* otherwise, you may inadvertently imply that people with disabilities are abnormal. Consider these more sensitive revisions:

Employees with vision impairments will receive company memorandums by voice mail.

The new elevator is for the exclusive use of employees who have disabilities.

To communicate that you are responsive to the differences of others, you must make a conscious effort to use bias-free (nondiscriminatory) language. Taking even a remote chance of offending someone is too great a risk. Using bias-free language permits the reader or listener to focus on your message rather than to raise serious questions about your sensitivity. Your concerted efforts to be caring and sensitive will yield tangible results: increased clarity and strong, lasting relationships—both measuring sticks for effective communication.

WORD CATEGORIES

In a book that discusses a wide variety of communication problems, a complete discussion of word usage is hardly possible. The following discussion touches on many of the word-selection problems encountered in business communication.

**What are the consequences
of making a grammatical
error?**

You don't have to use big, unusual words to convey the wrong message or cause human relations problems. Small, common words used incorrectly or ungrammatically can have the same effects.

Even when the correct message is received, a grammatical error can get more attention than the message itself. Such an error can cause the recipient to wonder about the sender's educational background or respect for others. Word-selection problems exist in all parts-of-speech categories.

Words That Label

Nouns—words that label people, places, things, or ideas—appear in all sentences. Using nouns effectively aids you in writing clearly and vividly.

Abstract and Concrete Nouns.   Pay special attention to the underscored words in each pair of sentences. Which do you prefer, the first sentence or the second?

Confirmation of the date will be received from the president.

The president will confirm the date.

Authorization of payment is the responsibility of the controller.

The controller authorizes all payments.

Excessive overtime and travel were listed by employees as their primary reasons for resigning.

Employees listed excessive overtime and travel as their primary reasons for resigning.

The first sentence in each pair uses an abstract noun as the subject; the second sentence uses a concrete noun as the subject. The subject is the main "actor" in a sentence. Therefore, the more vivid the subject is, the better. The abstract nouns "confirmation," "authorization," "overtime," and "travel" are hard to envision. Because "president," "controller," and "employees" are readily envisioned, the meaning of the second sentence in each pair comes through more clearly. Using an abstract noun as a sentence subject is certainly not an error; in fact, when an idea needs to be included but does not need emphasis, using an abstract noun as the subject may be desirable. Usually, however, writers and speakers will convey clearer messages if they *use concrete nouns as subjects*.

Abstract nouns *can* sometimes serve well as sentence subjects.

Possessive Nouns and Pronouns Before Gerunds.   Note the underscored words in the following pairs of sentences:

The supervisor will appreciate your help.

The supervisor will appreciate your helping the trainee.

We were concerned about his <u>adjustment</u>.

We were concerned about his <u>adjusting to flexible scheduling</u>.

In the first sentence of the first pair, "help" is used as a noun (it tells what is being appreciated). In the second sentence, "helping the trainee" is also used as a noun (another way of expressing "help"). Now note the words that precede "help" and "helping." Without thinking about it, a receiver knows that the word preceding "help" should be the possessive form ("your"). "The supervisor will appreciate you help" just does not sound right. Because "helping the trainee" serves the same purpose in the second sentence that "help" serves in the first, the word preceding "helping the trainee" must be possessive also. In the second sentence of the second pair, note the use of the possessive form "his" before "adjusting."

Can a verb be used as a noun?

The expressions "helping the trainee" and "adjusting to flexible scheduling" are called *gerunds* (verbs used as nouns and characterized by an *-ing* ending). Each of the following sentences contains a gerund. Of the two words that precede the gerund, determine which one is correct.

Busy executives appreciate (<u>you</u>, <u>your</u>) using simple, informal words.

His supervisor was concerned about (<u>him</u>, <u>his</u>) working such long hours.

(<u>You</u>, <u>Your</u>) highlighting customer benefits in the brochure created an ideal effect.

The interview will follow (<u>Jim</u>, <u>Jim's</u>) completing an application and brief employment test.

In each sentence, the second choice is correct. *Before a gerund use the possessive form of a noun or pronoun.* To a recipient who knows English well, failure to use the possessive form before a gerund is distracting.

Does a possessive noun or pronoun precede a gerund?

Words That Replace

In the following sentence pairs, note that a noun used in the first sentence has been replaced by a different word in the second:

When <u>Judge Margaret West</u> heard the SEC complaint, <u>Judge Margaret West</u> ruled that three executives had engaged in inside stock trading.

When <u>she</u> heard the SEC complaint, <u>Judge Margaret West</u> ruled that three executives had engaged in inside stock trading.

Brad Magee made a presentation on <u>adult illiteracy</u>. <u>Adult illiteracy</u> is projected to affect more than one-third of the adult population.

Brad Magee made a presentation on <u>adult illiteracy</u>, which is projected to affect more than one-third of the adult population.

Replacing "Judge Margaret West" and "adult illiteracy" (nouns) with "she" and "which" (pronouns) brings welcomed variety without decreasing clarity.

Sometimes careless use of pronouns can cause serious problems in communication. To avoid these problems, make sure you understand the rules and conventions for using pronouns.

Ambiguous Reference.   A pronoun must refer clearly to its antecedent (the noun it replaces) for the sentence containing the pronoun to be clear. Note the troublesome pronoun in the first sentence:

Not: Linda told Marsha that <u>her</u> report had been approved.

Instead: Linda told Marsha, "<u>Your</u> report has been approved."

The first sentence is not clear because the reader does not know whether "her" refers to Linda or Marsha. Can you locate the problem in the following sentences?

Illogical	*Logical*
The MIS manager removed the virus from the hard drive and protected it from future damage. (Is the virus or the drive being protected?)	The MIS manager removed the virus from the hard drive and protected the hard drive from future damage.
Jan found a fax on her desk that a sales manager had sent a week ago. (Did the manager send a fax or the desk?)	On her desk Jan found a fax that a sales manager had sent a week ago.
The accountant reminded the client that he could deduct for home mortgage interest. (Who could deduct? The accountant or the client?)	The accountant reminded the client that home mortgage interest is deductible.

Clarifying pronoun reference may be as simple as using a direct quotation, repeating the noun, repositioning the pronoun nearer to the antecedent, or recasting the sentence. *To achieve clarity, be certain that the pronouns refer clearly to only one antecedent positioned as closely to the pronoun as possible.*

First Person.   Sometimes, reaction to a message is strongly influenced by the choice of pronoun used. If the first-person pronoun *I* is used frequently, the sender may impress others as being self-centered—always talking about self. When *I* is used, it appears as the subject, and the sub-

COMMUNICATION MENTOR

A turn-off in any type of written correspondence is use of the word *I* and its sister words *me* and *us*. Try to eliminate these words from your vocabulary to prevent an *us* vs. *them* attitude.

Terence E. McSweeney
Director of Communications
PGA of America

---

ject of a sentence gets emphasis. Knowing that overuse of *I* is discouraged, some people try to circumvent its use by inserting such words as *the undersigned, yours truly, this researcher,* or *this reporter.* Use of these expressions is just as bad as or worse than use of *I.* They may be taken as a devious way of inserting self into the message without use of the first-person pronoun. *Avoid overuse of* I *and other words that identify self.*

Second Person.   Another pronoun that frequently interferes with correct interpretation is *you. You,* always referring to the person or persons being addressed, is called a *second-person pronoun.* In the following sentence, what does *you* mean?

<u>You</u> can't interpret these figures.

If the author of the sentence means "he" or "she" can't interpret, "you" should not be used. If "you" is intended to mean the specific person being addressed, it could be inaccurate or insulting. The person to whom the statement is directed *may be able* to interpret the figures and may be offended because the author underestimated his or her ability to interpret the figures. If "you" in the sentence means "no one" or "the average person," the message may be misunderstood. Because "you" in such sentences can be interpreted in three ways, *avoid "you"* when the person it stands for is not clear.

The following sentences use the second-person pronoun. In which sentence is "you" less advisable?

<u>You</u> typed a perfect copy.
<u>You</u> made numerous mistakes on this page.

The first sentence contains a positive idea. The person to whom the sentence is addressed can hardly resent being associated with perfection. The

> Second person designates the person *to* whom a remark is addressed.

second sentence contains a negative idea. Sensitivity about the mistake is heightened when the person addressed is directly associated with the mistakes. If the speaker's desire is to be diplomatic (at least to be no more negative than necessary), the second sentence could be revised to avoid the use of second person: "This page contains numerous mistakes." For better human relations, *use second person for presenting pleasant ideas and avoid second person for presenting negative ideas.* However, use of second person with negative ideas *is* an acceptable technique on the rare occasions when the purpose is to jolt the receiver by emphasizing a negative.

Normally, avoid second person in stating negative ideas.

Although use of *you* is discouraged when the antecedent is vague and when the idea is negative, the more common mistake is the failure to use *you* frequently enough. *You* (appropriately used) conveys to receivers a feeling that messages are specifically for *them.* Presenting ideas from the reader's viewpoint heightens interest and increases vividness. Compare the following examples of writer-centered and reader-centered statements:

I- or Writer-Centered	*Reader-Centered*
I want to take this opportunity to offer my congratulations on your recent promotion to vice president of commercial loans.	Congratulations on your recent promotion to senior vice president of commercial loans.
I like your willingness to revise the report until it is acceptable.	Your willingness to revise the report until it is acceptable is outstanding.
We have two laser printers compatible with your software.	Your software is compatible with two of our high-quality laser printers.
I am interested in ordering. . . .	Please send me. . . .
We allow a 2-percent discount to customers who pay their total invoices within ten days.	Customers who pay within ten days may deduct 2 percent from their total invoice.

"You attitude" increases clarity and builds relationships.

For success in human relations, a "you attitude" is essential. A "you attitude" involves thinking in terms of the other person's interests and trying to see a problem from the other's point of view. These habits assist people in getting along with others and make communication more effective. Those who have the "you attitude" find using *you* natural and easy.

Third Person. Like second and first person, third person has an influence on human relations. Note the difference:

<u>You</u> will soon learn that preparing the company's annual report is a tedious, time-consuming task.

<u>Carol Trevino</u>, who prepared last year's annual report, said <u>she</u> found the task to be tedious and time-consuming.

Whether the first sentence is preferred over the second depends on the speaker's purpose. If the intent is to warn that preparing the report is an arduous task, the use of second person is more effective. If the intent is to de-emphasize the tedious nature of the task, the use of third person is more effective. *Use second person to emphasize an idea and third person to de-emphasize an idea.*

Agreement.   Each of the following sentences contains an error in pronoun usage:

Because of increasing medical costs, <u>Carlson & Downer, Inc.</u> is revamping <u>their</u> employee benefits package.

<u>Everyone</u> must submit a tentative budget for <u>their</u> department by November 5.

The <u>recommendations</u> arrived today; the judge checked <u>it</u> thoroughly.

Because "Carlson & Downer, Inc." is the singular noun to which the pronoun refers, the pronoun "their" should be changed to a singular form, "its." In the other two examples, the pronoun should agree in number with the underlined noun. Substitute "his or her" for "their" and "them" for "it." Recognizing the lack of agreement, a reader or listener wonders whether more than one noun is involved or whether the wrong pronoun has been used. To avoid this confusion, *make sure pronouns agree in number with their antecedents.*

Use singular nouns with singular pronouns; use plural nouns with plural pronouns.

Case.   Pronouns may appear in almost any position in a sentence. Selecting the right form to use is seldom a problem when the pronoun is at the beginning. Without stopping to think about it, English-speaking people will say "I went" not "me went," "they went" not "them went." Errors are more likely to occur when the pronoun is at the end of a sentence or when the sentence involves two or more people. Understanding the forms and usage of pronouns will help you avoid these errors.

Let's start with the simplest usage: *the nominative case.* Always use a nominative-case pronoun (*I, you, he, she, we, it,* or *they*) in the subject of a sentence, regardless of whether the sentence has one subject or a compound subject:

<u>He</u> coordinated the computer conversion.

<u>He</u> and <u>Tom</u> coordinated the computer conversion.

<u>She</u> called in sick last Friday.

<u>She</u> and <u>Marie</u> called in sick last Friday.

<u>He</u> passed the CPA exam this summer.

<u>He</u> and <u>I</u> passed the CPA exam this summer.

    The first sentence of each pair has one subject and uses a nominative-case pronoun. The second sentence in each pair has a compound subject and also uses a nominative-case pronoun. Avoid the common error of using an objective-case pronoun in a compound subject ("Her and Marie called in sick"). Note that the compound subject in the last sentence is made up of two nominative-case pronouns ("he" and "I").

    An objective-case pronoun (*me, you, him, her, it, us,* or *them*) is used (1) following a preposition and (2) following words that show action (verbs). Note that some pronouns are the same in the nominative and objective cases.

    In the following pairs of sentences, observe that objective-case pronouns follow the underscored prepositions (words that show relationships between nouns or pronouns and other words in the sentence). The word that follows the preposition is its object so the objective case is used.

Wait <u>for</u> me to approve the changes.

Wait <u>for</u> the architect and me to approve the changes.

Send a fax <u>to</u> me.

Send a fax <u>to</u> the district managers and me.

Thank you for talking <u>with</u> me about your financial audit.

Thank you for talking <u>with</u> Mr. Chou and me about your financial audit.

Please make a guaranteed room reservation <u>for</u> me.

Please make a guaranteed room reservation <u>for</u> my spouse and me.

After verbs and prepositions, use objective-case pronouns.

    In the preceding pairs of sentences, the first sentence has one object and uses an objective-case pronoun. The second sentence in each pair has a compound object and also uses an objective-case pronoun. *Always use objective-case pronouns following prepositions.*

    In the following sentences, observe that objective-case pronouns follow words that show action (verbs):

Mr. Shaw is taking <u>me</u> to the Harbor Club for lunch.

The systems analyst helped <u>me</u>.

The president encouraged <u>us</u>.

Georgia assisted <u>them</u>.

The officer stopped Tom and <u>me</u>.

The noun or pronoun that follows a verb is called its object. *Use objective-case pronouns following verbs.*

Notice the use of "Tom and me" in the last sentence. Here "Tom and me" is the compound object of the verb "stopped"; therefore, the objective-case pronoun "me" is used. This does not mean that the objective case is always used when two people are involved. Recall the example: "He and Tom coordinated the computer conversion." Here the nominative-case pronoun "he" is used because "He and Tom" serves as the subject of the sentence.

Errors in pronoun usage seem to occur in sentences involving two or more people (such as the "Tom and me" example). Consider the following sentences:

Note: "Tom and *I* are waiting," but "Wait for Tom and *me.*"

The supervisor's reprimand was intended for Larry and <u>I</u>.

The marketing managers asked Karyn and <u>I</u> to attend the meeting.

Susan and <u>me</u> are in charge of the fax machine this week.

In the two first sentences, "I" should be changed to "me." Both sentences require objective-case pronouns. In the first sentence, the pronoun follows the preposition "for"; in the second sentence, the pronoun follows the verb "asked." In the last sentence, me should be changed to "I" because the compound subject requires the nominative case.

To avoid these errors, follow this simple rule: Use the same pronoun regardless of whether it stands alone or with another noun or pronoun. The position and function of the pronoun in the sentence determines which case to use, not the words that accompany the pronoun.

If a question arises about whether to use the nominative- or the objective-case pronoun, try reading the sentence without the words that accompany the pronoun. For example, read the first sentence without the words "Larry and." No one would say "The supervisor's reprimand was intended for I." One would say ". . . was intended for *me.*" The objective case "me" is used following the preposition "for," so the correct sentence is "The supervisor's reprimand was intended for *me.*"

Try this technique for the other two incorrect sentences.

Analyze the sentence structure carefully; sometimes the correct pronoun choice is less obvious than it seems. For example, which of the following sentences is correct?

Marla Garvin is more qualified for this job than *I.*

Marla Garvin is more qualified for this job than *me.*

Lance is just as interested in integrated software as *I.*

Lance is just as interested in integrated software as *me.*

"I" is correct in both pairs of sentences because "I" is the subject of the dependent clause "than (or as) I am"; the predicate ("am") is understood in both cases. *Use nominative-case pronouns as the subject of a clause with an understood predicate.*

"Myself" is a poor substitute for "I" or "me."

Sometimes, reflexive (self) pronouns are incorrectly used instead of nominative or objective pronouns:

Incorrect: Sue and <u>myself</u> will attend the desktop publishing training session.

Correct: Sue and <u>I</u> will attend the desktop publishing training session.

Incorrect: The note was signed by Jane and <u>myself</u>.

Correct: The note was signed by Jane and <u>me</u>.

Reflexive pronouns (such as *herself, himself, myself, themselves,* and *yourself)* re-identify a noun or pronoun for emphasis:

I <u>myself</u> am not alarmed.	Calls special attention to "I"; inclusion of "myself" has about the same effect as would underscoring "I."
The supervisor <u>herself</u> made the rule.	Use of "herself" indicates that the preceding word is especially significant.

Reflexive pronouns also reflect action on or by a subject:

Tim made <u>himself</u> a copy of the new procedures.

The visitor excused <u>herself</u>.

Use "self" words to (1) re-identify and thus achieve emphasis or (2) reflect action on or by a subject. Do not use them to replace nominative or objective pronouns.

Words That Show Action

Because every sentence includes an action or linking verb, correct use of verbs is especially important.

Correct: "One of the tires *is* flat."
Incorrect: "One of the tires *are* flat." Why?

Agreement.   For those whose native language is English, correct use of verbs is almost automatic: *they are, he is, she was, we were.* Whether to use *is* or *are* depends on whether the subject is singular or plural. Yet, because people are accustomed to using a plural form of the verb to accompany a plural noun or pronoun, they sometimes use the wrong verb when a noun appears between the subject and the verb. Observe the *misuse* of verbs in these sentences:

Only one of the consultants <u>are</u> present.

The board members, not the immediate supervisor, <u>is</u> accountable for this error.

Each of the following pages <u>have</u> been proofread carefully.

In the first sentence, note that the subject is "one," a singular form. "Consultants" is not the subject and therefore has no influence on the form of verb that is used: "Only one . . . *is* present." Likewise, "The *board members* . . . *are* accountable"; "*Each . . . has* been proofread."

Because subject-verb agreement is a principle of English, such errors are especially distracting. Even though recipients may be able to understand exactly what is meant, the message will not come through with the impact it deserves. Instead, the error may generate thoughts about whether it resulted from haste, lack of respect, or lack of knowledge. To avoid such possibilities, *use verbs that agree in number with the subjects of sentences.*

Agreement in person is also a necessity. The verbs in the following examples are used *incorrectly:*

He <u>don't</u> listen carefully to instructions.

Linda <u>don't</u> understand the importance of working as a team member.

You <u>was</u> notified of the July 9 production deadline.

"First person" describes a speaker or writer—*I* and *we*. "Second person" describes the one spoken or written to—*you*. "Third person" describes the one spoken or written about—*he, she, him, her, it, they, them*. In most usage, correctness is automatic: "I was," not "I were"; "she cooks," not "she cook"; and "they work," not "they works." The most common errors are in the use of *don't* with third-person singular ("Alice don't work here any more") and *was* with second-person singular ("You was a kid once yourself"). The correct forms of the previously displayed sentences are "He *doesn't* listen carefully," "Linda *doesn't* understand," and "You *were* notified." To avoid these grammatical errors that impede communication, *use verbs that agree in person with their subjects.*

Tense. In addition to revealing action, verbs reveal the *time* of action—past, present, or future. Observe the words that indicate time:

We <u>received</u> your report last week, we <u>are studying</u> it, and we <u>will make</u> a decision tomorrow.

Does "She don't drive" illustrate lack of agreement in number?

All three tenses are used in this example. Using three tenses in the same sentence is *necessary* if events are to be properly placed in time. However, *unnecessary* changes in tense sometimes cause confusion and distraction:

He studies^(present) the proposal and offered^(past) his reaction.

John offered^(past) to pay but fumbles^(present) for his wallet.

Which is right: (a) avoid changes in tense, or (b) avoid unnecessary changes in tense?

Such sentences cause listeners or readers to wonder which is to be thought of, a present event or a past event. Each sentence should use two present-tense verbs or two past-tense verbs, but not one of each. For consistency, *do not make unnecessary changes in tense.*

Infinitives. In English, two words are required for expressing verbs in infinitive form: *to be, to go, to write, to work, to study.* In other languages (French and German, for example), only one word is required for expressing infinitives: *aller* for "to go" in French, and *gehen* for "to go" in German. Even though the English infinitive consists of two words, it should be thought of as a unit and should not be split:

Incorrect

More data are necessary to accurately solve this complex problem.

We want you to seriously consider the proposal.

Correct

More data are necessary to solve this complex problem accurately.

We want you to consider the proposal seriously.

An infinitive: *"to go"*; a split infinitive: *"to quickly go"*

Avoid splitting infinitives. However, a split infinitive is acceptable in cases where wording is awkward or confusing by not separating the words. To prevent awkward construction, splitting the infinitive in the following sentence is acceptable: "The strategic plan calls for the company to more than double its retail outlets within the next five years."

Active and Passive Voice. In the following example, the sentence in the left column uses passive voice; the right, active voice:

Passive

Reports are transferred electronically from remote locations to the home office.

Active

Our sales representatives electronically transfer reports from remote locations to the home office.

Both sentences use the verbs correctly. In sentences in which the subject is the *doer* of action, the verbs are called *active*. In sentences in which the subject is the *receiver* of action, the verbs are called *passive*. Clarity of ideas is heightened when the subject is the actor. When sentences use passive voice, receivers get a less-distinct picture. In the left-hand sentence, the reader becomes aware that something was done to the reports, but who did it is not revealed.

Even when a passive sentence contains additional words to reveal the doer, the imagery is less distinct than it would be if the sentence were active:

> Reports <u>compiled by our sales representatives</u> are transferred from remote locations to the home office.

The word "reports" gets the most attention because it is the subject. The sentence seems to let a reader know the *result* of action before revealing the doer; therefore, the sentence is less emphatic.

Because active voice conveys ideas more vividly, senders rely more heavily on active voice than passive voice. Passive voice is useful, however,

1. In concealing the doer ("The reports have been compiled").
2. In placing more emphasis on *what* was done and what it was *done to* than on who *did* it ("The reports have been compiled by our sales representatives").
3. In subordinating an unpleasant thought.
   Both of the following thoughts are negative:

> You <u>failed</u> to proofread this bid proposal carefully.

> You <u>have not notified</u> the Shipping Department of this delay.

Both sentences are active. Because the subject "you" is the doer, the sentences are emphatic. Normally, negative thoughts should be de-emphasized. Presenting an unpleasant thought emphatically (as active verbs do) makes human relations difficult. When passive voice is used, the sentences retain the essential ideas, but the ideas seem less irritating:

> The bid proposal <u>was not proofread</u> carefully.

> The Shipping Department <u>has not been notified</u> of this delay.

Just as emphasis on negatives hinders human relations, emphasis on positives promotes human relations:

> You have proofread this bid proposal perfectly.

> You notified the Shipping Department of this delay promptly.

Some passive sentences reveal the doer; others do not.

Use passive voice with negative ideas.

Use active voice with positive ideas.

Because the subjects ("you") are the doers, the sentences are emphatic; pleasant thoughts deserve emphasis.

Sometimes the expressions *past tense* and *passive voice* are confused. *Past* and *passive* do have similar sounds, but they have different meanings. In the passive voice, the subject is the receiver of the action; that is, the subject is acted upon. Often the doer of the action is named in a prepositional phrase or omitted. The passive voice of a verb always consists of the appropriate form of the helping verb *be* plus the past participle of the main verb.

"Passive" and "past" have different meanings.

Passive: The report <u>was prepared</u> by the production control manager.

Passive: Unethical acts <u>are performed</u> by employees at all levels in an organization.

On the other hand, past-tense verbs appear in sentences in which events have taken place already:

Active voice, past-tense verb: John <u>has done</u> the work.

Passive voice, past-tense verb: The work <u>has been done</u>.

Note that such words as *have, had,* and *has* are frequently used in passive sentences, but they can be used as well when the sentences are active. Note the first sentence, in which the subject, John, is the doer of the action. A passive-voice sentence is not necessarily a sentence about a past event. In fact, a passive-voice sentence can be in the future tense:

Passive voice, future tense: The job <u>will be completed</u> before tomorrow afternoon.

When the subject is not the doer, the sentence is passive—regardless of whether the tense is past, present, or future. Out of concern for clarity and positive human relations, *use active voice to present important points or to present pleasant ideas; use passive voice to present less significant points or to present unpleasant ideas.*

Words That Describe

A word used to describe or give information about a noun is called an *adjective.* Compared with nouns and verbs, adjectives play a less-significant role in a sentence and present fewer problems in usage.

Overly Strong Adjectives.   One common problem is the use of adjectives that are too strong or too frequently used:

Sales have been <u>fantastic</u>.

Mr. Jones presented a <u>ridiculous</u> plan.

The difference between passive and active voice is similiar to the difference between playing tennis and watching television. In one situation, you, the subject, are in control of an activity, while in the other, action is being done to you.

Use of such adjectives can cause a receiver to wonder about a sender's objectivity. A person who wants to report a highly satisfactory sales program should avoid "fantastic" and, instead, give some details. Even though a plan may be worthy of ridicule, a person who comments on it is better off to point out areas needing improvement. By labeling a plan "ridiculous," a writer or speaker might risk being considered biased or overly negative. Communication is normally more effective if writers and speakers *avoid using adjectives that are used too frequently by others, are overly strong, or are overly negative.*

Compound Adjectives. Sometimes, writers or speakers search in vain for the right adjective. Not finding one that presents the right shade of meaning, they can form an adjective by joining two or more words with a hyphen. At first, a writer may put down, "We need *current* reports." Recognizing that "current" may be taken to mean "daily" or "weekly," the writer can use a compound adjective:

We need up-to-the-minute reports.

Because this report is stored on disk, last-minute changes are quite simple.

The compound adjective makes the description more precise. Note that "last-minute" is used in the same way as "recent"—to describe the noun that immediately follows it. When two or more words are used to form a single descriptor of the noun that follows, a hyphen is used to join the words and present them as one. In spoken language, "last-minute"

Before a noun, join the words of a compound adjective with a hyphen or hyphens.

would probably be spoken a little faster than other words in the sentence. The speeding-up technique helps to demonstrate that this compound adjective is used as one word. In written language, the hyphen serves the same purpose.

Using or failing to use the hyphen in a compound adjective is more than just a matter of mechanical correctness or punctuation. Improper use of the hyphen can cause serious differences in meaning:

All night seminars have been canceled.

All-night seminars have been canceled.

In the first sentence, "all" is describing "night seminars." The sentence means that every one of the seminars meeting at night has been canceled. In the second sentence, "all-night" is describing "seminars." The sentence means that seminars lasting the entire night have been canceled. Here are some further examples:

A new car salesperson	The phrase means a new person who sells cars.
A new-car salesperson	The phrase means a person who sells new cars.
His two base hits won the game.	The phrase means two hits, but they could have been singles, doubles, triples, or home runs.
His two-base hits won the game.	The phrase means doubles, but the number of such hits is not revealed.

Difference in meaning? "Two-day seminars" and "Two day seminars"

Hyphens are used to join descriptive words that *precede* a noun and are used as one-word descriptors. Hyphens are not always used when descriptors follow nouns.

The well-known consulting group was hired to solve the problem.

The consulting group hired to solve the problem was well known.

The boss made a spur-of-the-moment decision.

His decision was made on the spur of the moment.

For accurate communication, writers must *use hyphens to join words that form a one-word descriptor of a noun that follows.*

Use hyphens for compound adjectives; commas for coordinate adjectives.

Coordinate Adjectives.   When nouns are described in more than one way, the hyphen is not used. Observe the difference:

Introducing the product line was an exciting, challenging project.

Jane was asked to complete a long, complicated questionnaire.

The project was exciting; it was also challenging. Likewise, the questionnaire was long *and* complicated. In both cases, either adjective could be omitted and the sentence would still make sense. Such adjectives are called *coordinate* adjectives. They are alike in that each describes the following noun. Because each describes separately, they are not joined by a hyphen; rather, they are separated by a comma. Careful writers and editors learn to *place a comma between coordinate adjectives.*

Superlatives. Messages are sometimes influenced negatively by another form of adjective—the superlative:

This dryer is the <u>best</u> one on the market.

The factory has the <u>worst</u> odor imaginable.

Superlatives are very useful words. Frequently, the extreme unit in a series needs to be identified—the *highest* or *lowest* score, the *latest* news, the *most* qualified applicant. When superlatives are totally unsupported or unsupportable, however, their use is questionable. Furnishing proof that no other dryer is up to the standards of this one would be extremely difficult. Proving that one odor is the worst imaginable is practically impossible. Knowing that such statements are exaggerations, the receiver may not believe them at all. In fact, someone who has used a superlative to transmit an *unbelievable* idea may not be believed when offering support for a *believable* idea. For the sake of credibility, *use only supported or supportable superlatives.*

Adverbs. Like adjectives, adverbs describe or modify. Adjectives describe or modify nouns; adverbs describe or modify verbs, adjectives, or other adverbs:

Tim writes <u>rapidly</u>.	"Rapidly" describes a verb.
Sue is an <u>extremely</u> efficient operator.	"Extremely" describes an adjective.
Juan works <u>very</u> rapidly.	"Very" describes an adverb.

Superlatives can be either adjectives or adverbs. They are adverbs when they modify or describe verbs:

Ernie keys <u>fastest</u>.

This item sells <u>best</u>.

Whether a superlative is an adjective or an adverb, the same principle applies: *Use only supported or supportable superlatives.*

Define *superlative.*

Like adjectives, adverbs can arouse skepticism or resentment if they are used without care:

Our prices are <u>ridiculously</u> low.

Our forecasts have been <u>fantastically</u> accurate.

When adverbs are too numerous or too strong, the message may seem subjective.

For the sake of credibility, *avoid using adverbs that are used too frequently by others, are overly strong, or are overly negative.*

The position in which an adverb or adjective is placed can make a genuine difference in the meaning of the sentence:

<u>Only</u> John gets his vacation in summer.	"Only" modifies "John," meaning no other employee gets a summer vacation.
John gets his vacation in summer <u>only</u>.	"Only" modifies "summer," meaning John never gets a vacation at any other time.
John gets his <u>only</u> vacation in summer.	"Only" modifies "vacation," meaning John gets one vacation; it's in summer.
John gets <u>only</u> his vacation in summer.	"Only" modifies "gets," meaning John gets no other benefits.

For the sake of clarity, *place an adverb or adjective close to the word it describes.*

Words That Join

Conjunctions assist in joining ideas (words, phrases, or clauses). When the ideas are of about equal significance, *coordinate* conjunctions are used. In each of the following sentences, the coordinate conjunction joins the two clauses in the compound sentence.

Joyce Mitchell prepared the budget for the Wolverton case, <u>but</u> the advertising staff developed the brochures and advertisements.

Applicants must be able to operate a leading word-processing program proficiently, <u>and</u> they must have had exposure to desktop publishing and spreadsheet software.

When the clauses are not of equal significance, *subordinate* conjunctions are used:

The clerk checked out <u>when</u> the job was finished.

The reporter left <u>before</u> anyone could talk with her.

Note that the coordinate conjunctions "but" and "and" that connect two independent clauses in the first two sentences are preceded by a comma.

The comma is sometimes appropriately omitted when the coordinating conjunction joins two ideas that are exceedingly short ("He left *but* I stayed"). Note that the subordinating conjunctions "when" and "before" are not preceded by a comma.

Punctuation of adverbial conjunctions is different from punctuation of coordinate conjunctions:

The report arrived today, <u>but</u> it has not been evaluated.	Use a comma with conjunctions.
The report arrived today; <u>however</u>, it has not been evaluated.	Use a semicolon with adverbial conjunctions.

The words *however* and *therefore* appear frequently in business communication. Although they come between two related ideas, their relationship is a little closer to the second idea. The comma, which is a weak mark of punctuation, separates the adverbial conjunction from the second idea; the semicolon, a strong mark of punctuation, separates it even more definitively from the first. For accurate punctuation, then, *place a comma before coordinate conjunctions; place a semicolon before adverbial conjunctions and a comma after them.*

Words That Show Relationships

Prepositions are used to show a relationship between a noun or objective-case pronoun and some other word in the sentence (often the subject). Some examples are

The file is <u>in</u> the desk.
The file is <u>beside</u> him.

In the first sentence, "in" describes the relationship between the file (the subject) and the desk (the object of the preposition). In the second sentence, "beside" describes the relationship between the file (the subject) and him (the objective-case pronoun).

Prepositions normally do not appear at the beginnings or endings of simple sentences. Sometimes prepositions are unnecessarily attached to the ends of sentences.

Not:	Where is the Collier file <u>at</u>?
Instead:	Where is the Collier file?

Not:	What did he do that <u>for</u>?
Instead:	Why did he do that?

Equal ideas: coordinating conjunction, use a comma. Ideas of unequal significance: subordinating conjunction, don't use a comma.

Adverbial conjunctions: semicolon before, comma after

Which is better? "Where do you live at?" or "Where do you live?"

Yet prepositions can be effectively placed at the ends of sentences:

Jan was less concerned about what she was living <u>on</u> than what she was living <u>for</u>.

Before you can take anything <u>out</u>, you must put something <u>in</u>.

For purposes of contrast, the key words "for" and "in" need emphasis. Last-word position affords that emphasis. *Place prepositions at the ends of sentences only when doing so serves a useful purpose.*

Prepositions are sometimes repeated for purposes of clarity. Do these sentences have the same meanings?

All auditing staff must receive a satisfactory rating <u>in</u> technical competence, communication ability, and interpersonal skills.

All auditing staff must receive a satisfactory rating <u>in</u> technical competence, <u>in</u> communication ability, and <u>in</u> interpersonal skills.

In the first sentence, one rating is computed—an average of all ratings made in the three areas combined. The single preposition implies a single average. In the second sentence, the three prepositions imply that a satisfactory rating must be received in *each* of the three separate ratings. Under the terms of the second sentence, a staff member who had an unsatisfactory rating (2 points) in communication ability, an excellent rating (4 points) in technical competence, and a satisfactory rating (3 points) in interpersonal communication would not have satisfied the performance requirement. *Repeat the preposition before each word in a series if doing so conveys the precise meaning intended.*

For a more thorough treatment of word-usage consult an English reference book. For a list of words frequently misused, see Appendix B.

SUMMARY

Errors in word usage can result in lost meaning, lost time, distraction, and concern about the writer's or speaker's background. The following principles summarize the discussion of effective word usage:

Precise, Informal Words

- ◆ For vivid business communication, use specific words.
- ◆ For the informal writing that is practiced in business, use simple words instead of more complicated words that have the same meaning.

Parallelism

- ◆ Present multiple units in the same way grammatically.

Positive and Negative Words

◆ Rely mainly on positive words that speak of what can be done instead of what cannot be done, of the pleasant instead of the unpleasant.
◆ When the purpose is to sharpen contrast or when positive words have not evoked the desired reaction, use negative words.

Condescending Words

◆ Avoid using condescending words.

Euphemisms

◆ Use euphemisms when the purpose is to present unpleasant thoughts politely and positively.
◆ Avoid using euphemisms when they will be taken as excessive or sarcastic.

Compliments and Flattery

◆ Give sincere compliments.
◆ Avoid using flattery.

Demeaning Expressions

◆ Avoid using demeaning expressions.

Denotative and Connotative Words

◆ Rely mainly on denotative words or connotative words that will elicit a favorable reaction.

Gender-Biased Language

◆ Do not use the pronoun *he* when referring to a group of people that may include women.
◆ Avoid referring to males and females in stereotyped roles and occupations.
◆ Avoid expressions that reflect stereotypical characteristics.
◆ Avoid using gender-biased occupational titles or differentiating genders in an occupation.

Race and Ethnic Group, Age, Religion, and Disability

◆ Avoid referring to these groups in stereotypical and insensitive ways.
◆ Do not emphasize race and ethnic group, age, religion, or disability when these factors are not relevant.

Words That Label (Nouns)

◆ For clear, emphatic writing, choose concrete nouns as subjects of sentences.

◆ Before a gerund, use the possessive form of noun or pronoun.

Words That Replace (Pronouns)

◆ To achieve clarity, be certain that the pronouns refer clearly to only one antecedent positioned as closely to the pronoun as possible.

◆ Avoid using the word *you* when the person it stands for is not obvious.

◆ For better human relations, use second person for presenting pleasant ideas; and avoid using second person for presenting negative ideas.

◆ Cultivate a "you attitude"; it assists in effective use of second person.

◆ Use second person to emphasize an idea and third person to de-emphasize an idea.

◆ Make sure pronouns agree in number with the noun to which they refer.

◆ Use nominative-case pronouns as subjects of sentences; use objective-case pronouns to follow verbs and prepositions.

◆ Use reflexive (self) pronouns to re-identify and achieve emphasis or to reflect action on or by a subject.

Words That Show Action (Verbs)

◆ Use verbs that agree *in number* with the subjects of sentences.

◆ Use verbs that agree *in person* with their subjects.

◆ Avoid splitting infinitives unless keeping the two words together causes an awkward construction.

◆ Use active verbs to present important points or to present pleasant ideas.

◆ Use passive verbs to present less-significant points or to present unpleasant ideas.

◆ Do not confuse *past tense* and *passive voice*.

Words That Describe (Adjectives and Adverbs)

◆ Avoid using adjectives and adverbs that are used too frequently by others, are overly strong, or are overly negative.

◆ Use a hyphen to join words that form a single descriptor (compound adjective) of a noun that follows.

◆ Place a comma between coordinate adjectives.

◆ To maintain credibility, use only supported or supportable superlatives.

◆ For clarity, place an adverb or adjective close to the word it describes.

Words That Join (Conjunctions)

◆ For accurate punctuation, place a comma before a coordinate conjunction that combines the parts of a compound sentence.

- Do not use a comma before a subordinate conjunction.
- Place a semicolon before adverbial conjunctions and a comma after them.

Words That Show Relationships (Prepositions)

- Place a preposition at the end of a sentence only when doing so serves a useful purpose.
- Repeat the preposition before each word in a series if doing so conveys the precise meaning intended.

REFERENCES

Ehrlich, E. (1990, August 6). Anger, shouting, and sometimes tears. *Business Week*, p. 55.

McRitz, C. (Ed.). (1969). *Current biography yearbook 1968*. New York: H. W. Wilson.

Tyler, L. (1990). Communicating about people with disabilities: Does the language we use make a difference? *Bulletin of the Association for Business Communication, 53*(3), 65–67.

REVIEW QUESTIONS

Word Choice   For each pair of sentences, *which* is preferred? *Why* is it preferred?

1. **a.** We read about your *latest accomplishment.*
    b. We read about your *promotion to manager.*
2. **a.** We heard about *your injuries.*
    b. We heard about *your broken arm and multiple lacerations on your back.*
3. **a.** The final sales figures are *erroneous.*
    b. The final sales figures are *incorrect.*
4. **a.** By networking our microcomputers, we will improve our system for the better.
    b. By networking our microcomputers, we will improve our system.
5. **a.** The production manager *assessed* the problem.
    b. An *assessment* of the problem was made by the production manager.
6. **a.** Send one of the *gofers* to pick up that report from the Tenth Street office.
    b. Send one of the trainees to pick up that report from the Tenth Street office.
7. **a.** I *can't help* you until I finish this production report.
    b. I *can help* you just as soon as I finish this production report.

8. **a.** I've been promoted twice since I did your job, but I can help you for an hour.
   b. I'll be glad to help you for an hour.
9. **a.** The bonus checks have been received for distribution to employees.
   b. You can pick up your bonus check today.
10. **a.** Questions about in-service computer training should be directed to Leah Martin.
    b. Call Leah Martin for information about in-service computer training.

Word Categories   Each sentence violates a principle discussed in this chapter. Identify the error.

Example: You failed to sign the agreement.

The error: Uses second person and active voice to convey a negative idea.

11. The professor objected to us coming in late.
12. Each accountant must submit his time and expense report by the 15th of each month.
13. This researcher found no support for that hypothesis.
14. I have finished reading the research report; you can't tell whether the conclusions are valid.
15. You did not revise the report to include the latest sales projections for Model XL–31.
16. The Smythe proposal was prepared by the district manager and I.
17. The computer hackers completed the network system conversion several days ahead of schedule.
18. Each of the following employees are being promoted.
19. She don't proofread carefully enough to locate all grammatical errors.
20. Comprehensive writing exams are given to all job applicants.
21. You failed to sign the second copy of the engagement letter.
22. Evaluation of the proposal will be done by our production committee.
23. Our market share plunged to dangerous lows last year.
24. Our word processing software now includes the easy to use windows format.
25. The applicants expected a long stressful interview.
26. Our cafeteria serves the best coffee in the world.
27. John conducts the word-processing seminars and Cynthia conducts the spreadsheet seminars.
28. The project is to be completed three weeks earlier than originally announced, therefore we need to hire six additional operators.
29. Where will the new system be located at?
30. Newsome went to the meeting and leaves his presentation.

Exceptions   Give your answer to each question. Answers need not be in complete-sentence form.

31. Business writing is normally informal, but when is formal writing acceptable?
32. Simple words are normally preferred, but when would a difficult, technical term be justified?
33. In most situations, positive language is recommended. When is negative language more appropriate?
34. Euphemisms can make unpleasant ideas seem less unpleasant, but under what conditions would a euphemism be detrimental?
35. Generally, business writers are encouraged to use denotative words. Under what conditions would connotative words be acceptable?
36. Normally, concrete nouns serve well as sentence subjects. Under what condition would abstract nouns serve better?
37. For good human relations, use of *you* is encouraged. Under what condition should *you* be avoided?
38. Normally, active voice is preferred. When is passive voice better?
39. Superlatives are useful words, but when is their use detrimental?
40. The practice of ending a sentence with a preposition is usually discouraged, but when is a preposition appropriately used as the last word?

EXERCISES

Compose a sentence that has the characteristic described:

1. Uses parallel construction in a series of items.
2. Illustrates a euphemism.
3. Begins with a concrete noun.
4. Begins with an abstract noun and thus de-emphasizes an unpleasant thought.
5. Illustrates correct use of a possessive pronoun to precede a gerund.
6. Uses a third-person pronoun.
7. Uses a nominative-case pronoun.
8. Uses an objective-case pronoun.
9. Uses active voice to emphasize a positive idea.
10. Uses passive voice to de-emphasize a negative idea.
11. Illustrates correct punctuation of a compound adjective.
12. Illustrates correct punctuation of coordinate adjectives.
13. Illustrates acceptable use of a superlative.
14. Illustrates correct punctuation of a sentence that has a coordinating conjunction.
15. Illustrates correct punctuation of a sentence that has an adverbial conjunction.

Sales Development Associates

Words are abstract symbols that convey our thoughts, desires, and emotions. Words are the basic building blocks used in developing effective communication. Well chosen words can be powerful, tender, and expressive; inappropriate words can be empty, irritating, and meaningless.

The English language probably has about one million words; most people actively use about 10,000 words of them. A broad vocabulary allows the communicator to select the precise word needed for a given situation. Careful organization of words enables the originator to control the coherence, the tone, and the probable response to the message. Expert use of words is empowering because control over words is often the same as control over the ideas the words represent.

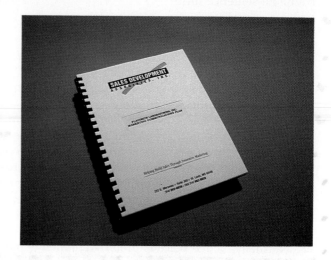

Discussion Questions

1. Pat Biggerstaff and Ken Hieronymus both discuss the importance of tone in effective communication. Define tone.
2. Pat Biggerstaff discusses the appropriateness of both formal and informal (conversational) tone. How are they different? Which would be used with more frequency in a typical business?
3. The business people interviewed mention several ways to improve readability of documents. Discuss three of them.
4. What is involved in preplanning a written communication? Why does Biggerstaff view this activity as so important?
5. What does Bill Shewman mean when he describes the necessity of using language with integrity?

Application

Your company markets a vitamin supplement called The Good Life. You must develop some preliminary materials for use in advertising the product. The product consists of five different vitamin and mineral tablets, individually packed for each daily dose. It costs $20 per month, payable by check, credit card, or C.O.D.; it is shipped in a month's supply; and it has a money-back guarantee.

1. Structure a topic sentence that embodies the main appeal of your product.
2. Brainstorm a list of words that could be used to produce the desired tone of your ad.
3. Structure three short paragraphs for inclusion in your brochure. Focus on (1) the need for the product, (2) a description of the product, and (3) the method of obtaining the product.

USING THE TECHNIQUES OF STYLE

OBJECTIVES

When you have completed Chapter 8, you should be able to

- Compose messages that are clear and concise.

- Compose messages that promote positive human relations.

- Identify factors affecting the readability of text.

- Use stylistic techniques to emphasize or de-emphasize points.

- Apply systematic proof-reading and revising procedures.

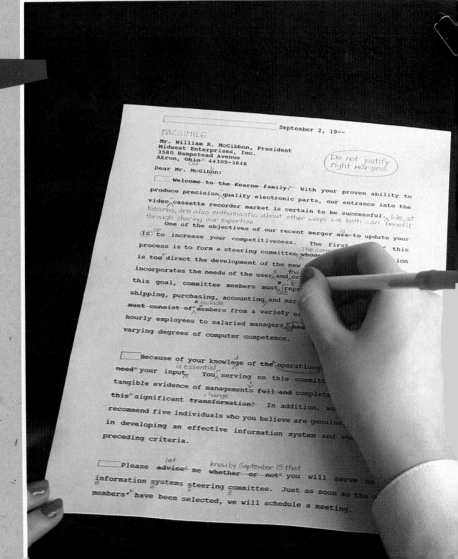

KEVIN, A RECENTLY HIRED MANAGER AT EMERSON-WHITMAN & CO., sits at his desk, staring into the blank face of his computer screen. He has just concluded a very important meeting with a prospective client and knows that his follow-up letter could have a great deal of influence on the prospect's decision. Although he realizes the importance of the letter, he does not allow the pressure to turn into a mental block. He outlines his letter and then begins to write, not paying attention to grammar or spelling. After he finishes his first draft, he goes back and places the information in the correct order; checks for grammar, spelling, and punctuation errors; and prints a copy. It looks clean; but as he begins to fold the letter, he notices that he has misspelled the client's surname. He re-reads the letter carefully, corrects his near-disastrous mistake, then places the final copy in the bin to be mailed. A few days later, the client calls Kevin's supervisor to accept the deal with Emerson-Whitman and mentions how promptly and efficiently Kevin had followed up after the meeting.

Writing is not easy for anyone. Even professional writers start with the same thing beginners do: a blank sheet of paper or a blank computer screen. Furthermore, no one should expect to write a perfect letter on the first try. Writing *is* revising. Author Dorothy Parker once said of her own

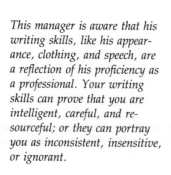

This manager is aware that his writing skills, like his appearance, clothing, and speech, are a reflection of his proficiency as a professional. Your writing skills can prove that you are intelligent, careful, and resourceful; or they can portray you as inconsistent, insensitive, or ignorant.

writing: "I can't write five words but that I change seven" (Charlton, 1985). Get accustomed to the idea that what you write will be changed. Learn to proofread your own work carefully and objectively, and don't rely solely on your computer to catch mistakes. And finally, take advantage of grammar handbooks, dictionaries, and thesauruses. Your writing, like your speech or clothing, is a reflection of you. Your writing can cause you to appear sloppy, insensitive, or even ignorant—or it can prove that you are intelligent, resourceful, and careful. What will your writing say about you?

ANALYZING WRITING STYLE

Computer programs are now available to help writers locate grammatical errors as well as improve their style—the way they express ideas. One writing-analysis program reportedly checks documents against 3,000 English principles. Typically, the writer (1) composes the document at the keyboard, (2) instructs the program to analyze the writing, (3) studies the writing analysis (which includes a readability index), and (4) revises the text incorporating valid suggestions only. For example, the computer may critique the sentence "Authorization of this procedure is recommended . . ." in this way: "Sentence begins with a long, abstract noun and uses passive voice. In rewriting, try 'Authorize' and active voice." Because these suggestions are valid, the writer can quickly input the changes and improve the style of the sentence. On the other hand, the writer would reject the suggestion to rewrite a sentence using active voice if the intention were to use passive voice to de-emphasize negative information.

How can writing-analysis software improve writing?

Figure 8-1 illustrates the feedback you might receive if you analyzed a document using *Grammatik*, a popular writing analysis software program. By allowing *Grammatik* to critique this document, you are able to correct an error in pronoun usage and to confirm the correct use of a commonly misused word. *Grammatik* provides definitions of *principle* and *principal* and allows the writer to select the appropriate word. Because *principle* is correct in this context, you select "Ignore Phrase" from the commands at the bottom of the screen. Among the stylistic errors that *Grammatik* detects are wordy sentences, passive voice, jargon, and gender-biased language. After reviewing the entire document, *Grammatik* displays a document summary showing a readability index, average sentence and paragraph length, and other useful statistics.

Using computer software to criticize writing can be extremely valuable if the writer recognizes that (1) the software is a tool to improve style and (2) the writer may overrule the computer critique to achieve specific objectives. Those who are familiar with the principles of writing will

You must understand basic writing principles to benefit from computer-generated writing critiques.

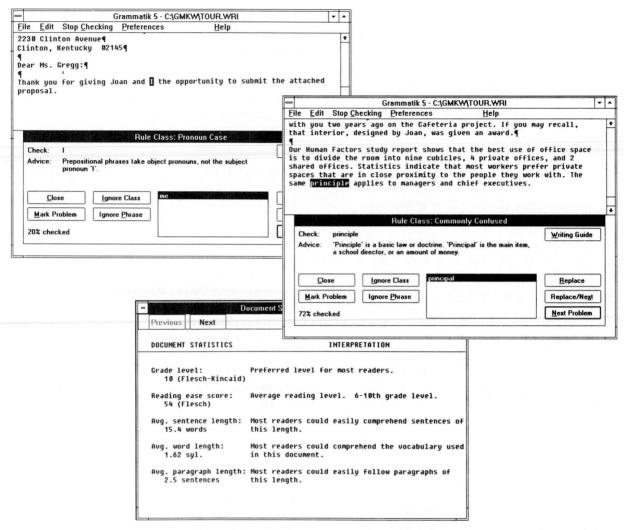

FIGURE 8-1 *Grammatik* **screens highlighting a pronoun error, commonly misused word, readability index, and other statistics.**

benefit most from writing-analysis programs. For example, how helpful would the critique "Uses long, abstract noun and passive voice" be if the writer does not understand what an abstract noun or passive voice is? Obviously, a writer who has an effective style will spend less time revising and will be more likely to understand and appreciate the computer's suggestions.

This chapter presents the writing principles most frequently violated and therefore those worth reviewing or learning for the first time. As a preliminary check to see whether you already know the stylistic principles discussed in this chapter, complete the following self-check.

SELF-CHECK

Cover the answers in the right-hand column with a sheet of paper. Identify the error(s) in the words used in each sentence in the left column. Slide the cover sheet down and read the answer. Do your revisions agree with the answers given? The numbers in parentheses following the correct sentences refer to the pages in the text where the principles that are covered in the sentence are discussed.

Example:

The top sales proposal was compiled by Maria.

The passive sentence shifts attention to the sales proposal and away from the creative sales representative. To place more emphasis on Maria's excellent work, use active voice: "Maria compiled the top sales proposal." (260)

---

1. I am sure you will agree that the seminar was exceptional.

The expression of certainty is unjustified. If the writer can be sure, the idea probably is known already and need not be stated. If the writer cannot be sure, the statement is not true. (242)

2. Enclosed please find our latest price list.

"Enclosed please find" is a worn expression that implies something is hidden. "Refer to the enclosed price list for prices on our high-quality exercise equipment" is more effective. (243)

3. Your credit application is unacceptable.

"Unacceptable" has a negative connotation. Simply explain what the reader must do to correct the situation. (263)

4. The writer appreciated your thoughtfulness.

"The writer" is a poor substitute for "I." It's longer and implies that the writer wants to insert self into the sentence without being discredited for using the first person. (246)

5. Provided, however, that we receive your application by April 17.

This group of words is not a complete sentence. (254)

6. Hanging from a tree, the children saw a monkey.

The participial phrase dangles; that is, it isn't attached to the correct noun. As written, the sentence literally means that the children are hanging from a tree. "The children saw a monkey hanging from a tree" more clearly conveys the meaning the writer truly intended. (257)

7. There are four likely reasons for the drop in sales.

The sentence begins with an expletive (the meaningless word "there") and thus presents the verb before presenting the noun. Better writing presents the noun first: "Four logical reasons for the drop in sales are . . ." (258)

8. Supervisors evaluate their employees' performance.

The idea in this sentence is known already. The reader could be insulted by this platitude. (259)

9. The computer consultants considered a very important criterion (processing speed) in their evaluation of new computer systems.

An appositive that deserves emphasis is de-emphasized through the use of parentheses. Dashes provide greater emphasis: ". . . a very important criterion—processing speed—in their. . . ." (264)

10. I endorsed your check and deposited it.

The sentence conveys an idea that need not be stated in words. The check was obviously endorsed or it would not have been deposited. "I deposited your check" is more effective. (251)

PHRASES

A phrase is a group of words that does not constitute a complete sentence. Grammar texts have more complete discussions of phrases, but those selected for discussion here commonly present problems in business writing.

Certainties

Read the following pairs of sentences, paying attention to the underscored phrases. Which sentence, the first or the second, is better?

I <u>am sure</u> you will agree that the instructions are clear.

Re-examine the instructions to see whether they are clear.

I <u>know</u> you will understand the importance of completing the designs by Friday.

The designs must be completed by Friday if we are going to meet the final deadline.

In each pair, the writer of the first sentence seems to be making a declaration of certainty when certainty is hardly possible. If through prior discussion the writer *can* be sure of agreement, the first sentence is unnecessary. If the writer really *knows* the designs have been completed, the listener is probably already aware of the idea contained in the sentence. When the phrases "I know" and "I am sure" *cannot* be true, the writer conveys a lack of empathy and respect for the reader. If the writer stretches the truth in this way often enough, the reader may question whether other statements are accurate or exaggerated, too.

The expression "as you know" is to be avoided for the same reasons: the receivers either already know that they know and the words are unnecessary, or the words are simply inaccurate. *Avoid expressions of certainty when certainty is hardly possible.*

> What is your reaction when "As you know" precedes an idea you don't know?

Clichés

Phrases that have become overused are called *clichés*. In each sentence, which phrase is well worn?

Pursuant to your request, the physical inventory was scheduled for May 3.

Please send a reply at your earliest convenience.

A booklet is being sent under separate cover.

Enclosed please find a copy of my transcript.

"Pursuant to your request," "at your earliest convenience," "under separate cover," and "enclosed please find" have been used so much that they

Monotonous clichés damage human relations.
Reprinted by special permission of King Features Syndicate, Inc.

no longer appear original. Now, look at the same sentences without the clichés:

As you requested, the physical inventory was scheduled for May 3.

Please send a reply by Friday, November 5.

The booklet is being sent in another mailing.

The enclosed transcript should answer most of your questions.

Clichés can make reading monotonous and can make the writer or speaker seem like a copier. On the other hand, less frequently used words capture the reader's attention because they are original, fresh, and interesting.

Clichés present a more serious problem. Consider the following scenario:

Kenneth is standing in line at a department store. As the two shoppers in front of Kenneth prepare to leave, the cashier says, "Thanks for shopping with us today; please come again." After Kenneth pays for his merchandise, the cashier uses the same line. Because Kenneth knows the line has been used before, he may not consider the statement genuine. The cashier has used an expression that can be stated without thinking and possibly without meaning.

A worn expression can convey such messages as: "You are not special" or "For you, I won't bother to think; the phrases I use in talking with others are surely good enough for you."

Clichés are common in business communications, as the following examples show:

According to our records, our records indicate

Everyone knows business firms keep records. The phrase "Our records indicate your last payment was due on January 5" is not necessary unless the person wants to contrast *his* or *her* records with others that are being discussed. If not, the same idea is communicated more simply and directly by saying, "Your last payment was due on January 5." However, if the purpose is to contrast records, the phrases may be useful: "According to the client's records, the account is paid; according to our records, it isn't."

at an early date

The expression is vague. Be specific. *Soon* is an improvement. Giving the exact date is more helpful.

at this time

The expression means *now*, so why not say *now*? It is shorter and less overused. Furthermore, the words may imply (without the writer's intent) that *another* time is being considered.

at this writing, at this point in time

When else could it be? Say *now* if an expression is necessary.

attached please find, please find enclosed, you will find

These expressions seem to imply that something has been hidden or that locating it may be difficult. In addition, they usually tell what is known already—that the letter accompanies other material. References to enclosures can be made in sentences that also say something else, such as "Refer to page 7 of the enclosed folder to see the basic steps of operation."

claim, complaint

In letters to customers, these words suggest negative thoughts. No one wants to learn that a letter asking for a legitimate adjustment has been branded as a *complaint*. And no one would be pleased to read a sentence that says, "You *claim* the cog was stripped when the drill was installed." To some people, the words *complaint* and *claim* suggest a request for something to which they are not entitled. "We appreciate your letter of March 18" is better than "We appreciate your complaint of March 18."

Avoid the word "complaint" with second person.

hereto, herewith, hereby, said, above, same, thereof, wherein, hereinafter

All these words are overused law terms. They convey an unnecessary tone of legality and formality.

I have your letter, your letter has been given to me for reply

These ideas will be understood without taking time to express them.

I remain

Who would think of saying, "I remain," or "I shall remain," if the expression had not been learned from others? In business letters, the expression is useless and should be omitted.

no problem

Although the words *deny* the existence of a problem, they are used in discussing something that *is* a problem. "If you don't have the cash, no problem; we accept credit-card purchases." Because a shortage of money is a problem, *no problem* is best omitted.

permit me to say, may I take this opportunity to say

Asking permission to make a statement is not necessary. Besides, asking permission and then immediately proceeding without it may imply that we are rude or are saying something that should not be said.

please contact me if you have any further questions

If this expression says exactly what is meant and if the receiver has not encountered it frequently before, its use is not especially objectionable. However, it does have these disadvantages: (1) It implies doubt about whether other questions have been answered adequately, (2) it is especially out of place if the preceding discussion has not been about *questions,* and (3) it may actually encourage needless correspondence.

pursuant to your request, referring to your request, in reference to your letter

These expressions often appear at the beginning of letters. Readers recognize them as coming from a person who says the same thing at the beginning of all letters. Such beginnings can have meaning when they identify the reply with a specific piece of correspondence. But referring to previous correspondence is more smoothly done in an indirect manner. Instead of saying, "Pursuant to your January 21 request for a catalog, we are sending it to you today," say, "The catalog you requested on January 21 was mailed today."

recent date

Be specific. State the exact date.

take this opportunity

Save time by getting right into the subject.

the writer, the undersigned

Such expressions suggest that we are trying to give the impression of modesty. Using *I* too frequently is monotonous; it also places greater emphasis on the writer than on the reader. But obvious attempts to circumvent *I* are just as bad. Instead of "I found that sales and collection departments actually have common goals" or "The writer found that sales and collection departments actually have common goals," rephrase to "The survey showed that sales and collection departments actually have common goals" or "Sales and collection departments, according to the survey, actually have common goals."

thanking you in advance

The expression seems to say, "I know you will do as I have asked you to do. After you do it, I will be grateful. Instead of sending a note of gratitude later, I'll just save time (and a stamp) by expressing my thanks now." To express gratitude for expected or requested action, "I would appreciate your (action)" or "If you will (action), I would be grateful" are less worn than "thanking you in advance."

this letter is for the purpose of, this will acknowledge receipt of, I am writing to

These words are usually just space fillers that warm up to the real message. Omit them and get right to the point.

COMMUNICATION MENTOR

The business world is full of people who can think and people who can communicate. We need to develop more people who can do both. Learning to think in our writing is difficult but important. To be able to organize our thoughts and communicate them to others is a worthwhile goal for all of us. It involves knowledge of vocabulary and grammar, organization skills, and conciseness. Communicating effectively does not mean writing or speaking volumes; it means conciseness and clarity.

The mission of the Financial Accounting Standards Board is to establish and improve standards of financial accounting and reporting for the guidance and education of the public, including issuers, auditors, and users of financial information. Decisions about the allocation of resources rely heavily on credible, concise, and understandable financial information. Everything the FASB publishes is geared toward making financial information *clearer to read* and *easier to understand.*

Dennis R. Beresford, Chairman
Financial Accounting Standards Board

trusting you will, trusting this is, we hope, we trust, I hope, I trust

Not only are these expressions overused, but they introduce the unpleasant idea of doubt as well. If we say, "We trust this is the information you wanted," we are suggesting our doubts; and the reader may also begin to doubt. The expression should be omitted in most cases.

under separate cover

Instead of using this nebulous expression, we can be specific by saying that a package is being sent by express, parcel post, or other means.

wish to, would like to

These words may convey *no* meaning, or they may convey the *wrong* meaning. "We wish to say that we have considered the idea" probably means "We have considered the idea." "We would like to recommend Mr. Clark" may be taken to mean either "We recommend Mr. Clark" or "Recommending Mr. Clark would be a pleasure, *if we could.*"

The following list contains many other expressions that have become clichés:

Can you add to this list?

---

above (as in "if the above is")	in regard to
acknowledge receipt of	in terms of
along this line	in the event that
are in receipt of	in the near future
as a matter of fact	inasmuch as
as the case may be	kindly (as in "kindly complete")
as to	meet with your approval
as yet we have not heard from you	party (as in "another party wants")
at all times	please be advised that
at an early date	previous to
avail yourself of the opportunity	prior to
due to the fact that	relative to
for your information	same (as in "have cashed same")
in accordance with	take the liberty
in due course	we feel
	we regret to inform
	would say

From a writer's or speaker's point of view, some of the preceding phrases are convenient; they can be used easily and quickly. But to avoid monotony, to keep from seeming to have no originality, and to avoid possible human relations problems, *avoid clichés.*

Conciseness

Concise messages are essential if today's information workers are to continue to process volumes of information. Some executives have reported that they read memos that are two paragraphs long but may only skim or discard longer ones. Of course, this survival technique has serious drawbacks: a vital message may be misinterpreted or never read. Learning to write concisely—to say in three words what others say in ten—will mark you as a highly effective communicator. Abraham Lincoln's two-minute Gettysburg Address is a premier example. Mark Twain alluded to the *skill* needed to write concisely when he said, "I would have written a shorter book if I had had time."

Concise messages save time and money for both the writer and the reader. The reader's attention is directed toward the important details and is not distracted by excessive words and details. To prepare a concise message, *include only those details that the reader needs; and state these details in the fewest possible words.*

The following techniques will help you learn to write in the fewest words possible:

1. Eliminate redundancies. A redundancy is a phrase in which one word unnecessarily repeats an idea contained in an accompanying word. In each sentence, which phrase contains a redundancy?

   The accident report was full and complete.

   The two twins are exactly identical.

   A personnel meeting has been scheduled for 3 p.m. this afternoon.

   Because "full" and "complete" convey the same meaning, both words are not needed. Because twins are understood to be two individuals, only "twins" is needed. "Exactly" and "identical" have the same meaning; "exactly" is not needed. Deleting "this afternoon" or revising the sentence to read "three o'clock this afternoon" would eliminate the redundancies "p.m." and "afternoon."

   The words in the right-hand column should be used in place of the redundancies in the left-hand column:

> In a paragraph, does use of a certain word for the third time constitute redundancy?

Redundant	*Not Redundant*
basic fundamentals	basics or fundamentals
end result	result
exact same	same
full and complete	full or complete
honest truth	truth

important essentials	essentials
looking forward to the future	looking forward
necessary requirement	requirement
other alternative	alternative
past history	history
personal opinion	opinion
true facts	facts or truth
serious danger	danger
severe crisis	crisis
whether or not	whether

**Redundancy is unaccept-
able, but repetition can be
very useful.**

*A redundancy is the unnec-
essary repetition of an idea
within a single phrase. The
words "exact same," "past
history," and "true facts" are
redundancies because both
words carry the same meaning.
Only one of the words in the
pairs is necessary; the other
word is useless and clumsy.
Similarly, wearing both
suspenders and a belt is
redundant because both serve
the same purpose.*

Redundancy is not to be confused with repetition. In a sentence or paragraph, we may need to use a certain word again. Repetition serves a purpose and *is not* an error. Redundancy serves no purpose and *is* an error. *Avoid redundancies;* they waste words and risk distracting from the idea presented.

2. Use active voice to reduce the number of words. Passive voice typically adds unnecessary words such as prepositional phrases. Compare the sentence length in each of these examples:

Active Voice

Passive Voice

The systems analyst wrote the user documentation.	The user documentation was written by the systems analyst.
The commercial loan officer revised the loan approval procedures for new business ventures.	The loan approval procedures for new business ventures were revised by the commercial loan officer.

3. Review the main purpose of your writing and identify the details that the reader needs to understand the message and to take necessary action. More information is not necessarily better information. Often we are so involved and perhaps so enthusiastic about our message that we believe the reader needs to know everything that we know. Or perhaps we just don't take the time to empathize with our reader by identifying the relevant details.

4. Eliminate clichés that are often wordy and not necessary to understand the message. For example, "Thank you for your letter," "I am writing to," and "May I take this opportunity" only delay the major purpose of the message.

5. Do not restate the ideas that are sufficiently implied. For example,

She <u>went to the bank</u> and made the daily deposit.

She <u>took the executive grammar course</u> and passed it.

<u>This is in response to your letter of June 25.</u>

In each case the underlined idea can be implied without affecting the meaning. Now examine the same sentences written more concisely:

She made the daily bank deposit.

She passed the executive grammar course.

Yes, I will be delighted to speak at the December meeting of the Boardtown Civic Club.

Notice how the following sentences are improved if the words that can be implied are eliminated:

Wordy	*Concise*
The auditor <u>reviewed the figures and concluded</u> that they are accurate.	The <u>auditor concluded</u> that the figures are accurate.
The editor checked the manuscript <u>and found</u> three spelling errors.	The <u>editor found</u> three spelling errors in the manuscript.

6. Shorten sentences by using suffixes or prefixes, making changes in word form, or substituting precise words for phrases. Note the differences in the following examples:

Wordy	*Concise*
She was a manager <u>who was courteous to others</u>.	She was a <u>courteous</u> manager.
He waited in an impatient manner.	He waited <u>impatiently</u>.
Accountants save time when they <u>use a spreadsheet</u> for complex calculations.	Accountants save time <u>by using a spreadsheet</u> for complex calculations.
the financial analysis <u>that they had not finished</u>	the <u>unfinished</u> financial analysis
the solution that we could debate <u>about the longest</u>	the <u>most debatable</u> solution
The production manager disregards methods he considers <u>to be of no use.</u>	The manager disregards methods he considers <u>useless</u>.

Omit details that are not relevant to the message.	Omit irrelevant details.
sale representatives with high energy levels	energetic sales representatives
arranged according to the alphabet	in alphabetical order
a design that was loaded with creativity	a creative design

The expressions on the right provide useful techniques for saving space and being concise. However, the examples in the left column are not grammatically incorrect or forbidden from use. In fact, sometimes their use provides just the right *emphasis*.

7. Use a compound adjective to help reduce the number of words required to express an idea.

Wordy	*Concise*
He wrote a report that was up to the minute.	He wrote an up-to-the-minute report.
Sid Hall, who holds the highest rank at Hooper Enterprises, is this year's Chamber of Commerce president.	Sid Hall, the highest-ranking official at Hooper Enterprises, is this year's Chamber of Commerce president.
His policy of going slowly was well received.	His go-slow policy was well received.

By using the compound adjective, you can reduce the number of words required to express your ideas and thus save the reader a little time.

Surprise, Doubt, and Judgment

Phrases that reveal a writer's surprise about a reader's behavior can cause problems in human relations. Why are the following sentences risky?

I am surprised that you did not accept.

I just cannot understand your attitude.

What would "I'm surprised you won" connote?

"I am surprised" risks conveying something like "I am accustomed to normal behavior. Yours is abnormal and therefore bad or totally unjustified." "I cannot understand" takes the same risks. Such expressions are particularly offensive to receivers because they seem to place them in a position of recognized inferiority.

Similarly, expressions that reveal judgment of recipients' emotional state are very risky. "I am so sorry you are upset" may be intended as a heart-felt apology, but the "I am sorry" can be completely overshadowed by "you are upset." It could mean, "Your conduct is such that I recognize your lack of self-control. Because of your condition, you could not be thinking rationally." *Avoid expressions of surprise, doubt, and judgment when they would be interpreted as insults.*

Could "Sorry to upset you" add to (instead of allay) irritation?

SENTENCES

For a complete review of sentences, consult an English handbook. The following discussion identifies problems and techniques business writers encounter frequently.

Structure

All sentences have at least two parts: *subject* and *verb.*

Sally	transferred.
(subject)	(verb)
The recession	continued.
(subject)	(verb)

In addition to subject and verb, a sentence may have additional words to complete the meaning. These words are called *complements:*

Sally	transferred	to another office.
(subject)	(verb)	(complement)
Pete	worked	in the luggage department.
(subject)	(verb)	(complement)
Sid	transferred	overseas.
(subject)	(verb)	(complement)

Observe from the preceding examples that a complement may be expressed in one word (the third sentence) or more than one word (the first and second).

A group of words that is not a complete sentence is called a *phrase* or a *clause*. A phrase does not include a subject and a verb; a clause does. In the following sentences, the phrases are underlined:

One of the workers was absent.

The people in that room have voted.

The electrician fell while replacing the socket.

In each of the following clauses, the subject is underlined once and the verb is underlined twice:

As the <u>president</u> <u>reported</u> this morning . . .

If <u>construction</u> <u>is</u> begun in January . . .

. . . if <u>I</u> <u>can pay</u> the rent.

Could a dependent clause serve as a complete sentence?

Clauses are divided into two categories: dependent and independent. A dependent clause does not convey a complete thought. The preceding illustrations are dependent. An independent clause does convey a complete thought; it could be a complete sentence if presented alone:

As the president reported this morning,	sales increased in May.
(dependent clause)	(independent clause)
If construction is begun in January,	the job can be completed in July.
(dependent clause)	(independent clause)
I can keep my apartment	if I can pay the rent.
(independent clause)	(dependent clause)

The independent clause "sales increased in May" can be stated as a separate sentence. The dependent clause "As the president reported this morning" does not convey a complete thought and should not be presented without the remainder of the sentence. When a *sentence fragment* (a portion of a sentence) is presented as a separate sentence, readers become confused and distracted.

Sentences fall into four categories: simple, compound, complex, and compound-complex. In the following examples, the independent clauses are highlighted in yellow and dependent clauses are highlighted in pink.

Simple: The union has gone on strike.

(an independent clause)

Compound: The union has gone on strike, and all manufacturing lines

have stopped production.

(two independent clauses)

Complex: Because contract terms cannot be reached, the union has

gone on strike.

(a dependent and an independent clause)

Compound-complex: Because contract terms cannot be reached, the union has

gone on strike; but a settlement is expected at the end of

the week.

(a dependent clause and two independent clauses)

In the preceding examples, note the use of punctuation to separate one clause from another. When punctuation is omitted or used incorrectly, the result is usually a *run-on* sentence. Run-on sentences also result from using too many clauses in one sentence.

Is a coordinating conjunction sometimes preceded by a *semicolon*?

Run-On Sentence

New forms have been ordered they should be delivered next Friday.

Corrected Sentence

New forms have been ordered. They should be delivered next Friday.

New forms have been ordered, and they should be delivered next Friday.

New forms have been ordered; they should be delivered next Friday.

The new forms, which were ordered last week, should be delivered next Friday.

New forms were delivered today, the number of questions has been reduced from 15 to 5, this simplification will reduce office work by 25 percent.

New forms were delivered today. Because the number of questions has been reduced from 15 to 5, office work will be reduced by 25 percent.

Misplaced Elements

A common problem in sentence structure is the placement of words, phrases, or clauses in the wrong position:

We have taken the check to the bank, which was unsigned.

The sentence is confusing (or amusing) because it seems to imply that the bank was unsigned. That impression is given because the "which" clause is placed closer to "bank" than to "check." Similarly, the following sentences have very different meanings:

Place pronouns close to the words they replace.

Confusing	*Clear*
The three-year budgets are being returned to the strategic planning committee, which have some serious defects. (Does the committee have serious defects?)	The three-year budgets, which have some serious defects, are being returned to the committee.
Susan displayed the financial ratios to upper-level managers on the screen. (Are the managers displayed on the screen?)	Susan explained to upper-level managers the financial ratios displayed on the screen..

Dangling Modifiers

The following sentences illustrate a very common (and sometimes very serious) type of error. What causes the confusion?

While making a presentation, a surge of electricity caused the projector bulb to blow.

Until unanimously convinced, a verdict was not reached.

To create that particular bar chart, the information must first be input into a spreadsheet file.

Although tired, the feasibility report had to be completed.

To "dangle" is to "hang loosely." A phrase dangles if it is not clearly attached to the appropriate noun or pronoun.

Re-examine the four sentences. Each begins with a modifier that precedes the independent (main) clause in the sentence. These modifiers speak of action without revealing who the doer is. "While making a presentation" does not reveal who is making the presentation. "Until unanimously convinced" does not indicate who is being convinced. "To create that particular bar chart" does not reveal who is preparing the chart. "Although tired" does not indicate who is tired.

Because the words *surge of electricity* come immediately after the idea of making the presentation, the surge seems to be making the presentation—not exactly the meaning the writer intends. The other sentences are also illogical: a verdict isn't convinced, information doesn't create a bar chart, and a feasibility report isn't tired.

When a sentence begins with a modifier that does reveal who the doer is, the subject of the independent clause gets credit for the action regardless of whether the credit is justified. These modifiers include

- ◆ Participial phrases (*while making a presentation, until unanimously convinced*).
- ◆ Infinitive phrases (*to create that particular bar chart*).
- ◆ Elliptical clauses in which the subject and perhaps the verb are understood (*although tired*).

Such sentences can be corrected in two ways:

1. Change the subject of the independent clause to a word that properly defines or describes:

Dangling	*Revised*
While making a presentation, a surge of electricity caused the projector bulb to blow.	While making a presentation, Clifford was interrupted when a surge of electricity caused the projector bulb to blow.
Until unanimously convinced, a verdict was not reached.	Until unanimously convinced, the jury did not reach a verdict.
To create that particular bar chart, the information must first be input into a spreadsheet file.	To create that particular bar chart, you must first input the information into a spreadsheet file.
Although tired, the feasibility report had to be completed.	Although tired, Sonia had to complete the feasibility report.

2. Recast the dangling modifier as a dependent clause:

Dangling	*Revised*
While making a presentation, a surge of electricity caused the projector bulb to blow.	While Clifford was making a presentation, a surge of electricity caused the projector bulb to blow.
Until unanimously convinced, a verdict was not reached.	Until the jury was unanimously convinced, a verdict was not reached.
To create that particular bar chart, the information must first be input into a spreadsheet file.	If you want to create a bar chart from this information, you must input it into a spreadsheet file.
Although tired, the feasibility report had to be completed.	Although she was tired, Sonia had to complete the feasibility report.

In the revised sentences, the intended meaning is much easier to understand. Because the subject of each independent clause is placed close to the action described in each modifier, the reader is certain who is performing the action.

  Dangling modifiers occur most often when the modifier precedes the independent clause, as illustrated in the preceding examples. Dangling modifiers may fall at the end of the sentence, as well:

Dangling	*Revised*
Stan had a car wreck rushing to an important job interview.	Rushing to an important job interview, Stan had a car wreck.
The selection was quite simple after considering the system's fast processing speed.	The selection was quite simple after the committee considered the system's fast processing speed.

Why is a dangling modifier a more serious error than a redundancy?

  Dangling modifiers are misleading because the introductory modifier is not properly positioned near its doer. The subject of an independent clause is presumed to be the doer of any action mentioned in a modifier that precedes it. *When the introductory modifier identifies action without revealing the doer, present the doer immediately after the modifier or recast the sentence so that the dangling modifier is a complete clause.*

Expletives

By definition, an *expletive* is a meaningless word. Find the meaningless word in the following sentence:

There is to be an addendum made to the policy.

Try to grasp the true meaning of "there." Since it is not being used in the sense of contrast with *here,* it does not mean "location." The same idea can be presented in fewer words:

An addendum is to be made to the policy.

What are the disadvantages of using expletives?

In addition to being shorter, the revised sentence has another advantage: It presents words in the normal sequence of the English sentence—subject, verb, complement. In the original sentence, a reader is exposed to the verb (*is*) before knowing what the sentence is about. Being unusual, such sentences make reading a little more difficult.

Are expletives considered grammatical errors?

  Expletive beginnings are not considered grammatical errors but are seldom advisable. Usually any sentence that begins with *there is, there are,* or *it is* can be improved.

Poor	*Improved*
There is a major problem with next year's budget.	Next year's budget has a major problem.
There are many complicated provisions within the new tax law.	The new tax law has many complicated provisions.
It is encouraging to note that sales have increased this month.	This month's increased sales are encouraging.

Each of the sentences at the left appears to use "there" or "it" that precedes the verb ("is" or "are") as the subject. Only after having read the entire sentence do we become aware of what "It" or "There" means. The revisions use fewer words in the more conventional subject-verb-complement pattern. *Avoid expletive beginnings.*

In some cases, the word *it* can serve as a first word when the antecedent is in a preceding sentence:

... of this document. It is being revised. ...

Seeing "It" before the verb "is", we know that "It" stands for "document." Such a pronoun can serve well as a coherence technique, and its use is not to be discouraged at all.

As a sentence beginning, "It is" is sometimes recommended: sometimes, not.

Platitudes

A platitude is a direct statement of an idea that almost anyone would know already:

Employees like to be well paid.

Team members should cooperate with one another.

Music is different from noise.

Because the message in such a sentence is so elementary, a receiver is insulted. The negative reaction could interfere with reception of the message from other sentences. *Avoid platitudes.*

Active and Passive Voices

If a sentence is in the *active voice*, the subject is a doer of action. If a sentence is in the *passive voice*, the subject is acted upon. (See the discussion of active and passive verbs in Chapter 7.)

Active voice: Angela wrote the report.
Passive voice: The report was written by Angela.

The active sentence draws attention to Angela. The passive sentence draws attention to the report. Active sentences normally are more vivid than passive sentences. The first sentence invites the reader to see a writer using a pen or a word processor. The second directs attention to a completed report. The choice of either active or passive voice is determined by the writer's purpose. *For most writing, use the active voice.*

From the discussion of tone, recall that positive ideas should be emphasized and negative ideas should be de-emphasized. Which sentence places more accent on the *positive* idea?

Jerry completed the job ahead of schedule.

The job was completed ahead of schedule.

Normally, use active sentences for pleasant ideas; use passive sentences for negative ideas.

Because a person (Jerry) is the subject of the first sentence and because people are easily envisioned in action, the first sentence is more vivid. *For presenting positive ideas, use the active voice.*

Which of the following sentences places greater emphasis on the *negative* idea?

Jerry completed the job two months behind schedule.

The job was completed two months behind schedule.

Again, the first sentence, which is active, is more vivid. Negative ideas, however, normally should be toned down. Because the idea is negative, Jerry would probably appreciate being taken out of the picture. Because the second sentence is in the passive voice, it places more emphasis on the job than on who failed to complete it. *For presenting negative ideas, use the passive voice.*

Subjunctive Mood

Does "We wish we could" *connote* **"We can't," or does it** *denote* **"We can't"?**

Sometimes, the tone of a message can be improved if the writer switches to the subjunctive mood. Subjunctive sentences employ such conditional expressions as *I wish, as if, could, would, might,* and *wish*. Subjunctive sentences speak of a wish, necessity, doubt, or conditions contrary to fact. Which of the following sentences seem more diplomatic?

Negative Tone	*Positive Tone*
I cannot approve your transfer to our overseas operation.	If positions were available in our overseas operation, I would approve your transfer.
I am unable to accept your invitation to speak at the November Chamber of Commerce meeting.	I could accept your invitation to speak at the November Chamber of Commerce meeting if I were to miss the annual stockholders' meeting.

I cannot accept the recommendations of the site-selection committee.	I wish I could accept the recommendations of the site-selection committee.

In all three pairs, a negative idea is involved; but the sentence in the right column transmits the negative idea in positive language. Positive language is more diplomatic. The revised sentences also include a reason. Because a reason is included, the negative idea seems less objectionable; and tone is thus improved.

Tone is important, but clarity is even more important. The revised sentence in each of the preceding pairs sufficiently *implies* the unpleasant idea without stating it directly. If for any reason a writer suspects the implication is not sufficiently strong, a direct statement in negative terms is preferable. *For tactful presentation of an unpleasant thought, consider stating it in the subjunctive mood.*

Emphasis

A landscape artist wants some features in a picture to stand out boldly and others to get little attention. A musician sounds some notes loudly and others softly. Likewise, a writer or speaker wants some ideas to be *emphasized* and others to be *de-emphasized*. Normally, pleasant and important ideas should be emphasized; unpleasant and insignificant ideas should be de-emphasized.

Normally, negative ideas should be subordinated.

Like clarity, emphasis is influenced by sentence structure. Which sentence places more emphasis on the idea of John's taking a job?

John took a job in insurance.

John took a job in insurance, but he really preferred a job in accounting.

The first sentence has one independent clause. Because no other idea competes with it for attention, its idea is emphasized. For *emphasis, place an idea in a simple sentence.*

Which of the following sentences places more emphasis on the idea of John's taking a job?

For stating an important idea, is a simple sentence better than a compound sentence?

John took a job in insurance, but he really preferred a job in accounting.

Although he took a job in insurance, John really preferred a job in accounting.

Note that the first sentence is compound; the second, complex. In the first sentence, the idea of taking a job is in an independent clause. Because an independent clause makes sense if the rest of the sentence is omitted, an independent clause is more emphatic than a dependent clause. In the second sentence, the idea of taking a job is in a dependent

Should significant ideas be placed in dependent clauses?

clause. By itself, the clause would not make complete sense. Compared with the independent clause that follows ("John really preferred . . ."), the idea in the dependent clause is de-emphasized. *For emphasis, place an idea in an independent clause; for de-emphasis, place an idea in a dependent clause.*

Which sentence places more emphasis on the idea of *success*?

The mission was successful because of . . .

The mission was successful; this success is attributed to . . .

In the second sentence a form of "success" is repeated. For *emphasis of a word, let it appear more than once in a sentence.*

In each pair, which sentence places more emphasis on the words *success* and *failure*?

The project was a success; without your efforts, it would have been a failure.

Your efforts contributed to the success of the project; otherwise, failure would have been the result.

Musicians, like writers, can project what they want their audiences to hear through a number of techniques. For example, the conductor can urge the musicians to play loudly throughout a portion of a symphony that he or she would like to emphasize, while directing them to play softly throughout a lesser part. In a similar manner, writers can employ several techniques to call attention to ideas they believe are important, while de-emphasizing unpleasant or insignificant ideas.

© Carlos Alejandro 1991.

Success resulted from your efforts; failure would have resulted without them.

The project was successful because of your efforts; without them, failure would have been the result.

In the first sentence, "success" and "failure" appear as the *last* words in their clauses. In the third sentence, "success" and "failure" appear as the *first* words in their clauses. For attention, words that appear first compete only with words that follow; words that appear last compete only with words that precede. *For emphasis of a word, let it appear first or last in a sentence or clause.*

Sometimes, the sting of an unpleasant thought can be reduced by placing that thought in the same sentence with a pleasant thought:

Negative Tone

Your personnel ratings in communication ability and interpersonal skills were unsatisfactory.

Positive Tone

Your personnel ratings in communication ability and interpersonal skills were unsatisfactory, but your rating in technical competence was excellent.

Why place a negative idea and a positive idea in the same sentence?

Because of increased taxes and insurance, you are obligated to increase your monthly payments by $50.

Because of increased taxes and insurance, your monthly payments will increase by $50; however, your home has increased in value at the monthly rate of $150.

For improved tone, place a positive idea in the same sentence with a negative idea.

In the following sentences, the ideas are the same; but the emphasis is different:

What is the effect of placing a number before each unit in a series?

The personnel problems have been narrowed into three categories: absenteeism, tardiness, and pilferage.

The personnel problems have been narrowed into three categories: (1) absenteeism, (2) tardiness, and (3) pilferage.

In the second sentence, the words preceded by numbers get special attention. They are easier to locate when the page is reviewed. If the preceding and following sentences on the page contain no numbers, the words with numbers take on special significance. The significance can be magnified even further:

The personnel problems have been narrowed into three categories:

- Absenteeism
- Tardiness
- Pilferage

When other ideas are in paragraph form, tabulated ideas are emphatic.

The preceding example uses a technique referred to as *tabulation*. Units of a series are placed in a column and indented (instead of being placed side by side). Because each unit in the series is on a line by itself (where it does not have to compete for attention) and because the arrangement consumes more space on the page, a tabulated series attracts attention. The items may be preceded by numbers, letters, asterisks, or various types of bullets (●, □, √, ◆, and so on), depending on the software being used. *For emphasis of units in a series, precede each element by a number or letter or bullet; for still further emphasis, tabulate the series.*

Describe four ways to punctuate an appositive.

Careful writers use punctuation marks for emphasis and de-emphasis, particularly when sentences contain appositives. An *appositive* is a word that purposefully repeats or explains a preceding word. After reading each of the following sentences, try to decide whether the appositive (leadership) is emphasized or de-emphasized.

Companies are seeking job applicants with a specific skill (leadership).

Companies are seeking job applicants with a specific skill, leadership.

Companies are seeking job applicants with a specific skill—leadership.

Companies are seeking job applicants with a specific skill: leadership.

Parentheses label an idea as parenthetical; it could be left out. An idea that could be omitted is not thought of as particularly important. Use of parentheses is like saying "The skill is not especially important, but just in case it is of interest, here it is." The comma in the second sentence implies neither emphasis nor de-emphasis. "Specific skill" and "leadership" are of about equal importance. The dash in the third sentence is considered a strong mark of punctuation. Requiring two strokes on the keyboard, the dash is longer and stronger than a comma. In oral presentation, a word preceded by a long pause gets special emphasis. Likewise, a dash attaches special emphasis to an appositive. The colon in the last sentence serves the same purpose as the dash. Requiring two dots and two keyboard spaces after it, a colon is a strong mark of punctuation; it serves to magnify the appositive. *For appositives, use parentheses for de-emphasis, a comma for neutral emphasis, and a dash or colon for emphasis.*

Another way to emphasize or de-emphasize an idea is to include words that label it:

But most important of all . . .

A less significant aspect was . . .

For emphasis or de-emphasis, attach words that label ideas as significant or insignificant.

Punctuation ✓

Speakers use pauses and voice inflection to assist listeners in extracting meaning from sentences. Similarly, writers use punctuation marks. Knowledge of punctuation is essential for both writers and readers. In the preceding pages, sentences used to illustrate other principles also illustrate principles of punctuation.

Place a comma before the conjunction in a compound sentence.

Jim's manager approved his transfer, but no positions were available.

The reports are ready for editing, and the statements are ready for checking.

Place a comma after a dependent clause that precedes an independent clause.

As I expected, production was behind schedule.

If work is begun in March, the job can be completed in July.

However, omit the comma when the dependent clause follows the main clause unless the dependent clause is nonessential.

Essential: The project was delayed because the equipment broke.
Essential: An outstanding candidate applied after we had made our decision.
Nonessential: The candidate's credentials arrived on May 1, after the screening committee had made their selection.

Place a comma before and after a parenthetical phrase.

The writer, not the typist, is responsible for proofreading a document.

Management does, as usual, plan to revise pay scales in January.

Place a comma between coordinate adjectives.

Jane was asked to complete a long, complicated questionnaire.

The system provides cold, dry air.

For appositives, determine the punctuation by the amount of emphasis desired.

We had one problem, quality control.	Neutral emphasis
We had one problem (quality control).	De-emphasis
We had one problem—quality control.	Emphasis
We had one problem: quality control.	Emphasis

Place a comma after the units in a series (except the final unit).

All accountants must achieve a satisfactory rating in technical competence, communication ability, and interpersonal skills.

Our primary problems are in absenteeism, tardiness, and pilferage.

Place a colon before a series if the series is preceded by a complete thought.

The problems have been narrowed into three categories: absenteeism, tardiness, and pilferage.

Three new employees have joined the company: an accountant, an administrative assistant, and a cost analyst.

In a compound sentence, place a semicolon before an adverbial conjunction and a comma after it.

The report arrived today; however, it has not been evaluated.

The project must be completed by the deadline; otherwise, the company will incur daily fines.

However, use commas before and after adverbial conjunctions that are not in a compound sentence.

Improving productivity, however, seems unlikely.

Omitting a conjunction is an acceptable practice.

Place a semicolon between independent clauses when the conjunction is omitted.

Joyce Mitchell prepared the budget for the Wolverton case; the advertising staff developed the brochures and advertisements.

The recommendations were presented today; management seemed receptive to these ideas.

Place a semicolon before the conjunction in a compound-complex sentence.

Because contract terms could not be reached, the union has gone on strike; but a settlement is expected at the end of the week.

As I expected, production is behind schedule; but the manager is confident that we will meet the September 15 deadline.

He reviewed the report; and as I expected, he made numerous changes.

Sales increased during the fiscal year; but the company did not attain a satisfactory net income, as the controller had projected.

Use hyphens to join words that form a compound adjective.

Today's health-conscious consumers prefer low-fat, cholesterol-free foods.

Diana has applied for a two-year overseas assignment in Helsinki.

For a more thorough review of punctuation, see Appendix B.

PARAGRAPHS

A paragraph is one or more sentences that discuss a single portion of a topic. For example, consider a pamphlet written to accompany a telephone answering machine that has been purchased. The overall topic is how to get satisfactory performance from the machine. One portion of that topic is assembly. Sentences that list the steps can appear as one paragraph, perhaps with steps numbered. Another portion (paragraph) discusses operation; another, maintenance. Within each paragraph, one of the sentences serves a special function.

Topic Sentence

Typically, paragraphs contain one sentence that identifies the portion of the topic being discussed and presents the central idea. That sentence is commonly called a *topic sentence*. For example. "To assemble your new answering machine, take the following steps: Step 1. . . ." In this illustration, the topic sentence *precedes* details. Such paragraphs are called *deductive* paragraphs. When topic sentences *follow* details, the paragraphs are called *inductive* paragraphs. Readers appreciate consistency in the placement of topic sentences. Once they catch on to the writer's pattern, they know where to look for main ideas.

When the subject matter is complicated and the details are numerous, paragraphs sometimes begin with a main idea, follow with details, and end with a summarizing sentence. But the main idea may not be in the first sentence; the idea may need a preliminary statement. For a writer, composition is simplified if a basic pattern (inductive or deductive) is selected and used. That consistency simplifies the reader's task as well.

Consideration of the reader determines whether to use the inductive or deductive paragraph. If a reader might be antagonized by the topic sentence in a deductive paragraph, antagonism can be avoided by leading up to the topic sentence (making the paragraph inductive). If a writer wants to encourage reader involvement (to generate a little concern about where the details are leading), inductive paragraphs are recommended. Inductive paragraphs can be especially effective if the topic sentence strikes the reader as confirmation of a conclusion the reader has drawn from the preceding details.

These suggestions seldom apply to the first and last sentences of letters. Such sentences frequently appear as single-sentence paragraphs. But

A topic sentence may be stated at the end of a paragraph.

If a paragraph is inductive, might a reader know the content of the topic sentence before reading it?

for reports and long paragraphs of letters, *strive for paragraphs that are consistently deductive or consistently inductive*. Regardless of which is selected, topic sentences are clearly linked with details that precede or follow.

Coherence

What are some of the techniques for achieving coherence?

Although the word *coherence* is used sometimes to mean "clarity" or "understandability," it is used throughout this text to mean "cohesion." If writing or speaking is coherent, the sentences stick together; and each sentence is in some way linked to the preceding sentences. The following techniques for linking sentences are common:

1. Repeat a word that was used in the preceding sentence.

   . . . to take <u>responsibility</u> for the decision. This <u>responsibility</u> can be shared. . . .

   The second sentence is an obvious continuation of the idea presented in the preceding sentence.
2. Use a pronoun that represents a noun used in the preceding sentence.

   . . . to take this <u>responsibility</u>. <u>It</u> can be shared. . . .

   Because "it" means "responsibility," the second sentence is linked directly with the first.
3. Use such connecting words as *however, therefore, yet, nevertheless, consequently, also, in addition,* and so on.

   . . . to take this responsibility. <u>However,</u> few are willing to. . . .

   "However" implies, "We're continuing with the same topic, just moving into a different phase." Remember, though, that good techniques can be *over*used. Unnecessary connectors are space consuming and distracting. Usually they can be spotted (and crossed out) in proofreading.

   Careful writers use coherence techniques to keep readers from experiencing abrupt changes in thought. *Avoid abrupt changes in thought, and link each sentence to a preceding sentence.* Coherent writing simplifies reading.

Readability

Even though sentences are arranged in a logical sequence and are written coherently, the reader may find reading the sentences difficult. Two factors contribute to the readability of a message: (1) length of the sentences and (2) difficulty of the words.

In an effort to determine the school grade level at which a passage is written, Robert Gunning (1968) developed a readability formula. This formula yields the approximate grade level a person would need to understand the material. For example, a grade level of 10 means a person needs to be able to read at the tenth-grade level to understand the material. Gunning referred to this formula as the *Fog Index.*

Today, many of the leading grammar and style software programs (for example, *RightWriter* and *Grammatik*) automatically calculate the grade level of the writing. These programs eliminate the laborious task of counting and calculating a readability index. If the readability level is considered inappropriate (too high or too low) for the audience, the writer must understand the two factors that affect readability: Short sentences and short words are easier to read. With this knowledge, the writer can input necessary revisions, recalculate the readability index instantaneously, and repeat the process until the reading level is appropriate for the audience.

To compute a Fog Index:

1. Select a passage of 100 words or more.
2. Find the *average sentence length* by dividing the number of words in the passage by the number of sentences. Count compound sentences as two sentences.
3. Find the number of *difficult* words per hundred. A *difficult* word is defined as a word with three syllables or more. Words are not to be counted as difficult if they (1) are compounded words made from smaller words, such as *however* or *understand;* (2) are proper nouns; or (3) are verbs that became three syllables by addition of -ed or -es, such as *imposes* or *defended.* Determine the number of difficult words per hundred by dividing the number of words in the passage into the number of difficult words and multiplying the resulting figure by 100.
4. Add the average sentence length and the number of difficult words per hundred.

COMMUNICATION MENTOR

Over the years, I have written many general notices to be posted on bulletin boards throughout a plant for all to read and understand. *Understanding* is the key word—the essence of communication. It makes no difference if the notice is grammatically correct if people with an eighth-grade reading level cannot understand it. The writer must always keep the reader in mind. Using simple words makes the message easier for the reader to understand.

Jere W. Hess, Jr.
Director, Personnel & Public Relations
Peavey Electronics

5. Multiply the resulting figure by 0.4 to arrive at the reading grade level of the passage.

The following passage illustrates the manual calculation of the Fog Index. Sentences are numbered, and difficult words are underscored.

> [1] Each successive development has changed society. [2] Early writings freed oral societies from limitations of time and space. [3] Their legacies were transmitted in writing; [4] therefore, anthropologists and historians have not had to rely on hieroglyphs, pottery, utensils, and religious artifacts to study our recent past. [5] However, the world was essentially illiterate until the development of printing. [6] Printing made literature available to other than the religious elite. [7] Printing multiplied the dimensions of communication; [8] those who weren't literate were encouraged to become so.
>
> [9] High-speed printing and inexpensive newspress paper overcame all previous limitations and led to mass communication. [10] With the advent of the telegraph, telephone, radio, and television, the world became a smaller place and instant communication commonplace. [11] What a milestone we achieved when millions of Americans (plus millions throughout the world) saw and heard Neil Armstrong begin his walk on the moon.

The passage contains 141 words in 11 sentences (two of the 9 sentences are compound) and 34 "difficult" words. *Transmitted* is not a difficult word because it is a verb that became three syllables by adding "-ed." *However, overcame,* and *commonplace* are not difficult words because they are made from two separate words compounded into one. *Americans* is not a difficult word because it is a familiar proper noun.

To compute the readability index:

1. Compute the average sentence length: $(141 \div 11)$ 12.8
2. Compute the percentage of difficult words:
  $(34 \div 141 \times 100)$ <u>24.1</u>
3. Add average sentence length and percentage of
  difficult words: $(12.8 + 24.1)$ 36.9
4. Multiply the resulting figure by 0.4: (36.9×0.4) 14.76

The Fog Index (reading grade level) of this passage is between 14 and 15.

The desirable Fog Index for most business writing is in the eighth-to-eleventh-grade range. A writer need not be overly concerned if the index is a little over 11 or under 8. Trying to write at the exact grade level of the recipient is inadvisable. The writer may not know the exact grade level, and even those who have earned advanced degrees appreciate writing they can read and understand quickly and easily.

A major word of caution is needed. Writing a passage with a readability index appropriate for the audience does not guarantee that the message will be understood. Numerous factors affect whether a message is communicated effectively. Chapter 2 explained how breakdowns in communication occur at all stages in the communication process. For example, the readability may be appropriate for the audience; however, the words used may not convey the precise meaning needed for understanding, gender-biased words may create barriers to understanding, unique expressions may not be understood by a reader in a different field or from a different background, and so on. Calculating the readability index, however, provides the writer valuable feedback about the average length of the sentences and the difficulty of the words. *For quick, easy reading (and listening), use small words and short sentences.*

Variety

Although a short *average* sentence length is desirable, keeping *all* sentences short is undesirable. The passage may sound monotonous, unrealistic, or elementary. A 2-word sentence is acceptable; so is a 60-word sentence—if it is clear. Just as sentences should vary in length, they should also vary in structure. Some complex or compound sentences should be included with simple sentences.

Variety is just as desirable in paragraph length as it is in sentence length. A paragraph can be from one line in length to a dozen lines or more. However, just as average sentence length should be kept fairly short, average paragraph length also should be kept short.

Paragraphs in business letters or memos are typically shorter than paragraphs in business reports. First and last paragraphs are normally short (one to four lines), and other paragraphs are normally no longer than six lines. A short first paragraph makes a letter or memo look more inviting to read than a long first paragraph. A short last paragraph enables a writer to emphasize the parting thoughts.

In letters, what is the advantage of writing short first paragraphs?

In business reports, the space between paragraphs comes as a welcome resting spot. Long paragraphs make a page look as if reading might be laborious. Depending on the subject matter, paragraphs approach the danger point when they exceed eight to ten lines.

Although variety is a desirable quality, it should not be achieved at the expense of consistency. Using *I* in one part of a letter and then without explanation switching to *we* is inadvisable. Using the past tense in one sentence and the present tense in another sentence creates variety at the expense of consistency—unless the shift is required to indicate actual changes in time. Unnecessary changes from active to passive voice (or vice versa) and from third to second person (or vice versa) are also discouraged. Generally, *strive for short paragraphs, but vary their lengths.*

Should consistency be sacrificed to achieve variety?

Where are the emphatic positions in sentences and paragraphs?

Emphasis

In sentences, the first and last words are in emphatic positions. In paragraphs, the first and last sentences are in emphatic positions. An idea that deserves emphasis can be placed in either position, but an idea that does not deserve emphasis can be placed in the middle of a long paragraph.

In sentences that contain a series, each element in the series can be emphasized if a number or letter is placed before it. In paragraphs, sentences can be numbered and tabulated with the same effect. For example, a long report could close with a concluding paragraph that restates four supporting reasons for a conclusion. The reasons can be emphasized by

◆ Placing each reason on a separate, indented line.
◆ Beginning each line (reason) with a number, letter, or bullet.
◆ Adding extra space (about one blank line) between each reason.

In the following example, note that the paragraph in the right-hand column places increased emphasis on the reasons:

Less Emphasis on Reasons	*More Emphasis on Reasons*
For our needs, then, the most appropriate in-service training method is computerized instruction. It is least expensive, allows employees to remain at their own workstations while improving their skills, affords constant awareness of progress, and lets employees progress at their own rates.	Computerized instruction is the most appropriate in-service training method because it ● Is least expensive. ● Allows employees to remain at their own workstations while improving their skills. ● Affords constant awareness of progress. ● Lets employees progress at their own rates.

Why should *I* be used sparingly?

In paragraphs, the first and last words are in particularly emphatic positions. The word *I*, which is frequently overused in letters, is especially noticeable if it appears as the first word. It is more noticeable if it appears as the first word in *every* paragraph. *However* and *but* are to be avoided as first words if the preceding paragraph is neutral or positive. These words imply that the next idea will be negative. Unless the purpose is to place emphasis on negatives, such words as *denied, rejected,* and *disappointed* should not appear as the last words in a paragraph. *Within paragraphs, emphasize a sentence by placing it first or last or by assigning it a number in a tabulated series.*

COMPOSITIONS

Sentences, paragraphs, and compositions all are formed from smaller units (words, sentences, and paragraphs, respectively). Regardless of whether a composition is a letter, a report, or a speech, problems encountered in sentence and paragraph construction are also encountered at the composition level.

Unity

If a letter has unity, it will cover its topic adequately but will not include extraneous material. The letter will have a beginning sentence appropriate for the expected reader reaction, paragraphs that present the bulk of the message, and an ending sentence that is an appropriate closing for the message presented.

What is unity?

If a report has unity, its introduction will identify the topic, reveal the thesis, and give a preview of upcoming points. The introduction may also include some background, sources of information, and the method of treating data. A unified report will also have a summary or conclusion that brings all major points together. Between the beginning and the ending, a unified report will have paragraphs arranged in a systematic sequence.

Sequence

The typical business message (letter, memorandum, or report) has (1) a major idea and (2) some accompanying ideas that are less significant. Prior to beginning, the writer must answer two questions: Should the major idea be stated first or last? What is the best sequence for presenting the accompanying ideas?

When messages begin with the major idea, the sequence of ideas is called *deductive*. When messages withhold the major idea until accompanying details and explanations have been presented, the sequence is called *inductive*. The decision about whether to write deductively or inductively is vital. It has a strong influence on the extent to which the message will be understood clearly and received favorably. Subsequent chapters discuss sequence-of-idea patterns more thoroughly. For now, simply remember that the most dependable guide is *anticipated reader reaction*. If the message will likely *please or at least not displease, write deductively*. If the message will likely *displease or if understanding of the major idea is dependent on prior explanations, write inductively*.

How can you determine whether to begin a letter with the main idea?

For determining the sequence of ideas that accompany the major idea, the following bases for paragraph sequence are common:

1. *Time.* In reporting on a series of events or a process, paragraphs proceed from the first step through the last step.
2. *Space.* If a report is about geographic areas, paragraphs can proceed from one area to the next until all areas have been discussed.
3. *Familiarity.* If a topic is complicated, the report can begin with a point that is known or easy to understand and proceed to progressively more difficult points.
4. *Importance.* In analytical reports in which major decision-making factors are presented, the factors can be presented in order of most important to least important, or vice versa.
5. *Value.* If a report involves major factors with monetary values, paragraphs can proceed from those with greatest values to those with least values, or vice versa.

Readers expect the first paragraph to introduce a topic, additional paragraphs to discuss it, and a final paragraph to tie them all together. If the ending cannot be linked easily to some word or idea presented in the beginning, unity has not been achieved. The effect is like that of an incomplete circle or a picture with one element obviously missing. *Make sure that compositions form a unit with an obvious beginning, middle, and ending and that in-between paragraphs are arranged in a systematic sequence. If the sequence is logical, coherence is easy to achieve.*

A good outline assists in achieving coherence and transition.

Transition

Just as sentences within a paragraph must adhere, paragraphs within a composition must also adhere. Connecting words, pronouns, repeated words, and orderly sequence are helpful. The *transition sentence* is especially helpful at the composition level.

Which is more likely to contain transition sentences: a *letter* or a *report*?

Unless a writer (or speaker) is careful, the move from one major topic to the next will seem abrupt. A good transition sentence can bridge the gap between the two topics by summing up the preceding topic and leading a reader to expect the next topic:

Cost factors, then, seemed prohibitive until efficiency factors were investigated.

This sentence could serve as a transition between the *cost* division heading and the *efficiency* division heading. Because a transition sentence comes at the end of one segment and before the next, it emphasizes the central idea of the preceding segment and confirms the relationship of the two segments.

Should transition sentences be used between *sub*topics?

Transition sentences are very helpful if properly used, but they can be overused. For most reports, transition sentences before major headings are sufficient. Normally, transition sentences before subheadings are unnecessary. Having encountered the previous subheading only a few lines back, a reader should readily see its relationship to the upcoming subheading. In addition, transition sentences typically summarize, and the discussion under a subheading of a report is seldom long enough to merit summarization. *Place transition sentences before major headings.*

Emphasis

Emphasis, a critical factor in composing sentences and paragraphs, is also critical at the composition level. The following techniques are commonly used:

By what techniques can parts of a composition be emphasized?

1. *Position.* Beginning and ending positions are emphatic. The central idea of a talk or a report appears in the introduction and the conclusion. Good transition sentences synthesize ideas at the end of each major division.
2. *Repetition.* A central idea is emphasized by transition sentences that repeat the essence of a discussion.
3. *Space.* The various divisions of a report or talk are not expected to be of equal length, but an extraordinary amount of space devoted to a topic attaches special significance to that topic. Similarly, a topic that gets an exceedingly small amount of space is de-emphasized.
4. *Headings.* Ideas that appear in headings get more attention than ideas that don't. Ideas that appear in subheadings are less emphatic than ideas that appear in major headings—a factor that should be taken into account at the outline stage. *Talking headings* (headings that reveal the conclusions reached in the following discussion) are more emphatic than general topic headings. For example, "Costs Are Prohibitive" is more emphatic than "Cost Factors."
5. *Nonverbal devices.* Ideas presented in graphs, charts, tables, or pictures are emphatic. Some ideas are more clearly presented in such devices, and the contrast in appearance is appealing.

Within a composition, achieve emphasis through position, repetition, space, headings, and nonverbal devices.

EDITING AND REWRITING

If writing and organizing are done simultaneously, the task seems hopelessly complicated. Writing is much easier if questions about the organization of the message are answered first: What is the message, what is the reader's likely reaction, and should the message begin with the main point? Once these decisions have been made, the writer can concentrate on expressing ideas effectively.

Normally, writing rapidly (with intent to rewrite certain portions if necessary) is better than slow, deliberate writing (with intent to avoid any need for rewriting portions). The latter approach can be time consuming and frustrating. Thinking of one way to express an idea, discarding it either before or after it is written, waiting for new inspiration, stopping to read and reread preceding sentences—these time-consuming habits can actually reduce the quality of the finished work.

Recall your own writing experiences. Which was more pleasant for you: (1) the time spent writing a sentence or (2) the time spent between sentences? Because the time spent between sentences can be unproductive or frustrating, that time should be reduced or eliminated. For most people, writing rapidly with the intent to rewrite certain portions if necessary is the better approach by far. Experienced writers believe that there is no such thing as good writing, but there is such a thing as a good rewriting.

An owner of a successful public relations firm reported that clients seldom returned work for revisions because the staff revised it as many as five or six times to be certain that the material was correct before it was submitted to the client. This business executive and countless others have learned the invaluable lesson that errors in business letters and reports reflect negatively on the reputation of the company. Errors distract the reader from the message itself and thereby reduce the effectiveness of the document. A message containing errors reflects negatively on the person who writes it. The writer is responsible for checking each document for accuracy before sending it.

With a computer, proofreading and revising can be done quickly and easily on the screen. In addition, the electronic spellcheck available with word-processing software is helpful in locating spelling and typographical errors. However, the spellcheck feature cannot be relied on to detect all errors. The software, for example, cannot distinguish between the use of *principle* for *principal* or determine whether a number should be written as a word or appear as a number. The electronic spellcheck aids but does not free the writer from the responsibility of carefully proofreading each document.

Following systematic revision procedures will help writers produce error-free documents that reflect positively on the company and themselves. These procedures require proofreading not once, but at least several times for a specific purpose each time. Writers using computers also should proofread using the electronic spellcheck and save the corrections in case the document is needed again. Because errors on the screen are sometimes difficult to locate, proofreading a printed page is essential. Regardless of the production method, the finished product should be free of errors in (1) content, organization, and style; (2) grammar; and (3) format and layout.

Content, Organization, and Style

Proofread the document first to locate errors in content, organization, and style. Ask yourself these questions:

1. Is the main idea presented appropriately based on the reader's likely reaction to the main idea (deductive or inductive organization)?
2. Are supporting ideas presented in a logical order?
3. Is all information complete? Have I included all the details the reader needs to understand the message and to take necessary action?
4. Is the information accurate? Have I checked the accuracy of any calculations, dates, names, addresses, and numbers?
5. Is the message clear? Will the reader interpret the information correctly?
6. Is the message concise and written at an appropriate level for the reader?
7. Does the message reflect a considerate, caring attitude? Is the message primarily focused on the reader's needs?
8. Does the message treat the reader honestly and ethically?

Grammar

Proofread a second time to locate the following errors:

1. Typographical, grammatical, capitalization, and punctuation errors.
2. Incomplete sentences.
3. Omitted and repeated words.
4. Word substitutions (*your* and *you*) and words that sound alike (*there* for *their*).

Proofread a third time *reading from right to left* to check again for any typographical or spelling errors. Reading in reverse requires reading slowly and concentrating deliberately on the text. Proofread carefully for potentially damaging errors that an electronic spellcheck cannot detect.

Format and Layout

Follow these steps to be certain the document adheres to conventional business formats:

1. Study the conventional business formats in Appendix A. Compare your document to the illustrations shown in Appendix A and make any revisions. Are all standard parts of the document included and presented in an acceptable format? Does the message begin on the correct line? Should the right margin be justified or jagged?
2. Proofread letter parts, including the date line, letter address, salutation, subject line, and closing lines. Research indicates that many errors appear in the opening sections of letters because writers typically begin proofreading at the first paragraph.

3. Be sure that all necessary special letter parts (mailing notation, attention line, subject line, enclosure, copy and mailing notations, second-page heading, and writer's address for a personal business letter) are included.

4. Check to be sure that numbered items are in the correct order; inserting and deleting text may have changed the order of these items.

5. Consider whether the text has the visual impact you desire. Could you increase the readability of long, uninterrupted blocks of texts by using enumerated or indented lists, headings, or different type styles (boldface, underlines, italics, or shadow type)? Could you increase the overall appeal by including graphics or using different fonts of various sizes and shapes? Could you partition the text into logical, easy-to-read sections by using graphic lines, boxes, and borders?

6. Be certain that the document is signed or initialed (depending on the document).

7. Print the document on high-quality bond paper. The envelope and second-page paper (if needed) should match the letterhead. The printing should read in the same direction as the watermark.

The letter in Figure 8-2 has been revised for (1) content, organization, and

COMMUNICATION MENTOR

Preparing a message free of grammatical and typographical errors is imperative. However, the writer's most important function is to assure that the reader fully understands the message.

Two of the most common barriers to clear writing are pseudo-sophisticated language and technical jargon. Some people mistakenly believe that their letters or reports will be considered more important if they are filled with long words and complicated phrases. Instead, writers should strive for clarity. The same can be said of those who rely heavily on technical jargon, including acronyms.

One of the easiest ways to avoid these pitfalls is to ask people unfamiliar with your work to review what you've written. Listen to their comments, and simplify the portions of the document that are confusing. The time spent editing and rewriting saves even more time—and confusion—in the long run.

Hugh B. Jacks
President
BellSouth Services

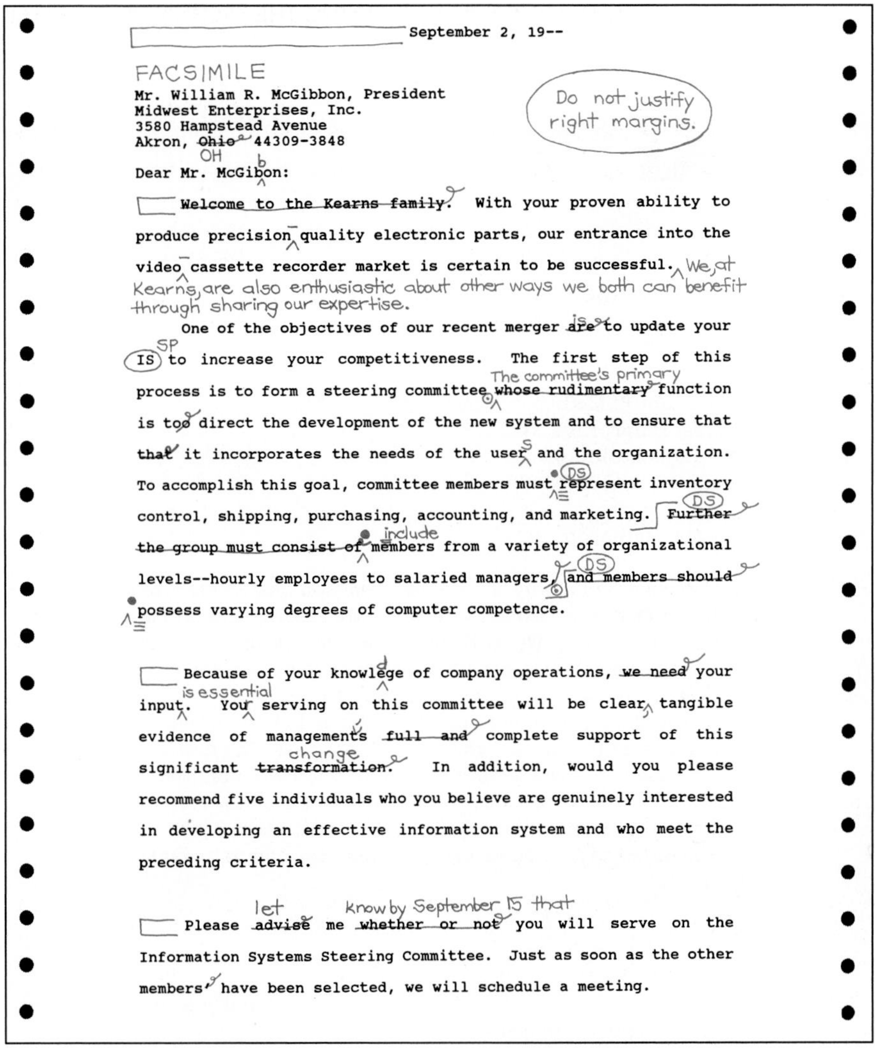

FIGURE 8-2 Rough draft

The rough draft letter reads (with handwritten editing marks):

```
                                    September 2, 19--

FACSIMILE
Mr. William R. McGibbon, President
Midwest Enterprises, Inc.
3580 Hampstead Avenue
Akron, Ohio  44309-3848          ( Do not justify
      OH   b                        right margins. )
Dear Mr. McGibon:
```

Welcome to the Kearns family. With your proven ability to produce precision quality electronic parts, our entrance into the video cassette recorder market is certain to be successful. We, at Kearns, are also enthusiastic about other ways we both can benefit through sharing our expertise.

One of the objectives of our recent merger are to update your IS to increase your competitiveness. The first step of this process is to form a steering committee whose rudimentary function *The committee's primary* is too direct the development of the new system and to ensure that that it incorporates the needs of the users and the organization. To accomplish this goal, committee members must represent inventory control, shipping, purchasing, accounting, and marketing. Further the group must consist of members *include* from a variety of organizational levels--hourly employees to salaried managers, and members should possess varying degrees of computer competence.

Because of your knowledge of company operations, we need your input. *is essential* You serving on this committee will be clear, tangible evidence of management's full and complete support of this significant transformation. *change* In addition, would you please recommend five individuals who you believe are genuinely interested in developing an effective information system and who meet the preceding criteria.

Please advise me whether or not you will serve on the *let   know by September 15 that* Information Systems Steering Committee. Just as soon as the other members have been selected, we will schedule a meeting.

Organization, Content, and Style

Eliminate clichés: "Welcome to Kearns" and "Please advise me."

Insert a smooth transition from the opening paragraph into ¶2.

Spell out "IS" to ensure understanding.

Break long sentence in ¶2 into two shorter sentences to increase readability.

Use simple words to increase clarity: Replace "rudimentary" and "transformation."

Eliminate redundancies: "full and complete" and "whether or not."

Write from the reader's viewpoint: "Your input is needed."

Write specific, action-oriented ending: "by September 15."

Grammar

Errors Undetectable by Electronic Spellcheck

Verify spelling of reader's name with source documents: "McGibbon."

Correct word substitutions: "too" for "to" and "you" for "your."

Omit repeated word: "that."

Add "s" to "user."

Other Errors

Spell "knowledge" correctly (frequently misspelled word).

Use a singular verb when "one" is the subject.

Use a possessive pronoun before gerund: "your serving."

Punctuation

Hyphenate the compound adjectives: "precision-quality" and "video-cassette."

Place comma after introductory dependent clause: "As you will recall."

Place comma between coordinate adjectives: "clear, tangible."

Use an apostrophe to show possession: "management's."

Omit apostrophe after plural noun: "members."

Format and Layout

Begin all lines at the left margin in block letter style.

Insert mailing notation: "FACSIMILE."

Format criteria in a bulleted list for emphasis.

Place comma after complimentary close in letter with mixed punctuation.

Use jagged right margins to improve appearance and readability.

Center letter vertically on high-quality letterhead.

September 2, 19—

FACSIMILE

Mr. William R. McGibbon, President
Midwest Enterprises, Inc.
3580 Hampstead Avenue
Akron, OH 44309-3848

Dear Mr. McGibbon:

With your proven ability to produce precision-quality electronic
parts, our entrance into the video-cassette recorder market is certain to be successful. We, at Kearns, are also enthusiastic about
other ways we both can benefit through sharing our expertise.

One of the objectives of our recent merger is to update your information system to increase your competitiveness. The first step of
this process is to form a steering committee. The committee's primary function is to direct the development of the new system and
to ensure that it incorporates the information needs of the users
and the organization. To accomplish this goal, committee members must

● Represent inventory control, shipping, purchasing, accounting, and marketing.

● Include a variety of organizational levels—hourly employees
to salaried managers.

● Possess varying degrees of computer competence.

FIGURE 8-3   Final draft

style; (2) grammar; and (3) format and layout . Changes are noted using
proofreaders' marks, a standard, simplified way to show where changes
or corrections need to be made. The detailed explanation will help you
understand how the revisions improve the quality of the final draft
(Figure 8-3). To aid you in editing your own documents, review the
proofreaders' marks in Figure A-1 in Appendix A.

Mr. William R. McGibbon
Page 2
September 2, 19—

Because of your knowledge of company operations, your input is
essential. Your serving on this committee will be clear, tangible
evidence of management's complete support of this significant
change. In addition, would you please recommend five individuals
who you believe are genuinely interested in developing an effective information system and who meet the preceding criteria.

Please let me know by September 15 that you will serve on the
Information Systems Steering Committee. Just as soon as the
other members have been selected, we will schedule a meeting.

Sincerely,

Lynda B. Kelly

Lynda B. Kelly, Manager
Information Systems

sl

FIGURE 8-3, *continued*

SUMMARY

In a discussion of writing, "style" means "the way ideas are expressed."
Even for those who can write well already, a review of basics can bring
about improvement (just as professional athletes frequently improve by
reviewing and drilling basic movements). For writers, computerized style-

improvement programs are available. They are most helpful to those who know basics. This chapter discussed stylistic problems that occur frequently in business writing. Basic as they are, the principles are frequently violated by business executives and students.

Phrases

- Avoid expressing certainty when certainty is hardly possible.
- Avoid using clichés.
- Be brief. (Avoid using wordy expressions.)
- Avoid expressing surprise, doubt, and judgment when they would be interpreted as insults.

Sentences

- When the introductory phrase identifies action without revealing the doer, present the doer immediately after the phrase.
- Avoid using expletive beginnings (sentences in which the verb appears before the subject for no other purpose except to postpone the subject).
- Avoid using platitudes (direct statements of ideas that almost anyone would know already).
- For presenting positive ideas, use the active voice.
- For presenting negative ideas, use the passive voice.
- For tactful presentation of an unpleasant thought, consider stating it in the subjunctive mood.
- For emphasis:
  a. Place an idea in a simple sentence.
  b. Place an idea in an independent clause; for de-emphasis, place an idea in a dependent clause.
  c. Use an important word more than once in a sentence.
  d. Place an important word first or last in a sentence.
  e. Precede each unit in a series by a number, a letter, or a bullet; for still further emphasis, tabulate.
- To de-emphasize a negative idea, place it in a sentence with a positive idea.
- For appositives, use parentheses for de-emphasis, a comma for neutral emphasis, and a dash or colon for emphasis.
- For emphasis or de-emphasis, attach words that label ideas as significant or insignificant.
- For a summary of the most commonly used punctuation, see Appendix B.

Paragraphs

- If a message will likely please or at least not displease, write deductively. If a message will likely displease or if understanding of the major idea is dependent on prior explanations, write inductively.

◆ Strive for paragraphs that are consistently deductive or consistently inductive.
◆ Avoid abrupt changes in thought, and link each sentence to a preceding sentence.
◆ For quick, easy reading (and listening), use simple words and short sentences.
◆ Strive for short paragraphs, but vary their lengths.
◆ Within paragraphs, emphasize a sentence by placing it first or last or by assigning it a number in a tabulated series.

Compositions

◆ Make sure compositions form a unit with an obvious beginning, middle, and ending and that in-between paragraphs are arranged in a systematic sequence.
◆ Place transition sentences before major headings.
◆ Within a composition, achieve emphasis through position, repetition, space, headings, and nonverbal devices.

Editing and Revising

◆ Organize before you write so that you can concentrate on expressing ideas effectively.
◆ Write rapidly with the intent to rewrite certain portions.
◆ Be willing to revise a document as many times as necessary to be certain that it effectively conveys the message and is error free.
◆ Follow systematic procedures for proofreading for (1) content, organization, and style; (2) grammar; and (3) format and layout.

These suggestions can assist in presenting clear, tactful messages that should be easily understood and positively received.

REFERENCES

Charlton, J. (Ed.). (1985). *The writer's quotation book.* Stamford, CT: Ray Freiman and Company.
Gunning, R. (1968). *The technique of clear writing.* New York: McGraw-Hill.

REVIEW QUESTIONS

1. Who is more likely to benefit from a computerized program that evaluates writing style, the person who (a) is very familiar with the basics of grammar or (b) knows little about the basics of grammar? Explain.

2. Which group of words is a phrase and which is a clause? (a) "Although I agree with you, . . ." or (b) "Under the circumstances, . . ." What is the distinguishing feature?
3. What are the disadvantages of using expressions such as "I *know* you will want to . . ." and "I am *sure* you have . . ."?
4. What are the disadvantages of using clichés?
5. (a) What do compound adjectives and coordinate adjectives have in common? (b) How are they different?
6. If a client or customer is obviously upset, what is wrong with your saying, "I'm sorry you are upset"?
7. Discuss five ways to prepare a concise message.
8. What is the difference between a dependent and an independent clause?
9. What is the difference between a complex sentence and a compound sentence?
10. Which provides more emphasis for an idea:
    a. A simple sentence or a complex sentence?
    b. An independent clause or a dependent clause?
    c. Parentheses or dashes?
    d. Tabulated arrangement or paragraph arrangement?
11. Which is the more accurate statement about sentences that contain dangling participial phrases? The reader may be confused about (a) when action was taken or (b) who took action.
12. List two disadvantages of beginning sentences with expletives.
13. Do platitudes affect human relations in a positive way? Explain.
14. Which is better for presenting a pleasant idea: (a) active voice or (b) passive voice? Explain.
15. What is the advantage of using a subjunctive mood for stating a negative idea?
16. For a word that deserves emphasis, which position in a sentence is better? (a) Use the word as the first or last word in the sentence. (b) Place the word in the middle of the sentence.
17. Does tabulation assist in achieving emphasis? Explain.
18. What is the difference between deductive sequence and inductive sequence?
19. List some techniques for achieving coherence (a) within paragraphs and (b) among major sections of a composition.
20. If the objective in revising a report is to reduce the readability level from 16 to 12, what editorial changes would you make?
21. Should paragraphs be uniform in length? Explain.
22. A report stops abruptly, without a "wrap-up" paragraph. Which principle has been violated: (a) unity or (b) coherence?
23. What are the advantages of including transition sentences in a long report?
24. What is the advantage of trying to anticipate a reader's reaction to a message before beginning to write?

25. Under what conditions would you recommend (a) deductive writing and (b) inductive writing?
26. What is the primary benefit of outlining before you write?
27. Is writing rapidly with intent to revise or writing slowly and deliberately more effective? Explain.
28. Provide a brief argument for editing and revising business correspondence carefully.
29. Outline the systematic steps for proofreading.
30. Discuss the limitations of electronic spellcheckers? Can they be relied on for proofreading?

EXERCISES

Each of the following sentences illustrates a weakness discussed in Chapter 8. (a) Using terminology presented in the chapter, identify the weakness. (b) Rewrite the sentence in such a way as to eliminate the weakness. The example illustrates the type of answer expected:

Example: We rode all day in a crowded noisy bus.

Answers: a. Omits comma between a coordinate adjective.
              b. We rode all day in a crowded, noisy bus.

1. I am sure you will understand our reasons for refusal.
2. The basic fundamentals are outlined in the manual.
3. At this point in time, we recommend cash purchases.
4. I wish to congratulate you heartily on your success.
5. John had a no care attitude about his work.
6. We realize that you are upset, but the fee is due on May 10.
7. Your report is being read by the department supervisor, which was received today.
8. While driving down the road, my car phone buzzed.
9. There is a meeting scheduled on May 15.
10. We conclusively consolidated our endeavors to revoke the capitulation in earnings.
11. Our main personnel problems are absenteeism, apathy, and the lowering of employee morale.
12. My tax forms were completed and mailed before March 15.
13. You did not record a personal greeting on your voice mail.
14. This innovative advertisement was designed by J. D. McKay.
15. I am writing in response to your recent claim letter.
16. A revision of the report is necessary.
17. Only one of the proposals are feasible.
18. The corrected order cannot be sent until March 5.
19. A manager must get to know his support staff.
20. The data have been compiled; it should be hear tomorrow afternoon.

Punctuation Application   Insert or make corrections in punctuation marks where needed.

21. The Pittman advertising campaign was completed yesterday but it has not been sent to the client.
22. The Public Relations Department handled the situation well we couldn't have done better ourselves.
23. If the merchandise is shipped March 1 it will be delivered before March 7.
24. The merchandise will be delivered before March 7, if it is shipped on March 1.
25. The vice president of commercial loans not the senior loan officer is responsible for developing loan approval procedures.
26. To increase accuracy, give short simple instructions.
27. The most important consideration (financing) will be discussed tomorrow.
28. Cohen Dairy's new ice cream is low in fat cholesterol and sodium.
29. The new system has three advantages costs less to install needs less maintenance and meets higher quality standards.
30. The consultant recommended a new marketing strategy it works much better than the strategy we formerly used.
31. When I carried a credit card I kept getting deeper and deeper in debt but I still could not resist buying.
32. As the Engineering Department predicted the prototype was not completed by the deadline.
33. This proposal for cutting communication costs is good, however, it isn't as cost effective as our present method.
34. Companies with strong benefit packages attract talented women but limited career opportunities and corporate culture are also decisive factors.
35. R. L. Pierce is the highest ranking official in the stencil division of Burton Glass.

Application of Emphasis Techniques   For each pair of sentences, *which* one is preferred? *Why* is it preferred?

36. In which sentence does "credit" receive more emphasis?
    a. On June 7, we applied for credit.
    b. We applied for credit on June 7.
37. In which sentence does the idea of denial receive more emphasis?
    a. Although our application for credit was denied, we were encouraged to make cash purchases.
    b. Our application for credit was denied, but we were encouraged to make cash purchases.
38. Which sentence is more emphatic?
    a. Tom hit a home run in the ninth inning.
    b. A home run was hit in the ninth inning.

39. Which sentence is more emphatic?
  a. Congratulations on your recent honor.
  b. Congratulations on your receipt of the "outstanding student" award.
40. Which sentence is less emphatic?
  a. We appreciate your letting us know about your condition.
  b. We appreciate your letting us know about your migraine headaches, your shingles, and your broken thumb.
41. Which sentence places less emphasis on the negative?
  a. I will not help you with your assignment.
  b. I wish I could help you with your assignment.
42. Which sentence places more emphasis on "excuses"?
  a. We are not allowed to make one thing, excuses.
  b. We are not allowed to make one thing—excuses.
  c. We are not allowed to make one thing (excuses).
43. Which sentence is more emphatic?
  a. George is expected to complete the plaster work tomorrow.
  b. The plaster work is expected to be completed tomorrow.
44. Which sentence is more emphatic?
  a. The building will be completed on or before June 8.
  b. Completion of the building is to be on or before June 8.
45. Which sentence places more emphasis on the units in the series?
  a. The firm has three needs: money, materials, and management.
  b. The firm has three needs: (1) money, (2) materials, and (3) management.

Proofreading Application Use proofreaders' marks to correct errors in spelling, grammar, word usage, punctuation, numbers, abbreviations, and formatting of the business letter on the next page. Do not revise a sentence and state its idea in an entirely different way. You should find approximately 15 errors.

Molcan Communications, Inc.
4300 North York Street
Atlanta, GA 30340-4300

Telephone (404) 555-3900 ———— *Fax (404) 555-0398*

February 31, 19—

Lowrey Manufacturing
1273 North Benton Avenue
Muncie, Indiana 47302-1273

Ladies and Gentlemen,

Congradulations on being selected to attend the two day seminar on effective listening. The seminar will be held in Atlanta, Georgia on March 15. These five guidelines for effective listening should be real helpful as you begin to analyze your own listening skills.

1. Learn to block out distractions that interfere with effective listening.
2. Take notes on the material to reinforce you memory.
3. Become sincrely interested in what the speaker is saying, this procedure will help you retain information.
3. Listen to the entire message before responding to be certain that you here everything.
4. Listen with an open mind, otherwise, you may miss key points.
5. Identify your weaknesses in listening and work to improve them.

We are eager for you to this professional development seminar. When you return please be sure to share this valuable information with others at Lowrey.

Sincerely,

Marla Hilliard
Consultant

Proofreading application

COMMUNICATING THROUGH LETTERS AND MEMORANDUMS

CHAPTER 9   Writing About the Routine and the Pleasant
CHAPTER 10   Writing About the Unpleasant
CHAPTER 11   Writing to Persuade
CHAPTER 12   Writing Special Letters

WRITING ABOUT THE ROUTINE AND THE PLEASANT

OBJECTIVES

When you have completed Chapter 9, you should be able to

- Use empathy to see your message from the point of view of the reader.

- Select the appropriate outline for developing messages by identifying the central idea and the likely reader reaction.

- State the steps in the deductive outline (the main idea, the details, and a pleasant or neutral close) and identify the advantages of using it for good news or routine information.

- Use deductive outlines in writing good news and routine letters and memos.

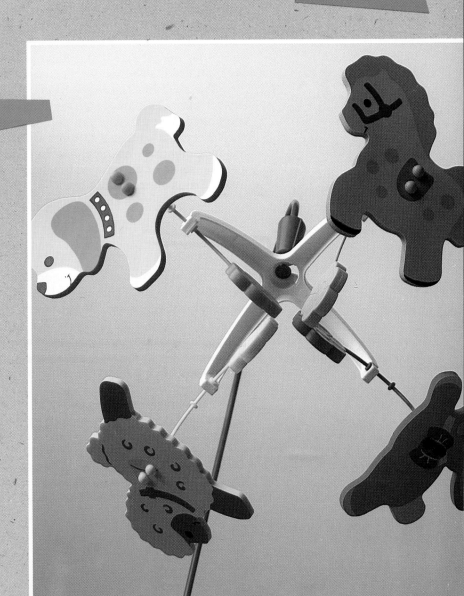

DO YOU EVER WONDER how toy designers know what a child will respond to with curiosity and pleasure? At Fisher-Price, toy designers actually test the products on themselves. Highly educated and creative adults get down on their hands and knees, play with plastic blocks, shake brightly colored balls to hear the objects inside it rattle, or lie under a mobile and look up at it.

Many behavioral scientists would say that such playful activity is productive and can help relieve stress and spark creativity; however, the people at Fisher-Price have something else in mind for all that child's play. They want their designers to develop new, sound ideas for toys, and they know that the only way an adult can produce a toy that a child will respond to is to understand or perceive that toy through a child's eyes. So for a short time, the Fisher-Price designers "become" children and experience their creations as children would. Through this experience, they may realize that colors need to be brighter, that the whistle in the train needs to be louder, or that the crib night-light is too bright.

The ability to *empathize*—to understand how others feel—is a necessity for business managers. This ability is especially important in written communication. Like the toy designers at Fisher-Price, a writer must always keep the audience in mind. Ignoring your audience can result in misunderstanding, hostility, and hurt feelings. Combining empathy with a strong sense of purpose and organization, however, leads to communication that is clear and positive.

EMPATHY

How does empathy aid in the communication process?

In an ancient fable, a vagabond quickly locates a horse that no one else in the village has been able to find. Asked to explain his success, the old man says, "It was easy; I simply went where I would have gone if I had been a horse." To find the horse, the vagabond used *empathy*—the ability to identify another's frame of reference (knowledge, feelings, and emotions) and to project or communicate understanding back to the person (or animal). In your efforts to solve interpersonal problems, you are aided by empathy.

The phrases "walking a day in your moccasins" or "putting myself in your shoes" imply that empathy requires us to experience another person's situation firsthand. Sharing an experience makes empathy easier. For example, a person who has recovered from a life-threatening disease can more easily understand the emotions and feelings of a person who has just received a similar diagnosis. The power of empathy is central to the success of self-help groups such as Alcoholics Anonymous, Narcotics Anonymous, Mothers Against Drunk Drivers (MADD), and many cancer support groups.

The film The Doctor, *starring William Hurt, showed how a doctor learned about bedside manner when he was diagnosed with a serious illness and became a patient. Empathy is essential for businesspersons as well; putting yourself in the position of others improves communication and builds strong business relationships.*

Fortunately, it is not always necessary to rely on firsthand experience to be able to provide genuine empathy. In situations when we cannot "walk in another's shoes," we can empathize by mentally projecting how we believe we would feel if that situation had happened to us. To illustrate this mental projection, Jess Lair once said, "Empathy is your pain in my heart" (Moody, 1987, p. 155).

How can being in touch with someone's feelings assist in business-related situations? In *How to Win Friends and Influence People* (1964), Dale Carnegie illustrated empathy with a story of a retailer standing behind a counter. To determine what to say to a customer who had just entered, the retailer would take an imaginary walk to the customer's side of the counter and mentally ask, "If I were this customer, what would I want a clerk to say to me?" This attempt at projection into the other's point of view enabled the retailer to advise clerks on how to communicate effectively and thus to increase sales. You have already seen how Fisher-Price uses empathy to perfect designs for its popular toys.

In today's competitive environment, no company can afford to alienate talented workers, and empathy is aiding companies in creating environments supportive of the needs of numerous diverse groups. For instance, recent efforts to involve workers in quality circles provide

List two ways empathy is used in a business-related situation.

management opportunities to see production through the eyes of the worker, the person closest to the operation, and give the worker an opportunity to be heard and appreciated. To illustrate their empathy for the needs of dual-career and single-parent homes, some companies are introducing flexible work schedules, strong family-benefit policies, extended leaves for mothers and fathers of newborns, assistance with child- and eldercare, and reductions in travel and relocation.

Companies serious about retaining and promoting women are making changes that lead to a corporate culture supportive of women. They are tackling discrimination and sexual harassment problems and responding to issues uncovered during frank discussions and gender-awareness workshops. For example, managers at Corning realized that they were cutting women out of the important elements of the company's informal corporate culture. Now co-ed executive groups frequently lunch together, allowing both men and women to benefit from the useful discussion and often creative problem-solving that occurs in an informal setting. U.S. West serves as an exemplary example of a company that is committed to breaking down barriers that impede women's success: U.S. women hold 21 percent of the jobs in the company's top 1 percent salary level, a rate higher than any U.S. corporation (Konrad, 1990).

Seeing a situation from the perspective of the reader/ listener is especially important when communicating with a person from another culture.

Because of increased foreign competition, companies must learn to use empathy to understand people who may not speak the same language; do not understand the culture's jargon, expressions, or nonverbal language; practice a different religion and customs; support a different political system; and apply entirely different management practices. A *Business Week* special report (Hoerr, Spiro, Armstrong, & Treece, 1990) highlighted the difficulty U.S. managers in Japanese subsidiaries are having functioning with Japanese managerial styles and worker relationships. For example, the top echelon management is reserved for the Japanese, causing U.S. managers to feel that they are *with* the organization but not *of* the organization; compensation for senior management is lower than in U.S. companies (mainly because foreign companies seldom give stock options, a large part of the U.S. senior executives' pay packages); and the traditional emphasis on collective values over individualism gives workers more power, which takes away power from the managers. For these managers, an important first step is to commit themselves to trying to use empathy to see the situation from the perspective of the Japanese.

Empathy is a useful tool in building positive interpersonal relationships, providing effective peer and professional counseling, selecting the correct response to a customer, marketing products that meet customer needs, and being sensitive to a multicultural workplace. Likewise, oral and written communication become more effective when the speaker or writer looks at the message from the point of view of the listener or reader.

Empathy enhances the communication process in several ways.

First, trying to understand the situation from another's point of view makes sense. Your readers/listeners will appreciate your attempting to understand their feelings; that is, your being in touch with them. The outcome may be mutual trust, which can greatly improve communication and people's feelings about you, your ideas, and themselves (as shown in the discussion of the Johari Window in Chapter 2). In other words, empathy is an excellent way to establish rapport and credibility and to build long-lasting personal and business relationships.

Second, seeing a situation or problem from the reader's perspective not only will permit you to address the reader's needs and concerns but will also enable you to anticipate the reader's possible reaction to the message. This understanding will help you tailor the message so that you are more likely to achieve the goal you desire. With your knowledge of the reader's likely reaction, you are better equipped to select relevant content, to determine the appropriate sequence of ideas, and to write in a suitable style. The following suggestions should help in achieving empathy.

Empathy helps us *anticipate* the reader's reaction to our message.

Cultivating a "You Attitude"

Readers find ideas more interesting and appealing if they are expressed from the reader's viewpoint. A letter reflecting a "you attitude" sends a direct signal of sincere concern for the reader's needs and interest. To cultivate a "you attitude," concentrate on the following questions:

Buy a gift that fits the receiver; design a message that fits the receiver.

- ◆ Does the message address the reader's major needs and concerns?
- ◆ Is information stated as truthfully, honestly, and ethically as possible?
- ◆ Will the reader perceive the ideas to be fair, logical, and ethical?
- ◆ Are ideas expressed clearly and concisely (to avoid the lost time, money, and possible embarrassment caused when messages are misunderstood)?

COMMUNICATION MENTOR

The best business writing is reader focused. Writing from your own point of view is easier; you know what you want to say. But reader-focused writing is more important. Ask yourself—what does my reader need to know? How can I most effectively and clearly convey the information to my reader? Get a picture of the reader in your mind. Think about your reader as you plan your communication.

H. Devon Graham, Jr.
Southwest Regional Managing Partner
Arthur Andersen & Co.

◆ Would the reader feel this message is reader-centered? Is the reader kept clearly in the picture?

◆ Does the message serve as a vehicle for developing positive business relationships—even when the message is negative? For example, are *please*, *thank you*, and other courtesies used when appropriate? Are ideas stated tactfully and positively and in a manner that preserves the reader's self-worth and cultivates future business?

◆ Is the message sent promptly to indicate courtesy?

◆ Does the message reflect the high standards of a business professional: quality paper, accurate formatting, printing quality, and absence of misspellings and grammatical errors?

Concentration on these points will boost the reader's confidence in the writer's competence and will communicate nonverbally that the reader is valued enough to merit the writer's best effort. For people who have practiced courtesy and consideration since childhood, the "you attitude" is easy to incorporate into a written message.

Using Your Knowledge of the Receiver

To help you see a situation from the point of view of the reader, focus on relevant information you know about the reader. The more familiar you are with the reader, the easier this task will be. When communicating with an individual, you immediately bring to mind a clear picture of the reader—his or her physical appearance, background (education, occupation, religion, culture), values, opinions, preferences, and so on. Most important, your knowledge of the reader's reaction in similar, previous experiences will aid you in anticipating how this reader is likely to react in the current situation.

You may find that empathizing with those you know well is often such a conscious action that you may not even recognize that you are doing it. On the other hand, empathizing with those you do not know well requires additional effort. Make a conscious effort to visualize the reader; add to your mental picture by thoughtfully considering all you know about the reader and how this information might affect the content and style of your final message. Consider the following major factors:

1. *Age.* A letter answering an elementary-school student's request for information from your company would not be worded like a letter answering a similar request from an adult.

2. *Economic level.* A banker's collection letter to a prompt-paying customer is not likely to be the same form letter sent to clients who have fallen behind on their payments for small loans.

3. *Educational/occupational background.* The technical jargon and acronyms used in a financial proposal sent to bank loan officers may be inappropriate in a proposal sent to a group of private investors. Similarly, a

message to the chief executive officer of a major corporation may differ in style and content from a message to one of the stockholders.

4. *Culture.* The vast cultural differences between people (language, expressions, customs, values, religions) increase the complexity of the communication process. A memorandum containing typically American expressions such as "The projections are *way off base,* and the prices are *out of our ballpark"* would likely confuse a manager from a different culture.

5. *Rapport.* A sensitive letter written to a long-time client may differ significantly from a letter written to a newly acquired client. The rapport created by previous dealings with this client aids understanding in this new situation.

6. *Expectations.* Because accountants, doctors, and lawyers are expected to meet high standards, a letter from one of these professionals containing errors in grammar or spelling would likely cause a receiver to question the credibility of the source.

7. *Needs of the reader.* Just as successful sales personnel begin by identifying the needs of the prospective buyer, an effective manager attempts to understand the reader's frame of reference as a basis for developing the message's organization and content.

Notice the use (or lack) of empathy in each of the following examples:

Sample Message	*Problem Analysis*
Example 1: Hurriedly as the store closed on Thursday evening, the store manager told sales clerks:	
Oh, by the way, it's time for our annual inventory. I want you here Sunday at 7 a.m. sharp and plan to stay until . . . And one other thing. Don't bother to embarrass yourself by giving me some flimsy excuse for not being able to work. I don't want to hear it. If I don't have this job done by Monday morning, the district manager will have <u>my</u> head. End of conversation.	Overuse of the pronoun I emphasizes the manager's self-centered attitude. Tactless, intimidating, and overly demanding tone eliminates the possibility of feedback. Insistence on one-way communication and the timing of the message highlight inconsideration for individual needs (arrangements for child- or elder-care and other extenuating circumstances).
Example 2: An excerpt from a letter sent to Mr. Adam Ritchey:	
Dear Mr. <u>Ritchie:</u> The desktop publishing software and the laser printer that you expressed an interest in <u>is</u> now available in our local	The misspelling of the reader's name and the grammar errors are unforgivable; the three other misspellings

stores. Both can be demonstrated at <u>you</u> <u>convience</u>. Please call your local sales representative to schedule <u>a</u> appointment. <u>I remain</u>

Respectfully yours,

Randall R. Flynn

Randall R. Flynn
District Manager

confirm incompetence (or carelessness) and disrespect for the reader (what other reason could explain this second-rate work?). The outdated closing reduces the writer's credibility further. Although the writer is purporting expertise in a technological field, his communication does not reflect modern conventions.

The writer does not anticipate the reader's need for the sales representative's name and phone number; omission of these important facts communicates unconcern for the reader.

Example 3: A U.S. manager's instructions to a new employee from an Asian culture:

Please get to work right away on <u>inputting</u> the financial data for the Smyth proposal. Oh, I need you to get this work out <u>ASAP</u>. Since this proposal is just a <u>draft</u>, why don't you just plan to give me a <u>quick-and-dirty</u> <u>job</u>. You can clean it up after we <u>massage</u> the <u>stats</u> and get final <u>blessings</u> from the <u>top dog</u>. Do you have any questions?

Can you imagine the confusion and intimidation caused by the acronyms and expressions peculiar to the U.S. environment? The final open-ended question indicates that the writer does not understand the importance of saving face to a person from an Asian culture. Deep cultural influences prevent this employee from asking questions that might indicate lack of understanding.

An untimely message may not get the attention it deserves.

Timing is one way of showing courtesy and consideration of your reader's needs. If a letter isn't delivered on the expected or promised date, the would-be recipient will react negatively. When it finally arrives, the letter automatically has a barrier to overcome. With empathy for the receiver, you probably would not want to time a message for delivery soon after the receiver has had a well-publicized emergency. Similarly, an income-tax accountant probably would not have much enthusiasm for an unsolicited sales letter delivered a few days before April 15.

Although knowledge about the recipient assists writers in developing empathy, they can practice empathy in communicating with people about whom they know little or almost nothing. From their knowledge of themselves and from their experiences with others, writers can predict (with reasonable accuracy) recipients' reactions to various types of messages. To illustrate, ask yourself these questions:

◆ Would I react favorably to a message saying my request is being granted?

COMMUNICATION MENTOR

Providing complete, well-documented information is critical in our business. Written communication, often a product of numerous verbal exchanges, serves as an official record of understanding between us and our customers and as a valuable point of future reference about details, decisions made, etc.

Accurate and thorough documentation is also an effective safeguard against potential legal or ethical questions. Receiving accurate information leaves our customers with a positive attitude toward our company—legitimate confidence in our ability to conduct business honestly and professionally. These satisfied customers, in turn, are our best source of public relations.

Beverly R. Kuehn
Branch Manager
CTX Mortgage Company
a division of Centex Corporation

♦ Would I experience a feeling of disappointment upon learning that my request has been refused?
♦ Would I be pleased when an apparently sincere message praises me for a job well done?
♦ Would I experience some disappointment when a memo reveals that my promised pay increase is being postponed?

Now, reread the questions as though you were another person. Because you know *your* answers, can you predict *others'* answers with some degree of accuracy. Such predictions are possible because of commonality in human behavior. Of course, each individual is unique; but each has much in common with others. Otherwise, psychology, psychiatry, and sociology would not have survived as disciplines. To practice empathy, ask yourself how you would react if you were in the other person's position. Asking that question *before* you write a message greatly simplifies the task of *organizing* your message.

ORGANIZATION

In a discussion of writing, the word "organize" means "the act of dividing a topic into parts and arranging them in an appropriate sequence." Before undertaking this process, the writer needs to be convinced that the message is the *right* message—that it is complete, accurate, fair, reasonable, ethical, and logical. If it doesn't meet these standards, it should not be sent. Good organization and good writing cannot be expected to compensate for a bad decision.

Why Organization Is Essential

When a topic is divided into parts, one part will be recognized as a central idea and the others as minor ideas (details). The process of identifying these ideas and arranging them in the right sequence is known as *outlining*. As used in this text, "outlining" and "organizing" have the same meaning. Typically, those who don't particularly enjoy writing care even less for outlining. Many people confess to having written outlines *after* writing assignments have been completed! Outlining *before* writing provides numerous benefits:

What is gained by taking time to outline before writing?

◆ Encourages brevity and accuracy. (Reduces the chance of leaving out an essential idea or including an unessential idea.)
◆ Permits concentration on one phase at a time. (Having focused separately on (a) the ideas that need to be included, (b) the distinction be-

For the architect or city planner, organization is essential; without it, buildings are constructed with poor materials or are missing vital components. Writers need organization as well to ensure that their ideas are presented clearly and logically, increasing the likelihood that the reader will react positively to their messages.

tween major and minor ideas, and (c) the sequence of ideas, the writer is now prepared for total concentration on the next problem—expressing.)

◆ Saves time in writing or dictating. (With questions about which ideas to include and their proper sequence already answered, little time is lost in moving from one point to the next.)
◆ Provides a psychological lift. (The feeling of success gained in preparing the outline increases confidence that the next step—writing—will be successful, too.)
◆ Facilitates emphasis and de-emphasis. (Although each sentence makes its contribution to the message, some sentences need to stand out more vividly in the reader's mind than others. An effective outline ensures that important points will appear in emphatic positions.)

The preceding benefits derived from outlining are writer oriented. Because a message has been well outlined, readers benefit, too:

◆ The message is more concise and accurate.
◆ The relationships among ideas are easier to distinguish and remember
◆ Reaction to the message and its writer is more likely to be positive.

> **When a message has been well-organized, do *both* writer and reader benefit?**

Reader reaction to a message is strongly influenced by the sequence in which ideas are presented. A beginnning sentence or an ending sentence is in an emphatic position. (For a review of other emphasis techniques, see Chapter 8.) Throughout this chapter and other chapters on letter writing, note that outlining (organizing) is an important factor.

How to Organize Letters and Memorandums

When planning your writing or dictating, you should strive for an outline that will serve the writer in much the same way a blueprint serves a builder or itinerary serves a traveler. When the goal is to produce a map or blueprint, thought precedes action. The same is true of outlining. Before listing the first point of an outline, you should answer the following questions:

> **An outline serves a writer as a blueprint serves a builder or an itinerary serves a traveler.**

◆ What will be the central idea of the message?
◆ What will be the most likely reader reaction to the message?
◆ In view of the predicted reader reaction, should the central idea be listed *first* in the outline; or should it be listed as one of the *last* items?

To answer the first question, think about the *reason* for writing. Is the purpose to get information, to answer a question, to accept an offer, to deny a request? If the letter were condensed into a one-sentence telegram, that sentence would be the central idea.

To answer the second question (predicted reader reaction), ask, "If I

> **What are the four reader reactions?**

were the one receiving the message I am preparing to send, what would *my* reaction be?" Because you would react with pleasure to good news and displeasure to bad news, you can reasonably assume a reader's reaction would be similar. Recall the twin goals of a communicator: clarity and effective human relations. By considering anticipated reader reaction, a writer facilitates achievement of the second goal. As shown in Figure 9-1, almost every letter will fit into one of four categories of anticipated reader reaction: (1) pleasure, (2) displeasure, (3) interest but neither pleasure nor displeasure, or (4) no interest.

After a letter or memorandum has been classified into one of the preceding categories, the next question is "Should the central idea be placed in the beginning sentence?" If so, present the message deductively; if not, present the message inductively (as discussed in Chapter 8).

Because the distinction between deductive and inductive writing is vital to an understanding of this and subsequent chapters, let's briefly recap what was said in Chapter 8. As messages in each category are discussed, these recommendations will be amplified:

FIGURE 9-1 Four reader reactions

Write Deductively (big idea first)	Write Inductively (details first)
When the message will *please* the reader	When the message will *displease* the reader
When the message is *routine* (will neither please nor displease)	When the reader *may not be interested* (will need to be persuaded)

Should you *always* begin with the central idea?

Although the principal focus is on writing, the same sequence-of-idea patterns are recommended for *oral* communication. These patterns are applicable in memorandums and reports as well as in letters.

Because deductive messages are easier to write and pleasant and routine messages follow similar outlines, they are discussed together in this chapter. Inductive messages are discussed in more detail in Chapters 10 and 11.

BUSINESS LETTERS

Letters that convey pleasant messages are referred to as "good-news" letters. Letters not likely to generate any emotional reaction are referred to as "routine" letters. As depicted in Figure 9-2, both outlines follow a deductive pattern in which the major idea is presented first, followed by supporting details. In both, the third point (closing thought) may be omitted without seriously impairing effectiveness; however, including it unifies the message and avoids abruptness.

The deductive sequence-of-ideas pattern has several advantages:

1. The first sentence is easier to write; it can be written with very little hesitation. After it, the details follow easily.

"Routine" letters are not likely to evoke an emotional reaction.

What are the advantages of the deductive pattern for good-news and routine letters?

COMMUNICATION MENTOR

Written communication is a prerequisite of any corporation. While a meeting can be a good communications tool, written correspondence is more effective—and permanent.

Terence E. McSweeney
Director of Communications
PGA of America

GOOD-NEWS
LETTER

ROUTINE
LETTER

States the
pleasant idea

States the
main idea

Provides details
or explanation

Provides details
or explanation

Reminds reader
of the good news
or includes a
future-oriented
closing thought

Reminds reader of
main idea or
includes a future-
oriented closing
thought

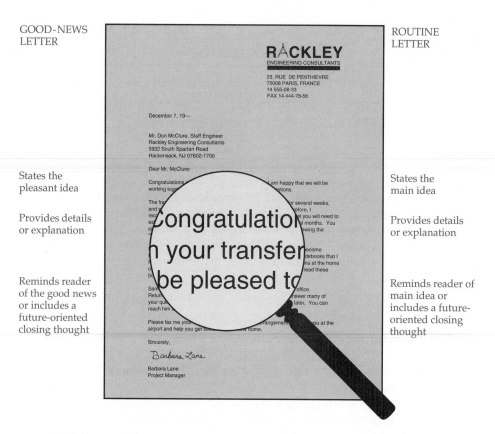

**FIGURE 9-2   Deductive sequence-of-ideas pattern used in good-news
and routine letters**

2. The first sentence is likely to attract attention. Coming first, the major idea gets the attention it deserves.
3. When good news appears in the beginning, the message immediately puts readers in a pleasant frame of mind; in this state, they are receptive to the details that follow.
4. The arrangement may save readers some time; once they get the important idea, they can move rapidly through the supporting details.

This basic plan is applicable in several business-writing situations: (1) routine claim letters and "yes" replies, (2) routine requests related to credit matters and "yes" replies, (3) routine order letters and "yes" replies, and (4) routine requests and "yes" replies.

Ineffective and effective applications of this outline are illustrated in the sample letters in this chapter. These letters are correctly formatted as acceptable business letters. Some sentences or sections of each letter are numbered and correspond to the numbers in the commentary beside the letter. The detailed comments will help you see how principles are applied or violated. The ⊘ is positioned beside poor examples for easy identification. When you see this familiar symbol, remember that you are about to read an example of what you should *not* do.

Typically, a rather poorly organized and poorly written example is followed by a well-organized and well-written example. The commentary on poor examples explains why certain techniques should be avoided. The commentary on well-written examples demonstrates ways to avoid certain types of mistakes. The well-written examples are designed to illustrate the application of principles discussed in Chapters 7, 8, and 9. They are not intended as models of exact words, phrases, or sentences that should appear in letters you write. At the conclusion of this chapter, you should be able to apply the principles you've learned and create your own well-written letters and memorandums.

To assist you in recognizing standard business formats, many of the examples are positioned correctly on letterhead and are formatted with appropriate letter parts. To become familiar with these important formatting conventions, study Appendix A, which provides a detailed explanation and illustrations of the standard formats and layout of business letters and memorandums. When you are confident you understand this information, return to this chapter to review the sample good-news and routine letters and memorandums. In addition to pinpointing writing principles, the commentary on the examples reinforces your understanding of the formats and layout in Appendix A. For example, the commentary may direct your attention to letters illustrating one of the three acceptable letter styles (block, modified block, and simplified), one of two punctuation types (open and mixed), or appropriate use and placement of special parts of the letter (e.g., subject line, attention line, and enclosure notations).

Routine Claims

A claim letter is a request for an adjustment. When writers ask for something to which they think they are entitled (such as a refund, replacement, exchange, or payment for damages), the letter is called a *claim* letter.

Should a routine claim letter *begin* with the main idea?

Claim Letter. These requests can be divided into two groups: *routine claims* and *persuasive claims*. Persuasive claims, which will be discussed in a later chapter, assume that the request will be granted only after explanations and persuasive arguments have been presented. Routine claims (possibly because of guarantees, warranties, or other contractual conditions) assume that the request will be granted quickly and willingly, without persuasion. Because you expect routine claims to be granted willingly, a forceful, accusatory tone is inappropriate.

When the claim is routine (not likely to meet resistance), the following outline is recommended:

Forceful, accusatory tone inappropriate for routine claims
Reprinted by special permission of King Features Syndicate, Inc.

1. Request action in the first sentence.
2. Explain the details supporting the request for action.
3. Close with an expression of appreciation for taking the action requested.

Figure 9-3 illustrates an inductive treatment and Figure 9-4 a deductive treatment of a routine claim letter. Written inductively, the letter in Figure 9-3 does transmit the essential ideas; but it is unnecessarily long and the main idea is not emphasized. Surely the builder intended to install 50-gallon heaters; otherwise, the building contract would not have been signed. Because a mistake is obvious, the builder would not need to be persuaded. Because compliance can be expected, the claim can be stated without prior explanation.

Without showing anger, disgust, suspicion, or disappointment, the claim letter in Figure 9-4 asks simply for an adjustment. The major point receives deserved emphasis. Reader response to it should be favorable.

An "adjustment" letter is a response to a claim letter.	**Favorable Response to a Claim Letter.** Businesses *want* their customers to write when merchandise or service is not satisfactory. They want to learn of ways in which goods and services can be improved, and they want their customers to receive value for the money they spend. With considerable confidence, they can assume that writers of claim letters think their claims are valid. By responding favorably to legitimate requests in *adjustment* letters, businesses can gain a reputation for standing behind their goods and services. A loyal customer may become even more loyal after a business has demonstrated its integrity.
Include a sales message in an adjustment letter.	Because the subject of an adjustment letter is related to the goods or services provided, the letter can serve easily and efficiently as a low-pressure sales letter. With only a little extra space, the letter can include resale or sales-promotional material. *Resale* is used in a discussion of goods or services already bought. It reminds customers and clients that they made a good choice in selecting a firm with which to do business, or it reminds them of the good qualities of their purchase. *Sales-promotional material* is used in a discussion of related merchandise or service. For example, a letter about a company's wallpaper might also mention its paint.

GONZALES PROPERTY MANAGEMENT CORPORATION

632 Houston Road, San Antonio, TX 78205-7323
(512) 555-5263

March 3, 19—

Mr. G. David Williams, Owner
Williams Plumbing & Heating Co.
78 Canterbury Street
San Antonio, TX 78205-1337

Dear Mr. Williams:

[1] MAYHEW STREET APARTMENTS

[2] Late yesterday evening, I stopped by the construction site of the apartments you are under contract to build for me. [3] At the present rate, you appear to be well ahead of schedule.

[4] According to our agreement, all requests and complaints are to be made in writing. [5] I noticed that water heaters had been installed in two of the apartments. [6] The units are 30-gallon heaters, but the specs call for 50-gallon heaters in each of the 12 apartments.

[7] For some families, the smaller size may be sufficient; but others may need the larger size. [8] Because the larger size is specified in the agreement we signed, I respectfully request that the two 30-gallon units be removed and that 50-gallon water heaters be installed in all the apartments.

[9] Thank you for your consideration in this matter. [10] I am enthused about the progress you have made.

Sincerely,

Edwin Gonzales

Edwin Gonzales
Contractor

[1] Subject line is too general to aid reader in understanding the subject.

[2] Begins with detail that will lead to the main idea. [3] Makes an observation that could be omitted (although it does show that the writer is willing to give credit where credit is due).

[4] States directly information that is already known. [5] Moves toward the main idea. [6] Continues with detail.

[7] Presents a reason for making the upcoming request. [8] States the main point of the letter that should have been presented in the first paragraph. Stating the claim in such a long sentence keeps the request from receiving the emphasis it needs.

[9] Uses a cliché. [10] Does close on a positive note but uses "enthused"; "enthusiastic" should be used instead.

FIGURE 9-3 Poor example of a routine claim letter

Mentioning the paint is using sales-promotional material. Subtle sales messages that are included in adjustment letters have a good chance of being read, but direct sales letters may not be read at all.

When the response to a claim letter is favorable, present ideas in the following sequence:

1. Reveal the good news in the first sentence.

GONZALES PROPERTY MANAGEMENT CORPORATION

632 Houston Road, San Antonio, TX 78205-7323
(512) 555-5263

March 3, 19—

Mr. G. David Williams, Owner
Williams Plumbing & Heating Co.
78 Canterbury Street
San Antonio, TX 78205-1337

Dear Mr. Williams:

[1] WATER HEATER SPECIFICATIONS FOR MAYHEW STREET
APARTMENTS

[2] Please replace the two 30-gallon water heaters (installed last week)
with 50-gallon units.

[3] Large units are essential for families with children. [4] For that reason,
the contract specifies a 50-gallon heater for <u>each</u> of the 12 apartments.

[5] The project appears to be well ahead of schedule; thanks for your
efforts.

Sincerely,

Edwin Gonzales

Edwin Gonzales
Contractor

[1] Subject line provides specific information about the subject.

[2] Emphasizes the main idea by placing it in the first sentence.

[3,4] Follow with explanation.

[5] Ends on a positive note.

Letter illustrates mixed punctuation; a colon appears after the salutation, and a comma appears after the complimentary close.

FIGURE 9-4   Good example of a routine claim letter

2. Explain the circumstances.
3. Close on a pleasant, forward-looking note.

Although the word *grant* is acceptable when talking about claims, its use *in* adjustment letters is discouraged. An expression such as "Your claim is being granted" unnecessarily implies that the writer is in a position of power.

Ordinarily, a response to a written message is also a written message. Sometimes, people write letters to confirm ideas they have already discussed on the telephone. Before reading the well-written deductive response in Figure 9-6, study the commentary on each sentence in the poorly written inductive response (Figure 9-5).

WILLIAMS PLUMBING &
HEATING CO.
78 CANTERBURY ST.
SAN ANTONIO, TX
78205-1337
(512) 555-2300 FAX: (512) 555-2525

March 7, 19--

Mr. Edwin Gonzales
Gonzales Property Management
  Corporation
632 Houston Road
San Antonio, TX 78205-7323

Dear Mr. Gonzales

¹ Thank you for your letter of March 3. ² It has been referred to me for reply.

³ Looking at our contract, I see that it does specify 50-gallon water heaters. ⁴ Therefore, we are complying with your request that the 30-gallon heaters be removed and that the 50 gallon units be placed in <u>all</u> your apartments.

⁵ Thank you for calling this matter to our attention.

Sincerely

G. David Williams

G. David Williams, Owner

[1]Uses a well-worn beginning. [2]States the obvious.

[3]Leads to main idea. [4]Presents main idea that should have been presented in the first paragraph.

[5]Uses a sentence that seems polite but is well worn.

Right margin should not be justified; the extra spaces placed between the words to achieve the straight margins are distracting and reduce the reader's comprehension.

FIGURE 9-5 Poor example of a favorable response to a claim letter

Figure 9-5 does reveal compliance with the request, but the main idea is not emphasized. In the absence of an explanation for the initial installation of 30-gallon heaters, the reader could become suspicious of the builder's intent. Although explaining is not obligatory, a builder who is honest and efficient would find out what happened. By investigating and

[1]The good news (main idea) receives emphasis. [2]Action is being taken already.

[3]Reaction to the report is positive. [4]Presents explanation.

[5]Closes with a look to the future.

Letter illustrates open punctuation. Notice that the colon is omitted after the salutation, and the comma is omitted after the complimentary close.

WILLIAMS PLUMBING &
HEATING CO.
78 CANTERBURY ST.
SAN ANTONIO, TX
78205-1337
(512) 555-2300   FAX: (512) 555-2525

March 7, 19—

Mr. Edwin Gonzales
Gonzales Property Management
   Corporation
632 Houston Road
San Antonio, TX 78205-7323

Dear Mr. Gonzales

[1]Each of your apartments will have a 50-gallon water heater. [2]The two 30-gallon units are being removed today.

[3]Thank you for reporting the problem before additional heaters were installed. [4]Clearly, "50-gallon" appears on the specs; clearly, "30-gallon" was keyboarded on the warehouse request form.

[5]Excellent progress is being made on this project; all plumbing should be complete by the original completion date.

Sincerely

G. David Williams, Owner

FIGURE 9-6   Good example of a favorable response to a claim letter

explaining, the builder may impress the reader as a manager who takes corrective and preventive measures.

In the revised letter in Figure 9-6, notice the deductive treatment and the explanation.

Confident that a routine request for an adjustment will be granted, the writer in Figure 9-4 simply asks for it (in the first sentence and without seeming to complain). Knowing that the recipient will be glad to learn that a request has been granted, the writer in Figure 9-6 simply states it (in the first sentence and without apparent reluctance). The details and closing sentence follow naturally and easily.

Routine Letters About Credit

Normally, credit information is requested and transmitted electronically or by form letters or simple office forms. When the response to a credit request is likely to be favorable, the request should be stated at the beginning.

Request for Information. The network of credit associations across the country has made knowledge about individual consumers easy to obtain. As a result, exchanges of credit information are common in business. Study the following outline for an effective letter request for credit information about an individual:

1. Identify the request and name the applicant early, preferably in the opening sentence or in a subject line.
2. Assure the reader that the reply will be kept confidential.
3. Detail the information requested. Use a tabulated-form layout to make the reply easy.
4. End courteously. Offer the same assistance to the reader.

In the letter in Figure 9-7, the credit applicant rather than the prospective creditor has written the request for credit information. Consequently, the credit reference is assured that the request is legitimate and that the applicant wishes to have credit information provided. Another desirable arrangement in this credit request is to include fill-in items within the letter. The desired information can be provided and the letter returned with a minimum of cost or effort.

Notice the subject line shown in the letter in Figure 9-7. The subject line serves as the letter's "title." If Seacoast Distributors (the prospective creditor) had written this letter to the credit reference, an acceptable subject line would be: CREDIT INFORMATION, COASTLINE CAFE.

Like a title to a report, the subject line is positioned directly above the first paragraph of the document. Placing the word *Subject* before the subject line is acceptable but is becoming less common because such labeling is unnecessary.

What is the outline for a credit-information request?

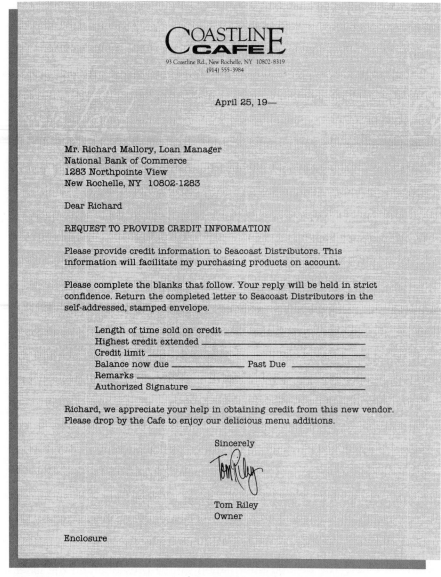

FIGURE 9-7   Good example of a request for credit information

Requests for credit information are acceptable with or without a subject line. The subject line does provide quick, emphatic identification of what the letter is about. Printed forms on which the names of the reference and applicant can be filled in are certainly desirable when the volume of credit requests is great.

Request for Credit. When people want to begin buying on credit and assume credit will be willingly extended, they can place their request in the first sentence and follow with details. This approach is recommended only when the writer's supporting financial statements are assumed sufficient to merit a "yes" response. Figure 9-8 shows a credit request that follows the deductive plan.

SOUTH PARK
ATHLETIC
C · L · U · B

June 3, 19—

Sanderson Athletic Clothing Co.
1377 Valerie Drive
Flint, MI 32094-1377

[1] Ladies and Gentlemen:

[2] Will you please fill the enclosed order on a credit basis? [3] We are eager to offer your popular line of athletic clothing to our customers.

[4] Established in 1974, we are the largest indoor athletic facility in Charlotte. [5] From aerobics and racquetball to a health-food cafe, our club offers members the most diversified selection of recreational activities available locally.

[6] The enclosed financial statements indicate that we purchase on account regularly from other vendors. [7] Credit references can be provided. [8] If you need additional information, please write to me.

[9] Many of our customers have been asking us to stock your line; therefore, we expect to place a similar order every six weeks.

Sincerely,

Edward Brooks

Edward Brooks
Manager

[10] Enclosures

1256 N. MACON ST., CHARLOTTE, NC 28202-1256
(704) 555-4910

[1] Uses an appropriate salutation for a letter addressed to a company.

[2,3] State the major idea and show interest in the company.

[4,5] Give background information about the company.

[6-8] Provide details needed for credit to be extended.

[9] Closes with a look to the future.

[10] Uses an enclosure notation to alert the reader that information is included.

FIGURE 9-8   Good example of a request for credit

Favorable Response to a Request for Credit. Effective "yes" replies to requests for credit should use the following outline:

1. Begin by saying credit terms have been arranged; or if an order has been placed, begin by telling of the shipment of goods, thereby implying the credit has been extended.
2. Indicate the foundation upon which the credit extension is based.
3. Present and explain the credit terms.
4. Include some resale or sales-promotional material.
5. End with a confident look toward future business.

Before credit managers say "yes" to a request for credit, they must answer two basic questions: (1) Will this potential customer have the money to pay when the bills become due? (2) Will the customer be willing to part with the money at that time? To answer the first question, they consider the prospective customer's financial status and earning power. To answer the second question, they consider character. Ordinarily, they get information from the following sources: (1) the potential credit customer; (2) credit-rating associations; (3) those who are presently selling or have previously sold to the potential customer; and (4) others who may have some knowledge of the potential credit customer's ability to pay.

Response to a Request for Information. Replies to requests for credit information usually are very simple—just fill in the blanks and return the letter. If the request does not include a form, follow a deductive plan in writing the reply: the major idea followed by supporting details.

To whom is the person who gives credit information obligated?

In credit-information letters, writers have an obligation to themselves as well as to the addressee and the credit applicant. Good advice is to stick with facts. Why say, "I'm sure he will pay promptly" when "His payments are always prompt" is a strong recommendation? Is there any need to say he *is* a good credit risk when all you know is that he had a good credit record when he purchased from you?

Most favorable replies to credit requests are form letters. If a firm uses word-processing software, an operator will retrieve the stored file containing the form letter and input information that will personalize the letter. For example, the loan applicant's name and address, amount of the loan, and terms are input in the appropriate location in the stored file. The revised file is printed and mailed to the loan applicant. Firms receive so many requests for credit that the costs of individualized letters are prohibitive. Typically, the form messages read something like this:

> We are pleased to extend credit privileges to you. Temporarily, you may purchase up to $2,000 worth of merchandise on time. Our credit terms are 2/10, n/30. We welcome you as a credit customer of our expanding organization.

Although such form messages are effective for informing the customer that credit is being extended, they do little to promote sales and goodwill. Whether to say "yes" by form letter or by individualized letter is a problem that each credit manager has to settle individually. If the list of credit customers is relatively short and few names are being added, individualized letters may be practical. A credit manager may choose to use individualized letters if the workload in the department is such that letters can be sent without overworking or adding personnel. But even when credit grants are tailor-made to fit the individual, they often fail to promote profitable business. Although the letter in Figure 9-9 is probably more effective than a form letter, it can be improved.

This chapter has discussed why you should tell of the shipment and credit extension in the first sentence, use resale and sales-promotional material, and write as if you expect future orders. Why should you discuss the foundation upon which you based your decision to extend credit? To prevent collection problems that may arise later. Credit managers should work to prevent collection problems. Indicating that you are extending credit on the basis of an applicant's prompt-paying habits with present creditors encourages continuation of those habits with you. It recognizes a reputation and challenges the purchaser to live up to it. When financial situations become difficult, the purchaser will probably remember the compliment and try to pay you first.

Why discuss the basis for granting credit?

Why would you discuss the credit terms? To stress their importance and prevent collection problems. Unless customers know exactly when payments are expected, they may not make them on time. Unless they know exactly what the discount terms are, they may take unauthorized discounts. Furthermore, the fact that you take time to discuss terms in detail suggests that terms are important and that you expect them to be followed. Figure 9-10, a revision of Figure 9-9, applies these principles.

Why should the credit terms be discussed?

Although the letter in Figure 9-10 was written to a dealer, the same principles apply when writing to a consumer. Each one should be addressed in terms of individual interests. Dealers are concerned about markup, marketability, and display; consumers are concerned about price, appearance, and durability. Consumers may require a more detailed explanation of credit terms.

What is the principal difference between a credit letter to a dealer and a credit letter to a customer?

The letter in Figure 9-10 performed a dual function: it said "yes" to an application for credit and "Yes, we are filling your order." Because of its importance, the credit aspect was emphasized more than the order. In other cases (if the order is for cash or if credit terms are already understood), the primary purpose of writing may be to acknowledge an order.

Routine Letters About Orders

Like routine letters about credit, routine letters about orders put the main idea in the first sentence. Details are usually tabulated, especially when more than one item is ordered.

[1]Illustrates a correctly formatted letter to a Canadian address.

[2]Delays the answer to the reader's question, "May I pay for them later?" [3]Implies the answer to the question of credit extension—if they are being shipped, credit must have been extended.

[4]"Pleased" and "investigated" could have been taken for granted. The applicant may feel under suspicion.

[5]Because this letter is to a dealer, the explanation of terms is probably sufficient. In letters to customers, more detailed explanation and interpretation are needed.

[6]Uses a cliché, which is probably meaningless. By sending an individualized letter that explains what the dealer wants to know, the writer could imply the welcome. [7]A good credit manager would not have ended the letter with a standard remark that was worn out long ago.

**Northern
Electronics
Corporation**

2910 Wilbanks Road
Fairfield, OH 45014-2910
(513) 555-1089
Fax: (513) 555-1123

August 15, 19—

[1]Space Age Electronics
MC2397 Succ. A
Montreal, Qué.
H3C 2J7 CANADA

Ladies and Gentlemen:

[2]Thank you for your order for 10 VISIONZ video cameras. [3]They are being shipped today.

[4]We are pleased to inform you that your credit rating was investigated and found to be satisfactory. [5]Our credit terms are the usual 2/10, n/30.

[6]Welcome to our growing list of satisfied customers. [7]We look forward to doing business with you in the future.

Sincerely,

Kenneth R. Stadalis

Kenneth R. Stadalis
Credit Manager

FIGURE 9-9   Poor example of a favorable response to a credit request

What outline should be used for an order letter?

Order Letter.   Order letters create one-half of a contract. They constitute the offer portion of a contract that is fulfilled when the shipper sends the goods, thereby creating the acceptance part of the contract. Therefore, if you seriously want to receive shipment, you should make your order letter a definite offer. The outline for order letters is deductive:

**Northern
Electronics
Corporation**

2910 Wilbanks Road
Fairfield, OH 45014-2910
(513) 555-1089
Fax: (513) 555-1123

October 15, 19—

[1]Attention Order Department
[2]Space Age Electronics
MC2397 Succ. A
Montreal, Qué.
H3C 2J7 CANADA

Ladies and Gentlemen:

[3]Ten VISIONZ video cameras were shipped by Fastgo Air
Express and should arrive in time for your Winter Fest.

[4]Because of your favorable current credit rating, we are
sending the shipment subject to the usual credit terms, 2/10,
n/30. [5]By paying this invoice within ten days, you save $150.

[6]The VISIONZ camera is known for its 8:1, fl .4 power zoom
lens and 2-lux light sensitivity—features that will allow your
customers to take high-quality pictures with a minimum of
light. [7]The display inside the viewer will give your customers
additional helpful information.

[8]See the enclosed folder for price lists and forms for ordering
additional cameras or other video or photography equipment.

Sincerely,

Kenneth R. Stadalis

Kenneth R. Stadalis
Credit Manager

Enclosure

[1,2]Illustrates correct Canadian address. Uses attention line in letter addressed to a company to assure efficient delivery.

[3]Presents good news. Indicates that the writer has some consideration for the problems of a dealer. Implies the credit extension.

[4]Recognizes the dealer for earning the credit privilege. Gives a reason for the credit extension; it was not extended arbitrarily. Introduces the credit terms. Addressed to a dealer, the letter does not need to explain what "2/10, n/30" means. [5]Encourages taking advantage of the discount in terms of profits for the dealer.

[6,7]Present resale.

[8]Looks confidently forward to future orders.

FIGURE 9-10 Good example of a favorable response to a credit request

1. Use order language in the first sentence. Say, "Please ship," "Please send," "I order," or some other suitable statement that assures the seller of the desire to buy. Avoid indefinite statements like "I'm interested" or "I'd like to."
2. Carefully detail the items ordered. Be specific by mentioning catalog

List two possible interpretations of "I would like to order. . . ."

numbers, prices, colors, sizes, and all other information that will enable the seller to fill the order promptly and without the need for further correspondence.

3. Include a payment plan and shipping instructions. Remember that the shipper is free to ship by the normal method in the absence of specific instructions from the buyer. Tell when, where, and how the order is to be shipped.

4. Close the letter with a confident expectation of delivery.

In large companies, the normal procedure is to use purchase-order forms for ordering. Most consumers buying from direct-marketing companies use the order forms enclosed with catalogs.

The most important thing you can do as a customer is to make sure your order letter or form is complete with every detail. If you sell by mail, you will want to use every work-simplification technique within your means to make the order system foolproof.

In addition to the application of the outline principles, note the physical layout in the order letter in Figure 9-11.

Favorable Response to an Order Letter.   When customers place an order for merchandise, they expect to get exactly what they ordered as quickly as possible. Most orders can be acknowledged by shipping the order; no letter is necessary. For initial orders and for orders that cannot be filled quickly and precisely, companies send *letters of acknowledgment*. Sending individualized letters of acknowledgment is not cost effective and letters do not reach the customer in a timely manner; therefore, companies typically send preprinted letters or a copy of the sales order. An example of a computer-generated sales order is shown in Figure 9-12. Although these forms are impersonal, customers appreciate the company's acknowledging the order and giving them an idea of when the order will arrive.

When are *form* acknowledgments inappropriate?

Nonroutine acknowledgments require individualized letters. Although initial orders can be acknowledged through form letters, the letters are more effective if individually written. If they are well written, these letters will not only acknowledge the order but also create customer goodwill and encourage the customer to place additional orders. Most people who write letters have no difficulty saying "yes"; but because saying "yes" is easy, they may develop the habit of making their letters sound too cold and mechanical (see Figure 9-13).

If a firm is truly grateful for clients' patronage, why not say, "Thank you for your patronage" as the last sentence in all letters to clients?

Is this letter good enough to create customer goodwill or generate future orders? Let's see how the same letter sounds when it confirms shipment of goods in the first sentence, includes concrete resale on the product and business establishment, and eliminates business jargon (see Figure 9-14).

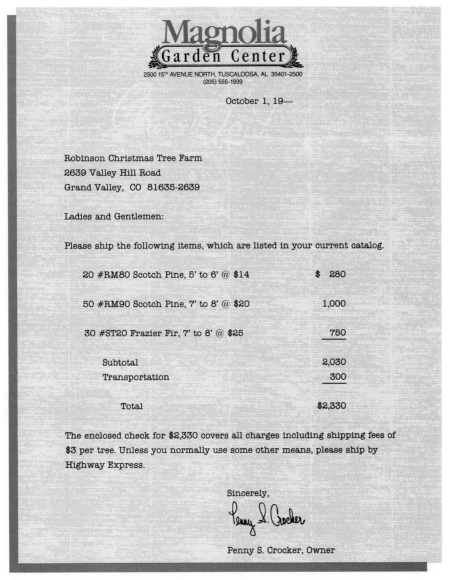

Magnolia
Garden Center
2500 15ᵀᴴ AVENUE NORTH, TUSCALOOSA, AL 35401-2500
(205) 555-1939

October 1, 19—

Robinson Christmas Tree Farm
2639 Valley Hill Road
Grand Valley, CO 81635-2639

Ladies and Gentlemen:

Please ship the following items, which are listed in your current catalog.

20 #RM80 Scotch Pine, 5' to 6' @ $14	$ 280
50 #RM90 Scotch Pine, 7' to 8' @ $20	1,000
30 #ST20 Frazier Fir, 7' to 8' @ $25	750
Subtotal	2,030
Transportation	300
Total	$2,330

The enclosed check for $2,330 covers all charges including shipping fees of
$3 per tree. Unless you normally use some other means, please ship by
Highway Express.

Sincerely,

Penny S. Crocker

Penny S. Crocker, Owner

FIGURE 9-11   Good example of an order letter

A major purpose of the acknowledgment letter is to encourage future orders. An effective technique to achieve this goal is to state that the
merchandise was sent, include resale, and imply that future orders will
be handled in the same manner. Don't expect to encourage future business by just filling the page with words like *welcome* and *gratitude*. They

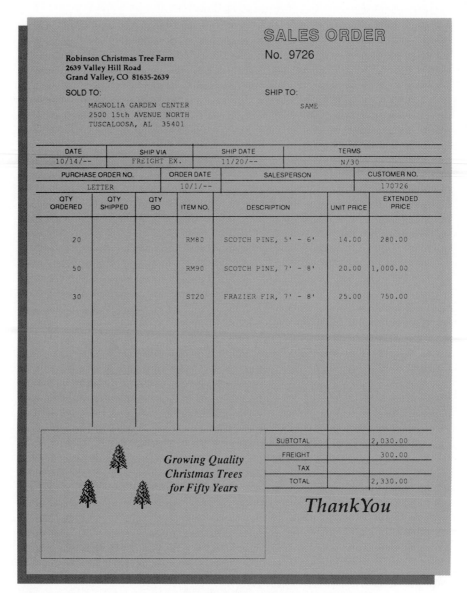

FIGURE 9-12   Good example of a computer-generated sales order

are overused words, and many people whose merchandise and services are poor overwork them. Appropriate action implies both gratitude and welcome. You can emphasize your appreciation by both action and words, but you should be careful. You should strive to make the words sound sincere and original.

**Northern
Electronics
Corporation**

2910 Wilbanks Road
Fairfield, OH 45014-2910
(513) 555-1089
Fax: (513) 555-1123

November 3, 19—

Central Electronics
DX3926 Succ. B
Toronto, Ont.
M5E 157 CANADA

Ladies and Gentlemen:

[1] Thank you for your order, which we really appreciate. [2] We sincerely welcome you to our ever-growing list of satisfied customers.

[3] We were delighted to send you 30 Porta-phone telephones. [4] They were shipped by express today.

[5] We are sure you will find our company a good one to deal with and that our telephones are of the finest quality.

[6] Please find our latest price list enclosed. [7] Thank you for your patronage.

Sincerely,

Vann R. Hamm

Vann R. Hamm
Sales Manager

Enclosures

[1] Begins with a cliché. [2] Says to this customer the same thing that has been said already to thousands of customers.

[3] Sounds exaggerated and thus insincere. [4] Presents main idea that should have been presented earlier.

[5] Includes unsupportable statement of certainty.

[6] Uses a cliché that states the obvious. [7] Ends with a cliché.

FIGURE 9-13   Poor example of a favorable request to an order letter

Letters About Routine Requests

Notice how routine requests and favorable responses to them use the same sequence-of-ideas pattern. Compared with persuasive requests (discussed in Chapter 11), routine requests are shorter.

Northern
Electronics
Corporation

2910 Wilbanks Road
Fairfield, OH 45014-2910
(513) 555-1089
Fax: (513) 555-1123

November 3, 19—

Central Electronics
DX3926 Succ. B
Toronto, Ont.
M5E 1S7 CANADA

Ladies and Gentlemen:

[1] Thirty CS 382 computer systems were shipped to your store by Fastgo Air Express today.

[2] Each unit has been customized according to your specifications. These modifications include **one 5 1/4" disk drive, one 3 1/4" disk drive, math co-processor,** and **memory expansion card to facilitate future memory needs.**

[3] With these distinctive features, these computers will provide your customers with leading-edge technology. [4] The flexibility of this system will allow your customers to take advantage of software innovations quickly and efficiently.

[5] With the custom features of these CS 382s, your customers can work optimally at the office. The NB-1 is available now. This notebook computer has the power your customers will need for work they take home or to other remote locations. [6] Its easy-to-use trackball and backlit liquid crystal display have made the NB-1 a popular portable.

[7] To make this preferred portable technology available to your customers, review the enclosed specifications and complete the enclosed order form. [8] Your order will be shipped immediately.

Sincerely,

Vann R. Hamm

Vann R. Hamm
Sales Manager

[9] Enclosures

[1] Sufficiently implies that the order has been received and filled. Refers to specific merchandise shipped and reveals method of shipment.

[2] Confirms the specific modifications for this customer order.

[3,4] Point out specific qualities of the merchandise (uses resale).

[5–6] Mention related merchandise (use sales-promotional material).

[7,8] Refer to enclosures without using an entire sentence. Imply additional orders are expected.

[9] Uses an enclosure notation to alert reader that other information is included.

FIGURE 9-14   Good example of a favorable request to an order letter

Routine Requests.   Most businesspeople write letters requesting information about people, prices, products, and services. Because the request is a door opener for future business, readers accept it optimistically. At the same time, they arrive at an opinion about the writer based on the quality of the letter. The following outline can serve as a guide for preparing effective requests that are expected to be fulfilled.

1. Make the major request in the first sentence.
2. Follow the major request with the details that will make the request clear. If possible, use tabulations for added emphasis.
3. Close with a forward look to the reader's next step.

Figure 9-15 is a vague request letter. Figure 9-16 is the same request handled more efficiently.

RÅCKLEY
ENGINEERING CONSULTANTS

5932 SOUTH SPARTAN ROAD
HACKENSACK, NJ 07602-1700
(201) 555-8134
FAX (201) 555-1234

December 3, 19—

Ms. Barbara Lane, Project Manager
Rackley Engineering Consultants
23, rue de Penthievre
75008 Paris
FRANCE

Dear Ms. Lane:

[1] For the past five years, I have worked as a staff engineer in the Environmental Group at Rackley. [2] Yesterday I received news of my impending transfer to Paris, France, to work in our plant location there.

[3] I am writing you to ask if you have any advice to help me make my transition to the Paris operation—my first overseas assignment. [4] Because you have been working in the Paris office for the past ten years, I felt you would already know the ropes and could be a great help.

[5] Any advice you can provide would be greatly appreciated.

Sincerely,

Don McClure

Don McClure
Staff Engineer

[1,2]Delay request (the main idea of the letter).

[3]Presents the request vaguely.

[4]The expression *know the ropes* may be difficult to interpret if the reader is from a culture other than the U.S.

[5]Superficial closing.

FIGURE 9-15   Poor example of a routine request

Note that the good example (Figure 9-16) starts with a direct request for specific information. Then it follows with as much detail as necessary to enable the reader to answer specifically. It ends confidently with appreciation for the action requested. The letter is short; but because it conveys enough information and has a tone of politeness, it is long enough.

[1]Illustrates the format of a French address; *rue* is the French word for street.

[2]Uses traditional U.S. salutation because the recipient is North American. *Monsieur* or *Madame* is an appropriate courtesy title when addressing a French man or woman, respectively. In French, *Dear* is used only when the recipient is known well.

[3,4]State request plainly.

[5-7]Ask specific questions; use enumeration for emphasis.

[8-10]Express appreciation and allude to action.

RACKLEY
ENGINEERING CONSULTANTS

5932 SOUTH SPARTAN ROAD
HACKENSACK, NJ 07602-1700
(201) 555-8134
FAX (201) 555-1234

December 3, 19—

[1] Ms. Barbara Lane, Project Manager
Rackley Engineering Consultants
23, rue de Penthievre
75008 Paris
FRANCE

[2] Dear Ms. Lane:

[3] Would you please assist me as I begin plans to transfer to the Environmental Group in the Paris operation—my first overseas assignment? [4] Because you have been working in this overseas location for several years, you may be able to give me some ideas on the following items:

[5]1. Can you suggest a strategy to help me optimize my purchase of francs, especially during the transition period?

[6]2. What degree of proficiency should I have in the French language? If I must speak French fluently, how can I manage until I learn the language?

[7]3. Can you suggest any books or other resources that will prepare my family and me for living abroad?

[8] I will arrive on May 26 to begin work on June 2. [9] Even though my transfer is six months away, my family and I wish to make our transition as smooth as possible. [10] Consequently, receiving this information from you will help us achieve that goal.

Sincerely,

Don McClure

Don McClure
Staff Engineer

FIGURE 9-16 Good example of a routine request

Favorable Response to a Routine Request. "Yes" is so easy to say that many people say it thoughtlessly. The letter in Figure 9-17 grants a request, but it reports the decision without much enthusiasm.

With a little planning and consideration for the executive transferring overseas, the letter in Figure 9-18 could have been written just as quickly.

Why grant a request in the very first sentence?

RĂCKLEY
ENGINEERING CONSULTANTS

23, RUE DE PENTHIEVRE
75008 PARIS, FRANCE
14 555-08-33
FAX 14 555-78-56

December 7, 19—

Mr. Don McClure, Staff Engineer
Rackley Engineering Consultants
5932 South Spartan Road
Hackensack, NJ 07602-1700

Dear Mr. McClure:

[1] I read your request hurriedly and hopefully my response will provide the logistics for your transition to the Paris operation.

[2] The exchange rate fluctuates rapidly; I'd say you will need at least $5,000 for starting expenses. [3] Your other questions are difficult to answer; you'll just have to work them out when you get here. [4] I will introduce you to some of the staff here and help you find your way around on the first day, but after that you're on your own.

[5] May we in the Paris office take this opportunity to welcome you to the overseas operation. [6] We look forward to your arrival on June 2.

Sincerely,

Barbara Lane

Barbara Lane
Project Manager

[1] Focuses on writer; tone suggests lack of interest in helping; vague; uses overly complex word.

[2-4] Not specific or helpful; not directly related to the questions asked.

[5,6] Uses too many words; is unconvincing because the rest of the letter is negative.

FIGURE 9-17   Poor example of a favorable response to a routine request

Occasionally, successful business or professional people are asked special favors. They may receive invitations to speak at various social or school groups. If they say "yes," they might as well say it enthusiastically. Sending an unplanned, stereotyped acceptance suggests that the talk will be in the same style.

RACKLEY
ENGINEERING CONSULTANTS

December 7, 19—

23, RUE DE PENTHIEVRE
75008 PARIS, FRANCE
14 555-08-33
FAX 14 555-78-56

Mr. Don McClure, Staff Engineer
Rackley Engineering Consultants
5932 South Spartan Road
Hackensack, NJ 7602-1700

Dear Mr. McClure:

[1] Congratulations on your transfer to the Paris office. I am happy that we will be working together and am pleased to answer your questions.

[2] 1. The franc has been declining against the U.S. dollar steadily for several weeks, and economists are predicting that this trend will continue. Therefore, I suggest you immediately purchase the francs you will need for the first several months. You can easily keep in touch with the fluctuating exchange rates by reviewing the "Money Rates" section of the Wall Street Journal each day.

[3] 2. English is used most often in the office. You will find it beneficial to become familiar with the French culture, customs, and economy. Several guidebooks are available from the director of International Operations at the home office. I recommend that you read these books thoroughly and share them with your wife and children.

[4] 3. Sam Cassidy has just left the Paris office to work in the Houston office. He would be able to answer many of your questions. You can reach him at (403) 555-1393.

[5] Please fax me your travel plans, and I will make arrangements to meet you at the airport and help you get settled in your new home.

Sincerely,

Barbara Lane

Barbara Lane
Project Manager

[1] Shows sincere interest in the request and the person.

[2, 3] Provide specific answers and guidelines.

[4] Provides additional helpful information.

[5] Specific offer to help communicates genuine interest in the person and his transition.

FIGURE 9-18 Good example of a favorable response to a routine request

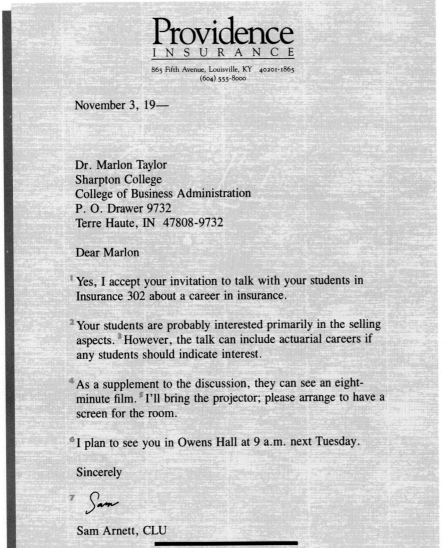

FIGURE 9-19   **Good example of a favorable response to an invitation**

The letter in Figure 9-19 accepts the invitation graciously, presents an idea of the contribution to be made, and ends with a reference to the event at which the speech is to be given.

If responses to invitations were frequent, the preceding letter could be stored on secondary storage (disk or hard drive) of a computer, retrieved, and revised to respond to the next invitation. Individualized form letters produced using computer-based technology enable businesses to communicate quickly and efficiently with clients or customers.

Form letters can save time and money.

Form Letters for Routine Responses.   Governmental agencies, savings and loan companies, banks, public utilities, and other organizations that serve a multitude of people use forms on which a variety of messages appear. To communicate a routine message, an office worker simply places a check mark beside the message that applies. The company's letterhead usually appears at the top of the form; and space is left for keyboarding in the date, recipient's name and address, and account number. The information to be keyboarded appears in parentheses in all-capital letters in the example form in Figure 9-20.

Instead of using forms similar to the letter in Figure 9-20, office personnel could use form paragraphs that have been stored in separate files on secondary storage (disk or hard drive). The originator selects the appropriate paragraphs according to the needs of the recipient. After assembling the selected files on the computer screen, the writer inputs variables (information that changes within the letter). In the example in Figure 9-20, the codes for the variables appear in all-capital letters in parentheses; namely, the inside address, salutation, and account number. A copy of this personalized form letter is printed on letterhead and sent to the recipient.

Form letters are a fast and an efficient way of transmitting frequently recurring messages to which reader reaction is likely favorable or neutral. When a form is designed for check marks in front of applicable sentences (as in Figure 9-20), the first sentence is of necessity introductory. Because the *main* idea is the one by which a check mark appears, the letter isn't in a strict sense deductive (as are the other letters illustrated thus far). For most "good-news" and routine letters, however, deductive writing is preferred. The same is true of memorandums that contain routine information or messages that will draw a favorable reaction.

MEMORANDUMS

Because letters go to people outside a firm and memorandums (commonly referred to as memos) go to people within a firm, their formats are different (see Appendix A for detailed format instructions). A memo needs no return address, inside address, salutation, or complimentary closing. Instead, a typical memo presents (on separate lines) (1) the name of the person *to* whom the message is addressed, (2) the name of the person *from* whom the message comes, (3) the *date,* and (4) the *subject.* When a memo is addressed to more than one person, all their names appear on

LandMark BANK

1900 West Fairway Drive   Lexington, KY   40523-1900
(606) 555-1751

Current Date

(TITLE) (FIRST NAME) (LAST NAME)
(COMPANY)
(ADDRESS)
(CITY), (STATE) (ZIP)

Dear (TITLE) (LAST NAME):

Account No. (ACCOUNT)

We appreciate your inquiry about the late charges assessed against your account. After checking your record of loan payments, we have the following report:

_____   The late charge has been waived because it resulted from circumstances beyond your control.

_____   The late charge appears to be valid; please add the amount to your next monthly payment.

_____   A late charge of $_____ has been waived; however, the following unpaid late charge remains on your account: $_____. Please add the amount to your next monthly payment.

_____Other_____

If your records disagree with ours, please use the enclosed envelope for sending us copies of receipts or checks (both front and back).

Sincerely,

Dennis A. Percy

Dennis A. Percy
Loan Officer

Enclosure

FIGURE 9-20   Good example of a form letter for a routine response

the "TO" line. If the list is long, a common practice is to write "Distribution" on the "TO" line. Then, beneath the last line of the memo, write the word *Distribution* and follow it with an alphabetized list of the names. In addition to simplifying interoffice mailing and reference, alphabetizing eliminates the risk of having someone on the list wonder whether names appear in order of importance.

People who sail for recreation have a language of their own. They communicate using terms like starboard, port, and jib. People who are unfamiliar with these terms cannot communicate without first understanding the jargon. When you communicate within your organization through memos, jargon is acceptable as long as everyone understands the terminology.

Principles of writing (see Chapters 7 and 8) that apply to business letters also apply to memos. An exception is the use of technical jargon, which is more likely to be useful in memorandums. Because people doing similar work are almost sure to know the technical terms associated with it, jargon will be understood, will not be taken as an attempt to impress, and will save time. For the same reasons, acronyms, abbreviations, and shortened forms, such as *typo*, *rep*, and *stat*, are more useful in memos than in letters.

Principles of organizing that apply to letters also apply to memos. In both, empathy is the basis for deciding whether to proceed deductively or inductively. In addition, memos may use other bases for determining the sequence of ideas; for example, time (reporting events in the order in which they happened), order of importance, and geography.

Graphics are appropriate whenever they strengthen your efforts to communicate, regardless of the medium—letter, report, or memo. Tables, graphs, charts, and pictures may be either integrated into the content of the memo or attached as supporting material. Tabulation and enumeration are also useful in memorandums.

The *subject line* (1) tells the reader what the following message is about and (2) sets the stage for the reader to understand the message. The following suggestions should be helpful in preparing subject lines:

1. Make the subject line as long as necessary to do the job. Some people view subject lines as though they were titles of books and try to make them as short as possible. If, for example, your subject is the report of a meeting, "Report of Meeting" is a poor subject line. "Report of June

10 Meeting on Relocation of Dublin Plant" is a better subject line. In addition to aiding understanding, subject lines provide information helpful to file clerks.

2. Take a suggestion from newspaper writers: Think of the five Ws to give you some clues for good subject lines: *Who, What, When, Where,* and *Why.* Key words help in the development of good subject lines.

3. Even though you may write a complete subject line, you should not assume the reader will remember it while reading your memorandum. Opening sentences should not include wording such as "This is. . . ." and "The above-mentioned subject. . . ." The body of the memorandum should be a complete thought in itself and should not rely on the subject line for elaboration; a good opening sentence might be a repetition of most of the subject line. Even if the subject line were omitted, the memorandum would still be clear, logical, and complete.

4. Keyboard the subject line in all-capital letters if additional emphasis is desired.

As you have learned to do in writing letters, write memorandums deductively when they contain good news or neutral information; write inductively when they contain bad news or when they are intended to persuade. (Inductive memos are discussed in greater detail in Chapters 10 and 11.)

COMMUNICATION MENTOR

Along with one-on-one contact with supervisors and peers and skill in group presentations and meetings, your memos will influence the way others view your leadership skills, judgment, and discretion.

The first mistake to avoid is writing too many memos. Avoid documenting events, solely to call attention to your own contribution. (It's better to remind your supervisor informally that you were "pleased to have a role" in the project.) Ask yourself if the information in the memo you are about to write can be communicated just as effectively with a phone call or a brief meeting.

Too many memos is a signal to others that you are overreaching and underachieving.

James F. Hurley
Senior Vice President
CalFed Inc.

Good-News Memorandums

By studying the commentary on well-written examples, you can see ways to avoid certain types of mistakes. To facilitate analysis, the memorandum examples are arranged in the same two-column format used in the discussion of letters.

MAXWELL
CORPORATION

TO: All Employees
FROM: Greg Hamlin, Director of Human Resources *GH*
DATE: December 15, 19—
SUBJECT: ADDITIONAL VACATION DAY

The board of directors has approved one additional vacation day for every employee.

This decision is our way of expressing gratitude for the most productive and profitable year in the history of the Maxwell Corporation. With the approval of your department head, you may select any day between January 2 and June 30. This day of vacation is in addition to year-end bonuses you will receive soon.

Thank you for all you have done to make the year successful, and best wishes for a healthy and happy new year.

329 SHEPARD ROAD ◆ BELLINGHAM, WA 98225-3983 ◆ (206) 555-4000

Commentary:

¹ Gets attention by placing good news in the subject line.

² Begins with the good news. Good news deserves the emphasis that first-sentence position provides.

³ Follows with an explanation.

⁴, ⁵ Continue with details.

⁶ Closes on a pleasant note.

FIGURE 9-21   Good example of a good-news memorandum

Like the letters, the examples are formatted according to standard business formats for memos. Study carefully Appendix A; it contains a detailed explanation and illustrations of the standard formats (traditional and simplified) and layout of memorandums. When you are confident you understand this information, return to this chapter to review the examples.

The memorandum in Figure 9-21 conveys good news. As a good-news message, this memo presents the main idea in the first sentence.

MAXWELL
C O R P O R A T I O N

August 10, 19—

Martha Pearson, Vice President of Operations

ITINERARY FOR GREG HAMLIN

[1] This month, I will be visiting the St. Louis plant to assist the plant manager in preparing next year's budget. [2] My itinerary for the trip follows:

[3] August 21
    Leave Bellingham at 8:15 a.m. by TWA. Arrive in St. Louis at 2:30 p.m.

[4] August 21 to 24
    St. Regis Hotel, St. Louis: (314) 555-3431; FAX (314) 555-6392.
Checkout: August 24, 8 a.m.

[5] August 24
    Leave St. Louis for Bellingham by TWA at 10 a.m. and arrive at 3:30 p.m.

[6] I expect to return to the office on August 25.

GH

Greg Hamlin
Director of Human Resources

[7] c Jim Keger, President

329 SHEPARD ROAD ◆ BELLINGHAM, WA 98225-3983 ◆ (206) 555-4000

[1,2]Begins with main idea. Leads to specifics.

[3—5]Begins by listing departure. List dates, names of hotels, phone numbers, and departure times.

[6]Provides useful information as well as a logical ending.

[7]Includes a copy notation to alert reader that a copy is being sent to someone else.

Illustrates simplified memorandum, a time-saving format.

Includes writer's name and title a quadruple-space below the body. Signature or initials appear in space provided.

FIGURE 9-22   **Good example of itinerary memorandum**

MAXWELL
C O R P O R A T I O N

TO: All Employees

FROM: Greg Hamlin, Director of Human Resources   *GH*

DATE: January 3, 19—

SUBJECT: POLICY FOR EMPLOYEE LOANS

[1] The ad hoc committee in charge of developing a procedure for handling short-term employee loans makes the following proposal:

[2] Policy: All full-time employees may request a loan of up to 25 percent of their normal net pay in case of an emergency.

[3] Procedure: Employees applying for loans take the following steps in the order presented:

[4] 1. Obtain a loan application form (Form PR-7) from the Office of Human Resources, Room 1620.

[5] 2. Complete all blanks in the Employee section of the form.

[6] 3. Submit a memo explaining the exact nature of the emergency and obtain a memo from your supervisor approving the loan.

[7] 4. Submit completed Form PR-7 and the two memos specified in step 3 to the Office of Human Resources, Room 1620.

329 SHEPARD ROAD ◆ BELLINGHAM, WA 98225-3983 ◆ (206) 555-4000

FIGURE 9-23   Good example of a policies and procedures memorandum

[1] Introduces the main idea.

[2] States the proposed policy.

[3] Introduces the upcoming list of steps.

[4–8] Note that time is the basis for sequence and parallelism—all five steps begin with a verb. Each is a complete sentence (subject "you" understood). Appearing in tabulated form with space before and after, each step gets attention. Enumeration both emphasizes and reinforces the desired sequence.

Routine Memorandums

The memo is the most frequently used method of communicating about itineraries, procedures, personnel, and other matters for which a written record is needed.

All Employees
Page 2
January 3, 19—

[8] 5. Pick up your check from the Payroll Department at the time designated in the memo informing you that the loan was approved.

[9] With your approval, we will incorporate this material in the Personnel Policy Manual.

[9]Seeks approval for inclusion in the manual. Because "this material" refers to the preceding statement of policy and procedural steps, its use adds unity to the message.

FIGURE 9-23, continued

Itinerary Memorandum. Before leaving on a long trip, an executive would probably list his or her itinerary in a memo. It would be distributed to the people who would most likely need to communicate with the executive before the travel ends. Figure 9-22 is an example of an itinerary memo.

Policies and Procedures Memorandum. When a proposed change is not controversial or when prior discussion indicates a reader's approval, a memo suggesting change is preferably written deductively, as shown in Figure 9-23.

Memorandums About Personnel Changes.   On or before a newly hired person's first day on the job, an introductory memorandum assists in getting the new relationship off to a good start. Although the memos about personnel changes in Figure 9-24 and Figure 9-25 are short, each would be keyboarded in single-spaced format on a full-size sheet of paper to facilitate efficiency.

Memorandum "To the File."   When information needs to be converted into written form and filed for future reference, the record may be made in memo form (Figure 9-26).

Lengthy memorandum reports may be divided into logical sections. Using headings to denote the divisions will alert the reader to the information that is ahead and make the information easier to comprehend. An example of a memorandum with headings is illustrated in Appendix A.

Although the format of memorandums differs from the format of letters, memorandums and letters use the same principles of style and organization.

Why use standard-size paper for a short memo?

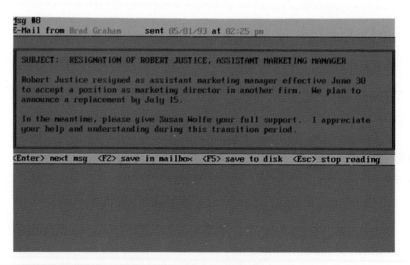

FIGURE 9-24   Good example of a memorandum
about personnel changes

April 2, 19--

All Sales Personnel

APPOINTMENT OF STEPHEN T. WHITE, COMMUNICATIONS
SPECIALIST

[1] I'm pleased to announce the appointment of Stephen T. White as
communications specialist in the corporate communications
department. [2] He will fill the position vacated by Kenneth Furniss
and begin work on May 6.

[3] Steve comes to us from Gynco Industries, where he was in charge
of mass-media relations for the firm. [4] His duties with us will
include long-range planning and liaison with our ad agency,
Smith and Moore. [5] He has college degrees in public relations and
marketing.

[6] Steve certainly merits your full cooperation and support. [7] We
wish him much success and extend a sincere welcome to our
organization.

Brad Graham

Brad Graham
Vice President of Operations

[1] Begins with the main idea. [2] Referring to the one being replaced gives
a general idea of the new employee's responsibilities. Includes
starting date.

[3–5] Provides relative background and
duties. Use of "Steve" suggests that
Mr. White probably prefers to be
addressed by that name instead of
"Stephen" or "Mr. White." Revealing previous responsibilities and educational background could add to
the new employee's initial credibility.

[6, 7] Encourage present employees to be
cooperative and to seek to make
the new employee feel appreciated.

FIGURE 9-25   Good example of a memorandum about personnel changes

April 2, 19—

File

ROD SPECIFICATIONS FOR SHIPPING DOCK,
HINESDALE WAREHOUSE

[1]By telephone today, I confirmed with A. J. Anderson and Son's chief engineer,
Harvey Milstein, that nothing less than 1 3/4-inch reinforcing rods be used in the
support wall of the Hinesdale Warehouse shipping dock. [2]An on-sight inspection
will be made to substantiate this agreement.

Mitchell Cook

Mitchell Cook
Transportation Manager

[1]Records details that may be needed when the subject is discussed later. The record will be discussed, and the act of writing the memo will assist the writer in remembering and using the information. [2]Includes additional information that affects future plans.

Illustrates the simplified memo, a time-saving format for such a routine memorandum.

FIGURE 9-26   Good example of a "to the file" memorandum

SUMMARY

Success in communicating is strongly influenced by a person's empathy. Before beginning to express ideas, the writer (or speaker) needs to answer several questions. What, exactly, is the message going to be? In view of what the message is, how will it affect the receiver? In view of its effect on the receiver, which sequence of ideas is best?

When the receiver can be expected to be *pleased* by the message, the main idea is presented first and details follow. Likewise, when the message is *routine* and not likely to arouse a feeling of pleasure or displeasure, the main idea is presented first (as illustrated in the letters and memorandums in this chapter). When the receiver can be expected to be *displeased* or *not initially interested,* explanations and detail precede the main idea (see Chapters 10 and 11).

From a writer's point of view, the task of writing is simplified if a prior decision has been reached about whether the message should be deductive (main idea first) or inductive (explanations and details first). From a reader's point of view, well-organized messages are easier to understand and promote a more positive attitude toward the writer.

The deductive approach is appropriate for the following types of letters: routine claim letters, routine letters about credit, routine letters about orders, routine requests, and favorable responses to all such routine letters.

The deductive approach is also appropriate for memos that contain good news as the central idea and memos that transmit such nonemotional information as itineraries, noncontroversial changes in policies and procedures, personnel changes, and various types of short reports.

The writing principles that apply to letters also apply to memos. Both are written informally; but memorandums normally make extensive use of jargon, abbreviations, acronyms, and graphics.

REFERENCES

Carnegie, D. (1964). *How to win friends and influence people.* New York: Simon & Schuster.

Hoerr, J., Spiro, L. N., Armstrong, L., & Treece, J. B. (1990, December 17). Culture shock at home: Working for a foreign boss. *Business Week,* pp. 80–81, 84.

Konrad, W. (1990, August 6). Welcome to the woman-friendly company where talent is valued and rewarded. *Business Week,* pp. 49–55.

Moody, P. G. (1987). *Skills for the electronic world—reach a little higher.* Cincinnati: South-Western.

CHECK YOUR WRITING

ROUTINE AND PLEASANT MESSAGES

Content
- ☐ Major idea is clearly identified.
- ☐ Supporting detail is sufficient.
- ☐ Facts or figures are accurate.
- ☐ Message is ethical and abides by any legal requirements.

Organization
- ☐ Major idea is in the first sentence.
- ☐ Supporting details are in the most appropriate sequence.
- ☐ Final sentence (in a letter) seems appropriate for an ending.

Style
- ☐ Words will be readily understood.
- ☐ Syntax is acceptable.
- ☐ Sentences are relatively short.
- ☐ Variety appears in sentence length and structure.
- ☐ Significant words are in emphatic positions.
- ☐ Significant or positive thoughts are stated in simple sentences or in independent clauses.
- ☐ Grammar is acceptable.
- ☐ Active voice predominates.
- ☐ First person is used sparingly or not at all.
- ☐ Ideas cohere (changes in thought are not abrupt).
- ☐ Expression is original (sentences are not copied directly from the definition of the problem or from sample letters in text; clichés are avoided).

Mechanics
- ☐ Keyboarding, spelling, grammar, and punctuation are perfect.
- ☐ Paragraphs are relatively short.

Letters
- ☐ Letter style is acceptable (block, modified block, or simplified).
- ☐ Letter is balanced on page.
- ☐ Letter parts are in appropriate vertical and horizontal position.
- ☐ Return address (if plain paper is used)
- ☐ Date
- ☐ Inside address
- ☐ Salutation (if needed for letter style used)
- ☐ Subject line (if needed)
- ☐ Complimentary close (if needed for letter style used)
- ☐ Keyboarded name (and title)
- ☐ Letter is signed legibly
- ☐ Reference initials (if needed)
- ☐ Enclosure notation (if needed)
- ☐ Other special letter parts (if needed)

Memorandums
- ☐ *TO, FROM, DATE,* and *SUBJECT* information is included.
- ☐ Side margins are consistent.
- ☐ Courtesy titles are omitted on TO and FROM lines.
- ☐ Lines are single spaced; blank space appears between paragraphs; paragraphs are not indented.
- ☐ Tabulated sentences or columns are indented.
- ☐ Handwritten initials are placed by name on the FROM line or signed in the space provided in the simplified format.

REVIEW QUESTIONS

1. What is your definition of empathy?
2. How does empathy assist in the organization of letters and memorandums?
3. To a writer, what are the advantages of outlining before beginning to write?
4. What is the distinction between deductive and inductive writing?
5. What questions should be answered before a writer decides whether to write deductively or inductively?
6. For a letter or memo that transmits good news, what are the advantages of placing the good news in the first sentence?
7. In the text, what word is used to label messages that are essential but convey neither bad news nor good news?
8. Are the outlines recommended for written messages applicable to oral messages?
9. What term is used to label responses to claim letters?
10. What is the difference between resale and sales-promotional material? Provide an example of each.
11. In which is tabulation more likely to be used: (a) a claim letter or (b) an order letter?
12. Why is business jargon more likely to be useful in memos than in letters?
13. What purpose is served by writing memos "to the file"?
14. Do principles of organizing applied in the writing of letters also apply in the writing of memos? Explain.
15. Are acronyms, shortened words, and graphics useful in memos? Why?

GENERAL WRITING GUIDELINES

In composing solutions to the exercises, applications, and cases in this and the remaining chapters about letters and memorandums, proceed in the following manner:

1. Study this chapter before composing your letters and memorandums. Look primarily for principles that can be applied (not for expressions or sentences that might possibly be paraphrased or used word for word in the letter to be composed).

2. Study the writing problem until you understand the facts.

3. Assume you are the person facing the writing problem.

4. Anticipate reader reaction, and jot down on scratch paper the outline you will use.

5. Compose rapidly without looking at the definition of the problem and without looking at sample letters from the text. A sentence written to *define* a letter-writing problem may not be appropriate in a letter designed to *solve* the problem. Concentrate on planning and expressing ideas in such a way as to achieve clarity and to promote good human relations.

6. Before keyboarding the letter, refer to the definition of the problem for such specifics as names, addresses, and amounts. The name and address that is to be used as an inside address on your letter appears at the end of each problem. Names and addresses are strictly fictitious. Unless otherwise instructed, keyboard your own name as the sender.

7. Exercise discretion in selecting the information that you will reveal to the reader. Identify the information the reader actually needs to respond to your message. Consider the confidentiality of the information revealed.

8. Consider the legal and ethical implications of your message. If necessary, investigate the problem to identify possible legal requirements for the message you are writing. Using the principles and ethical theories that parallel your own moral system, select an ethical action and write the appropriate message.

9. Reread your message carefully to be certain that you have expressed ideas clearly, stated unpleasant ideas tactfully and positively, included complete and accurate information, supported your ideas with objective facts, did not embellish or exaggerate the facts, and designed graphics to avoid distorting the facts.

10. Unless otherwise instructed, keyboard the letter or memo according to the formatting instructions provided in Appendix A. Review carefully the placement of the standard parts of the letter, the three acceptable business formats (block, modified block, and simplified), the two punctuation types (open and closed), and the special letter parts required in particular situations (return address needed for a letter written by consumer who would probably not have letterhead, attention line, subject, copy notations, and others). Other information that will be helpful from Appendix A are two-letter state abbreviations, word division rules, abbreviation rules, and keyboarding rules (number of spaces after punctuation), and proofreaders' marks.

GENERAL WRITING GUIDELINES

11. Before handing in an assignment, refer to the "Check Your Writing" checklist at the end of the chapter. By checking your letter against the list, you will either (1) gain confidence that your letter meets high standards, or (2) identify any changes that need to be made.

Thoughtful use of the checklist has the short-range effect of improving your grade on the assignment being handed in. Its use with all assignments has the long-range effect of indelibly stamping in your mind the four qualities that all of your subsequent writing should have:

◆ The *right* ideas with sufficient support (content).
◆ The best *sequence* of ideas for clear understanding and human relations (organization).
◆ The most appropriate ways to *express* ideas in words and sentences (style).
◆ High *standards* in putting words on paper—keyboarding, spelling, and punctuating (mechanics).

EXERCISES

1. Find an example of both a well-written and a poorly written good-news letter or memorandum. Analyze the strengths and weaknesses of each document. Be prepared to discuss them in class.

2. Analyze the effectiveness of the following sentences from a good-news message.
   a. The outstanding color graphics and charts were prepared and faxed to us by Jacob Hall, one of our staff accountants.
   b. We offer you the position effective November 1 provided you return these forms by October 12.
   c. After much deliberation, my office decided to approve your transfer to Dublin, Ireland.
   d. The convention agenda was prepared by the girls in the office.
   e. Enclosed please find a stamped, self-addressed envelope for returning the completed credit application.

3. Analyze the effectiveness of the following opening sentences for a good-news message.
   a. This letter is in response to your application for credit dated June 30; your application has now been received.
   b. Our company prides itself on its customer relations department; therefore, we have decided to return your payment for the merchandise in question.
   c. We are sure you will enjoy the requested introductory software package, even though it has been made obsolete by our latest line of programs.
   d. Although we have decided to grant your credit request, we caution you (along with all of our customers) to use your credit wisely.
   e. I am writing this informal memo to tell you that the controller, Peter Johnson, said that each department's final budget must be submitted by June 1.

4. Prepare a deductive outline to accept the invitation on the next page. You need to know the exact time the dinner will begin. Does a reception precede the dinner as it did two years ago? The earliest you can arrive is 6:30 p.m. The title of your speech will be "Social Security: Will It Be There When *You* Retire?"

5. Analyze the letter on page 346. Pinpoint its strengths and weaknesses and then revise the letter.

APPLICATIONS

ANCE	MANAGEMENT	MIS	CONS
Ethics	International	Legal	In

1. **Customized Drinking Cups Are Wrong Size.** Athletic concessions at Spinner College placed an order for 50,000 twenty-ounce plastic cups at 15 cents each from Custom Plastics Products. Each cup was to

MAXWELL

C O R P O R A T I O N

September 1, 19 __

Mr. Fred Thompson
P. O. Box 3783
Philadelphia, PA 19105-3783

Dear Mr. Thompson:

You can be extremely helpful to the members of the Lakewood
Civic Club. On October 17 at 6 p.m. we are holding our annual
interchapter meeting with three chapters in nearby cities.

We are excited at the prospect of having you speak on a
current topic of your choice as you did two years ago. We can
offer you good fellowship, a great audience, an excellent
dinner, and a $200 honorarium.

Please let me know that you will accept the invitation. I'd also
like to have a title for your talk to use in our program and in
our correspondence to the guest chapters. May I have your
response soon?

Sincerely,

Mrs. Marty St. Clair

Mrs. Marty St. Clair
Program Chair

329 SHEPARD ROAD ◆ BELLINGHAM, WA 98225-3983 ◆ (206) 555-4000

Exercise 4

be imprinted with the college's mascot and this year's basketball slogan, "Soaring to New Heights." When the concessions manager was
inspecting the order, he immediately noticed that the vendor had
sent 16-ounce cups and not the 20-ounce cups that were ordered. Because concession items must be priced in 50-cent intervals to expedite
service time, the regular drink price of $1.50 cannot be adjusted to
reflect the reduced quantity. After serious consideration, the manager

RICHARD LOCKETT
CERTIFIED PUBLIC ACCOUNTANT
P.O. Box 3943, DECATUR, IL 62525-3943
(217) 555-4528

June 21, 19—

Christopher Simpson, Manager
Magnum State Bank
P. O. Drawer 3919
Decatur, IL 62525-4312

Dear Mr. Simpson

This letter is in reply to your questions concerning the deductibility of your educational expenses. We have researched this tax question carefully.

According to Section 162 of the Internal Revenue Code, educational expenses (college tuition, books, supplies, etc.) are not deductible for a person who is acquiring skills to begin a new career. However, you explained that your employer is requiring you to take international business and computer applications courses to enhance your ability to work in your present field. Consequently, your educational expenses are deductible.

We look forward to working with you in the future.

Sincerely,

Richard Lockett

Richard Lockett, CPA

Exercise 5

decided that selling the 16-ounce drink for the same price would be inadvisable. Basketball season starts in only two weeks; therefore, the manager must act quickly.

Required: As the concessions manager, write the vendor explaining the error in the shipment and asking that the order be filled correctly and quickly. Address the letter to Custom Plastics Products, 1200 Ridgewood Road, Springfield, MO 65808-1200.

2. **Correct-Size Cups Are on the Way.** The claims manager at Custom Plastics Products was concerned when he learned of the error made in producing the plastic cups for Spinner College (Application 1). Working at peak levels for the past three weeks, the workers made a simple but rather costly mistake. However, the immediate problem is to give this order a priority rating and get it out to Spinner College, a long-standing customer, in time for the first basketball game.

Required: Write the concessions manager at Spinner College explaining the mistake and apologizing for the inconvenience. Assure him that the correct order will reach him on time and instruct him to return the 16-ounce cups at the company's expense. Address the letter to Dustin Blanton, Spinner College, Athletic Department, P. O. Drawer 2193, Topeka, KS 66601-2193.

MARKETING	PUBLIC RELATIONS	
erpersonal	Technology	Public S

3. **Volume Is Missing: Routine Claim.** Albert Waterson, a World War II veteran, responded to a magazine ad by placing an order for a 24-volume set of World War II encyclopedias. When they were delivered, Volume 18 was missing. Mr. Waterson feels sure the publisher will send Volume 18 as soon as the omission is called to its attention; no persuasion is necessary. He still has a copy of the shipping invoice, which was received with the other volumes. This document will provide needed details about the transaction.

Required: As Mr. Waterson, write a letter to the publisher mentioning that you are including the invoice. Include Mr. Waterson's return address: 412 East Jefferson Street, Wellsville, IA 50116-0412. Address the letter to Heritage House Publishers, Inc., 432 Edgewood Plaza, Meade, OH 43543-0432.

MENT	MIS	CONSUMER	HUMAN
Ethics	International	Legal	Ir

4. **Missing Volume Coming Soon: Favorable Response to Claim.** Heritage House Publishers (Application 3) had not included Volume 18 because it had not been released from the printer. Because of its complex graphics, the volume had required more production time than other volumes. A note of explanation (which Mr. Waterson had apparently overlooked) had been included in the shipment. The missing volume will be shipped within four weeks.

Required: Write a short letter, with which you plan to include a brochure about a soon-to-be-completed volume about the history of the U.S. Calvary. Use your name as manager of the shipping department. Mr. Waterson's address: 412 East Jefferson Street, Wellsville, IA 50116-0412.

MARKETING	PUBLIC RELATIONS	
iterpersonal	Technology	Publi

5. **Order Does Not Meet Minimum Standards: Routine Claim.** As standard procedure, the quality-control department at Walker Manufacturing, Inc. tested a randomly selected sample of an order of

RANCE	MANAGEMENT	MIS	CON
Ethics	International	Legal	I

10,000 ASTM A 325 connection pad bolts received from Sprigner Metals Corporation. Because these bolts connect the ends of the frame to the rafter of the company's prefabricated storage buildings, the reliability of the bolts is critical. To meet minimum standards, the connection pad bolts ($\frac{3}{4}$" by $2\frac{1}{2}$") must withstand 40,100 pounds of pressure per square inch. Of the 78 bolts tested, 5 bolts stripped; thus, the number of defective bolts exceeded the required 99-percent confidence level. Therefore, the entire shipment must be rejected and returned.

Required: As the manager of the shipping department, return the shipment. Mention the sales invoice (#73-31-3444) you are including to identify the order. Address the letter to Sprigner Metals Corporation, 1985 Northland Road, Chattanooga, TN 37401-1985.

NCE	MANAGEMENT	MIS	CONSU
Ethics	International	Legal	Ir

6. **Apology for Error in Order.**   As soon as Sprigner Metals Corporation received the letter from the shipping department manager (Application 5), the quality-control manager began investigating the problem. Finally, the manager discovered that the problem was quite simple: the order was inadvertently filled with bolts of a lesser quality than those ordered.

Required: Write the shipping department manager at Walker Manufacturing explaining the mistake and apologizing for the inconvenience. Because Walker Manufacturing is a long-time customer, you must attempt to regain the goodwill that has been lost. Address the letter to Walker Manufacturing, Inc., 8900 Blackburn Road, Windsor, NC 27983-8900.

MARKETING	PUBLIC RELATIONS	I
Ethics	International	Legal

7. **A New Business Venture: Request for Credit.**   Within three months, you will receive your degree in construction engineering. You plan to begin constructing new homes in a city 100 miles from your school. On your most recent trip to that city, you picked up credit-application forms from one of its building-supply stores. After completing the forms, you are confident you will be granted credit privileges.

Required: Write a letter to accompany the forms you are mailing to the store: Home Building & Supply, P. O. Box 21, Baxterville, KS 67891-3703.

MARKETING	PUBLIC RELATIONS	F
Interpersonal	Technology	Publi

8. **Credit Approval for Construction Engineer.**   The construction engineer's application (Application 7) has been approved. Initially, the engineer's credit limit is $100,000. As her construction projects expand, the limit can be raised if necessary. Home Building & Supply has prepared a pamphlet that gives details of the credit terms.

Required: As an official of the firm, write a letter conveying the good news. Call the engineer's attention to the enclosed credit-terms pamphlet. (Constructing the pamphlet is not part of your assignment; assume that it has been prepared already.) Ms. Carol S. Goodman, Room 347 Irish Hall, Southstate University, Woodland, NE 68451-9731.

9. **Credit Information Needed to Approve Line of Credit.** Burns Construction has requested a line of credit for building materials from your company, Thompson Building Supply.

Required: As the building supply manager, write a letter requesting Burns's credit records from its credit reference, Mobile Brickyard. The letter should adhere to all legal guidelines relating to credit requests. Mobile Brickyard, 1279 McKnight Road, Mobile, AL 36609-1279.

ELATIONS	FINANCE	ACCOUNTING
International	Legal	Interperso

10. **Order for Staff/Alumni Reception.** Nancy Martin, administrative assistant to the partner in charge, is responsible for planning the annual staff/alumni reception for Brooks and Lincoln, a regional accounting firm. Arrangements already have been made to hold this annual event at the Palm Garden Inn, one of the city's preferred hotels, on Saturday, June 27, from 7 to 9 p.m. During Nancy's initial tour of the facility, the restaurant manager gave her a complete menu including prices and asked that she place her order by May 30. He also reminded her to add to the order 7 percent sales tax and 17 percent service charge on all food and beverages.

NCE	MANAGEMENT	MIS	CONSU
Ethics	International	Legal	

   After reviewing the menu and consulting several others at the office, Nancy decides to place an order for the following items: 1 assorted international cheese tray with fruits and crackers at $125, 1 display of fresh garden vegetables served with assorted dips at $75, 1 iced jumbo gulf shrimp tray with cocktail sauce at $160, 1 baked Virginia ham tray with rolls and condiments (approximately 80 portions) at $150, 1 assorted gourmet cookie and candy tray at $50, 6 pounds of fancy mixed nuts at $14 per pound, 8 gallons of fruit punch at $18 per gallon, 1 gallon of regular coffee at $22.50, and 1 gallon of decaffeinated coffee at $22.50.

Required: Write the order letter that Nancy Martin sends to The Palm Garden Inn, 1083 Central Avenue, Winter Haven, FL 32789-1003.

11. **Error in Billing: Letter Requesting Correction.** When Ron McNeil, the accounts payable clerk at Metal Fabricators, Inc., paid the November 10 invoice to Newton Plastics on November 15, he deducted the 2-percent discount given when customers pay total invoices within 10 days (credit terms are 2/10; n/30). Today, Ron received a statement from Newton Plastics requesting payment for $159.30, the amount of the 2-percent discount.

NANCE	ACCOUNTING	INSURANCE
ersonal	Technology	Public Sect

Required: As Ron McNeil, the accounts payable clerk, write a letter of explanation to Newton Plastics Corp., 800 New Light Road, Appleton, WI 54911-2703. Mention the documents Ron will include to verify the company's right to the discount.

MARKETING	PUBLIC RELATIONS	
Ethics	International	Legal

12. **Successful Sales Campaign: Letter to Parent Company.**   You are the senior marketing consultant for an international computer company with offices in Finland, England, France, and Japan. Six months ago you initiated a new sales campaign for promoting your medical office software in the Finnish market. The results have been excellent; for example, measures of success have included increases in sales, in percentage of orders and personal calls resulting from receipt of demonstration disks, and in percentage of sales calls resulting in an order.

Required: Write a letter to the head of the U.S. office stating the good news and including specific details about the effectiveness of this campaign. Address the letter to Mitchell Grayson, Systems, Inc., 705 Westbrook Street, Evansville, IN 47711-7711.

IENT	REAL ESTATE	ADVERTISING
nal	Technology	Public Sector

13. **Video Presentations Expedite Real Estate Showings.**   Vintor Development Corporation is completing final stages of its prototype of a technological advance in the real estate business. Within the next two years, prospective buyers can view video presentations of available homes. At last, you, the marketing manager, have been given approval to begin initial promotion of this product. Because this technology will greatly affect the manner in which real estate transactions are conducted (video presentations in the office rather than endless hours transporting buyers from site to site), you realize that the first stage of promotion is educating realtors. In other words, your purpose is not to sell; instead, your purpose is to introduce the new technology, discuss its capabilities (benefits to realtor, buyer, and seller), and encourage realtors to consider this technology as they make long-range plans, especially in terms of computer capabilities.

Required: As the marketing manager, write a form letter to area realtors. Address the sample letter to Ms. Reed Hubbard, Broker-Owner, South Realty Company, 9837 22nd Avenue North, Champlin, MN 55316-9837.

CE	ACCOUNTING	INSURANCE	M
Interpersonal	Technology	Pu	

14. **Routine Request for Accommodations During an Annual Audit.** Laird and Herrington, CPAs, is preparing for its annual financial audit of Salina Processors, Inc. The staff will work in the client's office for three weeks beginning March 1. To facilitate an efficient and cost-effective audit, you as the audit manager plan to write to the controller at Salina requesting specific arrangements. The four accountants will need adequate work space during the three-week audit. A guided tour of the production facilities should be planned for the first day of the visit. For the first time, you are recom-

mending that the client arrange to have bills for the accountants' hotel accommodations sent directly to Salina. This procedure will save the client the 10 percent added to the audit fee to cover the cost of processing these charges.

Required: As the audit manager, write a letter to Douglas Webb, the controller, outlining these specific arrangements. Salina Processors, Inc., 9334 Tower Building, Wichita, KS 67202-9334.

15. **MIS Internships Are Available.** Cynthia Richton, college liaison officer for Oxford Petrochemical Corporation, is planning the search for applicants for the company's summer internship program in management and information systems. In the past, an announcement was sent to the department heads of the Management Information Systems departments of colleges and universities in a 12-state area. To create greater interest in the internship program (and hopefully attract more applicants), Cynthia intends to write a cover letter to accompany the announcement. The letter will highlight selected information on the announcement and suggest ways to communicate the internship opportunities to the students. Cynthia has just finished revising last year's announcement using the company's newly acquired desktop publishing software and laser printer; she is confident that this version is more appealing and will attract more attention than previous versions (see announcement on the next page).

NAGEMENT	MIS	CONSUMER	HUM
onal	Technology	Public Sector	

Required:

1. Decide which information contained in the announcement should be included in the cover letter to the department heads.
2. Compose the cover letter to department heads. Address the sample letter to Professor Ed Mitchell, Central State College, Management Information Systems, P. O. Drawer 1798, Dow, OK 74541-7931.

16. **Insurance Claim: Routine Information.** As Elda Smith, you must write a letter about her late husband's deferred compensation plan. She has already called the office where the plan is administered. Elda has a choice: (1) Leave the money on deposit and let it earn interest until her husband would have reached 65 (about 10 years from now), or (2) accept a check now for the current value ($15,586). Elda expressed preference for the first choice, but the office needs written authorization with Elda's signature.

NG	INSURANCE	MANAGEMENT	N
onal	Technology	Public Sector	

Required: As Elda Smith, write the letter. Address it to Charles Edwards, Manager, Missouri Deferred Compensation Plan, P. O. Box 1310, Jefferson City, MO 65314-1310.

17. **Investment Decision: Request for Information.** In response to an ad in a financial journal, George Wilson called a toll-free number and

C RELATIONS	FINANCE	ACCOUNT
onal	Technology	Public Sector

Internships in Management Information Systems

Available for Summer 19—

Oxford Petrochemical Corporation
Houston, Texas

Description

Petrochemical Corporation is a leading manufacturer of interactive computer graphics systems. Product lines range from microprocessors to workstations and specific systems for computer-aided engineering and manufacturing applications.

Interns will assist in the development of software for manufacturing applications and will report directly to the director of Information Systems.

Timeframe:	May 15 to August 15
Location:	Corporate headquarters, Houston, Texas
Provisions:	$15 per hour/35-hour week
	Three months' lodging in a one-bedroom efficiency suite within five miles of corporate headquarters at company expense.

Applicant Requirements

- Completed junior year of study with 3.5 (on a 4.0 scale) or better GPA in management information systems.
- Proficiency in DOS-based operating systems, word processing, spreadsheet, data base, and graphics software.
- Proficiency in software development using "C" and "C ' ' " in a Unix environment.

Application Procedures

Submit a resume, official transcript, and two letters of recommendation to the following address:

Ms. Cynthia Richton
College Liaison Officer
Oxford Petrochemical Corporation
2900 Commerce Parkway
Houston, TX 77002-2900
(713) 555-0311

All applications must be postmarked no later than March 30, 19—.

Application 15

asked that a prospectus be sent to him. As one of the vice presidents in charge of the Yield-Right Fund, you have decided to include a personalized letter with the prospectus. (This form letter is stored on disk and used in response to all requests for this prospectus.) Although the prospectus contains complete details of the proposed investment, one point is selected to be included in the letter (a point that deserves great emphasis): The *Delphi Money Fund Report* has rated Yield-Right as the top performer of all money-market funds (with similar investment criteria) for the 12-month period ending October 31 of the current year.

Required: Write the sample form letter. Address it to George Wilson, 454 North 37th Avenue, Weston, PA 13342-9454.

18. **Request for Product Information.** A recent publication has a picture of a product in which you have a special interest. If you had appropriate answers to certain questions, you might order the product.

MIS	CONSUMER	HUMAN RESOUF
ersonal	Technology	Public Sec

Required: Write a letter to the manufacturer. Ask at least three questions. Consider using enumerations to emphasize the questions. For example, number the questions or precede them with bullets (*, —, •, √, ▪, etc.) and indent the text five spaces from both margins.

19. **Survey of Customer Satisfaction.** The service department of Boykin Motors has noticed that a large percentage of car owners are not returning their cars for service after the initial warranty expires. In an attempt to determine the reason for this trend, the service manager has developed a questionnaire to send to car owners whose warranty has expired. Only five questions are asked; four of them require only a check-mark response and the fifth invites a written comment if the respondent chooses. A postage-paid envelope is included. As an incentive to complete the questionnaire, respondents are offered a free winterization checkup for their vehicles.

MARKETING	PUBLIC RELATIONS	I
cs	International	Legal	Interp

Required: Compose a form letter that invites car owners to complete and return the attached questionnaire. (Assume the questionnaire is already prepared; it is not a part of the writing assignment.) Address the sample letter to Ms. Reed Campbell, 2931 Sherwood Road, Rigby, ID 83442-2931.

20. **Employee's Ethical Action Boosts Company's Integrity: Memo of Support.** While involved in the annual financial audit of Longford Stores, Inc., Gail Ming, a junior accountant in your Chicago-based accounting firm, discovered massive embezzlement. As a result of this discovery, the people involved in the crime were convicted. Today, Longford Stores terminated the firm's audit services and engaged a new auditor. As the firm's audit partner, you are unsure how Gail might react to this news.

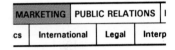

FINANCE	ACCOUNTING	INSURAN(
Ethics	International	Legal

Required: Write a memo to Gail commending her for her outstanding performance and assuring her that the firm's integrity will far outweigh this immediate financial loss.

21. **Memorandum Announcing Major Change in Operations.** On March, 19—, the board of directors approved the expenditure of resources to convert to optical scanners to track the flow of production

CE	MANAGEMENT	MIS	CONSUMI
onal	Technology	Public Sector

through the plant. After extensive research (including information from a quality circle of employees directly involved in the work flow), the vice president of information systems ordered the appropriate hardware. All equipment needed for the conversion has arrived. The vice president of information systems anticipates that approximately one month will be needed to install and test the equipment. To facilitate a smooth transition, he believes it is time for the supervisors to prepare the employees for the conversion.

Required

1. Consider the appropriate strategy (procedures) for informing employees of a major change in their day-to-day operations. Consult academic and practitioner journals for information related to employee resistance to change.
2. Write the memo to the supervisors.

22. **New Insurance Carrier Announced.** You are the director of human resources for Intertech, a computer manufacturer employing 1,300 people. You have changed insurance carriers recently (from Barnes & Ward to Thornton Insurance Company) to take advantage of lower premiums without reducing coverage. Thornton Insurance Co. will bill Intertech for its portion of the insurance premium on a quarterly rather than a monthly basis. In return for the reduced premium, Intertech will assume responsibility of verifying the validity of the policyholders and dependents. Unlike the previous carrier, Thornton requires pre-approval for nonemergency hospitalization; a brochure explaining detailed procedures will be distributed to each policyholder. With the new plan, the annual deductible is reduced from $500 to $250 annually (for the policyholder and each dependent).

Required:

1. Decide what information should be included in the memorandum informing employees of the change of insurance carrier.
2. Compose the memo to all employees.

23. **Steps to Minimize VDT Radiation Outlined in a Procedures Memo.** You are the office manager for a brokerage firm whose employees work at computer terminals for extended periods. Research you have recently read has drawn weak links between high exposure to the electromagnetic radiation from computer terminals and cancer or miscarriage in lab animals, but researchers are quite certain that a specific link will be identified in the years to come. The researchers suggested methods to minimize the exposure: redesign the office arrangement to prevent direct exposure to the backs of monitors, where radiation levels are highest; and test the actual radiation levels of terminals to see if they reach the intensity rated as most dangerous (2 to 3 units of strength, mG). By far, the easiest method of minimization is to counsel operators to move away from the monitor (an arm's length

is recommended), adjusting the placement of the keyboard as needed. Another option is to purchase new monitors with lower emissions.

Required: Concerned for the health of your employees but also aware of the financial condition of your firm, write a procedural memo to outline steps the company will initiate to minimize the effect of VDT radiation. You feel certain that options other than the ones listed are available if you research the topic more thoroughly.

24. **Approval to Hire Additional Sales Personnel.**   In the Ashland store of the Markens Art Company last season, business was exceedingly good, especially during the months in which theaters were open for staged productions of famous plays. This year's productions promise to be even more appealing. Many who come to see the plays will have an interest in art. In preparation for the busy season, Pauline Welch, store manager, has requested permission to hire two additional salespeople and an additional record keeper. She included convincing data about the workload, the amount of money spent for overtime last season, and other factors.

HUMAN RESOURCES MANAGEMENT		
onal	Technology	Public Sector

Required: As if you were Paul Adams, director of human resources at Markens, write a memo to Pauline Welch. Let her know that her request is approved, that the new employees can be placed on the payroll as soon as the theater season begins, and that the guidelines for selection (of which she has a copy) are still in effect.

25. **Memo Announcing Earthquake Preparedness Plan.**   Recently, earthquake tremors have been jarring your community of Evansville, Indiana. As personnel manager for Dorney & Associates, located in the high-rise Aldridge Building, you decide to communicate your company's earthquake preparedness plan to all employees. A documentary on public television offered several procedures on how to react during an earthquake. The following suggestions were included in the program: (1) Elevators should not be used. (2) Fire alarms or sprinkler systems may activate and startle people. (3) Earthquakes do not kill; buildings do. (4) If outside, open areas are safer than areas near wires, signs, buildings, or trees. (5) If people are in the office, they should drop to the floor, take cover under their desk, and ride out the tremor. (6) If no desks or tables are near, people should seek cover against an interior wall. (6) Windows, glass doors, tall furniture, and hanging objects should be avoided.

HUMAN RESOURCES MANAGEMENT		
International	Legal	Interpers

Required:
1. Consider the content of the memorandum. Which of the suggestions provided are pertinent to your company? Can you provide other suggestions? Consult professional literature related to earthquake preparedness to support your decision.
2. Write the memo to the employees communicating your company's earthquake preparedness plan.

CASE FOR ANALYSIS

UBLIC RELATIONS	FINANCE	ACCO
Ethics	International	Legal

Case 1.   Analyzing an Ethical Situation: A Sound Decision or a Clever Way Out?   In an effort to secure a large investment account, Harrelson Inc. has decided to host a weekend boating expedition for a select group of prospective clients.

Today you received the following electronic message from your supervisor.

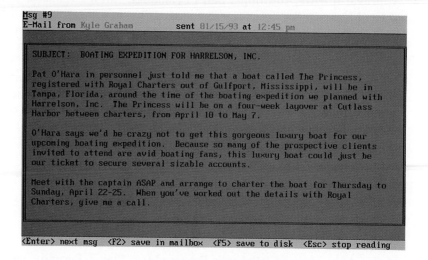

```
Msg #9
E-Mail from Kyle Graham          sent 01/15/93 at 12:45 pm

 SUBJECT:  BOATING EXPEDITION FOR HARRELSON, INC.

 Pat O'Hara in personnel just told me that a boat called The Princess,
 registered with Royal Charters out of Gulfport, Mississippi, will be in
 Tampa, Florida, around the time of the boating expedition we planned with
 Harrelson, Inc.  The Princess will be on a four-week layover at Cutlass
 Harbor between charters, from April 10 to May 7.

 O'Hara says we'd be crazy not to get this gorgeous luxury boat for our
 upcoming boating expedition.  Because so many of the prospective clients
 invited to attend are avid boating fans, this luxury boat could just be
 our ticket to secure several sizable accounts.

 Meet with the captain ASAP and arrange to charter the boat for Thursday to
 Sunday, April 22-25.  When you've worked out the details with Royal
 Charters, give me a call.


<Enter> next msg  <F2> save in mailbox  <F5> save to disk  <Esc> stop reading
```

When you reached the captain, he explained that the owner does not usually allow unscheduled charters. After you convinced him of the importance of chartering *The Princess* for this expedition, the captain offered to let you charter the boat for $1,000 a day (normal rate is $2,000). He assured you he would submit the money to the owner and explain the situation when he returned to the home port.

Required:
1. Decide whether it is ethical to accept the captain's offer. Consider these points:
   a. What are the relevant facts?
   b. What are the ethical issues raised by the decision to charter the boat under these circumstances?
   c. Who (which stakeholders) will be affected by this decision?
   d. What are the costs and benefits imposed by each alternative on each person listed in step (c)?
   e. What are the firm's obligations to each person listed in step (c)?
   f. What should you as the firm's representative do?
2. Based on your decision, complete *one* of the following:
   a. Write to the captain accepting the offer to charter the boat, confirming the $1,000 rate, and providing details about the dates.

Decide whether any other information should be included to ensure that the captain fulfills his side of this verbal contract. Address the letter to Bryan Martinez, 234 Sandy Beach Road, Tampa, FL 33602-2098.

b. Having decided to refuse the captain's offer, write a persuasive letter to the owner requesting a special charter. Based on your ethical analysis, decide whether to mention the captain's offer. Address the letter to Andrew Robinelli, Royal Charters, 4029 Beach Drive, Gulfport, MS 39507-0234.

c. Do any other options exist? If so, write the letter or memo to the appropriate person.

3. Awaiting a reply from the owner or the captain (depending on the decision made in step 2), write a persuasive memo to your supervisor (Kyle Graham) informing him of your action and including your analysis of this ethical situation.

Case 2. Communicating Concern for Employees. At this week's staff meeting, several of the managers commented that employee morale was quite low and that employees were producing at suboptimal rates. The controller quickly interjected that the financial condition of the company would not permit raises or additional fringe benefits.

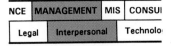

At this point you jumped in: "The answer to this situation is clearly not wages and fringe benefits. I am convinced that these employees need to feel as if the company cares about them as individuals, as members of a team. Other companies have been very successful in developing methods to communicate their concern for employees, and they have reaped the benefits in terms of increased employee morale and productivity."

Because of your interest in and knowledge of employee motivation, you were asked to research the situation and recommend action.

Required:

1. Based on your knowledge and experience, create a specific scenario: For example, select a particular business, identify the specific employee group involved, and generally describe the work environment of the group.

2. Identify something that management can do to symbolize concern for this group of people. To assist you, review the research related to employee motivation (e.g., management and human resource management textbooks and academic journals in the management field). Read current practitioners' journals to determine what ideas other companies have implemented successfully.

3. Write a memo to your supervisor (Jennifer Williams) convincing her to implement your idea. Use your research to provide evidence that the idea is theoretically sound or that it has been successful in another company (whichever is appropriate). Provide specific information about the benefits to be gained and the costs of implementation.

4. Assume your supervisor has enthusiastically supported your idea (memo written in step 3); the idea was theoretically sound, and she felt the company could only gain. For your supervisor's signature, write a memo to the employees telling them about the idea. Consider whether your description of the idea to the employees will be different from the description to your supervisor. If so, consider the changes you will make.

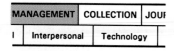

Case 3.   Is Providing Possible Faulty Swing Sets Unethical? For the last six months, you have been responsible for inspecting and approving the quality of swing sets (Model 2353) before they are shipped to customers. One afternoon as you were reviewing past records, you noted a change in the product specification and were curious about the reason for this change. Discussing this issue with the production manager, you learned that later product research indicated that the original metal used was not heavy enough.

You are upset because you know that at least 10,000 of these swing sets are still in use. You contend that if the reinforcement bars break while a child is swinging, an accident could occur. The production manager says, "Even our new swing sets will eventually break. It's been over two years and we haven't had any complaints yet. The problem's been solved; why bring it up now? It will not only cost money to recall the product but would damage our image." The production manager advises you not to bring the issue up again; otherwise, you may not be considered a team player.

Required:
1. Decide whether it is ethical to allow the swing sets that do not meet company standards to remain in use. Consider these points:
   a. What are the relevant facts?
   b. What are the ethical issues raised by the decision whether to recall the swing sets?
   c. Who (which stakeholders) will be affected by this decision?
   d. What are the costs and benefits imposed by each alternative on each person listed in step (c)?
   e. What are the company's obligations to each person listed in step (c)?
   f. What should you as the company's representative do?
2. Based on your decision, complete *one* of the following:
   a. Write a persuasive letter to the vice president of production advocating recall of these products. Include complete justification for your decision.
   b. Write a memo to the production manager stating that you have reconsidered your thoughts on the swing sets and believe the sets should not be recalled. Include complete justification for your decision.
   c. Do any other options exist? If so, write a letter or memo to the appropriate individual.

WRITING ABOUT
THE UNPLEASANT

OBJECTIVES

When you have completed Chapter 10, you should be able to

◆ Use empathy to see your message from the point of view of the reader.

◆ Select the appropriate outline for developing messages by identifying the central idea and the likely reader reaction.

◆ State the steps in the inductive outline (effectively introduce the topic, present details, report the bad news, and close pleasantly) and identify the advantages of using it to convey bad news.

◆ Use the inductive outline in writing letters and memorandums that convey bad news.

MARTIN HAS WORKED FOR YOUR COMPANY for several years. He was already here when you were hired as his manager. He and his wife have two children and recently announced that they are expecting a third child. You have noticed that Martin's work has shown signs of slackness lately. He recently made an error on a client's report that almost cost the company the entire account. At a meeting with you two weeks ago, he agreed with your observations about his work. He refused your offer of help and vowed to work harder and get back on track.

Despite his promise to do better, however, Martin's performance has not improved; and he has been habitually late for work. You feel you have no other choice than to notify him that his job is in danger. Although he has been a valuable employee in the past and has always been friendly and helpful, his recent actions are costly to the company. It is up to you to solve the problem. How will you handle this situation?

Nobody likes to give people bad news. Unfortunately, business people sometimes have to convey bad news. Employers have to turn down job applicants. Companies must tell employees and customers of unpopular changes; banks often have to refuse loans. Accountants must refuse audit engagements if a conflict of interest exists. Individuals and employees must alert companies of mistakes made in completing an order or handling an account. Finally, everyone (individuals and companies) at some point must refuse a request for a favor.

Knowing how to communicate bad news as delicately and clearly as possible is an essential business skill. A skillful manager will attempt to say no in such a way that the reader or listener supports the decision and is willing to continue a positive relationship with the company. To do this successfully, the manager must first have empathy; she or he must try to understand how the recipient of the unpleasant news will feel. If you are sending the information in a letter, you must first think how you would approach the news if the recipient were there to receive it in person. A letter is much less likely to be "cold" if you use empathy in addition to tact and effective writing skills.

Perhaps your personal response to a claim or a request, for example, would be much different from the tactful response needed to soothe negative feelings and ensure a harmonious relationship with the customer—especially when you doubt whether the request is legitimate or when you do not have the time required to write an effective bad-news letter. When this conflict exists, keep in mind that you are writing the letter on behalf of your company and that your response is a direct reflection on the company's image.

The importance of effective bad-news communication is illustrated by the story of a man who carried in his coat pocket a job-refusal letter he had received from a company some time past. Frequently he would show this superbly written letter to others and comment, "I'd accept a job from

COMMUNICATION MENTOR

Presenting a topic in a positive manner will always make the reader more receptive even when discussing sensitive issues. However, keep information realistic and resist the natural tendency to gloss over the intended message. Learning to balance the positive and realistic is important if your message is to be considered credible.

Beverly R. Kuehn
Branch Manager
CTX Mortgage Company
a division of Centex Corporation

this company any day because this letter made me feel *good* about myself even though the company couldn't hire me." Obviously, this letter was not an impersonal form letter, nor was it written in haste without genuine *empathy* for the reader's feelings.

The techniques and examples presented in this chapter will help you begin to refine your ability to convey bad news diplomatically so that you earn the respect and/or the continued business of the disappointed reader.

EMPATHY

Like a selfish player on a team, a selfish person in business operates under a severe handicap. Such a person's actions and words make cooperation hard to get, friends hard to keep, and decisions hard for others to accept. *Empathy* (as contrasted with selfishness) assists in escaping such hazards. Yet, even those who have genuine empathy for others often forget to ask themselves, "If I were the receiver of the message I am about to transmit, how would I react?" The answer to that question has an impact on the *sequence* in which the ideas are presented and the *style* in which they are expressed.

Sequence of Ideas

Just as good news is accompanied with details, bad news is accompanied with supporting details (reasons, explanations). If the bad news is presented in the first sentence, the reaction is likely to be negative: "They never gave me a fair chance," "That's unfair," "This just can't be." Hav-

Why avoid putting bad news in the first sentence?

Poorly written bad-news messages damage goodwill.
PEANUTS reprinted by permission of UFS, Inc.

ing made a value judgment on reading the first sentence, readers are naturally reluctant to change their minds before the last sentence—even though the intervening sentences present a valid basis for doing so. Having been disappointed by the idea contained in the first sentence, readers are tempted to concentrate on *refuting* (instead of *understanding*) supporting details.

From the writer's point of view, details that support a refusal are very important. If the supporting details are understood and believed, the message may be readily accepted and good business relationships preserved. Because the reasons behind the bad news are so important, the writer needs to organize the message in such a way as to emphasize the reasons. The chances of getting the reader to understand the reasons are much better *before* the bad news is presented than *after* the bad news is presented. If the reasons are presented afterward, the reader may not even read them.

People who are refused want to know why. To them (and to the person doing the refusing) the reasons are vital; they must be transmitted and received. The writer can simplify the process by using the outline shown in Figure 10-1.

The four steps shown in Figure 10-1 are applied in letters and memorandums illustrated in the pages that follow. Before reading them, consider the reasoning that supports each step.

Step 1: Introductory Paragraph. The first paragraph in a good-news letter contains the good news, but the introductory paragraph in the bad-news or refusal letter has a different function. It should (1) let the reader know what the letter is about (without stating the obvious) and (2) serve as a transition into the discussion of reasons (without revealing the bad news or leading the reader to expect good news). If these objectives can be accomplished in one sentence, that sentence can be the first paragraph.

What does the first paragraph seek to accomplish?

BAD-NEWS
LETTER

1. Begins with neutral idea that leads to the reason for the refusal.

2. Presents the facts, analysis, and reasons for the refusal.

3. States the refusal using positive tone and de-emphasizes techniques.

4. Closes with an idea that shifts emphasis away from the refusal.

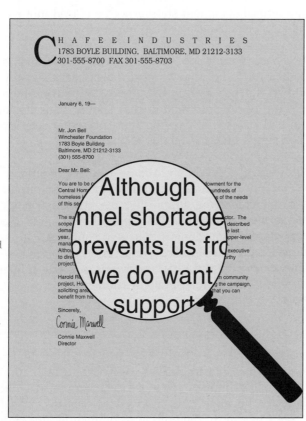

FIGURE 10-1 Inductive sequence-of-ideas pattern used in unpleasant messages

Putting bad news in the first sentence de-emphasizes reasons.

Step 2: Facts, Analysis, and Reasons.　Properly introduced, the essential information will be seen as related and important. If the bad news had preceded it, (1) the message might have been put aside before this important portion was even read, or (2) the disappointment experienced upon reading the bad news might interfere with comprehension or acceptance of the supporting explanation. Compared with explanations that *follow* bad news, those that *precede* have a better chance of being received with an open mind. By the time a reader has finished reading this portion of the message, the upcoming statement of refusal may be foreseen and accepted as valid.

Why not save the bad news for the final sentence?

Step 3: Refusal Statement.　Because preceding statements are tactful and seem valid, the sentence that states the bad news may arouse little or no resentment. If the writing were strictly inductive, the refusal statement would be last. Placing a statement of refusal (or bad news) in the last sentence or paragraph, however, would have the effect of placing too much emphasis on it. Preferably, *reasons* (instead of bad news) should remain uppermost in the reader's mind. In addition, placing bad news last would make the ending seem cold and abrupt.

The refusal statement should not be placed in a paragraph by itself; this arrangement would place too much emphasis on the bad news.

What does the final paragraph seek to accomplish?

Step 4: Closing Paragraph.　A closing paragraph that is about some aspect of the topic other than the bad news itself helps in several ways. It assists in (1) de-emphasizing the unpleasant part of the message, (2) conveying some useful information that should logically follow (instead of precede) bad news, (3) showing that the writer has a positive attitude, and (4) adding a unifying quality to the message.

Although the preceding outline has four points, a bad-news letter may or may not have four paragraphs. More than one paragraph may be necessary for conveying supporting reasons. In the illustrations in this chapter (as well as examples in Appendix A), note that first and final paragraphs are seldom longer than two sentences. In fact, one-sentence paragraphs (as beginnings) look more inviting to read.

The *sequence* of those paragraphs is strongly influenced by human empathy. So is the manner of expression.

Style

What are some stylistic techniques of subordination?

In messages that convey bad news, three stylistic qualities merit special attention: emphasis/de-emphasis, positive language, and implication.

A basic of human relations is "Emphasize the positive; de-emphasize the negative." For a review of *emphasis and subordination* techniques, see Chapter 8. The outline recommended for bad-news messages

COMMUNICATION MENTOR

Try to open and close any letter or memo on a positive note even if doing so requires some creative writing. The reader's tolerance level for negative news seems to increase when the bad news is sandwiched between some positive elements.

Terence E. McSweeney
Director of Communications
PGA of America

puts the statement of bad news in a subordinate position. Likewise, stylistic techniques work toward the same goal: subordinating bad news by placing it in the dependent clause, using passive voice, expressing in general terms, and using abstract nouns or things (instead of the person written to) as the subject of a sentence. Although a refusal (bad news) needs to be clear, subordination of it allows the reasoning to get deserved emphasis.

Positive language accents the good instead of the bad, the pleasant instead of the unpleasant, what can be done instead of what can't be done. Compared with a negative idea presented in negative terms, a negative idea presented in positive terms is more likely to be accepted. When you are tempted to use the following terms, search instead for words or ideas that sound more positive:

chagrined	failure	lied	overlooked
complaint	ignorant	misinformed	regrettable
disappointed	ignored	mistake	ridiculous
disgusted	inexcusable	neglect	underhanded
disregard	insinuation	nonsense	upset
error	irresponsible	obnoxious	wrong

Think of some other words that could be added to this list.

To businesspeople who conscientiously practice empathy, such terms may not even come to mind when communicating the unpleasant. Words in the preceding list evoke feelings that contrast sharply with the positive feelings evoked by words such as

accurate	cordial	freedom	pretty
approval	correct	generous	productive
assist	durable	gratitude	prosper
cheerful	energetic	happy	recommendation
commend	enthusiasm	health	respect
concise	fragrance	peace	true

To increase the number of pleasant-sounding words in your writing, practice thinking positively. Strive to see the good in situations and in others. Will Rogers professed to being able to see *some* good in every person he met.

Implication is often an effective way of transmitting an unpleasant idea. For example, during the noon hour one employee says to another, "Will you go with me to see this afternoon's baseball game?" "No, I won't" communicates a negative response, but it seems unnecessarily direct and harsh. The same message (invitation is rejected) can be clearly stated in an *indirect* way (by implication):

Must refusals be stated directly?

Which of these sentences illustrate use of the subjunctive mood?

I wish I could.	Other responsibilities forbid, but the recipient would *like* to accept.
I must get my work done.	By revealing the necessity of working instead, the worker conveys the "no" answer.
If I watched baseball this afternoon, I'd be transferred tomorrow.	By stating an undesirable consequence of acceptance, the worker conveys the idea of nonacceptance.
I'm a *football* fan.	By indicating a preference for another sport, the worker conveys nonacceptance.

By *implying* the "no" answer, the foregoing responses (1) use positive language, (2) convey reasons or at least a positive attitude, and (3) seem more respectful. These implication techniques (as well as emphasis/de-emphasis, positive language, and inductive sequence) are illustrated in letters that follow.

SAYING "NO" TO AN ADJUSTMENT REQUEST

Assume a seller of oriental furniture receives the following request for reimbursement:

Please reimburse me for the amount of the attached bill.

When I ordered my oriental chest (which was delivered yesterday), I paid in full for the price of the chest and the transportation charges. Yet, before the transportation firm would make delivery, I was required to pay $144. Recalling that our state does not collect sales tax on foreign purchases, and holding a purchase ticket (Sh-311) marked "Paid in full," I assumed an error that you would be glad to correct.

The $144 was a *federal* tax (import duties). Before placing the order, the purchaser had been told that purchasers were responsible for import duties that would be collected at the time of delivery. In addition, a statement to that effect was written in bold print on the buy-sell agreement of which she was given a copy. Maybe she didn't listen; maybe she lost or did not read her copy. Even though the purchaser is clearly at fault, the seller's response could be more tactful than that illustrated in Figure 10-2.

Southern Heritage Interiors
1508 Jefferson Drive
Biloxi, MS 39530-1508
(601) 555-3481

March 3, 19—

Ms. Joyce Rankin
1403 Greenbriar Lane
Gulfport, MS 39501-1403

Dear Ms. Rankin

[1] Your request for a $144 reimbursement has been received, and I am sorry to say it cannot be made. [2] Clearly, the charge is for import duties.

[3] In the discussion that preceded the purchase and in the documents you signed at the time, it was clearly pointed out that you would be responsible for import duties. [4] Duties are not collected at the time of sale because they cannot be accurately predicted.

[5] I am sure you can understand my position in this matter. [6] Thank you for doing business with us; and if you have any further questions, do not hesitate to call or write.

Sincerely

Marlon Bournazos

Marlon Bournazos
Manager

[1] Begins with an idea that is not needed (receipt of the request could be taken for granted). Apologizing for a justified decision hardly seems appropriate. Refusing in the first sentence places emphasis on the refusal. [2] Offers explanation that may not receive the emphasis it deserves, especially if reaction to the first sentence has been "They're crooks" or "It's totally unfair."

[3] Presents needed information; but if the reader is still smarting from reaction to the first sentence, the point may not register with sufficient impact. [4] Commendably presents a reason for the method of operation.

[5] Uses a cliché. [6] Uses another cliché. The words may seem polite but insincere. If taken literally, they could lead to unnecessary correspondence.

FIGURE 10-2   Poor example of a "no" response to an adjustment request

In the revised letter in Figure 10-3, note that the first sentence reveals the subject matter of the letter and leads into a presentation of reasons. Reasons precede the refusal, the statement of refusal is subordinated, and the final sentence is about something other than the refusal.

As we have seen, adjustment letters that say "no" follow a general sequence of ideas: (1) Begin with a neutral or factual sentence that leads to the reasons behind the "no" answer, (2) present the reasons and expla-

[1] Reveals the subject matter of the letter. Leads to a discussion of reasons. Includes a reminder of a positive quality (it's hand carved).
[2] Begins explanation.

[3] Presents reason for the procedure followed. [4,5] Complete the explanation.

[6] Reveals the refusal, which is stated in a compound sentence. The positive idea in the second clause takes some emphasis away from the you-must-pay idea in the first clause.

[7] Uses resale in the final sentence.

Uses open punctuation; the colon after the salutation and the comma after the complimentary close are omitted.

Southern Heritage Interiors
1508 Jefferson Drive
Biloxi, MS 39530-1508
(601) 555-3481

March 3, 19—

Ms. Joyce Rankin
1403 Greenbriar Lane
Gulfport, MS 39501-1403

Dear Ms. Rankin

[1] Your hand-carved, monkeywood chest was delivered about a month sooner than we had predicted when purchase papers were signed. [2] The invoice you received with the chest does show prepayment of cost and transportation.

[3] Because the import duty can only be calculated on the shipping date, the tax is paid when shipment is delivered. [4] Before sales contracts are written, buyers are told of their responsibility to pay for import tax. [5] (The sales ticket has a bold-face statement to that effect.)

[6] Responsibility for the tax is yours, but you have reason to feel good about your purchase. [7] By ordering directly from the overseas manufacturer rather than regional markets, you saved about 40 percent. You now have a beautiful chest that is exquisitely hand carved.

Sincerely

Marlon Bournazos

Marlon Bournazos
Manager

FIGURE 10-3 **Good example of a "no" response to an adjustment request**

nations, (3) present the refusal in an unemphatic manner, and (4) close with an off-the-subject thought. Naturally, the ending should be related to the letter or to the business relationship; but it should not be specific about the refusal. Although the same pattern is followed in credit, order, and favor refusals, those letters are sufficiently different to make a discussion of each helpful.

What is the outline for an adjustment refusal?

SAYING "NO" TO A CREDIT REQUEST

Once we have evaluated a request for credit and have decided "no" is the better answer, our primary writing problem is to say "no" so tactfully that we keep the business relationship on a cash basis. When requests for credit are accompanied with an order, our credit refusals may serve as acknowledgment letters. And, of course, every business letter is directly or indirectly a sales letter. Prospective customers will be disappointed when they cannot buy on a credit basis. However, if we keep them sold on our goods and services, they may prefer to buy from us on a cash basis instead of seeking credit privileges elsewhere.

In a letter that refuses credit, what is a good counterproposal?

When the credit investigation shows that applicants are poor credit risks, too many credit writers no longer regard them as possible customers. They write to them in a cold, matter-of-fact manner. They don't consider that such applicants may still be interested in doing business on a cash basis and may qualify for credit later.

In credit refusals, as in other types of refusals, the major portion of the message should be explanation. We cannot expect our reader to agree that our "no" answer is the right answer unless we give the reasons behind it. Naturally, those who send us credit information will expect us to keep it confidential. But if we give the reasons without using the names of those from whom we obtained our information, we are not violating confidence. We are passing along the truth as a justification for our business decision.

Why discuss reasons for a credit refusal?

Both writers and readers benefit from the explanation of the reasons behind the refusal. For writers, the explanation helps to establish fair-mindedness; it shows that the decision was not arbitrary. For readers, the explanation not only presents the truth to which they are entitled, it also has guidance value. From it they learn to adjust habits and as a result qualify for credit purchases later.

Including resale—favorable statements about the product ordered—is helpful for four reasons: (1) It might cause credit applicants to prefer our brand, perhaps being willing to buy it even on a cash basis; (2) it suggests that the writer is trying to be helpful; (3) it makes the writing easier—negative thoughts are easier to de-emphasize when cushioned with resale material, and by using resale material we seem confident of future cash purchases; and (4) it can confirm the credit applicant's judgment

Why use resale in a credit refusal?

(suggesting the applicant made a good choice of merchandise is giving an indirect compliment).

Assume a retailer of electronic devices has placed an initial order and requested credit privileges. After examining financial statements that were enclosed, the wholesaler decides the request should be denied. The letter shown in Figure 10-4 would be substandard.

[1] States ideas that could have been left to implication. [2] Reveals the negative decision before revealing the basis for it.

[3] Presents an explanation, but unnecessarily raises doubts about the applicant's knowledge of financial matters. [4] Continues with figures that should have preceded the statement of refusal. [5] Reveals that the writer has doubts about the strength of the explanation. [6] Uses worn expressions in referring to the enclosure.

[7] Does make a commendable effort to encourage additional orders.

★

L O N E S T A R
ELECTRONICS, INC.

1093 West Mae Street
Spokane, WA 99210-3922
(509) 555-3100

June 16, 19—

Hodges Office Supply
1600 Main Street
Austin, TX 78710-4981

Ladies and Gentlemen:

[1] Your order of July 6 has been received, and your request for credit privileges has been given to me for evaluation. [2] At this time, we do not believe it is in our best interest to sell to you on a credit basis.

[3] As you may be aware, many leaders in the field of finance recommend that businesses maintain a 2-to-1 ratio of current assets to current liabilities. [4] Because your current ratio is approximately 1 1/4 to 1, your orders will need to have payment attached. [5] We trust you will understand. [6] An envelope is enclosed for your convenience in sending your check for $1,487.53, after which your order will be shipped.

[7] For a look at the latest in video games, see the enclosed folder.

Sincerely,

Brian R. Spiegler

Brian R. Spiegler
Credit Manager

Enclosure

FIGURE 10-4   Poor example of a "no" response to a credit request

The credit refusal in Figure 10-5, in contrast, explains, refuses, and offers to sell for cash. Although credit references have been checked, it says nothing about having conducted a "credit investigation." It does not identify referents, and it makes no apology for action taken. Similar writing challenges occur in refusing orders.

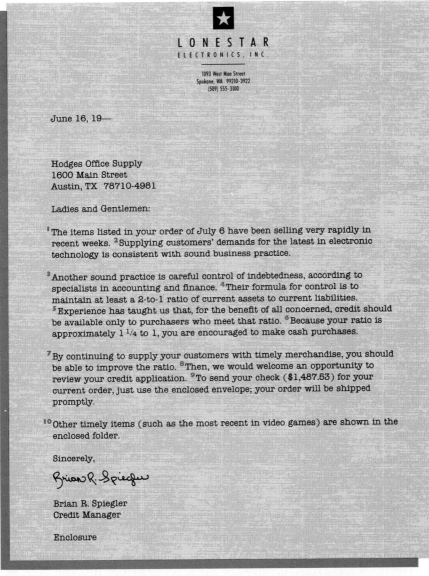

LONESTAR
ELECTRONICS, INC.

1093 West Mae Street
Spokane, WA 99210-3922
(509) 555-3100

June 16, 19—

Hodges Office Supply
1600 Main Street
Austin, TX 78710-4981

Ladies and Gentlemen:

[1] The items listed in your order of July 6 have been selling very rapidly in recent weeks. [2] Supplying customers' demands for the latest in electronic technology is consistent with sound business practice.

[3] Another sound practice is careful control of indebtedness, according to specialists in accounting and finance. [4] Their formula for control is to maintain at least a 2-to-1 ratio of current assets to current liabilities. [5] Experience has taught us that, for the benefit of all concerned, credit should be available only to purchasers who meet that ratio. [6] Because your ratio is approximately 1 1/4 to 1, you are encouraged to make cash purchases.

[7] By continuing to supply your customers with timely merchandise, you should be able to improve the ratio. [8] Then, we would welcome an opportunity to review your credit application. [9] To send your check ($1,487.53) for your current order, just use the enclosed envelope; your order will be shipped promptly.

[10] Other timely items (such as the most recent in video games) are shown in the enclosed folder.

Sincerely,

Brian R. Spiegler

Brian R. Spiegler
Credit Manager

Enclosure

[1] Implies receipt of the order. Leads to an explanation. [2] Introduces explanation. Implies approval of *one* of the applicant's practices (supplying most recently developed items).

[3] Leads to discussion of *another* practice that is the basis for subsequent refusal. [4] Provides further detail. [5] Continues with the explanation. [6] Uses positive language in expressing the refusal. Conveys "no" to credit purchases by recommending *cash* purchases—a counterproposal to the refusal. If a writer thought the statement of refusal should be more direct, the sentence could be expanded: "Because your ratio is approximately $1\frac{1}{4}$ to 1, the order will not be filled on a time-payment basis; but you are encouraged to make cash purchases."

[7] Looks confidently to the future and reminds the applicant of the commendable practice discussed in the second sentence. [8] Encourages subsequent application and thus implies expectation of continued business relationship. [9] Reminds the merchant of the desired action.

[10] Uses sales-promotional material as a closing sentence. Uses "timely" as a reminder of the applicant's commendable business practice and as a technique for developing unity.

FIGURE 10-5   Good example of a "no" response to a credit request

SAYING "NO" TO AN ORDER FOR MERCHANDISE

Why might you refuse to fill an order?

For various reasons, we may not be able to send the merchandise that people have ordered from us.

1. We may be able to send it, but there will be a waiting period. (At such times we would acknowledge the order and write a letter saying "Yes, you will receive the . . . by . . . . ")
2. We may not sell directly to consumers. (We would tell the customer where to buy the merchandise.)
3. We may not have what the customer ordered, but we have something that will serve his or her needs better. (We would wait to fill the order until we have made the customer understand that we have something better.)

For orders that cannot be filled, the inductive approach recommended for all "no" letters is preferred. The following request has to be refused because the manufacturer to whom it is addressed does not sell directly to consumers:

> Please send an OpticScan II laser printer. According to the fall catalog, the model number is 07-433-33. I don't have a price list; please send the printer c.o.d.

If a manufacturer received many similar requests, they would very likely be answered by form letter. But even form letters do not have to be so cold and indifferent as the letter in Figure 10-6.

People understand the practicality of form letters. They object to them not because they are forms but because they use indifferent, matter-of-fact language. When stored in disk files, form letters can be personalized for each recipient by adding variables (information that changes from one letter to another) to the standard text. The merge function of word-processing software will automatically insert the variables in the coded location and an individualized letter will be printed for each recipient. The variables that personalize Figure 10-6 include the inside address, salutation, merchandise ordered, and dealer's name and address. The codes for each variable appear boldface and in brackets.

The general plan of the revised letter in Figure 10-7 is to make customers' desire for the merchandise so strong that they will be willing to wait for it and to purchase it through conventional merchandising outlets.

If the merchandise involved in the letter in Figure 10-7 had been ex-

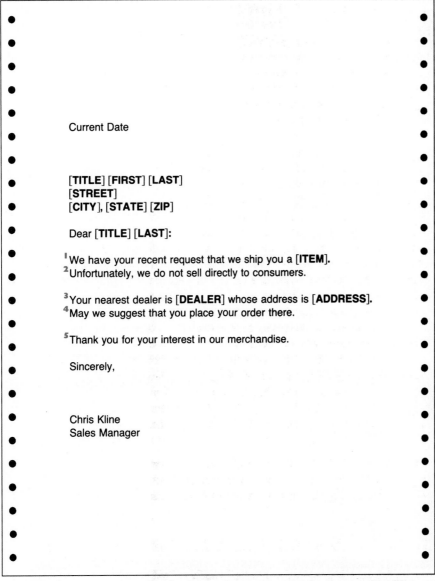

Current Date

[**TITLE**] [**FIRST**] [**LAST**]
[**STREET**]
[**CITY**], [**STATE**] [**ZIP**]

Dear [**TITLE**] [**LAST**]:

[1] We have your recent request that we ship you a [**ITEM**].
[2] Unfortunately, we do not sell directly to consumers.

[3] Your nearest dealer is [**DEALER**] whose address is [**ADDRESS**].
[4] May we suggest that you place your order there.

[5] Thank you for your interest in our merchandise.

Sincerely,

Chris Kline
Sales Manager

[1] The receipt of the order could have been implied; beginning with "we" places focus on writer. [2] Distribution through dealers has advantages; it isn't necessarily unfortunate.

[3] Giving the exact name and address of a local dealer is commendable. [4] This suggestion misses a chance for resale.

[5] The ending seems superficial.

Merge function inserts variables for each customer in the bracketed positions; each personalized letter is printed on letterhead and signed.

FIGURE 10-6   Poor example of a "no" response to an order for merchandise

pensive, or if orders sent directly to the manufacturer were rare, it would have been better not to use a form letter. Both form letters and individual letters can benefit from applying the following suggestions:

1. Imply receipt of the order and confirm the customer's good choice of merchandise.

¹ Introduces the subject and leads to an explanation.

² Provides resale on the item ordered. ³ Begins the explanation. ⁴ Reveals—in positive language—that sales are not made directly to consumers. Lets the reader see an advantage in the manufacturer's not selling to consumers directly.

⁵ Closes by providing needed information.

Jelinek **E**lectronics
1273 South Ogden Avenue
Portland, OR 97207-1273

(503) 555-9000
FAX(503) 555-2795

November 5, 19—

Mr. Stacy Schmidt
Schmidt Music Center
400 West Fifth Avenue
Ft. Collins, CO   80521-2365

Dear Mr. Schmidt:

[1]When we first began marketing the OpticScan II laser printer, we wanted to provide laser printer capabilities suitable for businesses of all sizes.

[2]Now available with ten scalable fonts, the OpticScan II will allow you to choose exactly the right style for any layout. [3]As manufacturers, we devote all our time to enhancing our current products and to developing innovative new products. [4]Because we concentrate solely on these efforts (and leave selling and advertising to retailers), we have been able to develop products that meet the ever-changing technological needs of today's businesses.

[5]To see our new OpticScan II printer in operation, visit your nearest OpticScan retailer—Moore Suppliers, 1000 Forest Hill, New Orleans, LA   70128-1000.

Sincerely,

Chris Kline

Chris Kline
Sales Manager

FIGURE 10-7   Good example of a "no" response to an order for merchandise

2   Wherever appropriate in the letter, use resale to make the customer willing to reorder through the proper channel.

3. Give reasons why sales are through dealers. Suggest or spell out how advantageously customers can buy through a dealer.

4. Use positive language to explain that the order is not being filled.

Form letters have earned a negative connotation because of their tendency to be insensitive and impersonal. However, you can effectively personalize a form letter to keep your reader from feeling like just another "address."

Sometimes, customers order one item when they can more profitably use another, as in the following order. The contractor has ordered light bulbs that are inappropriate for his use. Filling the order as submitted would be a mistake, and the customer is likely to be dissatisfied.

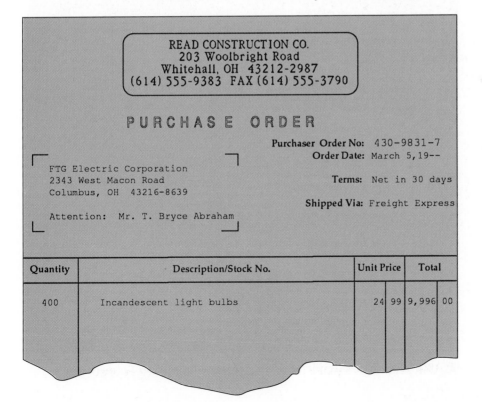

Although the form letter in Figure 10-8 may get the desired results (convince the recipient that the type of light bulb ordered is not the type needed), the letter in Figure 10-9 applies sound writing principles more effectively.

[1] Presents information that could have been implied; focuses on writer.
[2] Reveals the refusal before the explanation. "However" immediately lets the reader know that negatives follow.
[3] Provides no reasons; repetitive and vague. [4] Implies lack of expertise on part of customer. [5] Provides a major disadvantage but does not provide any benefits for making the substitution; uses "In the long run," a cliché.
[6] Presents needed information, but the idea of "holding" the order seems a little negative. "Hear from you" is worn and literally implies oral communication.

f t g e l e c t r i c c o r p o r a t i o n
2343 WEST MACON ROAD
COLUMBUS, OH 43216-8639
(614) 555-9383

July 3, 19—

Mr. Jim Read
Read Construction Co.
203 Woolbright Road
Whitehall, OH 43213-2987

Dear Mr. Read:

SUBJECT: Purchase Order No. 430-9831-7

[1] We received your order for 400 incandescent light bulbs (Stock No. 71731). [2] However, we need to explain why this particular bulb is inappropriate.

[3] The incandescent bulb is not appropriate for your intended use. [4] We have another product better suited to your purposes. May we have your permission to substitute halogen bulbs? [5] Although these bulbs are more expensive, we feel the benefits will far outweigh the costs in the long run.

[6] Your order will be held until we hear from you.

Sincerely,

T. Bryce Abraham

T. Bryce Abraham
Sales Manager

FIGURE 10-8 **Poor example of a "no" response to an order for merchandise**

Taking the time required to write such a long letter to a customer may at first seem questionable. The letter in Figure 10-9 is about a circumstance that occurs frequently. Storing a draft of the letter in the computer allows the company to adapt and reproduce a letter quickly and with little

ftg electric corporation
2343 WEST MACON ROAD
COLUMBUS, OH 43216-8639
(614) 555-9383

July 3, 19—

Mr. Jim Read
Read Construction Co.
203 Woolbright Road
Whitehall, OH 43213-2987

[1] Re: Purchase Order No. 430-9831-7

Dear Mr. Read:

[2] The incandescent bulb you ordered has been proven to be 10 percent brighter than others of its type and is ideal for occasional use for short intervals.

[3] According to our sales representative, Jeff Winter, you plan to install the bulbs in the parking lot lights of the new Cloverleaf Mall. [4] Because these bulbs will burn all night for security reasons, the halogen bulb designed for heavy-duty, long-term use is better suited for your needs.

[5] The longer life of the halogen will more than compensate for the larger initial investment required. [6] You will also benefit from the convenience and cost efficiency of replacing

[1] Reference line, not subject line, directs reader to source documents.

[2] Acknowledges order but is noncommittal about shipment. Includes resale on the contractor's choice, which also serves to begin the explanation.

[3,4] Continue with explanation by providing specific details about the needs of this reader.

[5,6] Reveal a disadvantage of the alternative, but de-emphasize it by putting it in a sentence that states primary advantages.

FIGURE 10-9 Good example of a "no" response to an order for merchandise

Mr. Jim Read   2   July 3, 19—

bulbs less frequently. [7]Refer to the enclosed pamphlet for additional details about the performance of the halogen bulb (Stock No. 97913).

[8]Instead of filling your order as requested, we would like permission to ship the long-lasting halogen bulb. [9]To authorize this shipment, simply check the appropriate square on the enclosed card and return in the enclosed envelope with your payment for the additional cost.

Sincerely,

T. Bryce Abraham

T. Bryce Abraham
Sales Manager

[10]Enclosures

[7]Includes an enclosure to present additional details and to reinforce ideas presented in the letter.

[8, 9]Seek permission to send what is needed instead of what was ordered. Make response easy. On the card, one of the squares (the options) could be to cancel the order. Mentioning this option in the letter would give it undesired emphasis, so no reference is made to it.

[10]Includes enclosure notation to alert reader that other information is enclosed.

FIGURE 10-9, (continued)

effort when the need arises. The following letter has been stored as RETAILER.LTR (closing lines wrapped to the next screen). When the need arises, the writer simply retrieves the file and personalizes the letter by inserting the customer's name and address and an appropriate salutation.

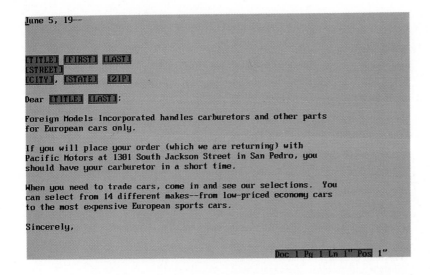

```
June 5, 19--

[TITLE] [FIRST] [LAST]
[STREET]
[CITY], [STATE] [ZIP]

Dear [TITLE] [LAST]:

Foreign Models Incorporated handles carburetors and other parts
for European cars only.

If you will place your order (which we are returning) with
Pacific Motors at 1301 South Jackson Street in San Pedro, you
should have your carburetor in a short time.

When you need to trade cars, come in and see our selections.  You
can select from 14 different makes--from low-priced economy cars
to the most expensive European sports cars.

Sincerely,

                                    Doc 1 Pg 1 Ln 1" Pos 1"
```

Remember, the sales-promotional material didn't cost anything as far as paper and postage are concerned—the company had to write anyway. And it's almost sure to be read—something that can't be said of all sales messages.

When people say "no" in a letter, they usually do so because they think "no" is the better answer for all concerned. They can see how recipients will ultimately benefit from the refusal. If the letter is based on a sound decision, and if it has been well written, recipients will probably recognize that the senders did them a favor by saying "no."

SAYING "NO" TO A REQUEST FOR A FAVOR

When a request for a favor must be denied, the same reasons-before-refusal pattern is recommended. To ensure positive relationships, the recipient of a request for a favor may offer a counterproposal—an alternative to the favor requested. In the letter in Figure 10-10, the writer explains why the company cannot lend an executive to direct a major community effort and recommends a member of the company's senior executive corps as a counterproposal.

The preceding letters—all of which are *responses* to prior correspondence—use the same principles of sequence and style that are recommended for letters that *initiate* communication about unpleasant topics. The same principles apply whether the communication is a letter or a memorandum.

What is an advantage of including sales-promotional material in an order refusal?

When you must give unpleasant news or reject an employee's ideas, offering an alternative instead of a flat "no" keeps communication open and avoids damage to egos.

1,2 Introduce the subject without re-vealing whether the answer will be "yes" or "no."

3–5 Give reasons.

6 Subordinates the refusal by placing it in the dependent clause of a complex sentence. Alludes to help in another form.

7–9 Close on a more positive note by offering a counterproposal. Summarizing the executive's responsibilities and providing his phone number increase the genuineness of the offer.

10 Signs first name only because she knows the reader well.

CHAFEE INDUSTRIES
1783 BOYLE BUILDING, BALTIMORE, MD 21212-3133
301-555-8700   FAX 301-555-8703

January 6, 19—

Mr. Jon Bell
Winchester Foundation
1783 Boyle Building
Baltimore, MD 21212-3133

Dear Jon

[1] You are to be commended for your commitment to create an endowment for the Central Homeless Shelter. [2] This much-needed project will aid the hundreds of homeless and increase the community's awareness of the needs of this sector of our population.

[3] The success of this project depends on a good project director. [4] The organizational, leadership, and public relations activities you described demand an individual with upper-level managerial experience.

[5] During the last year, Chaffee has decentralized its organization, reducing the number of upper-level managers to the minimal level needed. [6] Although our current personnel shortage prevents us from lending you an executive to direct the project, we do want to support this worthy project.

[7] Harold Roberts in our senior executive corps directed a similar short-term project, Homes for Humanity. [8] He organized the campaign, solicited area coordinators, and managed publicity. [9] If you can benefit from his services, call him at 555-8700, extension 791.

[10] Sincerely

Connie

Connie Maxwell
Director

FIGURE 10-10   Good example of a "no" response for a favor, including a counterproposal

INITIATING COMMUNICATION ABOUT THE UNPLEASANT

A personnel director wrote the memorandum in Figure 10-11 to communicate to employees a change in insurance premiums. The revision in Figure 10-12 reflects a more effective application of sound writing principles.

CONSOLIDATED ENTERPRISES

493 Baldwin Road
Honolulu, HI 96813-0493
(808) 555-7019

TO: All Employees

FROM: Jay R. Karnes, Human Resources Director

DATE: October 15, 19—

SUBJECT: CHANGE IN HEALTH INSURANCE PREMIUMS

[1] Effective August 1, payroll deductions for your Valley HMO Group health-insurance premiums will be increased between $15 and $30 per month. [2] This increase, although regrettable, is unavoidable.

[3] Premiums for our group policy have risen drastically in the last 24 months. [4] Consolidated Enterprises was able to absorb the smaller increases of previous years, but this is no longer possible. [5] We considered reducing other fringe benefits as an alternative to raising premium deductions, but the final conclusion was that such action would be unfair. [6] We *had* to raise premiums.

[7] To more precisely estimate the amount of your monthly deduction, we have attached a booklet. [8] On page 3, you will find a table from which your deduction can be determined.

[9] I trust you will understand this situation and assure you of our continued efforts to provide the best in health-care insurance.

[1] Begins with the bad news. [2] Uses negative language.

[3] Begins the explanation. [4] Uses negative language and a pronoun (this) that has an indefinite antecedent (the noun for which "this" stands is not used). [5, 6] Begin with "We'" and thus emphasize the writer. As the final word in a long sentence, "unfair" is emphasized. [6] Emphasizes the negative idea—simple, short sentence; first person; active voice.

[7] Uses third consecutive sentence with "we" as the subject. Includes a split infinitive. [7, 8] Could be combined and stated more concisely— "we have attached" and "you will find" could be left to implication.

[9] Introduces some doubt about whether the message will be clear. Unnecessarily shifts from use of "we" to "I." Commendably, includes a positive idea.

FIGURE 10-11   Poor example of a bad-news memorandum

[1] Introduces the topic (health insurance). Uses positive language—"pride" and "benefits."

[2,3] Use coherence techniques—"feedback" is about the "insurance" in (1), and "They" in (3) has antecedents in (2). *Before* the bad news (increased premium deduction) is presented, the paragraph reminds employees that experiences with their group policy have been very favorable. [4] Uses "high standards" (from which employees *benefit*) in the same sentence that uses "higher premiums" (for which employees will have to *pay*). In the same sentence with a positive, the negative is subordinated.

[5] Achieves coherence by repetition of "year" in sentence (4). Subordinates bad news ("share the cost") in a compound sentence. [6] Refers directly to the attached booklet without such unnecessary words as "attached is a booklet" and "you will find a table." [7] Achieves unity by using "employee-benefits package," which appeared in the first sentence. Assists in subordinating the premium increase by closing on another idea that is positive.

CIE CONSOLIDATED ENTERPRISES
493 Baldwin Road
Honolulu, HI 96813-0493
(808) 555-7019

TO: All Employees

FROM: Jay R. Karnes, Human Resources Director *JRK*

DATE: October 15, 19—

SUBJECT: CHANGE IN HEALTH INSURANCE PREMIUMS

[1] For six years, Consolidated has been able to point with pride to its employee-benefits package, especially its group health insurance.

[2] Overall, feedback from health-care institutions, physicians, and employees has been very favorable. [3] They like the speed and fairness with which claims are processed by Valley HMO. [4] To remain competitive and continue its high standards, Valley had to charge higher premiums last year; Consolidated Enterprises was able to absorb the cost.

[5] This year, Valley (like most other HMOs) has had to increase premiums again, but this time Consolidated must ask employees to share the cost. [6] The amount of your monthly deduction (which begins on December 1) can be determined from the table on page 3 of the attached booklet. [7] The booklet also summarizes other important features of Consolidated's complete employee-benefits package.

Attachment

FIGURE 10-12   Good example of a bad-news memorandum

Note that the revision is more concise, uses language that is more positive, and presents explanations before bad news.

In the memorandum in Figure 10-13, a supervisor informs an employee that the employee has done a poor job. The revision (Figure 10-14) would be more effective.

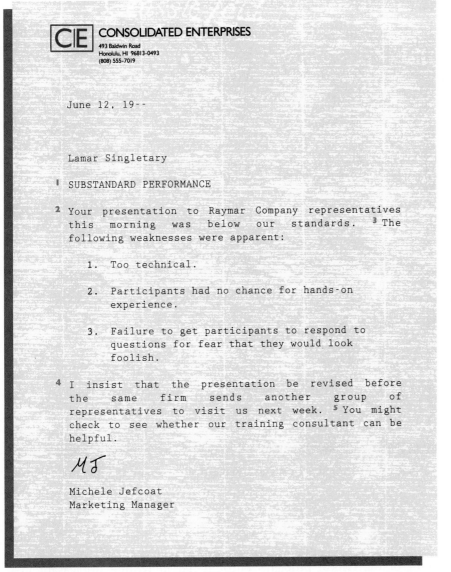

[1] As a subject line, these words immediately put the reader on the defensive.

[2] Emphasizes a negative thought by placing it in the first sentence and using negative language. [3] Emphasizes negatives with negative words (weakness and failure). Emphasizes unpleasant points by using tabulation and enumeration. Needs parallelism. (Point 2 is a complete sentence; 1 and 3 are phrases.)

[4] Seems unnecessarily demanding ("I insist"). [5] Seems unnecessarily weak in referring to action ("You might check").

Right margin should not be justified; the extra spaces placed between words to achieve the straight margin are distracting and reduce the reader's comprehension.

FIGURE 10-13   Poor example of a memorandum about poor job performance

1 As a subject line, these words assist in achieving a positive tone. A discussion of qualities desired in *next* week's presentation can have a much more positive tone than a discussion about the weaknesses of *this* week's presentation.

2 Uses positive language in introducing the subject. Use of "to me" assists in the transition to a discussion of others in the next paragraph.

3 Lets compliment precede criticism. By recognizing positive qualities, the supervisor establishes objectivity and reduces the sting of comments about negatives. **4** Identifies ways in which improvement can be made.

5, 6 Close with a helpful recommendation.

Illustrated simplified memorandum, a time-saving format, Includes writer's name and title a quadruple-space below the body. Signature (or initials) appear in space provided.

CONSOLIDATED ENTERPRISES
493 Baldwin Road
Honolulu, HI 96813-0493
(808) 555-7019

June 12, 19--

Lamar Singletary

1 NEXT WEEK'S SALES PRESENTATION TO RAYMAR COMPANY

2 Your presentation to Raymar Company representatives this morning was thorough and clear to me.

3 Because you were so well informed and organized, participants who were already somewhat familiar with our system could benefit greatly. **4** Most of them, though, would have gained more from a less technical discussion that involved hands-on experience and encouraged spontaneous questions.

5 Before next week's presentation, ask our training consultant (Carol Ried) for suggestions. **6** She has excellent ideas and access to the latest in audio-visual equipment.

Michele Jefcoat
Marketing Manager

FIGURE 10-14   Good example of a memorandum about poor job performance

The preceding analyses of letters and memoranda have highlighted most of the critical problems encountered in writing unpleasant messages. However, a few remain.

SPECIAL PROBLEMS IN WRITING ABOUT THE UNPLEASANT

While studying the preceding pages, you may have thought about the following questions:

1. *Is an inductive outline appropriate for* all *letters that convey bad news?* It is for *almost* all. Normally, the writer's purpose is to convey a clear message and retain the recipient's goodwill. In the rare circumstances in which a choice must be made between the two, clarity is the better choice. When the deductive approach will serve a writer's purpose better, it should be used. For example, if you submit a clear and tactful refusal and the receiver resubmits the request, a deductive presentation may be justified in the second refusal. Apparently, the refusal needs the emphasis provided by a deductive outline.

    Placing a refusal in the first sentence can be justified when
    a. The letter is the second response to a repeated request.
    b. A very small, insignificant matter is involved.
    c. A request is obviously ridiculous, immoral, unethical, illegal, or dangerous.

Although conveying unpleasant news to employees is not easy, your sensitivity and power of empathy will make the job easier and perhaps soften the blow.

d. A writer's intent is to "shake" the reader.

e. A writer-reader relationship is so close and longstanding that satisfactory human relations can be taken for granted.

f. The writer *wants* to demonstrate authority.

In most writing situations, the preceding circumstances do not exist. When they do, a writer's goals may be accomplished by stating bad news in the first sentence.

2. *Don't readers become impatient when a letter is inductive, and won't that impatience interfere with their understanding of the reasons?* Concise, well-written explanations are not likely to make readers impatient. They relate to the reader's problem, present information not already known, and help the reader understand. Even if readers do become impatient while reading well-written explanations, that impatience is less damaging to understanding than would be the anger or disgust that often results from encountering bad news in the first sentence.

3. *In inductive letters or memorandums, in which portions are mistakes most likely to be made?* Mistakes often occur in the first paragraph, the statement of bad news, and the last paragraph.

First Paragraph

The introductory paragraph should let the reader know the topic of the letter without saying the obvious. It should build a transition into the discussion of reasons without revealing the bad news or leading a reader to expect good news. The following introductory sentences do reveal the subject of the letter, but they have weaknesses:

I am writing in response to your letter requesting . . . .

The letter is obviously a response; omission of this idea would shorten the message. An *I* beginning signals that the letter may be writer centered.

COMMUNICATION MENTOR

Just as you are on the verge of signing a letter or memo, particularly one communicating sensitive information, force yourself to reread it slowly one more time. That final reading may yield inconsistencies, an unintentional breach of confidence, or even a typo!

You never know when something is the best it can be.

James F. Hurley
Senior Vice President
CalFed Inc.

Your letter of the 14th has been given to me for reply.

Obviously, the writer—instead of someone else—had the job of responding.

I can understand how you felt when you were asked to pay an extra $54.

Having requested a refund, a reader may be led to expect it. In the receiver's mind, the empathy displayed in the first sentence would be sufficiently strong to reveal the disappointment of subsequent denial; surely the request is to be granted. When a preceding statement has implied that an affirmative decision will follow, a negative decision is all the more disappointing.

Although the refund requested in your letter of May 1 cannot be granted, . . .

Immediate emotional reaction may cause the letter to be put aside at this point, or it may interfere with understanding of the explanations that follow.

Your request for an adjustment has been considered. However, . . .

The statement is neutral; doesn't reveal whether the answer is "yes" or "no." Such a beginning has about the same effect as an outright "no" beginning.

The following introductory paragraphs (1) identify the subject of the message and (2) serve as a transition into the discussion of reasons for a denial. (To illustrate transition/cohesion, the first words of the second paragraph are also presented.)

The double-indemnity feature of your policy has two provisions. In each, the words are "natural" and "accidental."

"Natural causes" are defined as . . .

To a policyholder who has submitted a double-indemnity claim, the topic of the letter is recognized immediately. "In each" relates the second sentence to the first; "natural" provides the transition from the introductory paragraph to the second paragraph, which begins the explanations.

Your application was reviewed separately by two loan officers.

Each officer considered . . .

To a would-be borrower who has applied for a loan, the subject of the letter is quickly established. Use of "officer" in the second paragraph is a coherence technique—an idea introduced in the first sentence is continued in the second. In the second paragraph, discussion of the officers' reviews will satisfy an expectation aroused in the first sentence.

After your request for permission to pick up leftover potatoes, we reviewed our experiences of recent years. Last year, two incidents . . .	An officer of a food-for-the-hungry mission would immediately recognize the letter as a response to a request that the mission be allowed to enter a grower's field and harvest potatoes left by the mechanical pickers. Note that repetition of "year" ties the second paragraph to the first and that the second paragraph intends to present details of the "experiences" mentioned in the introductory paragraph.

The preceding sentences illustrate effective introductory paragraphs that introduce a discussion without stating bad news or leading the reader to expect good news. Additional ideas can be incorporated into effective beginning paragraphs:

1. *A compliment.* A letter denying a customer's request could begin by recognizing that customer's promptness in making payments.
2. *A point of agreement.* If the letter being answered makes a statement with which you can agree, a sentence that reveals agreement could get the letter off to a positive discussion of other points.
3. *Some good news.* When a letter contains a request that must be refused and another that is being answered favorably, beginning with the favorable answer can be effective.
4. *Resale.* If the subject of correspondence is a product that has been bought, a refusal could begin with some favorable statement about the product.
5. *A review.* Refusal of a current request could be introduced by referring to the initial transaction or by reviewing certain circumstances that preceded the transaction.
6. *Gratitude.* Although an unjustified request may have been made, the reader may have done or said something for which you are grateful. An expression of gratitude could be used as a positive beginning.

Bad-News Sentence

In a sense, a paragraph that presents the reasoning behind a refusal at least partially conveys the refusal before it is stated directly or indirectly. Yet, one sentence needs to convey (directly or by implication) the conclusion to which the preceding details have been leading. The most important considerations are *positive language* and *emphasis*.

Your request is therefore being denied.	Being negative, the idea is not pleasant. Stated in negative terms, the idea is still less pleasant.

or

We are therefore denying your
request.

Both sentences seem to heighten abrasiveness
through use of emphasis techniques. The simple
sentences are emphatic. "Denied" stands out
vividly in the first sentence because it is the
last word. The second sentence is in first person and active voice, which are emphatic.

The preceding figures do not justify
raising your credit limit to $3,000
as you requested, but they do
justify raising the limit to $1,500.

The sentence uses negative language, but it
does use commendable techniques of subordination: It places the negative in a long, two-
clause sentence, and it includes a positive idea
in the sentence that contains the negative idea.

To soften the impact of a negative idea, a very helpful technique is
implication—an indirect statement, metacommunication. The following
sentences illustrate commendable techniques for *implying* a refusal:

Although the Bell Road
property was selected as the
building site, nearness to the
railroad was considered a plus
for the Hampton property.
[Statement made to the owner of
Hampton.]

Reveals what was *not* done by stating what *was*
done. Note also the passive construction and
the complex sentence, both of which de-
emphasize. "Bell Road property was selected"—the bad news—appears in the dependent clause, which is less emphatic than an independent clause. Inclusion of a positive
(nearness to the railroad) assists in
de-emphasizing the negative.

If the price were $15,000, the
contract would have been
accepted.

States a condition under which the answer
would have been "yes" instead of "no." Note
use of the subjunctive words "if" and "would."

By accepting the arrangement,
the ABC Company would have
tripled its insurance costs.

States the obviously unacceptable results of
complying with a request.

Last Paragraph

Having presented valid reasons and a tactful refusal, a writer needs a
closing paragraph that includes useful information and demonstrates empathy. It cannot do so by including statements such as these:

We trust this explanation is
satisfactory.

Could be taken as a confession of doubt about
the validity of the decision.

We hope you will understand our position.	May imply doubt about the receiver's ability to understand. Use of "position" seems to heighten controversy; positions are expected to be defended.
We are sorry to disappoint you.	Risks a negative retort: "If it made you feel so bad, why did you do it?" Can be interpreted as an apology for the action taken. If a decision merits apology, its validity is questionable.
Thank you for your interest.	This well-worn statement is often used thoughtlessly. Some refusals are addressed to people who have apparently *not* been interested enough to listen, read, or remember; otherwise, they wouldn't have made the requests. For them, the sentence is inappropriate. For others, it may seem shallow and superficial.
When we can be of further help, please don't hesitate to call or write.	This sentence is well worn and negative. *Further* help may seem especially inappropriate to someone who has just read a denial. The writer may see the *explanations* as helpful, but the reader may think the *denial* is being labeled as "helpful."

The final paragraph is usually shorter than the preceding explanatory paragraphs. Sometimes, a one-sentence closing is enough; other messages may require two or three sentences. The final sentence should seem like an *appropriate* closing; that is, it will bring a unifying quality to the whole message. Repetition of a word (or reference to some positive idea) that appears early in the letter serves this purpose well. Restatement of the refusal (or direct reference to it) would only serve to emphasize it.

Possibilities for the final sentence include reference to some pleasant aspect of the preceding discussion, resale, sales-promotional material, an alternative solution to the reader's problem, some future aspect of the business relationship, or an expression of willingness to assist in some *other* way. Consider the following closures, which use the preceding suggestions:

Your addition of the home-mortgage rider to your policy last year was certainly a wise decision.	Refers to something pleasant from the preceding discussion. "Home-mortgage" and other provisions had been mentioned in the early part of a letter to a client who was refused a double-indemnity settlement.
According to a recent survey, a four-headed VCR produces sound qualities that are far superior; it was an ideal choice.	Uses resale, a reminder that his four-headed VCR has a superior feature. His request for without-cost repair had been denied.

Mini-sized compacts and adapters are now available; see the enclosed folder.	Includes sales-promotional material. Request for without-cost repair had been denied.
Our representative will show you some samples when she calls next week.	Looks to a future event. The samples had been proposed as a possible solution to the recipient's problem.
If you would like to see the orientation film we show to management trainees, you would be most welcome.	Seeks to show a good attitude by offering to do something else. The reader had been refused permission to interview certain employees on the job.

In general, the same principles that apply to first, middle, and final sentences of a *written* message also apply to an *oral* message. The same principles that apply to all the letters in this chapter also apply to memorandums.

SUMMARY

Genuine empathy enables the writer to anticipate the reader's likely reaction to a message and, therefore, sequence the ideas in the most effective way. The inductive outline is recommended when the reader can be expected to be displeased by the message. As illustrated by the letters and memorandums in this chapter, the inductive outline places the main idea near the end of the letter. This sequence of ideas has the following advantages:

1. It sufficiently identifies the subject of the letter without first turning the reader off.
2. It presents the reasons *before* the refusal, where they are more likely to be understood.
3. It emphasizes the reasons by letting them precede the refusal.
4. It avoids a negative reaction. By the time the reasons are read, they seem sensible, and the refusal is foreseen. Because it is expected, the statement of refusal does not come as a shock.
5. It de-emphasizes the refusal by closing on a neutral or pleasant note. By showing a willingness to cooperate in some other way, the writer conveys a desire to be helpful.

In addition to using the inductive sequence, stylistic techniques help you to convey bad news effectively. For example, avoid overly negative words and statements or "red flags" that automatically set up barriers to your message. Instead consider more positive techniques such as stating what you *can* do rather than what you *cannot* do, including a positive fact in the same sentence with the negative idea, or offering a counterproposal to minimize the reader's disappointment.

Use sentence structure to help you de-emphasize negative ideas. Placing the negative message in the dependent clause of a complex sentence de-emphasizes the negative. Avoid using simple sentences to convey the refusal unless your intention is to emphasize the "no."

Using the inductive outline and reflecting a positive tone in your writing allows you to convey bad news diplomatically and to build lasting relationships.

UNPLEASANT MESSAGES

Content
- [ ] Major idea is clearly identified.
- [ ] Supporting detail is sufficient.
- [ ] Facts or figures are accurate.
- [ ] Message is ethical and abides by legal requirements.

Organization
- [ ] First sentence introduces the general subject
  - [ ] without stating the bad news.
  - [ ] without leading a reader to expect good news.
  - [ ] without making such an obvious statement as "I am replying to your letter" or "Your letter has been received."
- [ ] Details or explanations precede bad news.
- [ ] Main idea (unpleasant idea) emerges from preceding discussion.
- [ ] Closing sentences are about something positive (an alternative, resale, or sales promotion).

Style
- [ ] Words will be readily understood.
- [ ] Sentences are relatively short.
- [ ] Sentences vary in length and structure.
- [ ] Principal idea (the unpleasant idea, or the refusal) is sufficiently clear.
- [ ] Some techniques of subordination are used to keep the bad news from emerging with unnecessary vividness. For example, bad news
  - [ ] appears in a dependent clause.
  - [ ] is stated in passive voice.
  - [ ] is revealed through indirect statement.
  - [ ] is revealed through the use of subjunctive mood.
- [ ] First person is used sparingly or not at all.
- [ ] Ideas cohere (changes in thought are not abrupt).

- [ ] Expression is original (sentences are not copied directly from the definition of the problem or from sample letters in the text); clichés are omitted.

Mechanics
- [ ] Keyboarding, spelling, grammar, and punctuation are perfect.
- [ ] Paragraphs are relatively short.

Letters
- [ ] Letter style is acceptable (block, modified block, or simplified).
- [ ] Letter is balanced on the page.
- [ ] Letter parts are in appropriate vertical and horizontal position.
  - [ ] Return address (if plain paper is used)
  - [ ] Dateline
  - [ ] Inside address
  - [ ] Salutation (if needed)
  - [ ] Subject line (if needed)
  - [ ] Complimentary close (if needed)
  - [ ] Letter is signed legibly.
  - [ ] Keyboarded name (and title)
  - [ ] Reference initials (if needed)
  - [ ] Enclosure notation (if needed)
  - [ ] Other special letter parts (if needed)

Memorandums
- [ ] *TO, FROM, DATE,* and *SUBJECT* lines completed.
- [ ] Side margins are consistent.
- [ ] Courtesy titles are omitted in *TO* and *FROM* lines.
- [ ] Lines are single-spaced; blank space appears between paragraphs; paragraphs are not indented.
- [ ] Tabulated items are indented.
- [ ] Handwritten initials are placed by name on the *FROM* line (or signed in the space provided in the simplified format).

REVIEW QUESTIONS

1. How does empathy assist in organizing letters and memorandums?
2. List the four points that would appear in an outline for a letter or memo that conveys bad news. (List them in the best sequence.)
3. In planning a message, with which should a writer be concerned *first:* (a) the *organization* of the ideas or (b) the manner of *expressing* the ideas?
4. One disadvantage of stating a refusal in the first sentence is that the reader may stop reading at that point. State another disadvantage.
5. As a beginning sentence, what is wrong with "I am responding to your letter of the 25th"?
6. What would be the disadvantage of waiting until the last sentence to convey bad news?
7. List some stylistic techniques for achieving subordination.
8. Which is the more emphatic way to state a refusal: (a) positive language or (b) negative language?
9. Which will make a refusal stand out more vividly in a reader's mind: (a) a direct statement or (b) implication?
10. In which part of a refusal letter would sales-promotional material be most appropriate?
11. Under what condition should a memorandum be written inductively?
12. In the final paragraph, should a writer strive to achieve unity by referring to the statement of refusal? Explain.
13. List some conditions under which a writer would be justified in stating bad news in the first sentence.
14. How can writers reduce the risk that readers will become impatient while reading explanations that precede bad news?
15. Should the closing sentence apologize for action taken?

EXERCISES

1. Locate an example of both a well-written and a poorly written bad-news letter or memorandum. Analyze the strengths and weaknesses of each document. Be prepared to discuss in class.
2. Team up with a classmate to defend the use of the inductive or the deductive outline for bad-news messages. Consider whether your argument would vary if you were communicating with people of other cultures or other specific audiences. Consult the business literature to provide realistic examples and viewpoints that may strengthen your position.
3. Analyze the effectiveness of the following sentences as the opening sentences in bad-news messages.

a. Company policy does not allow me to approve the proposed transaction.

b. Tommy MacDougal received the promotion; you did not.

c. Our departmental award went to Charles Henning; you were our first runner-up.

d. We cannot grant you a refund. However, if you will agree to pay the shipping costs, we will send replacements for your defective spinning reels.

e. This letter is in response to your complaint of April 9.

4. Revise the following sentences to ensure positive tone.

   a. We cannot accept an application sent after May 9.

   b. Employees cannot smoke in the main office.

   c. I am sorry, but we cannot be responsible for the service charges on your car; the damage occurred at the dealership, not our factory.

   d. Your request for transfer to Kyoto, Japan, has been denied.

   e. We cannot accept this poorly organized report.

5. Analyze the letter on page 396. Pinpoint its strengths and weaknesses and then rewrite the letter.

APPLICATIONS

1. **Policy Covers Material Value Only.**   Continental Movers, a small moving company in Iowa, transported Charles and Linda Moore's belongings to Davenport. An oil painting that had belonged to Mr. Moore's great-grandmother was torn in transit; no other damage was done. When completing the required insurance claim forms, the Moores requested payment of $10,000, which they considered to be the value of this heirloom. However, the insurance policy covers only the material cost ($250). Before the Moores' possessions were moved, one of Continental's representatives carefully explained the policy to the Moores, and they signed the policy stating that they understood its stipulations.

   Required: As claims manager at Continental Movers, write an appropriate letter to Mr. and Mrs. Charles Moore, 873 North Spruce Lane, Davenport, IA 52802-8510.

RANCE	MANAGEMENT	MIS	CONS
Ethics	International	Legal	

2. **Refusal to Complete Free Repair.**   George Brandt bought a personal computer from one of the retail stores of a large computer-distribution center. He noticed its 90-day warranty for parts and labor and returned the manufacturer's certification-of-purchase form. Relatively unfamiliar with personal computers, he studied portions of the operator's manual and the first few frames of a tutorial software. He accidentally erased most of the tutorial. When he tried to get "Menu" to

NCE	MANAGEMENT	MIS	CONSUM
gal	Interpersonal	Technology	

1933 Southbend Road
Cedar Grove, IN 47016-1933
June 14, 19—

Mr. Marve Mitchell
619 Downey Street
Cedar Grove, IN   47016-0619

Dear Marve:

I am pleased and honored to have been asked to serve as
president of the Cedar Grove Jaycees for the coming year.

However, I regret to inform you that I cannot serve in this
important position. Last year, obligations kept me from attending
seven of the twenty-five meetings. Unfortunately, commitments
for the coming year are even greater than last year. The position
of president requires a tremendous amount of attention—much
more than I can give at this particular time.

Once again, I appreciate the confidence you have placed in me but
am sorry that my plans preclude my serving as president this
year. I look forward to actively participating in this year's
activities and am especially eager to chair the Goodwill Marathon
project again this year.

Sincerely,

Mark Ogletree

Mark L. Ogletree

Exercise 5

show up on the screen, the machine refused the command. He could
not find help in the manual. In panic, he took off the cover (with the
use of a screwdriver) and looked inside the monitor for possible
causes of the problem. No luck.

The retailer refused an adjustment because an unauthorized attempt at repair had invalidated the warranty. George wrote the main
office of the distribution center requesting permission to bring the
unit in for repair without charge. In all probability, George had not

given the machine appropriate instructions; and he certainly had ignored the boldfaced instructions on his manual: "Do not remove cover; only factory-trained specialists are authorized to do work."

Required: As a repair manager in the distribution center, write a letter refusing the repair-for-free request. Offer to inspect it and provide an estimate of the repair cost. George Brandt, 981 Hickory Lane, Scottsdale, AZ 85143-9081.

3. **Deductible on Insurance Policy Has Not Been Met.** Charles Dawson had insured his home with Security Insurance Company. During the Christmas holidays, a neighborhood child practiced target shooting with a BB gun he had received as a present. Two shots went through Mr. Dawson's front window. Knowing that such damages were covered by his policy, he had the window replaced, paid the $81.45 bill, and sent the statement to Security asking for reimbursement. Security cannot reimburse because the policy has a $100 deductible clause. He had chosen to include the clause because it made his premium payment lower. Possibly, the child's parents may have a policy that covers liability for such incidents.

ING	INSURANCE	MANAGEMENT
Interpersonal	Technology	Pul

Required: As a claims manager at Security Insurance, address an appropriate letter to Charles Dawson, 321 West 4th Street, Wilbur, KS 67543-9013.

4. **Damaged Blanket Improperly Washed.** Lt. Andrew Johnson wrote a letter to the manufacturer of an electric blanket asking that it be replaced under the terms of its two-year guarantee. It had been given to him as a wedding present 28 months ago. It had been used one season and then washed and stored for the next season while he had been overseas. It was guaranteed for two seasons, but it had been used for only one. When he returned home, the blanket would not heat; he returned it to the manufacturer. Although the washing instructions attached to the blanket stipulated that it be tumble washed, it apparently had been squeezed (either by wringer or by hand). As a result, the damaged wires will not permit current to flow. In any case, the guarantee has expired. It was not for two years of use; rather, it was for two years from the date it had been purchased by a consumer. The blanket is to be returned.

MANAGEMENT	MIS	CONSUMER
Ethics	International	Legal

Required: Write a letter to Lt. Andrew Johnson, P.O. Box 1234, Westview, OR 97654-3688.

5. **New Credit Policies Affect Real Estate Loans Adversely.** Kerwin Construction Corp. has requested $14 million from Colonial National Bank to build a 200,000-square-foot shopping center. Three major chains (department store, discount store, and electronics/video outlet) —adequate anchors for this size center—have already signed leases.

IONS	FINANCE	ACCOUNTING	INS
Interpersonal	Technology	Pul	

80 percent of the remaining space has been leased. Kerwin has presented budgets showing how the income from this center can service the loan, and the development itself is offered as collateral for the loan.

Under previous lending guidelines, the bank could grant a real estate loan if it had reasonable assurance that the borrower could repay the loan from either the income from operations or the sale of the development. Because of the current decline in the economy, lending guidelines for real estate loans have become stricter. The borrower must now provide assurance that the loan can be repaid from sources other than the development itself, typically the income or assets of other businesses or personal investments. Thus, these new guidelines are designed to ensure payment of the loan regardless of the success or failure of the proposed development.

Required: As the loan manager, write a letter to Bart Kerwin refusing to grant the loan. P.O. Box 9408, Eau Claire, WI 54703-9408.

6. **Customer Credit Too Risky to Obtain Loan.**   You are the director of loans at Wheaton State Bank in Cleveland, Ohio. You receive a letter from Peter Nelson, who applied for a loan to buy a bass boat. You denied his loan because his credit history revealed that he had three credit cards charged to the maximum with two months' payments overdue. In his letter, Mr. Nelson quoted the Ohio discrimination laws that require all creditors to make credit equally available to all creditworthy customers.

Required: Write to Peter Nelson restating reasons for denying credit and pointing out that the law emphasizes equal access to creditworthy customers. 910 Miller Court, Cleveland, OH 44101-8600.

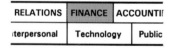

7. **Loan Denial for Poor Credit Customer.**   Having decided to build an addition to their home, George and Sandra Rustow made an application for a $15,000 loan from a personal finance company. The company's credit check revealed a consistent record of slow payment. Several times, they paid only after forceful attempts at collection.

Required: As manager of the local branch of the finance company, write a refusal letter. George and Sandra Rustow, P.O. Box 432, Baxter, WI 54321-5590.

8. **Family Too Financially Burdened for Store Credit.** Ernestine Bagota left an application for credit at your department store and was told that she would be informed by letter about the results of her application. These facts are apparent from the application. The family's income last year was $21,000. The family has four children, two of whom are in high school. The father is out of work but hopes to resume within three weeks. Obligated payments each month are $900. Additional obligations now would be a severe strain on Ms. Bagota's finances.

Required: Write a letter refusing Ms. Bagota's application but encouraging her to take full advantage of the seasonal sales your store offers. Some sales markdowns are as much as 50 percent. Ernestine Bagota, 917 West Hermosa Street, Wellville, TX 78540-1066.

9. **Dry Sprinkler System Is More Appropriate for Cold Climates.** As the owner of JPL Plumbing Contractors, you have reviewed the specifications for a new clubhouse at the Rolling Plains Golf Club. You are concerned that the plans include a traditional wet sprinkler system that carries water in the pipes to be used in case of fire. If exposed to subfreezing temperatures over extended periods, the water in the pipes will freeze and then break, causing water damage to the structure. This freezing problem has caused unnecessary damages to several of your previous contracts; therefore, you now recommend installation of a dry sprinkler system. In this system, the pipes contain pressurized air that opens a valve for sprinkler action when the fire is detected. Because the dry system is less conventional and more expensive than the wet system, few architects are including the dry systems in their blueprints.

   The client has three options: (1) authorize the architect to redesign the blueprint to include the dry system, (2) instruct you to install the wet system with a heat source in the attic to be used during subfreezing temperatures, or (3) arrange for another contractor to install the wet system (without the heat source). You are convinced that any dissatisfaction resulting from the unnecessary damages caused by broken pipes will more adversely affect your company than sacrificing the contract.

   Required: Write the letter explaining the need for the dry system and presenting the three options. Mention a brochure that you are including that explains and illustrates the dry system. Address the letter to Mr. Gary Myers, Manager, Rolling Plains Golf Club, Rolling Plains Boulevard, Springfield, IL 62701-3498.

INSURANCE	MANAGEMENT	MIS
Ethics	International	Legal

10. **No Refund for Damaged Sales Item.** You are in charge of sales returns for Uptown Styles, a mail-order catalog business. You receive a package containing scraps of material, a sales receipt, and a letter from Mary Phillips. She purchased the lightweight tropical skirt and coordinating blouse for $50 during a half-of-half-price sale two months ago, and the skirt simply fell apart after two washings. Your return policy states that sales of half price or more are final; the skirt was bought at a 75-percent reduction.

   Required: Write Mary Phillips a letter denying the adjustment. Mary Phillips, 102 Morning Lane, Greensboro, NC 58366-3107.

INSURANCE	MANAGEMENT	MIS
nterpersonal	Technology	Public

11. **Mail Order Catalog No Longer Free.** Atlanta Cost Distributors, a mail-order house, can no longer supply catalogs free of charge. The

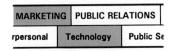

MARKETING	PUBLIC RELATIONS
rpersonal	Technology	Public Se

costs of designing, printing, and distributing have increased dramatically in recent years. The charge is now $5 per catalog.

Required: Write a form letter to people who have requested a catalog but have not included a check. Address the sample letter to Ms. Laura Tucker, 98 Layne Drive, Spartanburg, SC 29304-1957.

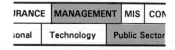

12. **Decision to Relocate Corporate Headquarters Is Final.**   Recently the board of directors of Royal Discount Stores decided to relocate its corporate headquarters from New York City to one of the city's suburbs. The mayor of New York, Cliff Vance, has written the board urging it to reconsider its decision to relocate. Despite the individual members' personal preference to keep the headquarters in the city, the board agreed that the decision to relocate was in the best interest of the company. The following factors led to the decision: (1) The lower tax rates in the suburbs would provide an economic advantage. (2) The company's salary structure is affected by the direct and indirect costs of commuting required of employees who live in the suburbs. (3) During the past few years, the company has had difficulty recruiting managerial talent, who prefer living in the suburbs. (4) Several major competitors are already located in the suburbs.

Required: As chairman of the board, write a letter to the mayor refusing his request. Address it to Cliff Vance, Mayor of New York, New York, NY 10001-7600. Consult a reference manual to identify the appropriate courtesy title and salutation for this public official.

13. **Parent Company Refuses to Continue Support of Not-for-Profit Program.**   ChemCon Engineering, a family-owned business, has underwritten an adult literacy program on public television for the past five years. The owners and the public relations director believe that the financial support of this worthwhile project has been a favorable public relations tool. Recently ChemCon was bought out by Petrol Corp. When approached by the television program director to renew financial commitment to the literacy program, the new president refused. The president is not opposed to efforts to increase adult literacy; however, top management at Petrol sees little if any merit in sponsoring public television programs. Therefore, no advertising dollars are channeled into projects such as this one.

Required: As the public relations director, write the letter to the television station refusing to contribute to the program. Address it to Patty Spencer, Program Director, WRMW Television, P.O. Drawer 93001, Salem, OR 97301-8461.

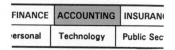

14. **Unable to Speak at Seminar.**   For several years, you as a civic-minded accountant have conducted seminars on investments for various organizations. This year, the Beta Alpha Psi chapter at the local university has asked you to assist with the annual VITA (Voluntary

Income Tax Assistance) program. Specifically, the group wishes you to devote two evenings to assist the accounting students as they complete income tax returns. The dates selected are at the end of March—a particularly inconvenient time for you. You need every moment that month if you are to satisfy the needs of your clients.

Required: Write a letter refusing the request. Dr. Jeff Johnson, Accounting Department, Central State College, P.O. Drawer 419, Oakwood, IA 63981-0532.

15. **Free Training for Additional Employees Is Not Available.** Computers, Incorporated sold a computer to a medical clinic. The sales agreement provided that an operator in the medical office would be admitted free to a five-day training class conducted on the seller's premises. Within a week after completing the training, the operator took a new job. The doctor now requests permission to enroll another operator for five days of free training. Space in the training sessions is scarce, and the cost of providing them free is excessive. Furthermore, the doctor bought the computer at a considerable discount.

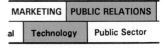

Required: Write a letter refusing the request for *free* training, but offer to provide it for $200. Dr. Anne Quinn, Room 302, Professional Building, Graham, UT 84312-7155.

16. **Informing Applicants Not Selected for Scholarship: A Challenge in Human Relations.** The founders of Bassett Communications are dedicated alumni of the College of Business at Walker College; consequently, the company awards an annual scholarship to an outstanding management or marketing major. As the human resources director, you chair the selection committee and have developed specific criteria: academic and leadership record and an essay outlining career plans. Previously you had written a form letter that was sent to all applicants who were not selected. After reviewing the rejection letter, you are convinced that it can be improved. Based on your past experience with this scholarship program, you have written several standard paragraphs to fit the various reasons each applicant may have been rejected. By selecting the appropriate paragraph, you can now send each applicant a personalized letter providing the specific reasons for his or her rejection and offering advice where appropriate.

Required: Write the appropriate letter to Mark Monterey, whose grade point average fell slightly below the criteria set by the committee and whose essay contained several major grammatical errors and misspellings. His address is Walker College, P.O. Box 190, Vero Beach, FL 32966-9583.

17. **Higher Price on Materials Forthcoming.** A manufacturer of fiberboard boxes needs a form letter that can be mailed to its customers. Its purpose is to inform that prices of fiberboard boxes will be

raised 10 percent effective two months from now. A revised price list is being prepared and will reach customers within two weeks. To hold prices down, the firm has tried every cost-cutting technique it can think of (such as labor-saving machinery, employee training, time-and-motion studies, and merit-rating systems). These efforts did help, but the increases are still necessary.

Required: Write the sample letter and address it to Harpole, Inc., 2500 Acadia Road, Blythedale, MO 64426-2500. Direct the letter to the attention of the purchasing department.

MANAGEMENT	MIS	CONSUMER
International	Legal	Interperson

18. **International Transfer Refused.**   Pat Cantrell has been with Carson TV Manufacturing for 15 years (7 as a plant worker, 6 years as crew supervisor, and 2 as plant manager in Houston, Texas). He and Charles Adams (plant manager in Des Moines) have been instrumental in establishing a branch plant in Heidelberg, West Germany, and both have applied to be manager of the German plant. Because Charles has been with the company for 20 years (9 as plant manager) and speaks German fluently, he has been selected for the transfer.

Required: As company president, write a memo to Pat denying his request for transfer.

HUMAN RESOURCES MANAGEMENT		
Ethics	International	Legal

19. **Insurance Premiums Are Increasing.**   Midland Timber Mill employs 1,000 workers. Sawmill workers operate in 12-hour shifts (6 to 6 night and day) and office personnel work 9 a.m. to 5 p.m. In the past, the company withheld $59.50 per month from workers' pay for health insurance premiums. Carey Life Insurance (the insurance carrier) has recategorized the night-shift workers as "high risk" because of the hazardous nature of the machinery and the stress of a nightly 12-hour shift. This change will raise the all workers' fee to $65.00 per week.

Required: As the business manager, write a memorandum to all employees outlining the reasons for the increase.

HUMAN RESOURCES MANAGEMENT			
Ethics	International	Legal	Int

20. **Written Disciplinary Action Required.**   You are the personnel director of a small rural hospital. Renee Visentin, one of the nurse's aides, has arrived several minutes late for work frequently over the past month; on each occasion she had a plausible reason for her tardiness. This week she has worked only one of the three shifts she has been assigned and has given no explanation for her absences.

Required: Write a memorandum to Renee, with a copy to her file, warning her that tardiness and unexcused absence are unacceptable. If such performance continues, further disciplinary action will be taken.

21. **Employee Must Pay Own Convention Costs.** Paul Adams, information systems manager for Seldane Enteprises, has decided to attend a national convention of information systems managers. Estimated cost of travel, registration fee, and lodging is $1,200, which he wants Seldane to pay. Precedent for paying such expenses is well established—for those who plan far enough in advance. In his five-year tenure with Seldane, Paul has not previously attended such a meeting. He should have made his intentions known last year when the accounting department sought estimates of each department's expenses for the coming year. Because the budget does not allow for such an expenditure this year, Paul will have to pay his own expenses if he goes. His personal accountant will probably confirm that the expense is deductible on his income-tax return.

    Required: As assistant controller, write a memorandum to Paul Adams refusing his request.

HUMAN RESOURCES MANAGEMENT		
Interpersonal	Technology	Publi

22. **Grade Earned Is Not Worthy of Full Tuition Reimbursement.** You are the human resources director for Young & Associates. For certain types of training (computer literacy, keyboarding, and communications), you encourage employees to enroll in night classes at a local college or university. For employees who earn an A, the firm pays 100 percent of the tuition; for a B, 75 percent; for a C, 50 percent. For lower grades, no reimbursement is allowed. Kathyrn Newsome has completed a small-group communication course and requested full reimbursement. Her grade was a C.

    Required: Write a memorandum that explains the reimbursement policy and refuses her request. Address it to Kathyrn Newsome, Operations Research Department.

HUMAN RESOURCES MANAGEMENT		
personal	Technology	Public Sec

23. **New Parking Garage Worth Dealing with Construction Problems.** Three weeks from the current date, the paved parking lot Herring Industries has been leasing for its employees will close. A multistory parking garage will be erected in its place. Construction will take about four months. During that time, employees will be able to park in the Third Street Parking Lot. The temporary site is a three-block walk to and from the office. When the new structure is completed, cars will be parked under a roof and thus shielded from the sun in summer and harsh weather in the winter. A covered walkway will be erected between the lot and the company's offices.

    Required: As the general manager, write a memorandum to all employees communicating this information about parking.

CE	MANAGEMENT	MIS	CONSUM
hics	International	Legal	Inte

HUMAN RESOURCES MANAGEMENT

| Ethics | International | Legal |

24. Offer of Early Retirement Instead of Paid Leave. Vinita Clark, chief of operations at the Markens Art Company, has received a memorandum from Ruth Hutchinson, the purchasing manager. Orally, Ruth had discussed the possibility of a year's leave of absence. Vinita had asked that the proposal be presented in written form. Ruth wants to be paid her salary for the year. The leave will allow her time to complete a book on which she has worked part-time for five years. In the book, which is about famous sculptors of America, she will devote considerable space to the work of Maynord Jenkins (the sculptor with whom MAC has an exclusive arrangement). By the time her leave is completed (and her book finished), Ruth will have reached the retirement age of 65. She plans to retire at that time.

Unquestionably, Ruth's background (both before and after coming to work for MAC 15 years ago) has prepared her well for writing the book she describes. Until about a year ago, her work as purchasing manager had been outstanding. Lately, she has seemed preoccupied; much of her work has been passed on to her subordinates. Instead of "working" on the book part-time for five years, she has probably been merely thinking about it. If her work of recent months is a valid indicator, Ruth will not complete the book. If it were completed, it would probably assist in the sale of Jenkins' work; but the advertising value would be far less than the cost of her year's salary.

After discussing the proposal with George Markens, president (who says there is no precedent for paid leaves), Vinita decides to refuse the request and offer early retirement instead. According to the MAC retirement policy, Ruth would be able to retire now at 60 percent of her base pay, only 2 percent less than she would receive if she retired at 65.

Required: As Vinita Clark, write the memorandum to Ruth refusing the request and offering early retirement. Assume Ruth and Vinita have discussed the leave and the possibility of early retirement verbally.

CASES FOR ANALYSIS

MANAGEMENT | MIS | CONSUMER

| al | Legal | Interpersonal | Techn |

Case 1. Plant Will Close for Two Weeks Economic troubles have hit the Hackney Forge Machinists Plant. Many employees have been laid off, and the grapevine has begun to promote rumors that additional employees will be laid off and that the company is going bankrupt. Communication related to the initial layoffs was poor and reactive. Top management is convinced that communication between employer and employees must be improved if the company is to survive this economic downturn.

As plant manager, you must announce to employees that the plant will close for two weeks at Christmas. Workers will be paid only 50 percent of their salaries for the two weeks the plant is closed.

Required:

1. To minimize employee fear and inaccurate rumors, research ways to communicate this negative information. Follow these suggestions: review the research related to communication crises, specifically employer-employee relations (e.g., public relations textbooks and academic journals in the communication field); and read current practitioners' journals to learn what approaches other companies have taken to improve communication with employees when the company is facing financial difficulty.

2. As the plant manager, use your research to write the memorandum informing employees of their reduced work schedule during Christmas.

3. As the plant manager, write a memorandum to the president (Cameron Sanford) providing general guidelines for improved employer-employee relations during a financial crisis. Include complete and accurate documentation of your sources. Your intention is that Mr. Sanford will distribute this memorandum (or the information within it) so that other managers can benefit from your research.

Case 2. Minimizing the Negative Publicity Associated with Product Recalls. Recently a new employee in quality control learned that the product description of the company's swing set (Model 2352) was modified because the metal used in the swing sets was not strong enough. Reinforcement bars could break under the weight of children swinging from them. When confronted, the production manager said there was no need to recall the 10,000 swings made from the inferior metal and insisted that the employee not mention the issue again.

MANAGEMENT	MIS	CONSUMER
ial	Technology	Public Sector

After careful analysis of this difficult ethical dilemma, the employee wrote a memorandum to you, the vice president of production, advocating recall of these dangerous swing sets. You are convinced that the swing sets should be recalled despite the negative publicity that will follow. This situation is new to you; you've never been faced with what public relations directors call "crisis communication." You must carefully consider the strategy you should take. You are certain of one thing; you have two equally important purposes: (1) You must disclose necessary information about the problem with the swing sets as honestly as you can and (2) at the same time, maintain the customers' confidence in the company's products and in its integrity.

Required:

1. Identify the important guidelines for communicating crisis information. Follow these suggestions: Review the research related to crisis communication (e.g., public relations textbooks and academic journals in the communication field), read current practitioners' journals to learn what approaches other companies have taken (e.g., product tampering, oil spills, and toxic waste contamination), and/or interview a public relations director of a company in your area or a public relations professor.

2. Based on your knowledge, write the recall letter to be sent to customers owning the swing sets. Inform the customer of what you believe to be the appropriate restitution (repayment) for the defective product. Address the sample letter to Mrs. Jean O'Toole, 1278 Webster Boulevard, Omaha, NE 68101-8100.

Case 3.   An Accountant's Knowledge of a Fraudulent Tax Return: What Action Is Legal? Is It Ethical?   As a tax accountant in a large accounting firm, you prepared Scott Harshaw's tax return last year. The return indicated that Mr. Harshaw was due a small tax refund; his business reported less net income than in the prior year. Now, more than a year later, Mr. Harshaw has asked your assistance in preparing a business plan to secure a loan. Immediately you notice that last year's income statement shows twice the net income of the income statement you used to prepare the tax return. When you question Mr. Harshaw about the discrepancy, his evasive response assures you that the understatement of net income for tax purposes was intentional.

Required:

1. Write a letter to Mr. Harshaw asking him to authorize you to file an amended tax return. The amended return will require your client to pay additional taxes, interest, and penalties. Address the letter to Scott Harshaw, 3300 Parkway Drive, Fresno, CA 91316-3300.

2. Assume the client refuses to authorize you to amend the tax return. Complete the following research to assist in making an informed response:
   a. Identify what action the IRS requires of tax preparers upon learning that a filed tax return was fraudulent. Consult tax references such as the circulars published by the Internal Revenue Service.
   b. Determine what action the Code of Ethics of the American Institute of Certified Public Accountants (AICPA) indicates is appropriate for a certified public accountant to take in this circumstance. For this information, refer to tax references such as the *Statements on Responsibilities in Tax Practice.*

3. After analyzing the research completed in step 2, write a memo to the tax partner communicating your analysis of the situation and the action you propose that the firm take. Cite the research to increase the credibility of your position.

4. The tax partner has approved your decision in the Harshaw case; he was impressed with your meticulous research and documentation. He has authorized you to prepare a letter to the client communicating the firm's action. Because of the sensitivity of the situation, he has requested that you prepare the letter for his signature; include your reference initials in all capital letters to identify the originator in the event of questions later. Address the letter to Scott Harshaw, 3300 Parkway Drive, Fresno, CA 91316-3300.

WRITING TO PERSUADE

OBJECTIVES

When you have completed Chapter 11, you should be able to

- Develop effective out-lines for messages that persuade.

- Develop a central theme for sales messages, per-suasive requests, and col-lection letters.

- Achieve unity, emphasis, and coherence in persua-sive messages.

- Write collection letters at various stages of the col-lection process.

IT'S SUNDAY NIGHT and you are reading the newspaper. You have the television on, although you are not paying particular attention to it. It's tuned to MTV, so it is almost like having the radio on anyway. Occasionally, you catch yourself humming a few stanzas of a song you like. Apparently, your conscious mind is reading while your unconscious mind is enjoying music. At some point during the evening, you hear the voice of a familiar vocalist, but she's not singing—later you seem to recall that she was talking about taking care of the environment. The next day, you actually watch the brief "commercial" on MTV and see the same vocalist telling you in detail things you can do to be more environmentally aware. The things she tells you to do are simple, and her argument is credible. You decide to tune up your bicycle and use it instead of your car for short errands on campus.

This example illustrates persuasion at work. Every day, we are targets of persuasion from advertisers on the radio, on television, in newspapers and magazines, on billboards, and even in the movies. We are bombarded with messages designed to convince us to buy the newest soft drink, see the latest Hollywood blockbuster, and support the best cause. In an election year, we are targets of the persuasive techniques of politicians. Persuasion is an effective sales technique—but it is also a strategy businesspeople must master to gain the support of others in important decisions. Persuasion involves the ability to win others to your point of view.

How do you learn to persuade others through written communication? Like other forms of writing, it requires practice and hard work. Have you ever written a cover letter, filled out an application for a job, or written an essay for college entry or a scholarship? If so, you already have experience with this type of writing.

For persuasion to be effective, you must understand your product or idea and your audience, anticipate the arguments that may come from the audience, and have a rational and logical response to those arguments. Remember, persuasion need not be a hard sell; it can simply be a way of getting a client or your supervisor to say "yes."

SALES LETTERS

A *sale* (exchange of goods or services for money) may or may not be preceded by prior discussion. Most grocery shoppers, for example, make their selections and pay without first discussing quality and price with the grocer. For most car shoppers, however, a discussion will precede the transaction. A transaction will take place only after the shopper is *convinced* that the exchange is favorable or at least equitable. This *act of convincing* is most commonly called "persuasion" or "selling." Selling is not an attempt to trap someone into taking action favorable to the seller. Instead, it is an honest, organized presentation of information upon which a prospective buyer may choose to act.

For those who will earn their living in a marketing-related field, knowledge of sales writing is especially beneficial. It is beneficial for those in other fields, as well. Although many of the examples and discussion in this chapter concentrate on selling *products*, very similar principles apply to selling an *idea* and *services*. Typically, achievement requires the setting of goals. Cooperation seldom results without exchange and acceptance of ideas. In all occupations and professions, rich rewards await those who can use well-informed and well-prepared presentations to persuade others to accept their ideas or buy their products.

Plan Before You Write

Success in *writing* is directly related to success in preliminary *thinking*. If the right questions have been asked and answered beforehand, the writing will be easier and the message will be more persuasive:

Preliminary planning is vital.

- What strong features does the product (or idea) have?

  How is it different from its competition?

  Who are the people to whom the message is directed, and what are their wants and needs?

  What specific action is wanted?

  Which writing principles will be especially helpful?

Before you can write an effective sales letter, you must know as much as possible about the product you are trying to sell. You must also be aware of the readers' needs and any doubts or questions they may have about your product.

Know the Product.   You cannot be satisfied with knowing the product in a general way; you need details. Get your information by (1) reading all available literature, (2) using the product and comparing it with others, (3) conducting tests and experiments, (4) watching others use the product, (5) observing the manufacturing process, and (6) soliciting reports from users. Before you write, you need concrete answers to such questions as these:

What questions must be answered before writing a sales letter?

1. What will the product do for people?
2. From what materials is it made?
3. By what process is it manufactured?
4. What are its superior features in design and workmanship?
5. What is its price?
6. What kind of servicing, if any, will it require?

Similar questions must be answered about competing products. Of particular importance is the question, "What is the major difference?" People are inclined to choose an item that has some advantage not available in a similar item at the same price. For example, some people may choose a brand of bread because it is high in fiber and contains no cholesterol; still others may choose bread because it is wrapped in two-layer paper.

Why is the major difference so important?

Know the Reader.   Is a sales letter to be written and addressed to an individual or to a group? If it is addressed to a group, what characteristics do the members have in common? What are their common goals, their occupational levels, their educational status? To what extent have their needs and wants been satisfied? (See the discussion of Maslow's needs hierarchy in Chapter 2.)

Envision yourself as the person receiving the letter.

Some people may respond favorably to appeals to physiological, security, and safety needs (to be comfortable, to be healthy, to save time and money, or to avoid danger). People with such needs would be favorably impressed with a discussion of such features as convenience, durability, efficiency, or serviceability. Others may respond favorably to appeals to their social, ego, and self-actualizing needs (to be loved, entertained, remembered, popular, praised, appreciated, or respected). Appeals to the second group of needs are usually referred to as "psychological" appeals. Because most North Americans' lower-level needs have been satisfied, appeals to psychological needs are more common. The more that is known about the reader, the more accurately an appeal can be selected.

What is an "appeal"?

Identify the Desired Action.   What do you want your reader to do? Fill out an order form and enclose a personal check? Return a card requesting a representative to call? Write for more information? Whatever the desired action, you need to have a clear definition of it before beginning to compose the letter.

Apply Sound Writing Principles. The principles of unity, coherence, and emphasis are just as important in sales letters as in other letters. In addition, some other principles seem to be especially helpful in sales letters:

1. *Use concrete nouns and active verbs.* Concrete nouns and active verbs help readers see the product and its benefits more vividly than do abstract nouns and passive verbs.
2. *Use specific language.* General words seem to imply subjectivity unless they are well supported with specifics. Specific language is space consuming (saying that something is "great" is less space consuming than telling what makes it so); therefore, sales letters are usually longer than other letters. Still, sales letters need to be concise; they should say what needs to be said without wasting words.
3. *Let readers have the spotlight.* If readers are made the subject of some of the sentences, if they can visualize themselves with the product in their hands, if they can get the feel of using it for enjoyment or to solve problems, the chances of creating a desire are increased.
4. *Stress a central selling point.* Few products have everything. A thorough product analysis will ordinarily reveal some feature that is different from the features of competing products. This point of difference can be developed into a theme that permeates the entire letter. Or, instead

Return to Chapter 8 for a quick review of coherence and emphasis.

Why are sales letters usually longer than other letters?

An expert salesperson keeps his or her attention focused on the customer. Likewise, when you write persuasive or sales messages, you should keep your reader (not yourself, your product or idea) in the spotlight.

of using a point of difference as a central selling point, a writer may choose to stress one of the major satisfactions derived from using the item. A central selling point *(theme)* should be introduced early in the letter and should be reinforced throughout the remainder of the letter.

5. *Use an inductive outline.* Well over eighty years ago, Sherwin Cody (1906, pp. 122–126) summarized the basic steps in the selling process. The steps have been varied somewhat and have had different labels, but the fundamentals remain relatively unchanged. The selling procedure includes four steps:

What are the four steps in the selling procedure?

   a. Getting the prospect's attention.
   b. Introducing the product and arousing interest in it.
   c. Presenting convincing evidence.
   d. Encouraging action.

These steps constitute the basic outline for sales letters. Each step is essential, but the steps do not necessarily require equal amounts of space. Good sales writing does not require that we have separate sentences and paragraphs for each phase of the letter—getting attention, introducing the product, giving evidence, and stimulating action. To follow such a plan would be to place our writing style in a straitjacket. Points (a) and (b) *could* appear in the same sentence. Point (c) could require many paragraphs.

Should a sales letter have four paragraphs—one for each phase of the selling process?

The four-point outline is appropriate for *unsolicited* sales letters. *Solicited* sales letters have been invited by the prospect; unsolicited sales letters have not. For example, a letter written to answer a prospect's question is *solicited;* a letter written to someone who has not invited it is *unsolicited.*

Why are unsolicited sales letters more difficult to write than solicited sales letters?

Someone who has invited a sales message has given some attention to the product already; an attention-getting sentence is hardly essential. Such a sentence is essential, however, when the recipient is not known to have previously expressed an interest. The very first sentence, then, is deliberately designed to make a recipient put aside other thoughts and concentrate on the rest of the message.

First Paragraph: An Attention Getter

Various techniques have been successful in convincing recipients to put aside whatever they are doing or thinking about and consider an unsolicited letter. Some commonly used methods:

The first sentence should arouse desire to read sentences that follow.

Writing-analysis software that identifies your mistakes helps you create error-free, professional documents.	A solution to a problem.
Warehouse sale at Westlake Office Furniture! Retail outlets offer wholesale prices!	A bargain.

A stitch in time saves nine.	A proverb.
Oil costs are projected to rise another 12 percent this year.	A news announcement.
More teens die as a result of suicide each month than die in auto accidents in the same time period.	Startling announcement.
Here's the typical day of a manager who uses Wilson Enterprises Voice Mail.	A story.
P. T. Barnum supposedly said, "There's a sucker born every minute." At Northland Candy Factory, we make the saying come true!	A quote from a famous person.
Conway—the Harvard of community colleges!	An analogy.
What if the boss announced, "We're going to increase efficiency in our department by 30 percent?"	A what-if opening.
An answering machine that lets you check messages in the office when you are hundreds of miles away on business!	An outstanding feature of the product.
A young boy approached his father. "What are you doing, Daddy?" "Watching the paint dry," his dad replied. "Want to help me?" "Won't that take too long?" questioned his impatient son. "Not long at all, Johnny. It's Walton's Quickdry."	An interesting anecdote.
Why are more businesses choosing Telefax over other leading facsimile machines?	A question.
Examine the enclosed custom-designed matching dividers, which are color-coded to decrease retrieval time. Notice	A comment on an enclosed product sample.
Ten free sheets of embossed personalized stationery are enclosed as a free sample.	A gift.

The World   A fake inside address. (These lines
Is Growing   would be arranged in the inside-address
Smaller   position, getting attention by location.)
Every Day

Dear Mr. Larkin:

You should see . . .   A split sentence.
the highly professional documents
produced on the Quick Print II laser
printer.

Regardless of the attention-getting technique we choose for any letter, we should ask ourselves some pertinent questions: (1) Is the attention getter related to the product and its virtues? (2) Does the first sentence introduce a central selling feature? (3) Is the attention getter addressed to the reader's needs? (4) Does the attention getter sound interesting? (5) Is the attention getter original? (6) Is the first paragraph short?

Start with the Product. The beginning sentence must suggest a relationship between recipient and product. It must pave the way for the remainder of the sales letter. The sentences that follow the first sentence should grow naturally from it. (See the discussion of coherence in Chapter 8.) If readers do not see the relationship between the first sentences and the sales appeal, they may react negatively to the whole message—they may think they have been tricked into reading.

Ordinarily, we have no difficulty in thinking of some way to get attention. But the main problem is getting attention in an appropriate manner. Is the following attention getter related to the product and its virtues?

When the first sentence exaggerates or seems to mislead, the remaining sentences may not be read.

Would you like to make a million?

We wish we knew how, but we do know how to make you *feel* like a million. Have you tried our latest mentholated shaving cream?

The beginning sentence is short and, being a question, emphatic. But it suggests that the remainder of the letter will be about how to make a million, which it is not. All three sentences combined suggest that the writer is using high-pressure techniques. The mentholated cream does have virtues and these virtues are important; one of them could have been emphasized by placing it in the first sentence.

Focus on a Central Selling Feature. Almost every product will in some respects be superior to the competing products. If it is not, such factors as favorable price, fast delivery, or superior service may be used as the primary appeal. This primary appeal (central selling point) must be emphasized, and one of the most effective ways to emphasize a point is by posi-

COMMUNICATION MENTOR

Presenting topics in a manner that will get immediate attention and be interesting to the reader is important regardless of the type of message—written or oral. One sure-fire way to ensure that the message is meaningful is to relate the topic to something relevant and important to the reader.

Beverly R. Kuehn
Branch Manager
CTX Mortgage Company
a division of Centex Corporation

---

tion. An outstanding feature mentioned in the middle of a letter may go unnoticed, but it will stand out if mentioned in the first sentence. Note how the following sentence introduces the central selling feature and leads naturally into the sentences that follow:

> A complete collection of Salvador Dali prints—only at PosterShop!
>
> You can select complete sets of prints by Doré and Monet, as well as Dali, at the PosterShop, the only fine arts poster dealer with this comprehensive selection of works of art by the "masters." PosterShop will also frame these prints professionally so you can display them in your home as proudly as you would the originals.

Select a major feature of the product or a primary user benefit; emphasize it throughout.

Address the Reader's Needs.   Few people will buy just because doing so will solve a problem for someone else. How would a student react to the following sales opening?

> After years of effort and expense, we have developed an electronic dictionary.

With the emphasis on the seller and the seller's problems, the sentence isn't particularly appealing. Revised, the beginning paragraph is changed to focus on a problem the reader has:

> Your first draft is complete. Time is short and your spelling must be perfect. You can use *Right-Spell* (an <u>electronic</u> dictionary) to meet your term-paper deadline.

Emphasize the reader, not the writer.

Empathy—an important factor in *all* communication—is especially important in persuasive communication. Before and during writing, think in terms of reader interests.

Use an Original Approach.   All the preceding attention-getting devices (and others, too) are useful. We can use any of them without being copyists. For example, beginning a sales letter with an anecdote is all right, but we should not use one with which many people are already familiar. Good sales writing often shows in the very first sentence how a product can solve a reader's problem. However, when mentioning the feature, don't use the same peculiar combination of words other people are known to use. That is a bad sales technique; it is also poor composition. People like to read something new and fresh; it gets their attention and interest. And writers should enjoy creating something new.

Keep Paragraphs Short.   The spaces between paragraphs serve three purposes: (1) They show the dividing place between ideas. (2) They improve appearance. (3) They provide convenient resting places for the eyes. What is your psychological reaction to a fifteen-line paragraph? Doesn't reading it seem an arduous physical and mental chore?

Should the first paragraph be the longest?

A reader is encouraged to take that first step if it is a short one. If possible, hold the first paragraph to three or fewer lines. A one-line paragraph (even a very short line) is very acceptable. You can even use paragraphs less than one sentence long! Put four or five words on the first line and complete the sentence in a new paragraph. Be careful to include key attention-getting words that either introduce the product or lead to its introduction.

Introducing the Product

A persuasive message is certainly off to a good start if the first sentences cause the reader to think, "Here's a solution to one of my problems," "Here's something I need," or "Here's something I want."

We may lead the addressee to such a thought by introducing the product in the very first sentence. If we do, we've succeeded in both getting attention and arousing interest in one sentence. If our introduction of the product is to be effective, we need affirmative answers to the following questions: (1) Is the introduction natural? (2) Is the introduction action centered? (3) Does the introduction stress a central selling point?

Be Cohesive.   If the attention getter does not introduce the product, it should lead naturally to that introduction. One sentence should grow naturally from another. Note the abrupt change in thought in the following example:

Strained eyes affect human relationships.

The Westview Association of Office Managers has been conducting a survey for the last six months. Their primary aim is to improve lighting conditions.

"Strained eyes" as first words of the first sentence are related to "lighting conditions"—the last words of the sentence. But the thoughts are too far apart. No word or phrase in the first sentence is readily identified with the words of the second sentence. The abrupt change in thought is confusing. The writer may have sought diligently for an attention getter; this one is not particularly related to the sales message that follows. Has the relationship between the two sentences been improved in the second example?

Strained eyes affect human relationships.

That's one thing the Westview Association of Office Managers learned from their six-month survey of office lighting conditions. For light that is easy on the eyes, they're switching to BA's Kold Kathode. When you flip on your Kold Kathode lights, you get . . . .

Let one sentence lead smoothly to the next.

The second sentence is tied to the first by the word "that's." The "light" of the third sentence refers to the "lighting" of the second. And the Kold Kathode is introduced as a solution to the problem of strained eyes.

Be Action Oriented. If we want to introduce our product in an interesting way, we won't simply bring it into the view of the reader and begin describing it. Remember, active voice is more emphatic than passive voice. Action is eye catching—it holds attention and interest more readily than description. Remember, too, that we normally expect *people* to act and *things* to be acted upon.

Place the product in your readers' hands and talk about their using it. They will get a clearer picture when they read about something happening than when they read a product description. And the picture is all the more vivid when the recipient is the hero of the story—the person taking the action. If we put readers to work using our product to solve problems, they will be the subject of most of our sentences.

In some sentences, use the *reader* as the subject.

A small amount of product description is necessary and natural; but too many sales writers overdo it, as in the following excerpt:

This VM600 Komcord is housed in a die-cast aluminum case. It has a 750-watt bulb, pitch-control knob, and easy-to-use, swing-out film gate.

See how each sentence has a *thing* as the subject. We're looking at a still picture. Now let's turn on the action. Let's let a *person* be the subject and watch that person *do* something with our projector.

Lift this Komcord. See how easy it is? That's because of the lightweight aluminum case. Now, swing the film gate open and insert the film. All you have to do is keep the film in front of the groove embossed on the frame. See how easily you can turn the pitch-control knob for the range of sound that suits you best. And notice the clear, sharp pictures you get because of the powerful 750-watt projection bulb.

Let readers see the *benefit* they derive from using the product.

In a sense, we don't sell products—we sell what they will do. We sell the pleasure people derive from the use of a product. Logically, then, we have to write more about that use than we do about the product.

Stress the Central Selling Point. If the attention getter doesn't introduce a distinctive feature, it should lead to it. We can stress important points by position and by space. As soon as readers visualize our product, they need to have attention called to its outstanding features; the features are therefore emphasized because they are mentioned first. And if we are to devote much space to the outstanding features, we have to introduce them early. Note how the attention getter introduces the distinctive selling feature (ease of operation) and how the following sentences keep the readers' eyes focused on that feature:

Your child can see vivid moving pictures of this year's birthday party—and from a machine so easy to use that your child can operate it.

Watch your child lift the Komcord combination video recorder. See how easy? We kept the weight down to four pounds by using an all-aluminum case. Let your youngster set it on a coffee table, chair, or kitchen table—easily.

Now, swing the film gate open and insert film. All you have to do is keep the film in front of the groove embossed on the frame. See how easily you can turn the pitch-control knob for the range of sound you like best. And notice the clear, sharp pictures you get because of the powerful 750-watt bulb.

Does stressing one point mean excluding other points?

By stressing one point, you do not limit the message to that point. For example, while *ease of operation* is being stressed, other features—pitch-control knob, swing-out film gate, 750-watt bulb—are mentioned. A good film presents a star who is seen throughout most of the film; a good term paper presents a central idea that is supported throughout; a school yearbook employs a theme—a sales letter should stress a central selling point.

Convince the Readers with Evidence

After we have made an interesting introduction to our product, we have to present enough supporting evidence to satisfy our readers' needs.

Emphasize the Central Selling Point. We should keep one or two main features uppermost in the readers' minds. When we present evidence, we should choose evidence that supports this feature or features. For example, it would be inconsistent to use appearance as an outstanding selling feature of compact cars while presenting abundant evidence to show economy of operation.

Use Concrete Language. Few people will believe us if we make general statements without supporting them with factual evidence. Saying a certain machine is efficient is not enough. We have to say *how we know* it's efficient and present some data to illustrate *how* efficient. Saying a piece of furniture is durable is not enough. Durability exists in varying degrees. We must present information that shows what makes it durable; we must also define *how* durable.

> **Why should we avoid unsupported generalities?**

Especially in the convincing-evidence portion of the sales letter, we need all the information we have gathered about our product. We can establish durability, for example, by presenting information about the manufacturing process, the quality of the raw materials, or the skill of the workers:

> **Why are facts and figures important in the evidence section?**

> KCC Publishing's *Garnet Classics* will last your child a lifetime—pages bound in durable gold-embossed hardback, treated with special protectants to retard paper aging, and machine-sewn (not glued) for long-lasting quality. The 100-percent cotton fiber paper can withstand years of turning the pages. The joy of reading can last for years as your children explore the world of classic literature with KCC's *Garner Classics*.

Evidence presented must not only *be* authentic; it must *sound* authentic, too. Facts and figures help. Talking about pages treated with special protectants to retard aging and machine-sewn pages suggests the writer is well informed. These facts increase reader confidence. Facts and figures are even more impressive if the reader can get some kind of internal verification of their accuracy. For example, the following paragraph presents figures and gives their derivation:

> We insulated 30 houses in Mesa last year. Before the insulation, we asked each homeowner to tell us the total fuel bill for the four coldest

months—November, December, January, and February. The average
cost was $408, or $102 a month. After insulation, we discovered the
fuel bill for the same four-month period was $296, or $74 a
month—a saving of $28 a month, or 25 percent.

Do not go overboard and inundate your readers with an abundance of
facts or technical data that will bore, frustrate, or alienate them. Never
make your readers feel ignorant by trying to impress them with facts and
figures they may not understand.

What are some signs of subjectivity?

Be Objective.   We must use language that people will believe. Specific,
concrete language makes letters sound authentic. Unsupported superlatives, exaggerations, flowery statements, unsupported claims, incomplete
comparisons, and remarks suggesting certainty all make letters sound like
high-pressure sales talk. And just one such sentence can destroy confidence in the whole letter. Examine the following statements to see
whether they give convincing evidence. Would they make a reader want
to buy? Or do they merely remind the reader of someone's desire to sell?

These are the best plastic pipes on the market today. They represent the
very latest in chemical research.

The way to tell which pipes are best is to gather information about all
pipes marketed and then choose the one with superior characteristics. We
know that the writer is likely to have a bias in favor of the product being
sold. We don't know whether the writer actually spent time researching
other plastic pipes or whether the writer would know how to evaluate
this information. And we certainly don't know whether the writer knows
enough about chemistry and chemical research to say truthfully what the
very latest is.

Gardeners are turning handsprings in their excitement over our new weed
killer!

Might an unsupported superlative in one sentence reduce confidence in subsequent statements?

Really? Doesn't that statement seem preposterous? And, if we don't believe in the handsprings, can we believe in the weed killer?

Stretch those tired limbs out on one of our luscious water beds. It's like
floating on a gentle dreamcloud on a warm, sunny afternoon. Ah, what
soothing relaxation!

The adjectives in every sentence suggest subjectivity. Even though some
people may be persuaded by such writing, many will see it as an attempt
to trick them.

Note the incomplete comparison in the following example:

Go farther on Duratread tires.

With which tires are Duratreads being compared? All *other* tires? With *most* other tires? With *one* unnamed brand? With *a few other* brands? Unless an additional sentence identifies the other elements in the comparison, we can't tell. Too often, the writer of such a sentence hopes the reader will assume the comparison is with *all* others. Written with that intent, the incomplete comparison is unethical. Likewise, statements of certainty are often inaccurate or misleading:

We are sure you will want to order the complete set of encyclopedias; but even if you don't, this first volume is yours to keep.

Can the writer be sure? "If you don't" conveys a connotation that the writer is *not* sure.

Interpret the Evidence.   Naturally, your readers will be less familiar with the product and its uses than you will be. Not only do you have an obligation to give information, you should interpret it if interpretation is necessary. Point out how the information will benefit the reader. For example:

And the new Karns refrigerator is frostproof as well as economical to operate.

Some prospects may not fully comprehend what "frostproof" means for them. If we make the most of this feature, we have to say *what* makes it frostproof and suggest *how* a frostproof refrigerator is superior to one that is not. The economy-of-operation feature should not have been introduced until the frostproof feature had been fully discussed. The following revision interprets this feature:

> Open the door to the frozen-food compartment of your Karns. No frost anywhere—even if the door has been opened several times during the day. The moment you open the door, a small fan concealed in the back wall begins to circulate the air. The air isn't still long enough to deposit frozen particles of moisture. Take frozen strawberries or juice from the new Karns and open the cans without first having to remove frost.

The following excerpt from a sales letter uses a pocket calculator as the subject of the sentence. Note how it states dimensions in cold figures without interpretation:

Can incomplete comparisons be misleading?

Why should we bother to interpret statements?

This calculator weighs 1/2 ounce. Its dimensions are 3 1/4 by 2 1/4 by 1/16 inches. It comes in black or ivory.

In what respect is a $\frac{1}{2}$-ounce unit superior to a 9-ounce one? Or is a 9-ounce unit actually better? If there is any advantage in having a calculator of these dimensions, what is it? What would be the disadvantage if it were twice as big?

Now see how interpretation makes the letter more convincing:

Let readers see the relationship of features and benefits.

> Compare the weight of this calculator with the weight of a credit card. The credit card may be heavier than the calculator's 1/2 ounce. See how easily it fits inside a billfold. That's because its dimensions are 3 1/4 by 2 1/4 by 1/16 inches—about the size of a playing card.

The revision shows what the figures mean in terms of reader benefits. It also makes use of a valuable interpretative technique—the comparison. We can often make a point more convincing by comparing something unfamiliar with something familiar. Most people are familiar with the size of a playing card, so they can now visualize the size of the calculator. Comparison can also be used to interpret prices. For example, an insurance representative might write this sentence:

> The annual premium for this 20-year, limited-payment policy is $219.00, or 60 cents a day—not much more than a cup of coffee.

Be Careful When You Talk About Price. Most sales letters should mention price. They should either tell what the price is or say something to assure the reader that the price is not unreasonable. Logically, price should be introduced late in the letter—after most of the advantages have been discussed. Few people want to part with their money until they have been shown how they can benefit by doing so.

Why should we introduce price late in the letter?

People are inclined to react negatively to price. They may think it's too high, even when it is actually low. So we have to find ways to overcome price resistance:

1. Introduce price only after presenting the product and its virtues.
2. Keep price talk out of the first and last paragraphs—unless, of course, price is the distinctive feature.
3. Use figures to illustrate how enough money can be saved to pay for the expenditure. (For example, say that a $60 turbo-vent that saved $10 per month on summer electric bills would save approximately $60 in two 3-month summers, and that the vent would last for many summers.)

4. State price in terms of small units. (Twelve dollars a month seems like less than $144 a year.)
5. If practical, invite comparison of like products with similar features.
6. If facts and figures are available, use them to illustrate that the price is reasonable.
7. Mention price in a complex or compound sentence that relates or summarizes the virtues of the product. In the sentence where price is mentioned, remind readers of what they get in return. The positive aspects (satisfaction from using the product) should be put beside the negative aspects (giving up money). If we have given convincing evidence, the positive features should remain uppermost in a recipient's mind; therefore, the emphasis is taken off the negative features. Note the following illustrations:

Why state price in a long sentence that is compound or complex?

> Small enough to fit in the palm and big enough to record a three-hour lecture, the voice-activated Minicord sells for $70 during March.

> For a $48 yearly subscription fee, *Medisearch* brings you a monthly digest of recent medical research that is written in nontechnical language.

> Purigard saves the average pool owner about $10 in chemicals each month; thus, the $150 unit completely pays for itself in 15 months.

8. Let the figure representing price appear in some position other than the first or last word of a sentence. (See the preceding illustrations.) First and last words are emphatic; but, unless it is the central selling point, price should be subordinated.

Give Supporting Evidence.   If we can present research evidence to support our statements, we have a good chance of convincing our readers to buy:

Results of research add to conviction.

> We asked 50 night-shift sawmill workers to wear Wilkers Steel-Toe Boots to work for one month. Fifty others wore Shilling boots for the same period of time. At the end of the month, we examined each pair of boots for wear. Twenty-five pairs of the Shilling boots had at least part of a sole missing, compared with only six pairs of the Wilkers boots. Another ten Shilling steel-toe tips were loose, compared with three on the Wilkers boots.

Relating the experiment takes more space and time, but it is well worth the effort. Experimental facts are much more convincing than general remarks about superior durability and appearance.

Be certain that in presenting your evidence you are ethical and abide by legal guidelines related to advertising. Overcome the temptation to embellish your product or source or exaggerate the evidence. Instead, use concrete evidence and objective language to create an accurate representation of your product (and competing products if mentioned).

Why avoid introducing the enclosure in the first paragraph?

Know How and When to Use Enclosures, Testimonials, and Guarantees. Ordinarily, the enclosure is less significant than the letter itself. The letter should make the recipient want to read the enclosure. Thus, the preferred technique is to refer to the enclosure late in the letter, after the major portion of the evidence has been given. Because readers have already seen the enclosure, we should not call attention to it by saying "Enclosed you will find" or "We've enclosed a brochure." An enclosure is easily referred to in a sentence that also says something else:

> Please compare the pictures on the enclosed folder.

If a product is really beneficial, some people are likely to report their satisfaction. If they don't write voluntarily, you can invite their comments through questionnaires or by attaching cards to the merchandise. Users are urged to fill out the cards after they have used the merchandise for a certain time. One way to convince prospective customers that they will like the product is to give them concrete evidence that other people like it. Tell what others have said (with permission, of course) about your product's usefulness.

Guarantees and free trial convey both negative and positive connotations. By revealing willingness to refund money or exchange an unsatisfactory unit if necessary, a writer confesses a negative: the purchase could be regretted or refused. However, the positive connotations are stronger than the negatives: the seller has a definite plan for ensuring that buyers get value for money spent. In addition, the seller exhibits willingness for the buyer to check a product personally and compare it with others. The seller also implies confidence that a free trial will result in purchase and that a product will meet standards set in the guarantee. If terms of a guarantee are long or complex, they can be relegated to an enclosure.

Last Paragraph: Motivating the Reader to Action

Regardless of the kind of evidence we give, we give it for the purpose of motivating action. If preceding paragraphs have been unconvincing, a well-written final paragraph has little chance of success.

Our chances of getting action are increased if we (1) state the specific action wanted, (2) allude to the reward for taking action in the same sentence in which action is encouraged, (3) present the action as being easy to take, (4) provide some stimulus to quick action, and (5) ask confidently.

Mention the Specific Action You Want. Unless specific instructions are included, such general instructions as "let us hear from you," "take action on the matter," and "make a response" are ineffective. Whether the reader is to fill out an order blank and return it with a check, place a telephone call, or return an enclosed card, define the desired action in specific terms.

Allude to the Reward for Taking Action. For both psychological and logical reasons, readers are encouraged to act if they are reminded of the reward for acting. If our letter has been well written, we will have chosen a distinctive selling feature (the reward for using our product). We will have introduced it early—perhaps in the very first sentence—and we will have stressed it in the following paragraphs. The distinctive selling feature is the big idea we've tried to put across. We want it to stick in the recipient's mind. Thus, we should also work it into our parting word, where it will be emphasized.

A distinctive selling feature is to a sales letter what a theme is to a speech. It's a thread of continuity running through every paragraph. To end without a final reference to the selling feature (theme) would be like ending a speech without summarizing remarks. The picture must be complete. Something in the ending should remind the reader of the beginning and the middle.

Present Action as Being Easy to Take. People naturally hesitate to attempt something that is difficult or time consuming. Instead of asking readers to fill in their names and addresses on order forms or return cards and envelopes, do that work for them. If action is easy or consumes little time, they may act immediately; otherwise, they may procrastinate.

Provide a Stimulus for Quick Action. We want action, fast or slow; but we prefer fast action because it's more certain. The longer the reader waits to take action on our proposal, the dimmer our persuasive evidence will become. Reference to the central selling point (assuming it has been well received) helps to stimulate action. Here are some commonly used appeals for getting quick action:

Buy while present prices are still in effect.

Buy while the present supply lasts.

Buy before Christmas (Father's Day, the end of the season, etc.).

What are some characteristics of the action ending?

Why allude to the reward for taking action?

What is one way to reduce the likelihood of procrastination?

Buy now while a rebate is being offered.

Buy quickly to get product benefits quickly.

Prospects will not necessarily act because we tell them to act. The following expressions seem to shout *too* loudly for action:

Act today.	Do it now.	Don't delay.
Hurry, hurry, hurry.	Why wait?	Don't wait another minute.

Why avoid *hope* and *if* statements in the action ending?

Ask Confidently for Action.   Sales writers who have a good product and have presented evidence well have a right to feel confident. Instead of *"If you want to save time in cleaning, fill in and return . . . ,"* writers can demonstrate confidence in favorable action by stating, "To save time in cleaning, fill in and return . . . ." Statements suggesting lack of confidence, such as "If you agree . . . ." and "I *hope* you will . . . ," should be avoided. (Recall the discussion of doubtful expressions in Chapter 8. "I hope you will" also connotes "In view of my weak presentation, I recognize that you *may not.*") Between the lines, such thoughts convey, "I have some doubts about my product or my selling ability." If such doubts exist in the mind of the writer, they are generated in the mind of the reader.

What ideas should appear in the final paragraph?

For good appearance and proper emphasis, the last paragraph should be kept relatively short. Yet the last paragraph has a lot to do: it must suggest the specific action wanted, refer to the distinctive selling feature, present action as being easy to take, encourage quick action, and ask confidently. Observe how the following closing paragraph accomplishes these tasks:

[1]The ease of operations makes CRR's new productivity software an asset for any busy executive. [2]The ease of ordering is just as attractive. [3]From a touch-tone telephone, simply dial 1-800-555-8341. [4]Then input the five-digit number printed in the top right-hand corner of the attached card. [5]Your name and address will be entered automatically into our system, an expedient way to get your productivity software to you within five working days along with a bill for payment. [6]Those who order by August 12 will also receive 10 high-density memory disks free with their order.

[1] Final reference to the central selling point.

[2-5] Make action easy; define definite action.

[6] Stimulus to quick action.

The following version is an improvement because it places the central selling point in the very last line:

From a touch-tone telephone, simply dial 1-800-555-8341. Then input the five-digit number printed in the top right-hand corner of the attached card. Your name and address will be entered automatically into our system, an expedient way to get your productivity software to you within five working days along with a bill for payment. Those who order by August 12 will also receive 10 high-density memory disks free with their order. CRR's new productivity software is as easy to use as it is to order!

Now that we have learned the strategy for writing the various parts of sales letters, let's read and analyze some complete letters. Note the inductive sequence of ideas.

Writing a Complete Sales Letter

The letters in this section illustrate the principles discussed in the preceding pages. Although they may seem long, each can be printed on a single page of letterhead. Typically, sales letters are longer than letters that present routine information or convey good news. Specific details (essential in getting action) are space consuming.

The letters in Figures 11-1 and 11-2 are illustrations of *unsolicited* sales letters. The same principles apply in writing a *solicited* letter, with one exception: because the solicited letter is a response to a request for information, an attention getter is not essential.

Some sales letters have no attention getters.

Printing and Mailing

A sales message (even though extremely well written) is ineffective if the would-be reader reacts negatively to the envelope in which it arrives or the paper on which it is printed. Such mechanical matters are less challenging than composing paragraphs, but they deserve careful attention. Some vital questions about paper and printing include

What is the most appropriate size, color, and weight of paper?

What size print is best? Would a different color be appropriate for words that deserve special emphasis?

Would some underlining that appears to have been done by hand be appropriate?

Should a personalized inside address be included?

Some vital questions about the envelope include

What is the most appropriate color and size? (If an enclosure is to be included, the envelope will have to be large enough to accommodate it.)

[1] Seeks to gain attention by introducing an experience the recipient has probably had. Presents "important business call" as central selling point.

[2] Introduces the product as a solution to a problem. Uses "important call" to achieve transition from the preceding sentence and to reinforce the central selling point. [3] Begins presentation of evidence. Uses a pronoun for coherence. Uses reader as subject of an active-voice sentence. [4], [5] Show how easy it is to solve the problem—the reason to buy.

[6] Continues presentation of the evidence. Uses active voice. [7] Presents price in a sentence that reinforces the primary reward for paying that price.

[8], [9] Associate action with reward for taking action, identify specific action desired, make action easy, and reward quick action.

SPACE AGE
ELECTRONICS, INC.

2677 Pinebrook Street
Oklahoma City, OK 73145-2677
(405) 555-0290

April 30, 19—

Dr. Dale Pittman
2900 Medical Plaza
San Antonio, TX 78207-2900

Dear Dr. Pittman:

[1] If you need an afternoon swinging a golf club, but you're worried you'll miss an important call, you need the ProCall pager.

[2] To make sure you will be able to catch that important call wherever you are, ProSystems is introducing the ProCall pager. [3] Wherever you go, you carry it with you. [4] When people need to reach you, they simply call ProCall's 800 number and key in your code. [5] Within seconds, our nationwide satellite system relays the message to your ProCall pager—and you never miss a call.

[6] The ProCall system reaches you almost anywhere in the United States and weighs less (2.5 ounces) than a golf ball driving down the fairway. [7] The ProCall pager keeps you on top of your game and in touch with your important calls for only $30 a month (about a dollar a day).

[8] To receive your ProCall pager, just initial the enclosed card. [9] Mail the card before June 1 and receive your first month of service free.

Sincerely,

J. Eugene Wright

J. Eugene Wright
Sales Manager

Enclosure

FIGURE 11-1   Good example of a complete sales letter

Is a window envelope appropriate? Should any of the message be visible through the window?

Should the return address appear on the front or on the back?

Should first-class postage be attached, or would metered postage be better? Can this letter be sent bulk rate?

Should addresses be keyboarded on envelopes, or would glued-on mailing labels be better?

Should such words as "Important" or "Immediate Attention Required" appear conspicuously on envelopes?

Answers to such questions vary, depending on the nature of the busi-

TA TRANSATLANTIC AIRLINES
P.O. Drawer 17033   New York, NY   10014-1703   (212) 555-5692   FAX (212) 555-8310

January 15, 19—

Ms. Martha Langford
378 South Bedford Street
Dallas, TX 75206-4891

Dear Ms. Langford:

[1] You've heard it before . . .

"FLY WITH OUR BONUS FLYER PLAN!"

[2] . . . of course, you end up flying 50,000 miles before earning discounts to places you don't want to go anyway and then only if the tickets cost under $200 normally.

[3] No longer! [4] With Transatlantic Airlines' EXECPLAN, fly only 20,000 miles and receive free tickets to anywhere in the continental United States! [5] And if you wish, save your unused free domestic tickets and receive free tickets to locations in Europe! [6] Our EXECPLAN is very flexible.

[7] Your options don't end when you leave the Transatlantic Airlines' terminal. [8] You not only gain mileage in flight; but with every car rental in conjunction with your Transatlantic flight, you earn 500 bonus miles!

[9] Then drive your rental car to your hotel room at VIP Accommodations or First Class Inns. [10] By selecting one of these hotels, you can earn an additional 500 bonus miles!

[1,2] Seek to gain attention by using a split sentence and introducing an experience the reader has probably had.

[3,4] Introduce the product as the solution to a problem. Use parallel items to first sentence for transition. [5,6] Emphasize central selling point (ease and flexibility).

[7,8] Present more features of the plan and repeat central selling point.

[9–12] Establish chronological transition and more evidence; involve the reader in the action by using active-voice sentences with the reader as the subject.

FIGURE 11-2 Good example of a complete sales letter

Ms. Martha Langford
Page 2
January 15, 19—

[11] Just give your EXECPLAN number from your blue-and-silver membership card when making hotel, car, or flight reservations and receive an instantly adjusted mileage credit! [12] Making reservations couldn't be easier!

[13] You will receive 1,000 bonus miles if you complete and return the enclosed application form by August 21. [14] Fly toward free tickets, discounts, and other benefits with Transatlantic Airlines' EXECPLAN now.

Sincerely,

Lance R. Moore

Lance R. Moore
Vice President of Sales

Enclosure

[13] Reinforces central selling point.
[14] Gives reader an incentive for specific action and restates the central selling point.

FIGURE 11-2,   continued

ness, the people to whom letters are addressed, and the cost. Help is always available from an advertising department or specialists in direct-mail advertising. Empathy is helpful: "If I received an envelope that looks like this one, would I react negatively? Would I open it?"

In general, the envelope should be consistent with the message. It should not violate principles of good taste, and it should not be misleading. Gimmicks such as putting "Personal" on an envelope when the letter is not personal, labeling it as urgent when it isn't, or arranging to have "Pay to the order of" appear through the window preceding the addressee's name (on a check that turns out to be phony) are inappropriate. A would-be reader who has been tricked into opening an envelope is almost sure to react negatively, even though the letter applies every principle previously discussed.

REQUESTS AND COLLECTION LETTERS

The preceding discussion of sales letters assumed the product was sufficiently worthy to reward the buyer for taking action. The discussion of persuasive requests assumes requests are reasonable—that compliance is *justified* when the request is for an adjustment, that compliance will (in some way) be *rewarded* when the request is for a favor.

A Persuasive Request for Action

Claim letters and letters that request special favors are common types of persuasive requests. Although their purpose is to get favorable action, the letters invite action only after attempting to arouse a *desire* to take action.

Making a Claim. Claim letters are often routine because the basis for the claim is a guarantee or some other assurance that an adjustment will be made without need of persuasion. However, when an immediate remedy is doubtful, persuasion is necessary. In a typical large business, the claim letter is passed on to the claims adjuster for response.

In modern businesses, any reasonable claim will probably be adjusted to the customer's satisfaction. Therefore, venting strong displeasure in the claim letter is of little value. It can alienate the claims adjuster—the one person from whom cooperation is sought. Remember, adjusters are human beings, too. And very likely, they have had little or nothing to do with the manufacture and sale of the product. They did not create the need for the claim letter.

From the point of view of the claims adjuster, claims should be welcomed. Only a small percentage of claims are from unethical individuals; the great bulk are from people who believe they have a legitimate complaint. The way in which the adjuster handles the claim determines, to a large extent, the goodwill of the company. For the adjuster, granting a claim is much easier than refusing it. Because saying "no" is one of the most difficult writing tasks, the writer of a persuasive claim letter has an advantage over the adjuster.

Like sales letters, persuasive claim letters should use an inductive sequence. Unlike routine claim letters, persuasive claims do not begin by

Why do businesses appreciate claim letters?

asking for an adjustment. The poor example in Figure 11-3 uses a deductive sequence. Two major changes would improve this letter: (1) writing inductively (to reduce the chance of a negative reaction in the first sentence), and (2) stressing an appeal throughout the letter (to emphasize an incentive for taking favorable action). In a persuasive claim letter, an *appeal* serves the same purpose that a *central selling feature* does in a sales let-

180 Spruce Lane
Boise, ID 83707-9013
April 19, 19—

Mr. Rodney Krinke
General Manager
ABC Auto
1200 Main Street
Boise, ID 83707-1200

Dear Mr. Krinke

I respectfully ask that you reimburse me for $105, the amount of the attached work order.

When my 510 hatchback failed the state's emission control test, I took it to your service department. Four hours later, the office called and informed me that the car was ready to be picked up.

Stopping at the cashier's window a few minutes before closing time, I paid the $105 your clerk said was due and received the keys. Then, I noticed the mechanic's comments on the work order. I needed a new carburetor. The cost new, I found out, was $516.

Talking with the service manager, I discovered that the $105 was for labor—all for taking the carburetor apart and putting it back together. He said that a previous owner had evidently replaced the original with one of inferior quality, that it could not be fixed, and that the car would still not pass the state's inspection.

I pointed out I had purchased the car new from your agency and the carburetor had never been repaired or replaced. For $105, I had received no value at all.

FIGURE 11-3   **Poor example of a persuasive claim**

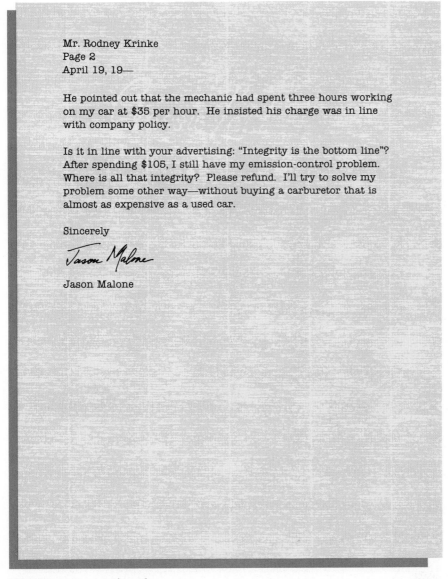

Mr. Rodney Krinke
Page 2
April 19, 19—

He pointed out that the mechanic had spent three hours working on my car at $35 per hour. He insisted his charge was in line with company policy.

Is it in line with your advertising: "Integrity is the bottom line"? After spending $105, I still have my emission-control problem. Where is all that integrity? Please refund. I'll try to solve my problem some other way—without buying a carburetor that is almost as expensive as a used car.

Sincerely

Jason Malone

Jason Malone

FIGURE 11-3, continued

ter. Both serve as a theme; both remind the receiver of a benefit that accrues from doing as asked. Note the application of these techniques in the revision (Figure 11-4).

Knowledge of effective claim writing should never be used as a means of taking advantage of someone. Hiding an unjustifiable claim under a cloak of untrue statements is very difficult and strictly unethical.

¹ 180 Spruce Lane
Boise, ID 83707-9013
April 19, 19—

Mr. Rodney Krinke
General Manager
ABC Auto
1200 Main Street
Boise, ID 83707-1200

Dear Mr. Krinke

² When I bought my 510 hatchback from ABC Auto two years ago, I was influenced by your advertising: "Integrity is the bottom line." ³ After the car failed this year's emission-control test, I took it to your service department. ⁴ You have serviced the car for four years, and I have had confidence that the job was being done right—with integrity.

⁵ After paying $105 for the repairs, I noticed the mechanic's comment on the work order: "Needs a new carburetor." ⁶ The charge on the work order was totally for labor—the three hours spent in taking the unit apart and reassembling it. ⁷ The service manager said a previous owner had evidently replaced the original carburetor with one of inferior quality that cannot be fixed. ⁸ The car still does not pass inspection, and a new carburetor will cost $516.

⁹ I bought this car new from ABC and have been its sole owner. ¹⁰ The car has needed no repairs other than normal servicing. ¹¹ ABC would not have exchanged carburetors before selling the

Side annotations:

¹ Provides return address because letter is printed on plain paper.

² Seeks attention by using the company's name and slogan. Reveals the subject of the letter (the writer's car) and introduces a central appeal. ³ Uses "car"—510 in (2)—for cohesion and transition. ⁴ Includes a further reminder of the central appeal. Adds emphasis to the appeal (integrity) by placing it last in the sentence and paragraph. Refers to the length of the relationship—the customer has demonstrated confidence in the company and contributed to its profits.

^{5–8} Continue with needed details.

^{9–11} Present further reasoning (if an inferior unit had been installed, ABC is responsible). Make further reference to the central appeal.

FIGURE 11-4   Good example of a persuasive claim

Adjusters are fair-minded people who will give the benefit of the doubt, but they are not give-away specialists who will satisfy a grumpy customer simply to avoid a problem. An ethical business follows the Golden Rule.

What are some common errors in asking a favor?

Asking a Favor.   Occasionally, everyone has to ask someone else for a special favor—action for which there is not much reward, time, or inclina-

Mr. Rodney Krinke
Page 2
April 19, 19—

car new—because of concern for integrity. [12]Yet the service manager explained that ABC was justified in charging for the employee's working time and is not responsible for replacing the carburetor.

[13]Please refund $105 and replace the carburetor free of charge, proving that integrity is your bottom line.

Sincerely

Jason Malone

Jason Malone

[12] Continues to lead up to the request for a refund.

[13] Connects the request with ABC's need to make actions and advertising consistent.

FIGURE 11-4, continued

tion. For example, suppose a professional association wants to host its annual fund-raiser dinner at an exclusive country club. The program chair of the association must write a letter to the club's general manager requesting permission to use the club. Will a deductive letter be successful? The letter in Figure 11-5 illustrates a direct request in what is really a persuasive-letter situation. Contrast this letter with the revision in Figure 11-6.

March 23, 19--

Ms. Emily Fuller
General Manager
Crystal Stream
P.O. Box 2383
Sacramento, CA 95813-2383

Dear Ms. Fuller:

[1] The Lakeside Medical Association (LMA) will hold its annual dinner/dance on Saturday, November 5.

[2] We would very much like to have this event at Crystal Stream. [3] We would like to hold the formal dinner/dance from 7 p.m. to 1 a.m. that evening. [4] We expect several hundred guests to attend.

[5] Will you let me know as soon as possible if we may hold the dance at Crystal Stream.

Sincerely,

Robin M. Vernon

Robin M. Vernon M.D.
Program Chair

---

[1] Begins with an announcement that may be of little interest to the recipient.

[2] Asks the favor before letting the person see any reason for accepting.

[3] Does not include important information such as the type of dance, food, and number involved. [4] Overuse of the first person pronoun *we* throughout letter.

[5] Sounds somewhat doubtful.

Right margin should not be justified; the extra spaces placed between the words to achieve a straight margin are distracting and reduce the reader's comprehension.

FIGURE 11-5   Poor example of a letter asking a favor

Note that the letter in Figure 11-6 uses an inductive approach. When a deductive approach is used in a persuasive situation, chances of getting cooperation are minimal. For example, what might be a probable reaction to the following beginning sentence?

Please send me, without charge, your $350 computerized instructional software package on office safety.

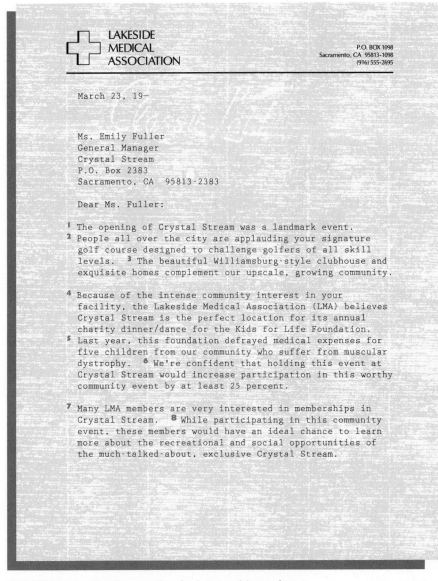

LAKESIDE MEDICAL ASSOCIATION

P.O. BOX 1098
Sacramento, CA 95813-1098
(916) 555-2695

March 23, 19—

Ms. Emily Fuller
General Manager
Crystal Stream
P.O. Box 2383
Sacramento, CA 95813-2383

Dear Ms. Fuller:

¹ The opening of Crystal Stream was a landmark event. ² People all over the city are applauding your signature golf course designed to challenge golfers of all skill levels. ³ The beautiful Williamsburg-style clubhouse and exquisite homes complement our upscale, growing community.

⁴ Because of the intense community interest in your facility, the Lakeside Medical Association (LMA) believes Crystal Stream is the perfect location for its annual charity dinner/dance for the Kids for Life Foundation. ⁵ Last year, this foundation defrayed medical expenses for five children from our community who suffer from muscular dystrophy. ⁶ We're confident that holding this event at Crystal Stream would increase participation in this worthy community event by at least 25 percent.

⁷ Many LMA members are very interested in memberships in Crystal Stream. ⁸ While participating in this community event, these members would have an ideal chance to learn more about the recreational and social opportunities of the much-talked-about, exclusive Crystal Stream.

¹⁻³ Begin on a point that is related and of interest to the receiver.
⁴ Reveals membership's enthusiasm for holding the dinner/dance at the club and presents benefits that help to increase the reader's enthusiasm for the proposal. ⁵,⁶ Provide additional benefits for saying yes.
⁷,⁸ Provide additional benefits for saying yes.

FIGURE 11-6   Good example of a letter asking a favor

If the first sentence gets a negative reaction, a decision to refuse may be made instantly. Having thought "no," the reader may not read the rest of the letter or may hold stubbornly to that decision in spite of a well-written persuasive argument that follows the opening sentence.

The letter illustrated in Figure 11-7 uses an inductive approach. (Note the extent to which it applies principles encountered earlier.) As

What outline should be used for a persuasive letter?

[9] This black-tie dinner/dance is scheduled for November 5, from 7 p.m. to 1 a.m. [10] Typically 400 guests have attended; however, we would expect at least 500 if the event were held at Crystal Stream. [11] A definite number can be confirmed two weeks prior to the event.

[12] We would appreciate your confirmation by May 1 that Crystal Stream will be the site of this year's dinner/dance. [13] Then we can finalize the details and promote this sure-to-be-spectacular event at the renowned Crystal Stream.

Sincerely,

Robin M. Vernon

Robin M. Vernon, M.D.
Program Chair

9–12 Provide details that will be useful if the reader accepts.

13 Seeks specific action.

FIGURE 11-6,   **continued**

this letter shows, if the preceding paragraphs adequately emphasize a receiver's reward for complying, the final paragraph need not shout loudly for action.

Requests for information are very common in business; and information for research reports frequently is obtained by questionnaire. Validity

___B & K___
Insurance Group

1897 20th AVENUE
TOLEDO, OH 43601-1897

(419) 555-2950

March 4, 19—

Software Solutions
1893 Alexander Street
Cambridge, MA 02138-5186

Ladies and Gentlemen:

The participants in our management-training program need to
know more about office safety, and they need to become familiar
with computerized instructional software.

Each year, about 50 new employees enter the training program.
Eventually, each is to assume a position of responsibility at the
home office or at one of our 39 branch offices. Many will at
some time be responsible for in-service training within their
departments.

Their present training provides some instruction in safety, but
not to the extent that you treat it in your CIS package. Many in
the program have yet to experience any form of computerized
learning. They need to learn from direct experience about its
potential.

If they could actually use your CIS-ST (the one described in the
current issue of Today's Office), they could begin to appreciate the

FIGURE 11-7   Good example of a persuasive request

and reliability of results are strongly influenced by the percentage of return. If the letter inviting respondents to complete the questionnaire is
written carelessly, responses may be insufficient.

The most serious weaknesses of the letter in Figure 11-8 are asking
too quickly for action and providing no incentive for action. The attitude

Software Solutions
Page 2
March 4, 19—

advantages of planned reinforcement. In addition, they could become real boosters of CIS as an alternative in in-service training.

In return for the opportunity to acquaint this select group with your CIS-ST, would you send a complimentary package? Every trainee would have an opportunity to use it and become sold on its advantages in training employees. Your sending the package will enable us to enrich our training and give your CIS-ST some well-deserved promotion.

Sincerely,

Cindi Johnston

Cindi Johnston
Production Manager

FIGURE 11-7   continued

Even when the reward for taking action is small or intangible, point it out.

conveyed by the letter is reminiscent of an ancient poet who wanted his calf to go through an open barn door. The calf refused and the poet hit it repeatedly with a stick. It still refused, until the maid let it drink milk from a pail. While it drank, the maid walked through and the calf followed. The maid provided incentive. Sometimes the reward for taking action is very small, but somehow the letter needs to make it evident. Note

COMMUNICATION MENTOR

Let's say you're preparing a memo to your supervisor; you're hoping for his approval of a cost-saving project you want to spearhead. Something fairly similar to it had been tried years ago; it failed miserably, embarrassing your supervisor and his supervisor. You *know* that seeking approval is an uphill battle, but you believe in yourself and the project. What tone should this sensitive memo take?

The temptation may be to position your project point-for-point in contrast to the old one, pounding on the relative merits of yours in an effort to convey its superiority.

Resist this temptation as you would a term paper over spring break. Turn from it as you would turn from Muzak. Never directly mention the other project in your memo; memories of its failure may be keen, and direct comparisons will be counterproductive to the objectivity you want to elicit in your readers. Rather, emphasize the strength of your plan by stressing features of it which are designed to avoid known pitfalls.

Your supervisor and his supervisor will get the message, and you will get your project. The moral to take away from all of this: don't stand on the grave of a bad idea to sell a new one.

James F. Hurley
Senior Vice President
CalFed Inc.

This executive has taken valuable time to respond to a questionnaire. If you expect such courtesies from others, you must be both persuasive and polite.

¹Invites action without having first given any incentive. ²Puts writer and reader on different levels by suggesting humility. Use of "impose" could serve as a reminder that the request *is* an imposition and therefore should be denied.

³Does reveal the nature of the research—a point that should have been introduced earlier. ⁴Risks alienation by introducing doubts about the reader's knowledge.

^{5, 6}Let the reader know what to expect but need to include some incentive for responding. ⁷Uses an action ending, but it seems a little demanding, especially when no incentive has been introduced.

15 Canterbury Apartments
Augusta, GA 31902-1910
February 1, 19—

Mr. Brian Bell
Purchasing Agent
City National Bank
2500 Center Street
Augusta, GA 31902-2500

Dear Mr. Bell:

¹Please complete the enclosed questionnaire and return it to me in the envelope provided. ²I dislike having to impose on the valuable time of a busy executive such as you, but in order for me to complete the research for my thesis at the university, I must seek first-hand information from business leaders.

³The study deals with the attitudes of purchasing agents toward vendor gratuities. ⁴As I believe you know, gifts from sellers to executives who do the buying for companies pose a problem of great concern. ⁵The questionnaire seeks information about practices in your firm and about your own opinions.

⁶Responses will be kept confidential, of course. ⁷Please return the questionnaire to me by February 20.

Sincerely,

John R. Pierce

John R. Pierce

Enclosure

FIGURE 11-8   Poor example of a request for information

Are routine requests shorter than persuasive requests?

the reward in the revision of the letter in Figure 11-9 (it appeals to the higher order of needs discussed by Maslow).

Persuasive messages are usually longer than routine messages. To provide enough information on which to base a decision, and to provide incentive for action, persuasive messages require more space. To a person

15 Canterbury Apartments
Augusta, GA 31902-1910
February 1, 19—

Mr. Brian Bell
Purchasing Agent
City National Bank
2500 Center Street
Augusta, GA 31902-2500

Dear Mr. Bell:

What if vendors continue making more and larger gifts to purchasing agents? For ethical and economic reasons, this question is of vital importance to purchasing agents. Yet it has not been answered in the literature, and recent purchasing journals have emphatically called for answers based on research.

For my master's thesis on purchasing behavior, I am seeking opinions from selected purchasing managers. Results will be shared with participants soon after the data are interpreted.

So the study will be complete and authoritative, please participate by completing the enclosed questionnaire and returning it to me in the envelope provided. Your answers, which can be indicated quickly by making check marks, will be confidential and reported only as part of group data. To get a report of the findings to you and other participating managers before school ends in early June, I need to receive the enclosed forms by February 20.

I appreciate your help and am eager to share with you a summary of what I learned about vendors and gratuities.

Sincerely,

John R. Pierce

John R. Pierce

Enclosure

Marginal annotations:

1. Writer provides return address because plain paper is used.
2. Seeks purchasing agent's attention. Use of "purchasing agents" establishes the letter as a document related to the recipient's work. Because the topic is current in the literature, agents may have already become interested. 3. Calls attention to the importance of the topic. At this point, the reader may think, "I've often wrestled with this problem, but I wish I could have found an answer." 4. Leads to an introduction of the questionnaire as one step toward finding answers.
5. Introduces the questionnaire.
6. Reminds managers of the *reward* for taking action. Professional managers who now have (or already had) an interest in the problem would see the sharing of results as a positive. Thus, they would be more inclined to say "yes" when the specific request is made.
7. Makes the request for action in a complex sentence that contains an additional idea that is positive.
8. Presents some needed assurance. With "quick marks," the effort is pictured as consuming little time.
9. Mentions a deadline in a sentence that reminds managers of the reward for complying.
10. Expresses gratitude, alludes to the reward for participating, and adds unity by using the words "vendors" and "gratuities," words that tie in with the first paragraph.
11. Includes enclosure notation to alert reader that information is enclosed.

FIGURE 11-9   Good example of a request for information

whose interest has been aroused in the first paragraphs, a long letter is more likely to be welcomed than resented. Some extremely effective sales letters have been as long as five pages (single spaced).

Like persuasive letters, persuasive memoranda need extra space for developing an appeal. The memo in Figure 11-10 *could* have been written

Use inductive approach to overcome resistance.

Select an appeal *before* beginning to write.

deductively, but the production manager recalled an experience of the preceding year. The president had implied his opposition to a change in work schedules. Therefore, the subject line does not reveal *how* reduction in congestion is to be achieved. (If the president reads "change in work schedule" in the subject line, the memo is off to a bad start.) Knowing the

COOPER *Industries, Inc.*

6395 Cooper Parkway
Naperville, IL 60566-2168
312-555-6320

TO: H. B. Smith, President

FROM: George Adams, Production Manager   *GA*

DATE: March 1, 19—

SUBJECT: Proposal to Reduce Parking Congestion at Peak Hours

Although employee morale is already high, we can do something to make it still higher.

Almost 1,000 of our employees come to work and leave at the same time. With more than 600 cars in our parking lot, about 30 minutes are required to clear it each evening. Having worked hard for eight hours without wasting any company time, employees experience a challenge to their morale when a half-hour of their time is wasted.

Many employees, especially production workers, begin their day with a negative pull on their morale: They must arrive at the parking lot a half-hour early so they can begin work on schedule.

The following schedule changes would go a long way toward solving the problem (without cost to Cooper Industries):

Production and Plant Staff

Change work hours of production and plant staff. Instead of beginning at 8 a.m. and leaving at 4:30 p.m., begin at 7:30 a.m. and leave at 4:00 p.m. This change would affect about 700 employees. It has support from the Employee Council.

FIGURE 11-10   Good example of a persuasive memorandum

H. B. Smith   2   March 1, 19—

<u>Office and Management Staffs</u>

Make no change in work hours for office and management staffs. By the time they arrive at the parking lot, production and plant workers would be already settled in their parking spaces. By the time they leave, traffic lanes should be clear for fast departure.

By making these changes, Cooper Industries would again demonstrate its concern for employees' problems. They would be appreciative, and we should detect a positive influence on their morale.

After you have considered this change, I would be pleased to survey production and plant personnel about their willingness to begin and leave work a half-hour early.

FIGURE 11-10, continued

president's concern about morale, and recognizing the problem's impact on morale, the production manager uses morale as an appeal. The word "morale" is used in the first sentence and near the end—as the last word in a paragraph where it gets emphasis. It also appears in the second and third paragraphs.

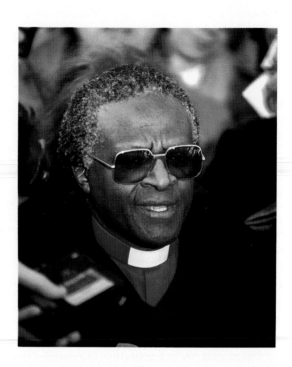

*Archbishop Desmond Tutu
helped direct worldwide
attention to the problem of
apartheid in South Africa, and
he created a large group of
supporters. However, he also
faced a great deal of opposition
to his ideas. When you are
trying to convince others to
adopt your ideas and you know
your reader is hostile toward
them, you must be diplomatic
and persuasive, which calls for
the inductive approach.*

The Collection Series

As in other persuasive letters, the primary purpose of a collection letter is to get action (payment). A secondary goal is to maintain a customer's goodwill.

Like other persuasive letters, collection letters are generally written inductively (exceptions are discussed later in this chapter); but they are shorter. Normally, customers know that they owe (no need to devote space to informing them); and they expect to be asked for payment (no need for an attention getter and no need for an apology). If a letter is short, its main point (pay is expected) stands out vividly. Compared with a long letter, a short letter has a greater chance of being read in its entirety. In a long letter, the main point could end up in the skipped-over portion or may have to compete for attention with minor points.

Knowing that slow-to-pay customers may not respond to the first attempts at collection, businesses that use collection letters normally use a series (if the first letter doesn't bring a response, a second letter is sent, then a third, and so on). An effective series of collection letters incorporates the following characteristics: timeliness, regularity, understanding, and increasing stringency.

1. *Timeliness.* A collection writer should not put off sending a letter. The longer debtors are given to pay, the longer they will usually take. Most people react favorably to deadlines. Deadlines stick in our minds and

provide the motivation to act. Effective collection efforts should be made promptly, and they should encourage payment by certain dates.

2. *Regularity.* Never let the obligation out of the debtor's mind. Although we can't send a collection letter every day, we can base the time lapse between letters on our previous experience with debtors and on a knowledge of the overall effectiveness of our collection practices. A regular system for mailings impresses on debtors the efficiency of collection practices.

3. *Understanding.* Understanding involves adaptability and skill in human relations. The collection series must be adaptable to the nature of the debtor. Good-pay risks should probably be given more time to pay than debtors with poor-pay reputations. We should recognize that many debtors have very good reasons for not having paid on time. They should be given every opportunity to meet their obligations or to explain why they are unable to do so.

   Understanding also influences the regularity of the collection series. Letters should not be sent so close together that the debtor won't have a chance to pay before the next letter arrives. No one likes to receive a collection letter after the bill has been paid. Some collection letters paradoxically accuse the debtor of trying to avoid payment and then end with a sentence that says, "If you have already paid, please ignore this letter." This notation is appropriate on friendly, printed reminders only.

4. *Increasing stringency.* The fourth characteristic of the collection series is increasing stringency in letter tone as the seriousness of the delinquency increases. Adverbs can add stringency to collection language. Instead of being *important*, a problem has become *extremely important.* Words and phrases such as *must, compelled,* and *no other alternative* are important in the later collection stages.

Most collection authorities classify the letters in the series according to the names that describe the seriousness of the problem. We can call these classes the *collection series.*

How many letters are in a collection series? The number of letters varies with the collection philosophy of the company and the nature of the debtor. Companies will have to write as many letters as necessary to collect the money or until collection is hopeless and must be attempted through legal action. The following stages are used: (1) reminder, (2) inquiry, (3) appeal, (4) strong appeal or urgency, and (5) ultimatum. Figure 11-11 illustrates the steps in a typical collection series.

Reminder. Many people will pay promptly when they receive a bill. Shortly after the due date, a simple reminder will usually bring in most of the remaining accounts. The reminder is typically a duplicate of the original statement with a rubber-stamped notation saying "second notice," "past due," or "please remit." To send a collection letter at this stage

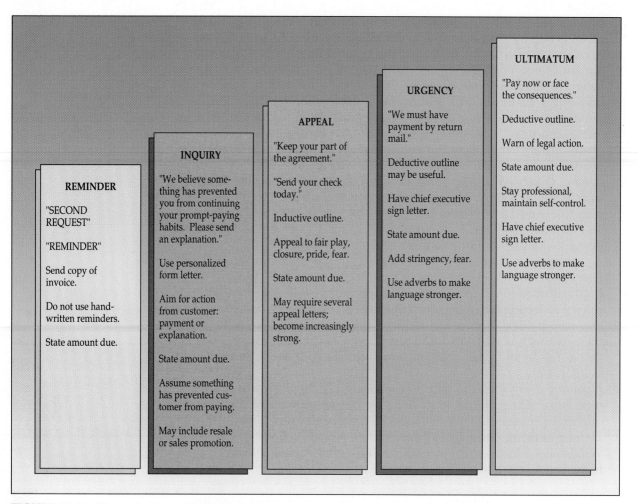

FIGURE 11-11   Stages in the collection-letter series

would be risky for goodwill. The assumption is that the obligation has been overlooked and will be paid when the reminder is received. Very often, companies will use two or three reminders before moving to the letter-writing stage. Remember, letters cost money. They should be used only when a company is reasonably sure collection is going to be difficult.

Colored gummed stickers may be attached to the statement for their attention-getting qualities. Some companies send reminders automatically generated by computers at specified intervals (for example, 30, 45, and 60 days past due). Other companies send a copy of the original statement produced on colored paper or stamped "second request." The aim at the reminder stage is to make sure the reader recognizes the reminder element. This step should be accomplished as though the reminder were a routine procedure (which it is); the debtor should not feel singled out for special attention. For that reason, avoid initialed handwritten reminders at this stage.

Inquiry. After sending the normal number of reminders without success, companies resort to letters. To increase efficiency, many organizations use form letters that may be initiated automatically by the computer or by a collector. In either case, the form letters are personalized by inserting the debtor's name and address, salutation, amount owed, and date payment is due.

In all letters at the inquiry stage, the assumption must be that something has prevented the debtor from paying. The aim is to get some action from the customer, in the form of either a check or an explanation. Follow these guidelines in writing effective inquiry letters:

1. Because reminders have failed to bring payment, something is wrong.
2. Action on the part of the debtor is necessary. Either a payment or an explanation is expected.
3. With empathy, think and write positively.
4. Make it easy for the debtor to reply, but do not provide excuses for nonpayment.

The inquiry should not provide an excuse for nonpayment or mention that the customer had merely overlooked paying. Inexperienced collectors often violate these two important principles. Inquiry letters often ask whether something is wrong with the goods purchased or service provided. If people are attempting to avoid payment as long as possible, they will be glad to tell you something was wrong with your product or service.

One letter of helpful inquiry is sufficient because additional letters may give the debtor the idea you will continue to wait. You must increase stringency by reducing the proportion of helpful talk as you proceed from one stage to the next. Helpful talk can be used in the appeal and ultimatum stages, but it should not predominate as it does in the inquiry stage.

Appeal. By writing a short letter restricted to one appeal, a collection writer (1) increases the chances that the entire letter will be read, (2) places emphasis on the appeal used, and (3) reserves something new to say if an additional letter is needed. Typically, collection letters use appeals selected from the following list:

◆ *Fair play.* Collectors often appeal to the debtor's sense of cooperation, loyalty, and honesty. For example: "The mutual contract we entered into was based on two things. The first was our ability to make delivery as agreed. The second was your ability to pay as agreed. We kept our part of the agreement, and the only way to complete the agreement is for you to send a check for $156 today."

◆ *Closure.* According to the closure principle in Gestalt psychology, people gain satisfaction from concluding that which they have begun; that is, from taking the final step—paying—in a business transaction. For example, "Send your check for $156 today so that we can mark your account 'Paid in Full.'"

◆ *Pride.* Many people wish to preserve their reputation and maintain a sense of prestige, accomplishment, and ownership. For example, "You must be proud of your excellent credit rating. Let us help you retain that pride by keeping your account in our 'preferred file,' Ms. Wright."

◆ *Fear.* Collectors know that many people fear loss of credit privilege, loss of possessions, and the possibility of litigation. For example, "So that you can continue to offer your customers the quality merchandise they demand, you must safeguard your good credit report. To do so, please send your check for $156 today."

Each of the preceding appeals can be used to help a customer see the advantage of paying. Certain appeals—a threat of physical violence and a statement of intent to destroy a credit reputation (by telling friends, relatives, employers, and others)—are illegal. Creditors are normally within legal limits when they provide facts about an account to firms or individuals entitled to receive such information. Appeals to fear, being negative, should be used only after more positive appeals have been given a chance to solve the collection problem.

For those debtors who have ignored the notices, reminders, and inquiries, the collection writer must select the appeal most suitable for the individual case and determine the best method of developing that appeal. The delinquent customer whose account has reached this stage must be persuaded to pay. Follow these two guidelines for the appeal letter or letters:

1. Keep in mind the personal nature of the appeal. It is written for one person or for one company. Personalize the letter by calling the reader by name if the use of the name falls naturally into place as you compose.
2. Write the letter from the reader's point of view. You shouldn't plead your own poverty as a reason why payment should be made. Instead, select an appropriate appeal and drive it home. Concentrate on one appeal. Multiple-appeal letters don't provide time or space to develop a single appeal properly.

Appeals in this stage intimidate only slightly, if at all. They suggest that the debtor might lose some tangible possession or be forced to become involved in a distasteful credit or legal entanglement. Typically, fear appeals are reserved for the strong-appeal or ultimatum letters.

4. Strong Appeal or Urgency. The strong-appeal letter emphasizes urgency. It says, in effect, "We must have the payment by return mail." By developing the basic appeals and insisting on payment for the debtor's own good, the writer adds stringency. Partial payments may be satisfactory, offers to accept time notes may be made, or full payment may be demanded. Comments about the cost of a lawsuit are common in urgency letters. Although implications about the loss of credit or possessions may be used, the best psychology is to let the reader know you are still willing to square things without undue embarrassment. To emphasize the crucial status of the delinquency, the strong-appeal or urgency letter may be signed by a top executive rather than by a member of the collection staff.

The appeal stages, both mild and strong, must of necessity involve human sensitivity, perhaps more than in any other communications issue. The deftness with which the writer handles the collection problem determines which customers are retained for the company. At the same time, the account has reached a crucial stage at which the assumption is that the customer will pay only after a persuasive challenge.

To develop the strong appeal from the mild appeal, follow these suggestions:

1. Change the appeal from one of challenging the debtor's *retention* of a favorable credit rating, a good reputation, or a prized possession to one of definitely implying that a debtor is about to *lose* something of value or *face a distasteful dilemma*.
2. Decrease the persuasive tone. Become more demanding.
3. Instead of discussing why the debtor *doesn't* pay, talk about why the debtor *must* pay.
4. Offer the debtor a choice between two or more things, none of which enables to debtor to get off the hook.
5. Let the debtor know clearly that the weight of evidence and the legal aspects definitely favor you and not the debtor.
6. Consider using the deductive approach.

Recall from Chapter 10 that sometimes bad news is appropriately placed in the first sentence. Late in the collection series, nothing (including the inductive approach) has worked. At this stage, the creditor may be justified in "shaking" the debtor or demonstrating some authority. Someone who has waited unusually long to pay a debt may respond to unusual treatment. By beginning with a direct request for payment or setting a time by which payment must be made, a deductive letter could get results when preceding inductive letters have failed. The action beginning is very emphatic. If it shocks a debtor into payment, good. If it doesn't, little is lost by trying the deductive approach.

5. Ultimatum. When strong appeals fail to do their work, the collection writer must take the only remaining course of action: a letter that says,

"You must pay now of your own volition or we will use every possible legal means to enforce collection." The debtor must pay or face the consequences. Whatever recourse you have to final collection must be mentioned in the letter. You must make the most of the fact that you will use the courts, a collection agency, or an attorney to enforce collection. Unfortunately, accounts that have reached this stage may be as costly to the lender as they are to the borrower. Furthermore, if payment is not made, you are sure to lose the customer. If payment is made, you would probably be hesitant about extending further credit to the customer.

Despite this dilemma, your letter should not use language that will make you susceptible to legal action by the customer. Keep your self-control, show some patience, and stay above the name-calling level. Any effort you can make to retain goodwill is worthwhile. Above all, avoid preaching because debtors who get to this stage do not react favorably to advice about how they should have acted. The ultimatum letter in Figure 11-12 shows that the tone has changed from "must pay" to "now or else."

Note how the ultimatum letter reviews the sequence of events, past and future, to indicate the seriousness of the matter. At this late stage, deductive writing is an option. To emphasize the ultimatum, the letter could have used the third paragraph as the beginning paragraph. If the ultimatum letter does not result in collection, the only resource is to tell the debtor you are taking the steps promised. The account is no longer in your hands.

SUMMARY

The purpose of a persuasive message is to get action. People are not inclined to act because they are told to do something; they will do something if they want to. The technique of persuasion, then, is to arouse desire.

When a writer's purpose is to sell a product or to request a special favor, ideas should be presented in the inductive sequence: Get the reader's attention, introduce the product or request, give evidence the reader gains by buying or complying, and encourage action. Effective persuasive letters build on a central selling point, just as a report develops a theme. The readers, rather than the product, serve as the subject of many of the sentences. Readers thus can envision themselves using the product or performing the request to satisfy their needs. The typical persuasive message is longer than the typical routine message because evidence of reader benefit is necessary and space consuming.

Compared with other persuasive letters, collection letters are shorter. Debtors already know that they owe money. A short letter that presents one good reason for paying has a better chance of success than a long letter that presents many reasons. In the collection series of increasingly stringent letters, each letter presents one appeal. If no response results, the next letter presents a different appeal.

MAIN STREET
AUTO SUPPLY

800 Main Street
Caspar, WY 82602-3703
(307) 555-3195

May 20, 19—

Mr. Jerome Brennan
Brennan Automotive Center
1873 25th Avenue
Caspar, WY 82602-1873

Dear Mr. Brennan:

When we agreed some three months ago to ship automotive supplies, you agreed that you would pay the $1,265 within 30 days. Yet the 30 days have gone by, then 60. Now more than 90 days have elapsed.

During this time, we have sent you several overdue notices and letters—all without a single reply from you. Because our overdue notices and letters have gone unanswered, our patience is exhausted; however, our interest in you and in your welfare is not.

As members of the National Retail Credit Association, we are compelled to submit your name as "nonpay" unless we receive your check for $1,265 by May 27. The effect of a bad report could very well restrict your ability to purchase supplies on credit. In addition, our legal department would be forced to bring suit for collection.

We have every right to enforce legal collection. You have until May 27 to retain your good record and to avoid legal embarrassment.

Sincerely,

Brian Garcia

Brian Garcia
President

FIGURE 11-12 Good example of an ultimatum

REFERENCE

Cody, S. (1906). *Success in letter writing: Business and social.* Chicago: A. C. McClurg.

CHECK YOUR WRITING

SALES LETTERS

Content
- [ ] Writer is convinced that the product or service is worthy of consideration.
- [ ] Letter includes sufficient evidence of usefulness to the purchaser.
- [ ] Price is revealed (in the letter or an enclosure).
- [ ] Central selling point is apparent.
- [ ] Specific action desired is identified.
- [ ] Message is ethical and abides by legal requirements.

Organization
- [ ] Sequence of ideas is inductive.
- [ ] First sentence is a good attention getter.
- [ ] Central selling point is introduced in the first two or three sentences and reinforced through the rest of the letter.
- [ ] Price is introduced only after reader benefits have been presented.
- [ ] Price (what the reader gives) is associated directly with reward (what the reader gets).
- [ ] Final paragraph mentions (a) the specific action desired, (b) the reader's reward for taking the action, and (c) an inducement for taking action quickly, and (d) the action as being easy to take.

Style
- [ ] Language is objective.
- [ ] Active verbs (instead of passive verbs) predominate.

- [ ] Concrete nouns (instead of abstract nouns) predominate.
- [ ] Sentences are relatively short.
- [ ] Sentences vary in length and structure.
- [ ] Significant words are in emphatic positions.
- [ ] Ideas cohere (changes in thought are not abrupt).
- [ ] Through synonyms or direct repetition, the central selling point is frequently called to the reader's attention.
- [ ] Expression is original (sentences are not copied directly from the definition of the problem or from sample letters in the text; clichés are omitted).
- [ ] Unity is achieved by including in the final paragraph a key word or idea (central selling point) that was introduced in the first paragraph.

Mechanics
- [ ] Letter parts are in appropriate positions; acceptable format is used.
- [ ] First and last paragraphs are short (no more than two or three lines).
- [ ] All paragraphs are relatively short.
- [ ] "Enclosure" is typed on the letter if a brochure or pamphlet is to be enclosed.
- [ ] Keyboarding, spelling, grammar, and punctuation are perfect.

CHECK YOUR WRITING

PERSUASIVE REQUESTS

Content
- ☐ Writer is convinced that the idea is valid, that the proposal has merit.
- ☐ Reader will benefit, and the way or ways in which the reader will benefit are pointed out.
- ☐ A primary appeal (central selling feature) is incorporated.
- ☐ The specific action desired is identified.

Organization
- ☐ Sequence of ideas is inductive.
- ☐ First sentence gets attention and reveals the subject of the message.
- ☐ The major appeal is introduced in the first two or three sentences and reinforced throughout the rest of the message.
- ☐ Reader benefits are pointed out.
- ☐ Desired action is associated with the reader's reward for taking action.
- ☐ Final paragraph includes a reference to the specific action desired and the primary appeal. The paragraph emphasizes the ease of taking action and (if appropriate) includes a stimulus for quick action.

Style
- ☐ Language is objective and positive.
- ☐ Active verbs and concrete nouns predominate.
- ☐ Sentences are relatively short but vary in length and structure.

- ☐ Significant words are in emphatic positions.
- ☐ Ideas cohere (changes in thought are not abrupt).
- ☐ Primary appeal is frequently called to the reader's attention through synonyms or direct repetition of a word.
- ☐ Expression is original (sentences are not copied directly from the definition of the problem or from sample letters in the text; clichés are omitted).
- ☐ Unity is achieved by including in the final paragraph a key word or idea (the primary appeal) that was used in the first paragraph.

Mechanics
- ☐ Letter parts are in appropriate position; acceptable format is used. In memorandums, the *TO, FROM, DATE,* and *SUBJECT* lines are properly completed.
- ☐ In memorandums, courtesy titles are omitted in the *TO* and *FROM* lines.
- ☐ Paragraphs are relatively short but vary in length.
- ☐ "Enclosure" is keyed on the letter/memo if a document other than the letter/memo is to be enclosed.
- ☐ Keyboarding, spelling, grammar, and punctuation are perfect.

CHECK YOUR WRITING

COLLECTION SERIES

Content
- [ ] Inquiry letter simply asks for explanation, may include resale or sales promotion, states amount due.
- [ ] Each appeal letter is limited to one appeal.
- [ ] Each appeal letter is a little more forceful than the preceding one.
- [ ] Each appeal letter states amount due.
- [ ] Urgency letter is signed by a higher official than the one who signed the appeal letters, reveals seriousness of delay, and states amount due.
- [ ] Ultimatum letter leaves the way open for payment by a certain date and time; states amount due.
- [ ] Compared with other persuasive letters, a collection letter is relatively short.

Organization
- [ ] Sequence of ideas is inductive; ultimatum letter may use deductive sequence.
- [ ] Inquiry leads up to request for explanation.
- [ ] Appeal letter reveals in the first sentence that letter is about the debt, introduces one reader benefit (appeal) for paying, requests payment, and mentions exactly amount due.

- [ ] Urgency letter (from a higher official) reveals that letter is about the account, gives a brief summary of the attempts to collect, urges payment, and states exact amount due.
- [ ] Ultimatum letter sets a date by which payment is expected and states action that will be taken if payment is not received; states exact amount due.

Style
- [ ] Verbs are active; nouns are concrete.
- [ ] Appropriate words at the appeals stage include *mutual*, *fair*, *cooperative*, and *agreed*.
- [ ] Adverbs are used to make language stronger at urgency and ultimatum stages (e.g., *very* important, *extremely* critical).

Mechanics
- [ ] Letter parts are in appropriate positions; acceptable format is used.
- [ ] Letters, though short, are balanced on the page.
- [ ] Spelling, keyboarding, grammar, and punctuation are perfect.

REVIEW QUESTIONS

Sales Letters

1. What is the text's definition of "selling"?
2. In selecting a central selling feature, what questions must be answered?
3. What is the difference between a physiological appeal and a psychological appeal?
4. What are the characteristics of a good attention getter?
5. Define "central selling feature."
6. Sales letters are normally longer than routine letters. Why?
7. List the four points in the outline recommended for sales letters.
8. Which has more need for an attention getter in the first sentence: (a) a solicited letter or (b) an unsolicited letter?
9. In a well-written sales letter, which pronoun would be used more frequently: (a) first person or (b) second person?
10. Which of the following sentences is more accurate? (a) The first paragraph should be one of the *shortest* in the letter. (b) The first paragraph should be one of the *longest* in the letter.
11. In sales letters, which is ordinarily the better technique? (a) Use things as subjects of sentences. (b) Use people as subjects of sentences.
12. Under what condition is use of superlatives acceptable in sales letters?
13. **a.** Compose a sentence that includes an incomplete comparison.
    b. In sales letters, why are incomplete comparisons to be avoided?
14. Ordinarily, which is the better spot for introducing the price of a product: (a) *before* discussing worthy features or (b) *after* discussing worthy features?
15. Ordinarily, which is the better way to reveal the price of a product: (a) in a simple sentence or (b) in a complex sentence?
16. Which is the better way to call a reader's attention to an enclosure: (a) "Enclosed you will find a brochure" or (b) "For additional features, see page 3 of the enclosed brochure"?
17. List some characteristics of an effective action ending.
18. Under what condition would referring to the product's price in the final paragraph be appropriate?
19. Are such expressions as "Act today," "Don't delay," and "Hurry, hurry" appropriate for inclusion in the final paragraph?
20. List some considerations in the preparation of envelopes that will carry sales letters.

Persuasive Requests and Collection Letters

21. What is the principal difference between a persuasive claim and a routine claim?

22. In a persuasive letter, what is meant by an "appeal"?
23. In the first paragraph of a persuasive request, what ideas should be included?
24. In a persuasive request, which should receive more emphasis: (a) the action desired or (b) the reward for taking action?
25. What would be the disadvantage of including "If you agree, please. . . " and "I hope you will be able to . . . ." in the paragraph that asks for action?
26. In a letter that introduces a long questionnaire and encourages the recipient to complete and return, should the writing be persuasive? Explain.
27. Ideally, should a persuasive request for action be stated in a simple sentence? Explain.
28. Why are collection letters normally shorter than other persuasive letters?
29. Give one example of how computers are being used to simplify the collection process.
30. Should an inquiry letter ask whether merchandise and service have been satisfactory?
31. In a collection series, how many letters should include a request for reasons for the delay in payment?
32. At the appeals stage in a collection series, how many appeals should each letter have?
33. Does the creditor's need for money serve well as a collection appeal? Explain.
34. A collection letter sets a date. If payment is not received by that date, the account will be turned over to a collection agency. After the date arrives and no payment is received, should a new date be set? Explain.
35. Which would have greater justification for use of negative terms: (a) an inquiry letter or (b) an ultimatum letter? Explain.

EXERCISES

1. Select an unsolicited sales letter you (or a friend) received. List (a) the principles it applies and (b) the principles it violates. Rewrite the letter retaining its strengths and correcting its weaknesses.
2. From a newspaper or magazine, clip a picture of an advertised product. Using the principles presented in this chapter, write an unsolicited sales letter. Attach the picture to the letter. Make sure your letter has a central selling point and presents evidence to convince the reader to buy.
3. Analyze the effectiveness of each sentence as the opening for a sales message.

    a. I am sending this letter to introduce you to our new line of PCs.

    b. The wave of the new millennium—Technocrat Integrated Software.

    c. You haven't lived until you've owned a Multi-Sound Compact Disc Storage Chest!

    d. We at Goldfield Surplus wish to have you as a customer.

    e. The enclosed folder shows our latest prices on chain saws.

4. Analyze the effectiveness of each sentence as the opening of a persuasive message. (The type of message is indicated in parentheses.)

    a. It is obvious that the merchandise is defective. (claim)

    b. I demand a refund of all charges. (claim)

    c. The merchandise you sent me on September 3 is defective, and I refuse to pay for it. (claim)

    d. This new policy I am proposing will revolutionize our sales figures within three months. (request)

    e. Anyone can see why I am qualified to be the next supervisor. (request)

5. Analyze the letter on page 460. Pinpoint its strengths and weaknesses and then revise the letter.

APPLICATIONS

1. Promoting a Product of Your Choice. Select a product that you own, assume you are its distributor, and write a sales letter addressed to others who are your age. Regardless of whether you select an item as expensive as a car or as inexpensive as a small pocket calculator, choose a product on which you are "sold." You have pride in it, you have benefited greatly from its use, you are well informed about it, and you could heartily recommend it to others. You may assume an accompanying picture, folder, or pamphlet is included with the letter.

MARKETING	PUBLIC RELATIONS		
ics	International	Legal	Interp

Required: Write the sales letter providing an inside address for a fictitious customer.

2. Selling the Cellular Phone to Select Customers. The XE300 is the newest cellular phone manufactured by Cartel, the long-distance company servicing the Washington, D.C., area. As the D.C. supervisor, you write an unsolicited sales letter to a mailing list of prospective buyers of the XE300. Special features include redial, home-to-car paging, and access to answering-machine messages at home or office from the car. Privacy coding and electronic lock of your frequency negate interference by other phones. The batteries operating the handset continuously recharge while the phone is in its mount. Installation and the phone unit cost $192.75. Several colors are available to match the phone to the car's interior.

MARKETING	PUBLIC RELATIONS	
nterpersonal	Technology	Public

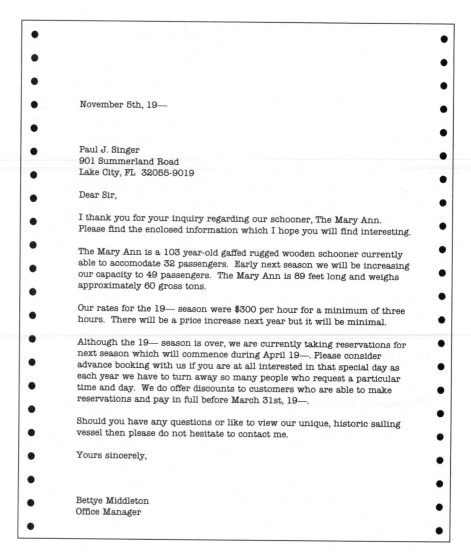

November 5th, 19—

Paul J. Singer
901 Summerland Road
Lake City, FL 32055-9019

Dear Sir,

I thank you for your inquiry regarding our schooner, The Mary Ann.
Please find the enclosed information which I hope you will find interesting.

The Mary Ann is a 103 year-old gaffed rugged wooden schooner currently
able to accomodate 32 passengers. Early next season we will be increasing
our capacity to 49 passengers. The Mary Ann is 89 feet long and weighs
approximately 60 gross tons.

Our rates for the 19— season were $300 per hour for a minimum of three
hours. There will be a price increase next year but it will be minimal.

Although the 19— season is over, we are currently taking reservations for
next season which will commence during April 19—. Please consider
advance booking with us if you are at all interested in that special day as
each year we have to turn away so many people who request a particular
time and day. We do offer discounts to customers who are able to make
reservations and pay in full before March 31st, 19—.

Should you have any questions or like to view our unique, historic sailing
vessel then please do not hesitate to contact me.

Yours sincerely,

Bettye Middleton
Office Manager

Exercise 5

Required: Write the sample letter and address it to Bart Collier, 114 South Meadowview Circle, Alexandria, VA 22313-0114.

3. **Promoting a New Book to Current Customers.**   You are the marketing director for Manuel Publishing. Your newest product is a reference work entitled *Down-Home Cures*. The book includes information arranged alphabetically on topics such as athlete's foot, earaches, insect bites, hay fever, toothaches, poison ivy, acne, and many more

ordinary hazards and maladies. The volume is bound in gold-embossed hardback. It costs $45.95, payable in three installments. Buyers also receive a free *Eat Smart Cookbook,* filled with recipes that can help reduce cholesterol, lower blood pressure, or prevent heart disease. You plan to mail letters to subscribers of your monthly magazine, *Wellness.*

Required: Write the sample letter and address it to Ann Carey, 101 Harris Drive, Chattanooga, TN 37416-0101.

4. **Promoting a Christmas Card/Photo Package.** Assume you are the owner of a local photo shop. This year you have an especially good offer on Christmas cards that include a family picture. You prefer to take four shots of a family and impose the best one on a card (the family selects the picture and card), or you can use a picture that has been taken already. Although processing will probably require only a few days, a family should allow a whole month for delivery to make sure the cards will be mailed in plenty of time for before-Christmas delivery. Prices are shown on an enclosed sheet.

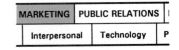

Required: Write the letter providing an inside address for a fictitious customer.

5. **Introducing a Credit Card to a Select Audience.** In an effort to expand its credit-card business, National Investors Trust Company wants you to write a letter to a select group of people who have outstanding credit ratings. Each respondent is invited to sign and return a form. Within a few days, the company will send a credit card that is good for credit purchases up to $3,000. Facts you may choose to include: The $25 annual fee will not be charged until the card is used. If the monthly statement is promptly paid in full, no finance charge is made. The annual percentage rate on a finance charge is 17.7 percent. Purchases can be made locally or in many foreign countries—at restaurants, hotels, motels, specialty stores, department stores, and so on. Cardholders can get cash at airports, banks, shopping malls, universities, and other locations. Each cardholder receives a checkbook. When one of the checks is used to pay for a purchase, only the writer is aware that a credit-card account is involved. When the card is used for purchasing an airline ticket, the traveler is automatically insured for $250,000.

Required: Write the sample letter to Arthur Sanderson, Box 123, Woodford Heights, MI 48765-0123.

6. **Earning a Finder's Fee for Exceptional British Stamps.** A client who wishes to start for his son a collection of high-quality European

MARKETING	PUBLIC RELATIONS	
thics	International	Legal	Int

stamps has asked you, a dealer in European stamps, to locate them. You have located a solid page of 100 stamps issued 10 years ago to commemorate British statesman Winston Churchill. This page is intact; no rows have been removed. Your own investigation has authenticated the dyes and inks on the stamps; you have also inspected the glue on the back and found no flaws. In short, the stamps are in mint condition. The owner paid 50 British pounds for the entire sheet and wishes to sell it for 200 pounds. You feel that the stamps are a very good buy for a beginning collector.

Required:

1. Locate the currency exchange rate so that you can give your client the price in U.S. dollars. Add 10 percent to the price for a finder's fee.
2. Write a sales letter to Glenn Marshall, 1103 Commerce Street, Denton, TX 76205-2955.

MARKETING	PUBLIC RELATIONS
nal	Technology	Public Sector

7. **Sold on European Tours: Request for Information.** As manager of a tour-service agency, you receive the letter on page 463. Although July is a busy month, the letter was received well in advance. A tour can be arranged for the last two weeks in July. Prices (listed on an enclosed folder) are based on a round trip from Denver, but any members who join the group in New York will receive a corresponding reduction. The tour includes Italy in addition to the three countries listed in the letter. All travel between countries is by air. A multilingual guide is provided. Tourists will stay in first-class hotels only. Other information (including suggestions about passports and visas) is included in the enclosed folder.

Required: Prepare a response to Professor Tate.

S MANAGEMENT	REAL ESTATE	A
thics	International	Legal	Int

8. **Exposing Potential Members to Resort Property and Privileges.** As the public relations director of Crystal Stream, an upscale residential/recreational development in Sacramento, California, one of your major responsibilities is to secure memberships. You believe people must be given an opportunity to experience Crystal Stream firsthand; that is, to see your signature golf course and to dine in your luxurious Williamsburg-style clubhouse. You intend to write a letter to prospects and include a certificate to be redeemed for 18 free holes of golf and a delicious appetizer and beverage in your dining room. Prospects will be instructed to call the pro shop to schedule a tee time. Accompanying the letter and certificate will be a four-color brochure that tells the history of the 712-acre development and includes pictures of the clubhouse, dining and meeting rooms, pool, and exercise rooms. The brochure also includes a detailed map of the course.

Required: Write the sample letter to Mr. and Mrs. David R. Denson, 373 Joline Avenue, Sacramento, CA 95813-0373.

Western State University
DEPARTMENT OF ENGLISH
P.O. BOX 2990
SALEM, OR 97308-2990
(503) 555-3789

February 1, 19—

Mr. David Tarpley
Tarpley Tours
1978 Crawford Plaza
Portland, OR 97208-1978

Dear Mr. Tarpley:

Please send information about your tours to Europe.

Fifteen members of my literary-study group would like to take a tour of Europe next summer, preferably in the last half of July.

We envision a trip of about two weeks' duration. Although we can't expect to see all of Europe's countries, we are especially interested in England, France, and Switzerland.

So that we can finalize tour plans, we would appreciate your sending information about your services—prices, itineraries, accommodations, etc.

Sincerely,

Lloyd R. Tate

Lloyd R. Tate
Professor of Literature

Application 7

9. **Party Time: Special Request.** The letter shown in Figure 11-6 is a persuasive request from the Lakeside Medical Association to Crystal Stream, an upscale residential resort. Refer to Application 8 for a description of the resort. The Lakeside Medical Association sought permission to hold a charity event at Crystal Stream. As social chairperson of your fraternity or sorority, you are certain Crystal Stream is the

GENERAL	EDUCATION	HOTEL MA
sonal	Technology	Public Secto

perfect place to hold your annual Christmas formal. Crystal Stream is a very exclusive club; consequently, its management may be reluctant to grant your request. Perhaps they have heard stories from other clubs about fraternity groups' holding wild parties on their grounds that resulted in thousands of dollars' worth of damage to the property.

Required:

1. Consider specific reasons why your fraternity/sorority should be allowed to use the club. What essential details should you provide about the dance?
2. Write a letter persuading management to allow you to hold the party at Crystal Stream. Refer to Figure 11-6 for the address.

10. **Using Effective Persuasion Techniques to Prevent a Hostile Takeover.** Robey-Huber, Inc. is attempting a hostile takeover of Waldron Industry by offering to buy stock at 55 when the current level is 40. As the chief executive officer of Waldron, you hope to prevent this takeover by communicating to the stockholders the benefits of not selling at the higher price. Two years ago Waldron Industries renegotiated its contract with union workers. That action positioned the company at a cost disadvantage to its competitors, thus reducing corporate profits. You have learned through reliable sources that your major competitors will renegotiate their union contracts within the year. Consequently, they will face the same increases in employee wages; and their current advantage will be dissipated. Management is confident that Waldron will quickly reap the benefits of taking the initiative and renegotiating labor contracts two years ago.

Required: As the chief executive officer of Waldron, write a letter to the stockholders persuading them not to sell their stock. Address the sample letter to Mrs. Helen Munson, 8311 Desert Lane, Tucson, AZ 85702-8311.

11. **Organ Donations: For a Good Cause.** As the public relations officer of a national organ donor association, you are initiating a campaign to recruit organ donors. One of your first efforts is to write a letter encouraging people to help alleviate the national shortage of available organs. Facts you may choose to include: The federal Uniform Anatomical Gift Act allows persons to authorize the use of their organs after death by simply signing a statement. Another way to communicate willingness to donate is to sign the donor card attached to driver's licenses in most states. The American Council on Transplantation estimates that on any given day 15,000 Americans are waiting for organs. About 25,000 healthy people die under circumstances that would allow their organs to be transplanted. According to a 1987

Gallup survey, 48 percent of those asked said they would be willing to donate their organs for transplantation; but fewer than 20 percent carry signed organ-donor cards.

Required:
1. Consider the possible emotional reasons for donating organs as well as the logical reasons provided in the application.
2. Write a persuasive letter encouraging the reader to commit to being an organ donor. Address the form letter to Mr. Jerry L. McDavid, 23 Queen Victoria Lane, Winchester, KY 40391-0023.

12. **Admissions Questions.** Typically, college students who apply for admission to professional schools are required to complete admission forms that ask (among other short-answer questions) an open-ended question: (a) "Why do you want to be a lawyer (or physician, dentist, therapist, nurse, engineer)?" Or (b) "Why have you selected *this* school instead of others?" Usually, a space limitation—one page or 200 or 500 words—is given. The answer gives students an opportunity to present pertinent information, to demonstrate skills in organizing and writing, and to persuade.

ENERAL	EDUCATION	HOTEL MAN
Ethics	International	Legal

Required: Using the principles of persuasion, write your answer to question (a) or to question (b). Assuming you are in your last semester as an undergraduate student, tailor your answer to your specific plans.

13. **Proposed Tax Hike: Persuasive Campaign.** A special election has been scheduled for a referendum on a 2-percent tax on prepared food and beverages. The tax has been proposed by the Tucson City Planning Board (the municipal government) as a means of providing public funding for the newly formed Tucson Development Council (TDC). Officials estimate the tax will produce approximately $900,000 in revenues. According to the bill, half of the funds would be used to fund the TDC, which will handle all local economic developmental projects. Twenty-five percent would be used by the Visitors and Convention Council for the development of tourism within the county, and 25 percent would be used to construct a welcome center. As president of the Tucson Chamber of Commerce, you are convinced that economic development, especially increased tourism, will benefit the entire community. Bringing more people to Tucson will create jobs and income for the people here. You have obtained current membership lists of the area civic clubs.

NCE	MANAGEMENT	MIS	CONSU
onal	Technology	Public Sector	

Required: Compose a form letter to be sent to members of the other civic clubs persuading them to support the tax. Address a sample letter to Alex Davies, 104 Duggar Acres, Tucson, AZ 85702-0104.

14. Information About Business Careers: Request for Mailing List. A national association of business managers wants to help high school seniors become more familiar with careers in business. The association has decided to publish a quarterly newsletter containing articles about business careers, profiles of people working in various business fields, and aptitudes and traits of successful business personnel. This newsletter will be sent to seniors in selected high schools.

Required: As secretary of the association, write a letter to high school counselors asking for names and addresses of their students; the list will be updated each year. A copy of the most recent newsletter is to accompany the letter. (Assure the counselors that the list of names will be used for no other purpose.)

15. Careers About Business: Cover Letter. As secretary of the national association of business managers (Application 14), you have acquired the names and addresses of high school seniors who will receive your quarterly newsletter.

Required: Write a cover letter to accompany the first newsletter and to explain your reasons for providing this publication. Address the sample letter to Ms. Frances Haggard, Route 3, Box 304, Duluth, GA 30136-0304.

16. Equipment Malfunction Justifies an Exchange. Six months ago you bought what was considered a top-of-the-line VCR from an electronics franchise in your town. After one week of use, it malfunctioned. It had a two-year warranty, so you returned it to the dealer for repair. One week later you took it home, and it broke again. After six months of continually returning the malfunctioning VCR for repair, you feel you deserve a new VCR. The local dealer will not give you a new machine, so you decide to write to the manufacturer.

Required: Write a persuasive letter explaining that you feel justified in asking for a new VCR because yours has been in the repair shop more than it has been available for use. Address the letter to Tele-video, 580 West Lakes Blvd., Milwaukee, WI 53202-0580.

17. Disappointing Services: Request for Adjustment. For his fifth wedding anniversary, Todd Gray decided to take his wife to one of New York City's top luxury hotels for a weekend. Although the price seemed to be very high ($295 per night), Todd felt that he had made a perfect choice for their fifth anniversary. The hotel did not live up to the couple's expectations. The service was slow and impersonal, the staff was unfriendly, and the room left much to be desired. They both thought they could have had a more pleasant stay at a mid-level hotel.

Required:

1. Consider these points: Do you believe that Todd is justified in asking for a full refund? What reasons support his justification? If the refund is not justifiable, what reasonable adjustment should he request?

2. As Todd Gray, write a letter to the hotel asking for the adjustment you feel is justified. Address the letter to James Parker, Manager, Anderson House, 708 East 26th Street, New York City, NY 10001-1708.

18. **Presenting a Case for a Year's Leave of Absence.** Ruth Hutchinson is purchasing manager for the Markens Art Company (MAC). She would like to take a year's leave of absence to complete an art book she has been writing. As an effective manager should, Ruth has for years practiced the art of delegation. Two assistants are very familiar with all phases of her work, and they are acquainted with the people from whom most of the folk art is purchased. Ruth requests that her salary be paid to her during her absence, and she thinks MAC will be well rewarded. Her book will devote about 20 pages to the work of Maynord Jenkins, a sculptor whose works are sold exclusively through MAC. Ruth thinks the book will increase demand for Jenkins' work. As a result, prices will increase, and MAC will profit. Because of Ruth's long years of interest in and study of American sculptors and her fame as a lecturer in the United States and Europe, she thinks the market for the book will be very good.

ANCE	MANAGEMENT	MIS	CONS
Ethics	International	Legal	Ir

Required: As though you were Ruth Hutchinson, write a persuasive memorandum to Vinita Clark, chief of operations at MAC. Ask for a leave beginning two months from now.

19. **Initiating a Change in Employee Pay Schedule.** For years, Hurley Company has paid its employees twice each month, on the 1st and the 15th. Occasionally employees (particularly those who are paid by the hour) have expressed a preference for checks every other Friday. When the matter was mentioned briefly last year, Charles Atwood, the controller, expressed opposition. In his mind, the change would not affect the total paid to each employee yearly. Such a change would need support from the company president, but without Atwood's approval, it has little chance.

ANCE	MANAGEMENT	MIS	CONS
nterpersonal	Technology	Public	

Required: As though you were Paul Adams (human resources manager), write a memorandum to Mr. Atwood. Try to get his support for paying employees every two weeks on Friday.

20. **Securing a Notable Speaker.** Hank Appleton (sales manager at Markens Art Company) is responsible for finding speakers for the monthly meetings of a civic club to which he belongs. Knowing of Ruth Hutchinson's background and interest in the history of Ameri-

ANCE	MANAGEMENT	MIS	CONSU
Ethics	International	Legal	I

can sculpture, he thinks she would be an ideal speaker. However, he knows how busy she is at her job at MAC; and he knows how much she cherishes her weekends. Speakers receive no fee. Several members of the club have backgrounds rich in art and literature.

Required: As Hank Appleton, write a memorandum to Ruth inviting her to give a presentation (30–45 minutes) on a Friday evening two months from now. Dinner at the Forum Club begins at 7 p.m.; her presentation would follow.

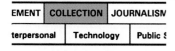

21. **Inquiring About Reasons for Nonpayment.**   When Stan Watson was campaigning for election as county sheriff, he had $1,500 worth of signs printed. He paid $1,000, and the printing shop agreed to accept the remaining $500 after the election. After losing the election, Stan paid $100—the first of what were to be five monthly payments. Two weeks have passed since his second payment was due, but no check has arrived. Write an inquiry letter to Stan Watson, P.O. Box 121, your city.

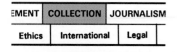

22. **The First Appeal for Payment.**   A month has passed and Stan (Application 21) has paid nothing. He now needs to pay $200. Write an appeal letter.

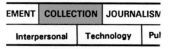

23. **The Second Appeal for Payment.**   Two weeks ago you sent the appeal letter to Stan (Application 22), and he has not yet responded. Write another letter with a different appeal.

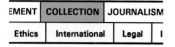

24. **A Stronger Appeal for Payment.**   Two weeks after sending the second appeal to Stan, you have received no response. Write another letter with a stronger appeal (see Applications 22 and 23).

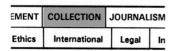

25. **The Ultimatum.**   Two weeks after sending the final appeal letter (Application 24), write Stan an ultimatum.

CASES FOR ANALYSIS

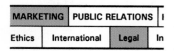

Case 1.   Determining the Legal Implications of Using a Person's Likeness in an Advertisement. During local television news coverage of a blues festival, the reporter and the camera crew shot some footage of a family of six (including four small children) arriving at the festival in a minivan. Your car dealership sells minivans of the same make, and you want to use the footage in your television commercials. The television station agrees to let you use its footage and gives you the name and address of the family involved.

Required:

1. Because you have never used pictures acquired in this way, the dealership owner (Anthony Coffin) wants you to research the legal guidelines for using a person's likeness. He has several concerns: What information must be included in the letter to meet these legal guidelines? How specific must you be in describing the use of the pictures? Should you offer to pay the family a fee for these pictures?

2. Write a memo to your supervisor providing the results of the research you conducted in step 1. Include complete and accurate documentation of your sources. This memo will serve as a record of your efforts to ensure legality on this issue.

3. Write the letter to the family asking permission to use their likenesses in your ad campaign and including the pertinent information identified in step 1. Address the letter to Mr. and Mrs. Curtis Alford, 4211 Main Street, Memphis, TN 38115-4211.

Case 2. Charitable Contributions or Shrewd Public Relations? As the president of a bottled water company, you have been looking constantly for a way to promote your product. The United States has just sent hundreds of troops to a foreign country to defend it against a possible military attack. Because soldiers will need plenty of water in this dry climate, you see this situation as a possible solution to your sales problem.

MARKETING	PUBLIC RELATIONS	
Ethics	International	Legal

Required:

1. As company president, write a persuasive letter to military officials asking them to purchase your bottled water for the military troops in this foreign country. Address the letter to the Procurement Department and use the simplified block format that omits the salutation.

2. Assume that the military officials refused to offer your company a contract to supply bottled water to the military troops. Your marketing/public relations department has proposed that the company donate 500,000 bottles of water to the military. Decide whether it is ethical to donate the bottled water. Consider these points:
   a. What are the relevant facts?
   b. What are the ethical issues raised by the decision to donate the bottled water?
   c. Who (which stakeholders) will be affected by this decision?
   d. What are the costs and benefits imposed by each alternative on each person listed in step (c)?
   e. What are the company's obligations to each person listed in step (c)?
   What should you as the company's representative do?

3. Based on your decision, complete *one* of the following options:
   a. As a stockholder, write a letter to the president voicing your dis-

senting opinion on the donation of the water. Address the letter to Michael Stevens, Sparkling Springs Water Company, 2731 North Lake Street, Chicago, IL 60607-2731.

b. As the public relations director, write a news release stating that your company has decided to donate 500,000 bottles of water to the military.

c. Do any other options exist? If so, write a letter, memo, or other document to the appropriate individual.

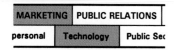

Case 3. Developing Support for a Worthy Community Effort. As a member of a local civic group, you are organizing an annual community project to provide holiday gifts to underprivileged children. Today one of the members of the committee gave you a draft of a letter soliciting support for the project. After reading the letter, you have two major concerns: (1) The basic principles of persuasive writing have not been applied; therefore, you are not certain how effectively the letter will be in drawing support for your worthy project. (2) You feel a more attractive, creative layout would increase the impact of the content. The draft you received appears on page 471.

Required:

1. Revise the letter incorporating the principles of effective persuasion.

2. Use desktop publishing capabilities available to you to design a creative, attention-getting layout, including a letterhead, for this document. Provide a fictitious name and address for the civic club. Use these page-design and layout principles as a guide:

   a. Keep it simple; don't clutter the page with too much information or too many fonts and graphics (lines, boxes, pictures). "Less is more" is a cardinal rule among professionals.

   b. When varying the typeface for emphasis (italics, bold, underline), keep the varied portions short for maximum effectiveness.

   c. Use plenty of white space to give the eye a break and to make the page more appealing to the reader.

   d. Don't use text lines that are too long for the eye to follow. Shortening the line of writing also opens up the page for more white space.

   e. Do not justify the right margin; a ragged-right margin opens up the page and creates a friendlier appearance.

   f. Use lines, boxes, shaded areas, or bullets (*, —, □, •, ✓, etc.) to emphasize particular items, to add spark, and to organize the page.

November 29, 19—

Mrs. Laura Ann Shaw
9655 Tenth Street
Cambridge, MA 02140-9655

Dear Mrs. Shaw

The Thirteenth Annual Holiday Store will be held in the lobby of the Main
Street Fire Station on Dec. 6, 7, and 8 from 3:00 to 6:00 p.m. New toys will
be given to the parents of approximately 400 underprivileged children at
this time.

If you can HELP any or all of the following afternoons, we will need YOU to
help set up and operate the store. We need volunteers on the afternoon of
Dec. 6, 7, and 8 to set up the store and work as clerks and gift wrappers.
We need you to please sign your name below, indicating the date you will
be able to help.

Name _____
Phone _____
Date & Time Available _____

Also, contributions to The Holiday Store are needed and will be greatly
appreciated.

Please return this form to either Mari Cooper, 3771 Abilene Street,
Cambridge, MA 02140-3771 (555-1043) or Frances Kuhnle, 101 Mangrove
Drive, Boston, MA 02184-0101 (555-9031). THANK YOU!

Sincerely

Rachele Saucier

Case 3

Tracy-Locke/Pharr Public Relations

Preparing effective, persuasive communication requires a carefully tuned set of skills. First, the writer must understand the needs and motivations of the intended audience and how to make the product or idea appealing. Second, the writer must be able to predict and overcome every reason the reader may have for rejecting the message, so as to assure the desired outcome. Third, the writer must be convincing yet courteous, persuasive yet polite.

Whether selling products, services, or ideas, a business's success or failure often rests on its employees' strengths of persuasion.

Discussion Questions

1. Cynthia Pharr likens the sales letter to a personal sales call. Explain how the two activities are similar.
2. Michael Fleming puts forth the idea that practicing conciseness shows concern for your reader/audience. Explain this concept.
3. What constitutes an effective opening for a sales letter? Give examples of techniques that may attract the attention of the reader. What should the writer guard against in structuring the opening?
4. Explain the concept of being receiver-oriented. How is this idea applied in sales letters?
5. How do surface characteristics, such as the envelope and stationery, impact the readers' responses to a sales letter?

Application

(This activity is a continuation of the application accompanying the Video Connection following Chapter 7, page 236.)

You must construct an effective sales letter to persuade your audience to purchase The Good Life, your company's vitamin supplement. Consider the facts previously presented; additionally, assume that your target market is young adults, age 20–30. Remember to include (1) an effective opening; (2) a concise, on-target discussion of your product; (3) convincing evidence that your product will meet your readers' needs; and (4) a courteous, effective call for action.

WRITING SPECIAL LETTERS

OBJECTIVES

When you have completed
Chapter 12, you should be
able to

◆ Recognize the benefits
   derived from writing special letters.

◆ Appreciate the impor-
   tance of intent in writing
   special letters.

◆ Write letters that congratulate, acknowledge congratulations, commend,
   console, invite, and
   thank.

◆ Write an effective news
   release.

◆ Write letters that identify
   situations needing im-
   provement.

MEGAN IS A TAX MANAGER for a large accounting firm. She worked several years to get into a management position, but she has not forgotten what an entry-level position is like. She remembers hearing the words, *good job,* and how those words seemed to encourage her to work even harder. Now that Megan supervises several accountants, she is busier than ever and has many responsibilities. Some days are so hectic that she finds it difficult to take a break or leave for a quick lunch. But no matter how crowded her day is, she always makes time to give the hard-working accountants in her department positive and sincere feedback. Megan knows that this feedback helps reinforce the workers' sense of worth and improve the quality of the work they produce.

Encouragement and sincere feedback are essential commodities for managers. Everyone benefits from being told that his or her work is appreciated and valued. In addition to an immediate boost in self-confidence and pride in their work, employees also feel compelled to do even better. Therefore, managers who are aware of their employees' hard work and frequently give them sincere recognition not only have a happier work force but a more productive one as well.

Quite often the manager will communicate this recognition orally. For some circumstances, however, the manager will want to put the message in writing—a permanent and tangible sign of the manager's praise. Empathetic managers do not overlook occasions to write letters and memorandums that create goodwill among employees as well as clients, customers, and various other groups. They use these opportunities to build strong, lasting relationships; they send genuine messages promptly; and they make sure that they follow the rules of professional protocol precisely.

COMMUNICATION MENTOR

In our company, we send preprinted thank-you notes telling customers we appreciate their business and offering assistance with any problems or questions about the loan closing. If problems have occurred during the process, we handwrite an additional comment to communicate our genuine apology. This goodwill letter has been quite effective in helping us assure customers that we are attempting to serve them honestly and well.

Beverly R. Kuehn
Branch Manager
CTX Mortgage Company
a division of Centex Corporation

Writing congratulatory messages to employees shows that you value their work and that you are pleased with their performance. The employees' likely response is a more positive attitude toward their jobs and motivation to set and work to meet challenging goals.

CONGRATULATIONS

Because the subject matter of congratulatory letters is positive, they are easy (and enjoyable) to write. Normally, they should receive a response.

Writing Congratulations

All too often we read about the election, promotion, or other significant achievement of a colleague or acquaintance and think that a note or telephone call of congratulations would be in order—only to procrastinate until it is too late. The successful executive takes advantage of the situation to build goodwill for the company and for herself or himself. Some executives accomplish this goodwill gesture by using one of a supply of note cards, which is always available. Although handwritten messages are acceptable, typed ones permit more to be said. The thoughtfulness of sending letters of congratulations is genuinely appreciated. And when your letter is the only one the person receives, it really stands out.

In addition to promotions and elections, such events as births, weddings, and engagements call for acknowledgment. We should always acknowledge the events when those involved are employees of our firm.

Here is an example of a short letter of congratulations on the occasion of a promotion:

How many times a year do you overlook an opportunity to congratulate someone?

What is your preference—handwritten or typewritten notes?

> Please accept my warmest congratulations and best wishes for your success. I just read of your promotion to sales division head in the monthly newsletter.

When a colleague wins an award or is elected to office, a congratulatory note is a lift for both the one who sends it and the one who receives it:

> Congratulations on your receipt of the Jaycees Community Contribution Award. The entire community and I recognize your commitment to serving the people in our community. Best wishes.

People don't get too old or too successful to feel good when their contributions are recognized by others.

For an engagement, the letter may take a warm and enthusiastic tone, as in the following example:

> Congratulations. I just heard of your engagement and wish you and Amy every happiness. She has always impressed me as a warm and friendly person. Best wishes to both of you in your life together.

Note the friendliness displayed in letters of congratulations. Because they are usually sent to friends and acquaintances, congratulatory messages and acknowledgments are casual, warm, and sometimes witty. We should not delay our message until it is too late to take advantage of the immediacy of the accomplishment.

Replying to Congratulations

Take time to acknowledge congratulatory messages.

In almost all cases, letters of congratulations should be answered. An acknowledgment might take the following form:

> Thank you for your good wishes concerning my promotion. I look forward to working more closely with you in the future. Thanks again for the note.

Some replies take a tongue-in-cheek tone, particularly when the promotion is to a rather high-pressure position:

> Many thanks for your nice words about my promotion and for the good wishes. I'll remember your confidence during some of those sure-to-be-trying days!
>
> The job is going to be demanding especially during this transition time. However, I'm going to give it my all. Your thoughtfulness will definitely help ease the burden. Again, I truly appreciate your support.

Letting a congratulatory message go unanswered is somewhat like failing to say "You're welcome" when someone has said "Thank you." Of course, the message and words used to convey it are important; but the act of responding conveys a positive metacommunication. Impact is reduced, though, if the tone implies self-confessed unworthiness or egotism:

I'm not sure I have the qualities you mentioned.	Unworthiness	**The response is no place for showing humility or feeding the ego.**
Others were more deserving than I.	Unworthiness	
Thanks for your note about my receiving Realtor of the Month award and for recognizing my energy, sincerity, and expertise.	Ego	

CONDOLENCES

A letter of sympathy to the family of a friend or business associate who has died should be written promptly. However, the sympathy message presents a difficult writing problem; and these messages are often put off until too late or are not sent at all. One way to solve the problem, although a little impersonal, is to send a card (called an *informal*), which may be purchased at any stationery store, and include a short handwritten message: "Deepest Sympathy" or "Deeply saddened by your loss. Sympathy to you and your family." Although etiquette now allows typed messages to be sent when the deceased is a business associate, a handwritten message provides a much more personal tone than does any other kind.

Are informals acceptable for condolences?

The simplest plan for such messages is to (1) start with a statement of sympathy, (2) follow with sentences about mutual experiences or relationships, and (3) close with some words of comfort and affection. The letter in Figure 12-1 is to the mother of a deceased acquaintance.

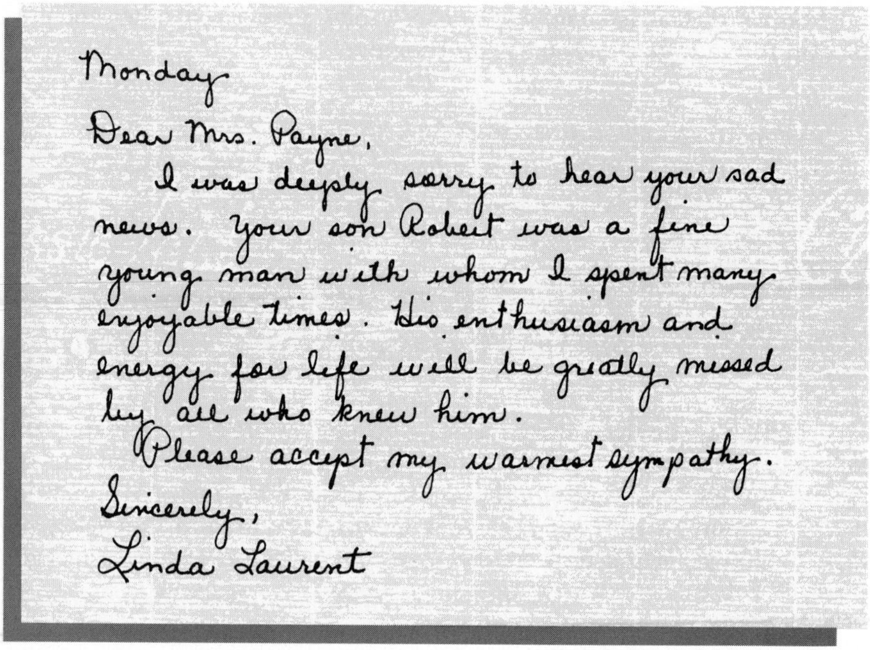

Monday

Dear Mrs. Payne,

I was deeply sorry to hear your sad news. Your son Robert was a fine young man with whom I spent many enjoyable times. His enthusiasm and energy for life will be greatly missed by all who knew him.

Please accept my warmest sympathy.

Sincerely,

Linda Laurent

FIGURE 12-1   Good example of a handwritten condolence

When a close relative (spouse, son, daughter, mother, or father) of a close friend dies, we should write the friend a letter of sympathy. Printed sympathy cards may also be used; but, in general, the closer the relationship, the greater the need for a personal written message of condolence.

INVITATIONS

Like most other special letters, invitations are deductive and relatively short. Responses to invitations should be handled similarly.

Writing Invitations

An informal invitation resembles a business letter. When sent from a business office, the letter is sometimes typed on executive stationery, which is smaller than the regular business letterhead. Wording should be conversational, as though the writer were extending the invitation orally. The letter in Figure 12-2 is an example.

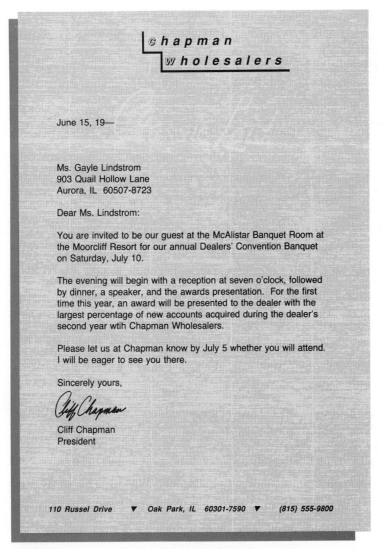

Chapman Wholesalers

June 15, 19—

Ms. Gayle Lindstrom
903 Quail Hollow Lane
Aurora, IL 60507-8723

Dear Ms. Lindstrom:

You are invited to be our guest at the McAlistar Banquet Room at the Moorcliff Resort for our annual Dealers' Convention Banquet on Saturday, July 10.

The evening will begin with a reception at seven o'clock, followed by dinner, a speaker, and the awards presentation. For the first time this year, an award will be presented to the dealer with the largest percentage of new accounts acquired during the dealer's second year wtih Chapman Wholesalers.

Please let us at Chapman know by July 5 whether you will attend. I will be eager to see you there.

Sincerely yours,

Cliff Chapman
President

110 Russel Drive ▼ Oak Park, IL 60301-7590 ▼ (815) 555-9800

FIGURE 12-2 Good example of an informal invitation

Replying to Invitations

All invitations should be acknowledged promptly. When a telephone R.S.V.P. is not mentioned, either a typed or a handwritten reply is satisfactory and should use the same conversational style as used in the invitation.

What is the meaning of R.S.V.P.?

Although many formal invitations are handwritten, especially for smaller groups, formal invitations are generally printed and follow formats provided by the printer, as shown in the example in Figure 12-3. When the affair includes formal wear, the invitation should include the notation "black tie."

The Board of Directors

Massachusetts Investment Company

requests the company of

_____

at dinner

on Saturday, the twelfth of June

at seven-thirty o'clock

744 North New York Avenue

Chicago, Illinois

FIGURE 12-3   Good example of a formal invitation

Replies to such invitations should follow a similar pattern:

> Ms. Gayle Lindstrom accepts with pleasure the invitation of Chapman Wholesalers to attend the Dealers' Convention Banquet on Saturday evening, July 10, at seven o'clock.

A simple, one-paragraph letter is satisfactory, particularly when the invitation is from a business concern and contains a fill-in line for the names of those invited. At the most formal level, however, the reply should be prepared in longhand and arranged in the same format as the invitation.

The refusal of an invitation is like the acceptance:

> Mr. and Mrs. Charles Longworth regret they are unable to accept
> the kind invitation of the Board. . . .

Although formal etiquette calls for handwritten replies to invitations, business protocol permits use of typewritten messages.

THANK YOUS

Following the receipt of a gift, attendance as a guest, an interview, or any of the great variety of circumstances in which a follow-up letter of thanks might be desirable, a thoughtful person will take the time to send a written message. As with all other special-letter situations, your message should reflect your sincere feelings of gratitude. When couples have been guests, one person usually sends the thank-you message for both. The message should be informal; a simple handwritten note is sufficient. When written in a business office to respond to a business situation, the message may be typed on letterhead. Here's a message of thanks for a weekend visit. Rather than the routine, thank-you-for-a-lovely-weekend thought, the letter includes something specific that the writer enjoyed:

> Ray and I thoroughly enjoyed our excursion this weekend
> on Lake Douglas. Since we moved here from Savannah,
> sailing has become a rare pleasure for us. You were kind to
> invite us. Thanks again for a delightful time.

A thank-you note covering a business situation might be sent electronically; see Figure 12-4.

In many cases, thanks could be conveyed as well by telephone calls. However, notes seem much more thoughtful.

All gifts received should be acknowledged by a thank-you note. Identify the gift, tell why you like it, and describe how you will use it:

> After conducting an in-service seminar for you, I was
> pleasantly surprised to receive the desk calendar. The
> convenience of being able to plan my week at a glance is an
> unexpected byproduct of my work with your company.
> Thanks for your kindness and for this useful gift.

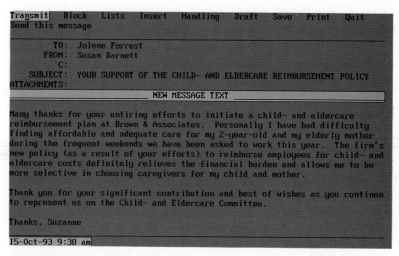

```
Transmit  Block  Lists  Insert  Handling  Draft  Save  Print  Quit
Send this message

       TO:  Jolene Forrest
     FROM:  Susan Barnett
        C:
   SUBJECT:  YOUR SUPPORT OF THE CHILD- AND ELDERCARE REIMBURSEMENT POLICY
ATTACHMENTS:
                        NEW MESSAGE TEXT

Many thanks for your untiring efforts to initiate a child- and eldercare
reimbursement plan at Brown & Associates.  Personally I have had difficulty
finding affordable and adequate care for my 2-year-old and my elderly mother
during the frequent weekends we have been asked to work this year.  The firm's
new policy (as a result of your efforts) to reimburse employees for child- and
eldercare costs definitely relieves the financial burden and allows me to be
more selective in choosing caregivers for my child and mother.

Thank you for your significant contribution and best of wishes as you continue
to represent us on the Child- and Eldercare Committee.

Thanks, Suzanne

15-Oct-93 9:30 am
```

FIGURE 12-4   Good example of a thank-you memorandum sent by electronic mail

Such letters are easy to write, and they require little time. Yet too many people put them off until later. The letter waits until tomorrow, then tomorrow, and is never sent.

NEWS RELEASES

Through newspapers, magazines, radio, and TV, businesses can inform communities on topics of mutual interest. In preparing news (press) releases, remember these points:

1. Use company letterhead (individuals should include a return address and phone number).
2. Include the preferred date on which the message is to appear.

Why begin with the main idea?

3. Include the name of the company official responsible for the release (or the name of the individual if the release is not from a company).
4. Give sufficient information (thinking of *who, what, when, where, why,* and *how* will help to ensure good coverage).
5. Write deductively with concern for brevity and clarity.

The example in Figure 12-5 illustrates these points.

Knowing that brevity is important to the media, submitters need to

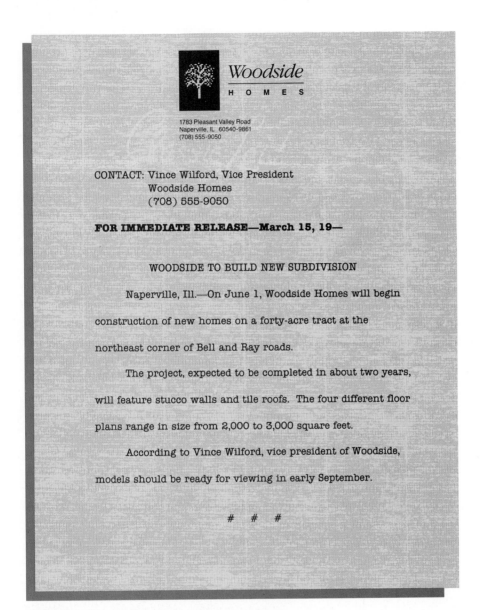

FIGURE 12-5   Good example of a news release

be very conscious of it, too. If a release has to be shortened, the media may eliminate the most important portion (to the submitter). If the phone number appears on the release sheet, the news media may take time to call about possible deletions or ask for more information.

SEASONAL MESSAGES

Many businesses send messages to their clients, customers, or employees at certain times of the year: Thanksgiving, Christmas, Hanukkah, birthdays, the beginning of a new concert season, the anniversary of an active account's opening, and so on. The intent is to demonstrate goodwill through an expression of good wishes or appreciation. Such messages remind recipients that they are important to the business and that they are remembered at a special time. For that reason, sales material (even very low-pressure sales messages) should not be included. It would reduce the impact of the primary message. Thinking they had been trapped into reading a sales pitch, readers might be resentful.

Such messages may be stored in the computer, retrieved, and sent on letterhead with the recipient's inside address and a salutation. More frequently, they are mass produced and written as though they were addressed to members of a group, as the example in Figure 12-6 illustrates.

To a valued customer, the following letter would be encouraging:

> One year ago today, you opened an account with us. Thank you for buying your building materials from us during the past year. Your promptness in paying has certainly been noticed, and we want you to know it has been appreciated.

Compared with the goodwill generated by such letters, the cost is likely to be very small.

WELCOMES AND FAREWELLS

Why *write* a note welcoming a new employee?

For most new employees, the first day on a job is trying—new tasks, new responsibilities, and new people. When introduced, many will extend an *oral* welcome. Those who bother to drop a *written* welcome into the mail box will make a special impact:

> Welcome to the Accounting Department!
>
> On this your first day, George has plans for a thorough orientation. Afterwards, if you have any questions about our facilities or procedures, just stop by Room 121. As soon as schedules permit, let's have lunch together. Best wishes for a long and happy tenure with us.

December 30, 19—

All Employees

APPRECIATION FOR OUTSTANDING YEAR

Bridges appreciates your efforts this past year. Thanks to you, every
goal has been reached or exceeded. As a token, a gift certificate
will be included in your next pay envelope.

May your holiday season be an enjoyable one.

CM

Clyde R. Mathison
President

FIGURE 12-6   Good example of a seasonal message

Positive as the impact of the *words* may be, the *thoughtfulness* demonstrated by taking time to write may have an even greater impact.

For those who are leaving a job, many colleagues and friends will
say some things that will make the departing employee feel good; but not
many will bother to *write*. The written message is likely to have a stronger
impact; it may be kept or shared with family members. To identify ideas

Will a *written* farewell have
a strong impact?

that might be included, reflect on experiences with the departing person. Brief reference to special interests, skills, accomplishments, or mutual problems may be appropriate. One who has demonstrated an appreciation for humor may enjoy a touch of it. In any case, the message ought to be brief, sincere, and personal:

> I will miss you, but I am glad to see you get the professional advancement you have earned.
>
> You leave an unmatched reputation for efficiency, punctuality, and integrity. But give me a little time; I'll find someone who can match your skills at backgammon during the lunch hour.
>
> Best wishes for success and happiness on the new job.

What to say in farewell letters (as well as other letters discussed in Chapter 12) is important. For most people, though, *taking time to write* them is the major challenge.

EVALUATIONS

Even though evaluation is not our intent, we can hardly escape noticing when the attitudes and performances of others are especially good or especially bad. For those who deserve high marks, letters can encourage; for those who deserve low marks, letters can alert.

Positive Qualities

How can a compliment be worth more than money?

When someone has performed exceptionally well or exhibited a commendable attitude, a tangible reward may not be possible or even advisable. From the bestower's point of view, an intangible reward (such as a letter) is easy and inexpensive. From the recipient's point of view, the value of an intangible reward can be much greater than any reasonable tangible reward. (Recall Maslow's hierarchy of needs.)

Why are *written* compliments so effective?

Letters that recognize positive qualities or performances are especially effective. People usually are not reluctant to *say*, "Thank you," "A great performance," "You have certainly helped me," and so on. Yet, because people seldom bother to *write* them, such messages are especially meaningful—even treasured. Compared with those who merely *say* nice things, people who take time to *write* them are more likely to be perceived as sincere.

Although a letter of commendation is intended to recognize, reward, and encourage the receiver, it also benefits the sender. Contributing to another's happiness, paying tribute to one who deserves it, encouraging that which is commendable—such feelings can contribute to the sender's own sense of well-being and worth. Such positive thinking can have a salutary influence on the sender's own attitude and performance.

Yet some of the potential value (to sender and receiver) is lost if a letter is mechanical, such as the following example:

> Your speech to our Business Breakfast Club was very much appreciated.
> You are an excellent speaker, and you have good ideas. Thank you.

To a speaker who has worked hard preparing and who has not been paid, such a letter may have *some* value. After all, the sender cared enough to write. Yet, such a letter could have been sent to any speaker, even if its writer had slept through the entire speech. A note closed with *sincerely* does not necessarily make the ideas seem sincere. Because the following revision is more specific, it is more meaningful:

> This past week I have found myself applying some of the time-management principles discussed at the seminar you conducted last week for the Association of Business Professionals.
> Prioritizing my tasks really helped me keep my perspective; and when I performed the time analysis, I easily identified some areas I can manage more effectively.
> Thank you for an informative and useful seminar.

The revision does not sound so much like a form letter. At least its writer was aware of the main points made and had already applied the information. The letter conveys gratitude, an intangible reward.

HAGAR THE HORRIBLE

Reprinted by special permission of King Features Syndicate, Inc.

In an intangible way, how do letters of commendation benefit their writers?

Should a letter that commends be couched in general terms?

Genuine motives for letters of commendation are essential.

Why write to an *employer* about an employee who has gone beyond the call of duty?

A different approach—a letter of commendation to the speaker's employer—could result in a tangible reward as well. Figure 12-7 illustrates an example. With such letters in his file, an employee's chances for promotion or other tangible rewards are increased. But the intangible reward alone makes the effort worthwhile.

Such letters should be written for the purpose of commending deserving people; they should not be written for the purpose of possible

---

ASSOCIATION OF BUSINESS PROFESSIONALS
P. O. Box 5433
Green Bay, WI 54301-5433
(414) 555-3000
◆ ◆ ◆ ◆ ◆ ◆ ◆

November 30, 19—

Mr. L. Eric Spencer
Spencer Electronics
1903 Front Street
Oshkosh, WI 54901-1903

Dear Mr. Spencer:

Mr. Bryan Daniel, human resources manager for your firm, gave a very interesting and useful seminar at last week's meeting of the Association of Business Professionals.

In a well-organized and interesting presentation, he offered several time-management techniques that, personally, worked very well for me. I observed the intense interest of the other members of the audience and the willingness of many individuals to voice their positive reactions to his comments on how disorganization causes stress. His seminar was very well received by this group.

Possibly Mr. Daniel told you that he led a seminar for our group; I wanted to let you know that he gave an outstanding presentation—totally consistent with the competence one sees in your employees.

Sincerely,

Michael L. Sims

Michael L. Sims
Vice President

c Mr. Bryan Daniel

FIGURE 12-7   Good example of a commendation letter sent to an employer

self-gain. Sometimes, however, those who take time to write such letters receive some unexpected benefits.

As an undergraduate student, Henry Kissinger wrote a letter of appreciation to a Prussian general who had spoken at his university. Touched by such thoughtfulness, the general invited Mr. Kissinger to dinner. Concluding that the young man had unusually keen insights into international affairs, the general was instrumental in getting Kissinger admitted to graduate study.

Although generous praise is seldom objectionable, a letter or memo of commendation may not fully achieve its purpose if it reaches the point of exaggeration or uses language that is hardly believable. The letter in Figure 12-8 is an example.

In the writer's mind, the statements may be true; but in the reader's mind, they may seem unbelievable. Because the language is strong and the statements are not supported, the letter could arouse thoughts about how bad other consultants were; or it could arouse questions about the writer's motives. The vice president would probably be more impressed with the letter in Figure 12-9.

Although the message does not use strong language, it conveys a stronger compliment than the other message did. Without the words "best" and "brilliant," it reveals *why* the staff's reaction was favorable.

The net effects of this letter are positive: (1) The writer feels good for having passed on a deserved compliment, (2) management gains some assurance that the consulting team's efforts are effective, (3) the team about whom the letter was written is encouraged to continue an effective technique, and (4) other divisions may have an increased likelihood of exposure to similar high-quality consulting.

Negative Qualities

A person who has had a bad experience as a result of another's conduct may be reluctant to write about that experience. Suppose, for example, the consultants in the preceding illustration had been ineffective. Before writing about the problem, a manager would recognize the following

> Is self-gain a legitimate motive for writing a letter that commends?

> Are exaggerations advisable?

> Does strong language strengthen a compliment?

> Who benefits from a commendation letter sent to the subject's employer?

> Why are people hesitant about writing letters that point out negatives?

Revenge is a popular theme in Hollywood movies. The capture of the "bad guy" makes a satisfying conclusion. Real life is more complex. If you must discuss someone's negative qualities, do so to facilitate cooperation or improvements, not to "get even," which will only make the situation worse.

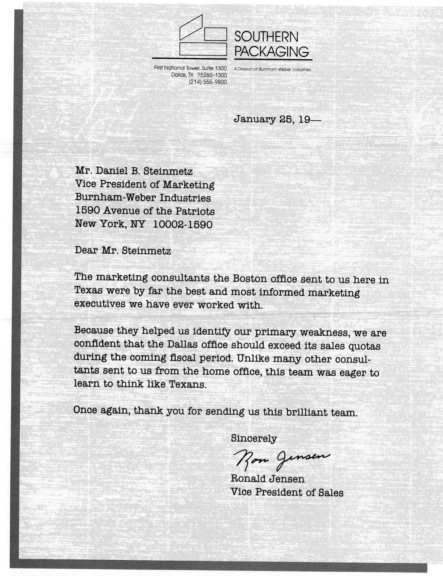

FIGURE 12-8   Poor example of a positive evaluation

risks: (1) being stereotyped as a complainer, (2) being associated with negative thoughts and thus thought of in negative terms, or (3) appearing to challenge one of management's prior decisions (choice of the consultants). Yet such risks may be worth taking because of the benefits: (1) The writer gets a feeling of having exercised a responsibility, (2) management learns of changes that need to be made, (3) the team about whom the let-

When another person has made or is making mistakes, what can be gained by writing a letter?

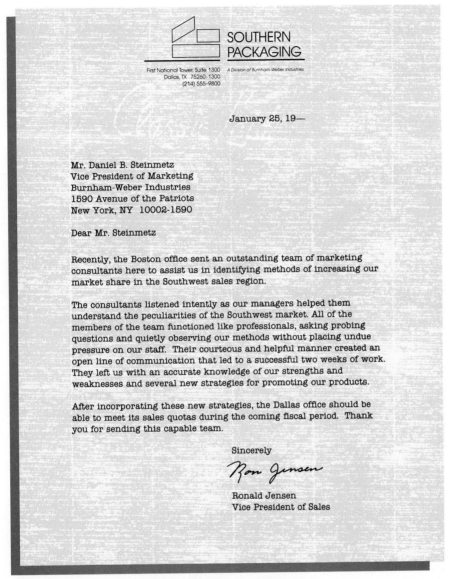

FIGURE 12-9 Good example of a positive evaluation

ter is written modifies techniques and is thus more successful, and (4) other divisions may be exposed to consultants who are more effective.

In the decision to write about negatives, the primary consideration is intent. If the intent is to hurt or to get even, the message should not be written. False information would be unethical and illegal.

In a written message that reports negative evaluation results, evalu-

Are letters that seek revenge advisable?

ative words are discouraged. Instead of presenting facts, the message in Figure 12-10 judges. In the mind of the writer, the first sentence may be fair and accurate; but in the mind of the reader, "complete waste of time" may seem overly harsh. It may convey the tone of a habitual fault-finder. Without details, the charges made in the second sentence lack force. If

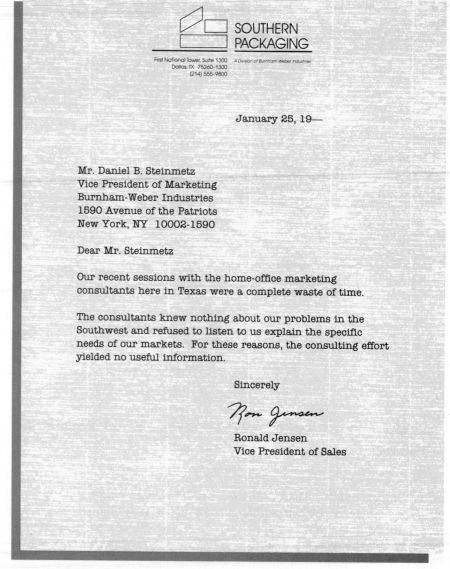

SOUTHERN PACKAGING
A Division of Burnham-Weber Industries

First National Tower, Suite 1300
Dallas, TX 75260-1300
(214) 555-9800

January 25, 19—

Mr. Daniel B. Steinmetz
Vice President of Marketing
Burnham-Weber Industries
1590 Avenue of the Patriots
New York, NY 10002-1590

Dear Mr. Steinmetz

Our recent sessions with the home-office marketing consultants here in Texas were a complete waste of time.

The consultants knew nothing about our problems in the Southwest and refused to listen to us explain the specific needs of our markets. For these reasons, the consulting effort yielded no useful information.

Sincerely

Ron Jensen

Ronald Jensen
Vice President of Sales

FIGURE 12-10 Poor example of a negative evaluation

"complete waste of time" strikes the receiver as an exaggeration, the whole message loses impact. Overall, the letter is short, general, and negative. By comparison, the revision in Figure 12-11 is long, specific, and positive.

Because one person took the time to write a letter, many could benefit. Although not always easy or pleasant, writing about negatives

SOUTHERN
PACKAGING

First National Tower, Suite 1300   *A Division of Burnham-Weber Industries*
Dallas, TX 75260-1300
(214) 555-9800

January 25, 19—

Mr. Daniel B. Steinmetz
Vice President of Marketing
Burnham-Weber Industries
1590 Avenue of the Patriots
New York, NY 10002-1590

Dear Mr. Steinmetz

[1] A team of Boston-based market consultants has just left our office. [2] They spent two weeks attempting to pinpoint weaknesses in our marketing strategies.

[3] Gaining insights from successful approaches used in other divisions of the company is an excellent idea; however, several aspects of this team's performance need to be called to your attention:

[4] 1. During their stay, the consultants seemed less interested in analyzing our problems and more concerned with instructing us in the strategies they have used in the Northeast. Although excellent in theory, many of these ideas are not applicable to our particular target market. When we attempted to provide essential information about our market, the team refused to listen.

[1,2] Introduce a discussion of the consulting project at the Dallas office.

[3] Tries to convey fair-mindedness and establish credibility by acknowledging good points in a letter that discusses bad points.

[4] Presents a statement of fact without labeling it in negative terms. Judgment is left to the reader.

FIGURE 12-11   Good example of a negative evaluation

Mr. Daniel B. Steinmetz
page 2
January 25, 19—

[5] 2. From the day they arrived, the team members clearly communicated their status as the experts. On one occasion, our marketing manager intervened to explain his perspective of a specific problem. The head consultant immediately reminded him that if we could have done the job ourselves, we wouldn't have asked for this team's help. Other similar situations occurred. Consequently, their attitude of superiority soon created a formidable barrier to communication, which obviously restricted the effectiveness of their efforts.

[6] The marketing department appreciates your efforts to help us identify ways to improve our marketing efforts. [7] In the spirit of helpfulness, I am passing this confidential information to you.

Sincerely,

Ron Jensen

Ronald Jensen
Vice President of Sales

[5] Includes a verifiable statement. If such conduct is deplorable, outrageous, or insulting, the reader will be aware of it without the writer's use of such terms.

[6] Ends on a pleasant note that seeks to add credibility to the preceding negatives. [7] Uses "confidential" as a safeguard; the information is intended for professional use only, not designed to hurt and not to be thought of as gossip.

FIGURE 12-11   continued

can be thought of as a civic responsibility. For example, a person who returns from a long stay at a major hotel might, upon returning home, write a letter to the management commending certain employees. If the stay had not been pleasant and weaknesses in hotel operation had been detected, a tactful letter pointing out the negatives would probably be appreciated. Future guests could benefit from the effort of that one person.

COMMUNICATION MENTOR

Personally, I have seen few letters, reports, or memos that didn't have a little room for improvement. Thus, as you prepare for a business career, take every opportunity to seek feedback and critique of your written communication and oral presentations. You may not like what you hear; however, swallowing your personal pride is a small price to pay for the chance to improve your communication skills and your potential for career success. And what's more, you may be surprised at just how willing people are to help you. All you have to do is ask.

Thomas G. Martin
Director of Corporate Development
Community Coffee Company, Inc.

Whether negative evaluations are presented in writing or in conversation, the same principles apply: have a positive intent, be factual, use positive language, and leave judgment to the recipient.

Why should you avoid use of judgmental terms?

REGRETS

The best way to handle an apology is to avoid the need for it. Sometimes, though, events don't turn out as planned and it's our fault. Looking back, our own conduct is regrettable, or some circumstance has prevented us from doing our best. In such cases, apologies are in order—for our own peace of mind and for good future relationships with an offended person.

The best way to handle apologies is to avoid getting into situations where you will need to make them. Milli Vanilli signed a contract with a record producer who instructed them to lip-sync only, allowing unseen vocalists to do the singing. When the fraud was uncovered, they apologized in a humiliating news conference. When you must apologize, be sincere, direct, and brief; avoid excuses and overly strong descriptions.

Whether to apologize face to face, over the phone, or in writing is a personal matter. The nature of the business, custom, seriousness of the infraction, personalities, and other factors are considerations. Regardless of the medium selected, the principles are the same: (1) Be sincere, (2) be direct, and (3) be brief. The memorandum in Figure 12-12 is better than

Should the main idea be in the final sentence?

[1] States a fact that is already known; focuses on writer. [2] Uses words ("terribly sorry") that seem overly strong and unnecessarily negative. Note four uses of "I" in the first three sentences.

[3] Offers an explanation; continues with an "I" orientation. [4] Presents a second apology; unnecessarily accents negative words. [5] Right margin should not be justified; extra spaces between words are distracting and reduce comprehension.

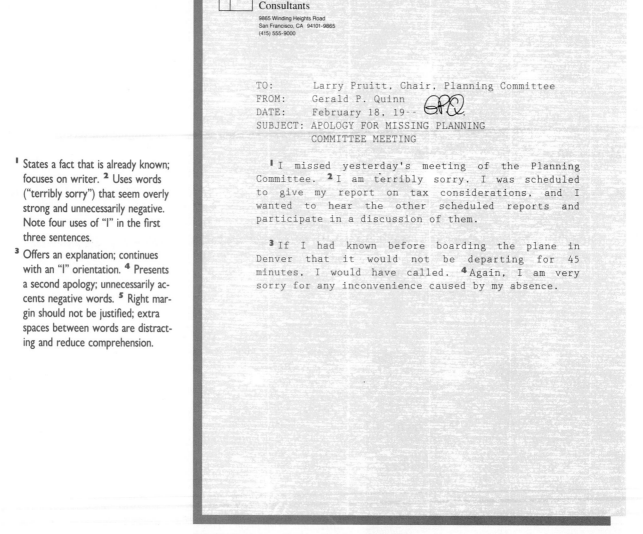

Interactive
Systems
Consultants

9865 Winding Heights Road
San Francisco, CA 94101-9865
(415) 555-9000

TO: Larry Pruitt, Chair, Planning Committee
FROM: Gerald P. Quinn
DATE: February 18, 19--
SUBJECT: APOLOGY FOR MISSING PLANNING
          COMMITTEE MEETING

[1] I missed yesterday's meeting of the Planning Committee. [2] I am terribly sorry. I was scheduled to give my report on tax considerations, and I wanted to hear the other scheduled reports and participate in a discussion of them.

[3] If I had known before boarding the plane in Denver that it would not be departing for 45 minutes, I would have called. [4] Again, I am very sorry for any inconvenience caused by my absence.

FIGURE 12-12   Poor example of an apology

no apology at all, but it has some weaknesses. Addressed to the committee's chairperson, the memorandum could have been more direct, shorter, and less writer centered, as illustrated in Figure 12-13.

In apologizing, people who have made mistakes are inclined to condemn themselves too severely or describe the mistake too vividly, as Fig-

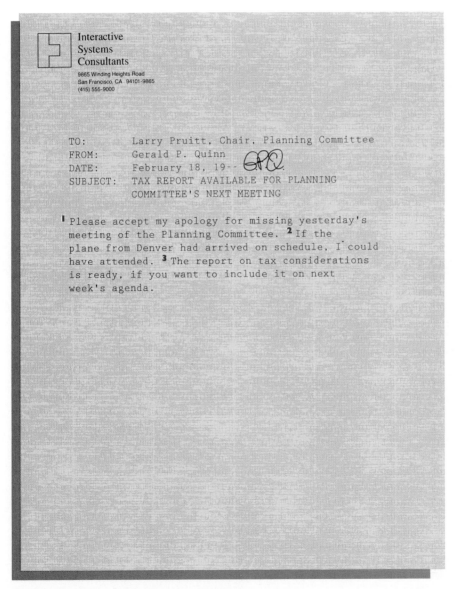

Interactive
Systems
Consultants

9865 Winding Heights Road
San Francisco, CA 94101-9865
(415) 555-9000

TO: Larry Pruitt, Chair, Planning Committee
FROM: Gerald P. Quinn
DATE: February 18, 19--
SUBJECT: TAX REPORT AVAILABLE FOR PLANNING
          COMMITTEE'S NEXT MEETING

[1] Please accept my apology for missing yesterday's meeting of the Planning Committee. [2] If the plane from Denver had arrived on schedule, I could have attended. [3] The report on tax considerations is ready, if you want to include it on next week's agenda.

[1] Presents the apology in the first sentence. Subordinates "apology" and "missing." [2] Explains, using the subjunctive mood, and thus uses positive language.

[3] Ends with a look to the future meeting.

FIGURE 12-13   Good example of an apology

ure 12-14 shows. Mr. Peaberry probably had noticed the errors in pronunciation but quickly dismissed them as rather common human errors, but suppose he *had* been irritated by them. Labeling them as inexcusable and using "horror" in talking about them (along with actual restatement of the incorrect words) would reinforce his irritation. That reinforcement

[1] Begins with a useless—and misleading—expression (would like to). Before the errors were *labeled* inexcusable, they may have been thought of in less harsh terms.

[2] Emphasizes the errors by use of specific language. Until now, the recipient may not have categorized the errors as horrible. [3] Emphasizes the errors by using a negative word as the final word.

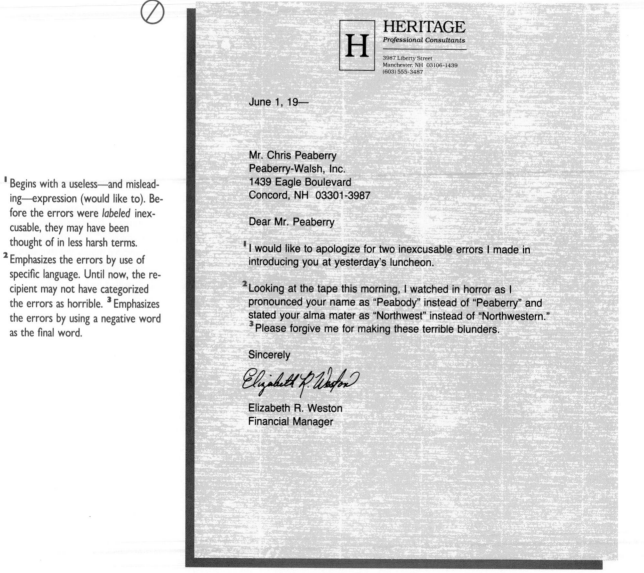

HERITAGE
Professional Consultants

3987 Liberty Street
Manchester, NH 03106-1439
(603) 555-3487

June 1, 19—

Mr. Chris Peaberry
Peaberry-Walsh, Inc.
1439 Eagle Boulevard
Concord, NH 03301-3987

Dear Mr. Peaberry

[1] I would like to apologize for two inexcusable errors I made in introducing you at yesterday's luncheon.

[2] Looking at the tape this morning, I watched in horror as I pronounced your name as "Peabody" instead of "Peaberry" and stated your alma mater as "Northwest" instead of "Northwestern." [3] Please forgive me for making these terrible blunders.

Sincerely

Elizabeth R. Weston

Elizabeth R. Weston
Financial Manager

FIGURE 12-14   Poor example of an apology

would work against the purpose of the apology. The revision in Figure 12-15 is better.

Of course, an apology without appropriate action is of little value. (Meeting Mr. Peaberry again and saying, "Hello, Mr. Peabody" would be fatal.) Without stooping to pick up a classmate's books, an apology for

Beyond apologizing, *do* something to make amends—if you can.

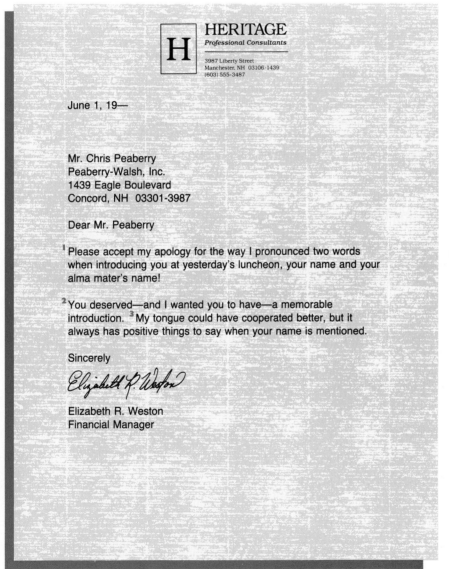

H HERITAGE
Professional Consultants

3987 Liberty Street
Manchester, NH 03106-1439
(603) 555-3487

June 1, 19—

Mr. Chris Peaberry
Peaberry-Walsh, Inc.
1439 Eagle Boulevard
Concord, NH 03301-3987

Dear Mr. Peaberry

[1] Please accept my apology for the way I pronounced two words when introducing you at yesterday's luncheon, your name and your alma mater's name!

[2] You deserved—and I wanted you to have—a memorable introduction. [3] My tongue could have cooperated better, but it always has positive things to say when your name is mentioned.

Sincerely

Elizabeth R. Weston

Elizabeth R. Weston
Financial Manager

[1] Apologizes directly. To avoid reinforcing an unpleasant thought, uses general terms instead of repeating the incorrect pronunciations.

[2,3] Seek to make amends.

FIGURE 12-15 Good example of an apology

causing them to fall is of little value. Again, empathy is the key: people who have the right attitude have the best chance of finding the right words.

Sometimes, an unsolicited letter of apology removes a barrier or even preserves a business relationship. For example, at the home office of a major firm, a client's representative parked in a space designated for the firm's officers only. Before reaching the entrance, the representative was stopped by a security officer who asked that the car be moved to the visitor's lot. According to the vice president of finance (who happened to observe the incident), the security officer was obviously angry and used vulgar language in asking that the car be moved. Cheerfully, the representative returned to his car and drove away (perhaps with the intent of terminating the business relationship).

Immediately the VP wrote an apology to the representative. By apologizing quickly, the VP may have avoided the necessity of responding to a strongly worded letter reporting the incident. Unfortunately, his letter (Figure 12-16) focuses on negatives and could make the matter worse. The revision (Figure 12-17) is more direct, more positive, and more detailed.

SUMMARY

Although routine business affairs dominate most of our time, special situations provide opportunities for us to put our best foot forward. The way in which we display our sensitivity to human relationships marks the kind of people we are. Special letters provide one way to demonstrate that sensitivity.

Moser & Associates

9800 West Roosevelt Road
Chattanooga, TN 37401-9800
(615) 555-3730

December 5, 19—

Mr. Juan Hernandez
South-Central Electronics
895 North Cass Avenue
Chattanooga, TN 37401-3109

Dear Mr. Hernandez:

[1]In the parking lot this morning, I overheard the discussion between you and the security officer. [2]For him and for our firm, I apologize for his vulgar language.

[3]He has been reprimanded, and we assure you that his conduct is regrettable. [4]Please accept our apology.

Sincerely,

Alex M. Dodd

Alex M. Dodd
Vice President of Finance

[1] Begins inductively. [2] Uses negative language. Emphasizes "vulgar language" by placing it at the end of a short paragraph.

[3] Uses negative language. Some details of the reprimand could make the statement more convincing. [4] Apologizes a second time. Emphasizes the word "apology" (and its negative connotations) by placing it at the end of the last sentence.

FIGURE 12-16   Poor example of an apology

[1] Emphasizes the apology by placing it in the first sentence. Reveals the purpose of the letter. "Manner" of speaking is more positive than "vulgar language." [2] Confirms the officer's right to ask that the car be moved and (through the subjunctive mood and positive words) condemns the officer's methods.

[3] Reports measures taken to avoid repetition of such incidents. By reporting something that has been *done*, the letter strengthens credibility of the apology *statement*.

[4] Closes with a positive look to future transactions.

Moser & Associates

9800 West Roosevelt Road
Chattanooga, TN 37401-9800
(615) 555-3730

December 5, 19—

Mr. Juan Hernandez
South-Central Electronics
895 North Cass Avenue
Chattanooga, TN 37401-3109

Dear Mr. Hernandez:

[1] Please accept my apology for the manner in which our security officer spoke to you this morning. [2] He had been instructed to keep certain parking spaces open for company officers, but he should have remembered his obligation to show genuine respect for you.

[3] The chief of security has already assigned the officer to (a) restudy his security manual and (b) attend the human-relations seminars now required of all newly hired employees. [4] When you call at our offices again, you can expect efficiency and courtesy, which have been our goals for the past twelve years.

Sincerely,

Alex M. Dodd

Alex M. Dodd
Vice President of Finance

FIGURE 12-17   Good example of an apology

CHECK YOUR WRITING

To check your writing of a message in one of the special-letters categories, first check the points listed under *special letters*. Then check the points listed under the category you're interested in. For example, check a letter of regret against the six qualities listed under *special letters* and the three listed under *regrets*.

Special Letters
- [ ] Convey the *right* message.
- [ ] Use the right *words* to convey the message.
- [ ] Use acceptable format.
- [ ] Achieve correctness in grammar, spelling, punctuation, and keyboarding.
- [ ] May be handwritten.
- [ ] Are characterized by directness, brevity, and sincerity.

Congratulatory Letters
- [ ] Are short.
- [ ] Are sincere.
- [ ] Are mailed immediately after the event.

Responses to Congratulatory Letters
- [ ] Do not sound egotistical.
- [ ] Do not seem to deny worthiness.

Condolences
- [ ] Begin with a statement of condolence.
- [ ] Refer to mutual experiences or relationships.
- [ ] Close with words of comfort or affection.

Invitations
- [ ] Informal invitations have a conversational tone.
- [ ] Formal invitations are generally printed.
- [ ] Replies to formal invitations have a tone similar to that of invitations.

Thank Yous
- [ ] Are specific about that which is appreciated.

News Releases
- [ ] Are written deductively.
- [ ] Give sufficient information (who, what, when, where, why, and how).
- [ ] Are brief but cover the essential points.

Seasonal Messages
- [ ] Do not include sales-promotional words.

Welcomes and Farewells
- [ ] Welcome letters try to convey an attitude of friendliness and willingness to help with adjustment to a new job.
- [ ] Farewell messages are tailor-made to the individual—a reference to a common experience, special skills and interests, accomplishments, or mutual problems.

Evaluations
- [ ] Are written for the right purpose.
- [ ] Are deductive if written about positives; inductive if written about negatives.
- [ ] Are factual (not judgmental) if written about negatives.

Regrets
- [ ] Apology appears only once in the message.
- [ ] Should not be overly self-critical.
- [ ] Should not describe a mistake too vividly.
- [ ] Includes a possible solution to the situation, if possible.

REVIEW QUESTIONS

1. Are messages in the "special" category longer or shorter than persuasive messages?
2. For most letters in the "special" category, which is preferred: (a) deductive presentation or (b) inductive presentation?
3. In expressing congratulations, which is more likely to have a strong impact: (a) an interoffice phone call or (b) a memorandum?
4. List two common pitfalls in the writing of responses to congratulatory messages.
5. In expressing condolence, what determines whether to send a printed card or a personalized letter?
6. Which is better for writing news releases: (a) deductive sequence or (b) inductive sequence? Explain.
7. Why should sales messages be omitted from seasonal messages?
8. Describe the appropriate points to include in a farewell message.
9. How are writers rewarded for the time they spend in writing letters of commendation?
10. What are the disadvantages of using superlatives and other strong adjectives and adverbs in a letter that commends someone for a job well done?
11. By writing a letter or memorandum that reports someone's failure to do a job well, what risks does a writer take?
12. In reporting someone's failure to do a job well, why should judgmental terms be avoided?
13. When the purpose of a message is to apologize, should it begin and end with the apology? Explain.
14. Which is the better expression? (a) "Please accept my apology for . . . ." or (b) "I would like to apologize for . . . ." Why?
15. In an apology, should a writer use strong adjectives to describe the mistake for which an apology is presented? Explain.

EXERCISES

1. In groups of three or four members, discuss the advantages and disadvantages of handwriting goodwill messages, keyboarding them, or sending commercial greeting cards. Initiate a formal discussion. Consult the business and business protocol (social etiquette) literature to support your views.
2. In groups of three or four members, discuss the role of goodwill messages in achieving the goals of an organization. Consult the business literature to support your views.

3. Analyze the effectiveness of the following sentences for goodwill messages.
   a. I would like to say congratulations on your recent honor.
   b. Even though my schedule was disrupted, thanks again for inviting me to your home.
   c. I just heard the supervisor finally gave you that promotion.
   d. The presentation at the dealer's meeting by Jason Embry was one of the worst I have ever attended.
   e. Amanda Beckell can come and lead another seminar for us any day!
   f. I am so sorry for the irresponsible way I handled your recent request.
   g. As a long-standing partner in Merrill and Crowder Sales, I always enjoy welcoming our new sales staff to the company.
4. Analyze the letter on page 506. Pinpoint its strengths and weaknesses and then rewrite the letter.

APPLICATIONS

1. **Congratulations on Completion of Spanish Course.** You are the president of a fashion design firm. You have heard through the grapevine that Margaret Ryan, one of your firm's sales representatives, has just completed an intensive course in conversational Spanish. Your company has recently expanded to sell your clothing overseas, and you feel that her skill will enable her to be an excellent sales representative to potential customers in Spain.

   Required: Write a memorandum of congratulations to Margaret Ryan.

ANCE	MANAGEMENT	MIS	CONSU
Ethics	International	Legal	In

2. **Response to Congratulations.** Yesterday Margaret Ryan received a memorandum of congratulations from her supervisor for her recent completion of a conversational Spanish course (Application 1).

   Required: As Margaret Ryan, write a memorandum to Tara Mason in response to the memorandum of congratulations.

E	MANAGEMENT	MIS	CONSUMEI
:rpersonal	Technology	Public Se	

3. **Praise to Well-Deserving Employees.** As president of Dixon Discount Stores, you have very much appreciated your employees' conduct during the peak sales season. With huge crowds attending, the days seemed hectic. Many employees worked overtime in the evenings and on weekends. No accidents occurred, very few customers complained, and sales were much larger than anticipated.

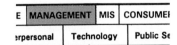

SURANCE	MANAGEMENT	MIS	CC
Ethics	International	Legal	

December 2, 19—

Bill Nowell, Supervisor, High-Cotton Pants Section

QUALITY PERFORMANCE AT McGOWAN ENTERPRISES

Being a sewing-machine operator in our plant is a very
demanding job. Boredom and fatigue often cause errors and
cut-rate products.

However, last month in your section, all the high-cotton pants
met our quality standards. We commend you on this achievement.
Thank you for making McGowan products better than ever!

Sam Conway

Sam Conway
Production Manager

EXERCISE 4

Required: Now that the heavy work season is over, write a memorandum to all employees expressing your appreciation.

4. **A Job Well Done.** Vinita Clark, operations manager for Markens
Art Company, attended one of Ruth Hutchinson's lectures on the his-

tory of American sculpture. Vinita liked the ideas presented, Ruth's subtle sense of humor, and the emphasis given to the work of Maynord Jenkins (the sculptor with whom MAC has an exclusive arrangement).

Required: As Vinita, write a memorandum to Ruth. Commend her for a job well done.

5. **Response to Commendation for High Ethical Standards.** As a sales representative for a fashion design firm, you have recently learned that one of your firm's designers has been "stealing" designs from another company. You brought this fact to the attention of the director of the design team, who ignored the problem. Finally, you explained the situation to the vice president. Yesterday you received an electronic message from the president commending you on your high ethical standards and your persistence in pursuing the issue regardless of the personal consequences.

URANCE	MANAGEMENT	MIS	CON
Ethics	International	Legal	I

Required: Write a memorandum in response to the president, Lance Moore.

6. **An Expression of Sympathy.** A friend with whom you had worked closely as a fellow officer in a community organization suffered a fatal accident.

NSURANCE	MANAGEMENT	MIS	C
Legal	Interpersonal	Technology	

Required: Write a letter of condolence to the friend's spouse (or closest relative).

7. **Thank you for. . . .** Your parents (or a special relative) have done something special for you to assist you in earning a college education.

URNALISM	PERSONAL	CAREER DE
terpersonal	Technology	Public S

Required: Write them a thank-you letter.

8. **Help from Overseas: Letter of Appreciation.** Marianne Brown lost her luggage in flight to a two-week international marketing seminar in Germany. To make matters worse, as she was leaving the airport to go to the hotel, she lost her traveler's checks in the taxi. Immediately Marianne called her German liaison contact, Anna Herpfer, who offered to handle the certain-to-ensue red tape. By the first day of the seminar, Anna had given Marianne replacement traveler's checks and had assured Marianne that the airline would deliver the luggage in two days. During the overseas stay, Anna was unfailingly courteous and polite.

MARKETING	PUBLIC RELATIONS	F
hics	International	Legal	Inter

Required:
1. As Marianne, you plan to write a thank-you letter to Anna. First consider these points: Should the letter be formatted as a traditional U.S.

letter or in an acceptable German format? If so, how will the letter appear? Do special requirements for addressing an envelope exist?

2. Write the thank-you letter to Anna Herpfer, Bahnhofstr. 9, 7000 Weinstadt 2, Germany.

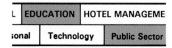

9. **A Political Stand for Education: Letter of Appreciation.**   On an education-reform bill, your local representative to the U.S. House of Representatives made an impressive speech to the House concerning the need for improvements in funding for public education. His words were quoted on national television. The bill in question eventually died in committee, but you appreciate his taking a stand on this issue.

Required: Write a letter to your representative expressing your appreciation and encouragement. Research needed to write this letter includes (1) locating the name and address of your representative and (2) consulting a reference manual to identify the appropriate courtesy title for this public official.

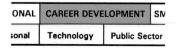

10. **Writing a Letter of Deserved Thanks.**   Jim Donovan, personnel director for a local firm, was invited to talk to your class about resume writing. Trying to incorporate his suggestions, you prepared a resume and submitted it to your college's career-services division. In subsequent interviews, you have been highly commended for having prepared an outstanding resume.

Required: Write a letter of appreciation to Jim Donovan, Southside Manufacturing, Inc., 189 South 29th Avenue, Portland, ME 04101-1897.

11. **Thank-you for Business Referrals.**   You own a photography studio and serve a small clientele, taking class pictures for area schools and ad pictures for small businesses. Mac Vickerson, a photographer who worked for you several months ago, recommended you to a couple to take pictures for their wedding. The couple, Mary and Stephen McCool, were so impressed with your work that they have recommended you enthusiastically to several other couples seeking a photographer for their weddings.

Required: Write Mac a letter of appreciation for his original referral. His address is 12 Main Boulevard, Downingtown, PA 19335-8100.

12. **Letter of Appreciation for Assistance in Job Placement.**   You graduated from college with a double major in marketing and fine arts and accepted a job with Heartbeats, a regional greeting card company. During your four-year stay, you worked closely with both the artists

and the sales personnel in marketing several new lines of cards. However, an illness in your family has required you to relocate to another state. The senior manager at Heartbeats was instrumental in helping you gain a similar position with a national greeting-card company.

Required: Write the manager a letter of appreciation. Dana Rollings, 715 McAdams Avenue, Thomasville, NC 27360-8601. Use plain paper and provide a fictitious return address.

13. **Employee Promotion: News Release.** You are a manager in a furniture factory in Minneapolis. Your company recently began sending news releases of events within the company to the Minneapolis *Daily Dispatch*. The past three releases, concerning a sales drive, a local community service award, and a special event recently sponsored by the company were reduced to minor items in a news-brief column in the weekly "Money" section. The next article you plan to submit announces Renée Hartman's recent promotion from production manager to vice president of product research and development.

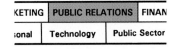

KETING	PUBLIC RELATIONS	FINAN
ional	Technology	Public Sector

Required: Write a news release to send to the *Dispatch*, carefully avoiding overt attempts to "sell" the company through the release.

14. **Welcome New Members.** As an officer of a business organization in your college, write a letter of welcome to be sent to new members.

ERAL	EDUCATION	HOTEL MANAG
International	Legal	Interpers

Required: Address the sample letter to Sam Wilkins, P. O. Box 1937, at your college.

15. **Welcome to the Club: A Public Relations Tool.** As a member of Gandy and Bowling Advertising in Silver City, you and your coworkers are encouraged to join civic clubs in the community to increase the company's visibility. Your membership in the Silver City Civic Club has enabled you to get to know many of the businesspeople coming to the city, and you are confident that these informal contacts have led to the acquisition of many of your advertising clients. Ray Schwartz, the owner of the new delicatessen on Clematis Drive, sat next to you at the meeting this week.

KETING	PUBLIC RELATIONS	FINAI
ional	Technology	Public Sector

Required: Write a personal letter welcoming Ray to the club and the city. Ray Schwartz, Goodtime Deli, 117 Clematis Drive, Silver City, NM 07120-0117.

16. **Farewell and Thanks For. . . .** You have worked for Watts, Taylor, and Winfield Brokerage Firm for seven years. When you entered the Wall Street company just out of college, your manager, Cecil Davis, became a mentor to you, helping you adjust to the firm's corporate

RELATIONS	FINANCE	ACCOUNTIN
International	Legal	Interpers

culture. He often gave you constructive criticism and generous "pats on the back" when they were deserved. You were especially appreciative of a powerful commendation letter he sent to your supervisor after your work led to the acquisition of a prominent client. Davis is retiring after 25 years of service to the company.

Required: Write a farewell letter to Cecil. His address is 112 Southaven Street, Brooklyn, NY 11223-0112.

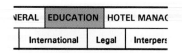

17. **To a Professor: A Job Well Done.** The semester is almost over. One of your professors taught an outstanding course.

    Required: Write a letter to that professor's department head. Your purpose is to commend a deserving person.

18. **Blowing the Whistle: A Positive Evaluation.** As publisher of a large metropolitan daily newspaper in Kansas City, you bear final responsibility for the financial health of the publication. Recently, Randy Howell, one of your advertising representatives, reported (with evidence) several instances over a one-year period in which the advertising manager intentionally failed to enter advertising revenues on the computer to cover up his embezzlement of the fees. Because Randy was willing to come forward with his concerns and with concrete evidence, management was able to initiate a full criminal investigation. The missing money was found invested with KC Lenders (a recently failed savings and loan in your city) in the ad manager's name; the advertising manager was convicted of embezzlement and fraud.

    Required: Write a memorandum of commendation to Randy for his part in the investigation.

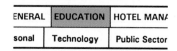

19. **An Attempt to Help Others: A Negative Evaluation.** Your semester will be concluding two weeks from now. One of your professors (use a fictitious name) has been exceedingly ineffective. You want to help the department, students who may be in that professor's class later, and the professor.

    Required: Write a letter to the professor's department head reporting objective, specific information about the professor's performance.

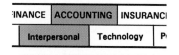

20. **Shortcomings in Professional Behavior Overshadow Strong Technical Skills: A Negative Evaluation.** Impressed with Michael O'Neill's excellent scholastic record and high scores on the CPA exam, Caldwell & Associates, a leading accounting firm, hired the new college graduate. Michael has been working on site for one of Caldwell's major audit clients for the past few weeks. The controller of the audit client has made the following observations about Michael's general

appearance and demeanor. Because Michael is very easy going, he often extends his casual attitude to his relations with clients, dressing too informally and blurring the distinctions between business and personal relationships. Michael does faultless work; he actually takes his work quite seriously.

Required: As the controller, write a letter to the audit manager. Your intent is to alert Caldwell of Michael's shortcomings so that steps can be taken to help Michael modify his actions. Address the letter to Derek Trelawney, Audit Manager, Caldwell & Associates, 609 Elliot Building, East Brunswick, NJ 08816-1834.

CASES FOR ANALYSIS

Case 1. Promoting International Understanding Rather than Reacting to Problems. Himco Oil is an offshore drilling company that has extensive dealings with oil concerns in Mexico. One afternoon the senior partner received a disturbing call from Carlos Mendez, a business associate at Fuentes Oil. Mendez was very upset and puzzled by the behavior of Robert Smith, one of Himco's production supervisors in Mexico City. Mendez had scheduled an appointment with Smith at 11:30 a.m. When Mendez arrived at 12:10, Smith had already gone to lunch. Very frustrated, Mendez returned to Smith's office at 2 p.m. (normal afternoon reopening in Mexico), but Smith didn't have time to discuss the matter and referred Mendez to the secretary to schedule another appointment.

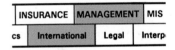

Very disturbed, the partner called Robert Smith for his side of the story. Smith said, "I assumed that Mendez was not planning to keep his appointment; otherwise, he would have called to explain that he had been detained but was on his way." Smith did not perceive his treatment of Mendez later that day as cold and unconcerned.

The partner realizes that Smith has not been in Mexico long enough to appreciate the importance Mexicans place on personal relationships and the relative casualness with which Mexicans regard time. However, since Smith's behavior has created ill will for Himco, an apology must be written.

Required:
1. As the partner, write a letter of apology to Mendez. Consider these points: Should the letter be formatted as a traditional U.S. letter or in an acceptable Mexican format? If so, how will the letter appear? Do special requirements for addressing the envelope exist? Address the letter to Carlos Mendez, Paseo Kulkulkan, 77500 Cancun, Q.R., Mexico.
2. The partner is optimistic that this carefully written apology will restore

the goodwill damaged by this unfortunate incident. As he signs the letter, the partner recalls three similar misunderstandings that occurred because newly transferred U.S. managers were unfamiliar with basic Mexican culture and customs. In each case, the partner reacted with a painstakingly written apology. He decides it is time to solve this problem proactively.

a. As the partner, write a memorandum to the U.S. managers who have been working in Mexico less than one year. Your purpose is to highlight major differences in culture and business practices between Mexico and the United States. Send a copy to Judith Sangalis, Director, International Assignments Division, in the home office. Conduct necessary research to prepare accurate, useful, and well-documented information. Provide a separate references page so that employees can locate your sources for additional study if needed. Refer to the references page as an enclosure to the memorandum. Use internal references (author, year) within the memorandum. *Keep in mind that you are attempting to solve a particular problem for a specific audience. You are not writing a general term paper on cross-cultural differences.*

b. Write a cover letter to accompany the copy of the memorandum being sent to Judith Sangalis. Explain the negative fallout being felt because U.S. managers are not prepared for assuming assignments overseas and encourage her to initiate efforts to alleviate this difficulty for future employees. Address the letter to Judith Sangalis, Himco Oil, 8633 Himco Road, San Bernardino, CA 92403-8633.

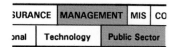

Case 2.   Gaining Support for a Plastics Recycling Plant. You are a member of the city council in Lucasville, a small town in rural Ohio. The mayor has asked you to chair a task force to evaluate the feasibility of building a plastics recycling plant in the city. Carpet yarn, fiberfill for parkas, floor tiles, wastebaskets, and "plastic lumber" for park furniture and decks are just a few of the materials that can be produced by recycling plastic containers and other plastic items. After completing extensive research including a tour of an existing plant and a meeting with the city's officials, you wholeheartedly support the plant in Lucasville. To determine the community's feelings, you've talked with a number of community leaders as well as individuals selected at random. For the most part, people are uninformed about the significant benefits gained from recycling, some are apathetic to the need to preserve our environment, and a few (at least three prominent business leaders) are adamantly opposed to building the recycling plant. Write the following letters as chair of the Environmental Preservation Task Force.

Required:

1. Write a letter to the mayor recommending that the plastics recycling plant be built in Lucasville. Support your decision with justifiable reasons. Your objective report should contain the pros and cons of the decision. Address the letter to Roger J. Scoffer, Mayor's Office, City Hall, Lucasville, OH 45648-1096. Be sure to include an appropriate salutation for this public official.

2. Assume the mayor has approved the construction of the recycling plant and has begun accepting bids from construction companies. Because of your intense interest and expertise in environmental concerns, the mayor has asked you to launch a public awareness campaign. Your purpose is not only to gain support for the plastics recycling plant but also to educate the public about the benefits of recycling. Complete *one* of the following options:

   a. Write a letter to the community leaders of Lucasville soliciting their support of the plastics recycling plant. Although this message is similar to the letter sent to the mayor, consider changes in the information included and the emphasis appropriate for this particular audience. Attempt to anticipate the public's reactions to the message. Include in the inside address: Community Leaders of Lucasville, Lucasville, OH 45648. Use an appropriate salutation for a letter addressed to a group, or use the simplified block format, which omits the salutation.

   b. Write a news release announcing the opening of the recycling plant and outlining the benefits it will bring to the community. Address it to the editor of *The Clarion*, P.O. Box 189-BC, Lucasville, OH 45648-6330. Because you do not know the editor's name, use the simplified block format, which omits the salutation.

   c. Develop a brochure to be included in the letter to community leaders (step 2a) and distributed by other means throughout the community. The brochure will focus on the benefits to be gained from recycling, particularly the many available uses of recycled plastics. If desktop publishing capabilities are available, design a creative, appealing layout for the brochure.

Case 3.   Is Overlooking a Vendor's Error to Your Advantage Ethical?

E	ACCOUNTING	INSURANCE	MA
Ethics	International	Legal	

John is responsible for checking the accuracy of invoices received from suppliers for purchases of inventory. A supplier recently shipped the company $5,000 worth of merchandise but neglected to include the merchandise on the invoice. Immediately John requested a revised invoice from the supplier. Learning of this request, John's supervisor severely reprimanded him for not overlooking the vendor's error, thus costing the company $5,000.

Functioning as plant manager, you hear nothing of this conversation from John or his supervisor. However, several comments filtering through the grapevine convince you that you must take appropriate action.

Required:

1. Decide whether it is ethical to overlook the erroneous billing. Consider these points:
   a. What are the relevant facts?
   b. What are the ethical issues raised by the decision whether to mention the erroneous billing?
   c. Who (which stakeholders) will be affected by this decision?
   d. What are the costs and benefits imposed by each alternative on each person listed in step (c)?
   e. What are the company's obligations to each person listed in step (c)?
   f. What should you as the company's representative do?
2. Based on your decision, complete *one* of the following options:
   a. Write a memorandum to John commending him for his ethical behavior. State that this document will be placed in his personnel file for use in future performance appraisals.
   b. You feel it is ethical to overlook the vendor's mistake. Write a persuasive memorandum to John explaining that overlooking similar errors in the future would be in his "best interest."
   c. Do any other options exist? If so, write a letter or memorandum to the appropriate individual.
3. Write a memorandum to John's supervisor, Bill McGhee, explaining the action that you took regarding John's behavior. The action taken in step 2 will affect the content and set the tone for this memo.

COMMUNICATING ABOUT WORK AND JOBS

CHAPTER 13   Preparing Resumes and Application Letters
CHAPTER 14   Job Interviews, Employment Messages,
             and Performance Appraisals

PREPARING RESUMES AND APPLICATION LETTERS

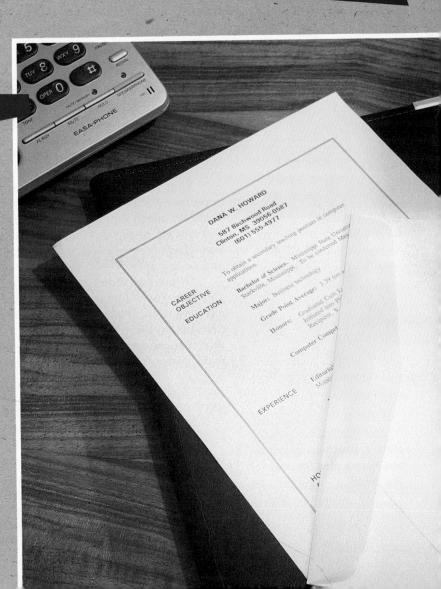

OBJECTIVES

When you have completed Chapter 13, you should be able to

- ◆ Complete systematic self-, career, and job analyses.

- ◆ Prepare an effective functional or chronological resume.

- ◆ Find information about employers' needs for workers.

- ◆ Write an application letter that effectively introduces an accompanying resume.

CARLOS SOON WILL GRADUATE from a major state university with a bachelor's degree in management. He is concerned about job opportunities, and with good reason. The job market is tight; and when Carlos gets his degree, so will thousands of other young people. He will be competing with other graduates for entry-level positions. Many companies advertise openings for ten positions and receive hundreds of inquiries and applications. Carlos knows that the competition is fierce, but he also knows he is intelligent and hard working and has good written communication skills. His writing skills may be the deciding factor in whether he will get a job or be just another applicant.

Carlos is now taking the first step toward securing employment: he is writing his resume. He has studied various formats and compared them with the information he plans to emphasize. After he drafts a resume accentuating his strengths and abilities, he spends a little extra time on its physical appearance: he varies bold and regular type, uses headings that are eye catching and easy to read, and prints the resume on high-quality paper in a tasteful color. And finally, before he sends it anywhere, he proofreads it carefully several times. He knows even the slightest mistake or typo may characterize him as sloppy or indicate to a possible employer he does not have adequate written communication skills. Carlos plans to send his resume to several different companies. Although he knows he may not get an interview, at least he knows he is in the competition and his resume won't work against him.

Your resume and accompanying application letter may be the most important documents you will write at this time in your life. A good resume can mean employment, success, and, with those things, happiness and a sense of self-worth. But a mediocre or flawed resume and application letter are only a waste of your time, the prospective employer's time, and good paper.

Before you write your resume, take some time first to know yourself and your goals, strengths, and weaknesses. Then study the many different formats in this chapter before deciding on one. And finally, never underestimate the importance of good grammar and accurate spelling and punctuation. Proofread carefully several times. Remember, your resume is what represents you to employers.

SETTING GOALS AND PLANNING

Have you set *your* goals? Do you have a plan for reaching them?

On his regular morning walk, an elderly counselor spoke to a young man who was raking leaves: "Good morning. How's it going today?" The response: "Well, I'm not getting anywhere raking these leaves." The counselor asked, "Not getting anywhere? Where do you want to get?" Reflecting for a moment, the raker said, "I have never thought much about that." "I'll be walking by here tomorrow at this same time," said the counselor, "and between now and then, why don't you do some thinking about it?"

As a result of the conversation, the leaf raker began to do some serious thinking about his life's goals—about what he wanted to get from life and the price he was willing to pay. Through subsequent encouragement from the counselor, the leaf raker analyzed himself, the careers in which he had some interest, and some specific jobs that would be better than raking leaves. Eventually, the young man found a rewarding career in the computer field.

Two things were vital to his success: (1) He set a goal and (2) he developed a plan for reaching it. For many years, a financial counselor conducted seminars for people who had very high economic aspirations. He asked participants to ponder the question, "How rich do I want to be?" He asked each person to write that figure on a small card, place it in his or her wallet, and look at it each night and morning. These daily reminders of the goal increased the likelihood of attaining it.

Goal setting does for individuals what management by objectives does for businesses. Setting goals forces people to consider these questions: What is to be accomplished? How is it best accomplished? How is progress measured? Are decisions congruent with goals? Important as such questions are, they sometimes do not get the attention they deserve. Many college seniors have confided to advisers, "I'm scared. About all I've ever done is go to school. Now I'll have to earn a living. How do I find a suitable job?"

Because the answer to that question can mean the difference between a pleasant life and an unpleasant one, it deserves careful attention. A suitable job satisfies needs at all of Maslow's needs levels, from basic economic needs to self-actualizing needs. During your working lifetime, you will spend about one-third of your nonsleeping time on the job (and probably much additional time thinking about your work). The right job for you will not be drudgery; the work itself will be satisfying. It will give you a sense of well-being; you can see its positive impact on others. The satisfaction derived from work has a positive influence on enjoyment of nonworking hours.

Life's happiness is directly related to life's work.

Students tend to devote too little time and thought to career decisions, or they unnecessarily postpone making career decisions. Of the many courses required to achieve your degree, how much time is devoted to one course? (Think of the daily reading assignments, doing research, preparing for tests, writing a term paper, and so on.) Are you willing to spend that much time gathering, recording, and analyzing information that will lead to a satisfying career? Would you be willing to start putting together a notebook of information that would guide you to the best career?

Research and analyze before choosing a career.

Just as finding the right career is important for you, finding the right employees is important for the employer. Before they can offer you a job, employers need information about you—in writing. Your resume is the written document that provides a basis for judgment about you. In preparing this vital document, your major concerns should be (1) gathering essential information, (2) planning the resume, and (3) constructing the resume.

GETTING ESSENTIAL INFORMATION

Why make a *written* record of career information? Recall from the discussion of sales letters that knowing the product is a prerequisite to writing. Likewise, knowing yourself is a prerequisite for preparing a resume. Although reading and thinking are beneficial, they are not enough. Career-related information should be written in a personal career notebook. Just as an accountant uses a worksheet when preparing a profit-and-loss statement and a balance sheet, job seekers can use a career notebook in preparing a resume. Keeping such a notebook (1) encourages the gathering of pertinent information, (2) makes review and summary easy, and (3) assists in analysis. Putting thoughts on paper helps in clarifying, remembering, and analyzing information.

To help you identify information about yourself and the job that is appropriate for including on a resume, you will complete a self-analysis, career analysis, job analysis, and company/job profile.

Self-Analysis

To be able to sell yourself in a resume, you must first identify your qualifications, focusing primarily on your capabilities that meet the employer's needs. Answering the questions in Figure 13-1 is a good way to begin your self-analysis. Write the questions (double- or triple-spaced) in your career notebook.

Make the career notebook thorough and neat; it's for *you*.

Making the notebook is good preparation for writing a resume and facing an interview.

After preparing these questions (and others you may want to add) for your notebook, write your answer beneath each question. Thoughtful answers to such questions will almost certainly point out some strengths (about which you can feel good) and some weaknesses (which you can begin to correct). The thinking required to answer the questions is excellent preparation for writing a resume. Having written thoughtful answers to these questions, you will have a good chance of providing ready answers for questions asked during an employment interview.

Career Analysis

The same technique—asking and answering questions—is helpful in career analysis. Try to answer the questions in Figure 13-2.

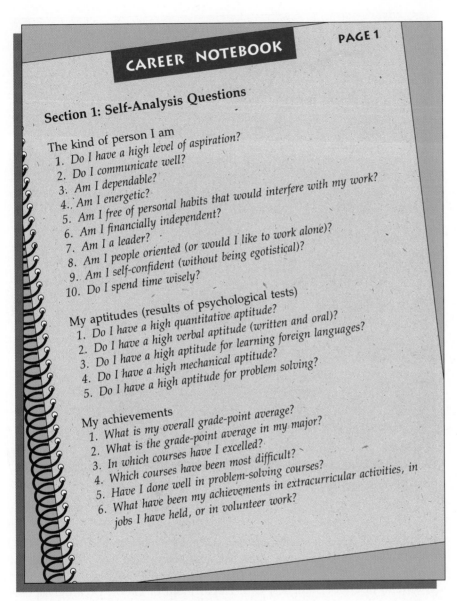

CAREER NOTEBOOK PAGE 1

Section 1: Self-Analysis Questions

The kind of person I am
1. Do I have a high level of aspiration?
2. Do I communicate well?
3. Am I dependable?
4. Am I energetic?
5. Am I free of personal habits that would interfere with my work?
6. Am I financially independent?
7. Am I a leader?
8. Am I people oriented (or would I like to work alone)?
9. Am I self-confident (without being egotistical)?
10. Do I spend time wisely?

My aptitudes (results of psychological tests)
1. Do I have a high quantitative aptitude?
2. Do I have a high verbal aptitude (written and oral)?
3. Do I have a high aptitude for learning foreign languages?
4. Do I have a high mechanical aptitude?
5. Do I have a high aptitude for problem solving?

My achievements
1. What is my overall grade-point average?
2. What is the grade-point average in my major?
3. In which courses have I excelled?
4. Which courses have been most difficult?
5. Have I done well in problem-solving courses?
6. What have been my achievements in extracurricular activities, in jobs I have held, or in volunteer work?

FIGURE 13-1   Self-analysis questions

To locate answers to the career-analysis questions, refer to the following sources. These and other books are available in school or community libraries and in many college and university career service centers.

◆ Bolles, R. N. (1990). *What color is your parachute? A practical manual for job hunters and career changers.* Berkeley, CA: Ten Speed Press.
◆ *Career opportunities.* Chicago, IL: J.G. Ferguson (published monthly).

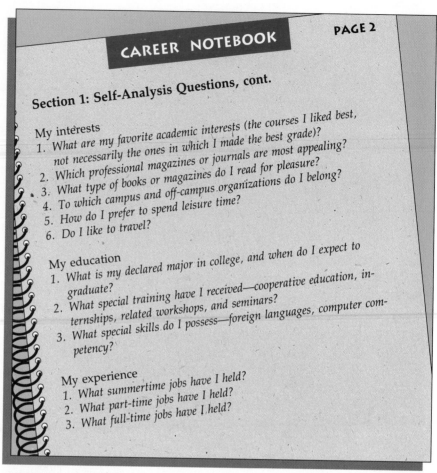

CAREER NOTEBOOK **PAGE 2**

Section 1: Self-Analysis Questions, cont.

My interests
1. What are my favorite academic interests (the courses I liked best, not necessarily the ones in which I made the best grade)?
2. Which professional magazines or journals are most appealing?
3. What type of books or magazines do I read for pleasure?
4. To which campus and off-campus organizations do I belong?
5. How do I prefer to spend leisure time?
6. Do I like to travel?

My education
1. What is my declared major in college, and when do I expect to graduate?
2. What special training have I received—cooperative education, internships, related workshops, and seminars?
3. What special skills do I possess—foreign languages, computer competency?

My experience
1. What summertime jobs have I held?
2. What part-time jobs have I held?
3. What full-time jobs have I held?

FIGURE 13-1, continued

◆ Bureau of Employment Security, U.S. Department of Labor. (1991). *Dictionary of occupational titles.* Washington, DC: U.S. Government Printing Office.

◆ Bureau of Labor Statistics, U.S. Department of Labor. *Occupational outlook handbook.* Washington, DC: U.S. Government Printing Office (published yearly).

◆ Powell, C.R. (1990). *Career planning today* (2nd ed.). Dubuque, IA: Kendall-Hunt.

After writing answers to the career-oriented questions in your notebook, you almost certainly will have either an increased enthusiasm for your chosen career or a feeling that you should consider other careers. Either way, the effort has been worthwhile. Once you have selected the right field for your career, you can begin to examine a specific job in that field.

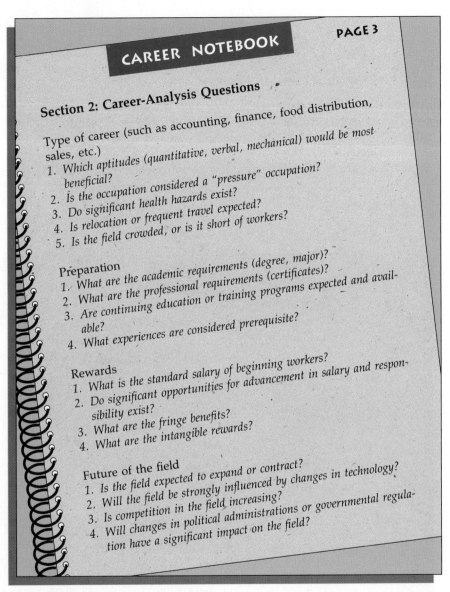

FIGURE 13-2 Career-analysis questions

The content of the career notebook reads:

CAREER NOTEBOOK   PAGE 3

Section 2: Career-Analysis Questions

Type of career (such as accounting, finance, food distribution, sales, etc.)
1. Which aptitudes (quantitative, verbal, mechanical) would be most beneficial?
2. Is the occupation considered a "pressure" occupation?
3. Do significant health hazards exist?
4. Is relocation or frequent travel expected?
5. Is the field crowded, or is it short of workers?

Preparation
1. What are the academic requirements (degree, major)?
2. What are the professional requirements (certificates)?
3. Are continuing education or training programs expected and available?
4. What experiences are considered prerequisite?

Rewards
1. What is the standard salary of beginning workers?
2. Do significant opportunities for advancement in salary and responsibility exist?
3. What are the fringe benefits?
4. What are the intangible rewards?

Future of the field
1. Is the field expected to expand or contract?
2. Will the field be strongly influenced by changes in technology?
3. Is competition in the field increasing?
4. Will changes in political administrations or governmental regulation have a significant impact on the field?

Job Analysis

Most college graduates with little or no experience expect to take what is commonly known as an entry-level position. Many businesses provide training or orientation programs for newly hired employees. Before preparing a resume, students need to ask and answer the questions in Figure 13-3.

Interview with a Career Person

If possible, interview more than one person in the field.

Before making the decision to embark on a certain career, you can profit greatly from interviewing someone who is already pursuing it. The interview is to your advantage, regardless of whether it increases your enthusiasm or reveals that the career is definitely not for you. For maximum benefit, prepare beforehand a set of questions such as those listed in Figure 13-4.

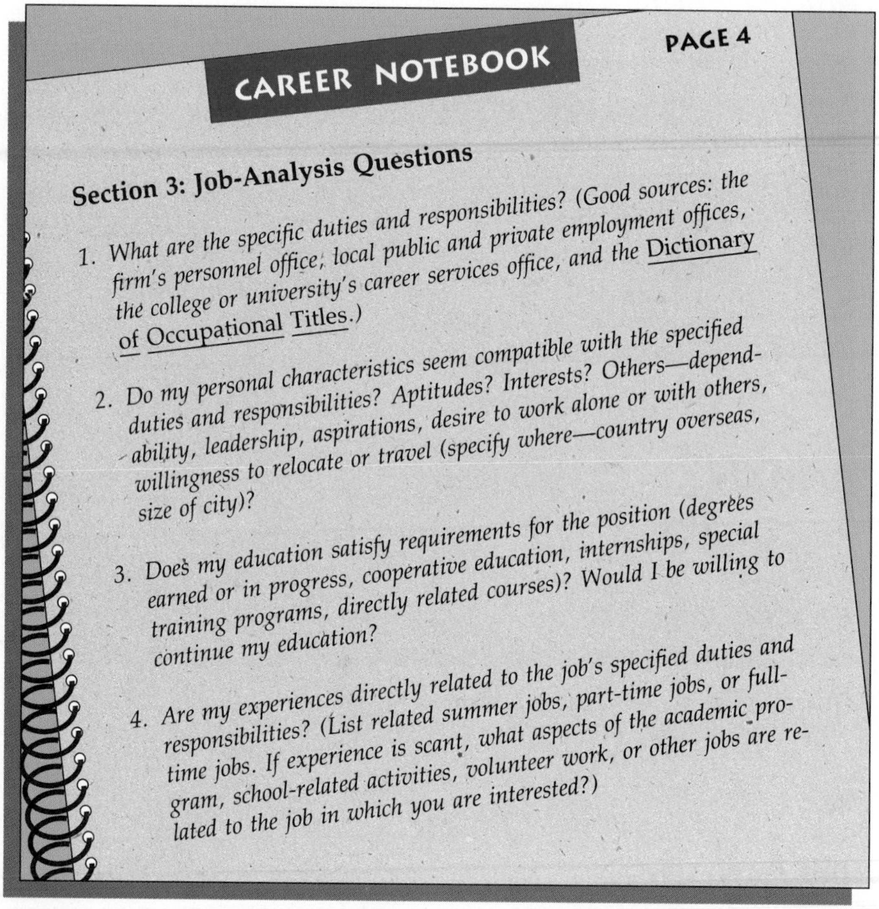

CAREER NOTEBOOK   **PAGE 4**

Section 3: Job-Analysis Questions

1. What are the specific duties and responsibilities? (Good sources: the firm's personnel office; local public and private employment offices, the college or university's career services office, and the <u>Dictionary</u> <u>of Occupational Titles.</u>)

2. Do my personal characteristics seem compatible with the specified duties and responsibilities? Aptitudes? Interests? Others—dependability, leadership, aspirations, desire to work alone or with others, willingness to relocate or travel (specify where—country overseas, size of city)?

3. Does my education satisfy requirements for the position (degrees earned or in progress, cooperative education, internships, special training programs, directly related courses)? Would I be willing to continue my education?

4. Are my experiences directly related to the job's specified duties and responsibilities? (List related summer jobs, part-time jobs, or full-time jobs. If experience is scant, what aspects of the academic program, school-related activities, volunteer work, or other jobs are related to the job in which you are interested?)

FIGURE 13-3   Job-analysis questions

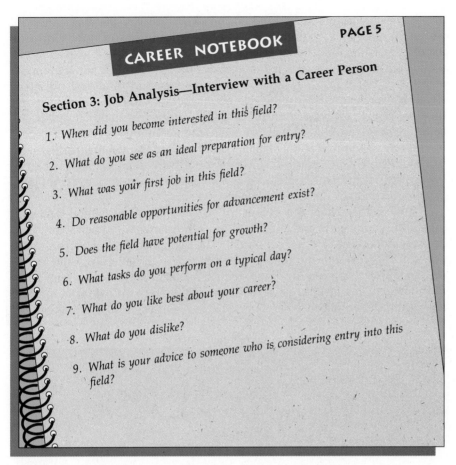

FIGURE 13-4   Job analysis: Interview with a career person

Company/Job Profile

Completing the self-, career-, and job analyses has allowed you to collect a great deal of information. The next step is to compile this information in a format that will allow you to compare your qualifications with the company and job requirements—to determine whether a match between you and the potential job is possible. Insert another page in your career notebook for this comparison of the company and job requirements with your qualifications and needs.

A company/job profile for an entry-level audit accountant in an international public accounting firm is shown in Figure 13-5. After completing the two columns, an individual can easily identify the exact areas in which company/job requirements and qualifications and needs do not match. Basic qualifications and salary and advancement expectations seem very compatible; the major differences are in work surroundings, amount of travel and overtime, and communication (oral and interpersonal) skills. By identifying the relative importance of these areas, the individual can decide whether pursuing a job in an international public accounting firm would be wise. Would he/she be willing to seek assistance in refining communication skills? Would he/she be willing to learn to work effectively in groups? How important are limited overtime and fewer travel requirements? Could he/she adapt to working in temporary locations without a desk of his/her own?

You will probably never find the job and the organization that will satisfy all your needs and meet all your requirements. Some factors will be more important to you than others. The benefits gained from this analysis will far outweigh the time and energy spent in gathering valid information about company and job requirements and in evaluating your qualifications and needs. This analysis may prevent you from becoming one of the increasing number of entry-level workers who are looking for

When job-hunting, apply to those companies whose needs match your qualifications. Getting a job with a company that does not value or utilize your talents or working for a company that needs resources you do not have will only create problems for everyone involved. Just as a puzzle piece won't fit in the wrong place in the puzzle, you won't fit in a job that is not right for you.

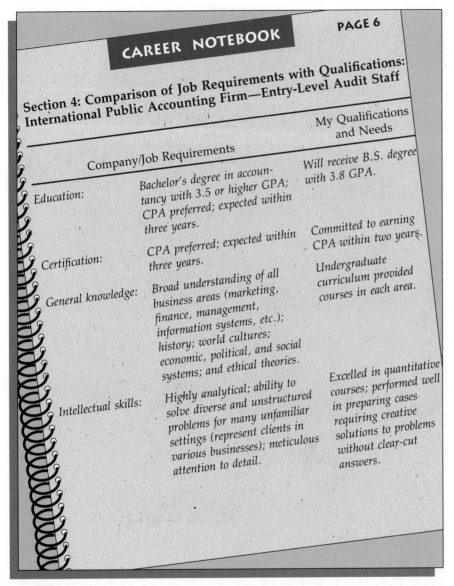

FIGURE 13-5 Comparison of company and job requirements with qualifications

another job after only six months because their qualifications and needs were not compatible with the company and job requirements.

With your self-, career, and job analyses recorded in your career notebook, you can quickly review information as necessary. Use the note-

Making a career notebook requires discipline; job success also requires discipline.

CAREER NOTEBOOK   PAGE 7

Comparison of Job Requirements with Qualifications: International Public Accounting Firm—Entry-Level Audit Staff, cont.

Company/Job Requirements		My Qualifications and Needs
Computer skills:	Proficiency in spreadsheet, word processing, and disk operating system; knowledgeable of general ledger and data management programs.	Proficient in the operation of Lotus 1-2-3, WordPerfect 5.1, and MS-DOS. Knowledgeable of leading general ledger programs and Paradox.
Communication:	Secure and transfer information easily; present and defend views formally and informally in writing or orally.	Proficient in written communication; attempting to overcome fear of speaking before groups; often reluctant to defend ideas if I encounter resistance.
Interpersonal skills:	Work efficiently in groups of diverse members to accomplish a task (e.g., with other members of the audit staff assigned to each audit and with the client); must withstand and resolve conflict (with peers and clients).	Prefer working independently; have had poor experiences completing class group projects.
Management skills:	Organize and delegate tasks; motivate and develop other people.	Part-time work and leadership roles in student groups provided opportunities to refine these management skills.
Work environment:	Work primarily on location at the client's office with temporary work sites (conference table, work room); may share a desk with other staff since days spent in the office rotate.	Must feel in control of my own work space; a desk organized for my sole use is important.

FIGURE 13-5, continued

CAREER NOTEBOOK PAGE 8

Comparison of Job Requirements with Qualifications: International Public Accounting Firm—Entry-Level Audit Staff, cont.

Psychometric profile:
Able to work on numerous audits simultaneously, to shift gears from one project to another readily, to set priorities and organize work to meet tight and often coinciding deadlines, and to meet any unexpected requirements; willing to revise work until it meets the high standards set by an international accounting firm.

Prefer to complete one project before moving to another; difficult to manage more than one major activity at once; often take criticism personally.

Ethical standards:
Must abide by the AICPA Code of Professional Conduct.

High moral standards as result of family background; willing to abide by code of ethics that upholds the high standards of the profession.

Salary range:
$26,000–$30,000 annually.

$24,000–$29,000 annually.

Travel:
Approximately 25%.

No more than 10%.

Overtime:
Average 15 hours per month; peaks between February 1 and April 1.

Limited overtime desired.

Career path:
Well-defined path; typically promoted from staff accountant to audit senior after 3 years; from audit senior to manager after 6 years; eligible for partner after 10 years.

Well-defined career path with frequent changes in responsibilities.

Prestige level:
High.

Medium to high prestige desired.

FIGURE 13-5, continued

book for other job-related information, too. Add pertinent questions and answers to the lists you have made. Occasionally review and update. Reserve some pages for clippings of career- and job-related information. Record addresses and phone numbers of firms for which you would consider working, employers and supervisors for whom you have worked (along with specific dates on which employment began and ended), and references. Include a copy of a transcript or a list of courses taken. Record notes taken during interviews.

Recording answers in your career notebook should have helped you (1) identify your qualifications as they relate to an employer's needs, (2) ensure that you have selected the right career, and (3) compare your qualifications with the duties and responsibilities of the job you are seeking. Because you have a record of this analysis in your career notebook, you can easily review this information to identify the information that should be included on your resume.

PLANNING YOUR RESUME

What purpose does a resume serve?

A job announcement that appeared in several midwestern newspapers described a career opportunity for someone with two years' sales experience to sell medical equipment to hospitals. John W. applied. He was well qualified and had sold medical equipment previously. He knew the territory, was willing to relocate, and had a proven track record of successful selling—but he didn't even get called for an interview. The same was true of Mary M., Bill T., and countless others. Of the nearly 200 people who applied for the position, fewer than a dozen were selected for interviews. This true story, told by Barnum (1987) in "Writing Resumes That Sell," occurs every day. Without a resume that sells your qualifications in terms of the employer's needs, you will never get an opportunity to sell yourself at an interview.

You have less than two minutes to convince the interviewer that you are the person for the interview.

Because an employer typically spends two minutes or less reading a resume (Holley, Higgins, & Speights, 1988), you have very little time to explain why you're the best person for the job. You must selectively choose *what* to say, *how to say* it, and *how to arrange* it on the page so that it can be read quickly but thoroughly. A concise, informative, easy-to-read summary of your relevant qualifications will not only get you an interview but also will tell the employer that you possess the straightforward communication skills demanded in today's information-intensive society.

The standard parts of a winning resume include

◆ Identification.
◆ Objective—job (or type of work) being sought.
◆ Summary of achievements (optional).

Olympic athletes know that a split second or a fraction of an inch often determines who wins. Today's job market is almost that competitive. Even a minor error can mean the difference between employment and joblessness.

- ◆ Qualifications (primarily your education and experience).
- ◆ Personal information (included only if it is related to the job duties and/ or strengthens the resume).
- ◆ References (often just a statement that references are available; however, references can be listed under certain circumstances).

Examples of resumes are provided in this chapter (Figures 13-8 to 13-12) to illustrate these standard resume parts and various resume formats. However, the format, content, and style of your resume depend on your specific qualifications, the job field (conservative or creative), and the individual personality you wish to portray. For example, you must make decisions about whether to include personal information and references and about which experiences are job related. The items you include are determined by personal preference, moral judgment, and your assessment of whether the receiver will want or need them.

Include information that increases your chances of getting an interview.

The goal of the resume is to get an interview, so ask yourself this question: "Does including this information increase my chances of getting an interview?" If the answer is "yes," include the information; if the answer is "no," omit the information and use the space to develop your qualifications.

When selecting information to be included, honestly ask yourself, "Does this information present my qualifications honestly and ethically, or does it inflate my qualifications to increase my chances of getting the job?" If you have the slightest inclination that including a piece of infor-

Murphy's Law No. 2

The _one_ little exaggeration on your resumé is the one they check!

PERSONNEL

HELLO... IS THIS THE WHITE HOUSE?

C86-4 The Drawing Board™ Box 660429 Dallas, Texas 75266 © Wheeler Group, Inc. 1985

Information included on resumes is verified.

mation will inflate your qualifications, omit it. This action allows you to uphold high ethical values.

What are the consequences of inflating your qualifications? First, the interviewer may uncover your "exaggeration" when verifying the information on a resume and can legally terminate your employment. Interviewers can tell numerous stories of applicants who claimed to have received degrees from schools they never attended, worked for nonexistent companies, or worked for companies that have no knowledge of the applicant. Second, if your employer becomes aware that you secured a job in an unethical manner, you probably will lose your employer's trust. This lack of trust may prevent you from advancing in the company. Third, if you are hired based on false qualifications, you may find yourself unable to perform the duties of a job for which you are not qualified.

What are the consequences of providing false information on a resume?

Identification

Be certain the interviewer can reach you by mail or telephone during regular office hours.

Your objective is to provide information that will allow the interviewer to reach you. Include your name, current address, and telephone number. To ensure that the interviewer can quickly locate this information, center it on the page. Most word-processing programs and printers allow you to increase the size of this and other information for added emphasis.

You may also include a permanent address (parents' address) if you are interviewing when classes are not in session. If you are rarely at home during typical office hours (the time the interviewer is likely to call), provide a phone number where messages can be left. Explain to those

532

taking messages that prospective employers may be calling; therefore, their accuracy in taking messages and the impression they make while taking the message could affect your job search. Evaluate the personal message on your answering machine to be certain that it portrays you as a person serious about securing a job.

Job and/or Career Objective

Immediately following the "Identification" section, state your job/career objective—the job you want. Interviewers can see immediately if the job you are seeking matches the one they have to offer. Therefore, a good job/career objective must be specific enough to be meaningful yet general enough to apply to a variety of jobs. The following example illustrates a general objective that has been revised to describe a specific job.

General Objective

A position that offers both a challenge and a good opportunity for growth.

A responsible position with a progressive organization that provides the opportunity for managerial development and growth commensurate with ability and attitudes.

Specific Objective

To secure an entry-level position in sales, leading to sales management.

To enter the management training program of a progressive firm that provides opportunities for advancement.

Some experts argue that a statement of your job or career objective may limit your job opportunities. Your objective should be obvious from your qualifications, they say. In general, however, making your objective clear at the beginning assures the interviewer that you have a definite career goal.

Summary of Achievements

Just as an abstract provides an overview of a report, the "Summary of Achievements" section summarizes your qualifications. By reading the career objective and a summary statement about your achievements, interviewers know *what* you want (whether your interests match theirs) and *why* the employer would want to hire you. Busy executives are finding this relatively new section of the resume to be exceptionally helpful (Barnum, 1987).

To be certain that you highlight all major qualifications, write the "Summary of Achievements" section after you have written the remainder of the resume. Barnum's three methods for summarizing qualifications are illustrated in the following examples:

If you are using an answering machine at the telephone number you provide, be sure the message is courteous, clear, and professional. Avoid music, jokes, and clever remarks.

What are the characteristics of a good job objective?

What purpose does a summary statement serve?

Separate Objective and Qualifications

OBJECTIVE:	To secure an entry-level position in international sales, leading to sales management.
SUMMARY OF ACHIEVEMENTS:	Bachelor of Science in Marketing including three semesters of cooperative education experience with a large retail store and three international business courses (one completed abroad); proficiency in Spanish and French; effective team worker and communicator.

Combine Objective with Qualifications in One Section

OBJECTIVE:	To secure a position in sales, leading to sales management. International sales/marketing executive with three years' successful experience in sales, marketing, advertising, and contract negotiation with international suppliers.

Link Objective and Summary in One Section

OBJECTIVE:	Position as a sales representative where demonstrated commission selling and hard work bring rewards.
Accomplishments:	• Three years' straight-commission sales. • Average of $35,000–$55,000 per year in commissioned earnings. • Consistent success in development and growth of territories.

Information in the resume *must* support the summary statement presented in the opening section.

    The "Summary of Achievements" section is optional. Some experts argue that this section is not beneficial unless your background is unusually varied. If you include a summary statement, be certain that the remainder of the resume supports the statement; otherwise, you may be eliminated from consideration ("Write a Resume that Works," 1990).

Qualifications

The "Qualifications" section varies depending on the information identified in the self-, career, and job analyses. This information is used to divide the qualifications into appropriate parts, choose appropriate labels for them, and arrange them in the best sequence. Usually, qualifications stem from your education and work experience (words that appear as headings in the resume). Arrange these categories depending on which you perceive as more impressive to the employer, with the more impressive category appearing first. For example, education is usually the chief qualification of a recent college graduate; therefore, education appears first. However, a sales representative with related work experience might list experience first, particularly if the educational background is inadequate for the job sought.

Education. Beginning with the most recent, list the degree, major, school, and graduation date. Include a blank line between schools so that the employer can see them at a glance. Using empathy for the interviewer's needs, determine the order for this information and follow that order consistently for each school attended. For example, the interviewer would probably want to know first whether you have the appropriate degree, then the institution, and so on. Recent or near college graduates should omit high school activities because that information is "old news." However, include high-school activities if they provide a pertinent dimension to the applicant's qualifications. For example, having attended high school abroad is a definite advantage to an applicant seeking employment in an international firm. In addition, high school accomplishments may be relevant for freshmen or sophomores seeking cooperative-education assignments, scholarships, or part-time jobs. Of course, this information will be replaced with college activities when the resume is revised for subsequent jobs or other uses.

Include overall and major grade-point averages if they are B or better—but be prepared to discuss any omissions during an interview. Honors and achievements that relate directly to education can be incorporated in this section or included in a separate section. Examples include scholarships, appearance on academic lists, and initiation into honor societies. If honors and achievements are included in the "Education" section, be sure to include plenty of white space or to use asterisks or bullets to highlight these points (see Figures 13-8 and 13-10).

The "Education" section could also include a list of equipment operated and special skills and abilities such as foreign language and computer competency. A list of courses typically required in your field is unnecessary and occupies valuable space. However, you should include any courses, workshops, or educational experiences that are not usual requirements. Examples include internships, cooperative-education semesters, "shadowing," "over-the-shoulder" experiences, and study abroad.

Information gained from self-, career, and job analyses will aid you in dividing this section into appropriate divisions.

Should information about high school be included? Explain.

Include GPA only if it strengthens your qualifications.

What do asterisks and bullets add to a resume?

Should you include educational experiences other than degrees earned? Explain.

Work Experience.   The "Work Experience" section provides information about your employment history. For each job held, list the job title, company name, dates of employment, primary responsibilities, and key accomplishments. The jobs may be listed in reverse chronological order (beginning with the most recent) or in order of job relatedness. Begin with the job that most obviously relates to the job being sought if you have gaps in your work history, if the job you are seeking is very different from the job you currently hold, or if you are just entering the job market and have little if any related work experience.

Arrange the order and format of information about each job (dates, job title, company, description, and accomplishments) so that the most important information is emphasized—but be sure all job information is formatted consistently. An applicant who has held numerous jobs in a short time should "bury" dates of employment within the text rather than surround them with white space. If the job relates directly to the job being sought, you might give the job title prominence by listing it first or surrounding it with white space.

Omit *obvious* job duties. The job title provides basic knowledge about what you did. By stressing what you accomplished on the job, you will set yourself apart from other applicants, who simply list a job description, by providing deeper insight into your ambition, capability, and personality. Recall instances when your personal involvement played a key role in the success of a project. Perhaps you uncovered a wasteful, labor-intensive procedure that was resolved through your innovation, or you bridged a gap in a communication breakdown. These instances neatly bulleted (see Figure 13-10) under the company name and job title "glitter like diamonds" (Charles, 1988).

Because interviewers spend such a short time reading resumes, the style must be direct and simple. Therefore, a resume should use crisp phrases to help employers see the value of the applicant's education and experiences. To save space and to emphasize what you have accomplished, use these stylistic techniques: omit pronouns referring to yourself (*I, me, my*), use subject-understood sentences, begin sentences with action verbs, and select adjectives carefully, as shown in Figure 13-6.

Because employers are looking for people who will work, action verbs are especially appropriate. In the subject-understood sentences in the right column of Figure 13-6, using action words as first words provides emphasis. The following list illustrates verbs that are useful in resumes:

accomplished	completed	drafted
achieved	computed	established
administered	controlled	expanded
analyzed	counseled	implemented
assisted	created	increased
compiled	developed	initiated

Accomplishments neatly bulleted so interviewers can readily locate them "glitter like diamonds."

What is the advantage of using subject-understood sentences and verbs as first words?

invented	prepared	scheduled
maintained	presented	sold
managed	proposed	studied
organized	recruited	supported
planned	researched	wrote

To give the employer a vivid picture of you as a productive employee, you may find some of the following adjectives helpful:

adaptable	efficient	reliable
analytical	forceful	resourceful
conscientious	independent	sincere
consistent	objective	systematic
dependable	productive	tactful

Instead of	*Use*
I had responsibility for development of new territory.	Developed new territory.
My duties included designing computer systems and writing user documentation manuals.	Developed computer programs to monitor accounting systems including carefully written documentation manuals that enabled users to operate these sophisticated systems effectively.
I was the store manager and supervised 8 employees.	Managed operations of store with sales volume of $1,000,000 and supervised 8 employees.
My sales consistently exceeded sales quota.	Earned average of $35,000–$55,000 per year in commissioned earnings. Received service award for exceeding sales quota two of three years employed.
I was a member of the Student Council, Society for the Advancement of Management, Phi Kappa Phi, and Chi Omega Social Sorority.	Developed effective interpersonal skills through involvement in numerous student organizations such as the Student Council, Society for the Advancement of Management, Phi Kappa Phi, and Chi Omega Social Sorority.

FIGURE 13-6 Use action verbs in sentences whose subject is understood.

To avoid a tone of egotism, don't use too many adjectives or adverbs that seem overly strong. Plan to do some careful editing after writing your first draft.

Honors and Activities.   Make a trial list of any other information that qualifies you for the job. Divide the list into appropriate divisions and then select an appropriate label. Your heading might be "Honors and Activities" unless you listed honors and achievements in the "Education" section. You might include a section for "Activities," "Leadership Activities," or "Memberships" depending on the items listed. You might also include a separate section on "Military Service," "Civic Activities," "Volunteer Work," or "Interests." If you have only a few items under each category, use a more general term and combine the lists. If your list is lengthy, divide it into more than one category; interviewers prefer "bite-size" pieces because they are easier to read and can be remembered more readily.

> *The title of this section varies depending on the items listed within the section.*

> *Ask yourself: Does the information relate to the job being sought?*

Resist the urge to include everything you have ever done; keep in mind that every item you add distracts from other information. Consider summarizing information that is relevant but does not merit several separate lines; for example, "Involved in art, drama, and choral groups." To decide whether to include certain information, ask these questions: How closely related is it to the job being sought? Does it provide job-related information that has not been presented elsewhere?

Personal Information

> *What types of personal information are best omitted?*

Because the resume should contain primarily information that is relevant to the applicant's experience and qualifications, personal information (not related to the job) must be carefully selected. The space could be used more effectively to include more about your qualifications or to add more white space to increase the appeal of the document. Personal information is commonly placed at the end of the resume just above the "References" section because it is less important than qualifications (education and experience).

> *Including information unrelated to the job being sought weakens job qualifications.*

PEANUTS reprinted by permission of UFS, Inc.

Under the 1964 Civil Rights Act (and subsequent amendments), employers cannot make hiring decisions based on gender, religion, age, marital status, handicap, or national origin. Employers prefer that this information be omitted from a resume because questions could be raised about whether the information were used in the hiring decision. Employers prefer that a photograph not accompany a resume because a photograph provides information about gender, age, and national origin—criteria employers are forbidden to use for hiring.

Such personal information as height, weight, and color of hair and eyes is not normally worthy of inclusion. Reveal ethnic background or physical handicap only if doing so is to your advantage. For example, certain businesses may be actively seeking employees in certain ethnic groups; that is, the ethnic background is a legitimate part of the job description. For such a business, ethnic information is useful and appreciated.

If personal information (other than the information covered by civil rights legislation) strengthens the resume, you may include it. Major categories include interests, hobbies, avocations, and willingness to relocate. For example, an applicant for a religious or political organization may benefit from revealing affiliation with such an organization. A nonsmoker may want to reveal that fact; it may be a favorable factor in the employer's decision to interview. On the other hand, the nonsmoking factor may raise the question of the applicant's compatibility with present employees who smoke. For the person who really wants a nonsmoking work environment, "nonsmoker" on the resume may restrict the number of interviews with employers who condone smoking and increase the number of interviews with employers who do not.

Would you reveal that you don't smoke or are affiliated with a particular religious or civic group?

In making a decision about whether to include certain personal information, consider these three criteria: (1) How closely is it related to the job being sought? (2) Does it portray me as a well-rounded, happy individual off the job? (3) Is it controversial?

Discuss the criteria used to select the personal information to be included on a resume.

If not included under some other heading in the resume, the following items are possibilities for inclusion under the "Personal Information" heading: oral and written communication skills, computer competency, foreign- or computer-language skills, military service, community service, scholastic honors, job-related hobbies, and professional association memberships. Favorite sports may be included, but be cautious. To an employer who plays golf regularly, your enthusiasm for it may be a plus. To one who does not, it could be a small but eliminating factor. Listing a sport that is stereotyped as dangerous or overly time consuming is risky.

References

A list of references (people who have agreed to supply information about you when requested) may be included. Listing names, addresses, and telephone numbers of people who can provide information about you

What are the advantages and disadvantages of including references?

adds credibility to the resume. Employers, former employers, teachers, and former teachers are good possibilities. Friends, relatives, and neighbors are not (because of their bias in your favor).

Recommendation letters include mostly positive information. Why?

In recent years, legislative acts and court decisions have diminished the value of recommendations from references. Employees in certain industries and businesses have the legal right to look at information in their personnel folders. People who write recommendations recognize the possibility of legal action (or ruined professional relationships) if they provide negative information. Thus, recommendation letters are inclined to concentrate on positives only, and their value to employers is restricted. Because of possible legal ramifications, some companies have policies against giving recommendations of any kind. These companies will merely confirm when an employee worked for them and in what capacity.

An applicant with good qualifications that are well presented will probably be invited to an interview, even if references are omitted completely. Practices vary; but in some businesses, interviews are conducted *before* communication with references. Therefore, instead of supplying a list of references on the resume, an applicant can include the statement, "References will be supplied on request."

Why register with your school's career services center?

Applicants may also include a statement such as "For references . . . . " or "For additional information . . . . " and give the address of the career services center of their college or university. As a service to graduates, the career services center will mail to prospective employers a complete employment portfolio including recommendation letters collected from your references. Students must register with the career services center to receive the numerous benefits it provides: on-campus interviews, workshops on resume writing and interviewing skills, and so on. The center can serve as an excellent resource for acquiring or refining job search skills.

As a courtesy, always ask your references if you may use their names as references before you put them on your resume or give them to an interviewer.

If references are not listed on the resume, a list of references can be provided after a successful interview. By withholding references until they are called for, an applicant may avoid unnecessary or untimely requests being sent to the present employer. The interview gives an applicant a chance to assess the desirability of the job. Until then, the applicant may not want the present employer to receive inquiries (which may be interpreted as dissatisfaction with the present job). In addition, withholding references until after the interview and until the applicant is certain about his or her interest in the job is a courtesy to the references. Even the most enthusiastic references may become apathetic after providing recommendations to endless interviewers. For this same reason, applicants should communicate with references if a job search continues longer than is expected. A letter of thanks and an update on the job search will assure references that their efforts are appreciated.

When preparing a separate list of references, place the word *REFERENCES* and your name in a visible position and balance the list (name, address, and phone number) attractively on the page. Use paper of the same size, color, weight, and texture as your resume because the two documents will be placed together. When asked for references at the end of a successful interview, you can immediately provide the references page to the interviewer. If you need additional time to consider the interview, you can mail the references page within a day or so. Whether it is handed to the interviewer personally or mailed, the references page professionally complements your resume. Furthermore, you have impressed the interviewer with your promptness in completing this task—a positive indicator that you will handle other duties similarly. An example of a references page is shown in Figure 13-9 page 549.

As a unique individual, you do not want your resume to look just like another person's or to contain the same information as a competitor's resume. Make your decisions about whether to include a statement of long-range career goals, certain personal information, and references.

Like any theme, letter, or memorandum you have written, your resume will need to meet high standards of content. All parts are important, but the most important portion is the one that covers your qualifications. If they seem compatible with job requirements, you have a good message to present. Confident that you have a good message, you are now ready to put it on paper—to construct a resume that will impress the employer favorably.

> **The references page should complement the resume. In what ways?**

> **What do you imply when you promptly submit a list of references in person or by mail?**

> **The career notebook helps provide the resume's content.**

CONSTRUCTING A RESUME

Instead of constructing a resume to suit *you*, try to make one that you think will suit the person who will read it. The acceptable resumes illustrated later in this chapter are not intended to restrict your own creativity. Your goal is to produce a resume that will emphasize the compatibility of your qualifications and the prospective employer's job requirements. You seek to achieve it through organization, style, and mechanics.

> **Use empathy; the resume is designed to impress the *employer*.**

Selecting the Organizational Plan

The general organization of all resumes is fairly standard: identification (name, address, and telephone number), objective, qualifications, personal information, and references. The primary organizational challenge is in dividing the qualifications section into parts, choosing labels for them, and arranging them in the best sequence. Reviewing your self-, career-, and job-analysis data, you will recognize that your qualifications stem mainly from your education and your experience. Your task is to decide how to present these two categories of qualifications. Resumes usually are organized in one of three ways: reverse chronological order (most

> **Should the "Education" section precede the "Experience" section?**

COMMUNICATION MENTOR

Be straightforward. Resumes should be complete, yet to the point. Too many attempts to create unique resumes backfire and do more harm than good. Including a concise recap of your course of study is important, as is listing significant work experience gained while in school. And don't underestimate the importance of referencing personal interests. Employers consider hobbies and leisure-time activities to get a sense of the individual behind the statistics.

Cynthia Pharr
President & CEO
Tracy-Locke/Pharr Public Relations

recent activity listed first), functional order (most important activity listed first), or a combination of chronological and functional orders. To determine which organizational plan to use, make trial outlines using each one.

Chronological Resume. The traditional way to organize a resume is chronologically. Two headings normally appear in the portion that presents qualifications: "Education" and "Experience." Which one should appear first? Decide which one you think is more impressive to the employer, and put that one first. Within each section, the most recent information is presented first (reverse chronological order). Reverse chronological order is easier to use and is more common than functional order; however, it is not always more effective.

The chronological resume is an especially effective format for applicants who have progressed up a clearly defined career ladder and want to move up another rung. The format is less effective for applicants who have gaps in their work history, are seeking jobs different from the job currently held, or are just entering the job market with little or no experience (Baxter, 1987; "Write a Resume that Works," 1990).

If you choose the chronological format, look at the two headings from the employer's point of view and reverse their positions if doing so is to your advantage. Under the "Experience" division, jobs are normally listed in reverse order. Assuming you have progressed normally, your latest job is likely to be more closely related to the job being sought than the first job held. Placing the latest job first will give it the emphasis it deserves. Include beginning and ending dates for each job.

Functional Resume. Listing jobs in chronological order is not a requirement. If listing jobs in order of their *relatedness* to the job sought or the

---

Why list jobs held in reverse chronological order?

Why list the experience most closely related to the job sought first?

value of experience provided is to your advantage, deviate from the time-oriented sequence. Begin with the job that will make the best impression. Including the dates is not a requirement.

A functional resume requires some analysis. However, preparing your career notebook has already forced you to analyze yourself, your career, and the job you are seeking.

Review the notebook and imagine an employer who has a stack of resumes and a limited amount of time for reviewing them and plans to invite two applicants for an interview. Looking through the resumes, the employer is trying to answer the question: "Who has what we're looking for?" The same questions may be phrased in different ways: "Who can do best what we want done?" or "Who has qualifications that match our requirements?" The major headings ("Education" and "Experience") of chronological resumes do not answer this last question. The answer is in the lines that appear beneath the headings; that is, the answer is subordinated. If the answer could be incorporated into the major headings, it would be emphasized—more likely to be seen and more likely to make a vivid impression. In functional resumes, the points of primary interest to employers—your transferable skills—appear in major headings.

Do functional resumes report experience and education?

Suppose, for example, that a person seeking a job as an assistant hospital administrator wants to emphasize qualifications by placing them in major headings. From the hospital's advertisement of the job and from accumulated job-appraisal information, the applicant sees this job as both an administrative and a public-relations job. The job requires skill in communicating and knowledge of accounting and finance. Thus, headings in the qualifications portion of the resume could be (1) "Administration," (2) "Public Relations," (3) "Communication," and (4) "Budgeting."

Do functional resumes use "Experience" and "Education" as major headings?

These headings highlight what the applicant can *do* for the employer—the functions that can be performed well. Under each heading, the applicant could draw from educational and/or work-related experience to provide supporting evidence. Under "Public Relations," for example, the applicant could reveal that a public relations course was taken at State University, from which a degree is to be conferred in June, and that a sales job at ABC Store provided abundant opportunity to apply principles learned. With other headings receiving similar treatment, the qualifications portion reveals the significant aspects of education and experience.

Order of importance is probably the best sequence for functional headings. If you have prepared an accurate job analysis and self-analysis, the selected headings will highlight points of special interest to the employer. Glancing at headings only, an employer could see that you have the qualities needed for success on the job. By carefully selecting headings, you reveal knowledge of the requisites for success on that job.

Should major headings be presented in alphabetical order?

Having done the thinking required for preparing a functional resume, you are well prepared for a question that is commonly asked in interviews: "What can you do for us?" The answer is revealed in your major headings. They emphasize the functions you can perform and the special qualifications you have to offer.

Do functional resume headings emphasize qualifications?

If you consider yourself well qualified, a functional resume is worth considering. If your education or experience is scant, a functional resume may be best for you. Using "Education" and "Experience" as headings (as in a chronological resume) works against your purpose if you have little to report under the headings; the format would emphasize the absence of education or experience.

Combination Chronological and Functional Resume. A resume that *combines* features of chronological and functional resumes may serve your purpose well. The qualifications portion could have headings such as these:

Combination chronological and functional resumes can give quick assurance that educational and experience requirements are met and still use other headings that emphasize qualifications.

Education	List the degree, major, school, and graduation date.
Experience	Briefly list jobs held currently and previously.
Administration	Give details drawn from education and/or experience.
Public Relations	Give details drawn from education and/or experience.
Communication	Give details drawn from education and/or experience.
Budgeting	Give details drawn from education and/or experience.

The preceding headings illustrate the types of headings that *could* be used; functional headings vary for different jobs. Moreover, two people applying for the same job would not be likely to choose the same headings or to list them in the same sequence. Select headings that are appropriate for you and that the employer will see as directly related to the job.

In planning the resume, take note of specific job requirements. They are good possibilities for functional headings. For example, for a job that requires bonding, "Top Security Clearance" gets deserved attention as a heading. Each of the following conditions, if it applies to the job sought, could be the basis for a heading: the work is in small groups, the work requires much overtime in certain seasons, travel is frequent, overseas assignments are a possibility, adaptability to rapid changes is desirable, ability to take criticism is essential, long and detailed reports are required,

In resumes as in outlines, choice of headings is critical.

or lateral transfers can be expected. Choosing appropriate headings is a critical decision in resume preparation.

Enhancing the Layout

Because first impressions are so powerful, the arrangement of the resume on the page is just as important as the content. If the page is arranged unattractively, is unappealing, or is in poor taste, the message may never be read. Errors in keyboarding, spelling, and punctuation may be taken as evidence of a poor academic background, lack of respect for the employer, carelessness, or haste. Many interviewers believe that the resume is an example of the applicant's best work. Hence, they believe that a person who submits a sloppily prepared resume will probably do the same type of work if hired. With this in mind, strive for perfection; give *110 percent* of your effort to this important task—one that could open the door to the job you really want.

As in writing other difficult documents, prepare a rough draft as quickly as you can and then revise as many times as needed to prepare an effective resume that sells you. After you are confident with the resume, ask at least two other people to check it for you. Carefully select people who are knowledgeable about resume preparation and the job you are seeking and can suggest ways to present your qualifications more effectively. After you have incorporated those changes, ask a skillful proofreader to review the document.

Knowing that you will prepare two or more drafts before finally producing the final resume, you should plan to produce it using word-processing software. You can easily revise the stored file, and you can experiment with various formats to determine which one will highlight your strengths most effectively. To make a good first impression, consider the formatting and layout guidelines in Figure 13-7.

For most students, a resume can be arranged on one page. As students gain experience, additional pages are needed. Some employers insist that the "best" length for a resume is one page. A one-page resume that includes irrelevant information is too long. A two-page resume that omits relevant information is too short.

A person with few qualifications applying for a lower-level job may be able to present all relevant information effectively on one page. A person with a great deal of experience applying for a higher-level job would struggle to include all relevant information on one page. The resume probably would appear dense and complicated because of narrow margins and large blocks of run-on text (multiple lines with no space to break them). This crowded resume reformatted onto two pages would have high initial impact. This easy-to-read format would simplify the interviewer's task of identifying the applicant's qualifications, and busy interviewers would appreciate the effort. As you gain more experience, you may need two or more pages to format an informative, easy-to-read resume.

Can poor mechanics counteract superior content, organization, and style? Explain.

Write several rough drafts and ask at least two people for advice and proofreading.

- Print the resume on standard-size (8 1/2" by 11") paper. Because an application letter will accompany a resume, use the large (No. 10) envelope. You may want to consider using a mailing envelope large enough to accommodate the resume and the letter unfolded. Unfolded on the reader's desk, the resume and letter may get favorable attention.
- Use high-quality paper, preferably 24-pound, 100-percent cotton fiber paper. Select a neutral color—white, buff, or gray. Be certain that the watermark (the design imprinted on quality paper) is positioned so that it can be read across the sheet in the same direction as the printing.
- Print the resume with clear, sharp type that will reproduce well. Modern electronic typewriters and typewriter-quality printers (*not* dot matrix) are acceptable. Preferably, use a laser printer to take advantage of the increased print quality. Use various sizes and styles of types to enhance your resume; however, limit the number of type styles and sizes so the page is not overwhelming and confusing. Keep the resume clean and simple to read.

  Laser printers and word-processing software with desktop publishing capability are readily available today, and your competitors will be exploiting these tools to make an outstanding first impression. Consequently, you will find the time and expense involved in gaining access to this equipment a necessity, not a luxury. The resume examples in this chapter illustrate graphic enhancements made using word-processing software.
- Balance the resume attractively on the page with approximately equal margins.
- Use generous white space so the resume looks uncluttered and easy to read.
  - Use ample margins even if you must use a second page.

- Use headings to partition major divisions so the interviewer can locate pertinent information easily and quickly.
- Use an outline format when possible to list activities and events on separate lines. Include bullets (■, ●, □, --) to emphasize multiple points.
- Use indentation, underlining, capitalization, font changes (size and appearance), and graphic lines and borders to enhance the style, readability, and overall impact.
- Be consistent throughout the resume. For example, if you double-space before the first heading and key it in bold print with all capital letters, key all headings in the same way. Select the order for presenting information about education and work experience; then be consistent with each school and job. Consistently include the information listed under each school or job unless you have a specific reason for omitting it; e.g., a grade-point average below B.
- Include your name and a page number at the top of the second and successive pages of a resume. With each new page, the interviewer is exposed to your name once again. If the pages of the resume are separated, they can be collated again if each page is identified.
- Consider adding a statement of your creativity and originality, but be certain that your creativity will not be construed as gimmicky and consequently distract from the content of the resume. For example, preparing a highly effective resume layout including borders, lines, and graphics communicates creativity as well as proficiency in use of computer-based technology. Demonstrating creativity is particularly useful for creative fields such as advertising, public relations, and graphic design and in fields in which computer competency is required.

FIGURE 13-7 Resume format and layout guidelines

ANGELA ROCHELLE

3172 West Fourth Street
Tallahassee, FL 32309-3172
(904) 555-6543

CAREER OBJECTIVE	To obtain a management position in the information systems division of a major corporation or consulting firm. Emphasis in developing applications and implementing programs.
SUMMARY OF QUALIFICATIONS	Bachelor's degree in Management Information Systems; proficient in operation of MS-DOS and Unix systems and primary applications software. Applied computer knowledge and acquired valuable work habits while completing cooperative-education requirements with a leading company. Willing to relocate.
EDUCATION	B.B.A. MANAGEMENT INFORMATION SYSTEMS, West State University. Anticipated graduation date: June 1993. Grade-point average: 3.6 (on a 4.0 scale). Financed 80 percent of education with scholarships, part-time work, and student loans.

Computer Systems:	MS-DOS and Unix
Languages:	COBOL, BASIC, and Pascal
Application Software:	dBase IV, Clipper, WordPerfect 5.1, Lotus 1-2-3, and Harvard Graphics

The centered format and larger type size emphasize the identification section.

Two-column format allows interviewer to locate specific sections easily. Bold type size is used for headings.

The statement of goals and qualifications reveals *what* type of work is sought and *why* the employer would want to hire Angela.

Educational strengths include high GPA (B or better) and a list of specific computer competencies.

FIGURE 13-8 Chronological resume with volunteer work and honors and activities in separate sections

EXAMPLES OF RESUMES

The resumes illustrated in Figures 13-8, 13-10, 13-11, and 13-12 demonstrate the organizational, formatting, and layout principles discussed so far. Figure 13-9 is an example of a references page.

Angela Rochelle   **Page 2**

RELATED EXPERIENCE	Management Assistant, Cooperative Education Program, Central Computer Services, Birmingham, Alabama, January 1992 to May 1992. Provided technical support to end users for hardware and software approved by the company. Applied knowlege of languages and application software in realistic MIS environment; assisted in the installation of a local area network; developed interpersonal skills while interacting with computer users.
	Courtesy Clerk/Cashier, Simpson Foods, Alabama, June 1990 to present. (Work 15 hours per week and full-time during summers.) Promoted from courtesy clerk to cashier in six months. Acquired valuable work habits—responsibility, dependability, time management, and human relations.
VOLUNTEER WORK	Served as unpaid assistant (candy striper) at Winiford Community Hospital, 15 hours per week, Summers 1987 to 1990. Served as president of candy stripers' group in 1990.
HONORS AND ACTIVITIES	Dean's Scholar (3.6 GPA or higher) Data Processing and Management Association Vice President Chair, Program Committee Assist others in selecting computer systems and learning applications software.
REFERENCES	Available on request.

Action verbs vividly portray work experience. Listing voluntary work indicates her service attitude and people-oriented experiences.

References will be provided after a successful interview.

FIGURE 13-8, continued

REFERENCES FOR ANGELA ROCHELLE

3172 West Fourth Street
Tallahassee, FL 32309-3172
(904) 555-6543

Mr. Paul J. Madison, Director
Management Information Systems
Central Computer Services
P.O. Box 47399
Birmingham, AL 35202-9876
(205) 555-9000

Mr. Rodney N. Locke
Associate Professor
Information Systems Department
West State College
P.O. Drawer MG
Jacksonville, FL 32203-0742
(904) 555-3490

Ms. Sharon Wells, RN
Winiford Community Hospital
1700 Lampkin Road
Tallahassee, FL 32309-1700
(904) 555-1939

Prepared at the same time as the resume, the references page can be provided *immediately* following a successful interview. Paper (color, texture, and size) and print type match the resume.

References include two former employers and a professor. The list does not include friends, relatives, or clergy.

Each reference includes courtesy title, full name, company affiliation, address, and phone number (where person can be reached during regular office hours).

FIGURE 13-9   References page

FINDING PROSPECTIVE EMPLOYERS

The career notebook is especially helpful for organizing information about job opportunities. Under the name, address, and phone number of each employer who has a job in which you have an interest, leave some space

Why alphabetize your list of prospective employers?

To ensure that the interviewer can reach him during school holidays, Kyle provides a school and permanent address.

Knowing that the corporations he has been considering have trainee programs designed for recent graduates, Kyle applies for acceptance.

Qualifications briefly summarize *why* the employer should hire Kyle.

Subdividing the "Education" section emphasizes major points and increases readability (eliminates large sections of run-on text).

Academic honors are integrated within the "Education" section and provide evidence of his ability to succeed. Other activities could be included in a separate section following "Experience."

KYLE D. RHODES

School Address	**Permanent Address**
P.O. Box 601	4173 West McClean Avenue
Alexandria State College	Oakdale, LA 71463-4173
Alexandria, LA 70711-3171	(318) 555-6789
(318) 555-4567	

CAREER OBJECTIVES

Immediate: To enter a management-trainee program.

Eventual: To specialize in human resources management in an international operation.

SUMMARY OF QUALIFICATIONS

B.S., Management with a concentration in human resources management; gained managerial experience, communication, and interpersonal skills through part-time employment; proficient in primary software applications; speak Spanish and exposed to other cultures through extensive travel and interaction with international students.

MANAGEMENT-ORIENTED EDUCATION

Bachelor of Science, Alexandria State College, Alexandria, Louisiana. To be conferred on May 1, 1993.

Major: MANAGEMENT, with a concentration in human resources management. Related courses: International Management, International Communication, Spanish (three semesters), and Computer Applications courses.

Grade-Point Average: Major: 3.8; overall 3.7 (based on 4.0 scale).

Honors: Beta Gamma Sigma (business honorary society).
Recipient of M. Thomas Suttle Academic Scholarship (ACT score above 30).
Listed on the Dean's or President's List for seven semesters (GPA 3.6 or better).

FIGURE 13-10   **Chronological resume with honors and achievements integrated within "Education" section**

for recording additional data. Record the date of each call (along with what you learned from the call), the date of each returned call, the name of the person who called, the date you sent a resume, and so on. By listing each prospective employer on a separate sheet and alphabetizing the

Kyle D. Rhodes	**Page 2**

Heading clearly identifies the second page of Kyle's resume.

MANAGEMENT-RELATED EXPERIENCE

Domeview Hotel	**Desk Manager**
Oakdale, Louisiana	**Summers 1991 to present**

Make room reservations, register guests, keep computerized records, and supervise bellhops and desk clerks.

- Promoted from desk clerk to desk manager after one year.
- Developed effective interpersonal skills through continuous interactions with guests and supervision of 12 employees.
- Gained computer competency and refined organizational skills.
- Initiated employee participation program; as a result of the ideas submitted, several more efficient procedures have been implemented.

Bullets (■) highlight accomplishments stated in brief phrases beginning with action verbs.

Alexandria State College	**Residence Hall Assistant**
Alexandria, Louisiana	**August 1990 to present**

Supervise 72 upper-class male residents from at least six different countries; enforce college regulations; provide individual and group counseling for academic and personal problems; prepare work schedules and handle payroll for 5 resident assistants and 13 desk assistants.

- Developed effective communication skills while counseling residents; learned the value of empathetic listening and seeing ideas from the other person's perspective—skills relevant to quality employee training.
- Designed computer-based work scheduling program that was adopted for use by all other residence hall directors.

Using horizontal lines to partition the resume into logical divisions simplifies the interviewer's ability to locate each major division.

PERSONAL INFORMATION

Developed cultural awareness through extensive travel throughout Europe and Mexico. Have a strong interest in physical fitness; exercise regularly—swim, jog, and play tennis. Certified as CPR and lifeguard instructor for the American Red Cross. Willing to relocate.

Only personal information that *strengthens* the resume is included.

ADDITIONAL INFORMATION

Letters from references and a transcript are available from Career Services Center, Alexandria State College, P.O. Box 3782, Alexandria, LA 70711-3783, (315) 555-8765.

Because the Career Services Center will provide recommendations from Kyle's references, references are not listed; the space is used to develop other qualifications.

FIGURE 13-10, continued

sheets, you can find a name quickly and respond effectively to a returned phone call.

Information about career and job opportunities is available from many different sources, including career services centers, employers' offices, employment agencies and contractors, help-wanted ads, libraries, and professional organizations.

Centered format and larger type size emphasize the identification section.

Horizontal line adds interest and partitions the identification section from the evidence that follows.

Two-column format allows interviewer to locate specific sections easily. Bold type size and all-capitals are consistently used to display headings.

Headings emphasize the qualities the applicant offers as a solution to the employer's problem. A quick look at the headings suggests that this applicant knows important requisites for success in sales.

In the material under each heading, Laura draws from education and/or experience for support.

References are listed on the second page (not shown here) because Laura is confident she wants to work for this company and believes providing them will strengthen her resume.

LAURA LINDHOLM

6173 North Gillespie
Anaheim, CA 92380-6173
(213) 555-6743

OBJECTIVE	To acquire a position in retail clothing sales with possible advancement to sales management.
SALES-ORIENTED CAREER	Since childhood, have had a strong interest in sales and fashion; began designing and making clothes for myself and others at age 14. Have had three years' part-time experience in fast foods. Currently a senior majoring in marketing at West State University. Subscribe to <u>Retail Selling</u> and <u>Fashions of the Year</u>. To graduate in May 1993.
PUBLIC RELATIONS SKILLS	Learned the value of tact in taking and filling orders in the fast-food business (C G's Quickburger, part-time from August 1990 to May 1992). Commended by manager for diplomacy with patrons and staff. Received an A in Interpersonal Communication and will take Public Relations next year. Volunteer work (as a counselor at Camp Seminole for three summers) provided experience in coping with various personality types.
RECORD-KEEPING SKILLS	Used cash register and balanced receipts against records each day at C G's Quickburger. Now taking two classes (Accounting and Computer Science) that emphasize keeping records electronically.
DEPEND-ABILITY	Am always on the job when scheduled for work. In three years, have never been late for work. Attend classes regularly. Open, close, and take cash to bank.
LEARNING CAPACITY	Commended for learning work procedures quickly. On the Dean's List for the last two semesters. Achieved 3.6 grade average (on a 4.0 scale) in major courses to date.

FIGURE 13-11   Functional resume

Career Services Centers

Register with your career services center.

Don't wait until your last semester to learn about the services provided by your college's or university's career services center. It may be listed under such names as "Career Services Department," "Career Services Division," or "Placement Center." Typically, the center has a browsing room loaded

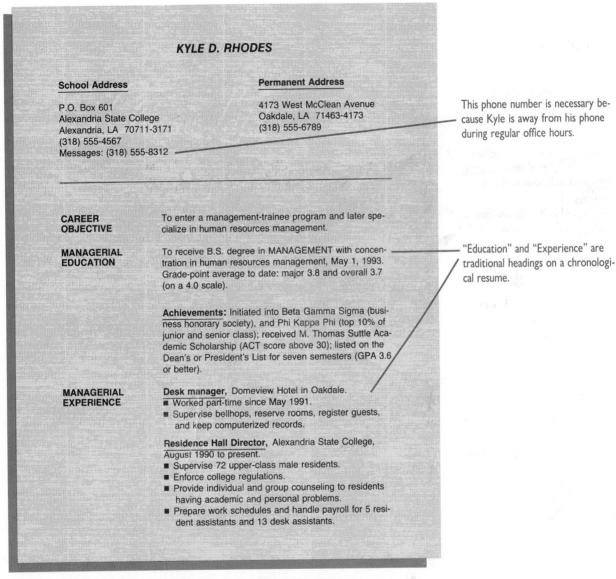

KYLE D. RHODES

School Address

P.O. Box 601
Alexandria State College
Alexandria, LA 70711-3171
(318) 555-4567
Messages: (318) 555-8312

Permanent Address

4173 West McClean Avenue
Oakdale, LA 71463-4173
(318) 555-6789

This phone number is necessary because Kyle is away from his phone during regular office hours.

CAREER OBJECTIVE	To enter a management-trainee program and later specialize in human resources management.
MANAGERIAL EDUCATION	To receive B.S. degree in MANAGEMENT with concentration in human resources management, May 1, 1993. Grade-point average to date: major 3.8 and overall 3.7 (on a 4.0 scale).

"Education" and "Experience" are traditional headings on a chronological resume.

Achievements: Initiated into Beta Gamma Sigma (business honorary society), and Phi Kappa Phi (top 10% of junior and senior class); received M. Thomas Suttle Academic Scholarship (ACT score above 30); listed on the Dean's or President's List for seven semesters (GPA 3.6 or better).

MANAGERIAL EXPERIENCE

Desk manager, Domeview Hotel in Oakdale.
- Worked part-time since May 1991.
- Supervise bellhops, reserve rooms, register guests, and keep computerized records.

Residence Hall Director, Alexandria State College, August 1990 to present.
- Supervise 72 upper-class male residents.
- Enforce college regulations.
- Provide individual and group counseling to residents having academic and personal problems.
- Prepare work schedules and handle payroll for 5 resident assistants and 13 desk assistants.

FIGURE 13-12   Combination chronological and functional resume

with career information and job-announcement bulletins. Career counseling is usually available. Through the center, students can schedule on-campus interviews with company recruiters who make regular visits to the campus.

The career services center can be especially helpful to students who

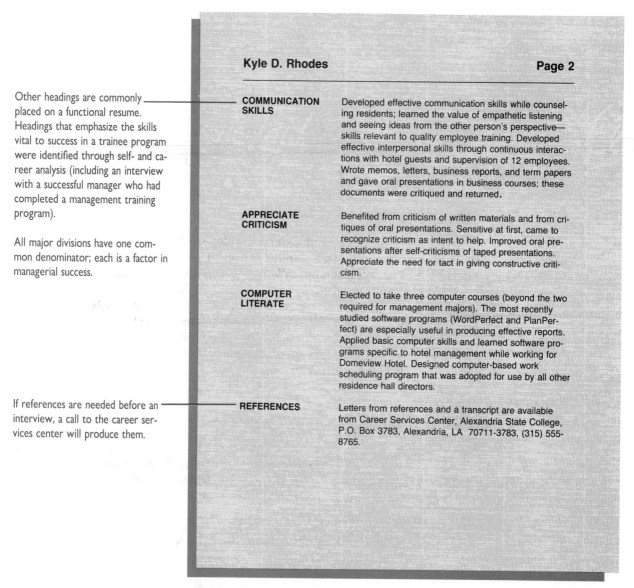

Other headings are commonly placed on a functional resume. Headings that emphasize the skills vital to success in a trainee program were identified through self- and career analysis (including an interview with a successful manager who had completed a management training program).

All major divisions have one common denominator; each is a factor in managerial success.

If references are needed before an interview, a call to the career services center will produce them.

Kyle D. Rhodes   **Page 2**

COMMUNICATION SKILLS
Developed effective communication skills while counseling residents; learned the value of empathetic listening and seeing ideas from the other person's perspective—skills relevant to quality employee training. Developed effective interpersonal skills through continuous interactions with hotel guests and supervision of 12 employees. Wrote memos, letters, business reports, and term papers and gave oral presentations in business courses; these documents were critiqued and returned.

APPRECIATE CRITICISM
Benefited from criticism of written materials and from critiques of oral presentations. Sensitive at first, came to recognize criticism as intent to help. Improved oral presentations after self-criticisms of taped presentations. Appreciate the need for tact in giving constructive criticism.

COMPUTER LITERATE
Elected to take three computer courses (beyond the two required for management majors). The most recently studied software programs (WordPerfect and PlanPerfect) are especially useful in producing effective reports. Applied basic computer skills and learned software programs specific to hotel management while working for Domeview Hotel. Designed computer-based work scheduling program that was adopted for use by all other residence hall directors.

REFERENCES
Letters from references and a transcript are available from Career Services Center, Alexandria State College, P.O. Box 3783, Alexandria, LA 70711-3783, (315) 555-8765.

FIGURE 13-12, continued

If you're registered, the career services center can provide an employer with *several* letters of recommendation in response to *one* call.

are looking for a job. Students complete a form, giving information about academic major, progress toward a degree, graduation date, career goals, and so on. Students then ask three to five people (professors, employers, or others who could provide valid information) to send letters of recommendation to the center. The form and letters are reproduced for sending to prospective employers when requested. With this arrangement, a reference submits only one letter of recommendation; but it can be sent to many different employers. By making one call to the career services center, a prospective employer can get three or more recommendations plus additional data.

Employers' Offices

Employers who have not advertised their employment needs may respond favorably to a telephoned or personal inquiry. The receptionist may be able to provide useful information, direct you to someone with whom you can talk, or set up an appointment.

Employment Agencies and Contractors

Telephone directories list city, county, state, and federal employment agencies that provide free or inexpensive services. Some agencies offer a recorded answering service; by dialing and listening, callers can get information about job opportunities and the procedure for using the agency's services. The fees charged by private agencies are paid by either the employee or the employer. The fee is normally based on the first month's salary and must be paid within a few months. Some agencies specialize in finding high-level executives or specialists for major firms. Employment "contractors" specialize in providing temporary employees. Instead of helping you find a permanent job, a contractor may be able to use your services on a temporary basis until you find a full-time job.

How can employment contractors help in finding a job?

Help-Wanted Ads

Responses to advertised positions should be made as quickly as possible after the ad is circulated. If your resume is received early and is impressive, you could get a favorable response before other applications are received.

Remember that many good jobs are not advertised in help-wanted ads.

If an ad invites response to a box number without giving a name, be cautious. The employer could be legitimate but doesn't want present employees to know about the ad or doesn't want applicants to phone or drop by the premises. However, you have a right to be suspicious of someone who wants to remain obscure while learning everything you reveal in your resume.

Libraries

The following library sources are useful in identifying firms in need of employees:

Annual reports from major firms

Black Enterprise (each year's June issue)

When you are looking for jobs, consider all avenues of information. Although some jobs can be found in the advertisement section of newspapers, most people find employment through business and personal contacts and placement services.

Career, The Annual Guide to Business Opportunities

College Placement Council (CPC) Manual

Company newsletters

Directory of American Firms Operating in Foreign Countries

Dun and Bradstreet's *Million Dollar Directory*

Encyclopedia of Careers and Vocational Guidance

Engineering Index

Forbes (Annual Directory Issue published May 15 each year)

Fortune

Moody's *Manuals*

National Business Employment Weekly

Science Research Associates' Occupational Briefs

Standard and Poor's *Register of Corporations, Directors, and Executives*

Trade or professional journals

United States Civil Service Commission

Wall Street Journal

Professional Organizations

Officers of professional organizations, through their contacts with members, are sometimes very good sources of information about job opportunities. Much job information is exchanged at meetings of professional associations. In response to help-wanted and position-wanted columns in journals of some professional organizations, interviews are sometimes arranged and conducted at hotels or schools in which the organization holds its annual meeting.

In addition to the professional growth that comes from membership in professional organizations, active participation is a good way to learn about job opportunities. Visiting lecturers sometimes provide job information. In addition, employers are favorably impressed when club membership is listed on the resume. They are even more impressed if the applicant is (or has been) an officer in the organization (implies leadership, community commitment, willingness to exert effort without tangible reward, social acceptance, or high level of aspiration). By joining and actively participating in professional, social, and honorary organizations for their majors, college students increase their opportunities to develop rapport with peers and professors. One of the benefits is sharing job information.

A student who expects to graduate in May should begin the search for prospective employers months beforehand. Waiting too long to begin and then hurrying through the job-search process could be detrimental to future employment.

APPLICATION LETTERS

When employers invite you to send a resume, they expect you to include an application letter. When they invite you to send an application letter, they expect you to enclose a resume. The two go together. The resume summarizes information related to the job's requirements and the applicant's qualifications. The application letter (1) seeks to arouse interest in the resume, (2) introduces it, and (3) interprets it in terms of employer benefits. One of its functions is to introduce, so the application letter is placed on top, where it will be seen first.

What is the purpose of an application letter?

As an instrument that seeks to arouse interest and to point out employer benefits, the application letter is persuasive. Written inductively, it is designed to convince an employer that qualifications are adequate (just as a sales letter is designed to convince a buyer that a product will satisfy a need). Like sales letters, application letters are either invited or uninvited. Job advertisements *invite* applications. Uninvited letters have greater need for attention getters; otherwise, invited and uninvited letters are based on the same principles.

Is an application letter a *sales* letter?

Uninvited application letters are sometimes referred to as "prospecting" letters. The same basic letter (perhaps with slight modifications) can be sent to many prospective employers. By sending uninvited letters, (1) you increase the possibility of finding employers who have employment needs, (2) you compete with fewer applicants than you would if let-

What are the advantages and disadvantages of sending "prospecting" application letters?

When you write your application letter, be sure that the letter is a reflection of your personality and not a copy of a standard application letter. You want your letter to stand apart and identify you as a unique individual.

ters were invited, and (3) you may alert employers to needs not previously identified. Impressed by the qualities described in an uninvited letter, an employer could create a job. The writer of an uninvited letter has demonstrated initiative, a quality most employers appreciate. However, sending uninvited letters has some disadvantages: (1) because the employer's specific needs are not known, the opening paragraph is likely to be more general than the opening paragraph in invited letters; and (2) depending on the ratio of responses to letters sent, the process could be expensive.

The job application letter is one of the most important letters you will ever write.

Because satisfaction derived from work plays a major role in life's total enjoyment and because the decision to interview is based primarily on reaction to the application letter and resume, these documents may be among the most important you will ever write. Even after an interview, the application letter and resume could receive further scrutiny and turn out to be deciding factors in your favor.

They represent *you*. They should be different from any other person's. Copying or paraphrasing someone else's resume or application letter is a serious mistake, but you can benefit from studying letters in which others have applied or violated principles. In evaluating application letters written by others (and in thinking about your *own* letter to be

COMMUNICATION MENTOR

The application letter should communicate your desire to obtain a position with this company and what you think you can "bring to the table" for the company. It should be formal in structure but contain some personal item that will help the prospective employer more readily identify you.

Another technique is to add a short one- or two-page biography to the employment package. This document will enable a prospective employer to learn more about you from your perspective.

Terence E. McSweeney
Director of Communications
PGA of America

written later), keep in mind the criteria by which any writing can be evaluated.

Content

If content is satisfactory, the letter will contain the *right ideas;* that is, the *message* will be appropriate. Do you think the following letter is effective?

> To Whom It May Concern:
>
> Wishing to be considered for an entry-level accounting position in your tax department, I submit the enclosed resume.
>
> After you have studied it, I shall appreciate your calling me to set up an interview.
>
> Sincerely,

The letter identifies the job sought, introduces the resume, and encourages action—but what is missing? Does it attempt to arouse the manager's interest? Does it lead the manager to expect something positive in the resume? Does it include anything that might cause the manager to think, "I'm eager to see *this* resume; it may lead to the solution of my employment problem"?

Length. Did you recognize the preceding letter as being too short to serve well as a sales letter? Remember, persuasive messages have to be long enough to give supporting evidence. Some human resources managers favor short letters, pointing out that only a few seconds can be spared for reading each letter. A short letter that is *read*, they argue, will do an applicant more good than a long one that is merely *skimmed*. They see brevity as a virtue that can be demonstrated in an application letter.

Employers are very busy. Is that a valid argument for keeping application letters short?

Others favor longer letters. They point out that good employees are hard to find and that longer letters provide (1) more information and (2) more opportunity to evaluate. If the first lines arouse interest, employers will thoroughly and eagerly read additional paragraphs if doing so will possibly resolve an employment problem.

By making paragraphs long enough to include interpretation of experiences on the present or previous job, you can give an employer some confidence that you are well prepared for your next job. For example, the following paragraph from an applicant whose only work experience was at a fast-food restaurant is short and general:

> For three months last summer, I worked at C G's Quickburger. Evaluations of my work were superior. While the assistant manager was on vacation, I supervised a crew of five on the evening shift.

As the only reference to the C G's Quickburger experience, the paragraph does convey one employer's apparent satisfaction with performance. Superior evaluations and the responsibility of some supervision are evidence of that satisfaction, but added details and interpretation could make the message more convincing:

To be convincing, include details.

> In my summertime job at C G's Quickburger, I could see the value of listening carefully when taking orders, making change quickly and accurately, offering suggestions if customers seemed hesitant, and keeping a cheerful attitude. Supervising a crew of five while the assistant manager was on vacation, I appreciated the need for fairness and diplomacy in working with other employees.

Apparently, the applicant's experience has been meaningful. It called attention to qualities that managers like to see in employees: willingness to listen, speed, accuracy, concern for clients or customers, a positive attitude, fairness, and tact. As a *learning* experience, the C G's Quickburger job has taught or reinforced some principles that the employer will see as vital in the job applied for.

For graduating students entering the world of full-time work for the first time, their educational background usually is more impressive than their work history. They can benefit from interpreting their education as a meaningful, job-related experience. An applicant for acceptance into an auditor's trainee program should do more than merely report having taken auditing theory and practice:

> In my auditing theory and practice class, I could see specific application of principles encountered in my human relations and psychology classes. Questions about leadership and motivation seemed to recur throughout the course: What really motivates executives? Why are auditors feared at many levels? How can those fears be overcome? How can egos be salvaged? "Consider the human element" was a frequent admonition. That element was the focus of my term paper, "The Auditor as a Psychologist."

Because the preceding paragraph included questions discussed in a class, don't assume that your application letter should do likewise. Or because this paragraph gives the title of a term paper, don't assume the same technique is a must for your letter. The techniques illustrated are commendable because they help to portray the educational experience as meaningful and related to the job sought. Recognizing that auditors must be tactful (a point on which the one reading the letter will surely agree), the applicant included some details of his class. That technique is a basic in persuasion: Don't just say a product or idea is good; say what makes it good. Don't just say that a certain educational or work experience was beneficial; say what made it so.

Your letter is approaching a desirable length if it succeeds in arousing interest and helps the reader see ways in which your services would be beneficial. One page is usually enough, especially for students and graduates entering the job market. Yet if circumstances seem to justify a longer letter, two- or three-page letters are not taboo.

Source of Job Information. Sometimes, referring to your source of job information may be to your advantage. For example, if a person well known in a large business spoke to your class and indicated a need for employees in a certain category, revealing that person's name in the first paragraph could serve as an attention getter. Or referring to the newspaper or magazine in which a job was advertised is an easy way to identify the job sought. The reference is easy to include in a beginning sentence.

Sidebar notes:

Write about a previous job as a *learning* experience.

Write about school as a *learning* experience.

To be convincing, be specific.

Sometimes, using the name of a person the employer knows is a good way to begin.

Knowledge of Employer's Activities. A thorough job search may have identified current trends in the industry you're entering. The company to which you are applying may have had a recent stock split, announced the upcoming opening of a new branch, or introduced a new product. Sentences that *imply* your knowlege of such matters may make a favorable impression. They show that you really are interested in the field, read widely, do more than you are required to do, gather information before making decisions, and so on.

Be informed, but don't sound like a private detective.

Knowledge of Job Requirements. Such statements as "The requirements of this job are . . . ." or "I understand that this job requires . . . ." are seldom necessary. Your knowledge of job requirements is usually assumed. They need not be stated directly (doing so takes up space and repeats what is known already). If a certain job is known to place special emphasis on certain requirements, however, your awareness of that emphasis could be a point in your favor. For example, a certain accounting job requires frequent and complicated written reports. Instead of writing, "I understand the job requires frequent reports" (which is already known), you could refer to writing experiences you have had or your preference for work that requires writing (if that's true). Your understanding is revealed without a direct statement.

Why not state job requirements directly?

Some ads for employment force respondents to include certain information: "Must provide own transportation and be willing to travel. Give educational background, work experience, and salary expected." These points must be discussed in the responding letter. Preferably, the question of salary is left until the interview; but if an ad requests a statement about it, the letter should include that statement. You may give a minimum figure or range, indicate willingness to accept a figure that is customary for work of that type, or indicate a preference for discussing salary at the interview.

Should a prospecting application letter mention salary?

Unless an ad requests a statement on salary, an application letter should not mention it. Like the price of a product in a sales letter, salary in an application letter is a negative. Don't emphasize what you want from the company (money); instead emphasize what you can contribute to it. Until after the interview, neither the employer nor the applicant knows whether the two are compatible. If they aren't, a discussion of salary is pointless. Like salary, the following ideas (sometimes found in application letters) should be omitted.

Discussion of Your Own Problems. Your need to earn more income, to be closer to your work, to have more pleasant surroundings, or to gain greater advancement opportunities are of little interest to the firm. The excitement you experienced upon learning about a job opportunity isn't worth mentioning. The possible implication is that, for you, jobs are re-

Use empathy. Think in terms of the employer's needs.

ally hard to find, perhaps because of your shortcomings. Use empathy and concentrate on reporting that which will meet the employer's needs.

Statements of the Obvious.   "This is an application," "I read your ad," and "I am writing to apply for" are sufficiently understood without making direct statements. With the letter *and* resume in hand, a reader learns nothing from "A resume is enclosed." Already aware of job requirements and requisites for success in a certain job, managers need not be told again. Such sentences as "An auditor should be able to . . . ." and "Sales personnel should avoid . . . ." seem to lecture. Although they may reveal familiarity with matters important to the job, they may be resented.

Current Employer's Shortcomings.   Regardless of how negatively you perceive your present employer, that perception has little to do with your prospective employer's needs. Also, if you knock your present employer, you could be perceived as someone who would do the same for the next employer.

Self-Deprecating Statements.   Concentrate on reporting your strengths. Surely, you would not apply for a job you thought you could not do. Just tell the aspects of your background that have prepared you for that job. Reporting failure or lack of aptitude at some other endeavor only weakens your case. Mentioning it could raise questions about your self-esteem. Instead of apologizing for some shortcoming, look for positive aspects of your education or experience. Reporting them may be to your advantage.

Boastful Connotations.   Self-confidence is commendable, but overconfidence (or worse still, just plain bragging) is objectionable. Like unsupported or unsupportable superlatives in sales letters, some self-judgmental terms can do more harm than good. Instead of labeling your performance as "superior" or "excellent," give supporting facts. A manager may think of them as evidence of superiority or excellence and react favorably.

Sound confident without bragging.

Flattery.   If a firm is well known for its rapid expansion, currently successful advertising campaign, competitive advantage, or superior product, conveying your awareness of these positive achievements is to your advantage. On the other hand, deliberate attempts at flattery will almost surely be detected. They are more likely to be resented than appreciated. For example, referring to the employer as "*the* leader in the field," "the best in the business," or "a company with an oustanding record" is risky. If such labels are inaccurate, they will be so recognized. If they are accurate, their use is still risky. Flattery could be taken as an attempt to get a favorable decision as a reward for making a complimentary statement.

Subtle, deserved compliments may help. Flattery won't.

Why avoid the narrative approach?

Biographical Discourse.   In certain situations, chronology is the best order in which to arrange items. Listing jobs in the order in which they were held is one legitimate sequence, but an application letter should not sound like a history of a job seeker's life. The narrative approach is likely to emphasize the individual too much and the employer's needs too little. For organizing an application letter, chronology is seldom the best sequence.

Organization

As a persuasive letter, an application letter uses the same sequence of parts as a sales letter:

Sales Letter	Application Letter
Gets attention	Gets attention
Introduces product	Introduces qualifications
Presents evidence	Presents evidence
Encourages action	Encourages action

Like a well-written sales letter, a well-written application letter uses a central selling feature as a theme. It is introduced in the first or second paragraph and stressed in paragraphs that follow. Two to four paragraphs are normally sufficient for supporting evidence. Consider order of importance as a basis for their sequence, with the most significant aspects of your preparation coming first.

Should the first paragraph introduce the resume?

A persuasive letter is designed to get action, which in this case is to get the reader to (1) read the resume and (2) invite you to an interview. Preferably, reference to the resume comes near the end of the letter. If you refer to it in the first or second paragraph, readers may wonder whether they are expected to put the letter aside at that point and look at the resume. Because your purpose in writing is to get an interview, the final paragraph is the logical place for making reference to it. Now that your message is complete, the next move is the reader's. The organizational decision about where to *place* reference to the interview is easy; the stylistic decision about how to *express* it is more challenging.

Style

Should the action be forcefully worded?

Stylistic principles that apply in other writing (especially in sales writing) also apply in application-letter writing. Some stylistic matters deserve special attention:

Use Language Used on the Job.   If the letter contains terminology commonly used by accountants, an applicant for an accounting job implies familiarity with the job and the language used. An applicant for a computer job would benefit from use of acronyms and other terms well known in the computer field but not altogether meaningful to others. Such language would communicate clearly, save space, and imply a computer background. The same principle applies to writing about other occupations.

Avoid Overused Words and Expressions. Some words that are useful in talking *about* letters of application are often used too frequently *in* them:

Are acronyms acceptable?

Try to avoid using words and sentences that have been overused by other applicants.

Applicant	If the letter shows how you are suited for the job sought, you need not label yourself as an "applicant." Obviously, you are.
Application	As a page that introduces a resume and discusses your preparation for a job, your letter is obviously an application.
I	Because the letter is designed to sell your services, some use of "I" is natural and expected; but try to restrict the number of times "I" is used. Empathy for the employer will help. "I" is especially noticeable if it is the first word of consecutive paragraphs.
Interview	The word "interview" is very commonly used in the final paragraph and connotes a formal question-and-answer session. The *idea* of a face-to-face meeting can be introduced without using "interview." "Talk with you," "discuss the work," and "come to your office" are possibilities.
Opening	Meaning "an unfilled position," "opening" is readily understood; but it seems abstract and is overused and usually unneeded.
Position	A "position" may be thought of as a title that someone *holds;* it does not necessarily apply to *work.* Compared with "job" or "work," it may sound more formal than you want.
Qualifications	Employers will recognize training, education, and experience as "qualifications" without a label. Leave the word to implication or use such words as "background," "preparation," or "record."
Vacancy	Like "opening," the word seems abstract, overused, and usually unnecessary.

Using some of the preceding words would not be an error, but they could take up space and make your letter sound like competitors' letters. The following examples illustrate overused sentences and phrases:

Consider me an applicant for the position.	The letter and resume sufficiently imply desire for consideration.
I would like to apply for	"Would *like* to" connotes desire to apply if conditions were different. Application is evident without use of "apply."
. . . to become associated with	The phrase seems vague, formal, and even condescending. The goal is to get a job, not to associate with an employer.
. . . your organization [your firm, your company].	Avoid these terms or use the *name* of the unit instead.
. . . interview at your earliest convenience.	Avoid or find other words to express the idea.

Tactfully Encourage Action. Because an invitation to interview is the object of the letter, the reader needs to be motivated to extend the invitation. Encouraging action is a delicate matter. The desired action is for the reader to (1) *write a letter* or (2) *place a phone call* inviting you to come for a face-to-face discussion. The choice (write or call) is best left to the employer. Asking for a written response when the employer prefers to call (or vice versa) could result in no response. The goal is to introduce the idea of action without seeming to apologize for doing so and without seeming to be demanding or "pushy." Find *your* words for achieving it, and try to avoid some frequently made errors:

An applicant with strong qualifications need not press forcefully for action.

1. *Setting a date.* "May I have an appointment with you on March 14." Grateful to have any appointment at all, you are better off to let the employer set the date. The date you name could be inconvenient; or even if it is convenient for the employer, your forwardness in setting it could be resented.

2. *Giving permission to call.* "You may call me at 987-6543." By making the call sound like a privilege (*may* call) you could alienate the reader. Implied meaning: You are very selective about the calls you take, but the employer does qualify.

3. *Reporting capability of response.* "You can call me at 987-6543." When a number or address is given, employers are well aware that they are capable of using it (*can* call).

4. *Expressing doubt.* "*If* you agree," "I *hope* you will," and "*should* you decide" use subjunctive words in which your awareness of possible negative results is implied. By showing lack of confidence, you may reduce reader confidence.

5. *Suggesting a one-way conversation.* ". . . when I can talk to you about the job." Use of "*with* you" (instead of "*to* you") implies a two-way conversation.

6. *Sounding overconfident.* "I know you will want to set up an appointment." If the writer doesn't know, the statement is inaccurate; if the writer does know, it seems unnecessary and egotistical.

7. *Sounding apologetic.* "May I take some of your time" or "I know how busy you are" may seem considerate, but the hoped-for interview should be thought of as advantageous to both people involved. Apology is totally out of place in a letter that discusses ways in which the employer *benefits* from hiring you.

If the final paragraph (action ending) of your letter is preceded by paragraphs that are impressive, you need not press hard for a response. Just mentioning the idea of a future discussion is probably sufficient. Compared with the action endings of sales letters, the endings of application letters have less need for forceful statements that define specific action. Surely, an employer who has just finished reading an impressive application would know what to do about it. Forceful statements about *when* and *how* to respond are unnecessary and could arouse resentment.

As closing sentences that refer to an invitation to interview, the following sentences are free of the weaknesses pointed out in preceding illustrations. They are not intended as model sentences that should appear in *your* letter. When the time comes to write your own closing sentence, write it, analyze it carefully, and rewrite it if necessary. Because finding the right job is so important to you, you will be well rewarded for the time and thought invested. Four active endings are critiqued in the following list:

1. *"When a date and time can be arranged, I would like to talk with you."* Passively constructed, "can be arranged" does not indicate *who* will do the arranging. If the work of extending the invitation is performed by an assistant, the employer's part

is fast and easy—just tell the assistant to schedule an interview and inform the applicant. If the employer's needs have been satisfied already or if the letter and resume are not impressive, the date and time for an interview are irrelevant; no action is requested or expected. In the independent clause, "I would like to talk with you," the meeting place and the subject of the conversation are understood.

2. *"I would appreciate an opportunity to discuss the loan officer's job with you."* Reference to action is not direct. If the opportunity arises, it will be as a result of the reader's action. Assuming preceding sentences have not overused "I," use of first person is appropriate. Appreciation is more emphatic when expressed in first person.

3. *With two days' notice, I could meet with you at any hour of your working day.* The indirect reference to action is not forceful; but assuming impressive qualifications, the reader will want an interview and will not need to be pushed. How the notice is given is the reader's choice. Intended to show consideration for the employer's time schedule, "at any hour" could imply an overabundance of free time or even lack of concern for getting the present employer's work done. Yet, the resume will show whether the applicant now has a job. The "two days' notice" could indicate a flexible working schedule. Or the applicant may need time to arrange for a replacement while the interview is being conducted.

4. *"To discuss your employment needs and my production-scheduling experience, I would appreciate an appointment."* When and if the appointment occurs is up to the employer. For an applicant who has had significant experience related to the job and has made that experience a central selling feature, incorporating it into the action ending adds unity and stresses the applicant's strongest qualification. To increase emphasis on the word "experience," the independent clause could be moved to the beginning of the sentence. As the last word in the final paragraph, "experience" would stand out vividly.

Mechanics

Compared with superior qualifications, physical arrangement on a page may seem insignificant. Yet, even before the letter is read, it communicates something about you. If it conveys a negative impression, it may not be read at all. The size, color, and quality of paper influence the readers' reaction; so do margins, letter format, keyboarding, and paragraphing.

Use plain paper for this personal-business letter. Using your present employer's letterhead is unacceptable because you are not representing your employer. If necessary, refer to Appendix A for letter formats and standard and special letter parts. Include your street address and city, state, and ZIP code above the date. Include "Enclosure" a double space below the signature block to alert the employer that a resume is enclosed. The proper letter format is shown in the good examples of application letters in Figures 13-14 and 13-15.

Because the letter will accompany the resume, the paper on which the letter is printed and the envelope must match the paper used for the resume in color, weight, cotton-fiber content, texture, and size. As with the resume, be certain the watermark is positioned so it can be read across the sheet in the same direction as the printing. Refer to the resume format and layout guidelines in Figure 13-7 for exact paper and high-quality printing requirements.

Errors in grammar, spelling, and punctuation are just as damaging in the letter as in the resume. They could imply that you pay little attention to detail, do your work hastily, have shortcomings in basic education, or lack pride or respect. Because the letter represents you and will be thought of as the best you can do, allow yourself time to do it well. Get opinions from others and make revisions where necessary.

Acronyms (such as OSHA and NASA) and abbreviations (such as FDIC and CPA) are sometimes very appropriate; they save space and are well known by businesspeople. An application addressed to a specialist in finance may profitably use CFA (for certified financial analyst), or a letter addressed to an insurance executive could use CLU (for certified life underwriter). Use such space savers only when you are confident they will be understood.

Examples of Application Letters

This section on application letters has given you an opportunity to think *separately* about content, organization, style, and mechanics. Analyzing some *entire letters* will enable you to synthesize, to understand why some practices should be avoided, and to see how principles can be applied. For each letter, (1) read each sentence carefully, (2) identify the principles you think it applies and violates, and (3) read the notation about the sentence. The thinking involved in such letter analysis will pay dividends when you later compose your own letter of application.

The letters in Figures 13-13 and 13-14 are designed to accompany the chronological resume in Figure 13-8. The letter in Figure 13-13 violates many of the principles discussed in this section. For example, it uses clichés and is "I" oriented. In the revision (Figure 13-14), "I" is not entirely eliminated; but it is used less frequently. The letter does not directly restate information that appears on the resume; rather, it attempts to

[1] Omits the sender's address, which is needed because plain paper is used.

[2] Does not address the letter to a specific individual; therefore, the letter is less effective than it could be.

[3] Salutation is impersonal and makes the letter sound like a form letter.

[4] Uses a cliché. [5] Emphasizes "I" by using it as the first word in a sentence.

[6–8] Continue to use "I" in self-oriented sentences. State the obvious but do not relate education or experience specifically to the job at Lincoln Express.

[9] Commendable attempt to interpret experiences as beneficial and related to the job sought. Passes judgment on her own qualifications. Judgment is best left to the employer.

[10] Refers to the resume by stating the obvious but does not call attention to the qualifications listed on the resume.

[11] Uses a cliché in the action ending. Misspells "convenience."

Omits the enclosure notation to alert the employer that a resume is enclosed.

[1] March 30, 19--

[2] Personnel Director
Lincoln Express, Inc.
1785 Lincoln Plaza
Spartanburg, SC 29301-1785

[3] To Whom It May Concern:

[4] Please consider me an applicant for the position in information systems. [5] I am currently a senior at West State University.

[6] Because I am planning a career in information systems, I have declared management and information systems as my major. [7] I have previously worked as a coop student in the information systems of a major corporation. [8] It gave me an opportunity to gain on-the-job experience while still attending classes.

[9] With this background of experience and my information systems major, I feel qualified for the position you advertised. [10] A resume is enclosed.

[11] May I have an interview at your earliest convience.

Sincerely,

Angela Rochelle

Angela Rochelle

FIGURE 13-13   **Poor example of an application letter to accompany a chronological resume**

[1] 3172 West Fourth Street
Tallahassee, FL 32309-3172
March 30, 19--

[2] Mr. Brannon Little
Personnel Director
Lincoln Express, Inc.
1785 Lincoln Plaza
Spartanburg, SC 29301-1785

[3] Dear Mr. Little:

[4] My thorough education and related experience have prepared me for an entry-level position in information systems.

[5] Earning a degree in Management Information Systems has provided me with an in-depth understanding of the field as well as an overall view of the major areas of business. [6] Upper-level courses have given me opportunities for gaining technical proficiency in structured programming, business applications software, and systems design. [7] My experience with Clipper, a major database management system, has involved developing applications and providing user support, including detailed documentation.

[8] Working as a coop student for Central Computer Services exposed me to the information systems operations of a major corporation and allowed me to apply knowledge and skills acquired in the classroom. [9] As part of a technical support group, I worked directly with users to solve both hardware and software problems.

[10] After you have reviewed the enclosed resume, I would welcome a chance to discuss career opportunities with Lincoln Express.

Sincerely,

Angela Rochelle

Angela Rochelle

[11] Enclosure

[1] Includes sender's address because plain paper is used.
[2] Addresses letter to a specific person within the company.
[3] Includes a salutation to a specific addressee.
[4] Identifies the job sought and introduces discussion of applicant's background.
[5] Includes career idea early—to set the applicant apart from others whose interests may be less serious.
[6-7] Lead to a presentation of ways in which skills gained have prepared for a job in information systems.
[8, 9] Point out experiences on the previous job that would be encountered on this job. Use words commonly used in the field; reveal an awareness of qualities essential for success.
[10] Introduces the resume. Uses an action ending without sounding pushy or apologetic. No preference is expressed about whether a call or a letter is expected in response.
[11] Includes enclosure notation to alert the employer that a resume is enclosed.

FIGURE 13-14 Good example of an application letter to accompany a chronological resume

point out ways in which educational and work experiences are directly related to the job being sought.

The letter in Figure 13-15 accompanies the functional resume in Figure 13-11. Note how the letter refers to the job being sought, the applicant's experience, and the enclosed resume without stating the obvious.

From reading the letter of application and the accompanying resume, the employer should be able to see the connection between the applicant's experiences and the job's requirements. That connnection needs
to be emphasized in the letter or the resume. In Figure 13-14, the letter of
application interprets experiences because its accompanying chronological
resume (Figure 13-8) does not.

Look back at the functional resume in Figure 13-11. It does point out

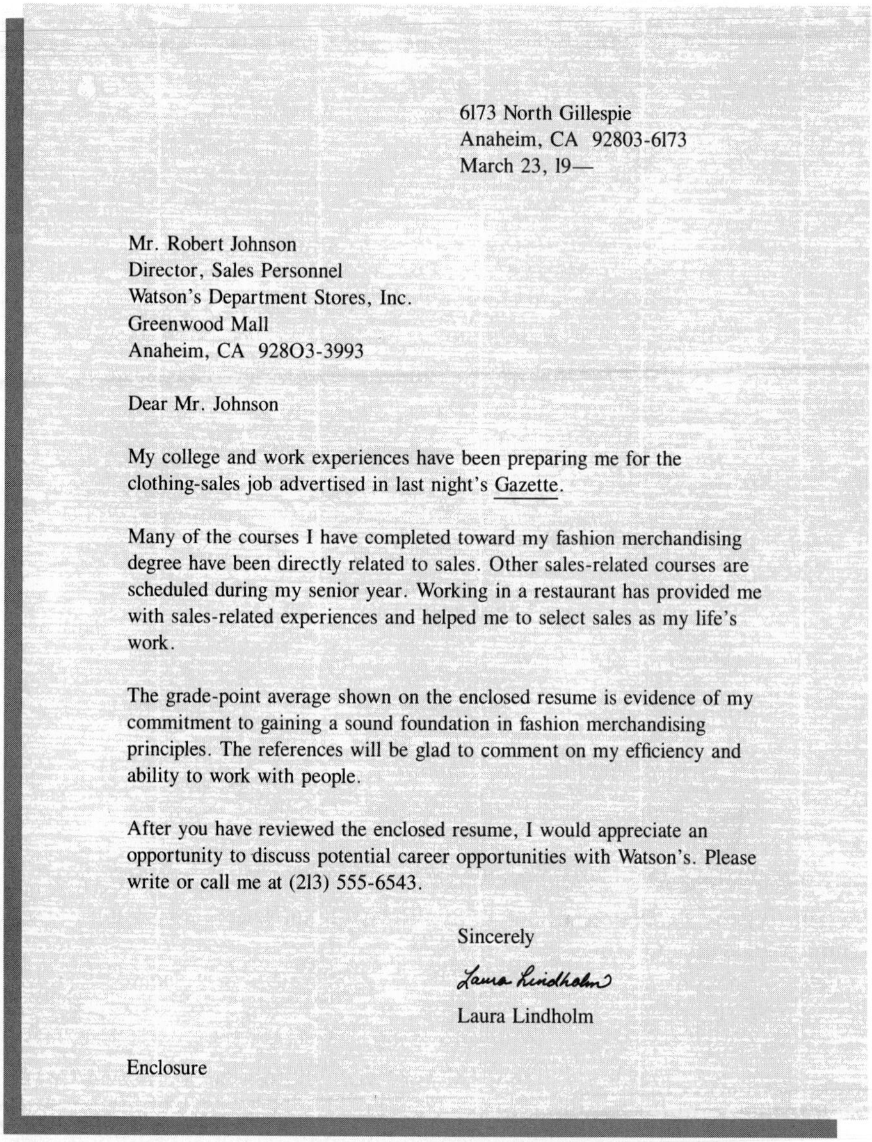

6l73 North Gillespie
Anaheim, CA 92803-6l73
March 23, I9—

Mr. Robert Johnson
Director, Sales Personnel
Watson's Department Stores, Inc.
Greenwood Mall
Anaheim, CA 928O3-3993

Dear Mr. Johnson

My college and work experiences have been preparing me for the
clothing-sales job advertised in last night's Gazette.

Many of the courses I have completed toward my fashion merchandising
degree have been directly related to sales. Other sales-related courses are
scheduled during my senior year. Working in a restaurant has provided me
with sales-related experiences and helped me to select sales as my life's
work.

The grade-point average shown on the enclosed resume is evidence of my
commitment to gaining a sound foundation in fashion merchandising
principles. The references will be glad to comment on my efficiency and
ability to work with people.

After you have reviewed the enclosed resume, I would appreciate an
opportunity to discuss potential career opportunities with Watson's. Please
write or call me at (2l3) 555-6543.

Sincerely

Laura Lindholm

Laura Lindholm

Enclosure

**FIGURE 13-15   Good example of an application letter to accompany a
functional resume**

the commonality of experiences and job requirements. The application letter, therefore, need not do so. The letter (Figure 13-15) identifies the job applied for, gives just enough highlights to generate interest in the resume, refers the reader to it, and makes an allusion to action.

In the resumes and letters illustrated, applicants have high grade-point averages. They suggest willingness to work hard, ability to learn quickly, and (possibly) skill in human relations. Compared with other professions, the accounting profession is reportedly most influenced by a high grade index. The reasoning is that knowledge of accounting principles and techniques is vital, and graduates who have the highest grades will know the most. Because students with 4.0 grade-point averages are sometimes stereotyped as "bookworms" or socially insensitive, such students should present personal information that depicts them as well rounded. The resume or the application letter could—by reporting special interests, activities, and accomplishments—counter the stereotype.

Most students who have a grade average between 2.0 and 3.0 (on a 4.0 scale) choose not to report their grades. Readers (most of whom are likely to be graduates themselves) are well aware that degrees are awarded only to students who have at least a 2.0 average. Applicants who choose not to report grade average can, instead, emphasize noteworthy school activities, offices held, volunteer work, or part-time work.

Either on the resume or in the application letter, students who have earned all (or a portion) of their school expenses are advised to report it. Employers tend to react favorably because they view the activity as evidence of hard work, thrift, organization, and determination.

SUMMARY

Because life's enjoyment is strongly influenced by success on the job, planning and preparing for a career are vital. Like other important decisions, career decisions are preceded by gathering information. Preferably, it is recorded in a career notebook for easy reference.

Ask questions about yourself such as these: What kind of person am I? What are my aptitudes? What have I achieved? What are my interests? Is my education pointed toward a career? About a possible career, ask questions such as these: Is it compatible with my aptitudes and interests? Is the field overcrowded? How much academic preparation is required? What are the rewards? About a specific job in the chosen field, raise questions about duties and responsibilities. Interview people already working at the job. Recording and analyzing results will assist you in selecting a satisfying career and preparing an effective resume.

Like other written documents, resumes and application letters should reflect high standards of content, organization, style, and mechanics. If errors are detected in any of these categories, an interview probably will not be granted.

Chronological resumes use "Education" and "Experience" as headings and list experiences in a time sequence. Functional resumes use functions you can perform or attributes you have as headings. Choose the one you feel most effectively presents your qualifications.

Names and addresses of possible employers may be obtained from career services centers at schools, employers' offices, employment agencies and contractors, help-wanted ads, libraries, and professional organizations.

An application letter accompanies a resume. The purposes are to introduce the applicant and the resume, arouse interest in the information given on the resume, and assist an employer in seeing ways in which the applicant's services would be desirable. As such, it is a persuasive letter—beginning with an attention getter and ending with a reference to action.

Length is influenced by the type of resume. If it is detailed enough to point out ways in which the employer benefits from the applicant's education and experience, the letter can be relatively short. If the resume lists degrees earned and jobs held without pointing out employer benefits, the letter will need to be relatively long.

The major portion of an application letter is devoted to evidence of compatibility between an applicant's qualifications and the employer's job requirements. Employers sometimes appreciate (at least they do not resent) a statement about the source of job information. They are pleased if the letter reveals some familiarity with the company's goals, services, products, or procedures. They react negatively to statements of the obvious, discussion of the applicant's problems, comments about the present employer's shortcomings, bragging, flattery, and a biographical emphasis. The following words are sometimes overused: *applicant, I, interview, opening, position, qualification,* and *vacancy.*

If an impressive background is well presented in the preceding paragraphs, the final paragraphs (action ending) need not be worded forcefully. Sounding neither apologetic nor pushy, it refers to future action. Whether the employer will call or write is left to the employer's preference.

REFERENCES

Barnum, C. M. (1987, September–October). Writing resumes that sell. *Management World,* pp. 10–13.

Baxter, N. (1987, Spring). Resumes, application forms, cover letters, and interviews. *Occupational Outlook Quarterly,* pp. 17–23.

Charles, P. J. (1988, September–October). Resumes without clutter. *Management World,* pp. 19–20.

Holley, W. H., Jr., Higgins, E., & Speights, S. (1988, December). Resumes and cover letters: What do HR managers really want? *Personnel,* pp. 49–51.

Write a resume that works: It's simple: Custom tailor each one to the job. (1990, June). *Changing Times,* pp. 91, 93, 95.

CHECK YOUR WRITING

RESUME

Content
- ☐ Is based on self-, career, and job analyses.
- ☐ Qualifications and requirements seem compatible.
- ☐ Includes only relevant ideas.
- ☐ Presents qualifications truthfully and honestly.

Organization
- ☐ Headings are arranged in appropriate sequence.
- ☐ Significant ideas are in emphathetic position.
- ☐ Experiences are listed consistently, either in time sequence or in order of importance.

Style
- ☐ Omits personal pronouns.
- ☐ Uses action verbs.
- ☐ Uses past tense for previous jobs; present tense for present job.
- ☐ Places significant words in emphatic positions.
- ☐ Uses parallelism in listing multiple items.
- ☐ Uses positive language.
- ☐ Uses simple words (but some jargon of the field is acceptable).
- ☐ Uses correct grammar.

Mechanics
- ☐ Is printed on high-quality (24-pound, 100-percent cotton-fiber content), neutral-colored paper.
- ☐ Is printed with clear, sharp print.
- ☐ Is well balanced on the page.
- ☐ Uses ample margins even if a second page is required.
- ☐ Includes a page number on all pages except the first.
- ☐ Positions headings consistently throughout.
- ☐ Uses an outline format or bullets (asterisks or dashes) to emphasize multiple points.
- ☐ Uses indentation, underlining, capitalization, font changes, and graphic lines and borders to enhance overall impact.
- ☐ Contains *no* typing, grammar, spelling, or punctuation errors.

CHECK YOUR WRITING

APPLICATION LETTER

Content
- ☐ Includes valid ideas (statements are true).
- ☐ From the first sentence, identifies the letter as an application for a certain job.
- ☐ Excludes nonessential ideas.
- ☐ Emphasizes significant qualifications.
- ☐ Makes reference to enclosed resume.
- ☐ Ends with action ending that is neither apologetic nor pushy.

Organization
- ☐ Begins by revealing the job sought in the attention getter.
- ☐ Presents paragraphs in most appropriate sequence (order of importance is possibly best).
- ☐ Ends with a reference to action employer is to take (call or write and extend an invitation to an interview).

Style
- ☐ Uses simple language (no attempt to impress with a sophisticated vocabulary; some professional jargon is justified).
- ☐ Uses relatively short sentences with sufficient variety.
- ☐ Places significant words in emphatic positions.
- ☐ Uses correct grammar.

Mechanics
- ☐ Includes writer's address above the date.
- ☐ Includes equal side margins (approximately one inch).
- ☐ Is well balanced on the page.
- ☐ Is printed on plain paper that matches the resume.
- ☐ Has first and last paragraphs that are relatively short; others are held to fewer than six or seven lines.
- ☐ Contains *no* typing, grammar, spelling, or punctuation errors.

REVIEW QUESTIONS

1. For a college student, what are the advantages of developing a career notebook?
2. If you want to learn about the duties and responsibilities of a certain job, what is a good library source?
3. What headings typically appear in a chronological resume?
4. Five years after graduation, which would probably appear first on a resume: (a) "Education" or (b) "Experience"? Explain.
5. What are the advantages and disadvantages of including personal information on the resume? What criteria are used to select which personal information to include, if any?
6. Under what conditions might you choose to include or not include references on the resume?
7. If you had little or no related experience, which resume would probably be better: (a) chronological or (b) functional? Explain.
8. What are the advantages of using subject-understood sentences in resumes? Action verbs? Crisp phrases? Descriptive but not overly strong adjectives?
9. Discuss five guidelines for formatting an attractive, highly professional resume.
10. List five sources from which prospective employers' names and addresses may be obtained.
11. Should an application letter and a resume contain the same information? Explain.
12. What do application letters and sales letters have in common?
13. In application letters, is flattery appropriate? Are acronyms? Explain.
14. List some words that are frequently overused in application letters.
15. As a sales letter, what action does an application letter seek?

EXERCISES

1. Study the application letter on page 578. As directed by your professor, complete one or more of the following tasks:
   a. Write a sentence-by-sentence critique.
   b. Make a list of ways in which the letter applies and violates principles discussed in this chapter.
   c. Rewrite the letter in a way that overcomes its principal weaknesses.
   d. Be prepared to discuss the letter in class.

April 5, 19—

Halligan Stores, Ltd.
Little Rock, AR 72099

Dear Sirs:

[1] Please consider me as an applicant for the buyer's position you advertized in last nights issue of the Gazette. [2] The primary advantage I would have as a buyer is my heavy educational background. [3] Among the courses I have taken are buyer behavior, retailing, marketing, public relations, and advertizing. [4] I am sure you realize the many ways in which these courses can prepare one for a career in marketing.

[5] In addition to my classes, my educational background includes work in the university bookstore, service on the school yearbook, and president of my fraternity. [6] I will be receiving my degree on May 5, 1993. [7] If you can use an energetic young man with my educational background, I will appreciate you studying the resume which you will find inclosed. [8] May I have an interview at your earliest convience. [9] So I can put my educational background to work for you.

Sincerely,

Eric Kritser

Eric Kritser

Exercise 1

2. Study the application letter on the next page. As directed by your professor, complete one or more of the following tasks:
   a. Write a sentence-by-sentence critique.
   b. Make a list of ways in which the letter applies and violates principles discussed in this chapter.

c. Rewrite the letter in a way that overcomes its principal weaknesses.

d. Be prepared to discuss the letter in class.

Kenneth S. Bender
P.O. Box 2334
Atlanta, GA 30345-2334
March 5, 19—

Mr. Stephen R. Ahlman
Beyer Associates, Inc.
9800 Parkview Avenue
Atlanta, Ga. 30327

[1] Please consider me for the insurance position you advertized in yesterday's paper. [2] As you can see from the attached resume, I have worked for a real estate firm for the last fifteen years. [3] As you know, real estate experience is very similiar to insurance experience.

[4] An insurance man needs (above all else) dependability. [5] He needs to be accurate, courteous, and understanding. [6] He needs to be able to communicate, both orally and written. [7] I have written many letters in connection with my work in real estate. [8] Actually, I do most of the correspondence for the other people in this office. [9] As a student in college, you will observe that I have been exposed to Marshall McLuhan's theories in various courses. [10] I have observed the influence of his thinking in all the writing I do.

[11] While in school (where I compiled a 3.621 average as a business major) I took some very valuable courses in insurance. [12] Work in real estate has kept me in constant contact with insurance matters.

[13] References (and details of my qualifications) are presented in organized form on the enclosed resume which is attached for your convenience. [14] I shall look forward to the opportunity of meeting you personaly and discussing my qualifications.

Sincerely

Kenneth S. Bender

Kenneth S. Bender

Exercise 2

APPLICATIONS

ONAL | **CAREER DEVELOPMENT** | SN
International | Legal | Interperson

1. **Getting Essential Information to Make a Wise Career Decision.** Prepare the career notebook described at the beginning of this chapter. At the top of separate pages, identify major sections: self-analysis, career analysis, job analysis, and interview with career person. Then, seek answers to the questions listed in each of the following categories:
   a. Self-analysis: Figure 13-1.
   b. Career analysis: Figure 13-2.
   c. Job analysis: Figure 13-3.
   d. Interview with a career person: Figure 13-4. Select a person currently working in the career field you have chosen. To validate the information you receive, you may wish to interview two people. Selecting a person who has worked in a particular field but is not currently involved might be more objective (for instance, an accountant in public accounting now working in private industry or teaching accounting).

ONAL | **CAREER DEVELOPMENT** | SN
al | Technology | Public Sector

2. **Preparing a Company/Job Profile.** Use the information obtained from completing Application 1 to prepare a company/job profile for the company/job in which you expect to be interviewing. Begin a new section in your career notebook: COMPANY PROFILE FOR _____ (supply company name). Insert the completed profile in your career notebook. Using Figure 13-5 as a guide, complete these steps:
   a. Review the completed profile and note the degree of compatibility between your qualifications and the company and job requirements.
   b. Compile a list of strengths and weaknesses (lack of a match between your qualifications and job requirements) as they relate to the job requirements.
   c. Consider carefully the deficiencies you must overcome before your qualifications fully match the job requirements. What are possible strategies for overcoming these deficiencies? Are any of these strategies feasible, or is overcoming these deficiencies out of your control?
   d. Analyze the final comparison and decide whether interviewing for this job would be wise.

. | **CAREER DEVELOPMENT** | SMALL
Ethics | International | Lega

3. **Preparing a Resume and an Application Letter for a Job of Your Choice.** Write a resume and an application letter for a job you would like to have. Use the information compiled in Applications 1 and 2 to identify the information that should be included in the resume and the application letter. Make the assumption you prefer:
   a. You are applying for an immediate part-time job.

b. You are applying for a full-time job for next summer.

c. You are applying for a cooperative-education assignment or internship.

d. You are applying for a full-time job immediately after you graduate. Look at the list of courses you plan to take and write as though you had taken them and satisfied the requirements for a degree.

Follow the guidelines presented in this chapter for preparing a resume. As a minimum, incorporate the valid comments of at least two others competent in proofreading and resume design. Use the desktop publishing capability available to you to produce a highly effective, professional document.

Address the application letter to the appropriate individual. After you receive comments from your professor, you can readily revise and mail the resume and letter or retain it until needed. If you had such a letter in your file (preferably stored on computer disk), you could revise it and mail it on short notice.

4. Preparing an Effective Application Letter for a Scholarship. Assume a $1,500 scholarship for students in your major field of study has been advertised in *Business Week.* The money comes from a national honor society in your discipline. The recipient must (a) have a B or higher grade average, (b) have more than 60 hours of college credit, (c) be free to attend a week-long, expenses-paid convention in Houston during the second week of May, and (d) write a satisfactory letter of application. Address your application letter to The Scholarship Foundation, 301 Skinker Boulevard, St. Louis, MO 63155-3038.

AL	CAREER DEVELOPMENT	SMALL
Interpersonal	Technology	Pul

CASES FOR ANALYSIS

Case 1.   Outplaced Workers Need Employment Advice. Flynn Mortgage Corporation has just completed radical reorganization and downsizing; consequently, approximately 50 top- and middle-level managers are seeking employment. Because many of these individuals have been with your company for ten years or more, they are finding the job-search process difficult. To assist these outplaced employees in finding jobs, the board of directors voted to open an Outplacement Center; and you have been hired to direct the center. Your first action was to set up an office with telephones, area newspapers (want ads), and current articles about job search for the use of the job seekers. After interviewing a few of these individuals, you realize they need basic information about preparing job credentials (resume and application letter). Immediately, you begin to develop a handout (flier or pamphlet) presenting concise, informative, and easy-to-follow guidelines for writing job credentials that will win an interview.

HUMAN RESOURCES MANAGEMENT		
erpersonal	Technology	Public S

Required:

1. Conduct needed research to locate relevant, up-to-date information. Cite a number of sources to be certain that your information is objective; use appropriate documentation within the document to protect yourself and your company against plagiarism and to assist the managers in locating your references for further research. Be creative in the way you direct your reader to the bibliography you will provide.

2. Review the research to determine the information that will be relevant to your particular audience. For example, giving guidelines about including high school activities or part-time work during college would be unnecessary to these veteran workers.

3. Write these relevant guidelines using the information gathered in steps 1 and 2.

4. Use desktop publishing capabilities available to you to design a creative, attention-getting layout for this document. Use these page-design layout principles as a guide:

   a. Keep it simple—don't clutter the page with too much information or too many fonts and graphics (lines, boxes, pictures). "Less is more" is a cardinal rule among professionals.

   b. When varying the typeface for emphasis (italics, bold, underline), keep the varied portions short for maximum effectiveness.

   c. Use plenty of white space to give the eye a break and to make the page more appealing to the reader.

   d. Don't use text lines that are too long for the eye to follow. Shortening the line of writing also opens up the page with more white space.

   e. Do not justify the right margin; use a ragged right margin to open up the page and create a friendly appearance.

   f. Use lines, boxes, or shaded areas to emphasize particular items, to add spark, and to organize the page.

HUMAN RESOURCES MANAGEMENT

| erpersonal | Technology | Public S |

Case 2. Preparing a Resume for an Outplaced Employee. As the director of the Outplacement Center for Flynn Mortgage Corporation, you help outplaced employees prepare professional resumes that reflect their abilities. Today, you are preparing a resume for Gregory De Angelo, who left the following narrative of his qualifications with you. He is interested in securing a position as a senior loan officer in a major banking firm.

EMPLOYMENT INFORMATION

Gregory De Angelo, 8901 Brookdale Road, Pueblo, CO 81002-8901.

Personal data: 38 years old, divorced, two children (John 8, Jeanne 5), 6'4" tall, in excellent health (wear glasses and hearing aid). Exercise regularly, primarily racquetball and lifting weights. Also enjoy golf.

I received a Bachelor of Science in Business at Westbrook University in May of 1975. My major was Finance and Real Estate; my overall grade-point average was 3.6. While in college, my activities included: Phi Kappa Phi, Beta Gamma Sigma, Dean's list for four semesters, recipient of the Du Bois Foundation Scholarship (awarded to outstanding finance majors), intramural football and tennis, president of the Student Association, Who's Who Among Students in American Colleges and Universities, Hall of Fame, president of the Banking and Finance Association. I graduated in the top 10 percent of a class of 100 at Blair High School in Pueblo, Colorado, in 1971.

My employment history includes the following: (1) Teller at Saguaro Bank during summers of 1972–74. I worked 20 hours per week and was promoted from Teller I to Teller III. (2) Completed a one-semester internship (gained three hours' credit toward degree) at Sunbelt Bank from September to December 1974. Selection process was very competitive. My primary responsibilities were to assist the branch manager and approve small consumer loans. (3) Commercial Loan Officer, Flynn Mortgage Corporation from June 1975 to November 1992. My duties included managing a $25 million loan portfolio, making substantial credit decisions for loans averaging $800,000 each, and striving to achieve realistic lending goals. I also arranged loans for various types of clients (importers and exporters, wholesalers, and manufacturers) with tremendous sales. Completed Flynn's intensive training program for commercial loan officers, which required me to pass an intermediate accounting examination before being admitted and to pass an arduous loan officer's examination when I finished.

Currently I volunteer as a Little League baseball coach (ages 6–8) and as a Boy Scout troop leader (ages 10–12).

The following individuals have agreed to provide additional information about my qualifications: (1) Paul J. Bryant, Head Teller, Saguaro Bank, 905 Courtland Drive, Pueblo, CO 81002-0905; (2) Ellyn Broome, Vice President, Sunbelt Bank, 3900 Central Avenue, Ft. Collins, CO 80521-3900; (3) James L. Hawthorne, Vice President of Commercial Loans, Flynn Mortgage Corporation, 2500 North Mesquite Drive, Pueblo, CO 81002-3728; (4) Cynthia M. Buntyn, Flynn Mortgage Corporation, same address as given above; (5) Rev. Joseph E. Kerns, Faith Church of Pueblo, 3710 Friar Lane, Pueblo, CO 81002-3710; and (6) Richard G. De Angelo, President, Chamber of Commerce, 9310 Commerce Street, Pueblo, CO 81002-9310.

Required:
1. Review the narrative and consider answers to the following questions:
   a. What is Gregory's career objective?
   b. What infonmation is relevant to Gregory's career objective?

    c. Has essential information been omitted? (Supply fictitious information if needed.)

    d. Which resume type would most effectively present Gregory's qualifications: chronological, functional, or combination chronological and functional? Explain.

    e. Would a "Summary of Qualifications" section strengthen Gregory's resume? Explain.

    f. Should Gregory list his references on the resume or state that a list is available? Should he prepare a separate references page? Which of the references are the most appropriate references (assuming all will provide positive recommendations)?

2. Prepare Gregory's resume (and references page if necessary) referring to the analysis prepared in step 1 and following the guidelines presented in this chapter. Incorporate the valid comments made by at least two others competent in proofreading and resume design. Use the desktop publishing capability available to you to produce a highly effective, professional document.

JOB INTERVIEWS, EMPLOYMENT MESSAGES, AND PERFORMANCE APPRAISALS

OBJECTIVES

When you have completed Chapter 14, you should be able to

- ◆ Participate in a variety of interview situations as both an interviewer and an interviewee.

- ◆ Reinforce your knowledge of the job-search process.

- ◆ Prepare effective answers to questions often asked in job interviews.

- ◆ Write other letters related to employment.

YOKO SITS IN THE RECEPTION AREA of the office. She has arrived a few minutes early for her interview to allow herself time to unwind and focus on what she will say. Although she feels confident, she is a little nervous; but she relaxes when she thinks of how well-prepared she is. She has researched the company and knows about its operations. In addition, she has rehearsed the interview, reviewing a list of possible questions. She has reviewed her resume to be able to answer any questions about it that may come up. And finally, she has chosen to wear a simple, conservative business suit so her interviewer will see her as a serious, professional candidate for the job. Yoko knows that her interviewer may conduct the interview in a number of ways: formally or informally, structured or unstructured. She is prepared for any of these formats. When the interviewer comes out to the reception area to greet her, she is ready with a smile and a firm handshake, certain that the interview will be a success.

Does the idea of a job interview cause you anxiety as it does many people? With some preparation and practice, you can be a successful interviewee or interviewer. In addition to the obvious oral communication skills you need for these tasks, you must possess impeccable writing skills for thank-you letters, acceptance letters, rejection letters, and requests for recommendations. Lack of preparation and poor communication skills cannot be hidden in an interview situation. Interviews allow you to "sell" yourself to a prospective employer; do not let carelessness cost you an important "sale."

TYPES OF INTERVIEWS

Interviews are interpersonal communication (see Chapter 1).

Interviewers and interviewees may meet for a variety of purposes: for hiring, firing, teaching, evaluating and appraising job performance, exchanging factual information, attempting to solve personal problems, or handling customer complaints. Here are examples of interview twosomes:

Seller and prospective buyer

Employment interviewer and job prospect

Marketing researcher and product buyer

Political pollster and voter

Employee and supervisor or in-service training director

Client and accountant, financial adviser, loan officer, lawyer, or computer consultant

Doctor and patient

Police officer and traffic violator

Newsmaker and reporter

Talk-show host and celebrity guest

Interviews fall into several broad categories based on their purposes. Within each category, interviews may be further classified by subject.

Employment Interviews

The employment interview will be of special importance to you. As a special category, it combines several interview purposes. It also involves the interviewer's goal of selecting someone who matches the employer's work needs and will fit effectively into the organization.

Review Chapter 2 for a refresher on listening.

Informational Interviews

Informational interviews are essentially fact-oriented meetings. In a doctor-patient meeting, the patient reveals information, which the doctor processes as part of the diagnostic function. The patient obtains information from the doctor about how to treat the diagnosed condition. Even though the exchange is primarily factual, both participants must listen for both *facts and feelings*.

Sales or Persuasive Interviews

Talk to many salespeople and you'll find that interviewing is the lifeblood of their business. Depending on the nature of the product or service offered, a salesperson may also have to be a problem solver for the potential customer. The appeals used in sales interviews are the same as those used in sales letters.

The key to persuasion in interviewing is in accepting, challenging, and rebutting the other person's arguments. Keep in mind that arguments are not quarrels; arguments involve exchanges of opinion and facts with each party attempting to win. If winning means making a sale, or in the case of a resistant buyer avoiding a purchase, that is the goal. Here are some suggestions:

1. Listen to detect a difference of opinion or an objection.
2. Restate the objectionable item in your own words. Debaters claim that such paraphrasing often causes the objection to sound less convincing. When you provide this feedback, the listener is able to analyze his or her own statements.
3. Use facts as evidence. Facts are provable items; misrepresentation can't be backed by facts.
4. In persuasive interviews, keep cool, don't raise your voice, don't rub it in when you win, and lose gracefully when you lose—your turn will come.

COMMUNICATION MENTOR

No matter what the setting or purpose for an interview, ground rules are important. The most essential of these revolve around the issue of privacy. A "zone of privacy" should be established between the parties in conversation either prior to an interview or as it develops, depending on the wishes of the person being interviewed.

The parties should understand at any given time in the interview what subjects (ethnic background, marketing strategies) are completely off limits and which may be discussed in general but not in detail (salary history, competitive advantages). In an employment interview, for example, privacy is far more easily established in advance than in a journalistic interview, where it should be established and re-established throughout.

We are not speaking only of personal privacy (self, family) but of organizational privacy (company, group) as well. Even if the interview is between friendly parties, the friendliness of parties privy to the contents of the interview over time should not be assumed.

Wherever there are sensitive issues to be discussed in any interview, you are not being paranoid to expect privacy for yourself and your firm.

James F. Hurley
Senior Vice President
CalFed Inc.

TYPES OF EMPLOYMENT INTERVIEWS

Depending on the goals of the interviewer, interviews may follow a formal structure or be allowed to take their own course. Both structured and unstructured interviews can be intentionally stressful—called "stress interviews."

Structured and Computer-Assisted Interviews

In structured interviews, the interviewer follows a predetermined agenda, including a checklist of items or a series of questions and statements designed to elicit the necessary information or interviewee reaction.

One type of structured interview is conducted by a computer. Companies are finding computer-assisted interviews to be a reliable and effective way to conduct preliminary job interviews. Applicants use a computer to provide answers to a list of carefully selected questions. Because expert computer systems can overcome some of the inherent problems

Computer-assisted interviews overcome typical human interviewer errors.

with traditional face-to-face interviews, the overall quality of the selection process improves. Typical human interviewer errors include forgetting to ask important questions, talking too much, being reluctant to ask sensitive questions, forming unjustified negative first impressions, obtaining unreliable and illegal information that makes an applicant feel judged, and using interview data ineffectively.

Research has shown that applicants prefer computer interviews to human interviews. They respond more honestly to a computer and are less likely to provide polite, socially acceptable responses (Mitchell, 1990).

By reviewing the comprehensive report generated by the computer, the human interviewer can reliably and quickly decide whether to invite the applicant for a second interview and identify the specific information that must be obtained from the applicant during a second interview.

The computer report contains standard, reliable information about each applicant, alerts the human interviewer to any contradictory responses (e.g., applicant indicated he was terminated for absenteeism but later indicated that he thought his former employer would give him an outstanding recommendation), highlights any potential problem areas (for example, applicant responded that he would remain on the job less than a year), and generates a list of structured interview questions for the human interviewer to ask (for example, "Mary, you said you feel your former employer would rate you average. Why don't you feel it would be higher?").

In light of the high costs of interviewing and the importance of selecting employees matched to the job, more and more companies will be using computer-assisted interviewing to screen applicants (Mitchell, 1990). Regardless of whether the interview is face-to-face or computer assisted, provide objective, truthful evidence of your qualifications as they relate to specific job requirements.

> **What types of information does the computer-generated interview report provide?**

> **Computer-assisted interviewing is an effective way to improve employee selection.**

Unstructured Interviews

Unstructured interviews are freewheeling exchanges and may shift from one subject to another, depending on the interests of the participants. Some experienced interviewers are able to make a structured interview seem like an unstructured one. The goal of many unstructured interviews is to explore unknown areas in search of new ideas.

Stress Interviews

Stress interviews are designed to place the interviewee in an anxiety-producing situation so an evaluation of the interviewee's performance under stress may be made.

In all cases, interviewees should attempt to assess the nature of the interview quickly and adjust behavior accordingly. As the following discussion of the role of the interviewer reveals, you, as an interviewee, can perform much better when you understand the interviewer's purpose.

> **Some interviewees create their own stress.**

JOB INTERVIEWER'S ROLE

The success of any interview depends on the communication skills of the participants and how strongly each wants to practice them. As a guide, the following four steps apply to almost all interviewing and vary with the types of interviews:

An interview: The ultimate in interpersonal communication.

◆ Preparation
◆ Interchange
◆ Evaluation
◆ Action

Preparing for the Interview

Preparation may be the most neglected of the four steps, yet it may be the most important. Preparation involves the following elements:

1. *Purpose.* What is the purpose of the interview? What are the expected outcomes? What style is most appropriate, and what atmosphere is best—relaxed or stressful?
2. *Physical arrangements.* Is the physical setup consistent with the purpose? Is privacy adequate? What distractions should be eliminated?
3. *Self-understanding.* Does the interviewer have an awareness of his or her own strengths and weaknesses, prejudices, biases, perceptions, and other possible barriers to effective communication?
4. *Understanding the other.* What is known or should be known about the interviewee? What are her or his values, aspirations, motives, and background?

Through effective preparation, the interviewer can set the stage for whatever kind of interview is desired. If the interview is to be structured, have items to be discussed been arranged in proper sequence? Will the nature of the questions elicit information-revealing responses? Will the sequence lead to a relaxed interview or to a stressful one?

When you, as a job applicant, plan for your interview, keep in mind that most personnel interviewers have probably gone through these preparatory steps. This reminder will help you determine the interview style, so you can adapt your behavior appropriately.

Meeting Face to Face—The Interchange

During the interview, both the interviewer and the interviewee should pay particular attention to the following factors:

Does a first impression last long?

1. *Rapport.* How well have you reached a common ground to establish a climate consistent with the purpose of the meeting? Does an air of mutual respect exist?

2. *Flexibility*. Can the interviewer redirect the flow of discussion when it strays from the purpose and disrupts the original plan?

3. *Two-way flow*. Are the participants engaged in two-way communication, or is one or the other turning it into a one-way situation?

As either the interviewer or the interviewee, you can become far more effective than the usual participant if you develop some simple techniques for providing feedback and for clarifying issues. Listening in the classroom, for example, is relatively easy to do because you assume a listening role as your primary activity. In an interview, however, you will be both a listener and a speaker; and some of your listening time will be spent preparing what you will say when it is your turn to speak.

Interviewing as a process is much like ordinary one-to-one conversation, differing primarily in the higher degree of tension that normally goes with interviewing. Thus, you should work to make your transition from listener to speaker as smooth as possible. If you haven't listened thoroughly enough to understand completely, your response to the other person will probably be inadequate. Effective, active listening involves mental concentration and good physical posture. Listening is not a passive activity as many people believe.

Questioning is one technique used by good conversationalists and interview participants to gain more information before making a complete response. Questioning can also encourage a shy person to participate more fully.

An example of a question to get more information:

Applicant: I had no idea I would be promoted so quickly.
Interviewer: What qualities do you think led to your promotion?

A question to clarify word meaning:

Applicant: Your answer is somewhat nebulous.
Interviewer: What exactly do you mean? (*Hint:* nebulous = unclear.)

A question to seek feelings:

Applicant: Then I was promoted to a job I didn't like.
Interviewer: How did you adjust to that?

Questions are effective forms of feedback and tend to keep the interview moving when it might otherwise fall flat. *Direct* questions can be answered easily and briefly. They ask for "yes" or "no" answers or for factual information. "Do you like to fly?" "When will you graduate?" "Have you traveled overseas?" Because they call for factual information, direct questions don't help much in encouraging the dialogue of the interview. *Indirect* questions, however, do contribute to dialogue because they call for answers that require thought on the part of the receiver. "Why do you believe accounting is the career for you?" "What experience have you had in working as part of a team or group?"

Feedback makes the interview!

The interviewer received clarification of the meaning.

Questions or statements are often a form of paraphrasing—restating the content or the intent of the sender's message to check your own understanding.

Applicant: My resume shows that I was actively involved in college student groups.

Interviewer: These activities must have provided an excellent opportunity to meet people.

Applicant: Yes, these activities provided me opportunities to interact with people of all types and to develop leadership skills.

We use the techniques of questioning and paraphrasing most of the time in conversation. The thoughtful use of these techniques can contribute much to interviewing situations and to two-way flow.

Evaluating the Interview

Decision-making time arrives at the interview. Is the interviewer prepared to analyze alternative actions? Should the decision be made or postponed? Should the interviewee be invited for further interviews? Should the interviewee be told a letter will be sent at a later time? The interviewer should know what action to take simply because arriving at some kind of decision or outcome was considered in the preparation step. Does each of the two participants know exactly what is to be done? Has a mutual understanding been developed?

Should an interviewee ask, "What happens next?"

Some Interviewer Guidelines

The interviewee should be told the interviewer's guidelines because they can help both parties in the meeting. If the interviewer plans to take notes during the interview, for example, the interviewee must be forewarned. Otherwise, the interviewee might freeze when the interviewer takes notes. On the other hand, if notes are not made, the job applicant in a personnel interview might feel that he or she is not receiving fair consideration. The interviewer should introduce the note-taking idea with a statement such as: "I like to take a few notes during the interview to jog my memory later and to make sure we cover everything we should. We can also use them near the end of the interview to make sure your comments and my understanding are in agreement. Do you mind?" Following agreement, note taking will not be a barrier of consequence, particularly if the notes are not considered secret and if they are for the interviewer's use only. Even leaving the notes in a visible place will help assure the interviewee. Of course, the interviewer can always add personal impressions to the notes after the interviewee leaves.

The interviewer can help establish the style of the interview by proper use of voice tone and volume. A friendly tone may put the applicant at ease. A harsh, aggressive tone may frighten the applicant and result in a stressful situation. In the same way, the interviewer can set the stage for a relaxed or stressful interview simply by organizing questions. Asking the most difficult question first, for example, may throw the applicant into a frenzied state. Body posture is also an important element. By paying attention through eye contact and by appearing interested through the use of acknowledging head motions and a general body posture indicating concern, the interviewer has a better opportunity to pursue the goals of the interview.

These guidelines have much to do with the effectiveness of the interview, but the kinds of questions asked can determine its success or failure. Questions that can be answered with a simple "yes" or "no" don't contribute much and may leave interviewees in a position of having to stray from the subject to put themselves in a better light. Questions that ask how or why provide openings for genuine discussion.

Some of these techniques must be practiced by both participants.

Interviewer Prohibitions

Interviewers must describe all working conditions to any job applicant. The applicant then must decide whether he or she is willing and able to meet those conditions. In addition, interviewers need to know if the applicant can do the job, is willing to do the job, and will fit in with others in the company.

In seeking answers to these questions, interviewers sometimes ask questions that invade the applicant's privacy and that violate the Equal Employment Opportunity Commission (EEOC) and Fair Employment Practices Guidelines. These EEOC guidelines prohibit discriminatory hiring based on race, creed, color, sex, national origin, handicap, and age. For example, turning down an applicant for any of the following reasons is illegal:

- Customers do not want to deal with a particular gender or ethnic group or a handicapped person.
- Coworkers might object.
- The position requires travel with members of the opposite sex.
- Working hours are unusual.
- Restroom facilities are lacking.
- Offering a lower salary than is offered to other applicants of equivalent background.

Interviewers must not introduce questions or information that might lead to discriminatory hiring. Access to such information could be used as evidence against the company in the case of litigation even if the information were not used in the hiring process.

To ensure fairness, interviewers should be absolutely certain that all questions and comments are relevant to the job for which the applicant is

Discuss at least three consequences of asking illegal interview questions.

being considered. If a question is not job related, it may not be legal; therefore, it should not be asked. Fairness of questions may vary depending on the job requirements. For example, the arrest/conviction record of a police officer could be highly relevant to the job; but the same information could be illegal for a person applying for a job as an engineer (Hunt & Eadie, 1987).

In general, the following subjects should not be introduced during an interview or during the small talk that precedes or follows an interview:

Avoid these illegal interview questions.

1. *Ethnic background.* "You have an unusual accent; where were you born?" "What religious holidays will require you to miss work?" "What is your immigration status?"
2. *Age.* "I see you attended Central State University; what years were you there?" "Could you provide a copy of your birth certificate?"
3. *Handicap.* "Do you have any problems with your eyesight or hearing?" "Can you manage a long flight of stairs?"
4. *Health.* "What is your general state of health?" "Have you ever had a major illness?" "Have you ever been treated by a psychiatrist?"
5. *Height and weight.* "Do you realize a more athletic person is usually hired for this job?"
6. *Marital status.* "Are you married?" "Who is going to watch your children if you come to work for us?" "Do you plan to have children?" "How many?" "Is your spouse employed?" "Do you realize that this job requires a great deal of travel and may require you to relocate?"
7. *Arrests/convictions.* "Have you ever been arrested other than for traffic violations? If so, explain." (Some states allow questions about convictions but not arrests.)
8. *Financial situation.* "Do you own your own home, rent, or live with your parents?" "How long have you lived at your present address?"
9. *Alcohol or drug use.* "Do you drink alcoholic beverages?" "Do you use or have you used drugs?"

James Nunan, vice president of human resources at SCICON Systems, a software company in Palo Alto, California, believes that most of today's managers may ask illegal questions accidentally, not purposely (Jenks, 1988). However, in view of increasing litigation and the court's decisive stand on discriminatory hiring, interviewers must be certain they are up to date on employment law. In addition, job applicants (especially those seeking jobs in high-market demand areas) who are well-informed about employment law will not tolerate such questions.

Following the guidelines discussed here will assure that the interviewer is thoroughly prepared for the interview. No matter how casual or how formal the interview may seem to be, you can be sure that considerable effort went into planning it. Obviously, interviews can never be identical.

Participants change as a result of each interview experience, and each experience gives them greater self-confidence. Competent interviewing is one of the most satisfying and rewarding management skills.

JOB INTERVIEWEE'S ROLE

Just as the interviewer proceeds through a step-by-step process, so should the interviewee. As the interviewee, you will want to engage in some pre-interview activities, prepare to perform well during the interview, and take appropriate action after the interview.

College students generally schedule on-campus interviews with representatives from various business organizations. Following the on-campus interviews, successful candidates often are invited for further interviews on the company premises. The purpose of the second interview is to give executives and administrators, other than the personnel interviewer, an opportunity to appraise the candidate. Whether on campus or on company premises, interview methods and practices apply to the situation. When the interview is with company executives, the candidate will probably encounter a wide variety of interview styles. Preliminary planning can pay rich dividends.

Preparing for the Interview

Pre-interview planning involves learning something about the company or organization, doing some studying about yourself, and making sure your appearance and mannerisms will not detract from the impression you hope to make.

Study the Company. Nothing can hurt the candidate more than knowing little about the organization. No knowledge probably indicates insincerity, and the interviewer doesn't want to waste precious interview time providing the candidate with information that should have been gathered long before.

Those with publicly traded stock are required to publish annual reports. Many business-school libraries have a file of annual reports and several financial service reports. Other information can be obtained from brokerage houses, from periodicals, and from financial newspapers. Employees of the company or other students who have been interviewed may be of particular help to the interviewee. Some major schools have prepared videotape interviews with various company recruiters and make the tapes available to students. Attempt to prepare a guide similar to that shown in Figure 14-1 for each company with which you interview. Place the guide in your career notebook.

Use your public library, too.

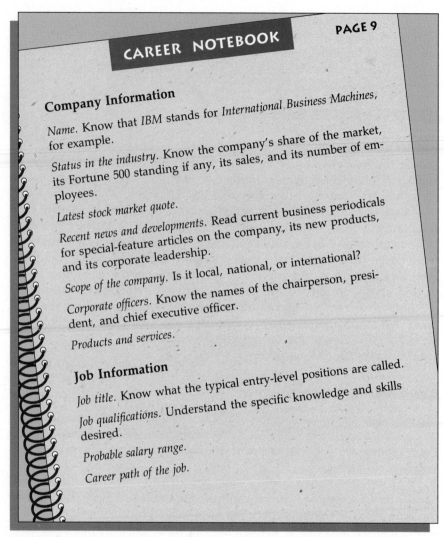

CAREER NOTEBOOK   PAGE 9

Company Information

Name. Know that IBM stands for *International Business Machines,* for example.

Status in the industry. Know the company's share of the market, its Fortune 500 standing if any, its sales, and its number of employees.

Latest stock market quote.

Recent news and developments. Read current business periodicals for special-feature articles on the company, its new products, and its corporate leadership.

Scope of the company. Is it local, national, or international?

Corporate officers. Know the names of the chairperson, president, and chief executive officer.

Products and services.

Job Information

Job title. Know what the typical entry-level positions are called.

Job qualifications. Understand the specific knowledge and skills desired.

Probable salary range.

Career path of the job.

FIGURE 14-1   Interviewee's guide for studying a company

Study Yourself.   When you know something about the company, you'll also know something about the kinds of jobs or training programs the company has to offer. Next, review your answers to the company/job profile (Figure 13-5). This systematic comparison of your qualifications with the company and job requirements helped you identify pertinent information (strengths or special abilities) to be included in your resume; it also will help you prepare for the employment interview. If you can't see a relationship between you and the job or company, you won't be able to demonstrate the interest or sincerity needed to sell yourself.

COMMUNICATION MENTOR

If a time-pressed business executive has granted you an interview, you should feel obligated to do enough preparatory work to make the interview meaningful. Research the industry and history of the business. Know some of the issues facing the company or its constituents. Have a few questions prepared that indicate you've done your homework.

Cynthia Pharr
President & CEO
Tracy-Locke/Pharr Public Relations

Plan Your Appearance. An employment interviewer once said that if the job applicant did not meet her *extremities* test, the interview might as well not take place. She went on to explain that the extremities were the candidate's fingernails, hair, and shoes. The fingernails had to be clean and neat, the shoes shined, or at least clean, and the hair clean and well groomed. Long hair on men met the standard, incidentally, if clean and well groomed. The interviewer felt that if the candidate did not take care of those items, the candidate could not really be serious about, or fit into, her organization. Another interviewer turned down an otherwise outstanding applicant because the applicant could not look him in the eye when he answered a question. Interviewers, like everyone else, are subject to personal perceptions and biases.

In terms of appearance, the applicant should

◆ Be as clean and well groomed as possible.
◆ Wear appropriate footwear.
◆ Select appropriate clothes for the interview.

For specific guidelines, read articles and books in current magazines. Talk with professors in your field, professors of professional protocol (business etiquette), personnel at the career services center, and graduates who have recently acquired jobs in your field.

If you must, borrow clothes from a friend. Research the company dress code—real or implied—ahead of time. And remember that if you *look* and *dress* like the people who already work at the company, the interviewer will be able to visualize your working there. Your college placement officer may be able to provide helpful hints.

Plan Your Time. One of the worst things you can do is be late for an interview. Another is to miss the interview entirely. Therefore, plan your time so you will arrive early. This planning allows you to unwind and

Many companies have "images" to maintain—Do you fit?

COMMUNICATION MENTOR

Go to the interview with a clear view of your objective.
If you are unfocused in career direction or unsure of your abilities, use family, friends, and career counselors to help you make decisions. Using a business interview to try to set basic career direction is a waste of both your time and the interviewer's.

Cynthia Pharr
President & CEO
Tracy-Locke/Pharr Public Relations

mentally review the things you plan to accomplish. At the same time, don't just sit in a waiting room making yourself nervous. Move around some to stay relaxed. But by *all* means, be on time. If something should happen to prevent your doing so, telephone an apology.

Meeting Face to Face—The Interchange

Now that you have gone through the planning stages, you are ready for the interview. Your job is to sell yourself so successfully that you are invited to proceed to the next step in the hiring process. If the first step were an on-campus interview, the next step would be an interview with company executives. You should not expect to receive a firm job offer in the first interview, but one may be made.

Repeating the interviewer's name will help you remember it.

Opening Formalities.   When you meet the interviewer, use the interviewer's name if you are sure you know how to pronounce it correctly. You may ask how to pronounce the name if necessary. Even if the interviewer calls you by your first name, always use the interviewer's surname unless specifically invited to do otherwise. Usually, the interviewer will initiate the handshake, although you may do so. In either case, apply a firm handshake. You don't want to leave the impression that you are weak or timid. At the same time, you don't want to overdo the firm grip and leave an impression of being overbearing. Once the introduction is over, wait for the interviewer to invite you to be seated. These common courtesies—using the correct name, applying a firm handshake, and waiting to be seated—can contribute to a favorable first impression. Use your body language to add to that impression. Sit erect with a slight forward lean to express interest. Avoid slouching, chewing gum, and fidgeting—none will help your image.

The interviewer will begin the conversation and effectively set the

Projecting a confident, mentally alert impression through your speech and appearance from the moment you walk into an interview is vital because most interview decisions are made in the first four minutes. Be prepared to provide quick, intelligent responses to questions about your education and experiences that required you to apply skills learned in the classroom.

stage for the interview. You might expect either some nonbusiness talk or a direct opening into the business of the interview.

A positive or negative impression is created during the first four minutes of an interview; this impression often determines, albeit unconsciously, the outcome of the interview. You should be able to determine quickly whether the interview will be structured or unstructured, nonstressful or stressful.

During these early minutes, make appropriate eye contact with the interviewer and be conscious of the nonverbal messages the two of you are sending. Some professional interviewers may look out the window while you are talking, stand up and stretch, or do other things early to detect your reaction. You can usually tell whether these actions are genuine; quite probably, they are acts. Retain your composure!

Can you smile under pressure?

As you proceed into the interview, keep in mind the barriers to communication in interviews shown in Figure 14-2. These barriers were revealed by a survey of 164 employment interviewers after they had interviewed undergraduate seniors at a major state university (Golen & Lynch, 1987).

Interviewing Guidelines. Much of the information about you will appear on your resume or company application form, already available to the interviewer. Thus, the interviewer most likely will seek to go beyond such things as your education, work experience, and extracurricular activities and will attempt to assess your attitudes toward work and the probability of fitting you successfully into the organization.

Know your resume thoroughly. It's a source for interviewer questions.

Rank	Barrier
1	Tendency not to listen
2	Lack of credibility
3	Lack of interest in subject discussed
4	Hostile attitudes
5	Use of profanity
6	Poor organization of ideas
7	Resistance to change
8	Know-it-all attitude
9	Lack of trust
10	Lack of feedback

FIGURE 14-2   Rank order of interview communication barriers

The best way to prepare for the interview discussion is to study the company and yourself. In addition, you can prepare to answer questions such as those listed in Figure 14-3. Having thoughtfully answered such questions *before* the interview, you can give smooth and confident answers *during* the interview. Practice by having a friend ask you these difficult questions.

Your education is your *major asset* if you are a student. You should point out its relationship to the job for which you are being considered. Even more important, the fact that you have succeeded in school indicates that you have the ability to learn. Because most companies expect you to learn something on the job, your ability to learn and thus to become productive quickly may be your greatest asset. So your most important response to the interviewer's questions may be about your ability to learn. Even lack of work experience may be an asset: You have acquired no bad work habits that you will have to unlearn!

Your *interpersonal skill*—getting along with others—may be an important attribute. What did you do in college that helped you get along with others? Were you a member, an officer, or president of an organization? What did you accomplish? How did others perceive you? Were you a leader? The extracurricular activities listed on your resume give an indication of these traits, but how you talk about them in your interview helps. "I started as corresponding secretary and was subsequently elected to higher office for four semesters, eventually becoming president" may be a statement that proves your leadership qualities. If at the same time your organization went on to greater heights, all the more power to you.

Humility pays off in all interviews. If you are being interviewed by a representative of General Motors, don't suggest that you can turn the company around. A candidate for the presidency of a university was not considered further when he said he could turn the university around; the

Do you have special training or out-of-the-ordinary background?

Can humility and confidence be combined?

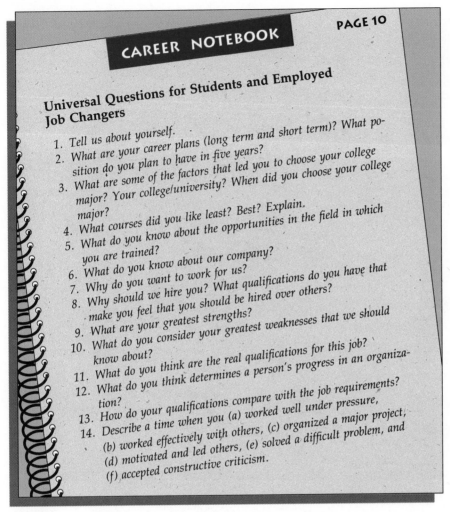

CAREER NOTEBOOK | **PAGE 10**

Universal Questions for Students and Employed Job Changers

1. Tell us about yourself.
2. What are your career plans (long term and short term)? What position do you plan to have in five years?
3. What are some of the factors that led you to choose your college major? Your college/university? When did you choose your college major?
4. What courses did you like least? Best? Explain.
5. What do you know about the opportunities in the field in which you are trained?
6. What do you know about our company?
7. Why do you want to work for us?
8. Why should we hire you? What qualifications do you have that make you feel that you should be hired over others?
9. What are your greatest strengths?
10. What do you consider your greatest weaknesses that we should know about?
11. What do you think are the real qualifications for this job?
12. What do you think determines a person's progress in an organization?
13. How do your qualifications compare with the job requirements?
14. Describe a time when you (a) worked well under pressure, (b) worked effectively with others, (c) organized a major project, (d) motivated and led others, (e) solved a difficult problem, and (f) accepted constructive criticism.

FIGURE 14-3   Frequently asked tough interview questions

university was already successful. Incidentally, he had been president of another university for only six months and claimed he had turned that university around. Obviously, the candidate hadn't become familiar with the problems of the university. He had failed to take even the first step toward a successful interview: Study the company.

"*Why do you want to work for us?*" is really not a difficult question to handle if you do some planning. In addition to your study of the company from the literature, you can usually locate someone who works for the company to tell you about it. You can sometimes visit a local office of the firm, as well. Then you can make a favorable impression simply by referring to the people you have talked with about the working conditions,

Get across the idea of "I like your company."

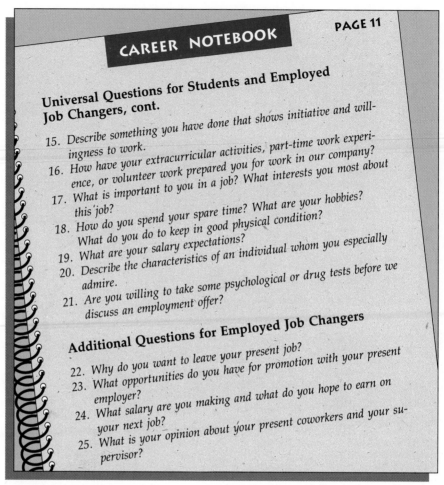

FIGURE 14-3, continued

company achievements, and career paths. You'll also show you are strongly interested in the company and not just taking an interview for practice. The interviewer not only attempts to develop an impression of you but also evaluates you in comparison with others being interviewed for the position. Your responses can indicate your sincere interest in getting a job with this company rather than just any company.

Your response to inquiries about why you should be hired will be a composite of some of the things already discussed. You have the proper education, you have proved you have the ability to learn, and you are enthusiastic about working for the company. If you really understand the job requirements, you should have little difficulty relating your skills and knowledge to the job. If the immediate job will lead to supervisory or management responsibilities later, make certain that you stress your skill in getting along with others and working successfully as part of a team.

A question about whether the company can offer you a career path is probably best answered with a question such as "I believe someone like me has a future with your company, but I would like to discuss the normal progression with the company. Can you tell me about it?" Most candidates for positions with public accounting firms are familiar with the steps from staff accountant to partner; but the steps are not so clearly defined in marketing, finance, and management paths. An open discussion can provide you with new information.

Everyone has a weakness. When asked about your greatest strengths and weaknesses, you can make an impression by acknowledging a weakness. To do otherwise may display a lack of appropriate humility. Avoid volunteering a weakness that will eliminate you from consideration for the job, however. An applicant for a controller's position revealed that his greatest weakness was his dislike for details. Because the controller's job requires meticulous attention to details, this applicant was immediately eliminated from consideration.

As a general rule, mention a weakness that can be perceived as a strength. For example, you may indicate that you occasionally become overcommitted to extracurricular activities, particularly if your resume shows a high level of extracurricular participation. But use this response only if you also have a strong academic record. Don't confess that your overcommitment resulted in a failure to pursue your education properly.

Your greatest strength probably is easy to identify: (1) the ability to learn, (2) the ability to work with others and to assume leadership roles,

Do you get the hint that weaknesses should border on being desirable traits?

HEATHCLIFF

" YOU HAVEN'T WON IT YET!"

Humility pays in a job interview.

(3) the ability to organize your time in such a way that you can achieve academically while still participating in nonclass activities or work, or (4) skill in problem solving. Because the question asks for your *greatest* strength, you should focus on a single point rather than brag about all of your strengths.

Questions about how you spend your spare time and about how your extracurricular activities have added to your education are designed to make you elaborate on resume items. Give some thought to these items so you can appear to have broad, balanced interests rather than a single, time-consuming avocation.

Develop a sincere, straightforward answer!

What's important in a job goes beyond financial reward. Although we are all interested in a paycheck, any job satisfies that need—some will pay more, some less; but the paycheck is a part of the job and should not be your primary concern. Intrinsic rewards such as personal job satisfaction, the feeling of accomplishment, and making a contribution to society are things you should think about discussing in the interview. You should like what you are doing. You should look forward to a challenge. A job that will satisfy these needs is important to almost everyone.

COMMUNICATION MENTOR

Take care to avoid overselling yourself in job interviews. This sounds so fundamental, yet it's the mistake that can put even experienced job applicants at an immediate disadvantage.

A candidate may think, for example, that a certain high-tech company's elite profile suggests that it would expect super-intelligence in applicants. The candidate then presents herself with a finger-snapping brashness that ill-suits her real personality and looks superficial to the interviewer. Another candidate for an administrative position in a health medical organization might try to demonstrate a sense of compassion and understanding for the sick, but he will come off as insincere to the interviewer.

Both candidates may genuinely possess the attributes they were attempting to project in the interview, but each may get the opposite reading. The point is, stick to what is natural for you in the way you act and react to the job interviewer. Don't try to paint the whole landscape of your character in one interview.

James F. Hurley
Senior Vice President
CalFed Inc.

One of the major reasons for college graduates' changing jobs is lack of challenge and the resulting dislike for the job. Research has shown that most of us change jobs two or three times before finding our career occupation. So, as you engage in the interview, look for things that will satisfy your immediate needs and lead to future challenges. Job changes usually involve hardships of some sort, and careful consideration of how the job and the company will meet your needs can prevent later problems.

Handling Illegal Interview Questions. As an interviewee, you must decide how you will handle illegal interview questions. Will you refuse to answer and inform the interviewer that the question is improper—and risk offending or embarrassing the interviewer? Or will you answer the question knowing that it is illegal and your answer is not related to the job requirements? Obviously, the latter option is more likely to keep you in the running for the job; but you may feel that you have compromised important principles.

A third and more effective alternative is to answer the legitimate concern that probably lies behind the illegal question rather than give a direct answer or refuse to answer the illegal question (Jenks, 1988). For example, an interviewer who asks, "Do you plan to have children?" is probably concerned about how long you might remain on the job. An answer to this concern would be "I plan to pursue a career regardless of whether I decide to raise a family." The interviewer who asks, "Have you ever been arrested other than for traffic violations?" is probably concerned about employee dishonesty. An appropriate answer to this concern is "Nothing I have ever done would give you any concern that I would breach your company's trust."

If you can see no legitimate concern in a question, such as "Do you own your own home, rent, or live with your parents?" answer, "I'm not sure how that question relates to the job. Can you explain?"

Asking Questions of the Interviewer. A new job is like a marriage: both the interviewer and interviewee must know as much as possible about each other before making a commitment to increase the likelihood that the relationship will be lengthy and mutually beneficial ("10 Interview Mistakes," 1990).

A good way to determine whether the job is right for you is to ask *pertinent* questions. Good questions show the interviewer that you have initiative and are interested in making a well-informed decision. For that reason, be certain not to say, "I don't have any questions." Focus on questions that help you gain information about the company and specifically the job that you could not learn from printed sources or persons other than the interviewer. Do not waste the interviewer's time asking questions that show you are unprepared for the interview (for example, questions about the company's scope, products/services, job re-

> How do you believe you could most effectively handle an illegal interview question?

> How is a new position similar to marriage?

> Good questions show initiative and genuine interest.

> What general guidelines should be followed for asking questions during an interview?

quirements, new developments). Having committed a block of uninterrupted time to talk with you, the interviewer will resent this blatant lack of commitment and respect for the company. Avoid questions about salary and benefits that imply you are interested more in money than in the contribution you can make.

To show further initiative, introduce questions throughout the interview whenever appropriate rather than waiting until you are asked whether you have questions. This approach will promote positive two-way interaction and should create a relaxed, unintimidating atmosphere. Just remember that the *interviewer* is in charge of the interview. Add your own questions to the typical interviewee questions shown in Figure 14-4.

Handling Salary Discussion. For most entry-level positions, the beginning salary is fixed. However, if you have work experience, excellent

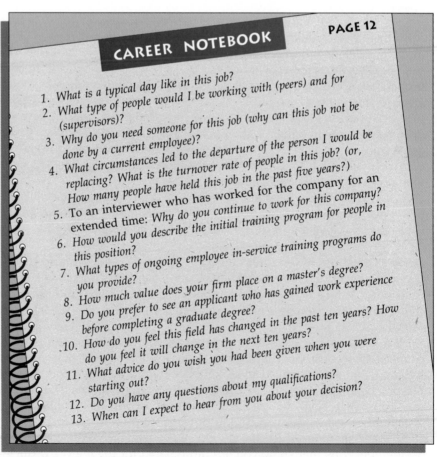

CAREER NOTEBOOK   **PAGE 12**

1. What is a typical day like in this job?
2. What type of people would I be working with (peers) and for (supervisors)?
3. Why do you need someone for this job (why can this job not be done by a current employee)?
4. What circumstances led to the departure of the person I would be replacing? What is the turnover rate of people in this job? (or, How many people have held this job in the past five years?)
5. To an interviewer who has worked for the company for an extended time: Why do you continue to work for this company?
6. How would you describe the initial training program for people in this position?
7. What types of ongoing employee in-service training programs do you provide?
8. How much value does your firm place on a master's degree?
9. Do you prefer to see an applicant who has gained work experience before completing a graduate degree?
10. How do you feel this field has changed in the past ten years? How do you feel it will change in the next ten years?
11. What advice do you wish you had been given when you were starting out?
12. Do you have any questions about my qualifications?
13. When can I expect to hear from you about your decision?

FIGURE 14-4   **Typical questions asked by interviewees during an interview**

COMMUNICATION MENTOR

Get yourself as well prepared as you can for the interview. Then relax and listen—*actively* listen. A question that springs from your genuine interest in and curiosity about what you're hearing will be much more impressive to your interviewers than standard, "canned" questions. And your genuine, honest response to a question you've heard correctly will be much more effective.

H. Devon Graham, Jr.
Southwest Regional Managing Partner
Arthur Andersen & Co.

scholarship records, or added maturity, you may be able to obtain a larger salary. The interviewer should initiate the salary topic. What you should know is the general range for candidates with your qualifications so that your response to a question about how much you would expect is reasonable. If your qualifications are about average for the job, you can indicate that you would expect to be paid the going rate or within the normal range. If you have added qualifications, you might say, "With my two years of work experience, I would expect to start at the upper end of the normal salary range."

If you have other job offers, you are in a position to compare salaries, jobs, and companies. In this case, you may suggest to the interviewer that you would expect a competitive salary and that you have been offered X dollars by another firm. If salary hasn't been mentioned, and you really want to know about it, simply ask courteously how much the salary would be for someone with your qualifications. In any case, though, if you really believe the job offers the nonmonetary things you seek, don't attempt to make salary a major issue.

Normally, an interviewer will introduce the subject of benefits without your asking about them. In some cases, a discussion of total salary and "perks" (perquisites) is reserved for a follow-up interview. If nothing has been said about certain benefits, you should take the liberty of asking, particularly when an item may be especially important to you. Medical insurance, for example, may be very important when you have children. Retirement planning, however, is less appropriate for a new graduate to discuss.

Should you stress opportunity over salary?

Closing the Interview. The interviewer will provide the cues indicating that the interview is completed by rising or making a comment about the next step to be taken. At that point, don't prolong the interview need-

COMMUNICATION MENTOR

Be clean, polished, and well presented when you arrive for your interview, at least 10 minutes early. Do not arrive more than 15 minutes early; it may appear you have nothing else to do or that you are rushing the interviewer who has better things to do than accommodate his or her schedule for you.

When answering questions, be brief but make sure you get your point across. Do not talk yourself into a grave when a yes- or no- answer will suffice. Always be upbeat, bright, cheerful, and never tired. Smile when possible, as personality counts a great deal in a job interview.

Do not be afraid to ask questions of your interviewer. Asking questions about an area where you have limited knowledge is a sure sign of intelligence. Remember, any prospective employer would probably like to hire you for life, not the next 18 months. Therefore, asking long-range questions only enhances your qualifications as a good candidate for a position.

Even if it becomes readily apparent that you are not the person for the job or the company is not for you, act cordial, interested, and positive. Many individuals have received job offers as a result of interviews they conducted somewhere else. Although you may not be the right candidate for Company A, you may be just the person for Company B. An interviewer's recommending a job candidate to a competitor for possible hiring is not uncommon.

Terence E. McSweeney
Director of Communications
PGA of America

---

lessly. Simply rise, accept the handshake, thank the interviewer for the opportunity to meet, and close by saying you look forward to hearing from the company. The neatness with which you close the interview may be almost as important as the first impression you made. Be enthusiastic. If you really want the job, you might ask for it!

Practicing for Interviews

Your display of sincerity is essential to presenting yourself favorably. Although most of us tend to be nervous during our first interview, we gain confidence with experience. Therefore, practice and rehearse your own interviewing style. Work with someone else in mock interviews, alternating roles as interviewer and interviewee. Then follow each practice interview with a constructive critique of each other's performance. A few such mock interviews will give you some experience and will make the first real interview more effective.

The job interview may be the most important face-to-face interaction you will have. You will be selling yourself in competition with others. How you listen and how you talk are characteristics the interviewer will be able to measure. Your actions, your mannerisms, and your appearance will combine to give the total picture of how you come across. Added to the obvious things you have acquired from your education, experience, and activities, your interview performance can give a skilled interviewer an excellent picture of you. Practice leads to perfection, so the time you devote to preparing for the interview may determine the payoff by making you stand a little higher than your competition.

You might use a third person as an observer.

PREPARING OTHER EMPLOYMENT MESSAGES

Preparing a winning resume and application letter is an important first step in a job search. You may be required to write several other employment letters throughout your career.

To expedite your job search, write follow-up letters to companies that do not respond to your resume. Sending a thank-you letter after an interview is not only courteous but also an absolute *must* because your competitors will be doing so. At some point, you must accept an offer and diplomatically reject others. A career change will require a carefully written resignation letter. Completing application and other employment forms correctly is yet another way to convey your qualifications and your high standards of accuracy and appearance.

Communicating with references is another critical area of employment communication. The quality of your request (written or oral) will affect the relevance and potency of the recommendation. Updating references when your qualifications change and keeping them informed of the status of your job search are courteous and beneficial actions. Later in your career, you may need to request recommendations from references and to provide both positive and negative recommendations.

Types of Employment Messages:

> **Follow-up letters**
>
> **Thank-you letters**
>
> **Job-acceptance letters**
>
> **Job-refusal letters**
>
> **Resignation letters**
>
> **Application forms**
>
> **Recommendation letters**

Follow-Up Letters

When an application and resume do not elicit a response, a follow-up letter may bring results. Sent a few weeks or months after the original letter, it includes a reminder that an application for a certain job is on file, presents additional education or experience accumulated, points out its relationship to the job, and closes with a reference to desired action. In addition to conveying new information, follow-up letters indicate persistence (a quality that impresses some employers). Figure 14-5 shows a good example of a follow-up letter.

Could a follow-up letter imply perseverance?

Thank-You Letters

Even though "thank you" was *said* at the close of the interview, should you *write* a "thank-you" letter?

After the job interview, a letter of appreciation is a professional courtesy and should be sent promptly. Even if during the interview you decided you do not want the job or you and the interviewer mutually agreed that the job is not for you, a thank-you letter is appropriate. It expresses grati-

[1] States main idea and clearly identifies the position being sought.

[2, 3] Refer to the enclosed resume; summarize additional qualifications.

[4] Assures employer that the applicant is still interested in the job.

1696 Bay Court
Windsor Locks, CT 06096-1696
September 15, 19—

Ms. Judith Webster
Personnel Director
Jensen Stores, Inc.
7800 Brookdale Road
Hartford, CT 06101-7800

Dear Ms. Webster:

[1] Having applied for a market-analyst job at Jensen Stores in April, I now have additional education and experience to report.

[2] The enclosed updated resume shows that I have taken a course in advanced statistical analysis this summer and have completed my third and final semester of cooperative education in the market research department of Nelson Department Stores. [3] The course and the experience have expanded my knowledge, increased my computer proficiency, and confirmed my interest in work as a market analyst.

[4] When Jensen Stores needs to add another market analyst, I would appreciate your calling or writing to me.

Sincerely,

Daniel W. Curtis

Daniel W. Curtis

Enclosure

FIGURE 14-5   Good example of a follow-up letter

COMMUNICATION MENTOR

Always follow up your interview with a thank-you note and a reminder of your interest, if applicable. Even if you have decided you would not want the position if offered, thank your interviewer for the opportunity and time given you. Recommendations can still be forthcoming through these individuals.

Terence E. McSweeney
Director of Communications
PGA of America

tude, refers to some point that was discussed in the interview, and closes pleasantly. It may mention the possibility of applying again after qualifications have been improved. If you were asked to submit some statement or further information, the prompt follow-up action becomes even more important.

After an interview has gone well and you think a job offer is a possibility, include these ideas in the letter of appreciation: express gratitude, identify the specific job applied for, refer to some point or points discussed in the interview, and close by making some reference to the expected call or letter that conveys the employer's decision (see Figure 14-6).

If the thank-you letter confirms that your enthusiasm for a job increased during the interview, the impact on the decision could be favorable. For maximum impact, send a thank-you letter as quickly as possible after an interview—the day of the interview or the following day.

A tardy thank-you letter has less impact.

The resume, application letter, and thank-you letter can be retained in a personal computer and adapted for submission to other firms when needed. Many job seekers keep a record of their efforts on a computer: dates on which letters and resumes were sent to certain firms, answers received, names of people talked with, facts conveyed, and so on. When a call is received, that firm's record can be retrieved and viewed on the monitor while the conversation is taking place.

Is your personal computer useful in the job search?

Application Forms

Before going to work on a new job, you will almost certainly complete the employer's application and employment forms. Some application forms, especially for applicants who apply for jobs with a high level of responsibility, are very long. They may actually appear to be tests in which appli-

A well-organized career notebook assists in giving quick, accurate information.

P.O. Box 601
Alexandria State College
Alexandria, LA 70711-3171
April 1, 19—

Mr. Dennis Payne
Personnel Director
Lennon Systems, Inc.
1180 North York Road
New Orleans, LA 70113-1180

Dear Mr. Payne:

[1] Thank you for taking time to talk with me on Tuesday about the management training program at Lennon Systems.

[2] Your description of your management-trainee program made me appreciate the case-method approach used in my advanced management classes. [3] You made me very glad I have taken courses in human relations and communications.

[4] The program is very appealing, and I am eager to receive a call from your office next week.

Sincerely,

Kyle D. Rhodes

Kyle D. Rhodes

[1] States the main idea: appreciation for the interview and information gained.

[2, 3] Include specific points discussed during the interview, increasing the sincerity of the letter and the likelihood the interviewer will remember the applicant.

[4] Assures the employer the applicant is interested in the job and politely reminds the employer he is awaiting a reply.

FIGURE 14-6   Good example of a thank-you letter

cants give their answers to hypothetical questions and write defenses for their answers. Increasing numbers of companies are designing employment forms to identify applicants' written communication skills. Review the guidelines in Figure 14-7 for completing application forms.

1. *Read the entire form before you begin completing it.* This procedure will prevent you from making careless mistakes caused by not understanding the form. Preparing a rough draft on a photocopy of the form is an excellent idea.

2. *Follow instructions.* If the form calls for last name first and you write your first name first, the damage could be fatal. If instructions clearly say "Print" and you write cursively instead, you could be stereotyped immediately as a bungler. When the form has multiple copies (NCR sheets or sheets with carbon paper between), place the form on a hard surface and put enough pressure on the pen to make the last copy clear. If instructions say, "Do not fold," honor them.

3. *Complete forms neatly.* If erasing is necessary, do it cleanly. Such techniques as marking through an original answer and squeezing another, or printing in all-capital letters in some blanks and in capital-and-lowercase letters in others may imply indecisiveness, carelessness, lack of respect, or haste. Unless instructions or circumstances forbid, type your answers for a neat, legible document.

4. *Respond to all questions.* For any questions that do not apply, write "NA" in the blank. If the form provides space for you to add additional information or make a comment, try to include something worthwhile. Competitors, especially those who habitually do no more than is required of them, will probably leave such spaces blank.

5. *Answer questions accurately.* If you have developed a career notebook (as described in Chapter 13), it will contain much information that would be called for on an employment form: transcripts of courses taken, dates of employment on other jobs, names and addresses of references, and so on. Carry it in a briefcase or portfolio and take it with you to employment offices and interviews. With a copy of your resume and application letter in the notebook, you can make sure all factual statements are consistent with statements on the form. Providing false information would be unethical and impractical. It could result in your being hired for a job you cannot do well or termination in disgrace when the misrepresentation is discovered.

6. *Keep a copy.* Save a copy of the application form for future reference. If you complete the application form before the interview, reviewing it prior to the interview could be to your advantage.

FIGURE 14-7 Guidelines for completing application forms

Job-Acceptance Letters

A job offer may be extended either by phone or by letter. Even though a job has been accepted by phone, the firm may also want a written acceptance. Note the deductive sequence of the letter shown in Figure 14-8: ac-

[1,2] Begin by stating the main news: job offer is being accepted.

[3] Continues with any necessary details.

[4] Confirms the beginning employment date.

1696 Bay Court
Windsor Locks, CT 06096-1696
April 25, 19—

Ms. Judith Webster
Personnel Director
Jensen Stores, Inc.
7800 Brookdale Road
Hartford, CT 06101-7800

Dear Ms. Webster:

[1] I accept your employment offer as a market analyst. [2] Thank you for responding so quickly after our discussion on Thursday.

[3] As requested, the enclosed employment forms have been completed in detail. [4] If you should need to communicate with me before I report for work on May 14, please leave a message at 555-6543.

Sincerely,

Daniel W. Curtis

Daniel W. Curtis

Enclosures

FIGURE 14-8   Good example of a job-acceptance letter

ceptance, details, and closing the letter also confirms the report-for-work date.

Job-Refusal Letters

Should job-refusal letters be organized like bad-news letters?

Like other messages that convey bad news, job-refusal letters are written inductively: a beginning that reveals the nature of the subject, explanations that lead to a refusal, the refusal, and a pleasant ending. Of course, certain reasons (even though valid in your mind) are better left unsaid: questionable company goals or methods of operation, negative attitude of present employees, possible bankruptcy, unsatisfactory working conditions, and so on. The applicant who prefers not to be specific about the reason for turning down a job might write this explanation:

> After thoughtfully considering job offers received this week, I have decided to accept a job in the actuarial department of an insurance company.

When your attitude toward the offering firm is positive, or when you recognize the possibility that at some later time you may want to reapply, you may want to be more specific about your reasons for refusal, as the letter in Figure 14-9 illustrates.

For follow-up, thank-you, acceptance, and refusal letters, use the personal business format illustrated in Appendix A. Letters of resignation, however, require a different format.

Resignation Letters

Resigning from a job requires you to communicate this fact appropriately. By the time you have reached the point of resignation, you will know whether your employer expects it to be in writing. You may have "given your notice" in person or written a formal resignation. Regardless of whether the resignation is given orally or in writing, show empathy for your employer by giving enough time to allow the employer time to find a replacement.

The memorandum format, illustrated in Appendix A, is appropriate when resigning from a job because the message is communicated between people *within* a company. However, some writers prefer the letter format to convey this formal message. Hence, this message is commonly referred to as a *resignation letter.*

Why emphasize positive ideas?

Thinking positively, treat a resignation letter as a bad-news letter. Because your employer has had confidence in you, has benefited from your services, and will have to seek a replacement, your impending de-

1923 Flock Avenue
Joplin, MO 64801-0893
October 21, 19—

Mr. Sherman Garvey, Loan Manager
Garvey Financial Services, Ltd.
1835 River Bend Drive
Joplin, MO 64801-1835

Dear Mr. Garvey:

[1] I appreciate your spending time with me discussing the loan officer's job.

[2] Thank you for your candid comparison of my background and opportunities in finance and insurance. [3] Having received job offers in both fields, I am now convinced that a career in insurance is more consistent with my aptitudes and goals. [4] Today, I am accepting a job in the actuarial department of States Mutual.

[5] Thank you for the confidence demonstrated by the job offer. [6] When I read reports of Garvey's continued success, I will think of the dedicated people who work for the company.

Sincerely,

Jeanne R. Anderson

Jeanne R. Anderson

[1] Begins with a neutral but related idea to buffer the bad news.

[2–4] Diplomatically present reasons that lead to the refusal.

[5, 6] End letter on a positive note that anticipates future association with the company.

FIGURE 14-9   Good example of a job-refusal letter

parture *is* bad news. As such, the letter is written inductively. It calls attention to your job, gives reasons for leaving it, conveys the resignation, and closes on a positive note (see Figure 14-10).

A resignation letter is not an appropriate instrument for telling executives how a business should be operated. Harshly worded statements could result in immediate termination or cause human-relations problems

JENSEN STORES, INC.

TO: Marilyn See, Director, Sales Personnel

FROM: Michele L. Wolfe, Manager, Women's Apparel

DATE: May 5, 19—

SUBJECT: PLEASURE OF SERVING JENSEN STORES

[1]My job as manager of Women's Apparel for the last two years has been a rewarding experience. [2]It has taught me much about the marketing of clothing and changing preferences in style.

[3]Predicting public acceptance of certain styles has been fascinating. [4]From the time I declared a major in fashion merchandising, I have wanted to become a buyer. [5]Before I accepted my present job in management, that goal was discussed. [6]Now, it is becoming a reality; I have accepted a job as buyer for Belton beginning one month from today. [7]If satisfactory with you, I would like May 31 to be my last day as manager here.

[8]This job has allowed me to grow professionally. [9]Thanks to you and others, I've had the privilege of trying new ideas and selecting sales personnel who get along well with one another and with customers. [10]Thank you for having confidence in me, for your positive rapport with the sales staff, and for your expressions of appreciation for my work.

[11]As I continue my career in fashion merchandising, I will always recall pleasant memories of my job at Jensen.

7800 Brookdale Road   Hartford, CT 06101-2700   (203) 555-1076

[1,2] Begin with appreciative comment about job to buffer the bad news.

[3-5] Present reasons that lead to the main idea, the resignation. **[6]** States the resignation. **[7]** Adds additional details.

[8-10] Convey genuine appreciation for the experience gained at Jensen.

[11] Ends on a cordial note.

FIGURE 14-10   Good example of a resignation letter

during your remaining working days. Remember, too, that your boss may subsequently review the resignation letter just before writing a recommendation letter for you.

Your letter of resignation may not come as a complete surprise to its reader. The new employer may have already asked the old employer for a letter of recommendation.

Recommendation Letters

Usually, letters of recommendation are written in response to a request. The request may come from the applicant or from the prospective employer.

Applicant's Request for Recommendation.   When prospective employers tell applicants to have recommendation letters sent, the normal procedure is to place a call to each reference. As the applicant, you would identify the job for which you are applying, give a complete address to which the letter is to be sent, and indicate a date by which the employer needs the letter.

In the conversation, you may need to remind the reference of a previously expressed willingness to supply employment information about you. By sharing some information about job requirements and reporting recent job-related experiences that are relevant, you may assist the reference in writing an effective letter. Indicate your gratitude, but don't apologize for making the request. (The reference has already agreed to write such a letter and will likely take pleasure in assisting a deserving person.)

Similar information is included when the request for a recommendation is made by letter, as the letter in Figure 14-11 shows.

People who have applied for jobs can greatly assist their references by alerting them to imminent requests for information, especially if considerable time has elapsed since the applicant and reference have last seen each other. Enclosing a recent resume and providing any other pertinent information (for example, name change) may enable the reference to write a letter that is specific and convincing. If the job search becomes longer than anticipated, a follow-up letter to references explaining the delay and expressing gratitude for their efforts is appropriate.

Employer's Request for Recommendation.   When businesses request information about prospective employees, use of forms is fairly standard. The forms normally allow space for responding to specific questions, and they either provide space for respondents to express themselves or invite them to attach a letter. When the request is by letter (instead of a form), the letter needs to identify the specific type of information wanted. Numbering and tabulating assist the writer in emphasizing and the reader in responding (see the letter in Figure 14-12).

Negative Recommendations.   Almost everyone who asks permission to use your name as a reference will expect your recommendation to be favorable. For a person whom you couldn't favorably recommend, you have the option of (1) saying "No" when asked for permission to use your name, (2) letting the request go unanswered, (3) responding with an objective appraisal, or (4) responding by letter and inviting a phone call.

When you must include negative information in a recommendation letter, be sure that you distinguish between opinion and fact. Including only the facts that can be supported is a foolproof safeguard against litigation and the temptation to retaliate for problems and losses caused by an employee's poor performance. Don't let opinions weigh you down like heavy packages.

1923 Flock Avenue
Joplin, MO 64801-0893
October 8, 19—

Dr. Lee Wing, Professor
Finance Department
South State College
P.O. Drawer FN
Joplin, MO 64801-1987

Dear Dr. Wing

[1] As one step in my application for a loan officer's job, States Mutual has asked me for letters of recommendation.

[2] Since receiving permission to use your name as a reference, I have completed the B.S. degree with a major in finance and real estate. [3] If a job offer is made, I would enter the loan-officer trainee program and later specialize in real-estate loans. [4] The enclosed resume will give you a summary of my academic and work experience as preparation for a job in the loan department.

[5] Please mail the recommendation to the following address by October 15:

> Mr. Lyle Richardson
> Human Resources Department
> States Mutual, Inc.
> 1835 River Bend Drive
> Joplin, MO 64801-1835

[6] I certainly appreciate your willingness to assist in my job search.

Sincerely

Jeanne R. Anderson

Jeanne R. Anderson

Enclosure

[1] States the main idea—request for recommendation.

[2, 3] Provide details. [4] Refers to enclosed resume, which will aid the reference in writing the recommendation.

[5] Provides needed information.

[6] Ends with an appreciative comment.

FIGURE 14-11   Good example of a request for a recommendation

Refusing permission may be difficult; but, for you, it is easier than writing a negative letter. For the applicant, your refusing to serve as a reference may be preferable to your accepting and subsequently sending a negative letter.

Failure to answer a request for information is in effect a negative response, even though the employer does not know whether you received

PIERCE FINANCIAL SERVICES
7900 North Center Street
Omaha, NE 68108-7900
(402) 555-9000

June 1, 19—

Ms. Ming Lin
Security Bank
1783 Main Street
Lincoln, NE 68501-1783

Dear Ms. Lin

Mr. Robert P. Grady has told us that you would be willing to provide information about his background for a job as a financial analyst at the Central State Bank.

Please give us your candid and confidential comments on each of the following job traits that are vital to the financial analyst's job:

- Dependability
- Tact (with clients and other personnel)
- Written and oral communication skills
- Knowledge of financial regulations
- Ethical standards

Add any other information you think would assist us in predicting his performance in this job. We would appreciate your comments by June 24.

Sincerely

Doug E. Beyer

Doug E. Beyer
Vice-President of Finance

FIGURE 14-12   Good example of an employer's request for a recommendation

the request. Nonresponse is legal and requires no effort; but (recognizing your responsibility to the applicant, the employer, and yourself) this option would probably be totally unacceptable to you.

Responding with an objective appraisal will give you the satisfaction of having exercised a responsibility to both applicant and employer. Because of your letter, an employer may escape some difficulty encountered after hiring an ill-qualified person. Your letter could spare an applicant the agony of going to work on a job that leads to failure. Figure 14-13 is an example of a well-written negative recommendation.

The word "confidential" in a request letter implies that the response

Protect yourself against possible lawsuits.

WEBB GROCERY
1575 JEFFERSON STREET
PITTSBURGH, PA 15219-1575
(412) 555-8392 FAX: (412) 555-8395

June 5, 19—

Ms. Kate M. Sanders
Store Manager
Pot Pourri Foods
3712 East Finch Avenue
Ironton, OH 45638-3712

Dear Ms. Sanders:

[1] JAMES WILSON'S EMPLOYMENT RECORD

[2] Webb Grocery provides the confidential employment information about James Wilson you requested in your June 1 letter.

[3] He worked from October 1 to December 13 as a courtesy clerk in our Greenwood store. [4] He had above-average skills at packing groceries, and he seemed to have good rapport with customers.

[5] On three occasions (each on a Monday morning), he did not report to work as scheduled; and he had not given the shift supervisor any notice of his absence. [6] He left the store at Webb Grocery's request.

[7] While he was on the job, his work was satisfactory.

Sincerely,

Eugene M. Wingler

Eugene M. Wingler
Store Manager

[1] Subject line clearly identifies the nature of the letter.

[2] States the main idea—request for employment information.

[3,4] Provide specific, objective information that can be verified easily.

[5,6] Provide additional objective information; omit opinions or value judgments. Can be easily verified.

[7] Describes Wilson's past performance but does not project how Wilson will perform on other jobs.

FIGURE 14-13   Good example of a negative recommendation

will be seen only by the person or persons who have responsibility for the hiring decision. Yet, after taking the job, the employee may have a legal right to inspect the personnel folder. Recognizing the possibility of hurt feelings, ruined friendships, and legal action, respondents are inclined to omit negatives or present them with extreme care.

Because of the threat of possible litigation, your letter must be written carefully so it can be defended if necessary. The following guidelines can help you write defensible recommendations:

1. *Provide only job-related information that will aid the reader in determining whether the applicant is employable.* If you are not familiar with the requirements of the job applied for, ask the requester to send you a job description. Use this document to include information that is *directly* relevant to the future job and to eliminate irrelevant information that could be defamatory.

2. *Avoid vague, general statements of the applicant's personal ability.* Instead, provide specific examples of performance and the situation in which the performance occurred. Include information such as the difficulty and complexity of the task, degree of applicant's control in the task, and the consequences of the performance, particularly rewards (Knouse, 1987).

3. *Report facts, not judgments.* For example, the number of workdays missed without prior communication with the supervisor is a verifiable fact. To label it as "a terrible record" or "irresponsible" is to pass judgment (which is best left to the reader). Avoid such defaming and judgmental words as *corrupt, crook, dishonest, hypocrite,* and *incompetent.*

4. *Include some positives, even if your overall recommendation is negative.* Conversely, including *no* more than one negative fact in a positive letter may make the letter appear more credible in the eyes of the reader (Knouse, 1987). Be certain to provide specific statements about the less-than-satisfactory performance and the overall context of the situation.

5. *Use an inductive sequence and stylistic techniques of de-emphasis* (unless your feelings are strong and you think emphasis of the negative is justified). Normally, the inductive sequence with de-emphasis techniques will seem considerate.

6. *Respond only to requests for specific information and indicate that your letter is written in response to a request.* Label your letter as confidential. These legal precautions indicate that your intent was not to defame but to give an honest answer to a legitimate request for information. In addition, studies show that employers prefer confidential letters rather than open letters that allow the applicant access to the letter. Employers perceive the letters to be a more honest evaluation of the applicant's employability (Knouse, 1987).

Responding by letter and inviting a phone call enable a reference to avoid putting negative ideas in writing. The letter is short, positive, and easy to write, as Figure 14-14 shows. Recognizing the possibility of negatives, the reference didn't want to state in written form, the recipient might not call. In response to such a call, abide by the same precautions that apply to writing letters of recommendation.

Positive Recommendations.   Fortunately, most people who invite you to write a recommendation are confident you will report positive information. Because it is designed to help a deserving applicant, your message should be believable. Believability may be questioned if the letter includes unsupported superlatives and adjectives or adverbs that are overly strong.

How could strong adjectives be detrimental?

Before requesting a recommendation, the employer has almost certainly seen the applicant's resume, application letter, and (possibly) application forms. Although the effect of your letter may be to *confirm* some of the information already submitted, do not devote all your space to *repeating* it. Instead, concentrate on presenting information the employer probably doesn't have. Your statements about proficiency and capacity to interact with others will be of special interest.

Regardless of whether a recommendation is for a promotion within the firm or for work in another firm, the same principles apply. For promotion within a firm, use the memorandum format, as shown in Figure 14-15.

Dear Mr. Pondel

CLIFFORD SMITH'S EMPLOYMENT RECORD

[1] Clifford Smith worked as a systems analyst for WEBCO from August 15, 1990, to December 30, 1992.

[2] The confidential information you requested will be provided by telephone: (601) 555-5432.

Sincerely

[1] States the main idea.
[2] Indicates preference to provide employment information by phone.

FIGURE 14-14   Good example of a letter inviting a telephone call to secure negative information

Westgate
NATIONAL BANK

1590 Central Avenue
Abilene, TX 79604-1590
Telephone (817) 555-9174
FAX: (817) 555-3809

TO: Tom Gray, Chair, Promotion Committee

FROM: Harold Mead, Chief Loan Officer

DATE: May 1, 19—

SUBJECT: FRANK JOHNSON'S PROMOTION
TO SENIOR LOAN OFFICER

[1] Frank Johnson would be an ideal senior loan officer. [2] For the following reasons, I recommend his promotion:

[3] ◆ *He is efficient.* Beginning with a $14 million loan portfolio, he now manages $25 million. In three years, the number of clients has grown from 16 to 26. Clients are astonished at the speed with which he completes paperwork.

[4] ◆ *He stays informed.* Daily, he spends time on the financial monitor and financial journals. Because of his knowledge, he has frequently made loans that would otherwise have gone to competitors.

[5] ◆ *He works well with the staff.* Colleagues communicate easily with him. His friendly, positive disposition contributes to our pleasant office atmosphere.

[6] ◆ *He helps maintain Westgate's public image.* Active in Kiwanis and in fundraising for the needy, he has frequent contacts with clients, prospective clients, and competitors in social situations. To me, he is an ideal person for reflecting the bank's image.

[7] A promotion would reward him for the part he has played in expanding our loans and would help us to keep him on our team.

"Serving your banking needs for over sixty years"

[1, 2] Introduce the main idea.

[3–6] Emphasize each reason the promotion is deserved. Each short sentence following the number has high impact.

[7] Restates the main idea.

FIGURE 14-15   Good example of a recommendation memorandum

PERFORMANCE APPRAISALS

Your ability to speak confidently and intelligently about your abilities will help you secure a desirable job. Effective interviewing skills will be just as valuable once you begin work. You will be involved in interviews with your supervisor for various reasons: to seek advice or information about

KPMG Peat Marwick

PERFORMANCE EVALUATION—PROFESSIONAL STAFF

Name _____ Staff Classification _____ Department _____

Engagement _____ Engagement Number _____

Interim _____ Final _____ Start Date _____ Release Date _____ Total Hours _____

Describe work assigned _____

_____
Is this person working (above at below) his/her current staff classification on this work assignment? *circle one*

Should work assigned be considered demanding? Yes_____ No_____ (Yes answer must be accompanied by an explanation)

Comments: _____

COMMUNICATION SKILLS

Above	At	Below		Above	At	Below
☐	☐	☐	Communicates and understands instructions	☐	☐	☐
☐	☐	☐	Contributes to the effective exchange of information	☐	☐	☐
☐	☐	☐	Prepares clear and concise letters, memos, proposals, and reports	☐	☐	☐
☐	☐	☐	Demonstrates effective oral expression when presenting ideas or tasks	☐	☐	☐
☐	☐	☐	Listens carefully to ensure own understanding of the ideas of others	☐	☐	☐
☐	☐	☐	Is tactful in both oral and written communications	☐	☐	☐
☐	☐	☐	Overall evaluation in this area	☐	☐	☐

The feedback you receive from your supervisor's routine evaluation of your performance is critical if you are to improve your performance. However, learning to evaluate your own performance objectively and being able to discuss your strengths and weaknesses openly with your supervisor will lead to even greater strides in job performance as well as higher levels of satisfaction and commitment to the job.

your work and working conditions, to receive informal feedback about your progress, to receive a deserved promotion, and to discuss other personnel matters. In addition, your supervisor will conduct a performance appraisal interview to evaluate your performance. This formal interview typically occurs annually on the anniversary of your start of employment.

Regardless of the job, employees need clear, direct feedback about their performance if they are to improve. This feedback also allows employees to fulfill important personal needs for accomplishment and success. Despite these crucial benefits, some employers hesitate to provide such feedback; and many employees are reluctant to participate effectively in appraisal interviews. The following sections identify the communication skills critical for an open, honest discussion about an employee's performance. Understanding and refining these skills should help you prepare for a relaxed and highly effective performance appraisal process.

Are interviewing skills important after you secure a job? Explain.

People need clear, direct feedback about their performance if they are to improve.

Guidelines for Employees

To increase your effectiveness during your performance appraisal interview, develop the following communication skills related specifically to this sensitive interview (Lehman, Taylor, & Forde, 1990):

1. *Ask that your employer evaluate your performance more frequently than at the end of the evaluation period.* Learn to accept constructive criticism from your supervisor and seek evaluation of your performance on a more frequent, informal basis if your supervisor does not readily provide it.
2. *Request a more informal review of your performance near the mid-point of the evaluation period.* The sole purpose of this developmental appraisal interview is to identify specific strategies for improvement by the end of the evaluation period. At that time, your supervisor will conduct a second appraisal interview for the purpose of evaluation that will be linked to promotions, pay raises, and terminations. Human resources management research supports two separate appraisal interviews; one interview *cannot* measure past performance and improve future performance (Novit, 1986; Schneier, Beatty, & Baird, 1986). Employers cannot function in two roles—counselors and judges—at the same time.

COMMUNICATION MENTOR

The job market is changing. Today, being able to reason, to read, and to communicate effectively—orally and in writing—is more important than ever before. For most of the new jobs in our economy, these attributes are absolute requirements. And this trend will continue.

Young men and women entering the labor force will need these skills to get and hold good jobs. They will be required to communicate about often increasingly technical matters in the office, on the plant floor, and in other worksites. And the ability of America to compete in a changing, competitive world will depend more and more on an educated work force. Workers will need to be productive and able to learn new, often complex processes, to follow difficult directions for these processes, and to communicate well with others.

As a former teacher, I am especially concerned that many young people today lack the basic skills needed to get ahead, and even to become self-supporting members of society. I have seen too many who can't read, can't spell, and can't express their own ideas clearly and concisely. We must do a better job educating the future work force. And the place to start—the basis of this educational challenge facing our nation—is to teach students good communications skills. Their future, and America's future, depends upon it.

The Honorable Lynn Martin
U.S. Secretary of Labor

3. *Learn to evaluate your own performance honestly.* Then you can be actively involved in developing strategies for improvement rather than reacting to your supervisor's appraisals. In a famous study by Herbert Meyer (1975) in which employees in a plant rated themselves, 95 percent considered themselves among the top 50 percent in job performance. Obviously, the first step in learning effective self-evaluation techniques is to be aware of a tendency to overrate your abilities!

List the weaknesses you perceive to be affecting job performance and try to pinpoint a reason for each of the weaknesses listed. If you are receiving frequent, informal feedback from your supervisor, this task will not be difficult. Identify a specific action that you are willing and able to take to overcome the weakness. Honestly answer these questions: Do I have any control over improving or eliminating the weakness? Am I willing to take the steps necessary? This example of a self-evaluation may help you to identify your own weaknesses:

> Julia has *no control* over completing client proposals by the deadline because the marketing staff is habitually late providing data needed for finalizing the budget. However, she may be *unwilling* to work independently to solve problems needed to complete work assignments (i.e., locate answers in policy manuals and reference books); instead, she will continue to rely on coworkers and her supervisor. Finally, she *is willing* to begin following standard proofreading procedures that will increase the quality of her work (eliminate the constant typographical and grammatical errors that others have noticed).

4. *Review the specific actions that you are willing and able to implement and prepare an overall plan for future performance.* With a clear understanding of your own performance and a detailed plan of action, you are well prepared to participate in setting performance goals for the next evaluation period. Participating in setting your goals will help you better understand what you must do and help you build a commitment to meet the goals (Latham & Wexley, 1981).

5. *Encourage your supervisor to help you set clear, specific,* measurable *goals.* "I will try to do better" is a poor goal because you cannot tell whether the goal has been met. With such a vague goal, you might try harder but not hard enough. Better goals are "I will produce all documents following standard policy and procedures," "I will meet all deadlines," or "I will not be tardy during the remainder of the period."

Guidelines for Supervisors

You will be able to perform better during the performance appraisal interview if you understand your supervisor's role. At some point in your career, you will be required to evaluate the performance of employees reporting to you. If you are working for a company with a well-defined career path, your opportunity to conduct an effective performance appraisal could occur quickly. Develop the communication skills presented in the following guidelines (Lehman & Taylor, 1991):

1. *Actively involve employees in the appraisal process.* They will find the process more beneficial if they are allowed to participate. Begin by building a positive, trusting relationship so that employees will be willing to disclose their weaknesses and work *with* you in developing a plan for improvement. Providing frequent, informal feedback (including praise) in a positive, constructive way is an excellent beginning.

2. *Create a warm, nonthreatening climate for the appraisal interview.* Sit in a chair facing the employee or at a round table rather than behind your desk to emphasize the counseling, participative nature of a developmental interview. If your office is pleasant and attractive, your employees are more likely to have positive feelings (Mintz, 1956).

   Begin the interview by stating its purpose. For example, "We're here today to find ways to improve your future performance—not to measure your performance" would be reassuring to an employee reporting for a developmental interview.

3. *Be prepared and highly organized.* Being disorganized and unprepared communicates that you are unconcerned about the importance of the process. For the same reason, allow no interruptions during the interview. Outline definite points to be made and issues to be discussed. Complete all paperwork before the interview. Invite the employees to share their weaknesses and possible strategies for improvement.

4. *Avoid generalizations, broad statements, and opinions.* For example, don't say, "Keep up the good work," "Just keep doing what you're doing," or "If you were a little more ambitious, you would meet deadlines." The fact is that the employee is not meeting deadlines. The reason for the less-than-satisfactory performance, lack of ambition, is your opinion. In addition, this statement emphasizes personal shortcomings rather than a deficiency in job performance.

5. *Offer specific, job-related behavioral comments.* For example, say "I liked the way you handled our refusal to manage the Larkin contract." Such comments tell employees that you value their work because you have observed their actions and know exactly what they are doing.

6. *Limit the number of weaknesses discussed during the interview to two or three.* Employees will become confused and defensive if you point out too many criticisms at once. Your informal feedback in the past should have included most of the problems already. After discussing weaknesses, offer praise about specific examples of good performance so the employee leaves on a positive note.

7. *Involve the employee in setting realistic performance goals.* Employees who help set goals are more committed to seeing that the goals are met. However, employees need some input from you; otherwise, they may overestimate their abilities and set goals too high.

COMMUNICATION MENTOR

Learn to approach sensitive issues such as a review of an employee's performance in a positive, objective manner. To make the performance review process valuable, be certain that the employee believes suggestions and discussions are constructive and are intended to enhance career opportunities. For example, rather than talking in weak generalities, communicate specific strategies for improvement. Involving the employee in honestly evaluating his or her own performance and helping you set goals for future performance are sure ways of increasing the employee's commitment to improve. Your ability to create an open, supportive climate will yield tangible benefits for everyone—the employee and the company.

Beverly R. Kuehn
Branch Manager
CTX Mortgage Company
a division of Centex Corporation

Following these guidelines will ensure that you are prepared for your first performance appraisal interview. Being able to communicate effectively during this important interview will pay handsome dividends. You are more likely to receive clear, specific feedback about your performance and to participate actively in setting goals for future performance. As an active participant in this process, you will better understand what is expected of you and will be more committed to meeting the goals you and your supervisor set.

SUMMARY

Job interviews, in many cases the graduate's final steps in getting the first job and beginning a career, are the focus for the discussion of interviewing in this chapter. Interviewers and interviewees can be looked at as buyers and sellers: interviewers want to know whether job candidates can meet the needs of their firms before making a "purchase"; interviewees want to sell themselves based on sound knowledge, good work skills, and desirable personal traits. When interviews fail, the reason usually lies in attitudinal shortcomings.

Good interviews seldom occur by accident. Both interviewers and interviewees have responsibilities for the success of the meeting. Just as actors practice their lines and roles, those engaged in interviews should plan and practice for their performances, too.

Follow-up letters either add information that has been accumulated since an application was sent or ask that an application be kept in the active file. After an interview, a thank-you letter is sent as a matter of courtesy regardless of whether a job offer is expected. Acceptance letters are written deductively; refusals, inductively.

Instructions on application forms should be followed carefully. Neatness, completeness, and accuracy are expected. If these qualities are evident and if the resume and application letter show a good match of qualifications and job requirements, the employer may be eager to schedule an interview.

Resignation letters normally satisfy a firm's requirement that resignations be submitted in writing; they confirm that termination plans are definite. Assuming a satisfactory employer-employee relationship, resignations are usually bad news for an employer. As such, they are written inductively, with emphasis on positive aspects of the job.

For job seekers with good qualifications, recommendation letters are written deductively; otherwise, inductively. Principal concerns are fairness and legality.

Effective interviewing skills are important in the performance appraisal interview, usually conducted once a year. Employees who actively participate in an honest evaluation of their performance are more likely to receive the clear, direct feedback they need to improve their performance. Employers must create an honest, nonthreatening climate that fosters open, honest communication and offer specific, job-related statements that lead to improvement.

REFERENCES

Golen, S. P., & Lynch, D. H. (1987, Spring). The seriousness of communication barriers in the interviewer-interviewee relationship. *Delta Pi Epsilon Journal, 29*(2), 47–55.

Hunt, G. T., & Eadie, W. F. (1987). *Interviewing: A communication approach.* New York: Holt, Rinehart and Winston.

Jenks, J. M. (1988, Spring). Tactful answers to illegal interview questions. *National Business Employment Weekly,* p. 37.

Knouse, S. B. (1987). Confidentiality and the letter of recommendation: A new approach. *Bulletin of the Association for Business Communication, 50*(3), 6–8.

Latham, G. P., & Wexley, K. N. (1981). *Increasing productivity through performance appraisal.* Reading, MA: Addison-Wesley.

Lehman, C. M., & Taylor, G. S. (1991). Participative appraisal of student performance + effective communication skills = long-run success. *Journal of Business and Technical Communication, 5*(3), 307–320.

Lehman, C. M., Taylor, G. S., & Forde, C. M. (1990). Experiential approach to performance appraisal. *Business Education Forum, 44*(5), 25–29.

Meyer, H. H. (1975). The pay-for-performance dilemma. *Organizational Dynamics, 3*(3), 39–50.

Mintz, N. L. (1956). Effects of esthetic surroundings: II. prolonged and repeated experience in a "beautiful" and an "ugly" room. *Journal of Psychology, 41,* 247–254.

Mitchell, B. (1990). Interviewing face-to-interface. *Personnel, 67*(1), 23–25.

Novit, M. S. (1986). Performance appraisals. In *Essentials of personnel management* (2nd ed.). Englewood Cliffs, NJ: Prentice-Hall.

Schneier, C. E., Beatty, R. W., & Baird, L. (1986). How to conduct a successful performance appraisal system. *Training and Development Journal, 40*(4), 38–42.

10 Interview Mistakes That Can Cost You the Job. (1990, March). *Tomorrow's Business Leader,* p. 19.

REVIEW QUESTIONS

1. How do structured and unstructured interviews differ?
2. Discuss how computer-assisted interviewing is being used to screen applicants.
3. How do responses to direct and indirect questions differ?
4. What is meant by paraphrasing?
5. Compose three statements or questions that might be considered discriminatory in employment interviews.
6. List some possible sources of information about a company.
7. What posture and body movements can the interviewee use to impress an interviewer?
8. If your education is your foremost attribute, how can you stress what it says about you and your potential value to an employer?
9. List four leading barriers to communication in employment interviews.
10. Discuss three ways an interviewee can handle illegal interview questions. What are the advantages and disadvantages of each?
11. What is a good strategy to use when you are asked about your major weakness?
12. What ideas are included in a follow-up letter?
13. In a thank-you letter, what is the advantage of referring to some point or points discussed in the interview?
14. List some suggestions for completing employment forms.
15. Which would be written deductively: (a) an acceptance letter or (b) a refusal letter?
16. Describe the ideas recommended for inclusion in a resignation letter.
17. Professor Adams agreed to serve as one of your employment references, but you have not talked with her for two years. Today, you

listed her name on an application form. Should you write to her? Explain.

18. An employee whom you fired last year has given your name as a reference. In the responding letter, would you include some positives *and* negatives? Discuss guidelines for writing a recommendation that you can legally defend.

19. In a negative recommendation, what is the advantage of labeling your letter "confidential" and reminding the reader that the information was requested?

20. What is the primary purpose(s) of a performance appraisal interview? Discuss important guidelines for employees being interviewed during a performance appraisal interview.

21. Discuss several important steps employers should take to ensure an effective performance appraisal interview.

APPLICATIONS

ιL	CAREER DEVELOPMENT	SMALL
Interpersonal	Technology	Pul

1. **Preparing to Answer Interview Questions Effectively.**   Turn to Figure 14-3 and prepare answers to the interview questions. Place your answers in your career notebook, and study them in preparation for an interview. As directed by your instructor, complete one or more of the following tasks:
   a. Be prepared to discuss your answers in class.
   b. Divide into small groups to discuss your answers. Revise your answers, incorporating relevant feedback and being sure that the answers are truthful and reflect your individual personality.
   c. Set up a mock interview with a friend serving as the interviewer. Having already stated your answers aloud to a receptive individual will ease the tension when you are asked the same questions during the interview.

ιL	CAREER DEVELOPMENT	SMALL
Legal	Interpersonal	Technolo

2. **Practicing Job Interviews.**   Form groups of four to practice job interviews. Each person should have available a copy of his or her resume. Alternatively play the roles of interviewer and interviewee, with the two additional people serving as critical observers. Change places until all four have had an opportunity to serve as interviewer and interviewee. You may assume the jobs being applied for are the ones you have selected and designed applications for. Alternatively, use one of the following positions:
   a. A part-time job visiting high schools to sell seniors on the idea of attending your school.
   b. A full-time summer job as a management intern in a local bank.
   This activity may be adapted for video taping and review.

3. **Accepting a Job Offer.** Assume you are offered the job (or internship) for which you have applied. Make the assumption you prefer:
   a. You applied for an immediate part-time job.
   b. You applied for a full-time job for next summer.
   c. You applied for a cooperative-education assignment or internship.
   d. You applied for a full-time job immediately after your graduation. Look at the list of courses you plan to take and write as though you had taken them and satisfied the requirements for a degree.

   Write a letter of acceptance for the job (internship) for which you have applied.

4. **Refusing a Job Offer Diplomatically.** Assume the job search identified in Application 3 was very successful; you were offered two positions. Write a letter refusing one of the job offers. Because you want to maintain a positive relationship with the company you are refusing to work for, provide specific reasons for your decision. Supply the needed address.

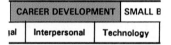

5. **Resigning from a Job.** Write a letter resigning from your current job. If you are not currently employed, supply fictitious information.

6. **Requesting a Letter of Recommendation.** Write a letter requesting a reference to provide information to prospective employers. Provide specific information about how your qualifications relate to the job requirements and enclose a resume. Supply an appropriate name and address.

7. **Informing a Reference of an Extended Job Search.** Your job search is taking much longer than you had hoped. Because your references have been providing recommendations for six months now, you must write expressing your gratitude and updating them on the status of your job search. If your qualifications have changed, include an updated resume. Address a sample letter to one of your references. Supply an appropriate name and address.

CASES FOR ANALYSIS

Case 1. Discrimination Hiring Needs Must Be Watched. As a standard procedure, applicants for jobs with Janicek Department Stores are interviewed by the manager and other selected employees. The home office has recently received some complaints from applicants who were not hired. True or not, the applicants have pointed out some possible violations of the Equal Employment Opportunity Commission's guidelines (which prohibit discriminatory hiring based on specified characteristics). Such topics are to be avoided in interviews, or in the "small talk" that precedes them. Direct or indirect questions about these specified characteristics (e.g., age or marital status) are not to be asked. Store managers need to review the guidelines themselves (in the *Policy and Procedures Manual* in each store manager's office) and make sure others who talk with job applicants are also familiar with the guidelines. Otherwise, Janicek could be severely embarrassed.

Required: As human resources director, complete the following tasks:

1. To ensure that the store manuals are up to date, research the current legal guidelines of the Equal Employment Opportunity Commission.
2. Write a memorandum addressed to the store managers urging them to adhere strictly to the guidelines, reviewing the basic guidelines, and informing them of recent changes. Cite a number of sources to be certain that your information is objective. Because of the timeliness of this problem, sources must be current. Use appropriate documentation within the memo to protect yourself and Janicek against plagiarism and to assist the managers in locating your references for further research.
3. Use desktop publishing equipment available to you to prepare an attractive, appealing flyer explaining the legal guidelines. You believe an attractive flyer will have greater impact and will be a more useful reference than the memo (step 2) that contains explanatory information.
4. Write a transmittal memo to the store managers explaining the attached flyer.

Case 2. A Negative Job Recommendation: What Is the Appropriate Course of Action? As the office manager of CompuTel, a computer systems consulting firm with relatively high personnel turnover, you often receive requests to write job recommendations for past employees. Last week, you received a letter from Mark Carlson, human resources director at Advanced Softworks, Inc. stating that Samuel Green listed your name as a reference on his job application.

After working for three years as a software developer, Green resigned to accept a similar job in a competing firm. You were pleased to see him leave for a number of reasons. He was often abrasive to coworkers and clients (he frequently received complaints) and was uncooperative and self-centered. He never considered his work as a part of an overall team effort. Other than his poor human relations skills, Green's job performance was outstanding; you can cite several examples of extraordinary work. He is a highly skilled programmer with a B.A. in computer engineering and an M.A. in management and information systems.

Required:

1. Decide whether you should provide a recommendation for Samuel Green. If so, what kind of recommendation should you write? Consider these points:

   a. What are the consequences if you ignore the request?

   b. What are the consequences of your writing a neutral recommendation (state dates of employment and job title) *or* acknowledging the request and inviting Mark Carlson to phone you for a confidential conversation?

   c. Would you consider it ethical to write a positive recommendation, ignoring Green's poor human relations skills?

   d. Should you mention Green's poor human relations skills as well as his competence? If you include the negative information, what precautions can you take as safeguards against possible legal action?

2. Based on your decision, complete *one* of the following tasks:

   a. Write a memo to the file stating that you are ignoring a request for a recommendation on Samuel Green and justifying your action.

   b. Write a recommendation letter including only the positive information. Write a brief memo to the file explaining why you chose to omit the negative facts.

   c. Write a letter including an objective appraisal of Green's performance (include positive and negative information).

   d. Write a letter responding to the request for a recommendation and inviting a telephone call to acquire confidential information. Write a dialogue of your anticipated telephone conversation with Mark Carlson.

   Address the letter to Mark Carlson, Advanced Softworks, Inc., 1015 Industrial Park, Birmingham, AL 35214-1015.

Venture Stores

Every job seeker desires to be effective in employment communication. The stakes are obvious and high. Preliminary analysis of one's strengths and weaknesses and careful planning of arrangement and format are essential to the development of an effective resume and application letter. In addition to planning and organization, originality is a plus, as the job seeker must somehow distinguish his or her resume from the countless others with which it competes. Success at this stage means that an interview is granted, at which time a candidate has the opportunity to sell himor herself to the company as well as to take a closer look at what the company has to offer.

Interviewing involves the use of numerous interpersonal communication skills, both verbal and nonverbal. The challenge of the interviewee is to relax, while realizing that every word, action, and response is being scrutinized. No small task!

Discussion Questions

1. Hyman Albritton suggests that a job seeker prepare two resumes. Explain the two and tell the purpose of each.
2. List three "dos" and three "don'ts" for resume preparation.
3. What is the "call to action" John Cripe mentions as essential in the application letter?
4. What advice does Marie Mulvoy have concerning dress for the interview?
5. Conducting a self-awareness activity is suggested as a helpful prelude to the employment search process. What is involved? How does it benefit the job seeker?

Application

Interview a business person who is involved in employment interviewing. Prepare a written summary that includes answers to the following questions: (1) What strategies are used for "weeding out" resumes of job applicants? (2) What are five questions most commonly asked by the interviewer? (3) What is the interviewer looking for in terms of the candidate's nonverbal communication skills?

COMMUNICATING THROUGH REPORTS

CHAPTER 15   The Report Process and Research Methods
CHAPTER 16   Managing Data and Using Graphics
CHAPTER 17   Organizing and Writing Short Reports and
             Proposals
CHAPTER 18   Writing a Formal Report

THE REPORT PROCESS AND RESEARCH METHODS

OBJECTIVES

When you have completed Chapter 15, you should be able to

- Analyze the possible approaches and methods used to solve problems.

- Take appropriate steps in the problem-solving process.

- Use sampling techniques.

- Develop survey questionnaires and other instruments.

WHEN COLIN MARSHALL GOT BEHIND THE CONTROLS at British Airways (BA) in 1983, the carrier was in a downward spiral financially and in popularity ratings. The airline's reputation for poor service had earned it the nickname "Bloody Awful." Marshall, determined to change its course, began with a simple strategy: he surveyed customers to find out what they thought BA should offer. The results showed that friendly, helpful employees topped the customers' wish list.

After the survey, all employees were trained to view customers as individuals, not numbers. In addition, Marshall learned that his largest group of customers consisted of business travelers. He acted on this knowledge and made changes in business-class flights. Since these improvements were initiated in 1987, revenues from business flights have increased at an impressive rate. Marshall also instituted a group of workers, called "hunters," who are stationed at London's Heathrow Airport. They keep their eyes open for customers in need of assistance and offer help with luggage, or directions, or any problems the customers may have. British Airways still has some problems, but it has come a long way since the early 1980s. Customer satisfaction has improved, and BA's future looks bright. (Maremont, 1990)

British Airways made a turnabout because it was aware of its problems. Airline executives conducted research to find out what those problems were and how to go about solving them. As a manager, you will probably have to deal with a situation that requires you to identify a trouble area as well as possible solutions. Unless you are equipped to communicate with employees and customers and to conduct research, you will be part of the problem instead of the solution.

KNOWING THE CHARACTERISTICS OF REPORTS

> Hello, Pete. This is Walters in customer services. The boss wants to know how things are going with the 400-case Sleepwell order. Are we going to make the 4 p.m. shipping deadline?

> Oh hi, Walt. We are going to make the deadline, with time to spare. We have about 250 cases on the loading dock, 100 on the box line, and 50 going through the labeling process. They'll all be ready for the loader at two o'clock.

This brief exchange illustrates a simple reporting task. A question has been posed; the answer given (along with supporting information) satisfies the reporting requirement. Although Pete may never have studied report preparation, he did an excellent job; so Walters, in turn, can report to his supervisor. Pete's oral report is a very simple illustration of five main characteristics of reports:

1. Reports are generally requested by a higher authority. In most cases, people would not generate reports unless requested to do so.

2. Reports typically travel upward in the organization structure. The upward direction of reports is a result of their being requested by higher authority.

Is a report feedback to downward communication?

3. Reports are orderly. Orderly, in this sense, means that reports are logically organized. In Pete's case, he gave Walt an answer to his question first and then supported the answer with evidence to justify it. Your study of the organization of letters showed you the difference between deductive and inductive organization. Pete's report was deductively organized. If Pete had given the supporting evidence first and followed that with the answer that he would meet the deadline, the organization of his reply would have been inductive and would still have been logical.

4. Reports stress objectivity. Because reports contribute to decision making and problem solving, they should be as objective as possible; when nonobjective (subjective) material is included, the reporter should make that known.

5. Reports are generally prepared for a limited audience. This characteristic is particularly true of reports traveling within an organization and means that reports, like letters, can be prepared with the receivers' needs in mind.

What Is a Report?

Based on those five characteristics, a workable definition of a report is "an orderly, objective message used to convey information from one organizational area to another or from one institution to another to assist in decision making or problem solving." Reports have been classified in numerous ways by management and by report-preparation authorities. The form, direction, functional use, and content of the report are used as bases for classification. However, a single report might be included in several classifications. The following brief review of classification helps explain the scope of reporting and establishes a departure point for studying reports and reporting.

What is the ultimate purpose of reports?

Formal or Informal Reports. The formal-informal classification is particularly helpful because it applies to all reports. Formal reports are carefully structured; they stress objectivity and organization, contain much detail, and are written in a style that tends to eliminate such elements as personal pronouns. Informal reports are usually short messages with natural, casual use of language. The internal memorandum generally can be described as an informal report. All reports can be placed on a continuum of formality, as shown in Figure 15-1. Later chapters will explain more fully the distinction among the degrees of formality of various reports.

See the dictionary definition of "formal."

Short or Long Reports. "Short-or-long" can be a confusing classification for reports. A one-page memorandum is obviously short, and a report of

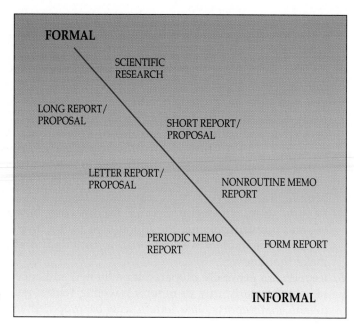

**FIGURE 15-1
Report formality
continuum**

twenty pages is obviously long. What about in-between lengths? One important distinction generally holds true: as a report becomes longer, it takes on more characteristics of formal reports. Thus, the formal-informal and short-long classifications are closely related.

Informational or Analytical Reports.   Informational reports carry objective information from one area of an organization to another. Analytical reports present attempts to solve problems. Company annual reports, monthly financial statements, reports of sales volume, and reports of employee or personnel absenteeism and turnover are informational reports. Reports of scientific research, real-estate appraisal reports, and feasibility reports by consulting firms are analytical reports.

Do you recall organizational control and coordination from Chapter 1?

Vertical or Lateral Reports.   The vertical-lateral classification refers to the directions reports travel. Although most reports travel upward in organizations, many travel downward. Both represent vertical reports and are often referred to as upward-directed and downward-directed reports. The main function of vertical reports is to contribute to management *control*, as shown in Figure 15-2. Lateral reports, on the other hand, assist in *coordination* in the organization. A report traveling between units of the same organizational level, as between the production department and the finance department, is lateral.

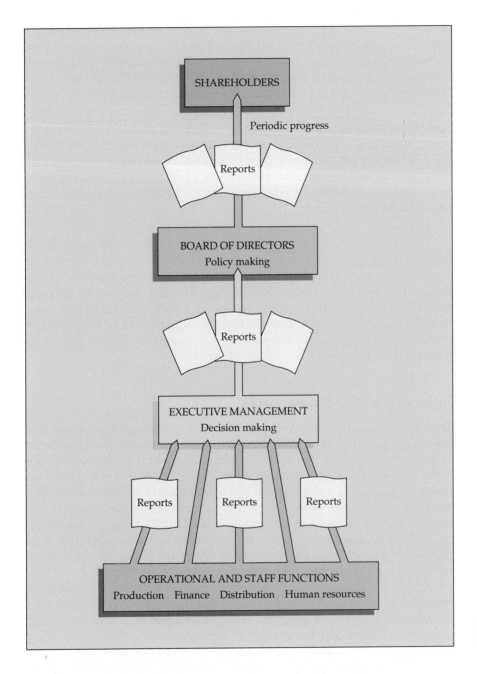

FIGURE 15-2 The general upward flow of reports

Internal or External Reports. Internal reports travel within the organization. External reports, such as annual reports of companies, are prepared for distribution outside the organization.

Periodic Reports. Periodic reports are issued on regularly scheduled dates. They are generally upward directed and serve management-control purposes. Daily, weekly, monthly, quarterly, semiannual, and annual time periods are typical for periodic reports. Preprinted forms and computer-generated data contribute to uniformity of periodic reports.

Functional Reports. The functional classification includes accounting reports, marketing reports, financial reports, personnel reports, and a variety of other reports that take their functional designation from the ultimate use of the report. For example, a justification of the need for additional personnel or for new equipment is described as a justification report in this classification.

Aren't these report classifications based on flow, time, and use?

As you review these report classifications, you will very likely decide—correctly—that almost all reports could be included in most of these categories. A report may be formal or informal, short or long, informational or analytical, vertically or laterally directed, internal or external, periodic or nonperiodic, functionally labeled, or any combination of these classifications. Although authorities have not agreed on a universal report classification, these report categories are in common use and provide a nomenclature for the study and use of reports.

Proposals as Special Reports

The proposal is a variation of problem-solving reports. A proposal is a document prepared to describe how one organization can meet the needs of another. Whenever you shop for a particular item, a salesperson may "sell" you on his or her merchandise by describing how it will meet your needs. If you are a conscientious shopper, you will probably visit more than one store before making a purchase. In effect, you are receiving oral proposals, weighing one against another, and finally making a selection.

Are newspaper ads proposals?

On a broader scale, most governmental agencies advertise their needs by issuing "requests for proposals," or RFPs. The RFP specifies a need, such as for architectural services. Potential suppliers prepare proposal reports telling how they can meet that need. Those preparing the proposal create a convincing document that they hope will result in their obtaining a contract. In addition, both public agencies and most private businesses issue "calls for bids" that meet the specifications established for proposed major purchases of goods and certain services.

In our information-intensive society, proposal preparation is a major activity for many firms. Chapter 17 presents proposal preparation in considerable detail. Although that chapter also discusses preparation of short proposals, keep in mind that a proposal to build a power plant would perhaps require many volumes.

Basis for a Report: A Problem

The upward flow of reports provides management with data that someone may use to make a decision. The purpose is to use the data to solve the problem. Some problems are recurring and, hence, call for a steady flow of information; other problems may be unique and call for information on a one-time basis. If we can accept the idea that a problem is the basis for a report, the preparation, organization, and writing of the report become much easier.

Whatever the problem—business or otherwise—human reason has developed the following steps for finding a solution:

1. Recognize and define the problem.
2. Select a method of solution.
3. Collect and organize the data.
4. Arrive at an answer.

These steps form the report skeleton.

Only after all four steps have been completed is the report written for presentation. Reports represent an attempt to communicate how a problem was solved and what the solution was. Let's take a closer look at the four steps in problem solving and in successful report preparation. Keep in mind that these problem-solving steps are completed *before* the report is written in final form.

COMMUNICATION MENTOR

Research (information gathering) is the single most important tool in communications. You must know a number of things:

Who is your audience? What are its perspective and specific needs?

What is your audience's level of understanding, interest, and receptiveness to your message?

Whom are you competing against and what are their strengths and weaknesses?

If you are in the information business, you will never run out of issues that need to be researched. The challenge is to do it in a manner that is efficient as well as effective.

David Martin
President
Sygnis, Inc.

RECOGNIZING AND DEFINING THE PROBLEM

Problem-solving research cannot begin until the researchers define the problem. Frequently, those requesting a report will attempt to provide a suitable definition. Nevertheless, researchers should attempt to paraphrase to ensure they will be on the right track.

Pinpoint your purpose.

Research studies often have both a statement of the problem and a statement of the purpose. For example, a real-estate appraiser accepts a client's request to appraise a building to determine its market value. The problem is to arrive at a fair market value for the property. The purpose of the appraisal, however, might be to establish a value for a mortgage loan, to determine the feasibility of adding to the structure, or to assess the financial possibility of demolishing the structure and erecting something else. Thus, the purpose may have much to do with determining what elements to consider in arriving at an answer.

In other words, unless you know why something is wanted, you might have difficulty knowing what is wanted. Once you arrive at the answer to *why* and *what* questions, write them down. You'll be on your way to solving the problem.

Using Hypotheses and Statements of Purpose

A *hypothesis* is a statement to be proved or disproved through some type of research. For example, a study of skilled manufacturing employees under varying conditions might be made to determine whether production would increase if each employee were part of a team as opposed to being a single unit in a production line. For this problem, the hypothesis could be formulated in this way: "The productivity will increase when skilled manufacturing employees are members of production teams rather than

COMMUNICATION MENTOR

Perhaps the greatest failure of researchers is in recognizing the real issues to be addressed. When beginning any information-gathering process, be sure you know *what* the real issue is and *how* the information you are gathering will be used in addressing this issue.

David Martin
President
Sygnis, Inc.

Before you can attempt to solve a problem, you must first realize what the problem is. This concert area could be empty for any number of reasons: poor publicity of the event, a bad choice of time or location, or the performers are simply unpopular in this area. Until the producers of the event carefully define the exact nature of the problem, the concert hall will likely remain empty.

single units in a production line." Because the hypothesis tends to be stated in a way that favors one possibility or a prejudice toward a particular answer, many researchers prefer to state hypotheses in *null* fashion: "No significant difference will exist in productivity between workers as team members and workers as individual production line units." The null hypothesis tends to remove the element of prejudice toward an answer.

Does the null form seem more objective?

Whether you develop hypothesis statements is not of great importance. But you should be familiar with the use of hypotheses and their statement in null style.

To restate the hypothesis as a problem and purpose statement, you might say, "The purpose of this study is to determine whether production will increase when employees are organized as teams as compared with their working as individuals in a production line." You have the option of using the hypothesis approach or the problem-purpose approach. In many ways, the purpose of a study is determined by the intended use of its results.

Limiting the Problem

One of the major shortcomings of research planning is the failure to establish or to recognize desirable limitations. Assume, for instance, that you want to study salaries of office support staff. Imagine the scope of such a task. Millions of people are employed in office support jobs. And perhaps a thousand or so different types of jobs fall into this classification. To reduce such a problem to reasonable proportions, use the *what*, *why*, *when*, *where*, and *who* questions to limit the problem. Here's what you might come up with as the human resources manager at a metropolitan bank:

The "W" words help narrow report scope.

What:	A study of salaries of office support staff.
Why:	To determine whether salaries in our firm are competitive and consistent.
When:	Current.
Where:	Our metropolitan area.
Who:	Office support staff employees in banks.

Now you can phrase the problem this way: "The purpose of this study is to survey salaries of office support staff in local banks to determine whether our salaries are competitive and consistent." Note that this process of reducing the problem to a workable size has also established some firm limits to the research. You've limited the problem to current salaries, to the local area, and to a particular type of business. Note, too, how important the *why* was in helping establish the limitations. Limiting the problem is "zeroing in on the problem."

Defining Terms Clearly

Vague terms contribute greatly to faulty communication. Clearly, in the study of office support staff salaries, a comparison of one bank's salaries with those paid by others would be meaningful only if the information gathered from other banks relates to identical jobs. A job description defining the duties performed by an administrative assistant, for example, would help ensure that all firms would be talking about the same job tasks regardless of the job title.

Definition: A statement of what something is.

In addition, the term *salary* requires definition. Is it hourly, weekly, monthly, or yearly? Are benefits included? A conversion table would probably be necessary to provide consistency in converting amounts to appropriate pay periods. In all research, terms must be defined if they could be misleading.

SELECTING A METHOD OF SOLUTION

After defining the problem, the researcher will plan how to arrive at a solution. One or a combination of the following recognized research methods can be used to collect necessary information:

◆ Library research.
◆ Survey research.
◆ Observational research.
◆ Experimental research.

Library research uses *secondary* sources—material already created. Surveys, observational studies, and experiments rely on methods designed to create their own information—*primary* sources.

Library Research

Library research, as a part of all research studies, provides information about what others have done previously in the same field. It saves researchers the wasted time and effort of duplicating research that has already been undertaken. For example, computer-program indexes, periodicals, and books provide information about available programs, making creation of those programs unnecessary. A scientist working in the area of airborne navigation systems knows others have been and are working in the same area. By engaging in library research, the scientist can determine the boundaries of knowledge before proceeding into the unknown.

Figure 15-3 illustrates the constant development of knowledge. Certain truths have been established within the confines (center, dark blue circle) of a field of knowledge. These truths are treated as principles and reported in textbooks and other publications. However, because knowl-

Does library research save time and effort?

Thorough research: A critical element in effective report writing
CALVIN AND HOBBES copyright 1989 Watterson. Dist. by UNIVERSAL PRESS SYNDICATE. Reprinted with permission. All rights reserved.

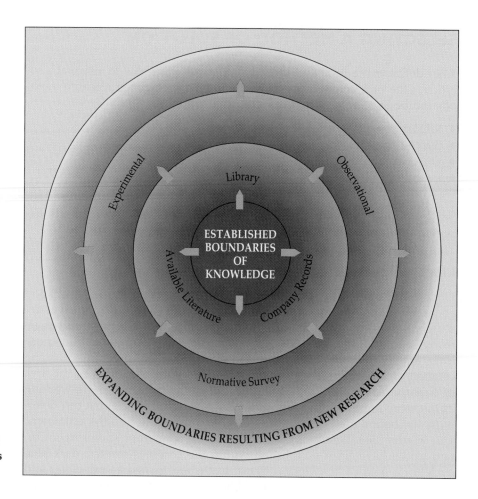

FIGURE 15-3   The constant expansion of the boundaries of knowledge

edge is not static and is constantly expanding, the researcher knows that new information is available. The job, then, is to become familiar with the library, canvass the literature of the field, and attempt to redefine the boundaries of knowledge (second circle). This redefinition is the function of library research. Researchers then explore the unknown (two outer circles). Through redefinition of boundaries, library research accomplishes the following objectives:

1. It establishes a point of departure for further research.
2. It avoids needless duplication of costly research efforts.
3. It reveals areas of needed research.

Why do universities have huge libraries?

One other point should be made: library research makes a real contribution to a body of knowledge.

Applied to business problems, library research involves the investigation of books, periodicals, and any records stored by the business because they might be needed for future information.

The availability of computer-assisted data searches has simplified the time-consuming task of searching through indexes, card catalogs, and other sources. Weekly and monthly updates keep electronic databases current, and they are easy to use. For example, by inputting the key term *cross-cultural*, a researcher received the computer printout shown in Figure 15-4, which is filled with information to facilitate the researcher's efforts. First, the researcher can quickly evaluate the relevance of each reference by simply reading the brief summary provided and highlighting each reference that appears to have merit. The next task is simple: locate each *useful* (highlighted) reference using the complete bibliographic information included in the printout. A research process that may have taken several hours can be completed in a matter of minutes.

When beginning to collect data for study, beware of one of the major deterrents to good reporting—the problem of collecting too much information. Although you want to be thorough, you don't want to collect and record such a large amount of information that you'll hardly know where to begin in your analysis. Try these suggestions to keep the volume at a minimum:

1. Use suggestive or cue notes.
2. Develop a card system.
3. Learn rather than accumulate.

Good advice: protect yourself against too much material!

```
Title:      The Boundaries of Business:  The Cross-Cultural
            Quagmire
Authors:    Hampden-Turner, Charles
Journal:    Harvard Business Review  Vol: 69  Iss: 5
            Date: Sep 1991  pp: 94-96  Jrnl Code: HBR
            ISSN:  0017-8012  Jrnl Group:  Business
Abstract:   Subtle but all-pervasive differences in cultural
            perspectives shape how managers from different
            societies conceive of their roles and their work.
            The problems that confront a cross-cultural
            manager are addressed.  Illustration.
Subjects:   Human resource management; management styles;
            cultural relations; multinational corporations
Type:       Commentary
Length:     Long (31+ col inches)


Title:      Communication Skills in Cross-Cultural Situations
Authors:    Knotts, Rose; Hartman, Sandra J
Journal:    Supervisory Management  Vol: 36  Iss: 3
            Date:  Mar 1991  pp: 12  Jrnl Code: SPM
            ISSN: 1045-263X  Jrnl Group:  Business
Abstract:   Some advice on how to handle cross-cultural
            communications is offered.  Some common problems
            and basics related to communicating with
            foreigners on business matters are discussed.
Subjects:   Cultural relations; interpersonal communication;
            professional relationships
Type:       Feature
Length:     Medium (10-30 col inches)
```

FIGURE 15-4   A sample computer assisted data search

Suggestive Note or Cue Note.   A suggestive or cue note is a reminder to you of something you wanted to recall. Whether you put these reminders on a single sheet of paper or on separate sheets or cards, the goal is to reduce bulky material to small, convenient-to-use data. Develop a system that satisfies your own needs.

Card System.   The card system is particularly useful for library work. Standard 3 × 5 or 4 × 6 cards are helpful. When library information is needed, go first to catalogs, readers' indexes, or electronic databases to compile a basic bibliography. Become familiar with sources such as those shown in Figure 15-5. By preparing a complete bibliographical entry for each reference on a separate card, you may save a trip to the library. Then you can use the abbreviated bibliographical entry on each note card, as shown in the samples in Figure 15-6.

After you have located the relevant sources, you can begin taking notes using various methods. Traditionally, researchers have read the article and immediately written notes on note cards. With photocopiers so readily available, many researchers prefer highlighting important points on a photocopy of the article; and then from the highlighted material, they write note cards or compose notes at the keyboard. In addition, some researchers are using portable computers to facilitate library research. Rather than spending time and money photocopying large volumes of information, researchers compose notes at the keyboard in the library and then return the reference material to shelf. This efficient method of gathering secondary data will grow as the price of portable computers decreases.

You can make notes from each reference in the form of direct quotes or as paraphrases (putting the information in your own words). Put quoted material in quotation marks as a reminder. When paraphrasing, be extremely careful not to change the author's intended meaning. Indicate on your card the page numbers from which cited material is taken. This step may save you another trip to the library. The call number of the reference is a time saver when you must return to the reference.

If you work with numerous references, develop a subject classification as a help in keeping like materials together. You might even begin a card file to be built over time. The note cards in Figure 15.5 are categorized under ethical decisions.

To safeguard your reputation against plagiarism charges, be certain to give credit where credit is due. Specifically, provide a citation (footnote, endnote, or in-text parenthetical reference) for each (1) direct quotation and (2) passage from someone else's work that you stated in your own words rather than using the original words (the words are your own, but the idea is not). Regardless of the note cards you choose to use in your report—the direct quote (shown at the top) or the paraphrased ver-

On Locating Information

Business Periodicals Index

Education Index

New York Times Index

Readers' Guide to Periodical Literature

Social Science and Humanities Index

Wall Street Journal Index

General Factual Information

Statistical Abstract of the United States and other Bureau of the Census publications

Dictionary

Encyclopedia (*Americana* or *Brittanica*)

Fortune Directories of U.S. Corporations

World Atlas

Almanacs

Biography

Who's Who in America (and a variety of similar directories for specific geographic areas, industries, and professions)

Report Style and Format

Gibaldi, J., & Achtert, W. S. (1988). *MLA handbook for writers of research papers.* (3rd ed.). New York: Modern Language Association.

American Psychological Association. *Publication manual of the American Psychological Association.* (1983). (3rd ed.). Washington, DC: Author.

Campbell, W. G., Ballou, S. V., & Slade, C. (1990). *Form and style: Theses reports and term papers.* (8th ed.). Boston: Houghton Mifflin.

University of Chicago Press. *The Chicago manual of style.* (1982). (13th ed.). Chicago: Author.

Turabian, K. L. (1973). *A manual for writers of term papers, theses, and dissertations.* (4th ed.). Chicago: University of Chicago Press.

FIGURE 15-5 Useful reference and source books

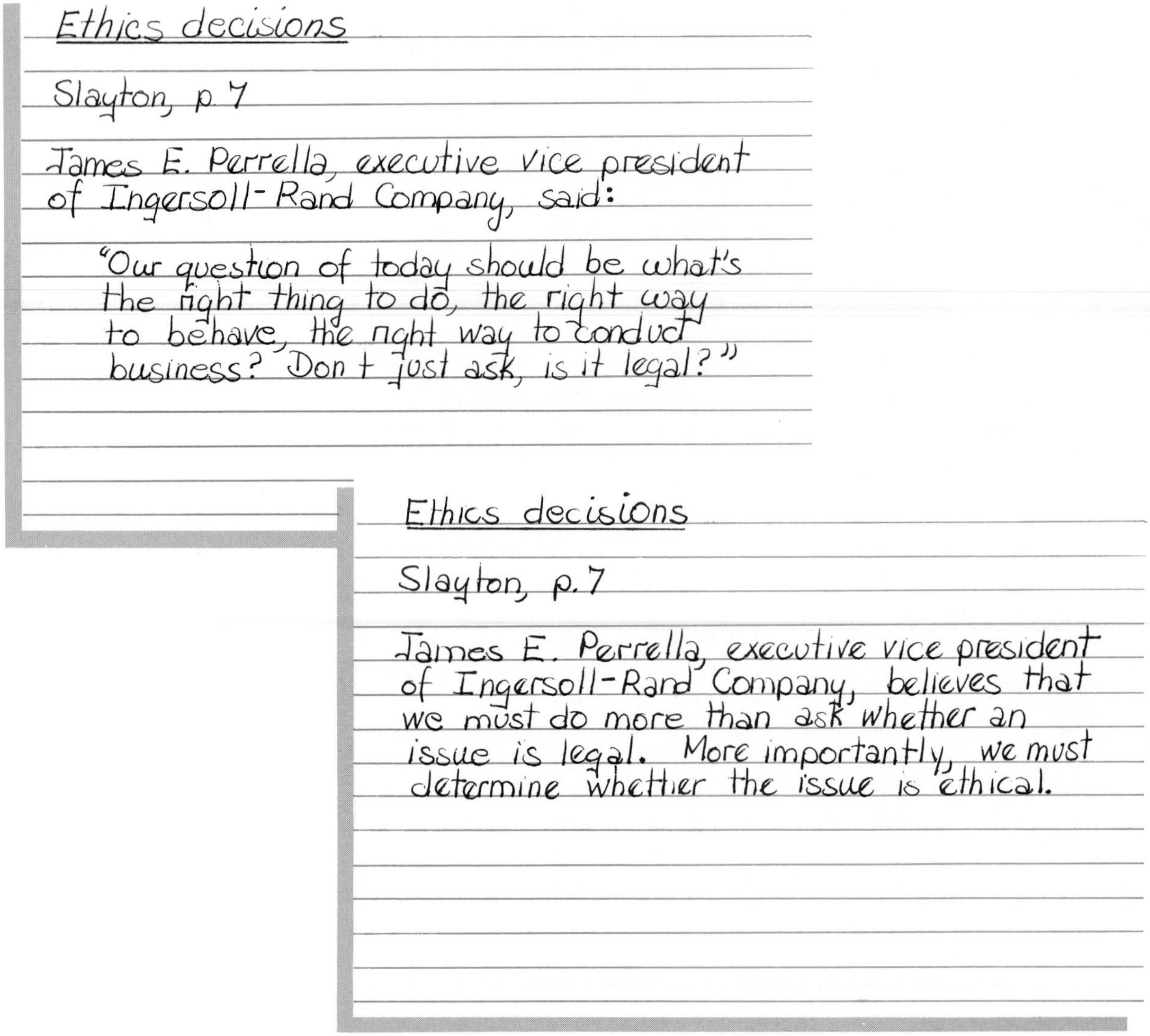

Ethics decisions

Slayton, p. 7

James E. Perrella, executive vice president
of Ingersoll-Rand Company, said:

"Our question of today should be what's
the right thing to do, the right way
to behave, the right way to conduct
business? Don't just ask, is it legal?"

Ethics decisions

Slayton, p. 7

James E. Perrella, executive vice president
of Ingersoll-Rand Company, believes that
we must do more than ask whether an
issue is legal. More importantly, we must
determine whether the issue is ethical.

FIGURE 15-6   Note cards showing abbreviated bibliographic reference and direct quotation (top) and paraphrased passage (bottom)

sion (shown at the bottom)—you must include a citation in your report so
that Perrella receives credit for his idea.

    After identifying the text that must be credited to someone else, de-
velop complete, accurate citations and a references page. Documentation
guidelines are discussed in Chapter 18.

Goal of Library Research. The primary purpose of library research is to *learn*, not to accumulate. The following technique is especially effective: (1) read an article rapidly, (2) put it aside, (3) list main and supporting points *from memory*, and (4) review the article to see whether all significant points have been included. Rapid reading forces concentration. Taking notes from memory reinforces learning and reduces the temptation to rely heavily on the words of others. If you really learn the subject matter of one source, you will (as research progresses) see the relationship between it and other sources. You will see yourself growing toward mastery of the subject.

Summarizing is a valuable skill.

Normative Survey Research

Normative survey research determines the status of something at a specific time. It uses survey instruments such as questionnaires, opinion surveys, checklists, and interviews to obtain information. Election-time opinion polls represent one type of normative survey research. The term *normative* is used to qualify surveys because surveys reveal "norms" or "standards" existing at the time of the survey. An election poll taken two months before an election might have little similarity to one taken the week before the election.

What is the primary purpose of normative survey research?

Surveys can help verify the accuracy of existing norms. The U.S. Census is conducted every decade to establish an actual population figure, and each person is supposedly counted. In effect, the census tests the accuracy of prediction techniques used to estimate population during the years between censuses. A survey of what employees consider a fair benefits package would be effective only for the date of the survey. People retire, move, and change their minds often; these human traits make survey research of human opinion somewhat tentative. Yet, surveys remain a valuable tool for gathering information on which to base policy making and decision making.

Validity and Reliability. Whether a survey involves personal interviewing or the distribution of items such as checklists or questionnaires, some principles of procedure and preplanning are common to both methods. These principles assure the researcher that the data gathered will be both valid and reliable. Data are *valid* (said to possess *validity*) when they measure what they are supposed to measure. Data are *reliable* (said to possess *reliability*) when they give assurance that they are reasonably close to the truth; that is, when they measure accurately.

What steps can you take to ensure that your data are valid and reliable?

Validity generally results from careful planning of the questionnaire or interview questions (*items*). Cautious wording, preliminary testing of items to detect misunderstandings, and some statistical techniques are helpful in determining whether the responses to the items are valid.

Reliability results from asking a large enough sample of people so that the researcher is reasonably assured the results would be the same even if more people were asked to respond. For example, if you were to ask ten people to react to a questionnaire item, the results might vary considerably. If you were to add 90 more people to the sample, the results might tend to reach a point of stability, where more responses would not change the results. Reliability would then be assured.

How large is the U.S. Census population? Would sampling be effective?

Sampling.   In all surveys, the research assumes that the people asked to respond either are representative of a larger group or constitute the entire group that is to be surveyed and about whom generalizations are to be made. The researcher normally can't survey everyone in the population. However, through sampling techniques, the researcher can be confident that a small part of the total population can fairly represent the total population. *Sampling,* then, is a survey technique that saves the time and trouble of questioning 100 percent of the population.

The sampling process is based on the principle that a sufficiently large number drawn at random from a population will be representative

A major factor affecting the value of a survey is the way in which it is conducted. The results of any survey are only as valid and reliable as the methods the researchers use to select and question a representative sample of the population.

of the total population; that is, the sampling group will possess the same characteristics in the same proportions as the total population. For example, public-opinion polls actually survey only a few people; but they are considered valid if the sample of people surveyed has the same percentage of butchers, housewives, Democrats, Republicans, computer programmers, teachers, retired persons, and so on, as the entire population does.

Sampling is thus a vital part of effective surveys. If, for example, you survey the members of the class on the value of this course, you will have surveyed the entire population—all members of the class. Results would be reliable because you would not plan to make generalizations about a larger population from this limited information.

When sampling methods may be necessary because of the size of the population involved, several options are available. These include (1) random sampling, (2) stratified random sampling, and (3) systematic random sampling.

1. Random sampling is perhaps the most desirable technique. To determine the career plans of a college student body, a researcher could use random sampling by putting the name of each student on a small piece of paper, tossing all the names into a container, mixing them, and drawing out a preselected number to include in the survey. Of course, the registrar's computer could be programmed to provide a random list as well. Because the entire student body is included, each name would have an equal opportunity to be drawn.

Does random imply chance?

2. Stratified random sampling is the method public-opinion poll organizations should use. In surveying the student body using this method, you would continue to draw names at random until you have the same percentage of seniors, juniors, sophomores, and freshmen as are in the total student population. Suppose the total student body of 10,000 is composed of 30 percent freshmen, 27 percent sophomores, 23 percent juniors, and 20 percent seniors. If you wanted to survey 1,000 students, you should draw names until you have 300 freshmen, 270 sophomores, 230 juniors, and 200 seniors. You could program other characteristics into your sample as well.

3. Systematic random sampling is a form of random sampling in which, to use our college survey as an example again, every tenth name might be drawn from the files of the registrar. To ensure randomness, you would place in a hat numbers 0–9 and then draw one. If 7 is drawn, for example, you would use the seventh name in the files, then the 17th, 27th, 37th, and so on until you have the number you want to include.

These techniques are used in surveys that attempt to determine shopper preferences, buying habits, attitudes, and similar marketing studies. Again, the researcher must be cautious about drawing conclusions from a sample and applying them to a population that might not be represented by the sample. For example, early-morning shoppers may differ from afternoon or evening shoppers, young ones may differ from old ones, men may differ from women. The good researcher defines the population as distinctly as possible and uses a sampling technique to ensure that the sample is representative.

Why are public opinion polls often inaccurate?

Achieving sophistication in surveys requires considerable study of the field. Findings are only as reliable and valid as are the methods of selecting and surveying the sample.

Even when the sampling technique results in a representative sample, the construction of the survey instrument—usually a questionnaire or interview guide—is critical to the process. Special attention is given to development of questionnaires and other survey instruments later in this chapter.

Observational Research

Observational, or statistical, research describes research involving statistical analysis of one or more sets of data. Suppose we wanted to know whether scores on college-aptitude tests really had any relationship to grades made in a college history course. We would gather the grades of students in the history class, obtain the college aptitude scores of those same students, and perform statistical correlations of the two sets of data to seek information about the relationship.

Frequently, businesses use both observational and survey methods to solve problems. Market analysts may use survey methods to determine buying habits of certain income groups. Then statistical analyses are used to determine the most desirable markets.

The name *observational research* is used because this type of analysis involves observing certain phenomena to assist in establishing new principles. Several studies have used the observational method to determine the differences between "good" or "bad" business letters. One study used a random sample of 500 letters obtained from the files of various companies. Copies of the 500 letters were sent to five experts in written communication who served as a rating jury. Each jury member was asked to sort the letters into five sets. The first set was to include the 100 best letters in the jurist's opinion; the second set, the second-best 100; the third set, the middle 100; and so on. The reports of the five jury members were then combined to determine the 100 letters with the highest ratings and the 100 with the lowest ratings. Three hundred letters fell in the middle and were discarded. Thus only the best and worst 100 remained. Then, the two groups of letters were analyzed in terms of planning, writing style, tone, sentence length, spelling, punctuation, and length. Statistical tests of significant differences between the two groups were used to determine the characteristic differences between good and bad letters. In this study, the observational method was used because certain phenomena were observed, counted, and analyzed statistically to help establish principles.

Experimental Research

Experimental research is familiar to most of us as the test-tube research conducted in a laboratory by a scientist. Scientists are conducting experimental research when they put exactly the same materials into two test tubes and then add one new ingredient to only one of the original tubes. After the new ingredient is added to one tube, the changes that take place in that tube are measured. Any change is due, of course, to the addition of the new ingredient.

Basically, then, *experimental research* involves two samples that have exactly the same ingredients before a variable is added to one of the samples. The differences observed are due to the variable.

How is experimental research used in business? As a simple example, assume an office has a great number of machinists doing the same routine job. Management decides to make a study of the effects of incentive pay (extra pay for production in excess of a minimum standard). It separates the machinists into two groups about equal in experience, skill, and previous productivity rates. Then one group is placed on an incentive-pay basis. During the period of the study, the difference in the two groups is noted. Because the incentive pay is assumed to be the only variable, any difference is attributed to its influence. Of course, we can criticize such a study; but the point is that business uses the experimental research method just as the laboratory scientist uses it.

Comparing results of treatment with medicines and results using placebos is experimental.

COLLECTING DATA THROUGH SURVEYS

Although selecting an appropriate population sample may seem difficult at times, obtaining responses to questionnaires and other survey instruments may seen even more difficult. For surveys conducted by mail, responses often represent only a small percentage of the total mailings. In some cases, a return of 3 to 5 percent is considered adequate and is planned for by researchers. In other cases, depending on the population, the sample, and the information requested, a return of considerably more than half the mailings might be a planned result. Researchers must consider many factors when conducting surveys:

Why is a 5-percent response sometimes adequate?

1. Questionnaire surveys by mail are inexpensive and not limited geographically. Respondents may remain anonymous, which might result

in honest answers, and a mailed survey removes difference-in-status barriers—a corporation president may respond readily when the researcher might never succeed in getting a response by phone or by personal interview. At the same time, mail-survey instruments must be concise; or they will end up in the wastebasket. Most people who respond have strong feelings about the topic, so this group of respondents might not be representative of the intended population. Researchers must prepare persuasive transmittal messages that indicate how the respondent can benefit by answering. That persuasion often takes the form of a gift for answering.

2. Personal interviews allow the interviewer to obtain answers in depth and perhaps to explore otherwise sensitive topics. But interviews are expensive in terms of time and money if interviewers are paid, and many people simply don't want to be interviewed.

3. Telephone interviews are inexpensive as a rule. But like mailed questionnaires, a low percentage of total phone calls will actually provide wanted information.

4. Participant observation is frequently used in consumer research with the observer simply noting how people seem to make selections. A problem, of course, is that observation is sight only and does not give clues about judgment or analytical processes.

No matter which survey technique or combination of techniques is used, the way in which the survey instrument is designed and written has much to do with response validity and reliability, percentage of response, and quality of information received.

Questionnaires

Before formulating items for a questionnaire or opinion survey, a researcher should visualize the ways responses will be assembled and included in a final report. Here are some suggestions for effective questionnaires:

1. The sequence of items should be logical; if possible, the sequence should proceed from easy-to-answer to difficult-to-answer items. Easy items get respondents involved and encourage them to finish; a difficult opening question might result in a wasted mailing.

2. Items that concern the same subject should be grouped for easy answering and tabulation. For example, demographic data such as name, age, gender, family size, and income are often requested. They are easy to answer and often provide background for analysis of other responses. If these items are not necessarily critical, you should indicate that answers to certain ones are optional.

3. Ask for factual information whenever possible. Opinions may be needed in certain studies, but opinions may change from day to day.

COMMUNICATION MENTOR

Clients typically push for the research to do more than it can be reasonably expected to do. As a researcher, you must constantly guard against promising too much. Instead, remind your client that research is but *one* source of information. The same principle applies to building a house. You wouldn't try to use a hammer as the only tool in constructing a home. Neither should a survey be the only tool in gathering information on any given issue.

David Martin
President
Sygnis, Inc.

As a general rule, too, the smaller the sample, the less reliable are conclusions based on opinions.

4. Short-answer items are easy to tabulate. Make answering easy, then. Respondents like items that may be answered by merely making a check mark or circling a response.

5. Provide enough space for respondents to answer essay-type questions. "What effect would an additional tax on oil and natural gas have on the economy?" may require a lengthy answer.

6. Ask for information that can be recalled readily. To ask for information going back in time may not result in sound data.

7. Test the wording of items by asking others to complete and/or read the questionnaire. Test for clarity, ease of answering, and quality of answers.

8. Mailed questionnaires have higher percentages of returns when a return envelope with postage paid is included.

Ease your own workload by making tabulating easy.

Gathering Demographic Data.   Researchers often find their studies require information about groups of respondents. For example, a survey of prospective buyers of Mercedes Benz automobiles would certainly be strengthened if the respondents all could afford luxury cars. Should you find yourself in need of such information as income and age, arrange your questionnaire items so you can arrive at an average age and income for the total population. For example, the following questionnaire item asks for household income:

Please check the box that best describes your household income:

Could these items also be
listed from high to low?

☐ $10,000–$19,999   ☐ $60,000–$69,999
☐ $20,000–$29,999   ☐ $70,000–$79,999
☐ $30,000–$39,999   ☐ $80,000–$89,999
☐ $40,000–$49,999   ☐ $90,000–$99,999
☐ $50,000–$59,999   ☐ $100,000 and over

Ten possible answers are included only for discussion purposes; normally a few with broader ranges would be adequate. By using ranges such as $50,000–$59,999, all the replies falling into that category would be assumed to be distributed equally throughout the range. In this case, the midpoint of the range—$55,000—could represent all incomes in the range.

People prefer to reply with check marks and within ranges simply because doing so is easy. Questions about age might be arranged in the following manner:

Indicate your age group:

☐ 20–29   ☐ 60–69
☐ 30–39   ☐ 70–79
☐ 40–49   ☐ 80 and over
☐ 50–59

In this example, people whose ages are between 20.0 and 29.99 years would check 20–29, and the assumed age for everyone in that group would be the midpoint, 25.0.

Wording of Items. Items requiring yes-no or agree-disagree responses should provide an opportunity for those who are undecided to respond, as in

Should the city have a sales tax?

☐ Yes
☐ No
☐ Undecided

Should items also be tested
for clarity?

Items should be tested to avoid wording that might put people in awkward positions, as in

Have you stopped abusing your spouse?

☐ Yes
☐ No
☐ Undecided

Avoid "skip-and-jump" instructions; such as, "If you answered yes to 4, skip directly to 9; if you answered no, explain your reason under 5 and 6." Note how the portion of a questionnaire shown in Figure 15-7 makes responding easy.

Rating Scales

Rating scales are similar to questionnaires because they pose problems or questions that can be responded to simply. Suppose you want to deter-

---

Marketing Survey of Stereo Purchasing Preferences

Please check the appropriate space for each item.

1. Age group:
☐ under 20
☐ 20–29
☐ 30–39
☐ 40–49
☐ 50–59
☐ Over 59

2. Occupation:
☐ Student
☐ White collar
☐ Blue collar
☐ Retired
☐ Unemployed
☐ Other

3. Gender:
☐ Female
☐ Male

4. Marital status:
☐ Married
☐ Single

5. Household income group:
☐ Below $10,000
☐ $10,000–$19,999
☐ $20,000–$29,999
☐ $30,000–$39,999
☐ $40,000–$49,999
☐ $50,000 and over

6. Do you presently own a stereo?
☐ Yes
☐ No

7. If you do not own a stereo, do you plan to purchase one?
☐ Yes
☐ No
☐ Undecided

8. If you own a stereo system, please check the appropriate spaces in the following items:

a. Do you plan to add to it within the next year?
☐ Yes
☐ No
☐ Uncertain

b. Estimate the value of your present system:
☐ Under $200
☐ $201–$400
☐ $401–$600
☐ $601–$800
☐ $801–$1,000
☐ $1,001–$1,200
☐ Over $1,200

FIGURE 15-7 Portion of a questionnaire

mine the most pressing problems facing employees in a production line. You could ask them to list the problems, but the responses might be so ambiguous that tabulating them would be impossible. A rating scale such as the following one would be an improvement:

Circle the degree to which each of the following factors affects your job satisfaction.

Acceptance by others

1	2	3	4	5	6

| Little effect | | Moderate effect | | | Great effect |

Interest in job

1	2	3	4	5	6

| Little effect | | Moderate effect | | | Great effect |

Note that six numbers have been used to indicate how respondents feel. When an odd number of choices, such as five, is provided, respondents tend to converge toward the middle number. This tendency to converge may create a bias in the responses.

Does convergence toward the middle say something about human nature?

Similar information could be obtained by listing the potential problems and by asking respondents to rank the problems in order of their importance:

Rank the following factors in order of their importance to you. Place a 1 in the space following the most important problem, a 2 in the space following the second most important problem, and so on until all have been ranked. Two blank lines have been left for you to write in problem areas that may have been omitted.

Acceptance by others	____
Interest in job	____
Economic security	____
Health	____
_____	____
_____	____

Even though most of us are familiar with rating scales because we encounter them both at work and at school, when we use them in research, we should first test them on a small sample to see if they are clearly understood and produce the kind of information we want.

To determine which of the factors is most critical to the production employee, a *forced answer* question can be used:

Of all the problems listed, which is the <u>single</u> most critical problem for you personally? _____

_____

This question could also have been posed in a multiple-choice form, much like the multiple-choice items used in academic tests:

Which of the following factors is the <u>single</u> most critical factor for you personally? Place a check in the space provided.

a. Acceptance by others   ____
b. Interest in job   ____
c. Economic security   ____
d. Health   ____
e. Other (specify)   ____ _____

Researchers must select from the several formats available the one best suited to the situation. Criteria for selecting one alternative over the others might include the following items: Which format leaves the least chance for misinterpretation? Which format provides information in the way it can best be used? Can it be tabulated easily? Can it be cross-referenced to other items in the survey instrument?

ARRIVING AT AN ANSWER

Even the most intelligent person cannot be expected to draw sound conclusions from faulty information. Sound conclusions can be drawn only when information has been properly organized, collected, and interpreted.

Organizing the Data

Having decided on a method, researchers must outline a step-by-step approach to the solution of the problem. The human mind is susceptible to digressions. Although these digressions may be short lived, they distract from the job at hand; and, if given free rein, they can lead to obliteration of the real object of the study.

Therefore, *keep on the right track.* Plan the study and follow the plan. Question every step for its contribution to the objective. Keep a record of actions. In a formal research study, the researcher is expected to make a complete report. Another qualified person should be able to make the same study, use the same steps, and arrive at the same conclusion. Thus, a report serves as a guide.

Tabulation techniques should be used to reduce quantitative data such as numerous answers to questionnaire items. Suppose we have made a survey and have collected several hundred replies to a 20- or 30-item questionnaire in addition to many cards or notes from library sources. What do we do next? As shown in Figure 15-8, the report process is one of reducing the information collected to a size that can be handled conveniently in a written message.

Visualize the report process as taking place in a huge funnel. At the top of the funnel, pour in all the original information. Then, through a process of compression within the funnel, take these steps:

1. Evaluate the information for its usefulness.
2. Reduce the useful information through the use of suggestive notes, card systems, or learning.

Does tabulating serve the same purpose as cue cards in library research?

Is it easier to read 300 separate questionnaires or a few tables?

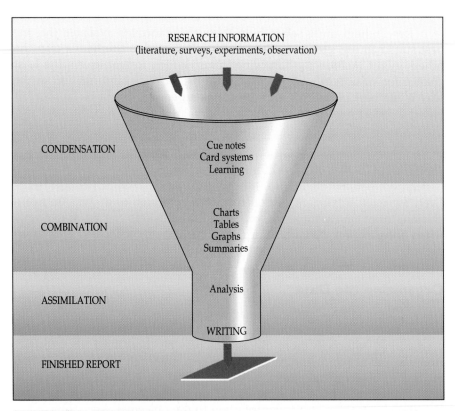

FIGURE 15-8   The report process

3. Combine like information into understandable form through the use of tables, charts, graphs, and summaries. (See Chapter 16.)
4. Report in written form what remains. (See Chapters 17 and 18.)

Collecting the Appropriate Data

If acceptable data-gathering techniques have been employed, data will measure what they are intended to measure (have validity) and will measure it accurately (have reliability). Some common errors at the data-gathering stage that seriously hamper later interpretation are

1. Using samples that are too small.
2. Using samples that are not representative.
3. Using poorly constructed data-gathering instruments.
4. Using information from biased sources.
5. Failing to gather enough information to cover all important aspects of a problem.
6. Gathering too much information and then attempting to use all of it even though some may be irrelevant.

Poor sampling spoils the analysis.

INTERPRETING DATA

Even valid and reliable data can be worthless if the interpretation is faulty. If we avoid data-collection errors, we are more likely to reach sound conclusions. But sound conclusions are unlikely if interpretation is faulty. Some common mental errors seriously handicap the interpretation of data:

1. *Trying, consciously or unconsciously, to make results conform to a prediction or desire.* Seeing predictions come true may be pleasing, but objectivity is much more important. Facts should determine conclusions.
2. *Hoping for spectacular results.* An attempt to astonish supervisors by preparing a report with revolutionary conclusions can only have a negative effect on accuracy.
3. *Attempting to compare when commonality is absent.* Concluding that a certain product would sell well in Arizona because it sold well in Massachusetts is risky. Because of differences in geography, climate, and economic factors, relationships might not be at all comparable.
4. *Assuming a cause-effect relationship when one does not exist.* A company president may have been in office one year and sales may have doubled. But the sales might have doubled *in spite* of the president rather than *because* of her.
5. *Failing to consider important factors.* A college professor returned from a tour of the educational institutions in Mexico. Speaking to a group of

The women's basketball team has won every game since you began attending. Is it a coincidence or your influence?

COMMUNICATION MENTOR

No research is perfect! You can always find ways to challenge research if your objective is to discredit the study. You should also remember that the same is also true if it is *your* study that you are trying to use on your own behalf.

My experience has been that the most common errors include (1) using inadequate sample sizes, (2) asking biased questions, (3) surveying the wrong audience, and (4) drawing inappropriate conclusions.

David Martin
President
Sygnis, Inc.

high school teachers, he cautioned against modifying the school curriculum to include four years of science and math, four years of foreign language, four years of social studies, and four years of English. That curriculum, he said, is Mexico's curriculum, and in Mexico last night two-thirds of the babies went to bed hungry. He apparently neglected to consider the influence of such factors as geography, climate, natural resources, tradition, and politics.

6. *Basing a conclusion on lack of evidence.* "We have had no complaints about our present policy" does not mean that the policy is appropriate. And, conversely, lack of evidence that a proposed project will succeed does not necessarily mean that it will fail.

7. *Assuming constancy of human behavior.* A survey indicating 60 percent of the public favors one political party over the other in March does not mean the same thing will be true in November. Because some people paid their bills late last year does not mean a company should refuse to sell to them next year. The reasons for slow payment may have been removed.

Keep in mind the differences in some research terms as you analyze your material and attempt to seek meaning from it. A *finding* from a research study is a specific, measurable fact:

. . . 67 percent of those interviewed preferred steel-belted, white-wall tires.

. . . average daily temperature in July is 89° in New Orleans and 70° in San Francisco.

A *conclusion* is derived from findings:

With the introduction of Coke II, market researchers aren't making the same mistake that contributed to the flop of New Coke in 1985—disregard for consumers' loyalty to the traditional flavor of Coke. Coca Cola Classic remains on the shelf and advertising emphasizes Coke II's "real cola taste."

. . . steel-belted, white-wall tires are preferred.

. . . the temperature of San Francisco meets the needs of XYZ Company.

When you select one item from among several, you may have findings about each related to cost, weight, manufacturer service after the sale, and any number of other criteria. Your conclusion from these findings may be "Item G meets my needs best."

A *recommendation* is a suggested action based on your research. Recommendations are not a part of every report and should be included only when requested or when they seem to be a natural outcome of the research. A finding is factual, a conclusion is drawn from findings, and a recommendation evolves from the conclusions and the nature of the problem.

SUMMARY

In arriving at an answer (a conclusion), report writers must have the results of their research before them. They should be able to see the problem as a whole. If they carefully defined the problem, selected an appropriate method of research, and gathered and analyzed the data, they can arrive at a sound conclusion. Throughout the entire process, however, researchers must protect themselves not only against their own human failings but also against their material. This process is the essence of objectivity. As you approach the report-writing task, your success will rest primarily on your ability to retain your objectivity.

REFERENCE

Maremont, M. (1990, March 12). How British Airways butters up the passenger. *Business Week,* p. 94.

REVIEW QUESTIONS

1. How do informational and analytical reports differ?
2. Why do reports generally travel upward in an organization?
3. In a bank, the internal auditing division performs semiannual audits of each branch. Then the audit reports are sent to the bank's chief executive officer and chief financial officer and to the manager of the audited branch. The purpose of the audits is to determine whether policies and practices are properly followed. Into what report classifications might the audit report fall? Explain.
4. How do the four steps in problem solving apply when the driver of an automobile realizes a tire is going flat rapidly?
5. How might a null hypothesis be stated for a research study attempt-

ing to determine whether television or newspaper advertising has greater influence on cereal sales?

6. How does library research make a contribution to all studies?

7. Gathering so much information that the researcher is "snowed under" by the amount is often a barrier to good reporting. How might researchers protect themselves against this possibility?

8. Distinguish between reliability and validity.

9. What is meant by random sampling?

10. What type of research is characterized by efforts to measure the effect of a variable added to one of two samples?

11. What questions might you ask of someone who wants assistance in planning a questionnaire survey to determine automobile-owner satisfaction with certain after-the-sale services provided by dealers?

12. Why is an even number of rating-scale responses supposedly better than an odd number?

13. Of the data-collection errors, which are directly related to construction of data-gathering instruments?

14. How does the assumption that human beings behave in consistent ways over time present a danger in data interpretation?

EXERCISES

1. For each of the following research topics, write a positive hypothesis and then restate it as a null hypothesis. Answers to topic (a) are given.

   a. A study to determine the relationship existing between the Fog Index readability rating of business textbooks and student interest in courses using the textbooks.

   Hypothesis: Students show more interest in courses using textbooks with low Fog Indexes than in courses using textbooks with high Fog Indexes.

   Null Hypothesis: Readability levels of course textbooks have no relationship to student interest in those courses. *Or:* No relationship exists between readability of textbooks and student interest in courses using those textbooks.

   b. A study to determine whether people's net worth at age 50 is directly related to education.

   c. A study to determine functional business areas from which chief executive officers advanced in their organizations. Functional areas are legal, financial, accounting, marketing, production, and other.

2. What factors might limit or influence your findings in any of the studies in Exercise 1? Could you apply the findings of Exercise 1 studies to a broader population than those included in the studies? Why or why not?

3. What research method would you use for each of the research problems included in Exercise 1?

4. If you were to conduct a survey of the 14,000 homeowners in a community of 40,000 people, describe how you might construct a sampling procedure to avoid having to survey the entire population.

5. "A course in economics should be taken by every college student" is a statement frequently made and also frequently challenged. Could this statement be tested through research? If so, what kind of research? Comment.

For the research studies in Exercises 6 through 10, prepare a one-page description of your attack on the problem. Use the following headings for the problem assigned:

Statement of the Problem

Research Method and Sources of Information

Nature of Data to Be Gathered and Analyzed

Hypothesis or Hypotheses to Be Proved or Disproved (if feasible)

Think ahead to the nature of the questionnaire or other type of research instrument or technique you might use.

6. As research director of Glow-Stern, a stock brokerage firm, you have the task of determining investment practices of your clients. Your goal is to learn how different age groups manage their investment or savings dollars. Because this subject could be quite sensitive to many clients, your survey is to be anonymous. You've also decided that your age groups should be adults under the age of 30, people between 30 and 50, and those over 50.

7. As marketing director of Club Carib, a chain of resort hotels in the Caribbean, you want to determine what former customers liked and disliked about their vacations at your resorts.

8. Burger Express plans to open a new outlet in one of three possible locations: (1) on an interstate highway, (2) in a downtown shopping district, or (3) in a neighborhood shopping mall. All locations are within a three-mile radius of the center of a city. You are to submit a recommendation.

9. As marketing-promotion director for the Ajax Cosmetics Company, you are planning to advertise your new line of high-priced cosmetics in either *Vogue* or *Cosmopolitan* magazine. Only one can be selected because of budget constraints. You plan to run full-page, color ads for the next 12 months. You are to submit a recommendation.

10. As promotion-advertising director of City First Thrift and Loan, you have the job of determining whether the firm should give gift certificates or actual gifts (items such as calculators, pens, or hand kitchen mixers) as incentives to encourage people to open accounts. In either case, the incentives cannot exceed a value of $5 for each $1,000 deposited in the new account.

Sygnis

Effective research is vital if a business is to respond to the changing requirements of customers and other interest groups. Various methods exist for obtaining necessary information. Secondary research yields results of information that already exists, while primary research reveals new information that cannot be obtained elsewhere. Primary research can be obtained in a variety of ways, each possessing advantages and limitations. Questionnaire design is critical to ef-fective data collection. Random sampling assures that the results obtained are representative of the larger population.

The written report brings all the elements of effective research into a readable format. Careful attention to organization, conciseness, visual presentation, and objectivity are essential as the report is the basis on which the research will be judged. It must respond to the readers' needs.

Discussion Questions

1. David Martin and Bruce Brown mention several primary research methodologies. List five and for each give a major consideration in choosing it for data collection.
2. How are the concepts of sampling and validity related?
3. What role do computers play in research report preparation?
4. List four characteristics of a well-designed questionnaire.

5. Explain the role of visual and written presentation in producing an effective research report.

Application

You are conducting marketing research on consumers of Jennas, an all-natural, low-fat yogurt. You are interested in the characteristics of typical purchasers and the reasons for their purchasing the product. Design a one-page questionnaire that might be used in a mall-intercept survey.

MANAGING DATA AND USING GRAPHICS

OBJECTIVES

When you have completed
Chapter 16, you should be
able to

- Manage quantities of
  data efficiently.

- Analyze quantitative data
  using the measures of
  central tendency.

- Design and integrate effective tables and graphics within reports.

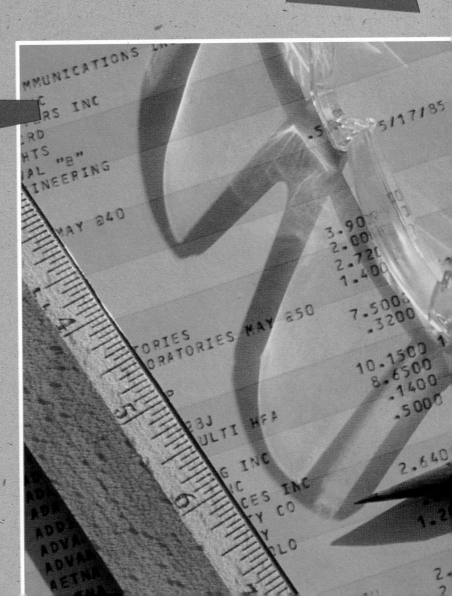

YOUR DESK IS LITERALLY COVERED with folders and stacks of papers relating to an advertising campaign your superiors are proposing to terminate. This project is important to you; it was partially your idea in the first place, and you really believe it will help launch your company's new frozen-food product. You have done months of research on the program's effectiveness and the public relations benefits of maintaining it. In less than a week, you must put all the data you have accumulated into a presentable report that will convince the company's top executives of the merit of the campaign. You begin sifting through the information, looking for the most impressive statistics before you sit in front of your computer to begin writing the rough draft of your report.

This same scenario occurs everyday in business. You, too, will have to write reports. A report's success depends largely on how well you have accessed information through research, processed the information through careful study of the data, and organized that information by putting it into a comprehensible format. What techniques can keep you from being overwhelmed by your data? How can you make important points stand out and complex data easy to understand?

MANAGING QUANTITATIVE DATA

In many studies, particularly those involving surveys, many of the data gathered lend themselves to statistical analysis. A number of people respond "yes," another number respond "no," and another number respond "no opinion" to a questionnaire item. Whether these responses are counted manually or by computer, the counting process is called *tabulation;* and tabulation must precede analysis. Assume, for example, that you have been given a stack of 200 or 300 questionnaires containing people's responses to several items. To tabulate the responses manually, you would probably make a list of the items, go through each questionnaire, and make a pencil mark to show the response to each item.

Tabulating would provide you with a single page showing total responses for each possible response to each item. For example, responses for employee training needs might appear like this following tabulation of 300 questionnaires:

Activity-based costing	15
Written communication	54
Computer technology	102
Just-in-time inventory	51
Human behavior	24
Legal environment	24
Workplace diversity	30
	300

The breakdown reduces 300 responses to a manageable size. The tabulation shows only seven items, each with a specific number of responses from the total of 300 questionnaires. Because people tend to make comparisons during analysis, the totals are helpful. But people generally want to know proportions or ratios, and these are best presented as percentage parts of the total. Thus, the number tabulations converted to percentages are

Training Need	Number	Percentage
Activity-based costing	15	5
Written communication	54	18
Computer technology	102	34
Just-in-time inventory	51	17
Human behavior	24	8
Legal environmment	24	8
Workplace diversity	30	10
	300	100

Now analyzing the data becomes relatively easy. Eighteen percent of the employees selected written communication, and 10 percent selected workplace diversity. Another observation, depending on how exactly you intend to interpret percentages, could be that just over one-third of the employees selected computer technology and approximately a quarter of the employees desire inventory-related training (activity-based costing and just-in-time inventory).

This analysis first reduced 300 questionnaires to seven tabulated categories. The total response of 300 was reduced to 100 percent, and the 100 percent was further divided into ratios or fractions. In research about people's opinions, likes, preferences, and other subjective items, rounding off statistics to fractions helps paint a clear picture for readers. In actuality, if the same group of people were asked this question again a day or two later, a few probably would have changed their minds. For example, an employee who had not indicated a desire for communication training may have received a negative rating on written communication skills during his annual performance appraisal; the next day he might indicate a desire for training in written communication.

Common Language

Fractions, ratios, and percentages are often called examples of common language. In effect, they reduce difficult figures to the "common denominators" of language and ideas. Although "102 of 300 prefer computer technology training" is somewhat easy to understand, "34 percent prefer computer technology training" is even easier, and "approximately one out of three prefers computer technology training" is even more understandable.

When you incorporate data into a report, be sure that you use language that your readers can understand. For example, stating numbers in ratios or percentages will help you clarify complex or unwieldy information in the same way Dow-Jones industrial averages help investors understand voluminous New York Stock Exchange figures.

Are school letter grades common language?

Common language also involves the use of indicators other than actual count or quantity. The Dow-Jones industrial averages provide a measure of stock market performance and are certainly easier to understand than the complete New York Stock Exchange figures for 2,000 stocks. "Freight car loadings" are weight measurements used in railroad terminology rather than "pounds carried," and oil is counted in barrels rather than in the quart or gallon sizes purchased by consumers. Because of inflation, dollars are not very accurate items to use as comparisons from one year to another in certain areas; for example, automobile manufacturers use "automobile units" to represent production changes in the industry. The important thing for the report writer to remember is that reports are communication media, and everything possible should be done to make sure communication occurs.

Measures of Central Tendency

Measures of central tendency are simple statistical treatments of distributions of quantitative data that attempt to find a single figure to describe the entire distribution. The three most commonly used measures are the mean, the median, and the mode.

COMMUNICATION MENTOR

Salt River Project (SRP) generally is perceived as meeting high ethical standards; yet, some users (particularly those who live on fixed incomes) perceive rate increases as unfair. They think a corporation set up by the state should subsidize low-income groups, but SRP does not. To minimize these misunderstandings, SRP readily provides users with facts and figures that clearly show that rate increases are justified. A recent proposal for a 2.9 percent increase, for example, was shown as being lower than the inflation rate.

Carroll M. Perkins
General Manager
Salt River Project

The Mean. The *mean* is the figure obtained when all the values in a distribution (table of values) are totaled and divided by the number of values. If, for example, eight people score values of 60, 65, 70, 75, 80, 85, 90, and 95 on a test, the total of these values is 620. Dividing 620 by 8 gives a mean of 77.5. Most people would call 77.5 the average score, but *mean* is a more accurate term.

When material is tabulated by classes, such as "10 people scored between 80 and 89," statisticians would take the midpoint—84.5—and multiply it by 10 to get a total score for that class. Doing the same for other classes would provide a total for all those in the tabulation. Dividing the total of all classes by the number of scores would provide a group mean. Grouping scores (placing them in classes) is not much different from totaling them separately. To determine the mean is simply the process of totaling all values and dividing by the number whether totaled by classes or by individual scores.

The Median. The *median* is the middle value in a distribution. For example, values of 20, 65, 70, 75, 80, 85, and 100 in a distribution would have 75 as the median. In this case, using the median might be more descriptive than would a mean because the very low score of 20 would not influence the measure of central tendency. In a case, for example, where nine people each earn $10,000 and a tenth person earns $110,000, the median is $10,000—a far better descriptive value for the ten people than a mean of $20,000.

When values are counted in classes, find the middle score or value

> **The mean is the arithmetic average.**

> **The median is the middle or midpoint.**

by counting from the top down or from the bottom up to the class containing the middle value. Roughly speaking, the class could then be described as the median class.

The Mode.   The *mode* is the value found most frequently in a distribution. For example, ten test scores of 65, 70, 75, 75, 75, 80, 85, 90, 90, and 100 would have a mode of 75—the most frequent score. The mean would be the total, 805, divided by 10, or 80.5. The median would be halfway between 75 and 80—the fifth and sixth scores of the ten—or 77.5. In this case, either the mean or the median would be an acceptable and more desirable measure than the mode.

The mode is the most common value.

In general, the mean is the most stable of these three measures and usually fluctuates less than the other two. As a result, the mean is used in calculating standard deviations (another measure of central tendency not covered in this text) and is extremely reliable when distributions are large. Even a person 150 years of age or with an income of $1,000,000 would not affect the mean very much in a distribution of several hundred people. In small distributions the median is often a good indicator, especially when some very high or very low extreme values would influence the mean.

These simple statistical measures help report writers describe the content and meaning of their tables and graphs. These measures are part of the common language of statistics and are especially efficient and effective in reporting to people who understand their meanings. Good judgment on the part of the report writer should determine which measure to use or whether to use one at all.

The Range.   When researchers first glance at a distribution, they probably look for the *range*—the difference between the lowest and highest values. For example, test scores of 20, 30, 75, 75, 75, 80, 85, 90, and 95 would have a range of 20 to 95, or 76 points (95 − 20 + 1, to count both the 20 and the 95).

High − low + one = range.

The range helps a researcher determine how many classes should be used in tabulating large numbers of values. In general, a first glance at the range reveals the extremes of values and assists in data analysis.

Some researchers use the *interquartile range*—the spread of the middle 50 percent of the values—as a form of central tendency measurement. For example, in a distribution such as 7, 19, 21, 23, 24, 25, 29, and 41, the interquartile range is 21 to 25. Because eight items are included, two are in each quarter of the distribution. The two middle quartiles, the middle half, have the figures 21, 23, 24, and 25. Even though the total range is 7 to 41, the interquartile range shows that most figures are grouped tightly. Thus, the extreme values of 7 (the low) and 41 (the high) become less important.

USING GRAPHICS

Managing data effectively protects a report writer from being overwhelmed by the data. To protect readers from being overwhelmed, report writers must select appropriate means of presenting the data. "One picture is worth a thousand words" is an old but meaningful saying. Material that can be reported in a table, picture, graph, or chart will make your written analysis of it clearer to the reader.

Imagine trying to put in composition style all the information available in a modern financial statement. Several hundred pages might be necessary to explain all of the material that could otherwise be contained in three or four pages of balance sheets and profit and loss statements.

Motion Picture & Television Photo Archive, Disney.

In the film Fantasia, *Walt Disney used clever graphics to interpret various selections of classical music, including casting Mickey Mouse in the lead role in* The Sorcerer's Apprentice. *Likewise, in your reports, use graphics to underscore or illustrate points that are important or difficult to explain with numbers or words alone.*

COMMUNICATION MENTOR

Absorption and retention of information are unquestionably enhanced by the use of graphics, whether you have time and budget to produce video or computer-generated 35mm slides, elect to hand-draw graphics on a flip chart, or use an overhead projector. (Perhaps you are considering graphics right now to support a term paper or research project.)

Don't be afraid to use graphics to present simple information. On the contrary, be afraid *not* to use them when you are tackling a complex subject. Readers and audiences expect them and will consistently reward you for your extra work.

James F. Hurley
Senior Vice President
CalFed Inc.

And even then, the reader would no doubt be thoroughly confused! Graphics go hand in hand with the written discussion to achieve clarity. As you proceed through the remainder of this chapter, ask yourself if the discussion would be effective if the accompanying graphic figures were not included.

Throughout our discussion of illustrations, the term "graphics" will be used to refer to all types of illustrations. In reports, the most commonly used graphics are tables, bar charts, line charts, pie charts, pictograms, maps, flowcharts, diagrams, and photographs. These graphic presentations are often used as aids during oral reports as well. In both written and oral reports, several questions can help you determine whether using a graphic presentation is appropriate and effective:

A picture may be worth a thousand words.

1. Does the graphic presentation contribute to the overall understanding of the subject? Would a graphic assist the reader?
2. Can the material be covered adequately in words rather than in visual ways? Graphics, both in written and oral reports, should be saved for things that are difficult to communicate in words alone.
3. Will the written or spoken text add meaning to the graphic display?
4. Is the graphic easily understood? Extreme use of color, complicated symbols, confusing art techniques, and unusual combinations of typefaces only detract from the impact of the material presented.
5. Is the graphic honest? The hand is often quicker than the eye; as we will discover later in this chapter, data can be distorted rather easily.
6. If the visual presentation is part of an oral report, can it be seen by the

entire audience? Flip charts, poster boards, overhead projector transparencies, and on-screen computer presentations are the visual means most often used to accompany oral reports.

Perhaps the most recent computer innovation to have an effect on business is computer graphics. With the proper software programs, managers can now produce at their desks almost any of the graphics discussed in this chapter. The graphics may be in black and white or in multicolored, three-dimensional style. Printing of computer graphics may require plotters and/or dot matrix or laser printers and special software.

The greatest advantage of computer graphics is their value to the individual decision maker who formerly had to battle through a maze of computer-printed output. Now the computer can produce a graphic after performing the data-management functions discussed at the beginning of this chapter. The information can be reproduced in a variety of ways for inclusion in reports. The great range of computer graphics is illustrated in Figures 16-1–16-15 in this chapter.

The figures illustrate acceptable variations in the graphic design: placement of the caption (figure number and title), with and without grid lines, the Y-axis labeled at the top of the axis or turned sideways, and others. When designing your graphics, adhere to the requirements in your company policy manual or the style manual you are instructed to follow. Then be certain that you design all graphics consistently throughout the report. When preparing a graphic for use as a visual aid (transparency or on-screen display) in an oral presentation, you may wish to remove the figure number and include the title only.

Tables

A *table* is a presentation of data in column form. Very simply, 2 plus 3 plus 5 plus 6 plus 11 equals 27 is better represented as

$$\begin{array}{r} 2 \\ 3 \\ 5 \\ 6 \\ \underline{11} \\ 27 \end{array}$$

Is the addition format also common language?

Typically, the preparation of tables is concerned with labeling techniques to make the content clear. Here are some helpful practices in table preparation:

1. Number tables and all other graphics consecutively throughout the report. This practice enables you to refer to "Figure 1" rather than to "the following table" or "the figure on the following page." Incidentally, the term *figure* should be used to identify all tables, graphs, pic-

COMMUNICATION MENTOR

Above all, technology provides options to business communications. Through revolutionized graphic techniques, almost limitless production capabilities are available via computers. As recently as the 1980s, use of professional typesetters for high-quality projects was the common practice. Now advancing technology offers businesses many alternatives—internally meet all or some of their graphics needs or continue to outsource graphics production for complex projects.

Cynthia Pharr
President & CEO
Tracy-Locke/Pharr Public Relations

tures, and charts. In this chapter, for example, note that all illustrations are identified as figures.

Detailed titles improve communication.

2. Give each table a title that is complete enough to clarify what is included without forcing the reader to review the table. Table titles may be quite long and even extend beyond one line. A two-line title should be arranged on the page so that neither line extends into the margins. The second line should be shorter than the first and centered under it. Titles may contain sources of data, numbers included in the table, and the subject; for example, "Base Salaries of Chief Executives of the 200 Largest Financial Institutions in the United States." Titles may be written in either uppercase or upper- and lowercase letters.

3. Label columns of data clearly enough to identify the items. Usually, column headings are short and easily arranged. If, however, they happen to be lengthy, use some ingenuity in planning the arrangement.

4. If the labels for the rows (horizontal items) require more than one line, indent the second line two or three spaces. Labels that are merely subdivisions of more comprehensive labels should be indented, and summary labels such as *total* should also be indented. The sample table shown in Figure 16-1 illustrates effective layout. Figure 16-2 illustrates this effective layout in actual use.

Arranging a great amount of data on one page can be challenging. Keep in mind that two-page tables often are necessary, scissors and tape may have to be used to make large tables, and material that won't fit on the page vertically might fit horizontally. In other words, a little creativity helps.

Figure Number			
TITLE			
Line Identification	**Caption Head**		
	Subcaption	**Subcaption**	**Subcaption**
Line caption	xxxx	xxxx	xxxx
Line caption	xxxx	xxxx	xxxx
Line caption	xxxx	xxxx	xxxx
Line caption	xxxx*	xxxx	xxxx
Line caption	xxxx	xxxx	xxxx
Line caption	xxxx	xxxx	xxxx
Summary or total caption	xxxx	xxxx	xxxx

* Footnote—explains one or more items in a table; use letters if the table includes more than one footnote.

Source: Identifies the source of the information in the table; follows the same format used for references.

FIGURE 16-1 Effective table layout identifying captions, labels, footnote, and source

Figure 1			
COMBINED FIRST-YEAR COSTS FOR THREE SITES			
Cost	**Location**		
	Main	**Linden**	**Palmeran**
Lease	$ 90,000	$ 75,000	$ 72,000
Property tax	14,000*	22,000	22,000
Trucking	64,000	60,000	64,000
Preparation	30,000	50,000	30,000
Totals	$198,000	$207,000	$188,000

* Real property on Main is to be reassessed in March. A 50-percent increase to about $21,000 is anticipated.

Source: Cattaneo Industries, Inc., *Annual Report,* 1992.

FIGURE 16-2 Effective table layout

Bar Charts

The *simple bar chart* (also called single-range bar chart) is perhaps the most effective graphic device for comparing quantities. The length of the bars, whether they are horizontal or vertical, indicates quantity, as shown in Figure 16-3. The quantitative axis should always begin at zero and be divided into equal increments. The width of the bars should be equal, or the wider bar will imply that it represents a larger number than the narrower bar. Here are further suggestions:

Bars emphasize relationships!

1. Shadings, cross-hatchings, or variations in color can be used to distinguish among the bars.
2. Even though the bars present relationships, readers will get a clearer picture when the specific dollar or quantity amount is printed at the top of each bar. Readers tend to skim the text and rely on graphics for details. Omit the actual amounts if a visual estimate is adequate for understanding the relationships presented in the chart. Excluding nonessential information such as specific amounts, grids, and explanatory notes actually increases the readability of the chart by reducing the clutter. Use your judgment in listing specifics in graphics.
3. Without making the graphic appear so complicated that readers will skip it, include enough information in your scale labels and bar labels to be understandable. Figure 16-4 shows production figures for three

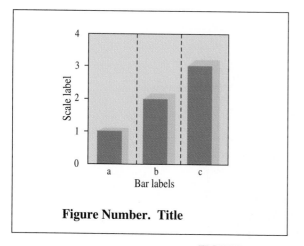

Figure Number. Title

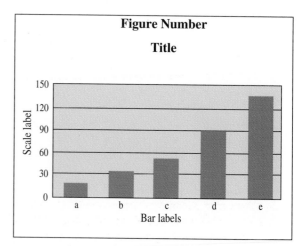

FIGURE 16-3   **Simple-bar chart layout variations**

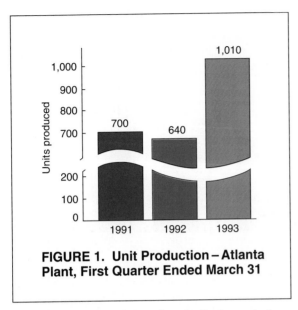

1,010
1,000
900
800
700
200
100
0
Units produced
700
640
1991
1992
1993
FIGURE 1. Unit Production – Atlanta Plant, First Quarter Ended March 31

FIGURE 16-4 Broken-bar chart indicates omission of part of the bar.

years; amounts appear in the vertical-scale labels and years in the horizontal-scale labels.

4. If some quantities are so large that the chart would become unwieldy, the bars may be broken to indicate omission of part of each bar, as shown in Figure 16-4.

Multiple-Range Bar Chart. The *multiple-range bar chart,* also called comparative or cluster bar chart, is useful for expressing data that change over time. The multiple-range bar chart is especially effective in comparing more than one quantity (set of data) at each point along the x-axis. Electronic spreadsheet software programs allow you to construct multiple-range bar charts comparing as many as six quantities. Figure 16-5 compares the frequency of reported injuries at three plants over an entire year. Because the chart was printed using a color printer, each quantity appears in a specific color to facilitate comparison. Patterns, also called cross-hatchings, differentiate the quantities if a color printer is not available.

Stacked-Bar Chart. The *stacked-bar chart,* also called component, 100 percent, or segmented bar chart, is shown in Figure 16-6. When you want to show how different facts (components) contribute to a total figure, the stacked-bar chart is desirable. This graphic is particularly useful when

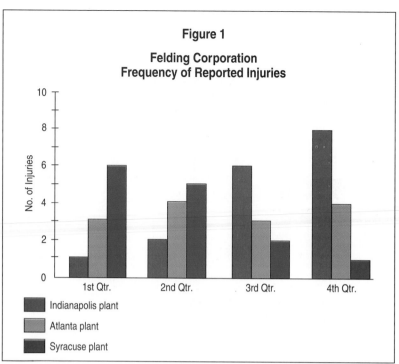

FIGURE 16-5 Multiple-range bar chart is useful for comparing more than one quantity over time.

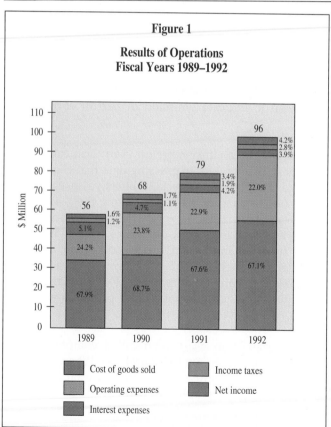

FIGURE 16-6 Stacked-bar chart shows how proportional relationships change over time.

components for more than one time period are being compared. Figure 16-6 shows the change in the five components of the results of operation over a four-year period. The actual percentage of each component is displayed in this example; however, these numbers can be omitted to reduce excessive clutter if you believe the reader's visual assessment of the proportions is adequate. Because this graph was printed using a color printer, colors distinguish the components, with a key included at the bottom of the chart. Patterns, also called cross-hatchings, differentiate the components if a color printer is not available.

Line Charts

Line charts, such as the one shown in Figure 16-7, depict changes in quantitative data over time and illustrate trends. When constructing line charts, keep these general guidelines in mind:

1. Use the vertical axis for amount and the horizontal axis for time.
2. Begin the vertical axis at zero. If the height of the chart becomes unwieldy, break it the same way the vertical scale was broken in Figure 16-4 or 16-9.

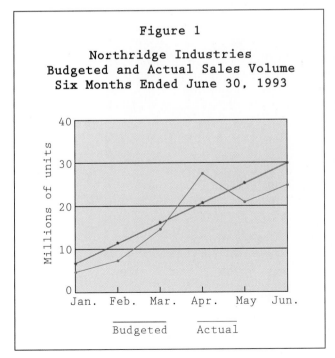

FIGURE 16-7 Line chart expresses changes over time.

Lines emphasize changes over time.

3. Divide the vertical and horizontal scales into equal increments. The vertical or amount increments, however, need not be the same as the horizontal or time increments as long as the line or lines drawn will have reasonable slopes. (Unrealistic scales might produce startling slopes that could mislead readers.)

Area charts, also called cumulative line charts or surface charts, are similar to component bar charts because they show how different factors contribute to a total. The area chart is especially useful when you want to illustrate changes in these components over time. For example, the area chart in Figure 16-8 illustrates the change in the components of a company's capital over a ten-year period. The cumulative total of contributed capital, retained earnings, long-term debt, and short-term debt is illustrated by the top line on the chart. The amount of each component can be estimated by visual assessment; labeling the vertical axis on the left and

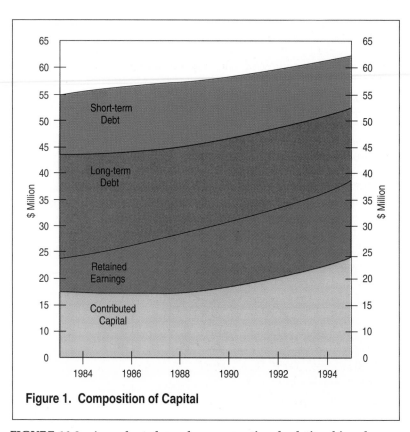

Figure 1. Composition of Capital

FIGURE 16-8   Area chart shows how proportional relationships change over time.

right sides helps the reader estimate amounts. Colors add visual appeal and aid the reader in distinguishing the components.

Unlike bar charts, which show only the total amount for a time period, line charts show variations within each time period. In oral presentations, an area (cumulative line) chart can be made more effective by having a separate transparency or graphic screen made for each component. During the presentation, each transparency could be laid over the previous one or each screen displayed in progression for a cumulative effect. In the example shown in Figure 16-8, for instance, the first transparency or screen may show only the contributed capital; the second, retained earnings; the third, long-term debt; and the fourth, short-term debt and the completed chart.

The chart in Figure 16-9 posed a particular challenge because the two quantities (sales and number of representatives) require scales of different intervals. The graphic is designed so that the reader can interpret the data easily, using the correct interval for each quantity. The bars use the left-hand vertical axis to depict sales, and the line uses the right-hand vertical axis to show the number of sales representatives. A line graph or a multiple-range bar chart could be used; however, this combination line and bar chart provides the contrast needed to interpret the relationship between sales and the number of sales representatives clearly.

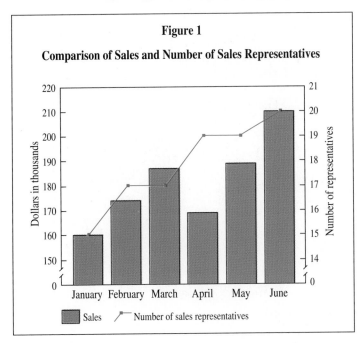

Figure 1

Comparison of Sales and Number of Sales Representatives

FIGURE 16-9 Combination bar and line chart facilitates interpretation of two quantities requiring different intervals.

Pie Charts

Like stacked-bar charts and area charts, pie charts show how the parts of a whole are distributed. As the name indicates, the whole is represented as a pie, with the parts becoming slices of the pie. Pie charts are effective for showing percentages (parts of whole), but they are ineffective in showing quantitative totals or comparisons. Bars are used for those purposes.

The pie chart in Figure 16-10 illustrates the information reported on a company income statement. The pie depicts sales; the slices represent various classifications of expenses. The net income slice is exploded to draw the reader's attention to this significant portion. Because Crocker's income statement was prepared using electronic spreadsheet software, the writer used the same spreadsheet file to prepare the pie chart, eliminating the need to rekey the data and allowing the spreadsheet to com-

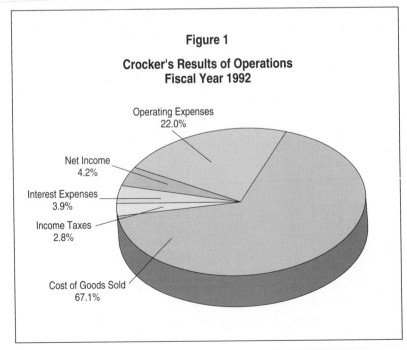

FIGURE 16-10   Pie chart with three-dimensional effect shows percentages of a whole.

pute each item's percentage of sales automatically. The three-dimensional effect and color enhance the appearance and appeal of the graphic.

Here are some generally used guidelines for constructing pie charts:

1. Position the largest slice or the slice to be emphasized at the twelve o'clock position. Working clockwise, place the other slices in descending order of size or some other logical order of presentation. Typically software programs automatically arrange the slices following their own guidelines. For example, if the pie contains many small slices, the program may intersperse the small slices with the larger slices to increase readability and enhance appearance. Some software programs allow you to organize the slices following your guidelines.
2. Label each slice and include information about the quantitative size (percentage, dollars, acres, square feet, etc.) of each slice. Note the labeling in Figure 16-10.
3. Draw attention to one or more slices if you wish by (a) exploding the slice(s) to be emphasized, (that is, removing it from immediate contact with the pie) or (b) displaying or printing only the slice(s) to be emphasized.
4. Use color or patterns (cross-hatchings) to aid the reader in differentiating among the slices and to add appeal.

Use your own judgment in constructing a pie chart. Your software may limit your ability to follow rules explicitly. Likewise, the nature of the data or the presentation selected may require slight deviations to increase the clarity of the graphic. For example, if you intend to explode the largest slice, placing it in the twelve o'clock position may not be desirable because the slice is likely to intrude into the space occupied by a title positioned at the top of the page. If your style manual or company policy requires that titles be positioned above the graphic, starting with a slice other than the largest is acceptable. For dramatic effect, many periodicals and reports vary from these general rules.

Pictograms

A pictogram uses pictures to illustrate numerical relationships. For example, the pictograms in Figure 16-11 use coins instead of bars to depict additions to personal savings. However, pictograms can be more dramatic than meaningful if they aren't planned properly. For example, doubling the height and width of a picture increases the total area four times. Therefore, all symbols must be the same size so that true relationships are not distorted. Note that the relative sizes of the coins in the pictogram on the left in Figure 16-11 are misleading and make the actual amounts and relationships hard to understand. In the pictogram on the right, use of the same size symbols makes both amounts and relationships instantly clear.

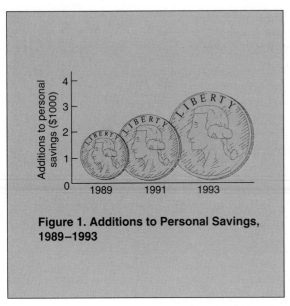

Figure 1. Additions to Personal Savings, 1989–1993

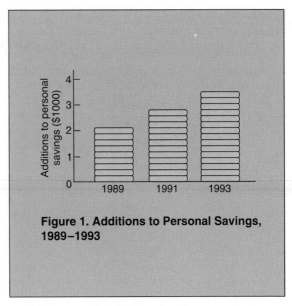

Figure 1. Additions to Personal Savings, 1989–1993

FIGURE 16-11   Relative-size symbols (left) distort data; same-size symbols (right) depict relationships accurately.

Maps

Maps help readers visualize geographic relationships and are especially useful when the reader may not be familiar with the geography discussed in the report. The map shown in Figure 16-12 is taken from an annual report. It effectively presents sales growth by state and shows the locations of the home office, distribution centers, and retail stores within the geographic region. The map gives the information visually and thus eliminates the difficulty of explaining the information in words. In addition to being less confusing, the map is more concise and interesting than a written message would be.

Flowcharts

A *flowchart* is a step-by-step diagram of a procedure or a graphic depiction of a system or organization. A variety of problems can be resolved by using flowcharts to support written analysis. For example, most companies have procedures manuals to instruct employees in certain work tasks. Including a flowchart with the written instructions minimizes the chances of errors.

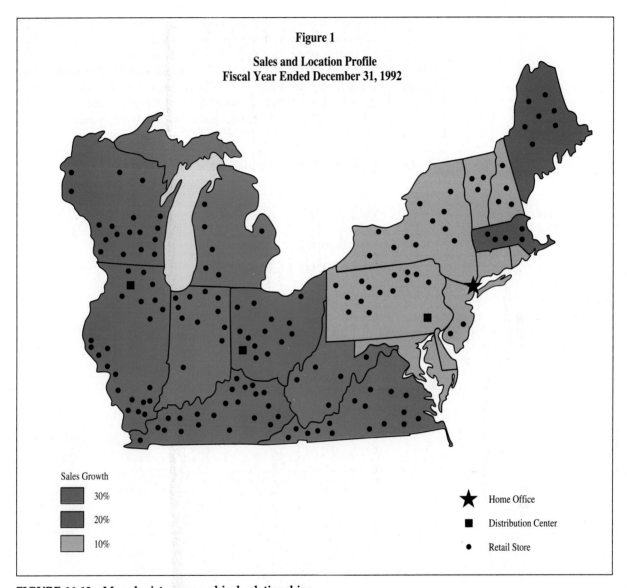

Figure 1

Sales and Location Profile
Fiscal Year Ended December 31, 1992

Sales Growth
30%
20%
10%

★ Home Office
■ Distribution Center
• Retail Store

FIGURE 16-12 Map depicts geographical relationships.

The flowchart traces a unit of work as it flows from beginning to completion. Symbols with connecting lines are used to trace a step-by-step sequence of the work. A key to the flowchart's symbols may be included if the reader may not readily understand standard symbols. For example, the flowchart in Figure 16-13 illustrates the procedures for verifying cash receipts. If this information had been presented only in a series of written steps, the chief accounting officer would have to rely not only on the accounting clerks' reading ability but also on their willingness to read and study.

Organizational charts are widely used to provide a picture of the authority structure and relationships within an organization. They provide

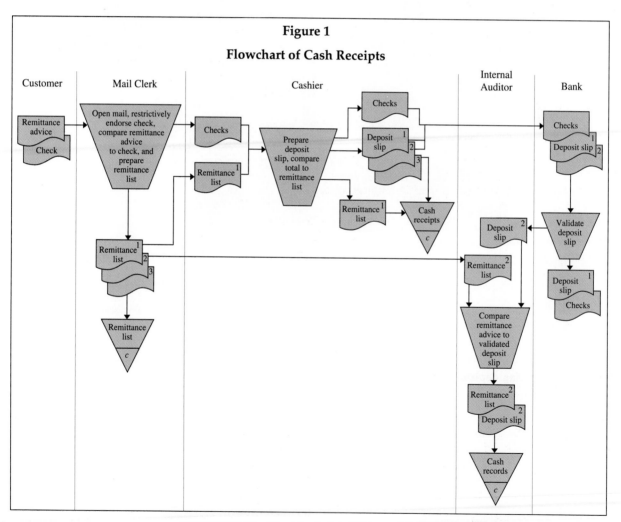

FIGURE 16-13   Flowchart simplifies understanding of work task.

employees with an idea of what their organization looks like in terms of the flow of authority and responsibility. Recall the organizational chart of The Home Center presented in Figure 1-1 (Chapter 1) as part of the discussion of the interdependence of individuals and units within an organization. When businesses change (because of new employees or reorganization of units and responsibilities), organizational charts must be revised. Revisions are simple if the organizational chart is prepared using graphics or drawing software and stored on disk to be retrieved when changes must be made.

Other Graphics

Other graphics such as floor plans, photographs, cartoons, blueprints, and lists of various sorts may be included in reports. The increased availability of graphics and sophisticated drawing software is leading to the increased inclusion of these more complex visuals in reports and oral presentations. Because managers can prepare these visuals themselves less expensively and more quickly than having them prepared by professional designers, these sophisticated graphics are being used increasingly for internal reports.

Advances in technology allow writers to prepare sophisticated graphics that give readers a concrete image of the concept being discussed.

Figure 16-14 helps company executives visualize a proposed floor plan for all staff offices. This diagram is much more effective than a written or oral description of the arrangement and relative size of each piece of furniture.

Photographs are used frequently in annual reports to help the general audience understand a complex concept and to make the document more appealing to read. The photographs from First Interstate Bank's annual report, shown in Figure 16-15, help stockholders visualize the employees' commitment to go beyond customer expectation to provide satisfaction.

Frequently, you will have some material that must be included in the report that would make the narrative discussion unwieldy. In this case, the material might be placed in an appendix and only referred to in the report, as explained in Chapters 17 and 18.

INTRODUCING TABLES AND GRAPHS IN THE TEXT

Under no conditions should a table or graph be included in the report without being referred to in the textual material. Text and graphics are partners in the communication process. If readers come to tables, graphs, or pictures in the text before they have been told about them, they will begin to study them and draw their own inferences and conclusions. If they are told about the graphic and its implications, the graphic will supplement what has been said.

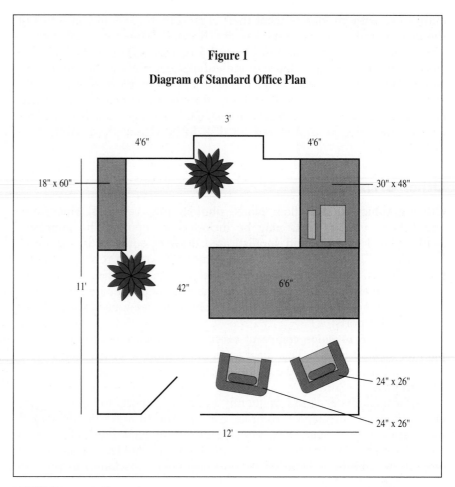

Figure 1

Diagram of Standard Office Plan

FIGURE 16-14   Floor plan helps readers visualize layout and dimensions.

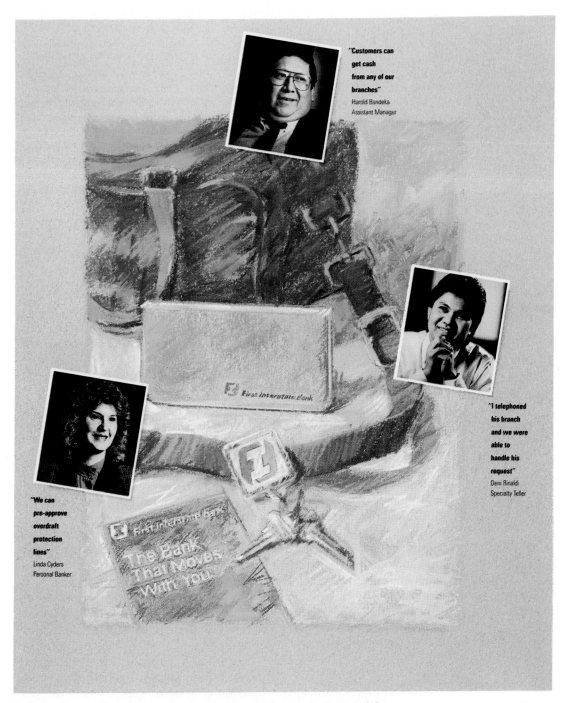

FIGURE 16-15 Photograph attracts attention and provides true-to-life, precise image.

Note how the language in the following sentences introduces graphic or tabular material:

Poor:	Figure 1 shows reader preferences for shopping locations.	This sentence is poor because it tells the reader nothing more than would the title of the figure.
Acceptable:	About two-thirds of the consumers preferred to shop in suburban areas rather than in the city. (See Figure 1.)	This sentence is acceptable because it does the job of interpreting the data, but it puts the figure reference in parentheses rather than integrating it into the sentence.
Improved:	As shown in Figure 1, about two-thirds of the consumers preferred to shop in suburban areas than in the city.	Although improved over the previous examples, this sentence puts reference to the figure at the beginning, thus detracting from the interpretation of the data.
Best:	About two-thirds of the consumers preferred to shop in suburban areas than in the city, as shown in Figure 1.	This sentence is best for introducing figures because it talks about the graphic and also includes introductory phrasing, but only after stressing the main point.

Does the reader get the point before turning to the graphic?

Ideally, a graphic should be integrated within the text material immediately after its introduction. If a graphic occupies an entire page, it should appear on the page following the page on which it is introduced. In this chapter, figures are placed as closely as possible to their introductions in accordance with these suggestions. However, in some cases, several figures may be introduced on one page, making perfect placement difficult and sometimes impossible.

Throughout the discussion of tables and graphics, the term "graphics" has been used to include all illustrations. Although your report may include tables, graphs, maps, and even photographs, you'll find organizing easier and writing about the illustrations more effective if you label all items as "Figure" followed by a number and number them consecutively. Some report writers like to label tables consecutively as "Table 1," etc., and graphs and charts consecutively in another sequence as "Graph 1," etc. When this dual numbering system is used, readers of the report may become confused if they come upon a sentence saying, "Evidence presented in Tables 3 and 4 and Graph 2 supports. . . ." Both writers and readers appreciate the single numbering system, which makes the sentence read, "Evidence presented in Figures 3, 4, and 5 supports. . . ."

Multiple labeling systems detract from communication.

SUMMARY

How difficult would it be to drive across the country for the first time without the aid of a road map? We'd probably have to ask directions frequently. And in a large city, finding a specific street address without assistance would be almost impossible. Tables and graphics add clarity to reports just as a map aids a traveler. Protecting ourselves against a deluge of data through good data management and use of tables and graphs has a great deal to do with effective report preparation.

Fortunately, we live in an age in which much of what we have discussed can be prepared by computers. If you plan to make a study involving the collection and analysis of considerable quantitative data, talk to an expert at your computer facility. Questionnaires and other data-gathering devices can be designed so that a respondent's answers can be fed to computers through optical scanning equipment directly from the answer sheet. A variety of easy-to-use programs are available for doing much of the data-management mathematics described earlier. Properly designed, the work of data management can be reduced hundreds, even thousands, of times. Many computers also have graphic capability; they can produce the tables and other graphic figures so important to reports.

For many reports, you will be able to prepare the tables and graphics on your own. You must know what you want and how to construct it; then you can either do the work on your own or tell the computer what to do.

The skilled report writer knows what graphics to use and when to use them. When people read about number relationships and ratios, they understand better when they have visualized in their minds what is involved. Your use of tables and graphics to complement your written words makes the visualization easy.

Although this discussion has emphasized the use of graphics in written reports, you'll also make use of them to support oral presentations. Often the writer of a report will be called on to make oral presentations about the written report. Many times, of course, graphic materials used in oral presentations will not have a research basis. Speeches designed to inform, to entertain, and to persuade often are built around the use of visual materials.

REVIEW QUESTIONS

1. In what ways does managing data help protect researchers from being overwhelmed by their material?
2. What is meant by common language? Provide several examples.
3. Which measure of central tendency do most people describe as the average? How is it calculated?

4. If a distribution consists of the amounts 12, 65, 68, 72, 73, 79, 81, 85, and 85, which measures of central tendency would be appropriate? Why?

5. What basic rules are used to determine whether a graphic should be used to present certain information?

6. Discuss the major principles involved in preparing effective tables.

7. Why should increments on the vertical axis be equal in a graphic? Can variation in the sizes of horizontal increments create the same problem?

8. What is meant by a "broken-bar chart"?

9. What is the difference between a stacked-bar (component) chart and an area (cumulative line) chart? Give an example of how each might be used.

10. Why can't pie charts do the same thing as simple line charts?

11. Must the writer prepare graphics according to ironclad rules (positioning graphic title at the top or bottom, slicing the pie beginning at twelve o'clock, and so on), or can the writer vary the arrangement for a specified purpose? Explain.

12. Why does a lack of consistency in the size of pictures create misleading pictograms?

13. Where should a graphic be placed in a report?

14. Must the writer introduce every graphic in the report? Is it necessary to interpret a self-explanatory graphic? Explain.

15. Discuss the appropriate way to introduce a graphic in a report.

EXERCISES

1. Select the most effective graphic means of presenting each of the following sets of data. Then prepare the graphic and write a sentence that would introduce the graphic effectively in a report.

    a. The profile of the various taxes paid by Edmonds Corporation during the last fiscal year is 30 percent federal income tax, 4 percent state income tax, 25 percent employment taxes, 13 percent real estate taxes, 23 percent sales tax, and 5 percent other taxes.

    b. Actual unit production as a percentage of maximum plant efficiency for the past ten years:

1981	67	1986	81
1982	71	1987	76
1983	75	1988	80
1984	72	1989	84
1985	78	1990	85

c. Dollar sales (in thousands of dollars) by division for Precision Electronics, Inc. during the last fiscal period were East, $27; South, $19; Northwest, $17; Northeast, $15; and Southwest, $22.

2. In thousands of dollars, the following figures represent salaries earned by chief financial officers of 25 local high-tech firms. Compute the mean, median, and mode.

36	48	66	74	82
38	49	68	74	87
38	53	70	78	90
42	57	74	80	92
42	62	74	82	96

3. To discover the differences between computing central tendencies from an array of individual items, and from grouped data, tally the scores in Exercise 2 in seven classes beginning with 30–39, 40–49, 50–59, and so on to 90–99. When you have tallied the scores, compute the mean and the median and indicate the modal class. How do you account for the differences between the answers here and those in Exercise 2?

4. Prepare a simple table for the data used in Exercise 3 and indicate the appropriate percentages for each class.

5. Prepare an introductory sentence for the table developed in Exercise 4.

6. Improve the following statements taken from reports:
   a. As can be seen in Table 5, the correlation between verbal scores on admission tests and achievement in English was .57.
   b. Land values in the southern part of the state have increased about 32 percent while those in the northern portion have increased 19 percent. (See Figure 6.)
   c. Take a look at Figure 3, where a steady decline in the price of farm products during the past quarter is shown.
   d. The data reveal (Figure 4) that only one of seven voters is satisfied with the performance of the City Council.

7. Obtain a copy of a corporate annual report. Prepare a one-page memorandum to your instructor telling how effectively the report incorporated graphics.

8. Evaluate the effectiveness of each of the graphics on the following page. Then revise the graphic incorporating the suggestions you generated in your evaluation.

a. Dollar sales (in thousands of dollars) for Newsome Reality, Inc. over a six-year period. Graphic is being prepared for inclusion in the annual report.

Figure 1. Annual Sales, 1985–1990

b. Unit production per plant during the second quarter of 19—.

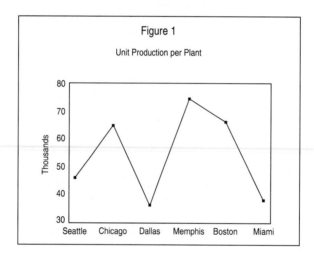

c. Number of customers by sales representatives during June 19—.

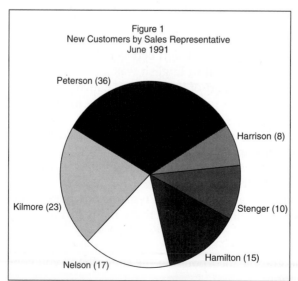

9. Prepare a graphic or table to show the *total* employer health insurance contribution for a fiscal period. Company data appear in the following paragraph:

> *Employee Health Insurance.* The following monthly premiums were paid by Linley Manufacturing Company for employee health insurance during the last fiscal period: single employees and no dependents, $45; employees and one dependent, $54; employees and two dependents, $60; employees and three or more dependents, $72. Linley employs 32 employees with no dependents; 26 with one; 18 with two; and 29 with three or more.

10. Prepare a graphic or a table to illustrate the following information:

> *Consumer Credit.* Total consumer credit at the end of March was $184.3 billion, of which $32.8 billion was noninstallment. The $151.5 billion of installment credit was composed of $51.6 billion for personal loans, $50.5 billion for automobiles, and $49.4 billion for other consumer goods.

11. Prepare whatever graphics or tables would be desirable for the following discussion involving fictitious information:

> *Urban Family Budgets.* Costs of three hypothetical family budgets for three urban families of four rose about 16 percent from the autumn of 1990 to the autumn of 1991, according to the Bureau of Labor Statistics. An average urban family consisting of a 38-year-old husband employed full time, his nonworking wife, a boy of 13, and a girl of 8 could expect the cost of living projected in an intermediate budget to amount to $25,866. Average costs projected in a low budget amounted to $16,080, and in the higher budget $33,412.
>
> Family-consumption items comprised 76 percent of the intermediate family budget with the remaining 24 percent composed of gifts and contributions, occupational expenses, life insurance, and social security and personal income taxes. Total family consumption at the lower- and higher-budget levels comprised 82 percent and 70 percent of the family budget, respectively. During the year, consumption costs rose by approximately 11.4 percent for all three budgets. Food costs accounted for 38 percent of total family consumption at the lower level, 33 percent at the intermediate, and 28 percent at the higher level. Food costs represented the largest single component for the lower and intermediate budget levels, but the largest component of consumption at the higher level was housing expenditures.

12. Prepare a graphic or a table for the following fictitious information:

> *Job Growth Rate.* The rate of government jobs opened and filled in the past decade was almost two times that in private industry, according to the Tax Foundation. The number of federal, state,

and local government workers increased 50 percent from 10.6 million to 15.9 million compared to a 27-percent job growth rate in private industry. Total nonfarm payroll employment in the U.S. rose from 62.0 million to 80.0 million in the ten-year period. Of this increase, 12.7 million jobs were added by the private sector and 5.3 million by the government.

13. Prepare a graphic or a table for the following fictitious information:

Costs of Higher Education. Median expected educational expenses per semester for full-time college students in September 19— varied from about $1,300 for those in community colleges to $11,000 for those in private universities. These costs cover tuition and fees, books and supplies, and transportation. For public institutions, the estimated medians were about $2,400 for four-year colleges, $3,200 for universities, $1,900 for vocational schools, and $1,300 for two-year colleges. For students attending private universities, median expenses were considerably higher than for those attending public schools: $11,000 for private universities compared with $3,200, $8,700 for four-year colleges compared with $2,400, and $9,000 for two-year colleges compared with $1,300. Board-and-room costs varied widely, but the median for those living at home and commuting was estimated at $4,200 a year. For those living at school, the median was $6,100.

14. Prepare a graphic for the following fictitious information:

How the Wealthy Invest. For families with net worths over $1 million in addition to residence equities, their assets were divided as follows: rental real estate, 15 percent; retirement savings programs, 10 percent; stock market equities, 30 percent; savings accounts, 5 percent; tax-exempt bonds and funds, 25 percent; government securities other than tax exempt, 15 percent.

ORGANIZING AND WRITING SHORT REPORTS AND PROPOSALS

OBJECTIVES

When you have completed Chapter 17, you should be able to

- Prepare reports in letter and memorandum formats.

- Prepare proposals for a variety of purposes.

- Construct formal reports consisting of several parts.

THE NAME STRADIVARI is synonymous with clarity and precision for all connoisseurs of classical music. Antonio Stradivari, who lived in Italy from 1644 to 1737, became a legend for building the finest violins the world has ever known, some of which still exist today. What made these musical instruments beautiful physically and tonally was the craft that went into every component of them. The artisans who constructed them put care into carving each piece of wood and preparing each string before all the pieces eventually were put together into one unique and perfect whole.

Like the violin, a business report also consists of several components. Each part must be carefully "crafted" and then reviewed to make sure it is as perfect as possible. If a part is missing, the report is incomplete and will not be effective. A complete, formal report should consist of preliminary parts, the actual text, and an addenda section. After gathering information for your report, be sure to check the style manual approved by your company to make sure that you have all the required components and to see how to organize those parts into a clear, complete whole.

PARTS OF A REPORT

Could a short report also be formal?

The differences between a formal report and an informal report lie in the format and possibly in writing style. The type of report you prepare depends on the subject matter, the purpose of the report, and the readers' needs. At the short, informal end of the report continuum described in Chapter 15, a report could look exactly like a brief memorandum. At the long, formal extreme of the continuum, the report might include most or all of the parts shown in Figure 17-1.

A business report rarely contains all of these parts. They are listed here simply to name all the possible parts. The preliminary parts and addenda are mechanical items that support the body of the report. The body contains the report of the research and covers the four steps in the research process. The organization of the body of the report leads to the construction of the contents page.

Because we usually write to affect or influence others favorably, we often add parts as the number of pages increases. When a report exceeds one or two pages, we might add a cover or title page. And when the body of the report exceeds four or five pages, we might even add a finishing touch by placing the report in a plastic cover or ring binder. Reports frequently take on the characteristics of the formal end of the continuum simply by reason of size. Note how the preliminary parts and addenda items increase in number as the report increases in size, as depicted in Figure 17-2.

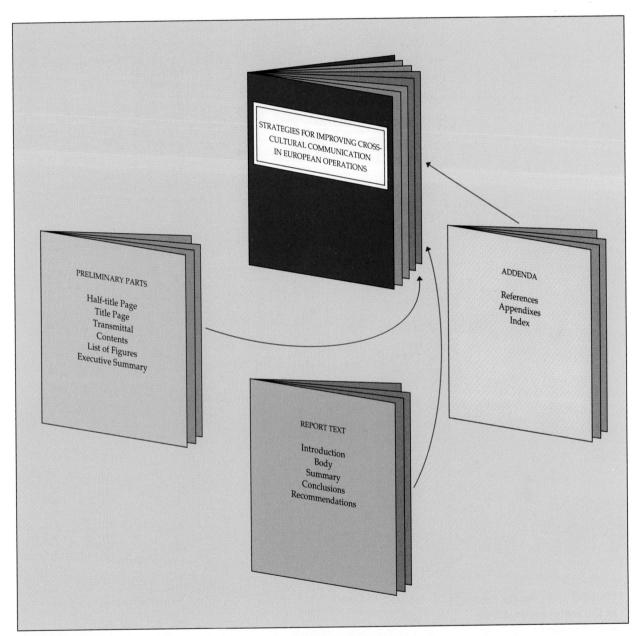

FIGURE 17-1 Formal reports are composed of preliminary parts, report text, and addenda.

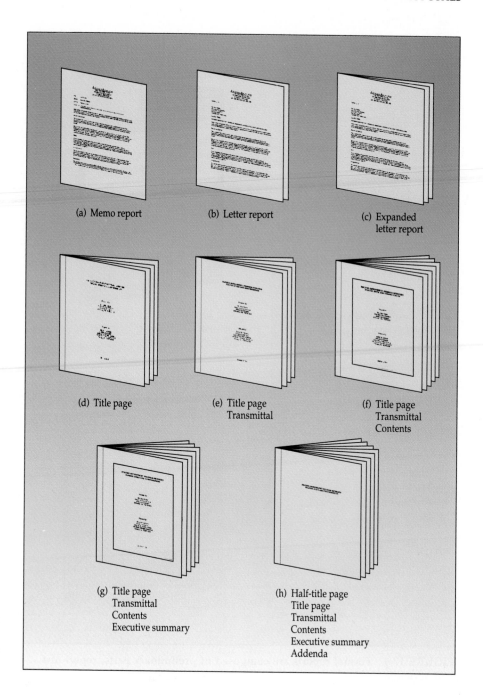

(a) Memo report

(b) Letter report

(c) Expanded
letter report

(d) Title page

(e) Title page
Transmittal

(f) Title page
Transmittal
Contents

(g) Title page
Transmittal
Contents
Executive summary

(h) Half-title page
Title page
Transmittal
Contents
Executive summary
Addenda

FIGURE 17-2 As the size of the report increases, so does the number of assisting items.

Memo and letter reports are seldom longer than a page or two, but they can be expanded into several pages. As depicted, long reports may include some special pages that do not appear in short reports. The format you select—long or short, formal or informal—may help determine how many of the supporting preliminary and addenda items to include.

To understand how each part of a formal report contributes to reader comprehension and ease of access to the information in the report, study the following explanations of each part in the three basic categories: preliminary parts, report text, and addenda. Figure 17-1 illustrates how these three sections are combined to prepare a complete formal report. In Chapter 18 you will study a sample long report to help you visualize the selected parts of a complete report.

Preliminary Parts

The preliminary parts are included to add formality to a report, repeat report content, and aid the reader in locating information in the report quickly and in understanding the report more easily. These parts include the half-title page, title page, authorization, transmittal, contents, list of figures, and executive summary. Preliminary pages are numbered with small Roman numerals (i, ii, iii, and so on).

Half-Title Page (Title Fly).   A half-title page, often called title fly, is a single page containing only the report title. This page simply adds formality and enhances the appearance of the report. In less formal reports, including letter and memorandum reports, the half-title page is omitted.

Title Page.   The title page includes the title, author, date, and frequently the name of the person or organization that requested the report. A title page is often added when the writer opts to use a formal report format rather than a memorandum or a letter arrangement.

Select a title that is descriptive and comprehensive; its words should reflect the content of the report. Avoid short, vague titles or excessively long titles. Instead, use concise wording to identify the topic adequately. For example, a title such as "Marketing Survey: Donuts" leaves the reader confused when the title could have been "Donut Flavor Preferences of Teenagers in Midville." To give some clues for writing a descriptive title, think of the "Five W's": *Who, What, When, Where,* and *Why.* Avoid such phrases as "A Study of . . . ," "A Critical Analysis of . . . ," or "A Review of. . . ."

Follow company procedures or a style manual to place the information attractively on the page. If the title is longer than one line, arrange it in the inverted pyramid format; that is, make each succeeding line shorter than the line preceding it. Arrange the title consistently on the half-title

What are several suggestions for writing an effective title?

page, title page, and the first page of the report. The inverted pyramid format also applies to titles of graphics. Note the arrangement of the following title of a graphic:

Incorrect: AVERAGE PER CAPITA INCOME IN 1992 FOR TEN STATES

AVERAGE PER CAPITA
INCOME IN 1992 FOR TEN STATES

Correct: AVERAGE PER CAPITA INCOME
IN 1992 FOR TEN STATES

Authorization.   If a report is authorized in writing, the letter or memorandum authorizing the report is included as a formal part of the report. This document follows the title page. If no written authorization is provided, authorization information may be included in the introduction. This information might include a clear description of the problem, limitations restricting the research, resources available, and deadlines.

Transmittal.   As the report becomes more formal, the writer may attach a letter or memorandum that serves two purposes. First, it presents the report to the one who requested it. Second, it typically provides the conclusion from an analytical study or highlights from an informational report. If the writer has prepared a report for a person or a department inside the company, the writer uses the memorandum format for the transmittal. A consultant preparing a report for another company arranges the transmittal in a letter format.

What information should be included in the transmittal?

This letter is the writer's opportunity to speak directly to the reader in an informal tone. Thus, the writer may include first- and second-person pronouns in the transmittal. If the report includes a synopsis or a detailed introduction, the transmittal is short. Use the deductive approach and follow these suggestions:

1. Let the first sentence present the report and remind the reader that he or she requested it.
2. Explain the subject of the report in the first paragraph.
3. Briefly present the conclusions and, if called for, the recommendations.
4. Close cordially. The closing paragraph also expresses appreciation for the cooperation given by the company.

Contents.   The contents provides the reader with an analytical overview of the report and the order in which information is presented. Thus, this preliminary part aids the reader in understanding the report and in locating a specific section of it. The list includes the name and location (beginning page number) of every report part except the half-title page, title page, and contents. Include the list of figures, transmittal, executive summary, report headings, bibliography, appendixes, and index. Placing spaced periods (leaders) between the report part and the page numbers helps lead the reader's eyes to the appropriate page number.

Word-processing software simplifies the time-consuming, tedious task of preparing many of the preliminary and addenda report parts including the contents. Because the software generates these parts automatically, report writers can make last-minute changes to the report and still have time to update the preliminary and addenda parts.

To generate the contents using word-processing software, simply "mark" each heading in the report and designate its level (major division, minor division, and so on). After a generate command is given, the headings, appropriately aligned leaders, and correct page numbers are displayed on a separate page. The headings are indented according to the level you designated when you marked the headings. For example, major headings appear at the left margin, minor headings are indented three spaces. Add the heading *Contents* and the page is ready to be printed.

List of Figures.   To aid the reader in locating a specific graphic in a paper with many graphics, the writer might include a list of figures separate from the contents. The contents and the figures can be combined on one

COMMUNICATION MENTOR

The executive summary is probably the most important part of reports being presented to top management. Summaries should be prepared with the needs of the specific executive readers in mind. For instance, a technically oriented executive may require more detail; a strategist, more analysis.

Executive summaries should "boil down" the report to its barest essentials, yet without brevity so severe that summaries are incomprehensible. If appropriate, the summary should offer a view or conclusion reached by the report. Essentially, summaries should enable top executives to glean enough information and understanding to feel confident making a decision.

Cynthia Pharr
President & CEO
Tracy-Locke/Pharr Public Relations

page if both lists are brief. Word-processing software can be used to generate the list of figures automatically.

Executive Summary.   Positioned before the first page of the report, the executive summary summarizes the essential elements in the entire report. This overview simplifies the reader's understanding of a long report. This summary may be called a *synopsis* or *abstract*.

Why is an executive summary useful?

Typically, an executive summary is included when the writer believes it will assist the reader in understanding a long, complex report. Because of the increased volume of information that managers must review, the tendency in business today is for managers to require an executive summary regardless of the length and complexity of the report.

The executive summary should (1) briefly introduce the report and preview the major divisions, (2) summarize the major sections of the report, and (3) summarize the report summary. The executive summary presents the report in miniature: the introduction, body, and summary as well as conclusions and recommendations if included in the report.

Report Text

The report itself contains the introduction, body, summary, conclusions, and recommendations. Report pages are numbered with arabic numerals (1, 2, 3, and so on).

Introduction.   The introduction orients the reader to the problem. It may include the following items:

1. What the topic is.
2. Why it is being reported on.
3. Scope and limitations of the research.
4. Where the information came from.
5. A preview of the major sections of the report to provide coherence and transition through the report:
   a. How the topic is divided into parts.
   b. The order in which the parts will be represented.

Body.   The body, often called the heart of the report, presents the information collected and relates it to the problem. To increase readability and coherence, this section contains numerous headings to denote the various divisions within a report. Refer to "Organizing Findings" later in this chapter and the "Using Headings Effectively" in Chapter 18 for an in-depth discussion of preparing the body.

Summary, Conclusions, and Recommendations.   An informational report ends with a brief summary that serves an important function: it adds unity to the report by reviewing the main points presented in the body.

The summary includes only material that is discussed in the report. Introducing a new idea in the summary may make the reader wonder why the point was not developed earlier. It may suggest that the study was not adequately completed or that the writer did not adequately plan the report before beginning to write. Finally, the summary, which is expected to be fairly short, does not provide enough space for developing a new idea.

Why is new information inappropriate in the summary?

Analytical reports, designed to solve a specific problem or answer research questions, may also include a summary of the major research findings, particularly if the report is lengthy. Reviewing the major findings prepares the reader for the conclusions that follow. The analytical report also includes conclusions the writer draws by inference from the findings. If required by the person/organization authorizing the report, recommendations follow the conclusions. Recommendations present the writer's opinion on a possible course of action based on the conclusions.

Analytical reports include conclusions and sometimes recommendations; informational reports contain only a summary.

For a long report, the writer may place the summary, the conclusions, and the recommendations in three separate sections. For shorter reports, the conclusions and recommendations can be combined into one section, or all three sections can be combined.

Is placing the summary, conclusions, and recommendations in separate sections acceptable?

Addenda

The addenda to a report may include all materials used in the research but not appropriate to be included in the report itself. The three basic addenda parts are the references, appendixes, and index. Addenda parts continue with the same page numbering system used in the body of the report.

References. The references (also called *works cited*) are an alphabetical list identifying the sources used in preparing the report. Because the writer may be influenced by any information consulted, some reference manuals require that the reference list include all sources that were consulted. When the references list includes sources not cited in the report, it is referred to as a *bibliography* or a *list of works consulted*. If a report includes endnotes rather than in-text parenthetical citations (author and date within the text), the endnotes precede the references. Using word-processing software to create footnotes and endnotes alleviates much of the monotony and repetition of preparing accurate documentation. Refer to "Documenting Reports" in Chapter 18 or a style manual for specific guidelines for preparing references and citations.

Should you include references consulted but not cited in the references?

Appendixes. Appendixes contain supplementary information that supports the report but is not appropriate for inclusion in the report itself. This information may include questionnaires and accompanying transmittal letters, summary tabulations, verbatim comments from respondents,

How do you decide whether to include an item in the text or an appendix?

complex mathematical computations and formulas, legal documents, and a variety of items the writer presents to support the body of the report and the quality of the research. Placing supplementary material in the appendix prevents the text from becoming excessively long.

If the report contains more than one appendix, label each one with a capital letter and a title. For example, the four appendixes in a report could be identified as follows:

Appendix A: Cover Letter Accompanying End-User Questionnaire

Appendix B: End-User Questionnaire

Appendix C: Means of 20 Technology Competencies

Appendix D: Number and Percentage of Ratings Given to 20 Technology Competencies

Each item included in the appendixes must be mentioned in the report. References within the report to the four appendixes mentioned in the previous example follow:

Mention in the text each item you include in the appendix.

A copy of the end-user questionnaire (Appendix A), along with a cover letter (Appendix B) and a stamped, pre-addressed envelope, was mailed to 1,156 firms on February 15, 19—.

Means were computed, and the total means were ranked to establish an order of importance for the 20 technology competencies as shown in Table 10. The means are shown in Appendix C, and the frequency distribution from which these means were computed is provided in Appendix D.

Index.   The index is an alphabetical guide to the subject matter in the report. The subject and each page number on which the subject appears are listed. To compile an index using word-processing software, you must first "mark" the key terms using special codes. The software generates the index by displaying on the screen each key term and the page number(s) on which each term appears in the report. Because the terms are displayed in the order they appear in the text, use the sort function to alphabetize the key words automatically. Each time a new draft is prepared, a new index with revised terms and correct page numbers is generated quickly and easily.

How can computer software help you prepare the index?

ORGANIZING REPORT FINDINGS

Because the body of the report discusses the four steps in problem solving—usually the items of most interest to readers—it represents the core of the presentation. Within the body, the purpose and method of the solution are minor items in terms of space and are considered part of an in-

When it decided to open for business, this company thought logically about the merits of several alternative locations. Managers carefully weighed the advantages and disadvantages of each location against a list of criteria (factors important to the success of this company). Their analytical report written to justify this site was organized using the same logic: the pros and cons of each alternative were presented in major sections that reflected (emphasized) the criteria used in making the decision.

troduction to a report. The findings leading to the conclusion or conclusions should consume the major portion of space.

Assume that you have the task of selecting a personal computer from among three alternative models—the Strad, the Amati, and the Beta. The purpose of your study is to select the computer that will best serve the record-keeping and word-processing needs of a small office.

You gather all the information available from suppliers of the three computers; you try each one personally and have two other people use them, and finally you compare the three against a variety of criteria. Your final selection is the Beta. Why did you select it? What criteria served as decision guides? When you write the report, you will have to tell the reader—the one who will put out the money to buy the machine—how the selection was made in such a way that the reader is "sold" on your conclusion.

If you organize your report so that you tell the reader everything about the Strad, then everything about the Amati, and finally everything about the Beta, the reader may have trouble making comparisons. Your content outline might look like this:

  I. Introduction
     A. The Problem
     B. The Method Used
 II. Strad
III. Amati
 IV. Beta
  V. Conclusion

Note that this outline devotes three of the roman numeral sections to the findings, one to the problem, and one to the method. This division is appropriate because the most space must be devoted to the findings. But the reader has difficulty comparing the storage of the computers because the information is in three different places. Would it be better to discuss storage capacity of all three in the same section of the report? Would prices be compared more easily if they were all in the same section? Most reports should be divided into sections that reflect the criteria used rather than into sections devoted to the "things" compared.

If you selected your computer based on cost, storage, service warranty, keyboarding ease, and availability of software programs, these criteria (rather than the computers themselves) might serve as divisions of the findings. Then your content outline would appear this way:

With page numbers added, the outline could be a contents page.

   I.   Introduction
      A. The Problem
      B. The Method Used
  II.   Cost Favors Strad
 III. Storage Capacity Points to Beta
 IV.   Service Warranties Are Equal
  V.   Keyboard Is Best on Beta
 VI.   Software Is Plentiful for Beta
VII.   Beta Is the Best Buy

The outline now has seven major sections and two subsections, with five of the major sections devoted to the findings. When the report is prepared in this way, the features of each computer are compared in the same section, and the reader is led logically to the conclusion.

Note the headings used in sections II–VII. These are called "talking headings" because they talk about the content of the section and even give a conclusion about the section. Page numbers following each outline item convert the outline into a contents page. Interestingly, the headings justify the selection of Beta. A knowledgeable reader who has confidence in the research might be satisfied by reading only the content headings.

Could logical order take several forms?

In addition to organizing findings by criteria, report writers can use other organizational plans. The comparison of three computers was an analytical process. When the report is informational and not analytical, you should use the most logical organization. Treat your material as a "whole" unit. A report on sales might be divided by geographic sales region, by product groups sold, by price range, or by time periods. A report on the development of a product might use chronological order. By visualizing the whole report first, you can then divide it into its major components and perhaps divide the major components into their parts. Remember, a section must divide into at least two parts or it cannot be divided at all. Thus, in an outline you must have a "B" subsection if you have an "A" subsection following a roman numeral or you should not have any subsections.

A final caution: beware of overdividing the sections. Too many divisions might make the report appear disorganized and choppy. On the other hand, too few divisions might create a problem for the reader. Note how the four steps of research have been developed through headings to the roman numeral outline and to a contents page for a report, as shown in Figure 17-3.

When developing content outlines, some report writers believe that readers expect the beginning of the body to be an introduction, so they begin the outline with the first heading related to findings. In our example, then, section I would be "Cost Favors Strad." Additionally, when they reach the contents page, they may eliminate the roman numeral or other outline symbols. A contents page for a report without the "Introduction," "Problem," and "Methods" headings would look like this:

CONTENTS

Cost Favors Strad... 3

Storage Capacity Points to Beta...................................... 4

Service Warranties About Equal 6

Keyboard Is Best on Beta.. 8

Software Is Plentiful for Beta....................................... 10

Beta Is the Best Buy... 12

The research process consists of inductively arranged steps:

1. Problem
2. Method
3. Findings
4. Conclusion

When the report is organized in the same order, its users must read through the body to learn about the conclusions—generally the most important part of the report to users. To make the reader's job easier, report writers may organize the report deductively, with the conclusions at the beginning. This sequence is usually achieved by placing a synopsis or summary at the beginning:

Inductive is indirect: the conclusion is presented last.

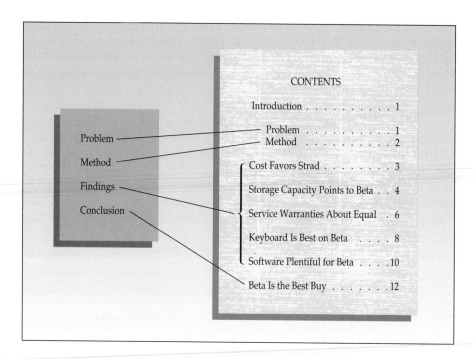

FIGURE 17-3   The basic outline grows to a contents page.

CONTENTS

Introduction 1
   Problem 1
   Method 2
Cost Favors Strad 3
Storage Capacity Points to Beta . . 4
Service Warranties About Equal . 6
Keyboard Is Best on Beta 8
Software Plentiful for Beta 10
Beta Is the Best Buy 12

Problem
Method
Findings
Conclusion

Deductive is direct: the conclusion is presented first.

  I. Conclusion reported in the synopsis
 II. Body of the report.
    A. Problem
    B. Method
    C. Findings
III. Conclusion

    This arrangement permits the reader to get the primary message early and then to look for support in the body of the report. The deductive arrangement contributes to the repetitious nature of reports, but it also contributes to effective reporting.

FORM REPORTS

Form reports meet the demand for numerous, repetitive reports. College registration forms, applications for credit, and airline tickets are examples of simple form reports. Form reports have the following benefits:

1. When designed properly, form reports increase clerical accuracy by providing designated places for specific items.
2. Forms save time by telling the preparer where to put each item and by preprinting common elements so the person filling in the form need not do any narrative writing.

Form reports are useful when numerous, repetitive reports are necessary. They may be pre-printed, which saves time and preserves accuracy.

3. Forms make tabulation of data relatively simple. The nature of the form is uni*form*ity.

Most form reports, like the bank teller's cash sheet in Figure 17-4, are informational. At the end of the teller's work period, cash is counted and totals entered in designated blanks. Cash reports from all tellers are then totaled to arrive at period totals and verified by computer records.

Do forms also tend to improve the quality of routine reports?

COMMUNICATION MENTORS

Use headings to draw your reader into the report. Readers prefer headings, so give them what they want. Most researchers follow a linear path of writing. They begin at *A* and continue to Z. However, most readers want to know *what* you found out—not how. In other words, tell your reader what time it is—not how to build the watch.

At Sygnis, we begin all reports with an executive summary that uses a "bullet point" style to highlight the key findings of the study. The complete report contains typical divisions—objectives, methodology, detailed findings, and conclusions and recommendations.

David Martin
President
Sygnis, Inc.

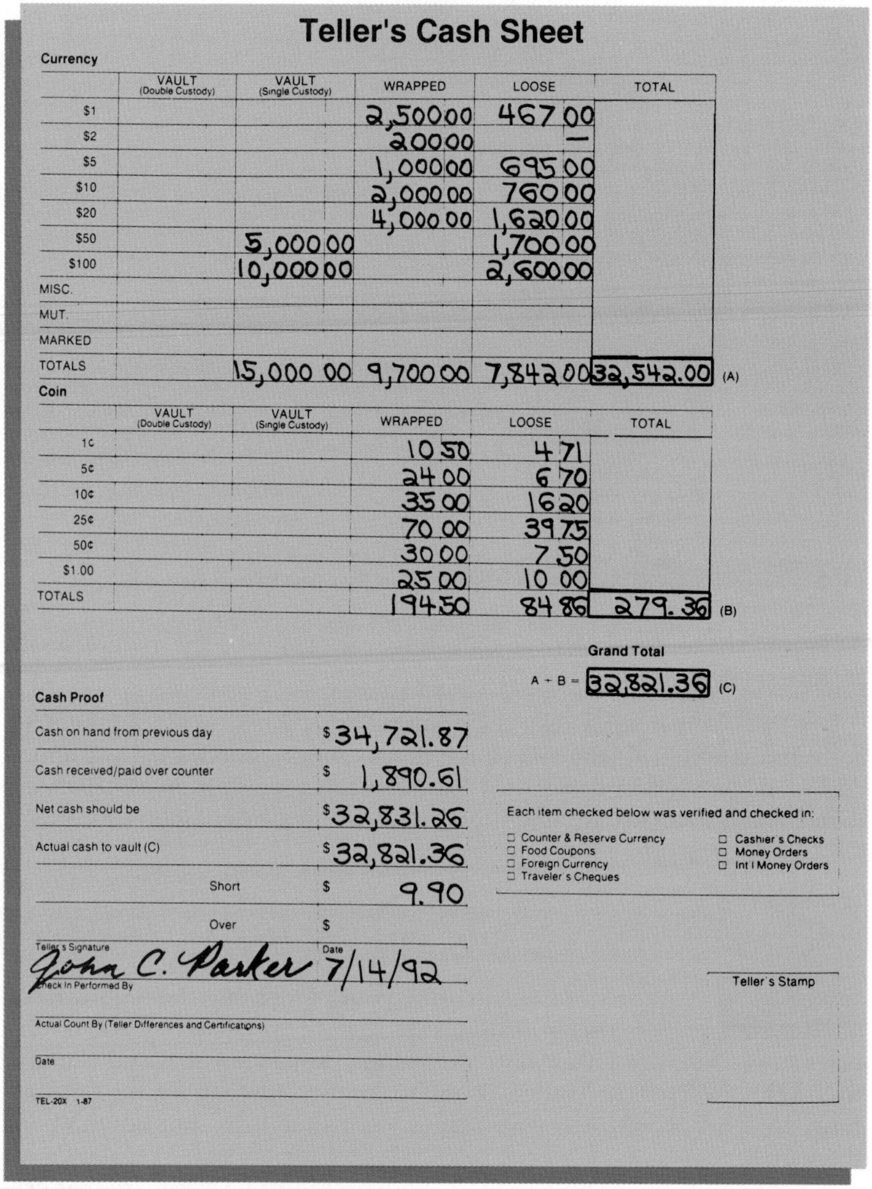

Teller's Cash Sheet

Currency

	VAULT (Double Custody)	VAULT (Single Custody)	WRAPPED	LOOSE	TOTAL
$1			2,500.00	467.00	
$2			200.00	—	
$5			1,000.00	695.00	
$10			2,000.00	760.00	
$20			4,000.00	1,620.00	
$50		5,000.00		1,700.00	
$100		10,000.00		2,600.00	
MISC.					
MUT.					
MARKED					
TOTALS		15,000.00	9,700.00	7,842.00	32,542.00 (A)

Coin

	VAULT (Double Custody)	VAULT (Single Custody)	WRAPPED	LOOSE	TOTAL
1¢			10.50	4.71	
5¢			24.00	6.70	
10¢			35.00	16.20	
25¢			70.00	39.75	
50¢			30.00	7.50	
$1.00			25.00	10.00	
TOTALS			194.50	84.86	279.36 (B)

Grand Total

A + B = 32,821.36 (C)

Cash Proof

Cash on hand from previous day	$ 34,721.87
Cash received/paid over counter	$ 1,890.61
Net cash should be	$ 32,831.26
Actual cash to vault (C)	$ 32,821.36
Short	$ 9.90
Over	$

Each item checked below was verified and checked in:

☐ Counter & Reserve Currency   ☐ Cashier's Checks
☐ Food Coupons   ☐ Money Orders
☐ Foreign Currency   ☐ Int'l Money Orders
☐ Traveler's Cheques

Teller's Signature   John C. Parker   Date 7/14/92

Check In Performed By

Teller's Stamp

Actual Count By (Teller Differences and Certifications)

Date

TEL-20X 1-87

FIGURE 17-4   Teller's cash sheet

In addition to their informational purpose, form reports also assist in analytical work. A residential appraisal report assists real-estate appraisers in analyzing real property. With this information, the appraiser is able to determine the market value of the property.

With today's technology, many form reports are generated by the computer. For example, the flowchart in Figure 17-5 illustrates a hospital's automation of repetitive patient reports. First, the admissions clerk inputs patient information using the carefully designed input screen. Note that the first item is the patient's social security number. If the patient has been admitted previously, the patient's name, address, and telephone number are displayed automatically, requiring the clerk to verify the accuracy of the information only. Likewise, as soon as the clerk inputs

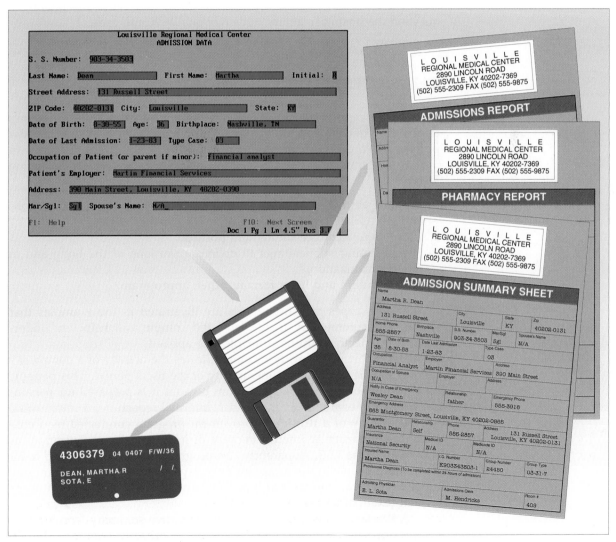

FIGURE 17-5 Computer-generated reports increase efficiency and accuracy.

the patient's date of birth, the computer calculates the patient's age, eliminating the need to ask a potentially sensitive question and assuring accuracy when people cannot remember their age. Second, all this information is stored on a computer file and retrieved as needed to generate numerous reports required during a patient's stay: admissions summary sheet, admissions report, pharmacy profile, and even the addressograph used to stamp each page of the patient's record and the identification arm band. In this case, using the computer leads to higher efficiency levels and minimizes errors because data recurring in more than one report are input only once. Preparing error-free reports is a critical public relations tool because errors, even minor clerical ones, may cause the patient to question the hospital's ability to deliver quality health care.

CHARACTERISTICS OF SHORT REPORTS

Most short reports include only the minimum supporting materials to achieve effective communication. Short reports focus on the body—problem, method, findings, and conclusion.

In addition, short reports might incorporate any of the following features:

1. Personal writing style using first- or second-person style. Contractions are appropriate when they contribute to a natural style.
2. Graphics to reinforce the written portion.
3. Headings and subheadings to delineate portions of the body and to reflect organization.
4. Memorandum and letter formats when appropriate.

Various types of short reports are illustrated in the examples that follow. The commentary in the left-hand column will help you understand how effective writing principles are applied.

The report in Figure 17-6 communicates the activity of a company's training department during one quarter of the fiscal period. This periodic report is formatted as a memorandum because it is prepared for personnel within the company and is a brief, informal report.

The study of a reading-improvement program conducted by a consultant is of particular interest because of its persuasive organization, as shown in Figure 17-7. Apparently, the program would be expanded to include more people in the company if the experimental (trial) program succeeded. The letter format is appropriate because a consultant is writing to a client (external audience).

A special kind of short report, the executive summary, condenses a complex or lengthy subject. For example, the executive summary in Figure 17-8 (on page 727) represents an abstract of a 150-page real-estate ap-

```
                    ┌────────┐ LAWRENCE ENTERPRISES, INC. ┌────────┐
                              8763 South Victoria Street
                                Newark, NJ  07109-8763
                             (201) 555-9030  Fax: (201) 555-3949
```

TO: Phillip Brierly, Vice President, Human Resources

[1]FROM: Abraham Frahm, Training Director TD

DATE: April 15, 19—

SUBJECT: Training Department Activity, Third Quarter, 19—

[2] _____

During the third quarter of our fiscal year, January 1 to March 31, the Training Department engaged in the following activities:

Training Programs, Third Quarter, 19--

Title	No. of Sessions	Total Participants	Classroom Hours
[3]Employee orientation	18	143	143
Ethics awareness	2	40	20
Management development	4	32	80
Workplace diversity	8	105	64
Written communication	5	60	20
Desktop publishing	6	25	48

Additionally, we prepared teaching-learning materials and videotapes for the training sessions that will take place during the next two quarters to bring the staff up to date on the new information systems. Copies of these materials are enclosed.

[4]Enclosures

FIGURE 17-6   Short report in memorandum format

[1]Includes headings to serve the function of the transmittal and a title page in a formal report.

[2]Includes horizontal line to add interest and to separate the transmittal from the body of the memo.

[3]Formats data in four-column table to facilitate reading. Table title and column headings are clear. The table is introduced in the text before the reader encounters it. Because the report contains only one table, it is not numbered.

[4]Attaches material to the memorandum. The enclosure would be an appendix item in a formal report.

praisal report covering a large office building. The summary concisely presents the major elements from the report. It gives clients what they are looking for in a one-page report that may be attached at the beginning of the complete report. When clients accept the appraiser's abstract, they may omit reading the total report.

Ability to summarize complex, lengthy reports is a critical skill needed to advance in your career.

JOHNSON AND ASSOCIATES
Suite 2410, Wilton Towers
440 North Michigan Boulevard
Chicago, IL 60607-4088
(217) 555-9500 FAX (217) 555-8529

October 1, 19—

[1]Ms. Jean Tobler
Executive Vice President
Noble Oil Company
P.O. Box 4521
Stillwater, OK 74074-4521

Dear Ms. Tobler

READING-IMPROVEMENT PROGRAM INCREASES
READING SPEED AND COMPREHENSION

[2]Sixty middle-management officials of Noble Oil have now completed the reading improvement program that began on September 1. I am pleased to explain the method used to conduct the study and to report the successful results of this experimental phase of the program.

[3]**Purpose and Method**

The purpose of the program was to improve the critical reading speed and comprehension skills of its management and supervisory personnel. In this program, each participant spent 15 one-hour sessions over a four-week period at the Controlled Reader, a machine that flashes printed material on a monitor at varying speeds.

My role was to present effective reading techniques and to help participants adapt to using the Controlled Reader at their individual study stations. Reading tests were administered to each member of the group at the beginning and at the end of the program. The tests consisted of material specially designed to reflect business and industrial language and difficulty. The effectiveness of the program was evaluated by comparing beginning and ending test scores.

FIGURE 17-7   Short report in letter format

[1] Letterhead, inside address, and subject line function as a title page and transmittal.

[2] Uses inductive organization to convince the vice president that the program should be continued.

[3] Includes headings that divide the report into logical divisions and add coherence.

Describe an effective way to condense information for quick, easy understanding.

The purpose of abstracts is to give busy people the gist of books, articles, conferences, and other meetings. Some executive assistants may find that preparing abstracts is a major part of their job assignments. These abstracts help keep busy executives up to date professionally and on conferences and meetings they are unable to attend. An effective way

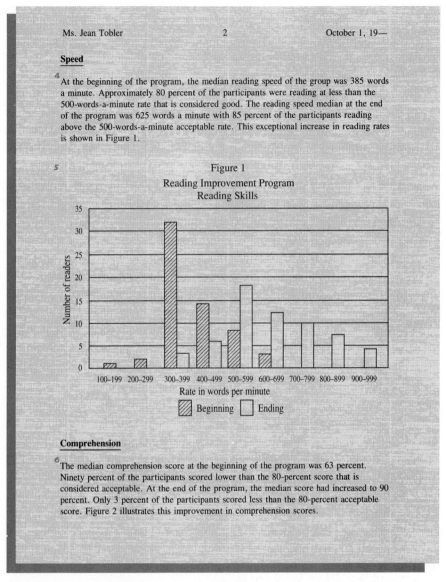

Ms. Jean Tobler   2   October 1, 19—

Speed

4 At the beginning of the program, the median reading speed of the group was 385 words a minute. Approximately 80 percent of the participants were reading at less than the 500-words-a-minute rate that is considered good. The reading speed median at the end of the program was 625 words a minute with 85 percent of the participants reading above the 500-words-a-minute acceptable rate. This exceptional increase in reading rates is shown in Figure 1.

5

Figure 1
Reading Improvement Program
Reading Skills

Number of readers

Rate in words per minute

▨ Beginning ☐ Ending

Comprehension

6 The median comprehension score at the beginning of the program was 63 percent. Ninety percent of the participants scored lower than the 80-percent score that is considered acceptable. At the end of the program, the median score had increased to 90 percent. Only 3 percent of the participants scored less than the 80-percent acceptable score. Figure 2 illustrates this improvement in comprehension scores.

4 Uses medians and percentages as common language in interpreting the quantitative data. The analysis logically leads to the conclusion that the reading program was successful. Introduces and interprets the data before referring the reader to the figure for additional detail.

5 Presents beginning and ending reading rates in a comparative (multiple-range) bar chart to simplify comparison.

6 Uses medians and percentages as common language in interpreting the quantitative data. The analysis logically leads to the conclusion that the reading program was successful.

FIGURE 17-7, continued

to assemble abstracts from formal reports is to pay special attention to topic sentences and to concluding sentences in paragraphs or within sections of reports. In many cases, this technique yields concise abstracts based on major ideas and reduces the use of supporting details and background information.

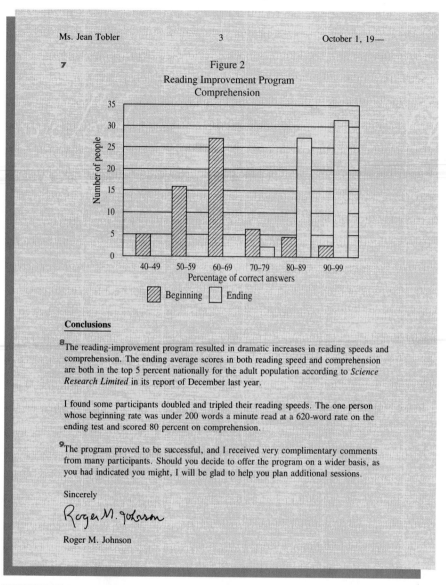

Ms. Jean Tobler   3   October 1, 19—

7

Figure 2
Reading Improvement Program
Comprehension

Beginning   Ending

7Presents beginning and ending comprehension scores in a comparative (multiple-range) bar chart to simplify comparison. Figure is placed as close as possible to the text introducing the data presented in the graph.

8Introduces evidence from an outside source to support the significance of the ending scores and the conclusion that the program was successful.

9Ends with the recommendation: the writer's offer (proposal) to continue to work for the company.

Conclusions

8The reading-improvement program resulted in dramatic increases in reading speeds and comprehension. The ending average scores in both reading speed and comprehension are both in the top 5 percent nationally for the adult population according to *Science Research Limited* in its report of December last year.

I found some participants doubled and tripled their reading speeds. The one person whose beginning rate was under 200 words a minute read at a 620-word rate on the ending test and scored 80 percent on comprehension.

9The program proved to be successful, and I received very complimentary comments from many participants. Should you decide to offer the program on a wider basis, as you had indicated you might, I will be glad to help you plan additional sessions.

Sincerely

Roger M. Johnson

Roger M. Johnson

FIGURE 17-7,   continued

PROPOSALS

Proposals are rapidly becoming prevalent in business, particularly in businesses engaged in high-technology activities and in producer relationships with governmental agencies.

A proposal is generated as the result of a potential buyer's "request

EXECUTIVE SUMMARY

Property Location: 2450 Market Avenue—east side between 51st and 52nd Streets.

Interests Appraised: Condominium complex including 100% of the basement, 1st, 2nd, and 20th through 38th floors, all land, and all common elements.

Current
Assessment:

	Land	$ 7,250,000
	Building	18,250,000
	Total	$25,500,000

Site: 58,110 square feet

Building Description: Modern, high-density office building with an efficient interior layout and an attractive facade.

Economic Status of Central City: (a) Former fiscal crisis seems manageable. (b) Corporate relocations have slowed. (c) Capital investment is increasing, reflecting investor confidence. (d) City encourages business with favorable tax rates.

Marketing Background: Approximately 80% of the available 3.5 million square feet of midtown office space is expected to be absorbed within the next year. Two years may be required to rent 92% of the rentable area of the subject property.

Financial Data: (a) About $4 million will be spent to bring the property up to normal operational standards. (b) Tenant installations may cost $8 million over three years. (c) Cash flows are estimated to be approximately as follows:

Year 1: $2.7 million   Year 4: $4.9 million
Year 2: $3.8 million   Year 5: $5.3 million
Year 3: $4.5 million

Capital value in five years is estimated to be $48 million and the pretax yield over ten years at 11.5%.

Uses appropriate title to designate this page clearly as the executive summary.

Uses headings to denote the major sections and to facilitate easy, quick comprehension.

Includes the *major ideas* presented in each of the major sections of the report and supporting details only when necessary.

FIGURE 17-8 Executive summary of a real-estate appraisal

for a proposal" (RFP). The request describes a problem to be solved and invites respondents to describe their proposed solution. The proposal includes (a) details about the manner in which the problem would be solved and (b) the price to be charged. By naming the price, the proposal "bids" on the project. Governmental agencies as well as major suppliers to the Department of Defense place most of their orders and contracts on

Many government agencies award contracts and orders to companies that submit the most desirable proposals. To earn contracts in this highly competitive market, managers quickly learn to prepare proposals that are well written, detailed, and organized effectively.

the basis of the most desirable proposals. Therefore, proposals receive intense attention as a critical part of the successful operation of many companies in a variety of industries.

The response to a proposal request often results in a lengthy report designed to "sell" the prospective buyer on the ability of the bidder to perform. However, a simple price quotation, such as that shown in Figure 17-9, also constitutes a proposal in response to a request for quotation (RFQ). In this case, the supplier is in the United States and the prospective buyer is in France, with facsimile transmission being the means of communication.

Parts of a Proposal

The format of a proposal will be a memorandum report when the proposal is short and travels within the organization; a letter report when it is short and travels outside the organization; and a formal report when it is long, whether it travels outside or remains within the organization.

Writers have much flexibility in preparing proposals. When they find a particular pattern that seems to be successful, they no doubt will adopt it as their basic plan. The ultimate test of a proposal is its effectiveness in achieving its purpose. The writer's task is to assemble the parts of a proposal in a way that "sells" the reader.

The following general parts or variations of them may be used as headings in a proposal:

Problem	Personnel/recommendations
Purpose	Follow-up/evaluation
Scope	Cost or budget
Method/procedures	Summary
Material	Addenda items
Equipment	

FELDSCO PRODUCTS, INC.
1001 Astralka Avenue
Fresno, CA 93721-6003
(209) 555-9800   FAX: (209) 555-7615

QUOTATION

To: M. B. Electronique
606 rue Fourny-Zac de Buc
B. P. 34, 87540 BUC
FRANCE

Part No.	Quantity	Description	Unit Price	Total
905R901	2	100 foot spool, 14 gauge wire	270.00	$540.00
153C906	2	250 foot spool, 11 gauge wire	570.00	$1,140.00
705C011	3	Wire couplings, 100 unit box	79.00	$237.00
			Subtotal	$1,917.00
			Freight	$145.00
			Tax	$115.02
			Total	$2,177.02

Date September 15, 19—	**Terms** Net 30 days	**Quotation firm for** 60 days
Method of Shipment Air Express	**Delivery can be made by** November 1, 19—	

FIGURE 17-9 Simple price quotation serves as a proposal.

Clear, concise writing is especially important in writing effective proposals.
Reprinted by special permission of King Features Syndicate, Inc..

Include these parts in addition to the normal preliminary report parts (title page, transmittal message, contents, and synopsis) and addenda (references, appendix, and index).

What is the objective of a proposal?

To put the proposal together expeditiously, determine the parts to include, select one part that will be easy to prepare, prepare that part, and then go on to another. When you have completed the parts, you can arrange them in whatever order you like, incorporate the transitional items necessary to create coherence, and then put the proposal in finished form. As with most report writing, you first prepare the pieces of information that you later assemble as the "whole" report. Trying to write a report by beginning on line one, page one, and proceeding to the end may prove to be frustrating and time consuming. Keep in mind that you should complete the research and planning before you begin to write.

Proposals often are written collaboratively as a team effort.

If you become part of a team producing a proposal of major size, you probably will be responsible for only a small portion of the total report. Someone will have the responsibility for putting all the parts together and creating the finished product. For example, a proposal team of sixteen executives, managers, and engineers might be required to prepare an 87-page proposal presenting a supplier's plan to supply parts to a military aircraft manufacturer.

Let's examine a few parts of a variety of proposals to see how they might eventually fit into a total proposal.

Problem and/or Purpose.   *Problem* and *purpose* are often used as interchangeable terms in reports. Here is the introductory statement, called "Project Description," in a proposal by a firm to contribute to an educational project:

Project Description

Mainline Community College has invited business and industry to participate in the creation of Business Communication, a television course and video training package. These materials will provide effective training in business communication skills to enhance the performance of individuals in business and contribute to organizational skills and profitability. In our rapidly evolving information society, skill in communication is integral to success.

Note how the heading "Project Description" has been used in place of "Purpose." In the following opening statement, "Problem" is used as the heading:

Problem

The board of directors of Heatherington Village Association has requested a proposal for total management and operation of its 1,620-unit permanent residential planned development. This proposal demonstrates the advantages of using Central Management Corporation in that role.

The purpose of the proposal may be listed as a separate heading (in addition to "Problem") when the proposal intends to include objectives of a measurable nature. When you list objectives such as "To reduce overall expenses for maintenance by 10 percent," attempt to list measurable and attainable objectives and list only enough to accomplish the purpose of selling your proposal. Many proposals have been rejected simply because writers promised more than they could ever actually deliver.

Scope. When determining the scope of your proposal, you can place limitations on what you propose to do or on what the material or equipment you sell can accomplish. The term *scope* need not necessarily be the

COMMUNICATION MENTOR

We've learned over the years that a written document, and especially a proposal, faces a great deal of competition for the reader's attention. It must compete, first of all, with the other proposals; then it must compete with all of the other papers on the reader's desk, ringing telephones, visitors, and many other distractions. This document, which we may have labored over for weeks, might get five minutes of the reader's attention. Thus, above all, the proposal must be cleanly written: very easy to read, free of jargon and buzz words, and to the point!

H. Devon Graham, Jr.
Southwest Regional Managing Partner
Arthur Andersen & Co.

only heading for this section. "Areas Served," "Limitations to the Study," and "Where XXX Can Be Used" are examples of headings that describe the scope of the proposal. Here is a "scope" section from a consulting firm's proposal to conduct a salary survey:

What the Study Will Cover

To assist ABDEC, Inc. in formulating its salary and benefits program for executives, Property Appraisers, Inc. will include an analysis of compensation (salary and benefits) for no fewer than 20 of ABDEC's contemporaries in the same geographic region. In addition to salaries, insurance, incentives, deferred compensation, medical, and retirement plans will be included. Additionally, Property Appraisers, Inc. will make recommendations for ABDEC's program.

Another statement of scope might be as follows:

Scope

Leading figures in business and industry will work with respected academicians and skilled production staff to produce fifteen 30-minute television lessons that may be used in courses for college credit or as modules dealing with discrete topics for corporate executives.

Method and Procedures. The method used to solve the problem or to conduct the business of the proposal should be spelled out in detail. In this section, simply think through all the steps necessary to meet the terms of the proposal and write them in sequence. When feasible, you should include a time schedule to indicate when the project will be completed.

Materials and Equipment. For large proposals, such as construction or research and development, indicate the nature and quantities of materials and equipment to be used. In some cases, several departments will contribute to this portion. When materials and equipment constitute a major portion of the total cost, include prices. Much litigation arises when clients are charged for "cost overruns." When contracts are made on the basis of "cost plus XX percent," the major costs of materials, equipment, and labor/personnel must be thoroughly described and documented.

Personnel and Recommendations. Assuming your proposal meets with acceptance in terms of services to be performed or products to be supplied, the prospective customer will buy if the "conviction" part of your proposal really convinces. As in a sales message, conviction plays a role in proposals. If everything outlined is acceptable, the "who" and "how much" sections may be critical. Conviction in proposals is based on past

---

Margin notes (left column):

Are problem, purpose, and scope related and introductory?

After scope tells "what," method tells "how" it will be done.

records of the bidder, the recommendations of its past customers, and the proposed cost.

A brief biography of the principal members in the proposal plays a strong part in conviction:

Following "what" and "how," proposals describe "who."

Principals

Engagement Principal: Harold M. Jones, M.B.A., M.A.I. Partner in Property Appraisers, Inc. consulting appraisers, since 1966. Fellow of the American Institute of Appraisers, B.A., M.B.A., Harvard University. Phi Kappa Phi and Beta Gamma Sigma honorary societies. Lecturer and speaker at many realty and appraisal conferences and at the University of Michigan.

In another related section, the proposal might mention other work performed:

Major Clients of Past Five Years

City of Denver, Colorado; Dade County, Florida; City of San Francisco, California; City of Seattle, Washington; Harbor General Corporation, San Francisco; Gulf and Houston, Incorporated, Houston, Texas. Personal references are available on request.

Follow up and/or Evaluation. Although your entire proposal is devoted to convincing the reader of its merit, clients are frequently concerned about what will happen when the proposed work or service is completed. Will you return to make certain your work is satisfactory? Can you adjust your method of research as times change?

If your proposal is for a research grant, don't promise more than you can do. If your study is to explore a promising new approach to medical cures for serious diseases, don't promise to solve all the world's problems. Not all funded research proves to be successful.

If you propose to make a study in your firm's area of expertise, you may be more confident. A public accounting firm's proposal to audit a company's records need not be modest. The accountant follows certain audit functions that are prescribed by the profession. However, a proposal that involves providing psychological services probably warrants a thoughtful follow-up program to evaluate the service.

Follow up and evaluation provide feedback.

Budget, Cost, and Summary. The budget or cost of the program should be detailed when materials, equipment, outside help, consultants, salaries, and travel are to be included. A simple proposal for service by one person might consist of a statement such as "15 hours at $200/hour, totaling $3,000, plus mileage and expenses estimated at $550." Present the budget or cost after the main body of the proposal.

In addition to a cost or budget, you might conclude the proposal with a summary. This summary may also be used to open the total proposal to put it in deductive sequence.

In selling, do you introduce price after you've convinced the reader to buy?

Most work resulting from proposals is covered by a working agreement or contract to avoid discrepancies in the intents of the parties. In some cases, for example, users of outside consultants insist that each consultant be covered by a sizable general personal liability insurance policy that also insures the company. Many large firms and governmental organizations use highly structured procedures to assure understanding of contract terms.

Addenda Items.   When certain supporting material is necessary to the proposal but would make it too bulky or detract from it, include the material as an addendum item. A bibliography and an appendix are examples of addendum items. References used should appear in the bibliography or as footnotes. Maps, questionnaires, letters of recommendation, and similar materials are suitable appendix items.

Sample Short Proposal

A short, informal proposal that includes several of the parts we've discussed is shown in Figure 17-10. It consists of three major divisions: "The Problem," "A Proposed Course of Instruction," and "Cost." The "Course of Instruction" section is divided into five minor divisions to facilitate understanding.

Wanting to increase his chances of winning the bid, the writer made sure the proposal was highly professional and had the impact needed to get the reader's attention. In other words, he wanted the proposal to "look" as good as it "sounds." To add to the overall effectiveness of the proposal, he incorporated appealing, but not distracting, page design features. Printing the proposal with a laser printer using proportional fonts of varying sizes and styles resulted in a professional appearance and an appealing document. The reader's positive impression of the high standards exhibited in this state-of-the-art proposal is likely to influence his or her confidence in the writer's ability to present the proposed communication seminar.

SUMMARY

As they increase in length from one page to several pages, reports also grow in formality with the addition of introductory and addenda items. As a result, reports at the formal end of the continuum tend to be repetitious. Title pages, transmittal messages, summaries, and contents all mention or discuss some elements included in the body of the report.

> **PROPOSAL FOR STAFF DEVELOPMENT SEMINAR:**
> **INTERPERSONAL COMMUNICATION SKILLS FOR**
> **SUPERVISORY AND MIDDLE MANAGEMENT**
>
> **by Gary D. Delaney, Staff Development Coordinator**
>
> **October 1, 19—**
>
> **The Problem**
>
> Management has perceived a need for improved communication performance on the part of supervisory and middle-management personnel to strengthen relationships between them and their employees. The proposed training course is designed to help participants develop effective interpersonal communication skills.
>
> **A Proposed Course of Instruction**
>
> Based on our experience, the following concepts should be effective in improving understanding and improved performance.
>
> **Teaching-Learning Method**
>
> The acquisition of interpersonal skills results from an activity-oriented training program where participants apply theory through role playing, case discussion, and feedback.
>
> In this approach, the instructor is a learning facilitator rather than a lecturer. Frequent use of our video playback accompanied by instructor and group feedback reinforces learning.
>
> **Content**
>
> The following topics constitute the content core of the program: perception and self-concept; a positive communication climate; sending, receiving, and nonverbal skills; reducing communication barriers; resolving conflict; interviewing; and small-group communication.

Describes the nature of the problem and presents the proposed plan as a solution to the problem.

Uses headings to aid the reader in understanding the organization of the proposal. Larger, boldface font adds emphasis.

Describes the course content, instructional method, and design in detail. Divides the "Proposed Course of Instruction" section into five minor divisions for easier comprehension.

FIGURE 17-10   Short proposal

Organizing the content of a report involves the ability to see the report problem in its entirety and then break it into its parts. Because reports are written after the research or field work has been completed, writers may begin writing with any of the report parts and then complete the rough draft by putting the parts in logical order.

Short reports usually are written in memorandum or letter format.

Learning Materials

Because participants seem to feel more comfortable when they have a textbook to guide them, we use the Verderber book, *Interact*. Additionally, case problem handouts are provided for role playing and discussion.

Length of Course

This course consists of 12 two-hour sessions over a six-week period.

Number of Participants

Because of the activity orientation of the program, a maximum of 12 participants is desirable.

Cost

All teaching-learning materials will be provided by us and include textbooks, handouts, and video camera and recorder. Based on a 12-session, 12-participant program, the total cost is $2,172. When two courses are offered on the same day, the total cost is reduced to $4,200. Exact charges:

Interact (12 copies @ $25)	$ 300
Case Problem Handouts (12 copies at $6)	72
Professional Fees (24 hours instruction at $75/hr., travel, subsistence, and lodging)	1,800
Total	$2,172

Includes a subsequent-page heading to identify the second page. The horizontal line is added to increase the professional appearance.

Itemizes costs so the reader understands exactly how the total cost was calculated. Disclosing this detailed breakdown gives the reader confidence that the cost is accurate.

FIGURE 17-10, continued

They are called "short" because they simply are not long enough to require the many supporting preliminary and ending parts of longer reports. Nevertheless, short reports require the same organizing and writing skills as long reports.

Proposals call for thorough organization and require writing methods that will be not only informative but convincing. Proposals often are written by teams; in this way, they typify the nature of reports as having discrete parts that writers can prepare in any order and then assemble into whole reports.

REVIEW QUESTIONS

1. What four terms could probably be used as headings for many reports?
2. What is meant by the concept that as reports become longer they grow in formality?
3. List each of the parts of a formal report and briefly discuss the purpose of each one.
4. Provide guidelines for writing an effective report title.
5. Discuss the proper format for arranging multiple-line titles for a report or graphic. Should a report title be presented in this style each time it is used in a report? Explain.
6. How does a report writer determine which preliminary or addenda parts to include in a report?
7. How are the pages of the three sections (preliminary, report text, and addenda) of a report numbered?
8. Briefly discuss the primary principles involved in writing a transmittal.
9. Describe how word-processing software can be used to simplify production of the preliminary and addenda parts of a report.
10. Briefly discuss the primary principles involved in writing an executive summary. What are other names given to this preliminary report part?
11. Discuss the major items that should be included in an effective introduction.
12. Should new ideas be presented in the summary? Explain.
13. Distinguish between findings, conclusions, and recommendations. Can the report summary, conclusions, and recommendations be presented in separate sections, or must they be combined into one section? Explain.
14. Differentiate between a references page (works cited) and a bibliography (works consulted).
15. Explain how appendixes are identified when more than one appendix item is included. Must the writer mention each item within the report text? Explain.
16. Explain why a report comparing alternatives should be divided into sections that reflect the criteria used to judge the alternatives.
17. How does an inductive organization become deductive when applied to reports?

18. How do form reports increase the accuracy of information?
19. Discuss how using the computer to generate form reports can increase a company's efficiency and accuracy.
20. Discuss several features that are incorporated into a short report.
21. What factor(s) determines whether memorandum or letter format should be used for short reports?
22. What is the primary purpose of a proposal? What is meant by RFQ?
23. When a lengthy, complex proposal is prepared in industry, is the original writing done by one person? Explain.
24. What factor(s) allows a writer to begin writing a report or a proposal with any part of the report?
25. Discuss at least three ways a writer can use word-processing software to improve the overall effectiveness of the final report.

APPLICATIONS

Prepare short reports or proposals as solutions for each of the following applications:

1. **Applying for a Franchise to Open a Miniature Golf Course.** Interested in opening a miniature golf course, Jason Flynn wrote Grand Lagoon, Inc., a franchiser of a popular miniature course, soliciting franchise information. In answer to his request, Jason received an extremely receptive letter requesting standard information designed to help Grand Lagoon determine the economic viability of the proposed location. After analyzing this preliminary information, Grand Lagoon will decide whether to accept Jason's franchise application.

   Grand Lagoon has requested preliminary information regarding the economic and social environment of the proposed site. Specifically, Jason must provide valid, objective data concerning the population of the service area, the economic status of the population, the impact of the climate on the operation of an outdoor business, the nature and extent of competing entertainment businesses, the local tourist industry, and any other information that would support the economic success of the proposed franchise.

   Required: As Jason Flynn, prepare a letter report to the franchiser. Address it to Grand Lagoon, 9700 Gulfside Drive, Pensacola, FL 32501-9700.

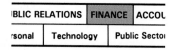

2. **Evaluating the Performance of a Stock Portfolio.** Select ten stocks listed on the New York Stock Exchange and reported in your daily paper or in *The Wall Street Journal.* Assume you will purchase 100

shares of each of the ten stocks at the prices listed at the market close on a particular day. You are going to keep a record of changes in the stocks for a one-week period—five trading days.

Required: Submit a memorandum to your instructor on the purchase date reporting your ten stocks according to the following format:

Name of Stock   *Price per Share*   *Total Cost (×100)*

At the end of the five-day period, submit another memorandum to your instructor detailing how your investments fared during the week. Record the Dow-Jones Industrial Average of thirty stocks for both your purchase date and the end of the five-day period. Compare your total performance—percentage gain or loss—with that of the Dow-Jones average.

3. **Selecting a Personal Computer.** Visit a computer store that handles more than one line or three stores that emphasize only a single line. Examine three brands of personal computers and select the one that you believe best serves your needs. Use whatever criteria you believe will enable you to make a selection.

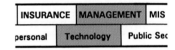

Required: Prepare a short report to your instructor.

4. **Preparing an Analytical Report.** Prepare a short report on the selection of an alternative in *one* of the following cases. Make any assumptions and create any background information needed to make an informed decision.
   a. Recommend one of three automobiles to be used as home-delivery vehicles for a food service. No trips are more than five miles from the company's food-preparation facility.
   b. Recommend how you would invest $2 billion of excess cash that the company will not need until the plant expands in two more years.
   c. Recommend a printer for a company installing a microcomputer-based information system. The company will use the printer for both internal and external correspondence; some correspondence requires graphics.
   d. Recommend whether a company of your choice should install a network computer system or stand-alone personal computers.
   e. You and six other investors are considering opening a restaurant in your city. Determine the most desirable form of organization for your business: sole proprietorship, partnership, or corporation. Consider the legal, tax, and other implications of each alternative.
   f. Your government agency has always purchased the automobiles used by its social workers. The cars are typically driven approxi-

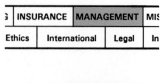

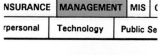

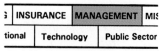

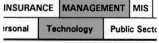

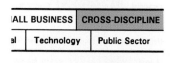

mately 30,000 miles per year and are sold for about 10 percent of their purchase value at the end of three years. Consider the cost effectiveness of the current policy and a car dealer's offer to lease the cars. Recommend whether the agency should purchase or lease the automobiles.

g. One of your sales representatives has provided literature that claims a sales representative's productivity can increase by as much as 30 percent when a cellular phone is used to make sales calls. Recommend whether the company should invest in the installation and use of cellular phones.

h. A family-owned business, having had substantial growth, is considering WATS-line service. The company currently incurs $3,000 of long distance phone charges per month. Evaluate the feasibility of the WATS-line service.

i. You have noticed a substantial increase in the number of employees who spend their lunch hour exercising at one of several health clubs in your community. Furthermore, your insurance agent has reported that claims of your company are increasing at less than the national average. Attributing this positive fact to your employees' commitment to physical fitness, you are considering either (1) installing exercise equipment in underutilized areas of your plant or (2) subsidizing membership dues. You're also thinking about extending the lunch hour to make exercising more convenient. Weigh the alternatives and make a recommendation.

j. You are the manager of a local restaurant, and your business is at maximum capacity. You have no more room to expand at the current location. Investigate whether to move to a new, larger location or to establish a competing restaurant.

k. Office support staff in each department of your company meter and prepare letters for mailing. Weigh the benefits and expenses of establishing a central mail room and make a recommendation.

l. Office support staff in each department of your company make all photocopies on convenience copiers in their departments. Weigh the benefits and expenses of establishing a central copy center.

5. **Analyzing Legal and Ethical Issues.** Select from the "Cases for Analysis" at the ends of Chapters 9–12 for additional topics requiring research to solve a particular business problem. Turn to the appropriate case and read the complete case problem.

a. *Chapter 10, Case 3.* Determine what action is appropriate when an accountant has knowledge that a client has filed a fraudulent tax return. Use a formal framework for analyzing ethical issues. You must determine the ethical and legal implications of this case: What behavior is ethical according to the standards of the Code of Professional Conduct of the American Institute of Certified Public

Accountants? What action, if any, does the Internal Revenue Service require? Communicate this analytical decision to two audiences, your superior and the client.

b. *Chapter 11, Case 2.* Identify the legal implications of using another person's likeness in a television ad. Write a memorandum to your supervisor providing a summary of your research to assure the supervisor that your actions are legally defensible. Based on your research, write the appropriate letter to the person whose likeness you wish to use.

c. *Chapter 6, Case 1.* Analyze the dilemma of whether hiring the homeless to purchase concert tickets is ethical. Communicate this analytical decision to your business partner and write a news release to the general public (content will vary depending on your decision). You may identify other letters needed to communicate your particular decision.

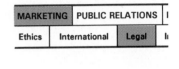

d. *Chapter 6, Case 2.* Analyze the dilemma of whether reducing the quality of engine parts to cut costs is ethical. Communicate this analytical decision to two audiences: your superior and engineers or quality control personnel.

e. *Chapter 9, Case 1.* Analyze the ethical dilemma involved in accepting a boat captain's offer to make an "unapproved" charter that is sure to cinch several sizable investment clients. Then communicate this analytical decision to superiors.

f. *Chapter 9, Case 3.* Determine whether prior products produced with less-than-adequate materials should be recalled using a formal framework for analyzing ethical issues. Then communicate this analytical decision to superiors.

g. *Chapter 10, Case 3.* See description in item b.

h. *Chapter 11, Case 1.* Using a formal framework for analyzing ethical issues, determine whether a company's donating bottled water to American military troops stationed abroad as a public relations maneuver is ethical. Then communicate this analytical decision to superiors and/or to the public in a news release.

i. *Chapter 12, Case 3.* Analyze the dilemma of whether overlooking a vendor's error to your advantage is ethical. Then communicate this analytical decision to superiors.

6. **Assessing the Feasibility of Constructing a Recreational Complex.** Central State University has established a committee to study the feasibility of constructing a recreational center for students, faculty, and staff. To help determine the interest of faculty and staff, the committee has administered a questionnaire. The findings will be combined with other aspects of the feasibility study in a presentation to the president. The committee believes the 668-person sample is representative of the faculty and staff. Here are the results of the survey:

1. On average, how often do you exercise each week?

136	0–1 day
274	2–3 days
197	4–5 days
61	6–7 days

2. During a week, in which of the following activities do you participate? Check all that apply.

171	Aerobic exercise
157	Jogging
147	Weightlifting
299	Walking
67	Tennis
42	Other

3. If you had access, in which of the following activities would you participate? Check all that apply.

196	Racquetball
361	Swimming
72	Basketball
126	Run or walk on an indoor track
165	Exercise machines

4. If a recreation center were constructed for employees, what is the maximum amount you would be willing to pay *per month* to provide use of the center to your immediate family members?

125	$0–$10
69	$11–$20
156	$21–$30
261	$31–$40
57	$41–$50

Required: As a member of the committee, prepare a short report for the president, Susan Chu. You asked respondents to estimate the amounts they would be willing to pay per month for their family to use the center as $0 to $10, $11 to $20, and so on. If you were to do mathematical computations, you'd probably use midpoints such as $5, $11.50, $25.50, and so on as values for each class. In this case, however, write in generalities simply using percentages. Measures of central tendency are not necessary.

NS	FINANCE	ACCOUNTING	INSU
personal	Technology		Public Se

7. **Determining the Perception of Occupations and Professions.** As vice president of Demographic and Social Research, Inc., you are the principal investigator for a study sponsored by your state society of Certified Public Accountants. The society is interested in determining what perceptions the general public has of CPAs compared with other occupations or professions. They would like to improve what-

ever image they present so more college students would investigate careers in public accounting.

The society contracted with your firm to make a study that could be used by a public relations firm to promote accounting as a career. Your job, therefore, is simply to determine how accountants are viewed by the general public. You are not hired to make recommendations about a public relations program or to study how the profession of accounting is viewed. The primary task is to get a view of how an accountant is perceived when compared with other professionals or practitioners of an occupation.

In particular, the society has asked you to assess how an accountant compares on four qualities: (1) honesty, (2) personality, (3) intelligence, and (4) physical appearance. The CPA society has consulted with public relations firms and determined that these four qualities lend themselves to effective image changing. Based on your results, the public relations firm will design a program to improve the perception of the professional accountant.

Using a stratified national sample of 6,000 people originally designed for national surveys by your firm, you obtained opinions on the public's perception of ten occupations/professions. These are listed on the left side of the following tabulation. The four qualities assessed are the column heads, and the columns contain the final ranking of each occupation/profession on each trait. Because you used a weighted, computerized method of arriving at the ranks, you should assume that you will attach the computer printouts in the appendix of your report. As you review the tabulation, note that some ties exist. These occur because the difference in the weighted perceptions was not significant enough to distinguish between or among ranks. For example, "honesty" shows a four-way tie among business executives, dentists, engineers, and medical doctors. They were all given rankings of 6 because ranks 4, 5, 6, and 7 were not significantly distinguishable.

Rank-order Perceptions of Professions by 6,000 People

	Honesty	Personality	Intelligence	Physical Appearance
Public accountants	2	9	5	6
Airline pilots	8	2	8	2
Business executives	6	4	6	1
Clergy	1	5	7	9
Dentists	6	7	4	7
Elected officials	10	1	9	4
Engineers	6	9	2	5
Lawyers	9	3	2	10
Medical doctors	6	6	2	8
Postal employees	3	9	10	3

Think about each of the four traits as a separate part of the findings. In this way, you can develop four separate simple tables as the basis for your discussion. You might point to similarities among rankings and professions on certain traits. These similarities, for example, could raise the question: "Does stereotyping play a part in public perceptions?"

Required: Prepare a short report in letter form. Use your own address or a fictitious one for your company. Address the report to J. J. Adams, Executive Director, State CPA Society, the capital city of your state.

MARKETING	PUBLIC RELATIONS	
erpersonal	Technology	Public S

8. **Surveying Opinions About Food Service.**   Preptech University is located in a community of 60,000 and has an enrollment of 8,500 students. As a private school with relatively high tuition, Preptech enrolls many students from upper-level income groups. At the same time, about 60 percent of the students receive some form of financial aid in the form of government loans, work-study funds, and university grants. Of the 8,500 students, about 6,000 live in campus residence halls, fraternities and sororities, and nearby off-campus apartments. The remainder are commuters living within about 25 miles of the campus.

The University Food Service operates a cafeteria, a deli shop, and a restaurant with a combined capability of serving about 3,000 people at each of the three daily meals. Meals at fraternities and sororities accommodate about 1,200 students. For those living in residence halls, the university has three room-and-board plans and a room-only plan. The room-only plan is $200 a month, and monthly room-and-board plans are as follows:

A. Room with 3 cafeteria meals daily, Monday–Friday: $500
B. Room with a cafeteria meal ticket worth $100 monthly: $300
C. Room with one meal daily, lunch or dinner, Monday–Friday: $320.

During the past four school terms (semesters), the number of people selecting the plans has been as follows:

	Room Only	*Plan A*	*Plan B*	*Plan C*
This term:	685	285	700	1280
Last term:	520	405	770	1140
1 year ago:	450	560	840	960
1½ years ago:	385	836	950	880

The University Food Service manager, Carla Perkins, is concerned about the decline in the use of campus food facilities and has been pressured from higher university administrators to do something about the problem. Overall, the total university enrollment has remained stable in the neighborhood of 8,500 during the four terms.

Although off-campus eating facilities have been around for a number of years, two years ago a McDonald's, a Taco Bell, a Joe's Pizza Parlor, and a full-service restaurant (the University Club) opened within a short walk of the campus.

Ms. Perkins has asked your business communication instructor for a group from your class to assist her by making a study of student opinion about the university food services compared with the off-campus eating facilities. The university will pay $1,200 for the study. Because your class is organized in four-person teams, your instructor decides that the teams should compete for the job by submitting proposals.

Your study plan is to determine the cost of meals for room-and-board plans A, B, and C and the cost of average meals in the four new eating facilities. Next, you plan to conduct a survey of student opinion using a rating scale for the eating facilities. You will sample about 20 percent of the student body during meal hours in the various eating facilities. The rating scale will make use of a five-point scale. Your team has decided to obtain student opinion about these items:

> Cost of meals
>
> Convenience
>
> Variety
>
> Food quality
>
> Atmosphere

Required: Prepare a proposal to compete for the project. You may make any assumptions you like in preparing the proposal.

9. **Applying for a Franchise to Open a Fast-Food Outlet.** A franchise for a fast-food outlet will be assigned in your community, and proposals have been requested. You'd like the franchise because it should yield about $50,000 a year for an owner who does not work actively in the operation and about $100,000 for one who does. Capital required is $150,000; you have $50,000 and have made arrangements for the remainder from financing sources. The franchiser, Frenchies, will supply initial staff training, the additional financing for the physical structure, and financial management advice.

Frenchies is a solid organization, similar to McDonald's, and has had few franchise failures. The firm operates on a percentage of the gross income of each franchise.

Required: Prepare a proposal to the Consumer Service Division of Frenchies. Make whatever assumptions you want to make about your background (qualifications).

NCE	MANAGEMENT	MIS	CONSUM
sonal	Technology		Public Sector

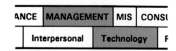

10. Proposal to Install an Office System.   As sales manager of Office Innovations, you are preparing a proposal to automate the Mortgage Department of City National Bank. The Mortgage Department consists of five office support staff, who prepare all mortgage forms and correspondence manually. Five loan officers advise customers on the implications of selecting various options available in making the loan such as interest rate, points, fixed versus variable rates, and term.

Required: Write a proposal that includes the following information: (1) an explanation of how the system described in your proposal would increase the efficiency and effectiveness of the Mortgage Department; (2) complete specifications for the hardware and software you believe will solve the Mortgage Department's problem; (3) a description of the installation procedures including a time line, if necessary, and the training included with the purchase; and (4) a budget for each item proposed in the system.

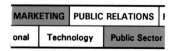

11. Bidding for a Convention Site.   The National Insurance Appraisers Association is planning an upcoming convention. This association of 500 members conducts a three-day conference during late October that includes at least one general session and as many as five breakout groups of 50–75 participants. The chair of this group's convention site committee has invited your city to submit a proposal bidding for the convention's 1997 national convention.

Required: As the executive director of the Economic Development Council, write a proposal including specific information to convince the group that your city can provide the needed meeting facilities, hotel accommodations, economical transportation from major U.S. cities, and a variety of social and recreational activities for members and guests.

12. Preparing Procedures for Reporting Payroll Mistakes.   As a member of the internal audit department of your firm, you have found that hourly-rate employees often believe their paychecks are incorrect. Misunderstandings and time-card mistakes are usually the problem. The current method of correcting mistakes is haphazard. Employees go to the payroll office during working hours and stand around waiting for the error to be checked and corrections to be made. Employees on hourly rates are paid every two weeks.

In cooperation with the payroll department manager, you have developed a similar procedure. When a payroll error is suspected, the employee should see the department head or supervisor to determine whether a mistake has been made. If so, the department head will fill out a Payroll Claim Form to be signed by the employee and the supervisor. The supervisor will send it to the payroll office by messenger.

Small adjustments will be paid in checks for the next pay period. For amounts exceeding $50, special checks will be issued the next day.

Required: Sort through the information presented and prepare a report presenting the new procedure. The memorandum will be distributed to all departments and supervisors. Steps in your procedure should be numbered and should be written for *employee* understanding.

CASE FOR ANALYSIS

Case 1. Are Cellular Phones Affecting Gross Profits at Presley Engineering? Today you received the following electronic message from the president and CEO concerning the impact of cellular phones on gross profit. Firmly convinced that cellular phones can increase the company's financial picture, you decide to take a closer look at last quarter's sales activity. Specifically, you want to compare the sales performance of each sales representative with his/her use of the cellular phone. Hopefully, this analysis will help explain the decrease in gross profits and give you the objective evidence you need to convince Mr. Presley to change his mind.

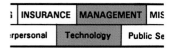

```
Msg #7
E-Mail from Ron Presley      sent 07/15/93 at 01:25 pm

   SUBJECT:   IMPACT OF CELLULAR PHONES ON GROSS PROFIT

   When we agreed to sink all that money into installing cellular phones, we
   were assured we'd see an increase in gross profit. All those studies
   clearly show that cellular phones can increase the productivity of a
   company's sales staff.

   But where are we three months after adding cellular? We've incurred
   exorbitant cellular phone charges, $25,000 last month alone. What's more,
   the second quarter financial statements show a decrease in gross profits.
   It's clear to me we've invested in some new fad that isn't yielding the
   expected returns. I've decided we'd better dump these cellular phones
   before we lose any more profits. Take the necessary steps to discontinue
   our service with Cellular 2000 immediately.

 <Enter> next msg  <F2> save in mailbox  <F5> save to disk  <Esc> stop reading
```

Required:
1. Study the accompanying spreadsheet carefully.
2. Compute the following calculations to help you analyze the data. To increase your efficiency, use an electronic spreadsheet. If software is not available, compute these calculations manually.
   a. Calculate the increase or decrease in gross profit from the first to second quarter without taking cellular phone costs into effect. Multiply the difference of first- and second-quarter sales by the company's 20-percent gross profit rate.

```
Worksheet Range Copy Move File Print Graph Data View System Quit    ↑↓
H14: +D14*0.2-F14
     A          B          C        D        E       F        G        H
1  Presley Engineering
2  Analysis of Sales by Sales Representative
3  For the Two Quarters Ended June 30, 19---
4
5       Sales Rep           Net Sales      Cellular Phone      Gross Profit
6
7                         First    Second   Phone           First    Second
8    No.    Name          Quarter  Quarter  Minutes  Cost   Quarter  Quarter
9    ----   --------      -------  -------  -------  -----  -------  -------
10   14  Davis, S.        $55,200  $78,600   4,190  $2,724  $11,040  $12,997
11    5  Evans, C.        $64,100  $84,900   7,895  $5,132  $12,820  $11,848
12   12  Franks, F.       $62,300  $61,200   1,322    $859  $12,460  $11,381
13   16  Greco, B.        $58,600  $60,400     917    $596  $11,720  $11,484
14   18  Holt, J.         $64,700  $62,200     488    $312  $12,940  $12,128
15    8  Miller, P.       $63,600  $82,800   3,390  $2,204  $12,720  $14,357
16    9  Peters, R.       $60,600  $77,200   7,745  $5,034  $12,120  $10,406
17    6  Reateg, V.       $52,300  $69,500   8,802  $5,721  $10,460   $8,179
18   10  Rehs, W.         $58,500  $53,000     475    $309  $11,700  $10,291
19   21  Shea, R.         $52,700  $58,100     800    $520  $10,540  $11,100
20   11  Wang, J.         $65,300  $84,900   3,922  $2,549  $13,060  $14,431
CELLULAR.WK1 [1]                                                     READY
```

b. Calculate the increase or decrease in gross profit including the cost of cellular phones. Calculate the difference of the first- and second-quarters' gross profit.

c. Calculate the total of each column.

d. Sort the information in the table in ascending order by each sales representative's phone minutes.

3. Prepare a combination bar-line chart using the spreadsheet completed in step 2 or graphics software. If spreadsheet or graphics software is *not* available, your instructor will provide you with a printed copy of the graph. Follow these instructions to prepare the graph:

x-axis	Identify each salesperson by number. Begin at the left listing staff in ascending order according to cellular phone use.
y-axis, left side	Plot the increase in gross profits from the first to second quarter including and excluding cellular phone costs; use comparative (multiple-range) bars.
y-axis, right side	Plot cellular phone use in thousands of minutes using a line graph.

Input a descriptive title for the graph labels (*x*-axis and *y*-axis, left and right), and a legend (identify the data shown in the two bars and the line). Input an explanatory note denoting the installation of cellular phone use at the beginning of the second quarter.

4. Analyze the data in the graph prepared in step 3 to determine the impact of cellular phones on gross profit.

5. Write a short memo report explaining your analysis to Mr. Presley. Integrate the graph into the memo to support your recommendation.

WRITING A FORMAL REPORT

OBJECTIVES

When you have completed Chapter 18, you should be able to

- ◆ Apply effective writing practices.

- ◆ Lend conviction to report writing.

- ◆ Use appropriate documentation methods.

- ◆ Develop your reports in an acceptable format and writing style.

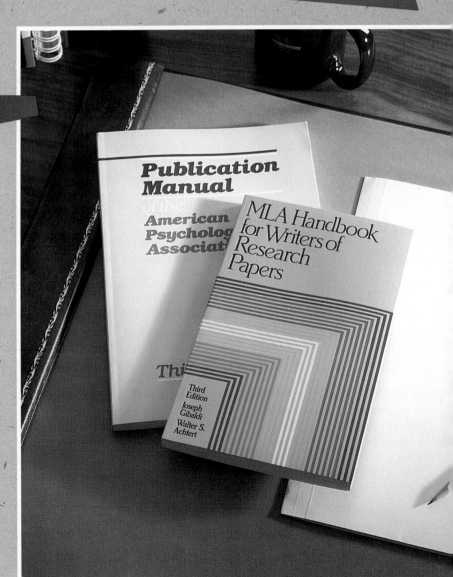

DEREK IS A FINANCIAL ANALYST for a chemical corporation. He was asked to head a committee to study the reasons behind the company's falling revenues. The losses began over five years ago and have increased each year. Derek and his colleagues have worked as a team for weeks brainstorming, researching, and taking notes about their findings. Now Derek is responsible for assembling the information into a final report. Because this formal report is the first he has written, he is a bit worried. He has had to write a number of short, informal reports during his career; and he knows that the only difference between those reports and this one is in length. He gathers all the notes and statistics that he and his colleagues have developed and organizes them in the order in which they will be used. Then he carefully reads the company's style manual before turning on his computer and beginning the first step.

Doing research and taking notes are only parts of the process of putting together a well-documented, acceptable report. Whenever you use ideas, thoughts, words, or statistics that were generated by someone other than yourself, you must document that information accordingly. Most companies have a style manual that gives examples of acceptable formats for documentation and assembly of reports. Take care to read your company's manual thoroughly, be sure to document your report thoroughly, and assemble all its parts into a cohesive and attractively formatted final document.

PROCEDURES FOR WRITING

A writing procedure that works well for one person may not work for another, but consider the following general suggestions:

1. Begin writing only after you have reached a conclusion and prepared a suitable outline.
2. Select a good writing environment. Avoid distractions. Some people can be creative in an environment that might be distracting to others.
3. Start planning early. "Burning the midnight oil" is sometimes necessary, but it doesn't always produce your best work. Give yourself more time than you anticipate using.

Which of these suggestions do you need to incorporate into your writing procedures?

4. Beginning with an easy section may help prepare you for more difficult ones later on.
5. Set aside long, uninterrupted blocks of writing time.
6. Write rapidly and plan to rewrite later. Do not attempt to edit as you go—you only waste time and lose your train of creative thought.
7. Skip difficult places when composing and return to them later. Usually they aren't so difficult then.

Writing a formal report is a major project; and for the report to be a success, you must begin planning early, work at a steady pace, and allow time after you have finished your draft to edit and rewrite. If you procrastinate, you may share the fate of the happy-go-lucky cricket in the fable, left out in the cold while the hard-working ants enjoy the fruits of their labor.

COMMUNICATION MENTOR

Clear, effective writing is usually the result of a great deal of rewriting. Rarely is the first draft the best that writing can be. Use a first draft just to transfer mental notes to paper. Then edit and rewrite stringently. When you've reached the point where almost every word works as well as possible, leave the text alone for a while. Later, go back and see if you can still find improvements. The best writing is almost always a product of many revisions.

Cynthia Pharr
President & CEO
Tracy-Locke/Pharr Public Relations

8. When you have finished the draft, let it sit for a day or two. To edit or rewrite immediately may not pay off. Something you have just written may look great; tomorrow you may see that it needs some work.

9. Review for possible improvement. Some points might need more supporting evidence. Reading your writing aloud reveals awkward grammatical construction and poor wording. Silent reading often misses these errors.

10. Rewrite where necessary. Rewriting is more than editing; sometimes you may have to rewrite weak material completely without reference to the original.

TECHNIQUES OF CONVICTION AND STYLE

Of all the qualities a report should possess, none is more important than conviction. If a report is convincing, readers will accept it as valid and reliable. You will write more convincingly if you have been careful in conducting the research and in interpreting the data. The following writing aids will also add to conviction:

1. *Avoid emotional terms.* "The increase was fantastic" doesn't convince anyone. "The increase was 88 percent—more than double that of the previous year" does convince.

2. *Identify assumptions.* Assumptions are things or conditions taken for granted. When you make an assumption, state that clearly. Statements such as "Assuming all other factors remain the same, . . ." let the reader in on the writer's starting point.

Use sound sources; readers may check your references.

3. *Label opinions.* Facts are preferred over opinion, but sometimes the opinion of a recognized professional is the closest thing to fact. "In the opinion of legal counsel, . . ." lends conviction to the statement that follows and lends credence to the integrity of the writer.

4. *Use documentation.* Footnotes and bibliographies are evidence of the writer's scholarship and honesty. These methods acknowledge the use of secondary material in the research.

For a thorough treatment of stylistic techniques, refer to Chapters 7 and 8. The following list summarizes some important principles of style:

Does first-person use the writer as sentence subjects?

1. *Avoid first-person pronouns as a rule.* In formal reports, the use of *I* is generally unacceptable. Because of the objective nature of research, the fewer personal references you use the better. However, in some organizations the first person is acceptable. Certainly, writing is easier when we can use ourselves as subjects of sentences. People who can change their writing by avoiding the use of the first person will develop a genuine skill.

2. *Use concrete nouns.* "Authorization was received from the IRS" might not be so effective as "The IRS granted authorization." Subjects that can be visualized are advantageous, but you should also attempt to use the things most important to the report as subjects. If "authorization" were more important than "IRS," the writer should stay with the first version.

3. *Use tense consistently.* Because you are writing about past actions, much of your report writing is in the past tense. However, when you call the reader's attention to the content of a graphic, remember that the graphic *shows* in the present tense. If you mention where the study *will take* the reader, you will use a future-tense verb.

4. *Use transition sentences.* Because you are writing a report in parts, you can show the connection between those parts by using transition sentences. "Although several advantages accrue from its use, the plan also presents problems" may be a sentence written at the end of a section stressing advantages and before a section stressing problems.

Transitions build bridges.

5. *Use tabulations and enumerations.* When you have a series of items, don't hesitate to give each a number and to list them consecutively. This list of writing suggestions is easier to understand because it contains numbered items.

6. *Define terms carefully.* When terms might have specific meanings in the study, define them. Definitions should be written in the term-family-differentiation sequence: "A dictionary (*term*) is a reference book (family) that contains a list of all words in a language (*point of difference*)." "A sophomore is a college student in the second year."

7. *Use a variety of coherence techniques.* Just as transition sentences bind portions of a report together, certain coherence techniques bind sentences together: repeating a word, using a pronoun, or using a conjunction. If such devices are used, each sentence seems to be joined smoothly to the next. These words and phrases keep you from making abrupt changes in thought:

Time Connectors	Contrast Connectors
at the same time	although
finally	despite
further	however
furthermore	in contrast
initially	nevertheless
meanwhile	on the other hand
next	on the contrary
since	yet
then	
thereafter	
while	

Similarity Connectors	*Cause-and-Effect Connectors*
for instance	as a result
for example	because
in the same way	but
just as	consequently
likewise	conversely
similarly	hence
	therefore
	thus

8. *Check for variety.* While you write, most of your attention should be directed toward presenting the right ideas and support. Later review may reveal that certain portions have a monotonous sameness in sentence length or construction. Changes are easy and well worth the effort.

The preceding stylistic techniques become habitual through experience. Without much awareness of them, you can simply use them while concentrating primarily on presenting and supporting ideas at the first-draft stage. Necessary improvements can be made later.

DOCUMENTING REPORTS

A crucial part of honest research writing is documenting sources fairly and accurately. Although time consuming and tedious, meticulous attention to documentation marks you as a respected, highly professional researcher. The *Publication Manual of the American Psychological Association* (1983, p. 112) points out the importance of documentation with a forceful quote by K. F. Bruner: an inaccurate or incomplete reference "will stand in print as an annoyance to future investigators and a monument to the writer's carelessness."

An important first step is to pledge that you will not, for any reason, present someone else's ideas as your own. Then, develop a systematic checklist for avoiding plagiarism. Carelessly forgetting to enclose someone else's words within quotation marks or failing to paraphrase another's words can cause others to question your ethical conduct. When you feel that the tedious work required to document sources fairly and accurately is not worth the time invested, remind yourself of the following reasons for documentation:

1. Citations give credit where it is due—to the one who created the material. People who document demonstrate high standards of ethical con-

COMMUNICATION MENTOR

If you want your report read, then make it readable. Research reports should be as inviting and easy to read as *USA Today*. To accomplish this goal, use ample visuals (charts, graphs, illustrations, and photographs) and train yourself to write for the reader.

David Martin
President
Sygnis, Inc.

---

duct and responsibility in scholarship. Those exhibiting this professional behavior will gain the well-deserved trust and respect of peers and superiors.

2. Documentation protects writers against plagiarism, which occurs when someone steals material from another and claims it as his or her own writing.

3. Documentation supports your statements. If recognized authorities have said the same thing, your work takes on credibility; and you put yourself in good company.

Why use documentation?

Many style guides are available to advise writers how to organize, document, and produce reports and manuscripts. Refer to Figure 15-5 on page 653 for a list of the most popular authoritative style manuals.

When repair workers work on power lines, they cannot simply rely on their knowledge and expertise. They are dependent on the physical stability and support of hydraulic lifts or safety belts. In reports, using and documenting the ideas and words of experts gives your own ideas a boost and helps support your main points.

The *Publication Manual of the American Psychological Association* (APA, 1983) has become the most-used guide in the social sciences and in many scholarly journals. The *MLA Handbook for Writers of Research Papers* (Gibaldi & Achtert, 1988), another authoritative source, is published by the Modern Language Association. In business reports and college papers, any of the various documentation methods is suitable. As you read professional literature and write business reports, you may need to become familiar with many methods.

Follow these suggestions for preparing accurate documentation:

1. Decide which authoritative reference manual to follow for preparing in-text parenthetical citations or footnotes (endnotes) and the bibliography. Some companies and most journals require writers to prepare reports or manuscripts following a particular reference manual. Once you are certain you have selected the appropriate style manual, follow it precisely as you prepare the documentation and produce the report.
2. Be consistent. If you are carefully following a format, you shouldn't have a problem with consistency. For example, one style manual may require an author's initials in place of first name in a bibliography; another reference requires the full name. The placement of commas and periods and other information varies among reference manuals. Consult the manual, apply the rules methodically, and proofread carefully to ensure accuracy and consistency. If you cannot locate a format for an unusual source in the reference manual you are using, use other entries as a guide for presenting information consistently.
3. If in doubt about whether to include certain information, follow the rule that it is better to include more than enough than too little.

Preparing Citations

Two major types of citations are used to document a report: source notes and explanatory notes. Depending on the authoritative style manual used, these notes may be positioned in parentheses within the report, at the bottom of the page, or at the end of the report.

Source Notes.   Source notes are designed to acknowledge the contributions of others. These citations might refer readers to sources of quotations, paraphrased portions of someone else's words or ideas, and quantitative data used in the report. Source notes must include complete and accurate information so that the reader can locate the original source if desired.

Explanatory Notes.   Explanatory notes are used for several purposes: (1) to comment on a source or provide information that does not fit easily in the text, (2) to support a statistical table, or (3) to refer the reader to another section of the report. The following sample footnote describes the mathematics involved in preparing a table:

*The weighted opinion was arrived at by assigning responses from high to low as 5, 4, 3, 2, 1; totaling all respondents; and dividing by the number of respondents.

In this case, the asterisk (*) was used rather than a number to identify the explanatory footnote both in the text and in the citation. This method is often used when only one or two footnotes are included in the report. If two footnotes appear on the same page, two asterisks (**) or numbers or letters are used to distinguish them. An explanatory note that supports a visual or a source note that provides the reference from which data were taken appears immediately below the visual.

Several citation methods are available: in-text parenthetical, bottom-of-the-page, end-of-report, and citation-to-bibliography link. Note the major differences among the methods in the following discussion.

In-text Parenthetical Citations. The APA *Manual,* MLA *Handbook,* and other documentation references eliminate separate footnotes or endnotes and refer the reader to a list of sources at the end of the report. To cite material within the text, place the author's name and the date of publication in parentheses. The list of sources at the end contains all publication information on every source cited in the report. This list is arranged alphabetically by the author's last name or, if no author is provided, by the first word of the title (not counting articles). The reader uses the author's name and date of publication and/or page number from the in-text parenthetical citation to locate the original source in the list of sources.

The citations contain the minimum information needed to locate the source in the complete list. Text citations prepared using the APA *Manual* include the author's last name and the date of publication; the page number is included if referencing a direct quotation. The MLA *Handbook* omits the date of publication. Note the following citations using the APA method:

One author not named in the text

"Good ethics, simply, is good business. Good ethics will attract investors. Good ethics will attract good employees . . ." (Perrella, 1991, p. 7).

Multiple authors or sources not named in the text

These founders firmly believed . . . (Langston & Smith, 1991).

A study of motivation . . . (Hansen et al., 1989).

. . . as the reward (Reardon, 1981; Smith, 1984).

Past research (Taylor, 1985, 1989) shows . . . .

For works by more than two authors and fewer than six, cite all authors the first time the work is referenced; use "et al." for subsequent references.

Reference to author(s) or date in the text

Marshall McLuhan (1965) coined the phrase . . . .

In 1986, Smith and Brown concluded . . . .

No author provided

. . . guidelines for effective writing ("Clear Writing," 1991).

One of two or more works by the same author(s) in the same year

Taylor (1985a) advocated . . . .

Bottom-of-the-Page Method.   Placing citations at the bottom of the page on which they are cited might be called the traditional method because of its long use. The reader can conveniently refer to the source if the documentation is positioned at the bottom of the page.

An example of a traditional footnote documenting a direct quotation taken from a book follows:

> "Comparisons between countries are always tendentious to
>
> some extent and thus suspect."[1]
>
> [1]Edwin J. Feulner, Jr., Congress and the New Economic Order (Washington: Heritage Foundation, 1976) 53.

Review the citations for a variety of publications using the Modern Language Association (MLA) format shown in Figure 18-1. Although MLA style recommends in-text parenthetical citations, the guide allows the traditional bottom-of-the-page citation.

Sophisticated word-processing programs have changed the formerly tedious task of preparing footnotes to a simple matter of instructing the computer to create a footnote. The software inserts the superscript number identifying the footnote and provides a special footnote-entry screen for keying the footnote. The software calculates how much space is needed at the bottom of each page for the footnotes and paginates each page automatically. The software also renumbers the notes automatically any time you add, delete, or move footnotes. The procedures for creating a footnote are illustrated in Figure 18-2.

Pick a method and stay with it.

Guide to Preparing Traditional Footnotes
MLA Style (3rd Edition)

A book reference with two authors and edition

Stefan Hyman Robock and Kenneth Simmons, International Business and Multinational Enterprises, 3rd ed. (Homewood: Irwin, 1983) 107.

Note: For more than three authors, use *et al.* (meaning "and others") after the name of the first author.

An edited book

Brent D. Rubin, ed., Communication Yearbook 1 (New Brunswick: Transaction Books, 1977) 48–50.

A report, book, or pamphlet from a private organization, corporate author

Bausch & Lomb, 1990 Annual Report (Rochester: Bausch & Lomb, 1990) 5–6.

Conference Board Antitrust Forum, The Future of a Business-Judgment Standard in Antitrust Law (New York: Conference Board, 1987) 23.

Common Sense & Everyday Ethics (Washington: Ethics Resource Center, 1980) 7–9.

A chapter in a book or section within a reference book

John Naisbitt, "National Economy—World Economy," Megatrends: Ten New Directions for Transforming Our Lives (New York: Warner, 1982) 61.

"Magnetek, Inc.," Moody's Handbook of Common Stocks (New York: Moody's Investors Service, 1991).

"Marine Holding Co.," Standard & Poor's Corporation Records, vol. 4 (New York: Standard & Poor's) 8503.

A journal article paginated by issue

Marvin H. Swift, "Clear Writing Means Clear Thinking," Harvard Business Review 51.5 (1990): 59.

FIGURE 18-1   Traditional footnotes, MLA style

Guide to Preparing Traditional Footnotes
MLA Style (3rd Edition)

An article in a periodical, with an author

Bruce Nussbaum, "A Career Survival Kit," Business Week 7 Oct. 1991: 99.

A periodical without an author

"Writing a Resume That Works: It's Simple: Custom Tailor Each One to the Job," Changing Times June 1990: 91, 93, 95.

An article in a newspaper

Kymberly K. Hockman, "The Last Barrier to the European Market," Wall Street Journal 7 Oct. 1991: A14.

A government publication

Equal Employment Opportunity Commission, Minorities and Women in Institutions of Higher Education (Washington: EEOC, 1991) 2.

Unpublished interviews, letters, and papers

Richard L. Wang, personal interview, 27 June 1992.

M. Allen Kline, letter to Donna Carlson, 31 Nov. 1990.

P. J. Forrest, "Factors That Influence Ethical Business," diss., Mississippi State U, 1989, 21.

Computer software

WordPerfect 5.1, computer software, WordPerfect Corporation, 1989.

Films, filmstrips, slide programs, and videotapes

Valuing Diversity, videocassette, Copeland Griggs Productions, 1987.

FIGURE 18-1,   continued

End-of-Report Citations.   The end-of-report style lists all citations in a list called "Notes" or "List of Notes" at the end of the report. A list of citations at the end of the report is obviously easier to prepare than bottom-of-the-page footnotes. However, readers will be forced to turn to the back

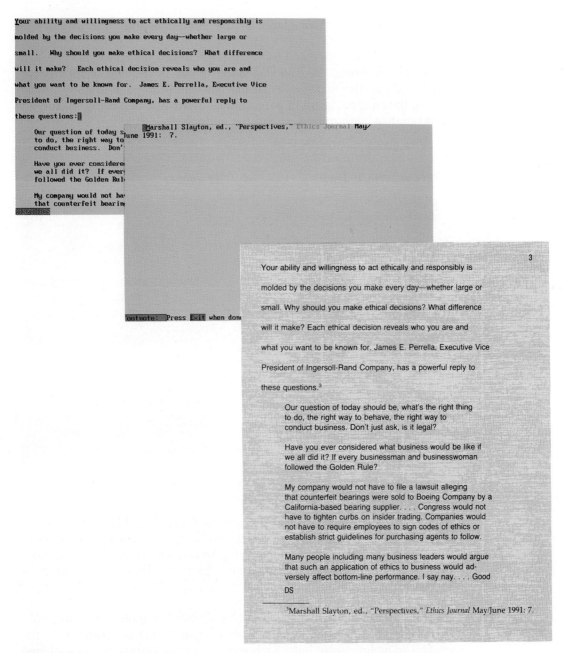

FIGURE 18-2 Footnoting feature of word-processing software simplifies report documentation.

of the report rather than glance at the bottom of the page to locate a source.

The endnotes are listed in the order in which the citations appear in the report. Indicate the in-text citation either by placing a superscript number above the text line as in the bottom-of-the-page method, or by placing the citation figure in parentheses on the line of writing. Examples of the citation within the text and the endnote follow:

Citation Within Text	*Endnotes*

"Comparisons between countries are always tendentious to some extent and thus suspect.[1]

16

NOTES

[1]Edwin J. Feulner, Jr., <u>Congress and the New Economic Order</u> (Washington: Heritage Foundation, 1976) 53.

or

or

"Comparisons between countries are always tendentious to some extent and thus suspect." (1)

(1) Edwin J. Feulner, Jr., <u>Congress and the New Economic Order</u> (Washington: Heritage Foundation, 1976) 53.

Word-processing software programs have simplified the task of preparing endnotes. The process is similar to that of preparing bottom-of-the-page notes except that you instruct the software to print the endnotes in the correct sequence on a separate page rather than at the bottom of each page.

Citation-to-Bibliography Link.   A method that ties footnotes to the bibliography and eliminates the need for a separate list of footnotes is the citation-to-bibliography link. Each entry in the bibliography is numbered consecutively. The citation in the text consists of the number corresponding to the entry in the bibliography and any page reference. The reader can locate the original source by turning to the bibliography. In the following example, the source for the citation is listed as number 2 in the bibliography; the page number is 53.

Citation Within Text

Bibliography

"Comparisons between countries are always tendentious to some extent and thus suspect" (2:53).

12

BIBLIOGRAPHY

1. Curtis, David. Personal interview. 25 May 1991.

2. Feulner, Edwin J., Jr. Congress and the New Economic Order. Washington: Heritage Foundation, 1976.

3. Jones, Harold R., Michael Smith, and Thomas Brown. Tomorrow. Chicago: Western Press, 1986.

Preparing a Bibliography

The bibliography is an alphabetized list of all the sources consulted when preparing a report. Each entry contains publication information necessary for locating the source. In addition, the bibliographic entries give evidence of the nature of sources the author consulted.

A researcher often uses sources that provide information but do not result in citations. To acknowledge that you may have consulted these works and to provide the reader with a comprehensive reading list, include these sources in the list of sources. The APA and MLA styles use different terms to distinguish between these types of lists:

	APA	*MLA*
Includes only sources cited	References	Works Cited
Includes works cited and consulted	Bibliography	Works Consulted

Your company guidelines or authoritative style manual may specify whether to list only works cited or all works consulted. If you receive no definitive guidelines, use your own judgment. If in doubt, include all literature cited and read and label the page with the appropriate title so that the reader clearly understands the nature of the list.

As noted earlier, in-text parenthetical citations contain just enough information to locate the source in the list of sources (author's last name and sometimes date of publication and page number). Footnotes and endnotes include complete publishing information in a form different from bibliographic entries. Note the difference between the traditional footnote/endnote, in-text parenthetical citations, and bibliographic entries. (Space limitations prevent showing indentations in this list.)

	MLA Style	*APA Style*
In-text parenthetical citation	(Feulner 53)	(Feulner, 1976)
Footnote or endnote	Edwin J. Feulner, Jr., Congress and the New Economic Order (Washington: Heritage Foundation, 1976) 53.	Not acceptable
Bibliography	Feulner, Edwin J., Jr. Congress and the New Economic Order. Washington: Heritage Foundation, 1976.	Feulner, E., Jr. (1976). Congress and the new economic order. Washington, DC: Heritage Foundation.

Three major differences exist between footnotes/endnotes and bibliographic entries:

1. Footnotes and endnotes are listed in the order in which they are cited in the text; bibliographic entries appear in alphabetical order.
2. Footnotes use given names of authors first; bibliographies use surnames first. In a bibliography, the alphabetical list of surnames aids the reader in locating an entry.
3. Bibliographic entries refer to the entire work cited and not simply to the specific page or pages from which the material came. Thus, an in-text citation or a footnote might cite a specific page, but the bibliographic entry includes the entire work. A bibliographic entry for a periodical lists the beginning and ending pages of the article.

To aid the reader in locating sources in lengthy bibliographies, include several headings denoting the types of publications documented; for example, books, articles, unpublished papers, and nonprint media.

Bibliographic styles for a variety of publications prepared using the MLA style are shown in Figure 18-3. The same entries prepared using the

Guide to Preparing Works Cited MLA Style (3rd Edition)

A book reference with two authors and edition

Robock, Stefan Hyman, and Kenneth Simmons. International Business and Multinational Enterprises. 3rd ed. Homewood: Irwin, 1983.

Note: For more than three authors, use *et al.* (meaning "and others") after the name of the first author.

An edited book

Rubin, Brent D., ed. Communication Yearbook 1. New Brunswick: Transaction Books, 1977.

A report, book, or pamphlet from a private organization, corporate author

Bausch & Lomb. 1990 Annual Report. Rochester: Bausch & Lomb, 1990.

Conference Board Antitrust Forum. The Future of a Business-Judgment Standard in Antitrust Law. (New York: Conference Board, 1987.

Ethics Resource Center. Common Sense & Everyday Ethics. Washington: Ethics Resource Center, 1980.

A chapter in a book or section within a reference book

Naisbitt, John. "National Economy—World Economy." Megatrends: Ten New Directions for Transforming Our Lives. New York: Warner, 1982. 59–78.

"Magnetek, Inc." Moody's Handbook of Common Stocks. New York: Moody's Investors Service, 1991.

"Marine Holding Co." Standard & Poor's Corporation Records. 4 vols. New York: Standard & Poor's Corp. 8503.

A journal article paginated by issue

Swift, Marvin H. "Clear Writing Means Clear Thinking. . . ." Harvard Business Review 51.5 (1990): 59. [51.5 = volume 51, issue 5]

An article in a periodical, with an author

Nussbaum, Bruce. "A Career Survival Kit." Business Week 7 Oct. 1991: 98–100, 104.

FIGURE 18-3   Works cited, MLA style

Guide to Preparing Works Cited MLA Style (3rd Edition)

A periodical without an author

"Writing a Resume That Works: It's Simple: Custom Tailor Each One to the Job." Changing Times June 1990: 91, 93, 95.

An article in a newspaper

Hockman, Kymberly K. "The Last Barrier to the European Market." Wall Street Journal 7 Oct. 1991: A14.

A government publication

Equal Employment Opportunity Commission. Minorities and Women in Institutions of Higher Education. Washington: Equal Employment Opportunity Commission, 1991.

Unpublished interviews, letters, and papers

Wang, Richard L. Personal interview. 27 June 1992.

Kline, M. Allen. Letter to Donna Carlson. 31 Nov. 1990.

Forrest, P. J. "Factors That Influence Ethical Business." Diss. Mississippi State U, 1989.

Computer software

WordPerfect 5.1. Computer software. WordPerfect Corporation, 1989.

Films, filmstrips, slide programs, and videotapes

Valuing Diversity. videocassette. Copeland Griggs Productions, 1987.

FIGURE 18-3, continued

APA style appear in Figure 18-4. Note that the APA format includes several distinct variations from the MLA and other traditional formats:

1. List the last names of all authors. Use initials for first and middle names. Use an ampersand (&) rather than "and" before the name of the last author in a series.
2. Place the date in parentheses after the author's name.
3. In titles of books and articles, capitalize only the first word of the title, the first word of the subtitle, and proper names. All other words begin with lowercase letters. In titles of journals, capitalize *all* significant words. Underline the titles of books and journals. Do not use quotation marks around the titles of articles.

Guide to Preparing References APA Style (3rd Edition)

A book reference with two authors and edition

Robock, S. H., & Simmons, K. (1983). International business and

multinational enterprises (3rd ed.). Homewood, IL: Irwin.

An edited book

Rubin, B. D. (Ed.). (1977). Communication yearbook 1. New

Brunswick, NJ: Transaction Books.

A report, book, or pamphlet from a private organization, corporate author

Bausch & Lomb. (1990). 1990 annual report. Rochester, NY:

Author.

Conference Board Antitrust Forum. (1987). The future of a

business-judgment standard in antitrust law. New York:

Author.

Ethics Resource Group. (1980). Common sense & everyday ethics.

Washington, DC: Author.

A chapter in a book or section within a reference book

Naisbitt, J. (1982). National economy—world economy. In J.

Naisbitt, Megatrends: Ten new directions for transforming our

lives (pp. 59–78). New York: Warner.

Moody's Investor Service. (1991). Magnetek, Inc. In Moody's

handbook of common stocks. New York: Author.

Standard & Poor's. (1991). Marine Holding Co. In Standard &

Poor's corporation records (p. 8305). New York: Author.

FIGURE 18-4   References, APA style

Guide to Preparing References APA Style (3rd Edition)

A journal article paginated by issue

Swift, M. H. (1990). Clear writing means clear thinking . . . Harvard

Business Review, 51(5), 59.

An article in a periodical, with an author

Nussbaum, B. (1991, October 7). A career survival kit. Business

Week, pp. 98–100, 104.

A periodical without an author

Writing a resume that works: It's simple: Custom tailor each one to

the job. (1990, June). Changing Times, 91, 93, 95.

An article in a newspaper

Hockman, K. K. (1991, October 7). The last barrier to the European

market. The Wall Street Journal, p. A14.

A government publication

Equal Employment Opportunity Commission. (1991). Minorities

and women in institutions of higher education. Washington,

DC: Author.

Unpublished interviews, letters, and papers

[Cite *interviews* in text as personal communications; do not

include in references.]

[Cite *letters* in text as personal communications; do not include in

references.]

Forrest, P. J. (1989). Factors that influence ethical business.

Unpublished doctoral dissertation, Mississippi State

University, Starkville, MS.

FIGURE 18-4, continued

> ### *Guide to Preparing References APA Style (3rd Edition)*
>
> *Computer software*
>
> WordPerfect 5.1. (1989). [Computer software]. Orem, UT:
>
>   WordPerfect Corporation.
>
> *Films, filmstrips, slide programs, and videotapes*
>
> Valuing Diversity. (1987). [Videocassette]. San Francisco: Copeland
>
>   Griggs Productions.

FIGURE 18-4, continued

4. Use a shortened form for the name of publishers. For example, omit "Co." and "Inc."
5. Double-space all entries. Indent all lines except the first line of each entry three spaces.

    Word-processing programs can be used to convert the endnotes into a properly formatted reference list. Simply use the block command to make another copy of the endnotes page. By inputting the necessary revisions on the copy (change the title to "References," reverse the order of the authors' names, add page numbers, and so on), you avoid having to re-key all the publication information. Finally, use the sort feature to put the entries in alphabetical order by author's last name or the first word of the title if no author is provided.

USING HEADINGS EFFECTIVELY

Headings are signposts along the way, informing readers about what is ahead. Headings take their positions from their relative importance in a complete outline. In a roman numeral outline, "I" is a first-level heading, "A" is a second-level heading, and "1" is a third-level heading:

  I. First-level heading
      A. Second-level heading
      B. Second-level heading
         1. Third-level heading
         2. Third-level heading
 II. First-level heading

Two important points about the use of headings also relate to outlines:

If an outline contains an
"A," must it also contain a
"B"?

1. Because second-level headings are subdivisions of first-level headings, you should have at least two subdivisions (A and B). Otherwise, the first-level heading cannot be divided—something divides into at least two parts or it is not divisible. The same logic applies to the use of third-level headings following second-level headings.
2. All headings of the same level should appear in the same physical location and type style, as shown in Figure 18-5.

As you review Figure 18-5, note that one blank line precedes first- and second-degree headings. This method is by no means universal, and you may follow any format you like—but follow it consistently to aid communication with the reader. A further suggestion, as you will observe in Figure 18-5 and in the sample report that follows, is to avoid placing two headings consecutively without any intervening text. For example, always write something following a first-level heading and before the initial second-level heading.

Two consecutive headings
with no intervening text is
unacceptable.

With word-processing programs, you can develop fourth- and fifth-level headings simply by using boldface and varying type fonts. In short reports, organization rarely goes beyond third-level headings; thoughtful organization can limit excessive heading levels in formal reports.

THE COMPLETE REPORT

A complete, long report is illustrated following the chapter summary and list of references. The notations next to the text will help you understand how effective presentation and writing principles are applied. APA style requires that reports be double-spaced and that the first line of each paragraph be indented five spaces; however, a company's report-writing policy may override this style and stipulate single spacing without paragraph indents. The sample report is single-spaced and paragraphs are not indented in order to save space and give a more professional look. The report may be considered formal and contains the following parts:

Title page

Transmittal

Executive summary

Contents

Figures

Report text (introduction, body, and conclusions and recommendations)

References

Appendix

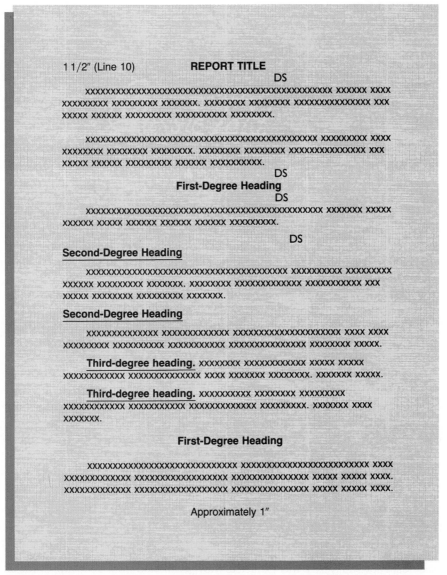

FIGURE 18-5 **Effective headings formats for reports divided into three levels**

This example should not be considered the only way to prepare reports, but it is an acceptable model. Following the sample report, the "Check Your Writing" section provides a comprehensive checklist for use in report writing.

SUMMARY

Although reports also grow in formality as they grow in size, writers determine whether to prepare a report in formal style and format before they begin writing. As they organize and make tentative outlines, writers learn quickly the format and style best able to communicate the intended message. This chapter presented general suggestions for writing effective formal reports.

First, you must develop specific writing procedures that work best for you. After completing complete, accurate research, attempt to write the report during long, uninterrupted writing sessions; begin with an easy section and write as quickly as possible knowing you will revise later.

Use a writing style that presents the findings and interprets the data clearly and fairly, convincing the reader to accept your point of view, but in an unemotional manner. Be certain you have labeled your opinions clearly and identified any assumptions. Document any idea that is not yours (direct quotation or paraphrased text) to avoid plagiarism and to demonstrate your high ethical standards. Follow an authoritative style manual for writing complete documentation that allows readers to locate your sources and portrays the work of a professional. Lay the first draft aside long enough to get a fresh perspective. Then revise the report with a genuine commitment to making all possible improvements.

The writing procedures, techniques, and documentation methods presented in this chapter and illustrated in the sample report also apply to short reports and proposals. Compare your report to the report-writing checklist shown in the "Check Your Writing" section that follows.

REFERENCES

American Psychological Association. (1983). *Publication manual of the American Psychological Association* (3rd ed.). Washington, DC: Author.

Gibaldi, J., & Achtert, W. S. (1988). *MLA handbook for writers of reserach papers* (3rd ed.). New York: Modern Language Association.

Note: Case for Analysis 1 was extracted with permission from Lehman, C. M. & Spencer, B. A. (1991). Creative thinking: An integral part of effective business communication, *Bulletin of the Association of Business Communication, 54*(1), 21–27.

INCREASING PARK MANAGEMENT EFFICIENCY AND RESIDENT AND COMMUNITY RESPONSIVENESS

Prepared for

Robert L. Kamden, President
American Mobile Home, Inc.
Scottsdale, Arizona

Prepared by

Marion and Associates
1227 Monmouth Avenue
Denver, CO 80202-1227

April 19--

Provides specific title to give the reader overview of topic covered in report.

Arranges information in appealing, professional format. Items appear to be centered horizontally between margins. Extra space allowed for binding at left (centered items slightly to the right of actual center).

States the name and title of reader—person who authorized report.

Includes the name and title of person and/or organization that prepared report. Including address is a matter of preference and company requirements.

Uses graphic design to enhance appearance and effectiveness:

◆ All capital letters and boldface, large font size to emphasize title.
◆ Different font for remaining items to add interest and to distinguish them from title.
◆ Double border to add professional flair.

Includes date report was submitted for later reference.

Omits page number but counts page.

Uses company letterhead.
Uses an acceptable letter format for the reports submitted to someone outside the company; uses memo format for reports prepared for someone inside the company.

Presents the report and reminds reader that he requested it.

Discusses methods used to solve the problem.

Summarizes major conclusions and recommendations. This information may be omitted if report includes an executive summary.

Expresses willingness to discuss the results further; may give thanks for cooperation given by the company or acknowledge assistance of others.

Uses informal, natural tone that involves the reader with writer and topic. Includes personal pronouns even though the report contains no first- or second-person pronouns.

Adds enclosure notation to alert reader that report is included.

Omits page number but counts page. If page number is used, a lowercase roman numeral is centered about 1 inch from the bottom of the page.

MARION and ASSOCIATES
1227 Monmouth Avenue
Denver, CO 80202-1227
(303) 555-9800 Fax (303) 555-1363

April 15, 19--

Mr. Robert L. Kamden, President
American Mobile Home, Inc.
P. O. Box 441
Scottsdale, AZ 85286-0441

Dear Mr. Kamden

I'm pleased to send you our report of the park management study you authorized in your letter of February 5.

The report reaffirms some of your observations and presents our conclusions and recommendations. We surveyed 2,400 residents for opinions about the weaknesses and strengths of park managers. We conducted audits of management performance in 40 parks.

Management weaknesses centered on interpersonal communication with residents and on certain office functions. Their strengths were primarily in the maintenance of physical facilities. Recommendations include focusing training programs on weaknesses.

When you have reviewed the report, Mr. Kamden, I'll be glad to discuss it further with you.

Sincerely

Leslie Marion

Ms. Leslie Marion
President

Enclosure

CONTENTS

1 ½" (Line 10)

DS

Transmittal ii

DS

Figures iv

Executive Summary v

Introduction 1

    Purpose of the Study 1
    Methods and Procedures Used 2

American's Role and the Park Manager 2

Residents' Views of Weaknesses and Strengths 5

    Weaknesses Involve People Skills 5
    Strengths Involve Visible Actions 6

The Management Audit 7

Conclusions and Recommendations 10

    Train Managers 11
    Develop Resident Associations 11
    Encourage Community Involvement 11
    Organize Regionally 12

References 13

Appendix 14

Adds leaders (spaced periods) to guide the eye from the heading to the page number.

Includes the page number on which each major and minor section begins.

Presents each heading exactly as it appears in the report. Includes "Introduction" even though the heading is not included in the report. For long reports containing numerous levels of headings (more than three), an abbreviated contents page that includes only two or three levels of headings provides an effective overview of the entire report.

Omits the outline numbering system (I, II, . . .) but arranges the outline to indicate the importance of the headings (main heads placed at left margin; minor ones indented).

Prepare the contents after completing the report. Use advanced word-processing features to generate the contents page automatically—including appropriately spaced leaders and correct page numbers. The contents can be updated quickly and submitted with each draft of the report.

Includes the list of figures on a separate page. If the contents and list of figures are short, they can be placed on one page.

Omits the word "list," an obvious fact.

1 ½" (Line 10)   **FIGURES**

DS

1. Ages of 40 Park Managers 3

2. Park Management Experience of 40 Managers 4

3. Top 5 Weaknesses as Viewed by 2,400 Residents 5

4. Top 5 Strengths as Viewed by 2,400 Residents 6

5. Audit Analysis of 5 Activities in 40 Parks 8

6. External Relations of 40 Managers 9

EXECUTIVE SUMMARY

1 ½" (Line 10)

DS

American Mobile Home, Inc. owns and operates 76 mobile home parks. Because of rapid growth, American has employed and installed park managers who may not have had adequate preparation or skills in all areas of their jobs. This study identifies areas of deficient managerial performance and recommends improvement. Robert L. Kamden, President of American, authorized the study.

Research was conducted in two ways: (1) A questionnaire survey of 2,400 park residents determined park managers' strengths and weaknesses as viewed by residents. (2) Two-person audit teams from Marion and Associates interviewed managers and examined practices at 40 parks.

Residents indicated managerial weaknesses primarily in interpersonal communication skills and in knowledge of and enforcement of rules. Strengths were managers' abilities to maintain the physical facilities.

The audits found managers' work inadequate in cost control, record keeping, and cash management. Managers were not as active in community involvement as American desired.

The study concluded that managers should participate in training programs designed to meet their needs and corporate needs. Recommendations also included preparing procedures manuals, underwriting costs of certain community activities for managers, and creating a method for better interaction between individual managers and corporate staff.

Summarizes essential elements in entire report to simplify understanding.

Uses title "Executive Summary"—a term widely used in business and industry; APA style uses "Abstract." Centers heading in all capital letters. Larger, boldface font adds emphasis.

Provides needed background and explains problems leading to need for the study. Presents purpose of study and identifies person authorizing it.

Describes method used to solve problem.

Synthesizes major findings focusing on specific findings needed to support conclusions that follow.

Highlights the conclusions and recommendations based on analysis of the findings.

Begins 1 ½ inches from the top of page. "Sinking" or adding extra space at the top adds appeal. Centers report title in all capital letters. Larger, boldface font adds emphasis; overrides APA format (capital and lowercase). The title appears *exactly* as on the title page and half-title page if required. If the title is more than one line, the arrangement should be identical on half-title page, title page, and first page of report.

Omits heading "Introduction"—the introduction obviously is the first material readers encounter.

Single-spaces and indents quotation from both margins for emphasis. Provides page number for direct quotation.

Uses side headings to move the reader from one minor division to another. These headings may be omitted in short reports. If headings are omitted, transitional words are used to help the reader move from one part of the introduction to the next.

Gives specific purpose of the study.

Centers the arabic numeral 1 approximately 1 inch from the bottom of the page.

---

1 ½" (Line 10) **INCREASING PARK MANAGEMENT EFFICIENCY AND RESIDENT AND COMMUNITY RESPONSIVENESS**

DS

> *In the past, zoning laws and citizens' groups have discriminated against the mobile home in much the same way the automobile was legislated off the highway and out of the cities when it first appeared. But these laws were not enforceable because the automobile provided a service that could not be given by the horse and buggy. Mobile and modular housing is essentially doing the same thing . . . as more people find their housing needs are harder to satisfy . . . they will begin to look for better solutions.*
> (Condon, 1976, p. 4)

As a leader in the residential mobile home park industry, American Mobile Home, Inc. relies heavily on the managers of its residential parks. American's rapid growth in the "sun belt" region has forced it to employ park managers who may not have had the preparation to assume managerial responsibilities.

Purpose of the Study

This study was requested by American Mobile Home, Inc. (American) and conducted by Marion and Associates to determine the effectiveness of park managers and to recommend ways in which their job performance might be enhanced. Answers were sought to the following questions:

1

1" (Line 6)   2

DS

1. What are the strengths and weaknesses of managers as viewed by residents of the parks?

2. How effective is the performance of managers in the technical aspects of their work and in their relationships in local communities?

Methods and Procedures Used

A questionnaire survey was conducted by mail to gather information from residents. Mailings were sent to every odd-numbered lot in each of the 76 mobile home parks operated by American. Of the 4,560 questionnaires that were mailed, 2,400 were returned and found to be usable. The relatively high return may be attributed to the confidentiality provided respondents and to the assurance that a response would not jeopardize their own park managers but would help improve park services. A copy of the questionnaire is included in the appendix to this report.

Four two-person management and audit teams spent a full day at 10 parks; thus, a total of 40 audits provided data that were considered representative of all 76 parks. Conclusions and recommendations developed from the analysis of the data are presented at the end of this report.

American's Role and the Park Manager

American Mobile Home, Inc. began business in 1965 with two parks in Phoenix, Arizona. Today it owns and operates 76 parks located in Arizona (16), California (16), Texas (12), Florida (12), New Mexico (10), Nevada (7), and Utah (3). According to *Woodall's Mobile Home and Park Directory* (1987), all of American's parks rate either

Numbers page 2 and the remaining pages with an arabic numeral at the top right-hand margin. Positions the number 1 inch from the top (or the default top margin of the word-processing software being used).

Uses enumeration to add emphasis to this important information.

Side headings are at the left margin, underlined, with the first letter of each significant word a capital letter. For added emphasis, uses a boldface font slightly larger than the text.

Provides methods and procedures used to add credibility. Readers with faith in method and sources of information have greater faith in findings.

Single-spaces report to save space and money and to give a polished appearance; company report-writing policy overrides APA's requirement to indent paragraphs. Always double-space in draft copy to allow space for revisions. Double-space and indent paragraphs five spaces in final report if company policy so specifies.

Uses centered heading to effectively move the reader from the introduction to the next major division. Keys all major division headings in capital and lowercase letters.

1" (Line 6) 3
DS

four or five stars, the top ratings given. One requirement for these ratings is that management must be available on a full-time basis.

American's managers and their families (spouse and children under 18) live in the parks. Their homes double as offices in several smaller parks; separate offices are provided in the 58 parks having over 100 homes. American has eliminated the landlord-tenant concept by using *managers* and *residents* as modern terms. Tustin (1986) says that *landlords* and *tenants* are medieval terms. Progressive managers refer to present-day tenants as occupants, residents, or lessees.

In addition to being the day-to-day manager of facilities and records, the modern manager may play several roles: counselor, financial advisor, home decorator, arbitrator, psychologist, confidant, and friend.

The median age of managers is about 58; a fourth are under 50, as shown in Figure 1.

Figure 1

Ages of 40 Park Managers

Age	Number	Percentage
30–39	4	10
40–49	6	15
50–59	13	32
60–69	17	43
	40	100

Summarizes major points in the table and refers the reader to the figure. The figure title is specific enough to assist readers who merely skim the report. If information presented in a graphic is extracted from secondary source, include source note. Refer to Chapter 16 for appropriate format.

To simplify identifying visuals, the five tables and the bar chart are labeled as figures and numbered consecutively with one numbering system. Formats tables consistently: centers figure number and title on separate lines separated by a double space. (Refer to Chapter 16 for specific guidelines for formatting tables.)

1" (Line 6) 4
DS

Over half of the managers can serve for some time before reaching 70, a usual retirement age; however, American does not practice mandatory retirement.

Despite their seeming maturity, managers have limited experience in the mobile home park industry. Over one-third are in their first three years, and the median tenure is about five years, as shown in Figure 2.

Figure 2

Park Management Experience of 40 Managers

Years	Number	Percentage
1–3	14	35
4–6	10	25
7–9	8	20
10–12	6	15
Over 12	2	5
	40	100

Most managers are able to relate to the residents of mobile home parks, who are generally their age peers. At the same time, younger managers in the 30–49 age range possess the potential to contribute continuity to American's operations. As this study shows, managers still have much to learn; fortunately, they are capable of learning and of benefiting from meaningful experiences on the job.

Places Figure 2 close to its textual reference.

Summarizes major section before moving to the next one.

1″ (Line 6) 5
DS

Uses centered heading to move the reader to the next major division.

Includes a lead-in paragraph that previews the information that will be presented in the next major section. A major and minor heading *never* appear together without an introductory sentence or paragraph separating them.

Uses side headings to divide the major section into minor divisions.

Uses a descriptive (talking) heading to reveal the conclusion to be drawn from the findings in the minor division.

Introduces the minor division and presents the conclusion to be drawn in this section.

Residents' Views of Weaknesses and Strengths

The survey questionnaire was designed to elicit responses from residents about their experiences with the managers. The weaknesses and strengths were indicated by residents by check-mark responses to listed items. Space was left for "other" items that may have been important to residents.

Weaknesses Involve People Skills

Most leading weaknesses of managers, in the view of residents, center on problems of an interpersonal nature and a lack of personal knowledge, as shown in Figure 3.

Figure 3

Top 5 Weaknesses as Viewed by 2,400 Residents

Weakness	Number	Percentage
Not readily available	1,425	59
Not consistent in rule enforcement	1,216	51
Doesn't seem to listen to residents	1,009	42
Unsure of laws and restrictions	828	34
Weak in settlement of disputes	658	27

Lack of availability to residents, failure to listen or seeming not to listen, inability to resolve disputes, and inconsistent rule enforcement indicate that managers need better communication with the corpor-

1" (Line 6) 6
DS

ation and with residents. Criticizing management for lack of availability is a common complaint inasmuch as all residents want to talk to the "top" authority. Unanswered telephone calls accumulate simply through volume and become a cause for complaints.

Some of these problems could be eased by developing residents' associations in all parks. Eight parks now have such associations. As Rejnis (1974, p. 163) said, "Whatever the practical/altruistic ratio in organizing (residents), the management that starts a resident organization is to be commended. Resident associations spot trouble before it explodes, develop friendships, help build morale, and can be effective sales tools."

Strengths Involve Visible Actions

Although weaknesses involved "people" aspects primarily, the leading strengths of managers, as viewed by residents, involved "things." Managers were complimented for their abilities to maintain facilities, as shown in Figure 4.

Figure 4

Top 5 Strengths as Viewed by 2,400 Residents

Strength	Number	Percentage
Maintenance of recreational facilities	2,100	87
Maintenance of streets and grounds	1,936	81
Concern for security and safety	1,550	65
Advice on appliance repairs	960	40
Attitude toward visitors	650	27

Uses a descriptive (talking) heading to reveal the conclusion to be drawn from the findings: strengths involve visible actions. Uses a side heading to indicate a minor division.

Moves the reader into this minor division by mentioning the conclusion drawn in the previous division: weaknesses involve people skills.

Places Figure 4 immediately following its textual reference.

1" (Line 6) 7
DS

Maintenance strengths received the two highest ratings—for maintenance of recreational facilities (87%) and streets and grounds (81%). Of the 14 possible areas, only one other (concern for security and safety) was mentioned by more than half the residents (65%). This concentration on the three leading strengths is significant. Weaknesses, on the other hand, received less concentrated emphasis, with no weakness being selected by as many as 60 percent of the residents. Strengths were related to visible actions, and weaknesses were identified as somewhat intangible people skills.

"Interview the manager, learn about management empathy for residents, ask about management-resident legislation; see if management is informed; ask for opinions; and check park rules" is the advice given prospective residents by Condon (1976, p. 11). This advice is pertinent today and pinpoints some of the items residents found wanting in their park management.

The Management Audit

In addition to the questionnaire survey of residents, the study included audit team analysis of management performance in 40 parks. In the areas of cost control, record keeping, and cash management, the audit teams rated management performance in half or more parks not satisfactory, as shown in Figure 5.

In the opinion of the audit teams, managers do a commendable job of working with suppliers and an adequate job of supplies control. In cost control, record keeping, and cash management, park managers have difficulty because of lack of training. An additional reason not articulated was that the record-keeping function was not considered particularly important when compared with maintenance of facilities.

Uses a centered heading to move the reader to the next major division.

Provides coherence by (1) reminding the reader information had been gathered from questionnaires (material presented in previous section) and (2) introducing the management audit, the topic to be discussed in this major section.

Completes the page with information appearing *after* mention of Figure 5 because the entire table will not fit on this page.

I" (Line 6) 8
DS

Figure 5

Audit Analysis of 5 Activities in 40 Parks

Activity	No.	Good Percentage	No.	Satisfactory Percentage	No.	Not Satisfactory Percentage
Supplier relationships	18	45	15	38	7	17
Supplies control	12	30	16	40	12	30
Cost control	6	15	14	35	20	50
Record keeping	3	7	12	30	25	63
Cash management	1	2	9	23	30	75

American wants its managers to play active roles in the communities where parks are located. This type of involvement occurs in such areas as church and service club membership, attendance at city council meetings, assistance to youth groups, and participation in such community affairs as celebrations, parades, anniversaries, and fund-raising benefits. Managers tend to be familiar with local suppliers and services, mildly knowledgeable about their communities, and less than satisfactory participants in community activities, as shown in Figure 6.

Begins the page with Figure 5 to place it as close to its textual reference (page 7) as possible.

Presents the comparative (multiple-range) bar chart as close as possible to the text interpreting the data. Figure number and title are placed above the figure; other placements are acceptable. (Refer to Chapter 16 for specific guidelines for preparing graphics.)

1" (Line 6) 9
DS

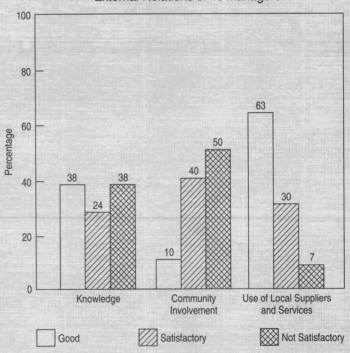

Figure 6

External Relations of 40 Managers

Corporate training programs can be designed to alleviate these weaknesses. Bernhard and Ingols (1988) suggest that training programs are successful when corporations do the following:

1. *Articulate a vision.* Let participants in training programs know about goals such as "Our goal is industry leadership through quality parks and quality park management."

1" (Line 6) 10
DS

2. *Analyze needs.* Be honest by letting participants know why they are in the program rather than having them ask one another, "Why are we here?"

3. *Involve top management.* Management's active involvement reveals corporate support.

Conclusions and Recommendations

Based on the findings of the resident survey and the audits of management performance, the following conclusions were drawn:

1. In general, current managers are young enough to be with American for several years.

2. Park managers are "new" to their jobs and relatively untrained for their tasks.

3. Major weaknesses of park managers, as perceived by residents, are in interpersonal relations and in the understanding and enforcement of laws and restrictions.

4. Major strengths of park managers, as perceived by residents, lie in their abilities to maintain the physical facilities, streets, and grounds.

5. Park managers, as revealed by the audit analysis, are inadequately prepared to handle record-keeping, cost-control, and cash-management tasks.

Uses a centered heading to move the reader to the next major division. Because this report is designed to solve a problem, "Conclusions and Recommendations" is an appropriate heading. The conclusions and recommendations could also be placed in separate sections for longer reports. "Summary" is used to label this section in an information report.

Enumerates conclusions for emphasis and clarity. The conclusions are broad generalizations drawn from the findings section of the report and do not repeat specific findings.

Ends the page a line or so short to prevent the page from ending with a single line of a paragraph. Instruct your word-processing program to paginate the report to avoid ending the page with a single line or carrying a single line to the top of the next page.

Ensures that the page does not begin with a single line of a paragraph appearing by itself. Instruct your word-processing program to paginate the report to avoid a single line of a paragraph at the top or bottom of a page.

Includes a lead-in sentence to introduce the recommendations that follow.

Presents the recommendations using side headings to focus the reader's attention on the four recommendations. Uses descriptive (talking) headings for added emphasis and clarity.

1" (Line 6) 11
DS

6. Park managers are familiar with local suppliers and services. They are not as knowledgeable about their surrounding communities nor as involved in community affairs as American would like them to be.

The following recommendations follow logically from the conclusions; and, if adopted, they should contribute to the development of a capable staff of managers.

Train Managers

Two types of training programs are recommended. The first should focus on office work and should emphasize cost and supplies control, record keeping, and cash management. The program should be built around a corporate park operations manual, with specific procedures included for various tasks. The second program should be devoted to improving the human relations and interpersonal communication skills of managers.

Develop Resident Associations

Residents want good parks, and they like to be heard. Many of the criticisms of managers' failures to listen can be allayed through resident associations. Association leaders could meet regularly with the manager and thereby reduce the number of individual resident-manager meetings.

Encourage Community Involvement

Park managers are currently inactive in community affairs to a large degree. Park residents contribute to the economy of the community; and as an economic force, the parks should be represented just as

1″ (Line 6) 12
DS

are other business concerns in affairs of community interest. American should consider underwriting the costs of manager membership in chambers of commerce and/or service clubs.

Organize Regionally

In addition to considering other recommendations, American should consider creating regional supervisors who would work closely with park managers.

Continues with the remaining recommendations.

These recommendations should be implemented with the idea that education and training for managers will be a continuing program. Responding to the training requirements of managers and the needs of the residents will require constant evaluation of existing training programs and vehicles for interacting with residents and the community.

Continues page numbering pattern used in the report body.

Centers heading in all capital letters. Larger, boldface font adds emphasis and is consistent with other similar headings: title on the first page, contents, executive summary, and appendix.

Presents sources cited in the APA format. Because the report contains in-text parenthetical citations, endnotes are not needed—only references. Titles of books and periodicals and volume numbers are italicized because software supports this special print feature.

Indents the second and subsequent lines of each entry to facilitate the reader's locating authors' surnames.

Single-spaces references to be consistent with the single spacing in the report. Standard report-writing policy overrides APA requirement to double-space. However, Marion policy allows double-spacing references on draft copies to provide space for adding revisions.

1" (Line 6) 13
QS

1 ½" (Line 10)   **REFERENCES**
DS

Bernhard, H. B., & Ingols, C. A. (1988). Six lessons for the corporate classroom. *Harvard Business Review, 66*(5), 40–48.

Condon, K. (1976). *Guide to mobile homes*. Garden City, NY: Doubleday & Co.

Rejnis, R. (1974). *Everything tenants need to know to get their money's worth*. New York: David McKay.

Tustin, M. (1986). Dealing with tenants. In R. Irwin (Ed.), *Handbook of property management* (pp. 1–14). New York: McGraw-Hill.

Woodall Publishing Co. (1987). *Woodall's mobile home and park directory*. Highland Park, IL: Author.

APPENDIX: COVER LETTER TO PARK RESIDENTS

Marion *and* Associates

1227 Monmouth Avenue
Denver, CO 80202-1227
(303) 555-9800 Fax (303) 555-1363

DS

March 1, 19--

[TITLE] [FIRST] [LAST]
[STREET]
[CITY], [STATE] [ZIP]

Dear [TITLE] [LAST]

We have been requested by American Mobile Home, Inc. to study the management of its residential parks. A part of that study is to ask residents for their opinions about the strengths and weaknesses of their park managers. Your opinion will help identify areas that may improve through training programs or through better assistance from the corporation.

Please help by taking just a few minutes to check your manager's strengths and weaknesses as listed below. Leave blank all items about which you are in doubt. Your response will be held confidential and will be included in group data so no reference will be made to your park manager. When you have finished, slip this page into the enclosed postage-paid envelope and drop it in the mail. We will be grateful for your help.

14

Centers "Appendix" and title in all capital letters. Letters are used to identify appendixes if more than one item is included (Appendix A, Appendix B, and so on).

Appendix title could be printed on a separate page.

Letter is coded to be merged with a mailing list. Using the merge feature of word-processing software and American's database of park residents, Leslie Marion prepared a personalized letter to each resident and efficiently and accurately followed up on nonrespondents. Researchers believe that these cost-effective procedures also are attributed to the high response rate of the questionnaire.

Only the first page of the letter is shown here.

CHECK YOUR WRITING

The following checklist provides a concise, handy guide for your use as you prepare a report.

Transmittal Letter or Memorandum
(Use the following points for a letter-style transmittal in reports going outside the organization. For internal reports, use a memorandum transmittal.)
- ☐ Carries a warm greeting to the reader.
- ☐ Opens quickly with a "Here is the report you requested" tone.
- ☐ Establishes the subject in the first sentence.
- ☐ Follows the opening with a brief summary of the study. Expands the discussion if a separate summary is not included in the report.
- ☐ Acknowledges the assistance of those who helped with the study.
- ☐ Closes the letter with a thank you and a forward look.

Title Page
- ☐ Includes the title of the report.
- ☐ Identifies the full authority for the report (the person for whom the report was prepared).
- ☐ Identifies the full preparer of the report.
- ☐ Includes the date of the completion of the report.
- ☐ Uses an attractive layout. (If the items are to be centered, leave an extra half-inch on the left for binding. In other words, make sure the point from which the items are centered is a little to the right of the actual center of the paper.)

Contents Page
- ☐ Uses *Contents* as the title.
- ☐ Uses a tabular arrangement to indicate the heading degrees used in the report.

- ☐ If many graphs or tables are used, list them separately. (Otherwise, the graphs or tables should not be listed because they are not separate sections of the outline but only supporting data within a section.)
- ☐ Centers the entire contents outline horizontally; begins on line 10 (1½").

Executive Summary
- ☐ Uses a brief title, such as *Executive Summary*, *Synopsis*, or *Abstract*.
- ☐ Is a condensation of the major sections of the report.
- ☐ Uses effective, generalized statements that avoid detail available in the report itself. Simply tells the reader what was done, how it was done, and what conclusions were reached.

Style in Report Text
- ☐ Avoids the personal *I* and *we* pronouns. Minimizes the use of *the writer*, *the investigator*, and *the author*.
- ☐ Uses active construction to give emphasis to the *doer* of the action; uses passive voice to give emphasis to the *results* of the action.
- ☐ Uses proper tense. Tells naturally about things in the order in which they happened, are happening, or will happen. Written as though the reader were reading the report at the same time it was written.
- ☐ Avoids ambiguous pronoun references. (If a sentence begins with *This is*, make sure the preceding sentence uses the specific word for which *This* stands. If the specific word is not used, insert it immediately after *This*.)

CHECK YOUR WRITING

☐ Avoids expletive beginnings. Sentences that begin with *There is, There are,* and *It is* present the verb before presenting the subject. Compared with sentences that use the normal subject-verb-complement sequence, expletive sentences are longer.

☐ Enumerates lists of three items or more if the tabulation will make reading easier. For example, a list of three words such as *Ivan, George,* and *Diana* need not be tabulated; but a list of three long phrases, clauses, or sentences would probably warrant tabulation.

☐ Attempts to incorporate transition sentences to ensure coherence.

Physical Layout

☐ Uses headings to assist the reader by making them descriptive of the contents of the section. Talking headings are preferred.

☐ Maintains consistency in the mechanical placement of headings of equal degree.

☐ Uses parallel construction in headings of equal degree in the same section of the report.

☐ Tries to incorporate the statement of the problem or purpose and method of research as minor parts of the introduction unless the research method is the unique element in the study.

☐ Uses the picture-frame layout for all pages. Recommended margins depending on the bindings are
Unbound: 1″ for all margins (top, bottom, left, and right).
Leftbound: $1\frac{1}{2}$″ left margin; 1″ for other margins.
Topbound: $1\frac{1}{2}$″ top margin; 1″ for other margins.
First page begins $\frac{1}{2}$″ lower than the other pages to add appeal to this first page.

☐ Numbers all pages, with the first page of the body of the report being page 1. For page 1, omit the number or place it in the center approximately 1″ from the bottom of the page. For all other pages, place the number on line 6 (1″).

Graphics or Tabular Data

☐ Numbers consecutively the figures used in the report.

☐ Gives each graph or table a descriptive title.

☐ Refers to the graph or table within the text discussion that precedes its appearance.

☐ Places the graph or table as close to the textual reference as possible and limits the text reference to analysis. (It should not merely repeat what can be seen in the graph or table.)

☐ Uses effective layout, appropriate captions and legends, and realistic vertical and horizontal scales that help the table or graph stand clearly by itself.

Report Analysis

☐ Questions each statement for its contribution to the solution of the problem. Is each statement either descriptive or evaluative?

☐ Reduces large, unwieldy numbers to understandable ones through a common language such as units of production, percentages, or ratios.

☐ Uses objective reporting style rather than persuasive language; avoids emotional terms. Identifies assumptions and opinions. Avoids unwarranted judgments and inferences.

☐ Tabulates or enumerates items when it will simplify the reading or add emphasis.

CHECK YOUR WRITING

Conclusions
- [ ] States the conclusions carefully and clearly, and makes sure they grow out of the findings.
- [ ] If necessary, repeats the major supporting findings for each conclusion.
- [ ] If recommendations are called for, makes them grow naturally from the conclusions.

Documentation
If citations are used:
- [ ] Includes a citation (in-text reference, footnote, or endnote) for any material used from another source.
- [ ] Adheres to an acceptable, authoritative style or company policy.
- [ ] Presents consistent citations including adequate information for readers to locate the source in the bibliography.

If a bibliography or list of references is used:
- [ ] Includes an entry for every reference cited in the text.

- [ ] Adheres to an acceptable, authoritative style or company policy.
- [ ] In cases of doubt about what to include for an entry, includes more information than might be necessary.
- [ ] Presents the bibliography in alphabetic sequence by authors' surnames.
- [ ] If the bibliography is lengthy, includes separate sections for books, articles, governmental publications, and unpublished references.

Appendix Material
- [ ] Includes cover letters for survey instruments, the survey instruments, maps, explanations of formulas used, and other items that should be included but are not important enough to be in the body of the report.
- [ ] Labels each item beginning with *Appendix A, Appendix B,* and so on.
- [ ] Identifies each item with a title.

REVIEW QUESTIONS

1. When using word-processing software, a writer should always expect to prepare final copy without working with a rough draft. Is this statement true? Discuss.
2. Why is reading your writing aloud an effective way to review?
3. Give two or three examples of emotional terms. Why should they be avoided?
4. Why is the use of the pronoun *I* generally unacceptable in formal report writing?
5. What is meant by "transition" in composition? By "coherence"?
6. Using the term-family-differentiation method, write definitions of *highway patrol*, *Senator*, and *elm*.
7. Identify each of the following terms as time, contrast, similarity, or cause-and-effect connectors: *because, for example, then, although.*
8. List three primary purposes of documenting reports.
9. List three suggestions for preparing accurate documentation.
10. Discuss the two major types of citations used to document a report.
11. How can a writer document a report if bottom-of-the-page and end-of-report citations are not used?
12. Explain how word-processing software simplifies preparing bottom-of-the-page and end-of-report citations.
13. What are the three major differences between a traditional (bottom-of-the-page or end-of-the-report) citation and a bibliographic entry?
14. Explain the relationship between the content outline of a report and the placement of headings within the body of the report.
15. Must formal reports be organized in only one way? Must they contain all the preliminary, report text, and addenda parts?
16. Should the contents outline and the figures always be placed on separate pages?
17. Is the heading *Introduction* essential on the first page of the report? Explain.
18. How many levels of headings does the sample report contain? Describe how each level of heading is presented to denote the various divisions within the report.
19. Explain how the graphics are positioned, numbered, and introduced in the sample report.
20. Summarize the techniques used to move the reader from one section of the sample report to the next.
21. List at least three ways the desktop publishing capabilities of sophisticated word-processing software can be used to enhance the appearance of a report.

APPLICATIONS

1. **Solving a Business Problem.**   Select one of the following problems to solve. Provide the necessary assumptions and background data. Then write a formal report of your analysis, conclusions, and recommendations. Alternatively, reviewing this list may help you identify a business-related problem you have encountered during your employment or cooperative education and intern experiences. If you choose to solve your own problem, provide the necessary assumptions and background data.

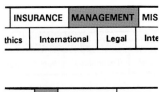

   a. While touring the manufacturing plant of a professional friend, you observe the use of universal product code (UPC) symbols to track the movement of inventory through the plant. Propose how UPC symbols could monitor the movement of employees within the manufacturing plant and investigate the implications of this action.

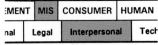

   b. Your data processing department soon will begin to analyze the current manual information system used in your department. Investigate effective methods of preparing your employees for the impending investigation (people asking drilling questions about their work) and later for the conversion to a computer-automated information system—a major change in employees' primary work tasks.

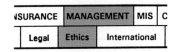

   c. Security concerns have prompted a security consultant to recommend that employees wear name tags (provide another procedure if you wish) while inside the facilities. Investigate potential personnel problems and present strategies for dealing with them.

   d. For some time you have recognized that drug abuse is present in your plant. The problem is becoming increasingly worse and the company is paying the price in extra health care, lost productivity, and absenteeism. Investigate strategies for coping with this problem.

   e. A committee of employees has recommended that the company establish a recycling center where employees can deposit recyclable items when entering the parking lot. The president has asked you to think the idea through and present a report of the cost, public relations implications, employee relations, and logistics of operating the recycling center.

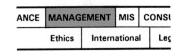

   f. Present a report on the cost and logistics of establishing a recycling procedure for computer paper used to prepare internal reports. Select a real or fictitious company.

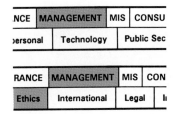

   g. You have received reports that several of your major competitors have installed electronic surveillance devices to monitor employees' performance. The president wants your immediate attention on this issue. Investigate the implications of using technology to monitor employees' performance. Will employees consider this procedure an invasion of privacy? Anticipate all possible problems and present strategies for dealing with them.

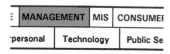

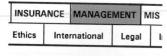

h. Although no employees have made formal complaints of sexual harassment in the workplace, information from the grapevine has convinced you that the company needs a formal policy concerning sexual harassment. To develop this company policy, research the legalities related to this issue and gather information (strategies) from other companies with sexual harassment policies.

i. The upcoming downsizing of your company will result in the displacement of approximately 10 percent of your middle- and upper-level managers. Investigate strategies for supporting these managers in their search for new employment. Many of these managers have worked for your company 15 to 20 years; therefore, they are quite apprehensive about the job-search process.

j. You are in charge of recruiting accounting graduates for entry-level positions in your firm. You believe your current approach needs improvement because too many of the top-notch students interview with you on campus but do not accept office interviews. Investigate the problem and identify effective strategies for recruiting quality students. For example, consider the following thoughts and anticipate many others: Should you hold a formal reception or casual party to get to know the interviewees? Should you take the accounting faculty to lunch to increase your contact with them? What can you do to make your recruitment effort cost effective?

k. Investigate the possibility of hiring senior citizens to fill selected positions in your company.

2. **Improving Cross-Cultural Understanding in International Operations.**   Dale's Burgers, a successful fast-food restaurant in the United States, has expanded its operations to Hong Kong, Paris, and now Moscow. In almost every case, U.S. managers were transferred to open and manage restaurants in the company's international operations. These highly competent managers continually make unintentional, yet costly, mistakes because they are so unfamiliar with the differences among the customs, culture, and business practices of these countries and the United States. The price being paid for these innocent mistakes is high: damaged or lost goodwill of customers, employees, and suppliers and eventually reduced profits.

When the company decided to expand its operation to Moscow, management agreed unanimously to establish an International Assignments Division. This division is charged with preparing managers transferring to overseas operations for functioning in a new culture. Although some misunderstandings cannot be avoided, a carefully designed orientation program is sure to improve cross-cultural understanding.

Required:

1. As the director of the International Assignments Division, one of your

first tasks is to prepare an informational report to the U.S. managers transferring to *one* of the company's three international locations: Hong Kong, Paris, or Moscow. Your purpose is to highlight the major cultural differences and business practices between the United States and the country you select. Conduct the research needed to provide these managers with accurate, useful, and well-documented information. Use in-text parenthetical citations unless your instructor requires another citation method. Use the following suggestions to help you organize your report:

a. Consider the specific information that managers would need to know to manage a fast-food restaurant in the country you select.

b. Consider whether the information can be classified. If it can, would headings be appropriate to subdivide this section? How would you present headings in the report?

2. Prepare the following preliminary and addenda parts to support the report prepared in step 1:

a. Title page.

b. Contents page if the report is long enough to require one.

c. Executive summary.

d. Transmittal letter. Address it to a manager (provide name and address) in the country you selected. Should the letter be formatted as a traditional U.S. letter or in an acceptable format of the country selected? If so, how will the letter appear? Do special requirements for addressing the envelope exist?

e. References page. Provide complete, accurate references so that managers are able to locate your sources for additional study if needed.

3. **Spiraling Health Costs: Do Employee Assistance Programs Help?** As director of human resources management of De Santo, Inc., you receive the following voice-mail message from Armando De Santo, president of the company:

ISURANCE	MANAGEMENT	MIS	C
Ethics	International	Legal	Ir

```
Hi.  I just finished reading your quarterly analysis
of benefits and compensation costs.  Frankly, I'm
overwhelmed with the consistent increase in health
claims since last year.  If this continues, we'll
have to eliminate employee health coverage or go out
of business.  I'm wondering:  Surely this problem is
not unique to us.  What are the other companies doing
to curtail health-care costs?  Do these employee
assistance programs I've been reading about in
business magazines really work?  Please complete a
thorough investigation so we can make an informed
decision should the situation get any worse.  Let's
schedule a meeting to discuss this issue later this
month.
```

Required:

1. To help you focus your research, select a particular business with which you are familiar. Then identify the major health problems that you believe employees in this type of company might have. Among the problems you might list are heart disease, high cholesterol, low physical fitness, substance abuse, stress and burnout, and physical problems caused by using computers or being exposed to other hazardous materials or equipment.

2. Using the problems you listed in step 1, conduct the necessary research to answer the president's question; provide accurate, useful, and well-documented information. Specifically, review the research related to employee assistance programs or methods of reducing health-care costs. In addition, read current general business magazines and practitioners' journals to learn about employee assistance programs at other companies and other relevant issues.

3. As the director of human resources management, write an informational report relating your research about employee assistance programs (relevant to De Santo's employee health problem profile) to the president. Include complete and accurate documentation of your sources; use in-text parenthetical citations unless your instructor requires another citation method.

4. Prepare the following preliminary and addenda parts to support the report prepared in step 3:

   a. Title page.

   b. Executive summary.

   c. Transmittal memorandum to President De Santo. Be sure to mention the attached references page.

   d. References page. Provide complete, accurate references so that you can readily relocate the information if the president requests a copy.

4. **Solving a Business Problem.** Refer to the "Cases for Analysis" at the end of Chapters 6 and 9–14 for additional topics requiring research to solve a particular business problem. Turn to the appropriate case and read the complete case problem.

   a. *Chapter 12, Case 1.* Research the cultural differences between business executives in the United States and Mexico. Write a memorandum report communicating this information to U.S. managers working in Mexico. Write another memo to the director of international assignments persuading her to develop other ways to promote international understanding in the company. You may vary this case by selecting a country of your choice.

   b. *Chapter 14, Case 1.* Research the current legal guidelines of the Equal Employment Opportunity Commission related to job interviewing. Write a memorandum report to store managers reviewing the major guidelines and focusing on recent changes.

   c. *Chapter 9, Case 2.* Review the research related to employee motivation and current practitioners' journals to identify ways to solve a company's problems with low morale and productivity. A basic scenario is provided. To make the case more meaningful to you, identify an employee group and environment with which you are familiar.

d. *Chapter 10, Case 1.* Review the research related to crisis communication, specifically employer-employee relations, to prepare for communicating information about a financial crisis to employees. You may vary this case; for example, communicating financial crisis information to stockholders or negative information about defective products, product tampering, environmental hazards, or ethical misconduct to clients and other groups.

e. *Chapter 10, Case 2.* Review the research related to communicating crisis information to prepare for writing a letter to customers announcing the recall of a faulty product.

f. *Chapter 12, Case 2.* Prepare an analytical letter report evaluating the feasibility of building a plastics recycling plant. Prepare a letter to community leaders, a news release to the general public, or brochure to gain support for the plastics recycling plant and to educate the public about the benefits of recycling.

g. *Chapter 13, Case 1.* Review current research related to preparing winning job credentials. Based on your research, prepare an informational report addressing the needs of a particular group (top- and middle-level managers outplaced by recent downsizing). If you wish, you may vary this case by writing guidelines for entry-level employees or others.

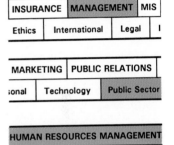

Report the following cases in formal style. Include preliminary and ending parts as you believe appropriate. Even though survey results are included in some of the cases, prepare a questionnaire in appropriate form. Sequences in questionnaire results and the discussion in the cases are purposely random. You must analyze and sort the data as part of the report process.

5. Selecting an Investment. As a client executive of Marshall Property Management, Inc., you, along with other members of the firm, serve as consultants to boards of directors of several condominium associations in your community. Additionally, a member of your firm serves full-time as general manager in many large associations. Boards of directors in these homeowner associations have the responsibility of making and enforcing policies and overseeing the funds of the associations.

  Several of your client associations have from 300 to 1,200 members, each owning a condominium or residence. As part of their membership initiation fees and monthly dues or assessments, associations set aside funds for replacement of roofs and improvements or repairs of other property common to all members. Because boards of directors must oversee their reserve funds—often amounting to several million dollars—they seek sound advice from your firm.

Legally, most boards of directors are restrained in their investment of reserve money by documents called Covenants, Conditions, and Restrictions (CC&Rs) effective upon formation of the associations. The restrictions generally require that money not be invested in risk ventures, such as common stocks, real-estate syndications, and corporate bonds. Rather, the money should be invested in secure, insured investments where the return would be less but the principal would be secure.

Required: Prepare a report on possible investments of this nature in banks; thrifts, such as savings banks and savings and loan associations; and insured funds of brokerages or other institutions. The report should be addressed to one association, Marlboro Country Homes; in your transmittal letter, however, you will say the report is also being sent to other client boards. Your report should be informational—a comparison of the amount of investments possible, the rates of return for varying amounts, the maximum amounts insured, the time restriction on accounts, and the availability of money if needed. Because most associations can space their needs for money, they can invest some amounts of $100,000 for as much as five years. Homeowners' associations must pay tax on taxable interest paid to them.

MARKETING	PUBLIC RELATIONS	
;onal	Technology	Public Sector

6. **Assessing Interest in a Far East Travel Tour.**   As summer-tour coordinator for the Beverly Hills Travel Bureau, you have to plan and promote vacation travel tours. The tours are usually made by charter flight to reduce travel costs. The Beverly Hills Travel Bureau is one of the largest firms of its kind in the nation. Before you can promote a tour, you submit a report to Beth Rosenfeld, president, for consideration by the executive committee. Once approval is given, you then work out the details of specific dates, travel itinerary, meal and hotel arrangements, and final costs. Prior to submitting the report, you survey a selected list of former tour customers about their desires. The survey helps establish interest in tours and the broad guidelines for specific travel. For the coming year, a tour of the Far East has been proposed. As a result, you surveyed by mail 600 former tour customers; 300 replied. Following are the cover letter, the questionnaire material, and the tabulated results of the 300 respondents:

Dear Traveler:

Because you have traveled with us before, we would greatly appreciate your taking the time to complete the following questionnaire. Your ideas will help us plan a charter trip to the Far East. As a seasoned traveler, your ideas are valued even though you may not be planning such a trip. Please simply respond as if you could plan your own trip.

When would you most like to leave on a tour of the Far East?

Late spring	75
Midsummer	200
Late summer	25

Which countries would you like to visit? Check all that apply.

Philippines	33	Mainland China	279
Vietnam	56	Taiwan	180
South Korea	234	Thailand	115
Maylasia	78	Borneo	54

Which do you prefer?

Air-sea tour   78   Air-land tour   222

Which cities would you prefer to visit? Check all that apply.

Seoul	234	Bangkok	115	Tokyo	283
Taipei	180	Singapore	60	Manila	30
Hong Kong	300	Beijing	276	Shanghai	144

Which hotel type would you prefer?

Luxury hotels	75	First-class hotels 180
Local tourist hotels	45	

How many meals would you prefer the tour to have together each day?

1 meal 45   2 meals 225   3 meals 30

How would you like your evenings?

Planned 45   Open 90   Some planned, some open 165

Which would you prefer?

Only American tour leaders	42
Native, English-speaking guides	36
A combination	222

What length trip would you prefer?

10–11 days	60	14 days	66
One month	39	21 days	135

Which price range is most acceptable to you for the trip you visualized in your responses?

	10–11 days	14 days	21 days	One month
$3,000–3,999	50	12	6	0
$4,000–4,999	10	54	16	0
$5,000–5,999	0	0	110	0
$6,000–6,999	0	0	3	39
	60	66	135	39

MARKETING	PUBLIC RELATIONS		
Ethics	International	Legal	Ir

7. Foreign Travel Package Tour. Using the design of the study in the preceding case as a guide, prepare your own questionnaire for a tour of any one of the following areas: Europe, the Mediterranean, South America, Scandinavia, Australia, or Africa. You may select either of these options to gather data: (1) survey members of your class and multiply responses by 10 to obtain a larger assumed sample or (2) make up your own distribution of 300 assumed responses.

Required: Prepare a report for Ms. Rosenfeld. You might do some outside research by visiting a couple of travel agencies.

MARKETING	PUBLIC RELATIONS	
onal	Technology	Public Sector

8. Determining Preferences in Housing Facilities. You have been hired by a major building firm, Watt Construction Company, to make a survey of what college students would prefer in nearby apartment complexes. The following data were developed as a result of your study, which included 200 students selected at random. The figures in parentheses following each item are the numbers of women's responses. Men's responses are in the figures preceding the parentheses. Thus, you have the data covering the responses of men and women separately; by combining them, you have the total response.

Required: Prepare the report for R. A. Watt, President.

I. Personal Data (check one alternative in each part of this section)

    A. Gender:
        Men: 112
        Women: 88

    B. Marital status:
        Married: 17(12)
        Single: 85(86)

    C. Age:
        18 and less: 4(6)
        19–21: 63(47)
        22–25: 27(17)
        26–30: 8(12)
        31–40:   6(6)
        41 and more: (10)

    D. Current residence:
        Residence hall: 23(24)
        On-campus apartment: 16(7)
        Fraternity or sorority: 38(26)
        Off-campus apartment: 13(11)
        With parents: 22(20)
        Other (specify):   0(0)

    E. School standing:
        Graduate: 16(8)
        Undergraduate: 96(80)

II. Recreational Facilities

    A. Outdoor facilities (check all that you would like to have provided)

        Pool: 85(80)
        Jacuzzi: 51(70)
        Tennis courts: 78(53)
        Badminton-volleyball courts: 40(37)
        Barbecue area: 25(67)

    B. Indoor facilities

        1. Recreation room (check one)

            Should be provided: 84(50)
            Should not be provided: 28(38)

            If you think that a recreation room should be provided, check all recreation room facilities that you would want:

            Billiards tables: 37(10)
            Ping-pong tables: 25(15)
            Television sets: 10(27)
            Lounging area: 55(36)
            Fireplace: 31(48)
            Cocktail area: 70(50)
            Party area: 78(50)
            Kitchen: 52(21)

        2. Gymnasium (check one)

            Should be provided: 60(30)
            Should not be provided: 52(58)

            If you think that a gymnasium should be provided, check all gymnasium facilities that you would want:

Weights: <u>45</u>(15)
Conditioning machines: <u>20</u>(30)
Ropes or rings: <u>50</u>(2)
Slant boards: <u>42</u>(30)

3. Sauna (check one)
Should be provided: <u>75</u>(31)
Should not be provided: <u>37</u>(57)

C. Organized recreation (check one)
Should be provided: <u>32</u>(20)
Should not be provided: <u>80</u>(68)

III. Parking Facilities

A. Number of parking spaces for each apartment that should be provided:

1. Spaces for each one-bedroom apartment (check one)
One: <u>57</u>(31)
Two: <u>54</u>(55)
Three: <u>1</u>(2)

2. Spaces for each two-bedroom apartment (check one)
One: <u>18</u>(16)
Two: <u>88</u>(71)
Three: <u>6</u>(1)

B. Type of parking lot that should be provided (check one)
Conventional: <u>75</u>(38)
Underground: <u>37</u>(50)

If you chose underground, check one:

Secured: <u>28</u>(40)
Unsecured: <u>9</u>(10)

IV. Security Facilities (check all that you would like to have provided)
None: <u>0</u>(2)
Locks on all doors to complex: <u>93</u>(80)
Watch dog: <u>16</u>(27)
Security guard: <u>79</u>(75)

9. **Identifying Effective Advertising Campaigns.** Assume you are involved in selecting advertising outlets and preparing advertisements for the Ajax Cosmetic Company. Your supervisor is Brian McDermott, director of sales promotion. He has asked you to select a national magazine from three magazines of your choice as a probable place to purchase advertising space for an initial new-product sales campaign. The product is a new line of women's competitively priced cosmetics. Ajax has long been a leader in low-priced facial cosmetics,

but this new product represents an attempt to break into the high-style field. Your new product line consists of skin, eye, and lip cosmetics.

Although you have been told to select from three magazines of your choice, you know that for proper exposure you should select from magazines such as *Vogue, Harper's Bazaar, New Woman, Working Woman, Cosmopolitan,* and other fashion-oriented magazines. From the three magazines you select for study, your final choice will be based on the nature of appeals used in advertisements in each magazine, the kinds of products advertised, and the cost of advertising. You can find information about cost of ads and circulation of all national magazines in the most recent issues of *Consumer Magazine* and *Farm Publication Rates and Data* or directories containing advertising rates and circulations.

Your plan is to use three recent issues of each of your three magazines to analyze the nature of advertisements. Ajax plans to use only full-page color or black-and-white ads. You plan to begin your study of each magazine with the inside cover and to analyze the first 30 or 40 ads of each of three issues until you have at least 100 ads in your total sample. Thus, you'll analyze at least 300 ads by the time you have covered three issues of each of the three magazines.

A couple of assumptions must be made. First, you are an expert in determining the basic appeal of an advertisement; second, a sample of 100 ads is adequate to determine the nature of products advertised and appeals used in each magazine.

Here are some of the product categories you may find convenient in tabulating your count of ads:

Automobiles	Travel
Cosmetics and beauty aids	Personal services (nonproduct)
Office equipment and supplies	Household appliances
Convenience items	Furniture
Clothing	Food

You may add others, of course. Some of the suggested product groups may not apply in certain magazines. If you find only a small number of ads in a product area, you may want to combine two or more areas such as household appliances and furniture. Should some ads not fit in any category, you could have a Miscellaneous or All Other grouping.

Advertising appeals typically fall into several categories:

Security	Beauty	Quality	Economy
Love	Health	Sex	Comfort
Safety	Pride	Elegance	Goodwill

Again, these are suggested appeal groupings only. Combining closely related appeals such as safety and security or pride and quality may be convenient.

After selecting your magazine, make a trial analysis to test the nature of the categories you will want to use. Keep in mind that the purpose of your study is to determine the products most advertised and the appeals most used for those products. For instance, your findings should indicate that the four or five most advertised product groupings were. . . . At the same time, you'll report that the four or five most used advertising appeals were. . . . To keep a record of which appeals were used for each product, you'll find a chart similar to the following one helpful for your initial tabulation of each magazine. All three issues of each magazine may be included in one chart.

PRODUCTS	APPEALS				
	Quality	Love	Economy	Beauty	•••
Autos	I		₩		
Cosmetics		II		₩ I	
Food	₩ II		III		
Travel	I				
•••					

To tabulate the ads, make a hatch mark for each ad in the appropriate cell. For example, an automobile advertisement using an appeal to quality would be recorded by making a mark in the Autos/Quality cell, as shown. After you have tabulated all the advertisements on the chart, you can total across each row to get the number of automobile ads, the number of cosmetic ads, the number of food ads, etc. By totaling down the columns, you can determine the total number of each appeal used. And by inspecting the cosmetic ads across the chart, you can determine the frequency with which each appeal was used in cosmetic advertisements.

Neat revisions of your three tabulating charts would be appropriate appendix items. You'll also use the totals in the charts for construction of tables and other figures to be used in the body of your report. For example, a figure showing the percentage of total ads devoted to cosmetic products from each of your three magazines would be an excellent table in the body of your report. As you study your tabulation charts, you will find an almost endless combination of items that lend themselves to tabular and graphic presentation.

You hope to be able to recommend a magazine and a major appeal or appeals to be used in the advertising campaign. The magazine and its readership should be compatible with your product.

Required: Prepare a formal report.

10. **Surveying Consumer Shopping Habits.** As part of a team selected from your class, make a one-hour survey of the nature of shoppers in your school bookstore. In addition, each member of your team will survey shoppers during a one-hour period, and you will pool your data to provide a comprehensive sample. The purpose of your study is to determine (a) what kind of people shop in the bookstore during certain hours, (b) what items seem to sell to certain categories of shoppers, and (c) what services or products not now offered would be desirable additions. In other words, your team will make a survey to determine how to provide better services. Organize your team in any way you like. Keep in mind sampling techniques. Don't survey only between 8 and 9 a.m. each day of the week. And don't limit your study to Friday afternoons. Outline the kinds of information you will need and can get. Your team will make an oral presentation to the class in addition to a written presentation to the instructor.

MARKETING	PUBLIC RELATIONS	
nal	Technology	Public Sector

Required: Prepare a formal report.

11. **Identifying Effective Communication.** Read the following studies concerned with communication. Complete each one individually or in a team and present your findings and conclusions in a formal report.
    a. Collect sixty copies of letters written by businesspeople as part of company business. You will have to ask for them personally to explain why you want them. You can offer each donor of letters a copy of your report when it is finished. Naturally, the letters will be held confidential; if the businesspeople prefer, you can take copies with no identifying information on them. For example, the inside address and the name of the writer may be deleted. When you have the copies, analyze them according to whatever criteria you can establish from earlier chapters in this book. For example, you might use organization, grammar and usage, spelling, consideration of the reader, Fog Index, and adequacy of detail as criteria. Keep track of the kinds of exceptions you find that would violate writing principles. Another approach would be to have a knowledgeable jury—a team of students in your class—select the fifteen best and the fifteen worst letters. Forget about the thirty letters that fall in the middle. Then attempt to determine what distinguishes good from bad letters. Prepare a report for your instructor.

NCE	MANAGEMENT	MIS	CONSUl
	Legal	Interpersonal	Techno

ANCE	MANAGEMENT	MIS	CONSL
thics	International	Legal	Inte

MARKETING	PUBLIC RELATIONS	F
ional	Technology	Public Sector

b. Collect several samples of news items and analyses from *Time, Newsweek,* and a local newspaper that discuss the same topic. Analyze each sample in terms of readability, visual presentation, and quality of writing. You might again use the jury approach. Attempt to use some quantitative basis—for example, a rating scale as described in Chapter 15—to determine which publication is best in terms of your study.

c. We are bombarded constantly with sales slogans and the use of personalities to promote products and services advertised on television. Develop a list of slogans and personalities with a matching list of products. Then attempt to determine from people in your age group which seem to be the best-known ads by having people attempt to match the products with the advertising theme or personality. Analyze why some are better recognized than others. You may find help in advertising or marketing textbooks and periodical literature. You can also ask respondents to indicate the amount of time they watch television each week; which television shows, games, and news reports they watch most; and whether they are really conscious of television advertising.

CASE FOR ANALYSIS

ANCE	MANAGEMENT	MIS	CONSL
thics	International	Legal	Inte

Case 1. The Riverside Cafe. Around eight o'clock on a warm, summer evening, you and your date arrive at the Riverside Cafe and stop for a moment to watch a barge slowly make its way down the Arkansas River. You are eagerly greeted by Mr. James Becker, the owner, who has asked you to visit the restaurant and recommend some changes.

Mr. Becker explains, "I opened the restaurant two years ago with the purpose of attracting the young singles market. You know, a group who will come in around seven in the evening, have several drinks and some appetizers, and visit with their friends until about midnight. We're earning a reasonable rate of return, but I'm concerned that our earnings are falling short of the projected."

As you find a cozy table for two facing the river, you notice about six young couples with children ranging from tot-size to about ten years. While you are munching on your hamburger, a disc jockey starts playing records, but no one goes to the dance floor. In addition, your date brings to your attention the provocative pictures hanging on the wall over the bar.

Around ten o'clock the restaurant is practically empty except for a lone couple. Mr. Becker returns to see if you have any questions and says, "I'm leaving tomorrow on a camping trip in the Ozark Mountains—no phones, a great getaway. Could we meet as soon as I return? I'm eager to get some feedback."

Required:

1. What is Mr. Becker's problem? You can look at this situation in several ways. What do you think is wrong here? Write your answer in the form of a problem statement using clear, specific language.

2. What are three alternative solutions to the problem you defined in step 1? In developing your solutions, be open minded and consider every idea presented—even what may seem to be the most bizarre, off-the-wall idea. Use the following guidelines to evaluate each solution:

   a. Does each alternative solution solve the problem as defined?

   b. Is each alternative solution different, or has the solution simply been rephrased using different language?

3. Write an analytical report to Mr. Becker including the following points:

   a. State the problem as you see it.

   b. Briefly describe the three alternative solutions you identified.

   c. Based on your objective analysis of each solution, state the solution you believe will best solve the problem.

   d. Discuss the factors that led to your decision.

   e. List and explain several recommendations Mr. Becker should take to implement your solution. Explain each recommended change thoroughly.

4. Prepare a title page and transmittal letter. Address the letter to Mr. James Becker, Riverside Cafe, 151 Riverside Road, Little Rock, AR 72204-0151.

5. Congratulations! Mr. Becker was very impressed with your recommended changes and wants to get started right away. Although you may not be able to develop every aspect of your recommended solution, you can help Mr. Becker communicate these recommendations to the appropriate group(s). You may use any technology available to you; for example, word processing, spreadsheet, desktop publishing, graphics, sign/banner maker, and other software programs.

   a. Develop your solution.

   b. Write a letter of transmittal to Mr. Becker explaining how each item relates to the solution. Use your professional judgment to determine the manner in which you will physically present the letter and the documents to Mr. Becker.

6. You have arranged to present your ideas to Mr. Becker tomorrow at 8 a.m. in his office at the Riverside Cafe. Develop a ten-minute oral presentation to explain your recommended changes to Mr. Becker. Carefully follow these pointers:

   a. Have I analyzed my audience and designed my message accordingly?

   b. Do my nonverbal communication cues agree with my worded messages?

   c. Have I prepared the visual aids needed to present my message effectively?

DOCUMENT FORMAT AND LAYOUT GUIDE

APPENDIX A

Appearance
Proofreaders' Marks
Paper
Placement of Text
on the Page
Justification
Spacing
Word Division

Punctuation Styles and Letter Formats
Mixed and Open
Punctuation
Letter Formats
Block
Modified Block
Simplified Block

Standard Letter Parts
Heading
Inside Address
Salutation

Body
Complimentary Close
Signature Block
Reference Initials

Special Letter Parts
Mailing Notation
Attention Line
Reference Line
Subject Line
Second-Page Heading
Company Name in
Signature Block
Enclosure Notation
Copy Notation
Postscript

Memorandum Formats
Formal
Simplified

Envelopes

FIRST IMPRESSIONS ARE LASTING ONES, and the reader's first impression of your letter is its appearance and format. Preparing an error-free, attractive document is a basic requirement for maintaining credibility with your reader. This section presents techniques for producing an appealing document. In addition, you will learn the standard and special parts of a letter, the standard letter formats, punctuation styles, and envelope addressing formats accepted in business.

APPEARANCE

To convey a positive, professional image, the letter should be proofread carefully, prepared on high-quality paper, and balanced attractively on the page. Other factors that affect the overall appearance of your document are justification of margins, spacing after punctuation, abbreviations, and word division. Review the following guidelines to ensure that your documents are accurate in these areas.

Proofreaders' Marks

Carefully proofread for three overall factors: (1) organization, content, and style; (2) grammatical errors; and (3) format errors. In addition, check your document with the electronic speller. Refer to Chapter 8 for a detailed explanation of systematic proofreading procedures. Become familiar with standard proofreaders' marks shown in Figure A-1.

Paper

The quality of paper used reflects the professionalism of the company and allows a company to control communication costs effectively. Paper quality is measured in two ways: cotton-fiber content and weight.

High-cotton bond paper has a crisp crackle, is firm to the pencil touch, is difficult to tear, and ages without deterioration or chemical breakdown. Most business letters are produced on company letterhead that is printed on paper with 25-percent cotton-fiber content.

The weight of paper is based on the weight of a ream consisting of approximately 1,000 sheets of 17- by 22-inch paper (equivalent to 4,000 sheets of $8\frac{1}{2}$- by 11-inch paper). If the ream weighs 20 pounds, the paper is said to be 20-pound weight. The heavier the paper, the higher the quality. Most business letters are produced on company letterhead that is printed on 16- or 20-pound bond paper.

Extremely important external documents such as reports and proposals may be printed on 24-pound paper with 100-percent cotton content. Memorandums, business forms, and other intracompany documents

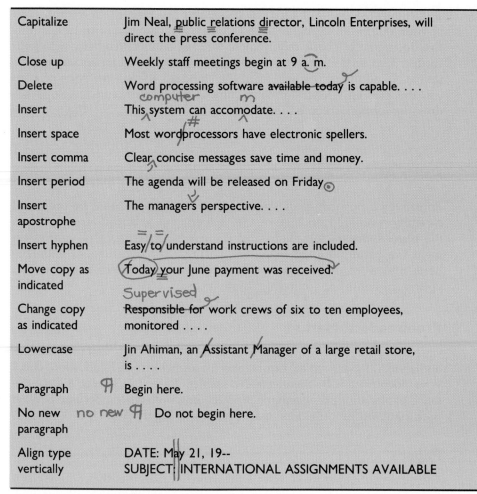

Capitalize	Jim Neal, public relations director, Lincoln Enterprises, will direct the press conference.
Close up	Weekly staff meetings begin at 9 a. m.
Delete	Word processing software available today is capable. . . .
Insert	This system can accomodate. . . .
Insert space	Most wordprocessors have electronic spellers.
Insert comma	Clear concise messages save time and money.
Insert period	The agenda will be released on Friday
Insert apostrophe	The managers perspective. . . .
Insert hyphen	Easy to understand instructions are included.
Move copy as indicated	Today your June payment was received.
Change copy as indicated	Responsible for work crews of six to ten employees, monitored . . . .
Lowercase	Jin Ahiman, an Assistant Manager of a large retail store, is . . . .
Paragraph	¶ Begin here.
No new paragraph	no new ¶ Do not begin here.
Align type vertically	DATE: May 21, 19-- SUBJECT: INTERNATIONAL ASSIGNMENTS AVAILABLE

FIGURE A-1   Standard proofreaders' marks

may be printed on lighter-weight paper with lower cotton-fiber content. Envelopes and plain sheets to be used for the second and successive pages of multiple-page letters should be of the same weight, cotton-fiber content, and color as the letterhead.

The standard paper size for business documents is $8\frac{1}{2}$ by 11 inches. Some top executives use executive-size ($7\frac{1}{4}$ by $10\frac{1}{2}$ inches) letterhead printed on 24-pound paper with 100-percent cotton content. However, this smaller size could easily be misfiled and may require special formatting that adds to the document cost.

Another characteristic of high-quality paper is the watermark, the design imprinted on the paper. Hold the paper up to the light to see this

Spell out	(8) boxes of No. 10 envelopes
Transpose	The Japanese beleive . . . .
Center line	ctr Systematic Proofreading Procedures
Use italics	ital <u>Business Communications</u>
Use bold	bf <u>SITE SELECTION FOR MEMPHIS PLANT</u>
Let the original material stand	Schedule an intercultural communication seminar. . . .
Move down; lower	June 2, 19--
Move up; raise	May 15, 19--
Move to left	1. Begin the date on line 10.
Move to right	Indent paragraphs within double-spaced text.
Single-space	SS Mr. Jay R. Albright
	President
Double-space	DS Enclosures c Mr. Keith Chan
Quadruple-space	QS October 1, 19--
	Mrs. Sandra Pierce

mark clearly. The watermark may be the trademark of the company using the paper or the brand name of the paper. Watermarked paper has a right side and a top edge; therefore, it must be placed in the printer or typewriter correctly. The watermark is positioned so that it can be read across the sheet in the same direction as the printing.

Placement of Text on the Page

Letters should be balanced on the page with approximately equal margins. Companies using word-processing software set standard line lengths. To increase efficiency, the standard line length is often the same as the default margins set by the software. One-inch side margins, which produce a $6\frac{1}{2}$-inch line of writing, is a typical standard line. The date is printed on lines 14–16, depending on the length of the letter. Side margins are usually adjusted to improve the appearance of extremely short letters.

Many software programs will allow you to center a page of text vertically with one simple command; in that case, execute the center page command. This placement, which creates approximately equal margins on all sides of the letter, is often referred to as fitting the letter into a picture frame. With the proper equipment, the exact centering process is simple and creates a highly professional effect.

Justification

Word-processing software makes justified margins possible; that is, all lines start at the left margin and end at the right margin. Extra spaces are added between words so that the line ends exactly on the right margin. These extra spaces are visually distracting and make the document difficult to read. Research has shown that reader comprehension is reduced when the copy is justified. In addition, justified margins give the document a computer-generated appearance, as if it were just another form letter. For these reasons, use the jagged right margin as shown in the examples throughout this text.

Justified documents look very professional when they are printed with proportional spacing (the size of the letters varies and the extra space between words is minimized). Proportional printing and scalable fonts (different print styles whose size and appearance can be altered) are available with many laser printers. These enhancements increase your ability to prepare highly professional letters, reports, and proposals.

Jagged Right Margin (Left Justified)

ESSENTIAL COMPUTER SKILLS

Currently employees at all levels of our organization are using primary computer applications to increase their productivity and are eager to expand their knowledge to other more advanced areas. A primary need is to implement a telecommunications system that will allow our staff to transmit reports from the field to the home office. Other areas of interest include desktop publishing and electronic mail.

Justified Margins (Left and Right)

```
                    ESSENTIAL COMPUTER SKILLS

         Currently employees at all levels of our organization are using
         primary computer applications to increase their productivity
         and are eager to expand their knowledge to other more
         advanced areas.    A primary need is to implement a
         telecommunications system that will allow our staff to
         transmit reports from the field to the home office. Other areas
         of interest include desktop publishing and electronic mail.
```

Justified Margins Using Proportional
Print with Scalable Fonts

```
                    ESSENTIAL COMPUTER SKILLS

         Currently employees at all levels of our organization are
         using primary computer applications to increase their pro-
         ductivity and are eager to expand their knowledge to other
         more advanced areas.  A primary need is to implement a tele-
         communications system that will allow our staff to transmit
         reports from the field to the home office.  Other areas of in-
         terest include desktop publishing and electronic mail.
```

Spacing

Proper spacing after punctuation is essential in preparing a professional document. The rules of spacing apply to *business letters* and *reports*. They do not necessarily apply in the printing of books, magazines, and newspapers.

1. Space twice after a period, question mark, or exclamation point (terminal punctuation) or after a colon. (However, if you are printing with a proportional font and justifying the right margins, space only once after terminal punctuation. This is an example of the slight differences between typography—typesetters' rules—and normal keyboarding.)

```
Step two was completed.  Then....
When will he arrive?  Regardless of the time....
We have three questions:  (1) Where is....
```

2. Space once after a comma or a semicolon.

When the end of the month comes, we will be prepared.

The operator left at three o'clock; he was ill.

3. Space once after a period following an initial.

Mr. Warren H. Ragsdale

4. Space once after a period following such abbreviations as *No.*, *Co.*, and *Corp.*

Word Division

Often word division is necessary to avoid extreme variations in line length. Word-processing software automatically wraps words that will not fit within the margins to the next line. If a long word is wrapped to the next line, the previous line will be extremely short (jagged right margin) or will have large spaces between words (justified right margin). In either case, the result is distracting. A divided word at the end of the line would be less distracting.

Try to avoid dividing words at the ends of lines. If words must be divided, follow acceptable word division rules. Word-processing software will allow you to make hyphenation decisions. In addition, upgrades to industry's most popular word-processing programs are now capable of automatic hyphenation based on accepted word-division rules. These rules do not necessarily apply in the printing of books, magazines, and newspapers. Apply the following word-division rules:

1. Divide words between syllables only. (Words with only one syllable cannot be divided: *through, hearth, worked*).
2. Do not divide a word if it has fewer than seven letters. (Lines on a printed page can vary as much as six or seven letters in length; therefore, dividing short words such as *letter* or *report* is pointless.)
3. Do not separate the following syllables from the remainder of a word:
   a. A syllable that does not include a vowel: *would/n't*.
   b. A first syllable that contains only one letter: *a/greement*.
   c. A last syllable that contains only one or two letters: *pneumoni/a, apolog/y*.
4. Divide a word after a single-letter syllable, unless the word contains successive single-letter syllables: *semi-nary, congratu-late, extenu-ate, semi-aquatic*.
5. Avoid dividing hyphenated words at any place other than the hyphen: *self-employed, semi-independent*.
6. Do not divide proper names.
7. Avoid dividing a word at the end or top of a page, because these positions receive added emphasis.

PUNCTUATION STYLES AND LETTER FORMATS

Just as a speaker's appearance has an impact on an oral message, page layout (format) has an impact on a written message. Many companies have policies that dictate the punctuation style and the letter format used.

Mixed and Open Punctuation

Two punctuation styles are customarily used in business letters: open and mixed. Letters using mixed punctuation style have a colon after the salutation and a comma after the complimentary close. Open punctuation omits both the colon after the salutation and the comma after the complimentary close. Mixed punctuation is the traditional style; however, cost-conscious companies are increasingly adopting the open style (and other similar format changes), which eliminates unnecessary keystrokes.

Mixed Punctuation

January 24, 19—

Mr. John L. Smith
1938 South Welch Avenue
Northwood, NE 65432-1938

Dear Mr. Smith:

Sincerely,

Sally Ingram

Sally Ingram
Program Chair

Open Punctuation

January 24, 19—

Mr. John L. Smith
1938 South Welch Avenue
Northwood, NE 65432-1938

Dear Mr. Smith

SALUTATION

Sincerely

Sally Ingram

Sally Ingram
Program Chair

COMPLIMENTARY CLOSE

Letter Formats

The three letter formats that are commonly accepted by business include block, modified block, and simplified block.

Block.   Companies striving to reduce the cost of producing business documents adopt the easy-to-learn, efficient block format. All lines (including paragraphs) begin at the left margin; therefore, no time is lost setting tabs and positioning letter parts. Study carefully the letter in block format with open punctuation shown in Figure A-2.

Modified Block.　Modified block is the traditional letter format still used in many companies. The date line, complimentary close, and signature

DATE LINE

INSIDE ADDRESS

SALUTATION

BODY

COMPLIMENTARY CLOSE

SIGNATURE BLOCK

REFERENCE INITIALS

The Society of
REAL-ESTATE APPRAISERS
S O U T H E A S T　C H A P T E R
P.O. BOX 9687 INDIANAPOLIS, IN 46206-9687 (317) 555-0012

February 24, 19—
QS

Mr. John L. Smith
1938 South Welch Avenue
Northwood, NE　65432-1938
DS
Dear Mr. Smith
DS
Your recent article, "Are Appraisers Talking to Themselves?" has drawn many favorable comments from local real-estate appraisers.
DS
The Southeast Chapter of the Society of Real-Estate Appraisers has felt a strong need for more information about appraisal report writing. About 200 members will attend our annual seminar dinner meeting. They would be glad to meet you and interested in hearing you discuss "Appraisal Report Writing."

By accepting this invitation, you'll be able to assist the appraisal profession. You will meet several new members of our group. The meeting will be at the Tilton Hotel on Thursday, May 23, at 7 p.m. We promise you a pleasant evening and an attentive audience.

We would appreciate having, with your acceptance, a photograph to be printed in the program.
DS
Sincerely
QS
Sally Ingram

Sally Ingram
Program Chair

tw

FIGURE A-2　Block format with open punctuation

block begin at the horizontal center of the page. The paragraphs may be indented five spaces if the writer prefers or the company policy requires it; however, the indention creates unnecessary keystrokes that increase the cost of the letter. All other lines begin at the left margin. Study carefully the letter in modified block format with block paragraphs and mixed punctuation shown in Figure A-3.

DAVE'S SMALL ENGINES | 900 Tanglewood Road Charlotte, NC 28228-8328 (704) 555-3719

February 4, 19— — DATE LINE

QS

Mr. Ben Wood
4513 East Colton Street
Charlotte, NC 28228-8328 — INSIDE ADDRESS

DS

Dear Mr. Wood: — SALUTATION

DS

Johnson Motors are among the most dependable small electric motors manufactured in the United States today. Here at Dave's Small Engines, we believe that the right size Johnson engine for the particular job is critical.

DS

The three-month warranty with the Johnson motors applies only if the motor is used under normal operating conditions. Your pipe size (3/15 inch), the large distance between your pool and the filtering system (100 feet), and the size of your pool (50 by 60 feet) placed undue stress on the 2.5-horsepower motor. Your sales receipt indicates that a 3.5-horsepower motor was recommended based on our evaluation of your needs. — BODY

Our sales force will be happy to show you the 3.5-horsepower Johnson motor. This powerful motor should provide clear, sparkling water for outdoor enjoyment for your family.

DS

Sincerely, — COMPLIMENTARY CLOSE

QS

Jon L. Carr

Jon L. Carr
Manager — SIGNATURE BLOCK

DS

ms — REFERENCE INITIALS

FIGURE A-3 Modified block format with mixed punctuation

Simplified Block.   The simplified block format is an efficient letter format. Like the block format, all lines begin at the left margin; but the salutation and complimentary close are omitted and a subject line is required. Place the subject line a double space below the inside address and a double space above the body. Study carefully the letter in simplified block format with block paragraphs shown in Figure A-4.

DATE LINE

INSIDE ADDRESS

SUBJECT LINE

BODY

SIGNATURE BLOCK

REFERENCE INITIALS OMITTED

Riverside
Cable Television

Telephone: (302) 555-8155
Telex: (302) 555-9873

1983 River Oak Drive   Wilmington, DE 19850-8502

February 15, 19—
                    QS

Mr. Pierre Reed
2987 West Wakefield Court
Wilmington, DE 19850-8871
                    DS
Changes in Cable Service
                    DS
Some important changes in your cable television service will begin March 1, 19—. We will rearrange our channel line-up and institute a rate change. These changes are necessary to maintain quality service and to meet new federal guidelines for programming selection.
                                            DS
Our new monthly rates are as follows:

Basic Service $12.50
Extended Service. 18.00
Premium Service. 32.00

With these changes, the cost of our extended package (all channels except premium for pay) is still only 60 cents per day, less than the cost of the cup of coffee and doughnut.

Our employees are committed to providing you with the best quality and variety of cable television, including education, sports, religion, and public affairs programming. Please call us if we can be of additional service to you.
                                    QS
Dennis Hunter

Dennis G. Hunter
Systems Manager

FIGURE A-4   Simplified block format

STANDARD LETTER PARTS

Business letters include six standard parts. Other parts are optional and may be included when necessary. The standard parts include (1) heading, (2) salutation, (3) body, (4) complimentary close, (5) signature block, and (6) reference initials. The proper placement of these parts is shown in Figures A-2, A-3, and A-4; a discussion of each standard part follows.

Heading

When the letterhead shows the company name, address, telephone and/or fax number, and logo, the letter begins with the date line. Use the month-date-year format (May 2, 19—) unless you are preparing government documents, writing to an international audience who uses the date-month-year format, or company policy requires another format. Abbreviating the month or using numbers (9/2/—) may portray a hurried attitude.

If the letter is prepared on plain paper, the writer's address must be keyed immediately above the date; otherwise, the recipient may be unable to respond if the envelope is discarded. The heading consists of three single-spaced lines: (1) the writer's street address; (2) the writer's city, two-letter state abbreviation, and 9-digit ZIP code; and (3) the date. The writer's name is omitted because it appears in the signature block.

Inside Address

The inside address begins a quadruple space after the dateline. It includes a personal or professional title (e.g., Mr. or Ms.), the name of the person and company to whom the letter is being sent, and the complete address. Refer to Figure A-5 for appropriate formats for inside addresses.

Letterhead Heading

**Graphic Design
Advertising**
2630 East Lee Avenue
Charlottesville, VA 22906-2630
(703) 555-4700

August 12, 19—

Ms. Sharon Cory
Cory & Associates
2988 St. Charles Road
Alameda, NM 87184-2988

Dear Ms. Cory:

Heading on Plain Paper

1800 Brookdale Road
Albuquerque, NM 87125-1800
August 12, 19—

Ms. Sharon Cory
Cory & Associates
2988 St. Charles Road
Alameda, NM 87184-2988

Dear Ms. Cory:

Inside Address	Appropriate Salutation	Explanation
A Specific Person		
Mr. Shawn Tate, President Bank of Commerce P.O. Box 3902 Lincoln, NE 68506-3902	Dear Mr. Tate:	If the person is a business associate, use a courtesy title and the last name.
	Dear Shawn:	If you know the person well, use the person's first name or the name you would use greeting the person face to face.
	Dear Shawn Tate: or use the simplified format (Figure A-4) that omits the salutation.	If you do not know whether the person is male or female, use the whole name or omit the salutation to avoid offending the reader.
A Company		
Bank of Commerce P.O. Box 3902 Lincoln, NE 68506-3902	Ladies and Gentlemen: or use the simplified format (Figure A-4) that omits the salutation.	This salutation recognizes the presence of males and females in management. Do *not* use "Dear Ladies and Gentlemen." You may use "Ladies" if you are sure that management is all female or "Gentlemen" if you are sure that management is all male.
A Company and Directed to a Specific Individual		
Attention Mr. Shawn Tate Bank of Commerce P.O. Box 3902 Lincoln, NE 68506-3902	Ladies and Gentlemen: or use the simplified format (Figure A-4) that omits the salutation.	The letter is officially written to the company; therefore, "Dear Mr. Tate" is *not* acceptable. The salutation matches the second line of the inside address when you direct attention to a specific person.

FIGURE A-5   Appropriate formats for inside addresses and salutations

Inside Address	Appropriate Salutation	Explanation
A Specific Position Within a Business		
Purchasing Officer United Brokerage Firm 876 Addison Road Toledo, OH 43692-7832	Dear Purchasing Officer: or use the simplified format (Figure A-4) that omits the salutation.	Because the name of the person is unknown, the simplified block format would be especially useful. A subject line is used rather than the salutation.
A Group of People		
Institute of Public Accountants 2958 Central Avenue Baltimore, MD 21233-2958	Dear Accounting Professionals:	
Form letter to a potential customer or policyholders (inside address may be omitted)	Dear Customer:	When form letters are merged with available databases, the letter is personalized by inserting the recipient's inside address and a specific salutation such as "Dear Mr. Smith." This automated procedure eliminates the need for these less-personal salutations.
A Public Official		
The Honorable (first and last name of U.S. Senator)	Dear Senator (last name):	
The Honorable (first and last name of U.S. Representative)	Dear Mr. or Ms. (last name):	This form is also used for state senators and representatives.
The Honorable (first and last name of state governor)	Dear Governor (last name):	
Refer to an up-to-date reference manual or professional protocol guide when writing to other public officials.		

Salutation

The salutation is the greeting that opens a letter and is placed a double space below the inside address. The salutation is omitted in the simplified block style shown in Figure A-4.

To show courtesy for the individual, be sure to include a personal or professional title (Mr., Ms., Dr., Senator). To determine an appropriate salutation, refer to the *first line* of the inside address. In the previous example, "Dear Ms. Cory" is an appropriate salutation for this letter addressed to Ms. Sharon Cory (first line of inside address). If the first line of the inside address were "Cory & Associates," "Ladies and Gentlemen" would be an appropriate salutation. Use the examples shown in Figure A-5 as a guide when selecting an appropriate salutation.

Body

The body contains the message of the letter. It begins a double space below the salutation. Paragraphs are single-spaced with a double space between paragraphs. Because a double space separates the paragraphs, paragraph indention, which requires extra startup (setting tabs) and keying time, is not necessary. However, some companies may require paragraph indention as company policy. If so, you must use the modified block style (Figure A-3) with the addition of indented paragraphs.

Complimentary Close

The complimentary close is a phrase used to close the letter in the same way that you say good-bye at the end of a conversation. To create goodwill, choose a complimentary close that reflects the formality of your relationship with the reader. Typical examples are "Yours truly," "Sincerely yours," "Sincerely," "Cordially," and "Cordially yours." "Sincerely" is considered neutral and is thus appropriate in a majority of business situations. Capitalize only the first word of the complimentary close and position it a double space below the body. The complimentary close and the salutation are omitted in the simplified block style (Figure A-4).

Signature Block

The writer's name is keyed a quadruple space (three blank lines) below the complimentary close (or body in the simplified block letter). The writer's name is signed legibly in the space provided. A female may include a courtesy title to indicate her preference (e.g., Miss, Ms., Mrs.), and a female or male may use a title to distinguish a name used by both males and females (e.g., Shane, Leslie, or Stacy) or initials (E. M. Goodman). The business or professional title may be placed on the same line with the writer's name or directly below it. Use the following examples as guides for balancing the writer's name and title:

Title on the Same Line	*Title on Next Line*
Ms. Shawn Tate, President	Ms. E. M. Goodman
Paul Warner, Manager	Assistant Manager
Quality Control Division	Raymond Fitzpatrick
	Personnel Director

Reference Initials

The initials of the keyboard operator are keyed in lowercase a double space below the signature block. The writer's initials are not included because the name appears in the signature block. The reference initials and the signature block identify the persons involved in preparing the letter in the event of later questions. Reference initials are omitted when the letter is keyed by the writer—a common practice now that many executives compose documents at a computer terminal both in the office and from remote locations. However, company policy may require that the initials of all people involved in writing a letter be placed in the reference initials line to identify accountability in the case of litigation.

SPECIAL LETTER PARTS

Other letter parts may be added to the letter depending on the particular situation. These parts include (1) mailing notation, (2) attention line, (3) reference line, (4) subject line, (5) second-page heading, (6) company name in signature block, (7) enclosure notation, (8) copy notation, and (9) postscript.

Mailing Notation

A mailing notation, such as REGISTERED, CERTIFIED, OVERNIGHT DELIVERY, or FACSIMILE, provides a record of how the letter was sent. CONFIDENTIAL, PERSONAL, or PLEASE FORWARD gives instructions on how the letter should be handled. Key these notations in all capitals a double space below the date at the left margin.

Attention Line

The attention line directs a letter to a specific person ("Attention Ms. Laura Ritter"), position within the company ("Attention Human Resources Director"), or department ("Attention Purchasing Department"). The attention line appears as the first line; the company name appears on the second line of the inside address. Because the envelope format also requires the attention line to appear on the first line of the inside address, the word-processing block-print function can be used to prepare the envelope without rekeying the address.

Reference Line

A reference line ("Re: Contract No. 983-9873") directs the reader to source documents or to files. Key the reference line a double space below the inside address.

Subject Line

The subject line tells the reader what the letter is about and sets the stage for the reader to understand the message. The simplified block letter requires a subject line; in other letter formats, the subject line is optional. Key the subject line a double space below the salutation. Use either lowercase and capitals or all capitals for added emphasis. If modified block style is used, the subject line can be centered for added emphasis. To increase efficiency, the word *subject* is omitted because its position above the body clearly identifies its function.

The mailing notation, attention line, reference line, and subject line are illustrated in Figure A-6.

Second-Page Heading

The second and successive pages of multiple-page letters and memorandums are keyed on plain paper of the same quality as the letterhead. The second and successive pages need a heading that identifies them as a continuation of the first page. The three-part heading includes: (1) name of person or company to whom the message is sent (identical to the first line of the inside address), (2) page number, and (3) date.

Place the heading one inch (six lines) from the top edge of the paper. Double-space after the heading to continue the body of the letter. Both vertical and horizontal formats are acceptable.

With all three lines beginning at the left margin, the vertical format is compatible with the block and simplified block formats but can be used with the modified block format. The horizontal format is more complex to keyboard but looks attractive with the modified block style and is especially effective when using the vertical heading would force the letter or memorandum to additional pages:

SPENCER & TAYLOR, LTD., CPAs
3702 Hawkins Building, Suite 275
Oakland, CA 94621-2645
(510) 555-3095

January 19, 19—
DS
FACSIMILE   MAILING NOTATION
DS
Attention Ms. Jeanne M. Neal   ATTENTION LINE
Communications Systems, Inc.
Shuman Building, Suite 250
Atlanta, GA 30311-5309
DS
RE: Engagement No. 39-29-3773   REFERENCE LINE
DS
Ladies and Gentlemen:
DS
ENGAGEMENT AGREEMENT   SUBJECT LINE
DS
Spencer & Taylor is pleased to confirm our arrangements
to audit the financial statements of Communication
Systems, Inc. for the year ended June 30, 19—.

FIGURE A-6   Special letter parts

Vertical Format

Mr. John L. Smith
Page 2
February 24, 19—
DS
We would appreciate having, with your acceptance, a
photograph to be printed in the program.

Sincerely,

Sally Ingram

Sally Ingram
Program Chair

Horizontal Format

Mr. John L. Smith   2   February 24, 19—
                                                       DS
We would appreciate having, with your acceptance, a photograph to be
printed in the program.

Sincerely,

Sally Ingram

Sally Ingram
Program Chair

Company Name in Signature Block

The company name as a part of the signature block is commonly omitted
because the company name appears on the letterhead; however, some
companies prefer to see the company name in the signature. The company line is beneficial when the letter is prepared on plain paper or is
more than one page (the second page of the letter is printed on plain paper). When the writer wishes to emphasize that the document is written
on behalf of the company, a company line may be useful. For example,
the company line might be included when the nature of the letter is a

Sincerely,
              DS
PRESTON DATA SERVICE, INC.
                                                   QS
Jerome S. Fuja

Jerome S. Fuja
Financial Manager

ek

contract such as an engagement letter to a newly acquired client. Key the company line in all capitals a double space below the complimentary close and a quadruple space (three blank lines) above the signature block.

Enclosure Notation

If a letter contains an item other than the letter (brochure, price list, resume) in the same envelope, key an enclosure notation ("Enclosure") a double-space below the reference initials (or signature block if no reference initials appear). Use the plural form ("Enclosures") if more than one item is enclosed. You may identify the number of enclosures ("Enclosures: 3") or the specific item enclosed ("Enclosure: Bid Proposal"). Avoid the temptation to abbreviate ("Enc.") because abbreviations may communicate that you are in a hurry or that a thorough job is not necessary for this particular person. Some companies use the word "Attachment" on memorandums when the accompanying items may be stapled or paperclipped and not placed in an envelope.

Copy Notation

A copy notation indicates that a copy of the document was sent to the person(s) listed. Include the person's personal or professional title and full name. Progressive companies no longer use "cc" for carbon copy, instead, they use terms that accurately reflect the company's modern communication practices. These terms include "pc" for photocopy, "c" for copy, or simply "copy." Key the copy notation at the left margin a double space below the enclosure notation, reference initials, or signature block (depending on the special letter parts used).

The copy notation is omitted when a copy of a letter is sent to someone without the recipient's knowledge. A blind copy notation ("bpc" or "bc") is keyed on all file copies a double space below the last printed line.

Postscript

The postscript, appearing as the last item in the letter, traditionally included anything that was omitted from the letter. Postscripts that are added because the writer did not outline the document effectively reflect negatively on the writer. Furthermore, the editing capabilities of word-processing software have eliminated the need for adding postscripts. Even if the letter has already been printed, retrieving the letter, inserting the needed information at the most logical point, and reprinting it is a simple task.

Today the most common use of postscripts is to emphasize information. A postscript in a sales letter, for example, is often used to restate the central selling point; for added emphasis, it may be handwritten or printed in a different color. Researchers have noted an increased trend toward handwritten postscripts of a personal nature as individuals attempt to keep in touch with people in our high-tech society. Key the postscript a double-space below the last notation or signature block if no notations are used. Treat the postscript as any other paragraph; indent only if the other paragraphs in the letter are indented. Because its position clearly labels this paragraph as a postscript, do not begin with "PS."

The second-page heading, reference initials, copy notation, enclosure notation, and postscript are illustrated in Figure A-7.

MEMORANDUM FORMATS

Memorandums are messages sent to offices or individuals *within* a business. To increase productivity, companies use formats that are easy to input and thus save time. Memorandums, or memos, may be prepared on preprinted memorandum forms, plain paper, or letterhead depending on the preference of the company. Follow these general guidelines in formatting memos:

1. Set one-inch margins or the default set by your word-processing software.
2. Follow these guidelines for determining the starting line:
   Plain paper: Line 10.
   Letterhead: A double space below the letterhead.
3. Single-space paragraphs and double-space between paragraphs. Do *not* indent paragraphs. A single or a double space between the TO, FROM, DATE, and SUBJECT lines is acceptable.
4. Include a subject line in all memos to facilitate quick reading and filing. You may key the subject line in all capitals for added emphasis or begin the first word and all other words except articles, prepositions, or conjunctions with capital letters.
5. Omit personal and professional titles (Mr., Mrs., Dr.) on the *TO* and *FROM* lines because of the informality of this intercompany communication. Include job titles or department names.
6. Handle reference initials, enclosure and copy notations, and postscripts just as you would in a letter.
7. Include a second-page heading on the second and successive pages of a memorandum just as you would in a multiple-page letter.
8. Place memos in special envelopes designated for intracompany mail or in plain envelopes. If you use plain envelopes, key "COMPANY MAIL" in the stamp position so that it will not be inadvertently

Communications Systems, Inc.   Line 6
Page 2
January 19, 19—
                    DS
Sharon Hampton has been assigned as the audit manager in
charge of your audit examination. Please review the enclosed
preliminary time schedule she has developed and direct your
questions to her at 555-3095, extension 25.

We at Spencer & Taylor look forward to providing these and other
quality professional services to you.
                        DS
Sincerely,
        QS

Richard L. Anderson

Richard L. Anderson
Audit Partner,
            DS
cf
    DS
Enclosure: Audit Agreement
                    DS
c Mr. David Banks
            DS
Our annual tax update has been scheduled for March 5–6, 19—.
You will receive an agenda from the tax department just as soon
as all details have been finalized.

SECOND-PAGE HEADING

REFERENCE INITIALS

ENCLOSURE NOTATION

COPY NOTATION

POSTSCRIPT

FIGURE A-7   Special letter parts

stamped and mailed. Key the recipient's name and department in the
address location and any other information required by company policy. Large companies may require use of office numbers or other mail
designations to expedite intracompany deliveries.

Many variations of memorandum formats are used in business. The
formal and the simplified memorandum are illustrated.

Formal

The formal memorandum format begins with a standard heading that contains the recipient's name, writer's name, date, and subject. To save input time, some companies use a preprinted form that identifies the document as a memorandum and contains the basic information: *TO, FROM, DATE, SUBJECT*. The writer's initials are typically handwritten to the right of the writer's name. Double-space before the beginning of the body. Figure A-8 is an example of the formal memorandum format.

Simplified

Similar to the simplified block letter format, the simplified memorandum format is designed to save input time. The guide words (*TO, FROM, DATE, SUBJECT*) are omitted, and all lines begin at the left margin. Key the subject line in all capitals a double space below the recipient's name and a double space above the body of the memorandum. Key the sender's name a quadruple space below the body, leaving enough space for the writer's signature. Figure A-9 is an example of a simplified memorandum format.

ENVELOPES

The U.S. Postal Service recommends a specific format for addressing envelopes so that the address can be read by optical character readers used to sort mail quickly. The recommended format requires that the envelope be keyed in all capital letters with no punctuation (all caps, no punctuation).

Proper placement of the address on the large envelope (No. l0) is shown in Figure A-10 and the small envelope (No. $6\frac{3}{4}$) in Figure A-11. Note these specific points:

◆ The address matches the inside address on the letter.
◆ The address contains at least three but no more than six lines.
◆ All lines of the return (writer's) address and the inside (recipient's) address are keyed in block form (flush at the left).
◆ All lines are single-spaced.
◆ A personal or professional title (Mr., Ms., Dr.) is included on the envelope as well as in the inside address of the letter.
◆ The last line contains three items of information *only:* (1) city; (2) two-letter abbreviation for state, territory, or province; and (3) 9-digit ZIP code.

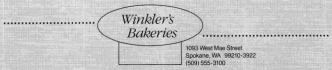

DS

TO: Mark R. Sloan, Vice President

FROM: Lora A. Glaze, Marketing Director *LG*

DATE: March 31, 19—

SUBJECT: Marketing Activity Report for March

The marketing division reports the following activities for March.

DS

Advertising

Three meetings were held with representatives at the Bart and
Dome agency to complete plans for the fall campaign for Fluffy
Buns. The campaign will concentrate on the use of discount
coupons published in the Thursday food section of sixty daily
newspapers in the Pacific states. Coupons will be released on the
second and fourth Thursdays in June and July.

Estimated cost of the program is $645,000. That amount includes
2.2 million redeemed coupons at 20 cents each ($440,000).

A point-of-sale advertising display, shown on the attached sheet,
was developed for retail grocery outlets. Sales reps are pushing
these in their regular and new calls. The display may be used to
feature a different product from our line on a weekly basis.

Sales Staff

We have dropped one sales rep from the northern California
section and divided the area between the southern Oregon and
Sacramento reps.

Attachment

FIGURE A-8   Formal memorandum format

♦ Two spaces appear between the two-letter state abbreviation and the
   ZIP code.
♦ The writer's name is keyed in the half-inch of space above the com-
   pany's address when preprinted company letterhead is used.
♦ Place special notations for the addressee ("Please Forward," "Hold for
   Arrival," "Personal") a double space below the return address. Place

Line 10

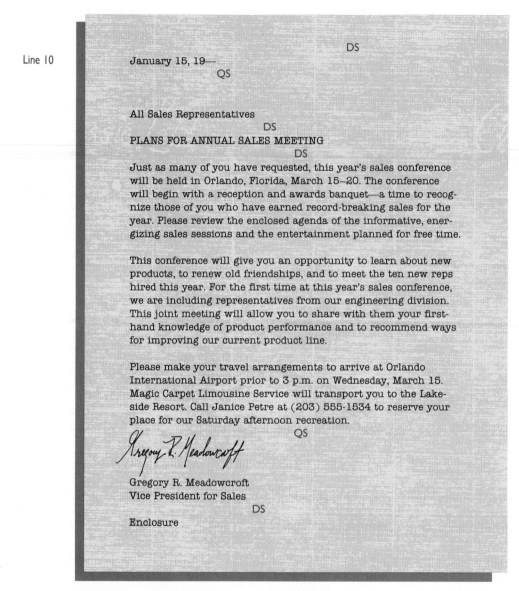

DS

January 15, 19—
QS

All Sales Representatives
DS
PLANS FOR ANNUAL SALES MEETING
DS
Just as many of you have requested, this year's sales conference will be held in Orlando, Florida, March 15–20. The conference will begin with a reception and awards banquet—a time to recognize those of you who have earned record-breaking sales for the year. Please review the enclosed agenda of the informative, energizing sales sessions and the entertainment planned for free time.

This conference will give you an opportunity to learn about new products, to renew old friendships, and to meet the ten new reps hired this year. For the first time at this year's sales conference, we are including representatives from our engineering division. This joint meeting will allow you to share with them your first-hand knowledge of product performance and to recommend ways for improving our current product line.

Please make your travel arrangements to arrive at Orlando International Airport prior to 3 p.m. on Wednesday, March 15. Magic Carpet Limousine Service will transport you to the Lakeside Resort. Call Janice Petre at (203) 555-1534 to reserve your place for our Saturday afternoon recreation.
QS

Gregory R. Meadowcroft
Vice President for Sales
DS
Enclosure

FIGURE A-9   Simplified memorandum format

mailing notations for postal authorities ("Overnight" and "Registered") a double space below the stamp position. Underline or use all capitals for special notations.

Many businesses use word-processing software to print envelopes and mailing labels using the inside address in the letter. To eliminate the need to key the address twice—once for the letter and again for the enve-

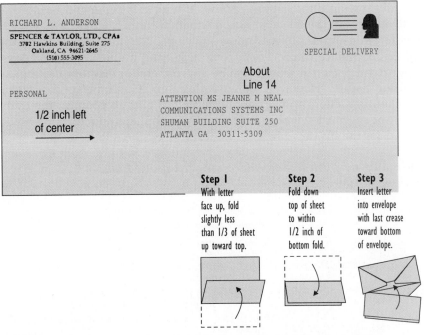

FIGURE A-10   Large envelope (No. 10) format and folding instructions

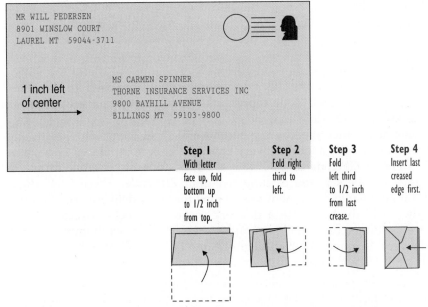

FIGURE A-11   Small envelope (No. 6¾) format and folding instructions

lope (all caps, no punctuation)—some authorities recommend keying the inside address in the all-caps, no punctuation format. Obviously, if a letter is to be inserted into a window envelope, this format will assist the U.S. Postal Service in processing and delivering it quickly. The all-caps, no punctuation format would also be appropriate for quantity mailings of a routine nature. However, because this format may make documents look like form letters and is only beginning to gain acceptance, the traditional upper- and lowercase letters with appropriate punctuation should be used for the inside address in nonroutine business letters.

Routine Letter with Inside Address Keyed in All Caps, No Punctuation

Northside Insurance Co.
1249 Heritage Drive
Norfolk, VA 23511-1249
(804) 555-3700

January 19, 19—

MS MAJORIE VAN DYKE
215 NORTH THIRD STREET
NORFOLK VA 23511-3100

RE: Life Insurance Policy No. 89-392-12

Dear Ms. Van Dyke

The two-letter state abbreviations (see Figure A-12) and the 9-digit ZIP code assigned by the U.S. Postal Service should be used for all letters. The first digit in a ZIP code represents one of ten national areas. Within these areas, each state is divided into an average of ten smaller geographic areas, identified by the second and third digits. The fourth and fifth digits identify a local delivery area. The U.S. Postal Service now uses an extended ZIP code called ZIP + 4, which adds a hyphen and four additional numbers to the existing five-digit ZIP code. These "+4" digits permit automated equipment to sort mail for faster delivery. The first two of the "+4" digits denote a delivery section of blocks, streets, several office buildings, or a small geographic area. The last two numbers denote a delivery "segment," which might be one floor of an office building, one side of a street, a firm, a suite, or a group of post office boxes.

Alabama	AL	Montana	MT
Alaska	AK	Nebraska	NE
Arizona	AZ	Nevada	NV
Arkansas	AR	New Hampshire	NH
American Samoa	AS	New Jersey	NJ
California	CA	New Mexico	NM
Canal Zone	CZ	New York	NY
Colorado	CO	North Carolina	NC
Connecticut	CT	North Mariana Islands	CM
Delaware	DE	Ohio	OH
District of Columbia	DC	Oklahoma	OK
Florida	FL	Oregon	OR
Georgia	GA	Pennsylvania	PA
Guam	GU	Puerto Rico	PR
Hawaii	HI	Rhode Island	RI
Idaho	ID	South Carolina	SC
Illinois	IL	South Dakota	SD
Indiana	IN	Tennessee	TN
Iowa	IA	Texas	TX
Kansas	KS	Trust Territories	TT
Kentucky	KY	Utah	UT
Louisiana	LA	Vermont	VT
Maine	ME	Virginia	VA
Maryland	MD	Virgin Islands	VI
Massachusetts	MA	Washington	WA
Michigan	MI	West Virginia	WV
Minnesota	MN	Wisconsin	WI
Mississippi	MS	Wyoming	WY
Missouri	MO		

FIGURE A-12   State, district, and territory two-letter abbreviations

GRAMMAR REVIEW AND EXERCISES

Self-Check

Words Frequently Misused

Nouns

Pronouns

Verbs

Adjectives and Adverbs

Sentence Structure

Abbreviations

Capital Letters

Numbers

Punctuation

Spelling

Self-Check

Review Quiz

IF MESSAGES DO NOT MEET high standards of grammar and mechanics, they have negative consequences. The receiver may (1) misunderstand the message, (2) lose time by stopping to review the message, (3) think more about the error than the message, or (4) think negatively about the sender's background or lose respect for the receiver.

The following pages review some of the common problems that confront business writers. Regardless of job level (from the lowest entry-level to the highest managerial level), a knowledge of basics is beneficial. The rules and principles on the following pages should be mastered by both administrative personnel and correspondence personnel.

The following review of basics seeks to answer frequently encountered questions about word usage, grammar, spelling, and punctuation. For more thorough reviews, consult standard reference books on grammar or transcription.

SELF-CHECK

To measure your knowledge of grammar, spelling, and punctuation, follow these steps for sentences 1–10:

a. Place a covered sheet over the right-hand column.

b. Examine the numbered sentence for errors in word usage, spelling, punctuation, and manner of expressing numbers.

c. Make the needed corrections on a separate page. Do not attempt to revise a sentence and state its idea in an entirely different way. Do not divide a sentence into two sentences.

d. Move the cover sheet down and check your answer against the corrected sentence (or sentences). Making an unnecessary change is a mistake; failing to make a necessary change is a mistake. If a sentence can be corrected in more than one way, two corrected sentences appear in the right-hand column.

e. Record the number of mistakes in the spaces provided at the left.

_____ **1.** Only one of the applicants have completed the employment tests; but three have submitted resumes.

Only one of the applicants <u>has</u> completed the employment tests<u>,</u> but three have submitted resumes.

_____ **2.** The managers presented their recommendations last week, they will submit their research on May 10th.

The managers presented their recommendations last week<u>; they</u> will submit their research on <u>May 10.</u>

The managers presented their recommendations last week<u>, but they</u> will submit their research on <u>May 10.</u>

_____ **3.** Because the project had not been completed, Margaret could not give her report but the meeting was held anyway.

Because the project had not been completed, Margaret could not give her report; but the meeting was held anyway.

_____ **4.** The supervisor was enthused about the suggestion, it was very unique.

The supervisor was enthusiastic about the suggestion; it was unique.

The supervisor was enthusiastic about the suggestion; it was very unusual.

_____ **5.** Although technical skills are important effective communication magnifies the over-all value of those technical skills.

Although technical skills are important, effective communication magnifies the overall value of those technical skills.

Technical skills are important, but effective communication magnifies the overall value of those technical skills.

_____ **6.** One applicants' employment test was postponed for two hours, this may have impacted the test score.

One applicant's interview was postponed for two hours; this delay may have affected the test score. (Some other noun, such as postponement, could be used instead of "delay.")

_____ **7.** Matthew's grin and bear it attitude is his fundamental principal of survival.

Matthew's grin-and-bear-it attitude is his fundamental principle of survival.

_____ **8.** Supervisors discussed one criteria for promotion during annual performance interviews with full time personal.

Supervisors discussed one criterion for promotion during annual performance interviews with full-time personnel.

_____ **9.** I appreciate you waiting on us to submit a proposal, it will be forwarded to your office by the controller and I.

I appreciate your waiting for us to submit a proposal; it will be sent to your office by the controller and me.

I appreciate your waiting for us to submit a proposal; the controller and I will send it to your office.

_____ **10.** Neither Senator Blake nor Representative Cox oppose the recently-proposed education legislation, however, the operating budget will not support these reforms.

Neither Senator Blake nor Representative Cox opposes the recently proposed education legislation; however, the operating budget will not support these reforms.

The preceding self-check exercise provides approximately 30 opportunities for error. The more errors you made, the more profitably you can study the following pages.

Because this review is intended for study or for reference, the terminology found in English textbooks is used. For those who have forgotten, many of the basic grammatical terms are defined. Principles are followed by illustrations. For best results, follow these suggestions for studying this material:

1. Read the principle and examine the illustrations that follow.
2. Reread the principle. Returning to the principle after reading the illustrations increases the clarity of the principle and reinforces learning.
3. Complete the 17 exercises positioned throughout this review. They are designed to test your understanding of the principles.
4. Complete the Self-Check review exercises 18–20 on pages B-48 to B-56 designed to assess how well you have mastered the grammar principles presented in Appendix B. Analyze any questions you may have answered incorrectly to identify specific areas in which you need further study. Then reread these principles.
5. Complete the Review Quiz at the end of Appendix B at your instructor's direction.

WORDS FREQUENTLY MISUSED

1. *Above and below.* In referring to material that comes before or after, avoid use of *above* and *below*.

   Not: The <u>above</u> statement . . . .
   But: The <u>preceding</u> . . . .

   Not: The graph <u>below</u> . . . .
   But: The <u>following</u> graph . . . .

   Above and *below* are especially distracting when they appear in unfortunate positions on a printed page. Too often, *below* appears in the last paragraph of a page and the reference is *not* in fact below (it's at the top of the next page); or *above* appears in the first paragraph of a page and the reference is *not* in fact above (it's at the bottom of the preceding page).

2. *Accept, except.* *Accept* means "to take what is offered," "to accede," "to assent"; *except* means "to exclude," or "with the exclusion of."

   I <u>accept</u> your offer.

   All columns have been added <u>except</u> one.

3. *Accompanied by, accompanied with.* *Accompanied by* is used when *people* are involved. *Accompanied with* is used when *objects* are involved.

   She was <u>accompanied</u> by her agent.

   The letter was <u>accompanied</u> with a check.

4. *Advice, advise.* *Advice* is a noun meaning "suggestions or recommendations about a course of action." *Advise* is a verb meaning "to give advice; to caution or warn."

The supervisor's <u>advice</u> to John was to abide by safety rules.

Supervisors <u>advise</u> employees of the consequences of safety rules violations.

5. *Affect, effect.* *Affect* is a verb meaning "to influence"; *effect* is a noun meaning "result"; *effect* is also a verb meaning "to bring about."

The change does not <u>affect</u> his pay.

What <u>effect</u> will the change have?

The manager wants to <u>effect</u> a change in the schedule.

6. *Aid, aide.* *Aid* is verb that means "to assist"; it is also a noun that means "assistance" or "help." *Aide* is a noun that means "a person who serves as an assistant."

The potion will <u>aid</u> digestion.

The potion serves as an <u>aid</u> to digestion.

The governor's <u>aide</u> made a statement to the press.

7. *All right, alright.* *Alright* is considered substandard usage.

The answers were <u>all right</u>.

That's <u>all right</u> with me.

8. *Among, between.* Use *among* to discuss three or more, *between* to discuss two.

Divide the earnings <u>among</u> the six workers.

Divide the earnings <u>between</u> the two workers.

9. *Amount, number.* Use *amount* when speaking of money or of things that cannot be counted; use *number* when speaking of things that can be counted.

The <u>amount</u> of grumbling has been troublesome to the supervisors.

The <u>number</u> of workers has been increased.

10. *Anxious, eager.* Use *anxious* only if great concern, doubt, worry, or anxiety is involved.

The manager is <u>eager</u> to participate.

He is <u>anxious</u> about the lack of security.

11. *Anyone, any one.* Use *anyone* if the *any* is to be accented; use *any one* if the *one* is to be accented. *Any one* is often followed by *of*.

Does <u>anyone</u> have a pencil?

<u>Any one</u> of our machines will be satisfactory.

12. *As to, about,* and *on.* Use *about, on,* or some other single-word preposition instead of *as to*.

Do you have any remarks <u>about</u> the contract?	Not "as to the contract?"
May we have your comments <u>on</u> the proposal?	Not "as to the proposal?"

13. *Bad, badly.* As an adjective, *bad* modifies a noun. *Bad* also follows a linking verb (*be, become, feel, seem*). As an adverb, *badly* modifies a verb, adjective, or adverb.

We received a <u>bad</u> report.

Fred feels <u>bad</u> about the outcome.

The fender was bent <u>badly</u>.

14. *Balance, remainder.* Use *balance* to refer to the difference between the debit and credit sides of a ledger account or to refer to an amount of money owed. Use *remainder* to refer to that which is left over.

The unpaid <u>balance</u> is $60.

Our staff can complete the <u>remainder</u> of the work in an hour.

15. *Biannual, biennial.* *Biannual* is the label for an event that happens twice in a year; *biennial* is

the label for an event that happens once in two years.

Your biannual payments are due in January and July.

Members of Congress are eager to adjourn for their biennial campaigns.

16. *Can, may.* *Can* indicates capability or power. *May* indicates permission or possibility.

We can do this work easily.

You may talk with the superintendent now.

The weather may change.

17. *Capital, capitol.* *Capital* is money, property, or a city in which state or national government is located. A *capitol* is a building in which the government meets.

One business partner provided the capital; the other provided the expertise.

The capitol is at the intersection of Jefferson Street and Tenth Avenue.

18. *Cite, sight, site.* *Cite* means to quote or mention. *Sight* refers to the sense of seeing, the process of seeing, or a view. *Site* is a location.

Marianne cited several authorities in her report.

Working at the computer is affecting her sight.

Market Avenue is the site of the new store.

19. *Coarse, course.* *Coarse* means "lacking in fineness," "rude," or "rough." *Course* means "a school subject," "the ground designated for a race," "a portion of a meal served at one time," "a series of successive proceedings."

The gravel was too coarse for use in the concrete mixture.

She is taking a course in mathematics.

That issue has now run its course.

20. *Compare to, compare with.* Use *compare to* in pointing out similarities; use *compare with* in pointing out differences as well as similarities.

He compared Kennedy to Lincoln.	He pointed out similarities.
He compared Kennedy with Lincoln.	He pointed out differences as well as similarities.

21. *Complement, compliment.* *Complement* means "to complete" or "that which completes or suits another." *Compliment* means "words of praise."

This shipment is a complement to our latest series of orders.

The clerk was complimented for his success.

22. *Complete, perfect, unique.* These adjectives have neither comparative nor superlative forms. *Unique* means "the only one of its kind"; therefore, something that is unique is not comparable. Anything is either complete or not, perfect or not, unique or not.

His report is complete.	Not "fairly complete."
Her score is perfect.	Not "more perfect" or "most perfect."
The plan is unique.	Not "very unique."

23. *Continual, continuous.* If an action is *continual*, it will have planned-for breaks in continuity; if an action is *continuous*, it will be constant, without breaks.

The mechanism for raising and lowering the garage door has given continual service for four years.	It provided service over a four-year period, but it did not raise and lower the door constantly.
The clock has run continuously for four years.	It has not stopped.

24. *Correspond to, correspond with.* If one thing *corresponds to* another, it matches or has a similarity. To *correspond with* is to write, to exchange letters.

His recommendations <u>correspond</u> to mine.

Mr. Woods has <u>corresponded with</u> us about a job.

25. *Council, counsel.* *Council* means "an advisory group." *Counsel* means "advice," "one who gives advice," or "to advise."

<u>Council</u> members will meet today.

First, seek legal <u>counsel</u>.

The defendant and his <u>counsel</u> were excused.

An attorney will <u>counsel</u> the suspect.

26. *Credible, creditable.* *Credible* means "believable." *Creditable* means "praiseworthy" or "worthy of commercial credit."

The explanations were <u>credible</u>.

Mr. Jones did a <u>creditable</u> job for us.

27. *Criteria, criterion.* A *criterion* is a standard for judging, a yardstick by which something is measured. The plural form is *criteria*.

The most important <u>criterion</u> was cost.

Three <u>criteria</u> were developed.

28. *Data, datum.* *Datum* is a singular noun meaning "fact," "proposition," "condition," or "quantity" from which other facts, etc., may be deduced. *Data* is the plural form.

This <u>datum</u> suggests . . . .

These <u>data</u> suggest . . . .

Use of *data* as a singular form is gaining some degree of acceptance. Some people use the word in the same way they use *group*. Although composed of more than one, *group* is singular:

The group has decided.

Until (and if) *data* becomes generally accepted as a singular, the word should be used carefully. Because *data is* may sound incorrect and distracting to some and *data are* equally incorrect and distracting to others, an alternative expression may be preferred. Instead of "This data is," or "These data are," such expressions as "This *set* of data is," or "These facts are," "This information is," or "These figures are" can be used to avoid the risk of alienating cetain readers or listeners.

29. *Deal. Deal* is not a good substitute for *transaction or exchange.*

We reaped a profit   Not "deal."
from the
<u>transaction</u>.

30. *Decent, descent, dissent.* *Decent* means "respectable" or "good." *Descent* means "a movement downward." *Dissent* means "to disagree."

We were served <u>decent</u> meals.

Fasten your seat belts; the plane is beginning its <u>descent</u>.

The motion passed; only one member <u>dissented</u>.

(*Words Frequently Misused* continues after Exercise 1.)

Exercise I

Select the correct word.

1. If you agree with the (preceding, above) statement, please write your initials in the space provided.
2. The governor was accompanied (by, with) two body guards.
3. All questionnaires were returned (accept, except) one.
4. Exactly how will the change (affect, effect) us?
5. The governor brought two of his (aids, aides) to the hearing.
6. Is the proposal (alright, all right) with you?
7. The consultants' (advice, advise) is to downsize the organization.
8. The commission is to be divided equally (among, between) the three sales agents.
9. We were astonished by the (amount, number) of complaints.
10. The employees were (anxious, eager) for a raise in the hourly wage.
11. Does (anyone, any one) have a suggestion?
12. Do you have a question (about, as to) procedures?
13. The waitress felt very (bad, badly) about the way the meal was cooked.
14. Most of the work is finished; the (balance, remainder) will be completed next week.
15. Members of the U.S. House of Representatives are elected (bi-annually, biennially).
16. You (can, may) take your coffee break now.
17. The (capital, capitol) will be repainted before the legislature convenes in January.
18. The (cite, sight, site) of Jim's receiving the service award was exhilarating.
19. Because of conflicting instructions, the employees hardly knew which (coarse, course) to pursue.
20. In this research, the scores of smokers will be compared (with, to) the scores of nonsmokers.
21. Thank you. I consider that remark a (compliment, complement).
22. Your demonstration was very (unique, unusual).
23. Sam was (continually, continuously) asking for a raise.
24. Because your information corresponds exactly (with, to) mine, the decision will be easy.
25. The suspect declined to accept legal (council, counsel).
26. Because the suspect's statements were (credible, creditable), no charges were filed.
27. The conclusion was based on only one (criteria, criterion).

28. This (data, set of data) will be fed into our computer.
29. We are eager to bring this (deal, transaction) to a conclusion.
30. The measure was passed without (descent, dissent).

WORDS FREQUENTLY MISUSED (continued)

31. *Differ from, differ with.* Use *differ from* in discussing characteristics; use *differ with* to convey the idea of disagreement.

This machine <u>differs from</u> that machine.

The manager <u>differs with</u> the president.

32. *Different from, different than.* *Different from* is correct; *different than* is to be avoided.

That machine is <u>different from</u> mine.

33. *Each other, one another.* Use *each other* when referring to two people; use *one another* when referring to more than two.

The two employees competed with <u>each other</u>.

The members of the group helped <u>one another</u>.

34. *Eminent, imminent.* *Eminent* means "well known." *Imminent* means "about to happen."

An <u>eminent</u> scientist will address the group.

A merger seems <u>imminent</u>.

35. *Enthused, enthusiastic.* *Enthusiastic* is preferred. *Enthused* is colloquial.

The gentleman is   Not "enthused."
<u>enthusiastic</u> about
his work.

36. *Envelop, envelope.* *Envelop* is a verb meaning "to surround" or "to hide." *Envelope* is a noun referring to a cover for a letter.

A fog was about to <u>envelop</u> the island.

Just use the enclosed <u>envelope</u> for your reply.

37. *Equable, equitable.* *Equable* means "uniform throughout," "steady," "even," or "without variation." *Equitable* means "just," "fair," or "impartial."

For an <u>equable</u> mixture, use an egg beater.

The wage-scale proposal was considered <u>equitable</u>; therefore, it was accepted.

38. *Farther, further.* Use *farther* when referring to distance. Use *further* when referring to extent or degree.

Let's go one mile <u>farther</u>.

Let's pursue the thought <u>further</u>.

39. *Fewer, less.* Use *fewer* with items that can be counted; use *less* with items that cannot be counted.

<u>Fewer</u> than half the employers approved the proposed pay plan.

Maria spent <u>less</u> time writing the report than Michael because she had spent more time organizing her data.

40. *Fiscal, physical.* *Fiscal* means "financial" or "pertaining to revenue." *Physical* pertains to nature or to the parts of the human body.

The budget director stressed the need for <u>fiscal</u> responsibility.

Ten minutes were devoted to <u>physical</u> exercise.

41. *Following, preceding.* These words are not nouns; they are adjectives and should be followed by nouns. Avoid "the following is" or "the preceding is." Instead, write

    The <u>following</u> list is up to date.

    The president has approved the <u>preceding</u> idea.

42. *Formally, formerly.* Use *formally* in discussing that which is ceremonious or done according to an established method. Use *formerly* in discussing that which has preceded in time.

    The award will be <u>formally</u> presented at tomorrow's convocation.

    Tom <u>formerly</u> worked for the department of revenue.

43. *Forward, send.* Use *send* to convey the idea of *initiating* movement of an item toward its receiver; use *forward* to convey the idea of *redirecting* an item that has already been sent on its way to the receiver.

    After the contract is signed, I will <u>send</u> it you.

    The package came to my address, but I <u>forwarded</u> it to you.

44. *In, into.* Use *in* to denote location. Use *into* to denote action.

    The keys are <u>in</u> the vault.

    He fell <u>into</u> the water.

45. *Infer, imply.* *Infer* means "to draw a conclusion"; readers or listeners infer. *Imply* means "to hint" or "to set forth vaguely"; speakers and writers imply.

    I <u>infer</u> from your letter that conditions have improved.

    Do you mean to <u>imply</u> that conditions have improved?

46. *Ingenious, ingenuous.* An *ingenious* person is clever or skillful in inventing. An *ingenious* device has been cleverly conceived or designed. An *ingenuous* person is honorable, frank, or free from disguise.

    The superintendent is <u>ingenious</u>; he can always find a way to solve such problems.

    The superintendent is <u>ingenuous</u>; he never makes excuses.

47. *Insure, ensure.* To *insure* is to contract for payment of a certain sum in the event of damage or loss. To *ensure* is to make certain that a specified event or result will occur.

    We plan to <u>insure</u> the house for $150,000.

    To <u>ensure</u> a passing score, study systematically.

48. *Irregardless.* Avoid this word. Use *regardless* instead.

49. *Its, it's.* *Its* is a possessive pronoun; *it's* is a contraction for "it is."

    The phrase has lost <u>its</u> meaning.

    <u>It's</u> time to quit.

50. *Kindly.* Avoid using *kindly* for "please."

    <u>Please</u> fill out the attached form.   Not "Kindly."

51. *Later, latter.* Use *later* as an adverb or as an adjective; use *latter* only as an adjective that precedes a noun.

    The minutes will be read <u>later</u>.   Adverb

    The frost will be <u>later</u> than usual this year.   Adjective

    Our first frost usually comes in the <u>latter</u> part of October.   Adjective

52. *Latest, last.* Use *latest* to refer to something that is still in effect; use *last* to refer to something that came after all the others.

The latest model has an 80-mb hard drive.	The series has not necessarily ended; other models could follow.
The last model had an 80-mb hard drive.	The series has ended; no other models will follow.

53. *Lay, lie.* In the present tense, *lay* means "to put" and *lie* means "to rest."

Lay Present:	She lays the book on the table.
Past:	She laid the book there yesterday.
Past participle:	She has laid it there many times.

Lie Present:	He lies on the sofa.
Past:	He lay down for an hour.
Past participle:	He has lain there for an hour.

54. *Lend, loan.* *Lend* is a verb meaning to let another use something temporarily. *Loan* is a noun referring to the thing given for the borrower's temporary use.

The bank has agreed to lend us the money.

The bank has approved our loan.

55. *Lose, loose.* *Lose* means "to fail to keep"; *loose* means "not tight."

Don't lose the moneybag.

The cap on the fountain pen is loose.

56. *Majority.* Avoid use of *majority* in referring to a singular.

Not:	The majority of the contract is acceptable.
But:	The major portion of the contract is acceptable.
Or:	The majority of the provisions are acceptable.

57. *Marital, martial.* *Marital* pertains to marriage; *martial* pertains to the military (army, navy, air force, marines).

After years of marital problems, the couple divorced.

For two years after its defeat, the country was governed by martial law.

58. *Media, medium.* A *medium* is a means for transmitting a message. Letter, telephone, radio, newspaper, and telegraph are examples. The plural form is *media*.

The best medium for advertising this product is the radio.

The news media are very objective in their coverage.

59. *Miner, minor.* *Miner* means "one who works in mines." *Minor* means "inferior in importance or size" or "one who has not reached adulthood."

Our miners struck a rich lode at 2,000 feet beneath the surface.

Too much time was spent discussing minor points.

As a minor, Steve was ineligible to vote.

60. *Moral, morale.* A *moral* person meets generally accepted high standards of personal conduct; such a person is considered virtuous or ethical. *Morals* is often used as a noun to mean "principles of ethical conduct." *Morale* is a level of cheerfulness or confidence.

The applicant has high moral standards; I would trust him completely.

People enjoy working there; morale is high.

(Words Frequently Misused continues after Exercise 2.)

Exercise 2

Select the correct word.

1. Late in the discussion, the manager and supervisor differed (from, with) each other over the wage issue.
2. Your answers are different (than, from) mine.
3. The three panelists were constantly interrupting (each other, one another).
4. Completion of Project A is six months away, but completion of Project B is (eminent, imminent).
5. The president was (enthused, enthusiastic) about the proposal.
6. Remember to include return (envelops, envelopes) with your questionnaires.
7. Union members rejected the proposal because it was not considered (equable, equitable).
8. The issue will be discussed (further, farther) at our next meeting.
9. Our finance department will check the report from a (fiscal, physical) point of view.
10. Limit your discussion to five or (fewer, less) points.
11. The trend is depicted in the (following, following graph).
12. Stan (formerly, formally) worked for the health department.
13. Please (send, forward) a copy of your report to me.
14. Insert the key (in, into) the lock.
15. From his statements to the press, I (infer, imply) that he is optimistic about the proposal.
16. Production has increased 300 percent since we adopted this (ingenious, ingenuous) labor-saving device.
17. Fred forgot to (ensure, insure) his car.
18. (Regardless, Irregardless) of weather conditions, we should proceed.
19. The storm seems to be losing (its, it's) force.
20. If you agree, (kindly, please) sign and return the enclosed form.
21. We planned to incorporate (latter, later) in the year.
22. The story appeared in the (last, latest) issue of *Time*.
23. Perhaps you should (lie, lay) down and rest for a while.
24. Please, (lend, loan) me a copy of today's *Wall Street Journal*.
25. Do not (loose, lose) sight of your primary objective.
26. I agree with the (majority, major portion) of his argument.
27. If your (marital, martial) status is single, turn immediately to page 3.

28. Only one news (media, medium) was present for the announcement.
29. Except for a few (miner, minor) points, the contract is acceptable.
30. Employees are complaining; (moral, morale) seems to be very low.

WORDS FREQUENTLY MISUSED (continued)

61. *Myself, me.* *Myself* is used to intensify *I* or *me*. It should not be used in place of these words.

I <u>myself</u> would like to have a vacation.

The manager and <u>I</u> have investigated this plan.   Not "myself."

Give the report to Ms. Smith and <u>me</u>.   Not "myself."

Use of such pronouns as *myself, herself,* and *themselves* is appropriate when the pronoun has been used already in the sentence.

I taught <u>myself</u> to type.

She sees <u>herself</u> as a perfectionist.

They were criticizing <u>themselves</u>.

62. *Nor, or.* Use *nor* with *neither*; use *or* with either. (*Or* is also used in sentences that don't contain *either*.)

Use <u>neither</u> pen <u>nor</u> pencil.

Use <u>either</u> pen <u>or</u> pencil.

You may pay now, <u>or</u> you may wait until January.

63. *Only.* Place *only* as close as possible to the word it is intended to modify.

<u>Only</u> Dana monitors advertisements.   No one else monitors advertisements

Dana <u>only</u> monitors advertisements.   She does nothing more than monitor advertisements.

Dana monitors advertisements <u>only</u>.   Monitoring advertisements is the only thing she does.

64. *Party.* Except in legal documents, do not use *party* as a synonym for *person*. Technically, a *party* is a group of people.

Another <u>person</u> is interested in buying this house.   Not "party."

65. *Passed, past.* *Passed* is the past tense of the verb *pass*. *Past* is an adjective when used to describe a time period that has ended; it is also used as a noun to identify time that has gone by.

Mary <u>passed</u> her test. A car <u>passed</u> us on our right.

We had several inquiries in the <u>past</u> week.

In the <u>past</u>, the system worked beautifully.

66. *Personal, personnel.* *Personal* means "concerned with a person" or "private." *Personnel* means "people" or "employees."

Omit the questions about family background and musical preference; they're too <u>personal</u>.

All advertising <u>personnel</u> are invited to participate in the workshop.

67. *Practical, practicable.* *Practical* means "useful" or "not theoretical." *Practicable* means "capable of being put into practice." Do not use *practicable* in describing a person.

The manager is a <u>practical</u> person.

This a <u>practical</u> tool.

The plan appears to be <u>practicable</u>.

68. *Principal, principle.* *Principal* means "a person in a leading position," "main," or "primary"; *principle* means "rule" or "law."

The <u>principal</u> scheduled an all-day faculty meeting.

The <u>principal</u> purpose is to gain speed.

The <u>principal</u> plus interest is due in thirty days.

The theory is based on sound <u>principles</u>.

69. *Provided, providing.* *Provided* means "on condition that." *Providing* means "supplying" and takes an object. Do not use *that* after provided.

Robin will supervise advertising <u>provided</u> we win the contract.

<u>Providing</u> portable computers to the sales staff is an excellent idea.

70. *Quiet, quite.* *Quiet* means "silent"; *quite* means "entirely" or "completely."

This room is <u>quiet</u>.

The instructions are <u>quite</u> clear.

71. *Raise, rise.* *Raise* means "to lift up" or "to move something upward." *Rise* means "to go up" or "to come up."

Raise	Present:	We do not want to <u>raise</u> prices.
	Past:	We <u>raised</u> our prices last year.
	Past participle:	Our prices have been <u>raised</u> this year.
Rise	Present:	I do not expect prices to <u>rise</u>.
	Past:	Prices <u>rose</u> slightly last year.
	Past participle:	Prices have <u>risen</u> this year.

72. *Reason is because.* *Because* means "for the reason next presented"; therefore *reason is because* is a redundancy.

Not: The <u>reason is because</u> losses from bad debts tripled.

But: The reason is <u>that</u> losses from bad debts tripled.

Or: Profits decreased <u>because</u> losses from bad debts tripled.

73. *Respectfully, respectively.* *Respectfully* means "with respect." *Respectively* means "in the sequence presented."

The speaker is eminent; please listen <u>respectfully</u>.

The highest scores were 99, 96, and 95, made by Ruby, Gil, and Carrie, <u>respectively</u>.

74. *Set, sit.* *Set* is "to place"; *sit* is "to rest one's body on the buttocks."

Set	Present:	<u>Set</u> your briefcase on the counter.
	Past:	She <u>set</u> the briefcase there yesterday.
	Past participle:	She <u>has set</u> the briefcase there previously.
Sit	Present:	Please <u>sit</u> on the bench.
	Past:	He <u>sat</u> there yesterday.
	Past participle:	He <u>has sat</u> there for ten minutes.

75. *Shone, shown.* *Shone* is the past and past-

participle form of *shine*. *Shown* is the past-participle form of *show*.

The sun had <u>shone</u> for two hours.

This article was <u>shown</u> in last week's exhibit.

76. *Sometime, some time.* Use *sometime* to refer to a point of time on the clock or calendar. Use *some time* to refer to an indefinite number of time units.

Come to the office <u>sometime</u> this afternoon.

Try to pay the account <u>sometime</u> next month.

We have not seen him for <u>some time</u>.

<u>Some time</u> has elapsed since we saw him.

77. *Stationary, stationery.* *Stationary* means "without movement" or "remaining in one place." *Stationery* is writing paper.

The machine is to remain <u>stationary</u>.

Order another box of <u>stationery</u>.

78. *Statue, stature, statute.* A *statue* is a molded or sculptured figure. *Stature* means "height" (with respect to the human body), "rank," "reputation," or "status." A *statute* is a law.

A <u>statue</u> of the king stands in the park.

<u>Stature</u> was a primary consideration in the recruitment of basketball players.

Because of Mary's <u>stature</u> in the insurance field, she was invited to testify.

According to the judge, only one <u>statute</u> had been violated.

79. *Steal, steel.* *Steal* means "to commit theft." *Steel* is iron in modified form (contains a certain amount of carbon).

A vagrant tried to <u>steal</u> from the supply room.

The concrete is to be reinforced with <u>steel</u> rods.

80. *Suit, suite.* A *suit* is a set of garments to be worn together; it is also the act or process of bringing a disputed matter to court. A *suite* is a group of connected rooms; it is also a set of furniture.

The players will soon receive warmup <u>suits</u>.

The <u>suit</u> will be heard by Judge Jones.

We leased a <u>suite</u> in the Medical Arts Building.

We ordered a dining-room <u>suite</u>.

81. *Sure, surely.* *Sure* is an adjective; *surely* is an adverb.

I am <u>sure</u>.

We <u>surely</u> appreciate　Not "sure."
that attitude.

82. *That, which.* Use *that* when a relative clause is essential in conveying the basic meaning of the sentence. Use *which* when a relative clause is not essential in conveying the basic meaning of the sentence.

The books <u>that</u> were on the shelf have been sent to the bindery.

The apparent purpose of the sentence is to identify certain books as having been sent to the bindery; therefore, "that were on the shelf" is essential. Because the clause restricts the discussion to certain units, it is called a *restrictive* clause.

Multigrade oil, <u>which</u> is only slightly more expensive than one-grade oil, will serve your purpose better.

The apparent purpose of the sentence is to convey the superiority of multigrade oil; therefore, "which is only slightly more expensive than one-grade oil" is not essential. Because the clause does not restrict the discussion to certain units, it is called a *nonrestrictive* clause. Note that nonrestrictive (*which*) clauses employ punctuation; restrictive (*that*) clauses do not. Note the difference in meaning:

| Return the papers that are marked "passing." | Return "passing" papers only; keep the others. |
| Return the papers, which are marked "passing." | Return all papers; incidentally, they are marked "passing." |

83. *Their, there, they're.* *Their* is the possessive form of "they." *There* refers to "at that place" or "at that point." *They're* is a contraction for "they are."

The president accepted their proposal immediately.

The final copy must be there by May 1.

They're eager to complete the renovation in time for the spring selling season.

84. *To, too, two.* *To* is a preposition or the beginning of an infinitive. *Too* is an adverb meaning "also" or "excessive." *Two* is a number.

Jose organized the campaign to initiate flexible scheduling.

Twenty percent overtime is too demanding.

The entire department shares the two laser printers.

85. *Very, real.* *Very* is an adverb; *real* is an adjective. Do not use *real* to modify verbs, adjectives, or adverbs.

| The report was very effective. | Not "real." |

86. *Wait for, wait on.* *Wait for* means "to await." *Wait on* means "to serve."

We are waiting for the report.

The waitress will wait on us next.

87. *Was, were.* Use *was* with the singular and *were* with the plural. However, use *were* with the singular when the mood is subjunctive (when the sentence speaks of doubt, probability, sorrow, wishfulness, or conditions that do not actually exist).

She was present.

They were present.

| I wish the story were true. | Not "I wish the story was true." |
| If I were old enough, I would apply. | Not "If I was old enough...." |

88. *Weather, whether.* Use *weather* in discussing conditions of the atmosphere. Use *whether* in discussing alternatives.

In January, weather conditions made construction difficult.

I don't know whether to invest in stocks or bonds.

89. *While.* *While*, meaning "at the same time that," should not be used as a synonym for such conjuctions as *but, though, although, and,* and *whereas.*

You do the worksheet while I type a stencil.	Concurrent activities.
One man likes his work, but the other doesn't.	Not "while."
Although we realize your account is overdue, we think you should not pass up this opportunity.	Not "while."

90. *You.* Do not use *you* to mean "I" or "people in general." "You can scarcely interpret these data" is incorrect if it is intended to mean "I can scarcely interpret these data" or "People can scarcely interpret these data." Such misuses of *you* can make a reader think his or her abilities have been underestimated.

Exercise 3

Select the correct word.

1. The contract must be signed by a notary public and (me, myself).
2. Neither the morning shift (nor, or) the afternoon shift will be affected.
3. Which sentence, (a) or (b), reveals that John makes deliveries in no area other than the south side?
   a. John makes deliveries on the south side only.
   b. Only John makes deliveries on the south side.
4. One (party, person) spoke under conditions of anonymity.
5. The incident occurred three times in the (past, passed) month.
6. This employee is entitled to examine her (personal, personnel) folder.
7. For our purposes, this machine is very (practical, practicable).
8. The system's (principal, principle) advantage is monetary.
9. The contract is acceptable (provided, providing) these changes are made.
10. Will you please be (quite, quiet)!
11. The college plans to (raise, rise) entry standards.
12. The reason is (because, that) legislative appropriations have been stalled.
13. The supervisor listened (respectfully, respectively) to the operator's complaints.
14. Before turning on the switch, (set, sit) the dial at 12.
15. The device will be (shone, shown) to the committee on May 13.
16. You will need (some time, sometime) to relax before the demonstration begins.
17. Please have (stationary, stationery) printed for our new address.
18. The jury decided no (statue, statute) had been violated.
19. Construction is to be of (steal, steel) and concrete.
20. Because of the dispute, a (suit, suite) will soon be filed in superior court.
21. The attorney (sure, surely) appreciates the information I provided.
22. We sold only the mowers (that, which) were in the demostration booth.
23. (Their, There, They're) planning to complete (their, there, they're) strategic plan this week.
24. The supervisor expects us (to, too, two) complete (to, too, two) many unnecessary reports.
25. Your demonstration was (very, real) effective.

26. We are waiting (on, for) our accountant to verify the figures.
27. If the story (was, were) true, I would resign.
28. When (weather, whether) conditions improve, construction will begin.
29. (Although, While) my findings are similar, my conclusions are dissimilar.
30. From the back of the large lecture hall, (you, students) could hardly hear the speaker.

NOUNS

Nouns (words that indicate people, places, or things) may be either specific or general, concrete or abstract, proper or not proper.

1. **Specific Versus General.** For most business writing, use *specific* nouns because they let a reader see exactly what is meant. "The dean objected" gives a clearer picture than "An administrator objected"; "A $2\frac{1}{2}$-ton truck is missing" is clearer than "One vehicle is missing."

   When you do not want (or need) to convey a vivid mental picture, you can use general words. "I appreciated your letting me know about the accident" is less vivid (and better) than ". . . about your sprained ankle, your broken ribs, and the smashed-up car."

2. **Concrete Versus Abstract.** *Concrete* nouns are word labels for that which is solid—something that can be seen, touched, and so on. *Abstract* nouns are word labels for that which is not solid—something that cannot be seen, touched, and so on. *Tree* is a concrete noun.

Thought, *confrontation*, and *willingness* are abstract nouns.

   As sentence subjects, concrete nouns are normally preferred because they help to present ideas vividly. "Joe explained the procedure" is more vivid than "Explanations were given by Joe." Because "explanations" are harder to visualize than "Joe," the idea in the second sentence is more difficult to see. However, if a writer does not want an idea to stand out vividly, an abstract noun can be used as the subject of a sentence: "His weakness was well known" is less vivid than "He was known to be weak."

3. **Proper Versus Common.** A proper noun begins with a capital letter; other nouns do not. Capitalize special names of geographic locations: the *Near East*, the *South*, the *Great Plains*.

   Do not capitalize words that simply indicate direction: *southern* Arizona, *west* of Kansas City, an *easterly* direction.

Exercise 4

For each pair of sentences, (l) select the better sentence and (2) give your reason for thinking it is better than the other sentence.

1. **a.** Mr. Edwards called me yesterday.
   b. A man called me yesterday.

2. **a.** George was driving 40 mph in a 25-mph zone.
   b. George was exceeding the speed limit.
3. **a.** We appreciate the explanation of your financial circumstances.
   b. We appreciate the information you gave about your losses from bad debts and your shrinking markets.
4. **a.** An explanation of the procedures was presented by Mary Lewis.
   b. Mary Lewis explained the procedures.
5. **a.** The plant will be constructed about 30 miles South of St. Louis.
   b. The plant will be constructed about 30 miles south of St. Louis.

PRONOUNS

Pronouns (words used in place of nouns) enable us to make our writing smoother than it would be if no pronouns were used. For example, compare these versions of the same sentence:

Without pronouns: Mr. Smith had some difficulty with Mr. Smith's car, so Mr. Smith took Mr. Smith's car to the corner garage for repairs.

With pronouns: Mr. Smith had some difficulty with his car, so he took it to the corner garage for repairs.

Grammatically, selecting pronouns of the appropriate gender is simple. Socially, the problem is more complicated (see Chapter 7). Pronouns do present three grammatical problems: (1) how to get agreement in *number*, (2) how to use the appropriate *case*, and (3) how to use *relative* and *interrogative* pronouns.

1. **Agreement in Number.** (*Number* indicates whether a pronoun involves one or more than one. An *antecedent* is the specific noun for which a pronoun stands.)
   a. When a pronoun represents two or more singular antecedents connected by *and*, the pronoun must be plural:

   The secretary <u>and</u> the treasurer <u>will</u> take <u>their</u> vacations.

   The article "the" before the word "treasurer" indicates that the sentence is about two people.

   The secretary <u>and</u> treasurer will take <u>his</u> vacation.

   Lack of the article "the" before the word "treasurer" indicates that the sentence is about one person who has two sets of responsibilities.

   b. Parenthetical remarks (remarks that can be omitted without destroying the basic meaning of the sentence) that appear between the pronoun and its antecedent have no effect on the form of the pronoun:

   Daniel Brown, <u>not</u> <u>the secretaries</u>, is responsible for <u>his</u> correspondence.

   Because "his" refers to Daniel and not to "secretaries," "his" is used instead of "their."

   c. *Each, everyone, no,* and their variations are singular and take singular pronouns:

   <u>Each</u> student and <u>each</u> teacher will carry his or <u>her</u> own equipment.

   <u>Everyone is</u> responsible for <u>her or his</u> work.

d. When two or more singular antecedents are connected by *or* or *nor,* the pronoun must be singular:

Neither David nor Bill can complete his work.

Ask either Mary or Sue about her in-service training.

e. When a noun represents a *unit* made up of more than *one* person or thing, use a singular pronoun:

The company stands behind its merchandise.

The group wants to retain its goals.

f. Collective nouns take pronouns that agree in number with the intended meaning of the collective noun:

The accounting staff has been asked for its contributions.	Here the staff is thought of as a *unit*; thus, the singular "its" is appropriate.
The accounting staff have been asked for their contributions.	Here the *staff* is thought of as more than one individual; the plural pronoun "their" is appropriate.

2. Pronouns and Case. *Case* tells whether a pronoun is used as the subject of a sentence or as an object in it.

a. Use nominative-case pronouns (*I, he, she, they, we, you, it, who*) as subjects of a sentence or clause:

The manager and he are working on the report.

You and I must work together.

b. Use objective-case pronouns (*me, him, her, them, us, you, it, whom*) after transitive verbs (active verbs requiring an object):

Mrs. Kellegher telephoned him.

Mrs. Kellegher telephoned Mr. Horn and me.

c. Use objective-case pronouns after prepositions:

The information is valuable only to you and me.	You is still *you* regardless of whether it is used in the nominative or objective case.
This secret is between you and me.	
The increase in salary is for the manager and her.	

d. When forms of the linking verb *be* require a pronoun to complete the meaning, the pronoun must be in the nominative case.

It was he who received credit for the sale.

It is she who deserves the award.

Because "he" and "she" in these sentences are equal in meaning with the subject "It," these pronouns are correctly expressed in nominative case. Yet the correct constructions "It was he," "It is she," etc., may to some people sound just as distracting as the incorrect constructions "It was him" and "It is her." Express the ideas in a different way to avoid the error and an expletive beginning.

He was the one who received credit for the sale.

She deserves the award.

e. Use the possessive form of a pronoun before a gerund (a verb used as a noun):

Incorrect: We were delighted at him taking the job.	"Taking the job" is used here as a noun. "His" in this sentence serves the same purpose it serves in "We are delighted at his success."
Correct: We were delighted at his taking the job.	

Incorrect: I would appreciate <u>you</u> helping me.

Correct: I would appreciate <u>your</u> helping me.

Problems with possessive pronouns involve apostrophes, so possessive pronouns are discussed in the punctuation section.

3. **Interrogative and Relative Pronouns.** An *interrogative* pronoun is used to form a question.

<u>Who</u> is there?

<u>Which</u> is correct?

A *relative* pronoun joins a subordinate clause to its antecedent.

The woman <u>whom</u> we choose must have experience.

"Whom we choose" is the subordinate clause; it is less significant than "The woman must have experience." "Whom" is the relative pronoun that joins "woman" and "we choose"; it is "whom" because it is the object of the choosing.

a. Place relative pronouns as near their antecedents as possible.

Incorrect: The <u>members</u> were given receipts <u>who</u> have paid.

Correct: The <u>members who</u> have paid were given receipts.

Incorrect: The agreement will enable you to pay <u>whichever</u> is lower, <u>6 percent or $50</u>.

Correct: The agreement will enable you to pay <u>6 percent or $50, whichever</u> is lower.

b. Use *who* as the subject of the sentence; use *whom* as an object:

<u>Who</u> does the work?

Those <u>who</u> work will be paid.

Although "who" is not itself the subject, "who" refers to the subject.

We are working for <u>whom</u>?

To <u>whom</u> should we send the report?

"We" is the subject; "whom" is the object of "for" in the preceding question and of "to" in this question.

c. To determine which pronoun to use, restate the subordinate clause introduced by *who* or *whom*:

She is the type of manager <u>whom</u> we can promote.

Restating "whom we can promote" gives the proper form of the pronoun: "We can promote *her (whom)*.

She is the type of manager <u>who</u> can be promoted.

Restating "who can be promoted" gives the proper form of the pronoun: "*She (who)* can be promoted."

Note in the first example the pronoun is the object; in the second example, the pronoun is the subject.

d. To determine the correct form of an interrogative pronoun such as *who, whom, which,* or *what,* change the question to a statement:

<u>Whom</u> did you call?

You did call *whom?*

<u>Whom</u> did you select for the postion?

You did select *whom* for the position?

e. Use *who* or *whom* to refer to persons; *which* to refer to things or animals; and *that* to refer to things, animals, or persons.

f. Instead of risking a vague pronoun reference, restate a noun:

Vague: The patrolman captured the suspect even though <u>he</u> was unarmed.

Clear: The patrolman captured the suspect even though <u>the patrolman</u> was unarmed.

Or: Even though the patrolman was unarmed, <u>he</u> captured the suspect.

g. Do not use a pronoun by itself to refer to a phrase, clause, sentence, or paragraph. (*A pronoun should stand for a noun, and that noun should appear in the writing.*)

Incorrect: He expects to take all available accounting courses and obtain a position in a public accounting firm. <u>This</u> appeals to him.

Correct: He expects to take all available accounting courses and obtain a position in a public accounting firm. <u>This plan</u> appeals to him.

Exercise 5

Select the correct word.

1. The president and the chief executive officer (is, are) earning an exorbitant salary.
2. The copy editor, not the keyboarders, (were, was) at fault.
3. In the boys' class, everyone was asked to share (his, their) opinion.
4. Of all the employees who took the test, only one had brought (her, their) calculator.
5. Melissa and Helen were recognized for (her, their) contribution.
6. Neither Melissa nor Helen was recognized for (her, their) contribution.
7. Our company is revising (their, its) statement of purpose.
8. The committee presented (its, their) recommendation to the president yesterday.
9. Elaine asked me to take a picture of her husband and (her, she).
10. The instructor asked Dan and (I, me) to leave the room.
11. Lucille requested that proceeds be divided equally between Calvin and (her, she).
12. These supplies were intended for James and (me, I).
13. I would appreciate (you, your) returning the form by June 1.
14. The speaker did not notice (me, my) leaving early.
15. We were surprised about (him, his) leaving so soon.
16. To (who, whom) should we appeal?
17. (Who, Whom) is calling?
18. She is an employee in (who, whom) we have great confidence.
19. He is the one (who, whom) arrived twenty minutes late.
20. (Who, Whom) will take her vacation first?
21. (Whom, Who) should we invite?
22. (Whom, Who) was invited last year?
23. We are betting on the horse (that, who) won last week's race.
24. Mr. Smith forgot to retain his expense vouchers; (this, this oversight) caused a delay in reimbursement.
25. Interest rates have been steadily declining. (This, This decline) caused us to reconsider the venture.

VERBS

Verbs present problems in mood, number, person, tense, and voice.

1. **Mood.** *Mood* reveals the writer's attitude toward the idea expressed, indicating whether the idea is to be thought of as a fact; a command; or a supposition, desire, or possibility.

   The *indicative* mood makes a statement of fact or asks a question:

   The merchandise <u>arrived</u> today.

   When <u>is</u> the delivery date?

   The *imperative* mood states a request or a command:

   <u>Send</u> us your check today.

   <u>Wait</u> until the end of the month.

   The *subjunctive* mood talks of conditions that do not necessarily exist. It suggests doubt, supposition, probability, wishfulness, or sorrow.
   a. In the subjunctive mood, use *were* for the present tense of *to be:*

Incorrect:	I wish the story <u>was</u> true.
Correct:	I wish the story <u>were</u> true.
Incorrect:	If I <u>was</u> he, I would try again.
Correct:	If I <u>were</u> he, I would try again.

   b. Consider the subjunctive mood for communicating negative ideas in positive language:

I wish I <u>were</u>.	In response to someone who asks if you are going to the company picnic, the sentence sounds better than "No, I am not."
We <u>would</u> make a refund if the merchandise had been used in accordance with instructions.	The sentence conveys "Because the merchandise has *not* been used in accordance with instructions, we are *not* making a refund" but avoids negative words.

2. **Number.** *Number* is used to describe how many people, things, items, and so on are being discussed.
   a. Do not switch unnecessarily from singular to plural:

Incorrect:	We would appreciate your returning the contract to <u>me</u>. I am glad you are joining Burdon's.	
Correct:	I would appreciate your returning the contract to me. I am glad you are joining Burdon's.	Both "I" and "we" are frequently overused, but changing from one to the other just for variety may cause confusion about whether one is speaking for oneself only or for oneself and others.

   b. If the subject is singular, use a verb form that fits the singular; if the subject is plural, use a verb that fits the plural:

Incorrect:	Good material <u>and</u> fast delivery <u>is</u> essential.
Correct:	Good material <u>and</u> fast delivery <u>are</u> essential.
Incorrect:	The <u>gentleman</u> <u>and</u> his son <u>is</u> in charge of the business.
Correct:	He <u>and</u> his son <u>are</u> in charge of the business.

   c. Remember that parenthetical words coming between the subject and the verb have no effect on the verb used:

Incorrect:	<u>You</u>, not the carrier, <u>is</u> responsible for the damage.
Correct:	<u>You</u>, not the carrier, <u>are</u> responsible for the damage.

Incorrect: The manager, as well as her three support staff, were inclined to agree with the statement.

Correct: The manager, as well as her three support staff, was inclined to agree with the statement.

d. When *or* or *nor* comes between two subjects, determine the verb form by inspecting the number of the noun closer to the verb:

Incorrect: Only one or two questions is necessary.

Correct: Only one or two questions are necessary.

Incorrect: Several paint brushes or one paint roller are necessary.

Correct: Several paint brushes or one paint roller is necessary.

e. Determine the verb by the subject, not by modifiers that come between the verb and the subject:

Incorrect: The attitude of these people are receptive.

"Attitude" is the subject; "of these people" is simply a phrase coming between the subject and the verb.

Correct: The attitude of these people is receptive.

Incorrect: One of the clerks were dismissed.

"One" is the subject; "of the clerks" is simply a phrase coming between the subject and the verb.

Correct: One of the clerks was dismissed.

f. Use singular verbs with plural nouns that have a singular meaning:

The news is good.

Economics is a required course.

Mathematics is to be reviewed.

g. Use a singular verb with plural subjects that are thought of as singular units:

Twenty dollars is too much.

Ten minutes is sufficient time.

h. Even if titles of articles, firm names, and slogans are plural, use a singular verb:

"Understanding Computers" is an interesting article.

Stein, Jones, and Baker is the oldest firm in the city.

In each sentence, the subject is singular: one article, one firm, and one slogan.

"Free lunches for all" is our campaign slogan.

3. Person. *Person* is used to describe the quality of the verb that indicates whether the subject is (1) speaking, (2) being spoken to, or (3) being spoken about:

First person:	I am, we are.	Writer or speaker
Second person:	You are.	Receiver of message
Third person:	He is, she is, they are.	Person being discussed

a. Choose verbs that agree in *person* with their subjects:

Incorrect: She don't attend class regularly.

Correct: She doesn't attend class regularly.

Correct: They don't attend class regularly.

b. For vivid, emphatic writing, choose second person instead of third person:

Less vivid: Next, the operator takes the film in his right hand, swings the gate open with his left, and . . . .

More vivid: Next, you take the film in your right hand, swing the gate open with your left, and . . . .

c. Try to avoid second person in formal reports.

Poor: You would have difficulty interpreting such data.

Improved: Such data would be difficult to interpret.

To the reader, "you" could have three different meanings: the one who asked for the report, all readers of the report, or the writer of the report.

d. Try to avoid third person in referring to yourself. In business letters, *I* is preferable to *the writer* or *the undersigned*. However, *I* should be used sparingly because its overuse usually places too much emphasis on the one who writes. In formal business reports, *I* is avoided; it has the effect of emphasizing the writer and thus taking emphasis away from the subject matter.

4. Tense. *Tense* indicates time. Tenses are both simple and compound.
  a. Simple tenses:

Present:	I see you.	Tells what is happening now.
Past:	I saw you.	Tells what has already happened.
Future:	I will see you.	Tell what is yet to happen.

  b. Compound tenses:

Present perfect:	I have seen you.	Tells of past action that extends to the present.
Past perfect:	I had seen you.	Tells of past action that was finished before another past action.
Future perfect:	I will have seen you.	Tells of action that will be finished before a future time.

  c. When something *was* and *still is* true, write about it in present tense:

Incorrect: The speaker reminded us that Rhode Island was smaller than Wisconsin.

Correct: The speaker reminded us that Rhode Island is smaller than Wisconsin.

d. Avoid unnecessary shifts in tense:

Incorrect: The deliveryman brings my package but left without asking me to sign for it.

Correct: The deliveryman brought my package but left without asking me to sign for it.

Verbs that appear in the same sentence are not required to be in the same tense.

The contract that was prepared yesterday will be signed tomorrow.

5. Voice. *Voice* is the term used to indicate whether a subject *acts* or whether it *is acted upon*. If the subject of a sentence acts, the verb used to describe that action is called an *active verb:*

The typist made an error.

The woman asked for an adjustment.

If the subject of the sentence is acted upon, the verb used to describe that action is called a *passive verb.*

An error was made by the typist.

An adjustment was asked for by the woman.

For most business writing, active voice is preferred. But sometimes passive voice is more appropriate. Use passive voice in the following situations:
  a. To emphasize the receiver of action more than the doer:

Say: Dinner is now being served.

Not: The waiters are now serving dinner.

b. To avoid an accusing tone:

Say: Three errors <u>have been made</u> on this page.

Not: You <u>made</u> three errors on this page.

c. To avoid revealing names:

Say: The procedure <u>has been criticized</u>.

Not: President Huckaby <u>has criticized</u> this procedure.

Exercise 6

Select the correct word.

1. Mrs. Walls and her son (was, were) invited.
2. If he (was, were) over 18, he would have been hired.
3. Only one of the graphs (was, were) usable.
4. The typesetters, not the editor, (was, were) responsible for these errors.
5. The typesetter, not the editors, (was, were) responsible for these errors.
6. Neither the players nor their coach (was, were) invited.
7. Neither the coach nor the players (was, were) invited.
8. Both John and Steven (was, were) promoted.
9. Only one of the statements (was, were) audible.
10. The news from the rescue mission (is, are) encouraging.
11. *Ten Steps to Greatness* (has, have) been placed in the company library.
12. Two of the booklets (has, have) been edited.
13. Kelley & Smith (was, were) the only firm to submit a bid.
14. Apparently, "Do unto Others" (is, are) John's motto.
15. About one child in ten (inherit, inherits) left-handedness.
16. A child reminded me that the earth (rotates, rotated) on its axis.
17. Only one of the issues (has, have) been discussed.
18. Tim (don't, doesn't) ask for favors.
19. The president studied the page for a minute and (starts, started) asking questions.
20. Sally wrote rapidly and then (revises, revised).

Exercise 7

Change each sentence from passive to active voice.

1. The booklet was edited by Susan Woodward.
2. The figures have been checked by our accountant.
3. Ms. Jackson was recommended for promotion by the supervisor.

4. The applications are being screened. (In revising, assume that a committee is doing the screening.)
5. Your request for a leave has been approved. (In revising, assume the manager did the approving.)

Exercise 8

In revising each sentence, (a) use passive voice and (b) conceal the doer.

1. Wesley made three computational mistakes on this page.
2. Meredith reported Tom's absence to the personnel office.
3. The committee has denied Willard's application for promotion.
4. You should have proofread the report more carefully.
5. Students have completed their reports.

ADJECTIVES AND ADVERBS

Adjectives modify nouns or pronouns. *Adverbs* modify verbs, adjectives, or other adverbs. Although most adverbs end in *ly*, some commonly used adverbs do not end in *ly*: *there, then, after, now, hence,* and *very*. Most words that end in *ly* are adverbs; but common exceptions are *neighborly, timely, friendly, gentlemanly*. Some words are both adjective and adverb: *fast, late,* and *well*.

1. **Adjectives**
   a. Use an adjective to modify a noun or pronoun:

   She wrote a <u>long</u> letter.

   I prefer the <u>little</u> one.

   b. Use an adjective after a linking verb when the modifer refers to the subject instead of to the verb. (A linking verb connects a subject to the rest of the sentence. "He *is* old." "She *seems* sincere.")

The salesperson seemed <u>enthusiastic</u>.

The president looked <u>suspicious</u>.

The adjective "enthusiastic" refers to "salesperson," not to "seemed."

The adjective "suspicious" refers to "president," not to "looked."

c. Use comparatives and superlatives carefully:

Incorrect: She is the <u>fastest</u> of the two workers.

Correct: She is the <u>faster</u> of the two workers.

Correct: She is the <u>fastest</u> of the three workers.

Incorrect: He is the <u>best</u> of the two operators.

Correct: He is the <u>better</u> of the two operators.

Correct: He is the <u>best</u> of the three operators.

d. Exclude a person or thing from a group with which that person or thing is being compared.

Incorrect: **He is older than anyone in his department.**

Correct: **He is older than anyone else in his department.**

As a member of his department, he cannot be older than himself.

Correct: **He is older than any other person in his department.**

"The XD600 is newer than any machine in our department" is illogical if the XD600 is in "our" department. It can't be newer than itself. It can be newer than any *other* machine in our department or newer than any machine in some *other* department.

The salesperson looked enthusiastically at the prospect.

The adverb "enthusiastically" refers to "looked," not to "salesperson."

The president looked suspiciously at the cash register.

The adverb "suspiciously" refers to "looked," not to the "president."

b. Use an adverb to modify an adjective:

The committee was really active.

The adverb "really" describes the adjective "active." Because it is an adjective, "real" could not be used to modify "active" or any other adjective.

2. Adverbs

a. Use an adverb to modify a verb:

c. Use an adverb to modify another adverb:

Worker A progressed relatively faster than did worker B.

The adverb "relatively" modifies the adverb "faster."

Exercise 9

Select the correct word.

1. Our supply is being replenished (frequent, frequently).
2. Chester works (enthusiastic, enthusiastically) and never asks for time off.
3. Chester looked (angry, angrily).
4. Chester looked (eager, eagerly) for help.
5. Help arrived (real, very) quickly.
6. The lecture seemed (really, real) long.
7. Of the two people who were interviewed, Jane made the (better, best) impression.
8. Hazel is the (youngest, younger) of the three daughters.
9. The waitress moved (quick, quickly) from table to table.
10. Of the two keyboarders, John was the (fastest, faster).
11. John is faster than (any, any other) keyboarder in his department.
12. Although John is in the accounting department, he is faster than (any, any other) keyboarder in the presentation department.

SENTENCE STRUCTURE

1. Be sure to state the subject of each sentence (unless the sentence is a command):

   Incorrect: <u>Received</u> the supervisor's request today.

   Correct: <u>I received</u> the supervisor's request today.

   In such imperative sentences as "Return the forms to me," the subject (*you*) is understood and therefore appropriately omitted.

2. Rely mainly on sentences that follow the normal subject-verb-complement sequence:

   <u>We</u> <u>withdrew</u> for three <u>reasons</u>.
   (subject) (verb)   (complement)

   People are accustomed to sentences stated in this sequence. Sentences that expose the verb *before* revealing the subject have three disadvantages: they slow down the reading, they present less vivid pictures, and they employ more words than would be required if the normal sequence were followed:

   Original: <u>There</u> are <u>two reasons</u> for our withdrawal.

   Better: <u>Two reasons</u> for our withdrawal are. . . .
   <u>We</u> withdrew for two reasons.

   Original: <u>It</u> is important that we withdraw.

   Better: <u>Our withdrawal</u> is important.
   <u>We</u> must withdraw.

   There and *it* are called *expletives*—filler words that have no real meaning in the sentence.

3. Do not put unrelated ideas in the same sentence:

   The <u>coffee break</u> is at ten o'clock, and the company plans to purchase additional <u>parking spaces</u>.

   These ideas have little relationship. Therefore, they should certainly not be introduced in the same sentence; they should be discussed in different paragraphs or in different messages.

4. Put pronouns, adverbs, phrases, and clauses near the words they modify:

   Incorrect: I saw his <u>performance</u> at the Christmas party, <u>which</u> I certainly enjoyed watching.

   Correct: I saw his <u>performance, which</u> I certainly enjoyed watching, at the Christmas party.

   Correct: I certainly enjoyed watching his performance at the Christmas party.

   Incorrect: He <u>only</u> works in the toy department for $3.25 an hour.

   Correct: He works in the toy department for <u>only $3.25</u> an hour.

   Incorrect: The <u>secretary</u> stood beside the fax machine <u>in a white dress.</u>

   Correct: The <u>secretary in a white dress</u> stood beside the fax machine.

   Incorrect: He put a new type of <u>oil</u> on his hair, <u>which</u> he had just purchased at the drugstore.

   Correct: He put a new type of <u>oil, which</u> he had just purchased at the drugstore, on his hair.

5. Do not separate subject and predicate unnecessarily:

   Incorrect: <u>He</u>, hoping to receive a bonus, <u>worked</u> rapidly.

   Correct: Hoping to receive a bonus, <u>he worked</u> rapidly.

6. Attach an introductory phrase to the subject of an independent clause. Otherwise, the phrase dangles. Correct the dangling phrase in one of two ways: Change the subject of the independent clause, or make the phrase into a subordinate clause by assigning it a subject:

Incorrect: **When** a little boy, **my mother** took me through a milk-processing plant.

Implies that the mother was once a little boy.

Correct: **When I was a little boy**, my mother took me through a milk-processing plant.

Correct: **When** a little boy, **I** was taken through a milk-processing plant by my mother.

Incorrect: **Working** at full speed every morning, **fatigue** overtakes me in the afternoon.

Implies that "fatigue" was working at full speed.

Correct: **Working** at full speed every morning, **I** become tired in the afternoon.

Correct: **Because I work** at full speed every morning, **fatigue** overtakes me in the afternoon.

Incorrect: **After working** four days on the financial statements, **they** were finally completed.

Implies that "financial statements" were "working four days."

Correct: **After working** four days on the financial statements, the **accountants** finally completed the task.

Correct: **After the accountants** had worked four days, the financial statements **were** finally **completed**.

Incorrect: **To function** properly, **you** must oil the machine every hour.

Implies that if "you" are "to function properly," the machine must be oiled hourly.

Correct: **If the machine** is to function properly, **you** must oil it every hour.

Correct: **To function** properly, the **machine must** be oiled every hour.

7. Express related ideas in similar grammatical form (use parallel construction):

Incorrect: The machine operator made three resolutions: (1) to be <u>punctual</u>, (2) <u>following</u> instructions carefully, and <u>third, the reduction</u> of waste.

Correct: The machine operator made three resolutions: (1) to be <u>punctual</u>, (2) to <u>follow</u> instructions carefully, and (3) to <u>reduce</u> waste.

Incorrect: The personnel manager is concerned with <u>the selection</u> of the right worker, <u>providing</u> appropriate orientation, and <u>the worker's</u> progress.

Correct: The personnel manager is concerned with <u>selecting</u> the right worker, <u>providing</u> appropriate orientation, and <u>checking</u> the worker's progress.

8. Do not end a sentence with a needless preposition:

Incorrect: Where is the plant to be located <u>at</u>?

Correct: Where is the plant to be located?

Incorrect: The worker did not tell us where he was going <u>to</u>.

Correct: The worker did not tell us where he was going.

9. End a sentence with a preposition if for some reason the preposition needs emphasis:

I am not concerned with what he is paying <u>for</u>.
I am concerned with what he is paying <u>with</u>.

The prospect has everything—a goal to work <u>toward</u>, a house to live <u>in</u>, and an income to live <u>on</u>.

10. Avoid clumsy split infinitives. (Two words are required to express an infinitive: *to* plus a *verb*. The two words belong together. An infinitive is split when another word is placed between the two.)

Incorrect: **The superintendent used <u>to</u> occasionally <u>visit</u> the offices.**

Correct: **The superintendent used <u>to visit</u> the offices occasionally.**

Incorrect: **I want <u>to</u> briefly <u>summarize</u> the report.**

Correct: **I want <u>to summarize</u> the report briefly.**

Exercise 10

For each sentence, write an answer to the question "What weakness in structure does the sentence illustrate?" Then write an improved version of the sentence.

1. Have reconsidered your proposal.
2. It is essential that you sign and return the enclosed form.
3. There is no need to refurnish this room.
4. When a small girl, my brother taught me to play basketball.
5. Mary only works on Sunday; Ruth works Monday through Friday.
6. I am submitting an article to *Time*, which I wrote last summer.
7. Almost all of my time is spent in planning, organizing, and the various aspects of control.
8. While driving 30 miles an hour, my dog jumped out the window.
9. Where is the personnel department at?
10. We want to quickly bring the project to a conclusion.

ABBREVIATIONS

As a general rule, avoid abbreviations because they are visually distracting to the reader, are difficult to understand, and may send the mistaken message that you are too hurried to do a complete job. Some personnel directors have reported that the use of unnecessary abbreviations is a criterion for eliminating applicants from consideration for a job. Style manuals generally agree on the following abbreviation rules:

1. Abbreviate
   a. Titles that come before proper names: Dr., Mr., Mrs., Ms.

   b. Titles that come after proper names: D.D.S., Esq., Jr., M.D., Ph.D., Sr.

   c. Commonly known government agencies: FDIC, FCC, FHA, TVA.

d. Commonly known organizations, businesses, or institutions: AAUP, NEA, UN, GE, IBM, MIT, UCLA.

e. Commonly used business expressions: f.o.b., C.O.D., a.m., p.m. (Note: Use a.m. and p.m. only when a specific time is mentioned. Small letters—a.m. and p.m.—are preferred.)

Incorrect: Come to the office this a.m.

Correct: Come to the office at 10:15 a.m.

Correct: Come to the office this morning.

f. The names of businesses when their own letterheads contain abbreviations: Smith & Company; Jones and Smith, Inc.; The John C. Andrews Co.

g. The word *number* when it is used with a figure to designate something:

Go to room No. 7.

May we have a carton of No. 10 envelopes.

Refer to Policy No. 384862.

h. The names of states when they appear as parts of envelope addresses or inside addresses. The U.S. Postal Services prefers use of two-letter abbreviations for states, districts, and territories (as shown in Appendix A, Figure A-12).

2. Do not abbreviate

a. The names of cities, states (except in envelope and inside addresses), months, and days of the week.

b. The words *avenue, boulevard, drive,* and *street.*

c. Points on the compass:

Tom has been in the West for seven years.

Go east one block and turn south.

d. The word *Christmas.*

CAPITAL LETTERS

Style manuals are in general agreement on the rules of capitalization.

1. Capitalize
a. Names of people, animals, places, geographic areas, days of the week, months of the year, holidays, deities, publications, and other special names.

b. The first word of a direct quotation:

The sales representative said, "We leave tomorrow."

c. The first word of a title (book, magazine, article, theme) and all other words of a title or heading except conjunctions (*and, for, but*),

articles (*a, an, the*), and short prepositions (*in, on, of, to*):

"The Story of My Life"	Article
The Prince and the Pauper	Book
"Cost of the Land"	Heading in a report

d. The first word following a colon when a formal statement or question follows:

Here is an important rule for report writers: Plan your work and work your plan.

Each sales representative should ask himself or herself this question: Do I really look like a representative of my firm?

e. Pronouns that refer to the deity:

The clergyman asked His guidance.

f. *Father, mother, brother, sister* when used as names:

Make the suggestion to my father.
Make the suggestion to Father.

g. Only the first and last words in salutations and only the first word in complimentary closes:

My dear Madam:
Sincerely yours,

h. The names of documents and historical events:

Missouri Constitution
Battle of Bunker Hill

i. Titles that come before a name:

Editor Smith
President King

j. A one-word sentence:

Yes!
Certainly.

k. *No.* when used with a figure to designate something:

Policy No. 8746826

2. Do not capitalize
   a. The first word of an indirect quotation:

He said that the report must be submitted by the end of the week.

b. Such words as *father, mother, uncle,* or *cousin* when they are preceded by a possessive pronoun:

He has taken the position formerly held by his father.
Please mail the check to my mother.

c. The names of school courses that are not proper nouns:

The student is taking French, mathematics, science, and English.

d. The names of seasons (except when they are personified):

We make most of our profits during the winter.

Note: When a season is used to designate a particular school term or semester, the season is ordinarily capitalized:

Summer Session 1993
Spring Semester 1993

e. The first word in the last part of an interrupted quotation:

"We will proceed," he said, "with the utmost caution."

f. The first word of a parenthetical sentence:

The president said (you will probably agree) that production could be increased by 10 percent.

Exercise 11

Copy each of the following sentences, making essential changes in abbreviation and capitalization.

1. The summer season is much slower than the rest of the year.
2. When I was interviewed on monday, the first question was "why do you want to work for us?"
3. Was *The Power of Ethical Management* advertised in the Sept. 7 issue of *Time*?
4. We paid by check no. 627 on December 10.
5. The P.T.A. meeting will be moderated by Carl Smith, jr.
6. Mister Raferty will address the assembly this A.M.
7. The NCAA will meet in Boston in 1993 and in N.Y. in 1994.
8. Mister and Mistress Smith plan to spend Xmas. in MO.
9. As soon as he arrived, father asked, "when do we eat?"
10. A retirement ceremony is being planned for president Schwada.

NUMBERS

Businesspeople use quantiative data often, so numbers appear frequently in business writing. *Accuracy* is exceedingly important. The most frequent problem in expressing numbers is whether to write them as figures or spell them out as words.

1. Use figures
   a. In most business writing because (1) figures should get deserved emphasis, (2) figures are easy for readers to locate if they need to reread for critical points, and (3) figures can be keyed faster and in less space than spelled-out words.

      Regardless of whether a number has one digit or many, use figures to express dates, sums of money, mixed numbers and decimals, distance, dimension, cubic capacity, percentage, weights, temperatures, and chapter and page numbers:

   May 10, 19—

   $9 million (or $9,000,000)

   25% (or 25 percent)

   165 pounds

   Chapter 3, page 29

   With the preceding exceptions, numbers one through ten are normally spelled out if no larger number appears in the same sentence:

   Only <u>three</u> people were present.

   We need <u>five</u> machines.

   Send <u>5</u> officers and <u>37</u> men.

   b. With ordinals (*th, st, rd, nd*) only when the number precedes the month:

   The meeting is to be held on <u>May 10</u>.

   The meeting is to be held on the <u>10th of May</u>.

   c. With ciphers but without decimals when presenting even-dollar figures, unless the

NUMBERS

figure appears in a sentence with another figure that includes dollars and cents:

He paid $30 for the cabinet.

He paid $31.75 for the table and $30.00 for the cabinet.

d. Without a colon when expressing times of day that include hours but not minutes, unless the time appears in a sentence with another time that includes minutes:

The reception began at 7 p.m.

The award program began at 6:30 p.m. with a reception at 7:00 p.m.

2. Spell out
a. Numbers if they are used as the first word of a sentence:

Thirty-two people attended.

b. Numbers that represent time when *o'clock* is used:

Please be there at ten o'clock.

Meet me at 10:15 p.m.

c. Names of streets up to and including twelve:

Fifth Street, Seventh Avenue

d. One of two adjacent numbers, preferably the smaller of the two:

The package required four 17-cent stamps.

We shipped nine 180-horsepower engines today.

Note also that a hyphen joins the second number with the word that follows it, thus forming a compound adjective that describes the noun "stamps."

e. Numbers that are indefinite or approximate:

Several hundred boxes were shipped.

The incumbent won by about ten thousand votes.

f. Numbers in legal documents, following them with figures enclosed in parentheses:

For the sum of four hundred dollars ($400), . . .

For the sum of four hundred (400) dollars, . . .

. . . including forty (40) acres, more or less.

Exercise 12

Assume the following sentences appear in a letter or a report. If a number is presented in appropriate form, write "correct." If a number is presented in inappropriate form, change the number to correct form as you copy the sentence.

1. The question was answered by sixty-one percent of the respondents.
2. The meeting will be at 9:00 a.m. on February 21st.
3. Three figures appeared on the expense account: $21.95, $30, and $35.14.

4. Go to the service station at 5th Street and Hardy Drive.
5. We ordered five sixteen-ounce hammers.
6. This MIS manager ordered 10 40-mb hard drives.
7. 21 members voted in favor of the motion.
8. The cost will be approximately $1,000,000.00.
9. Mix two quarts of white with 13 quarts of brown.
10. Examine the diagram on page seven.

PUNCTUATION

Punctuation is basically the same in business writing as in other writing. Clarity is a primary consideration. Convention is another.

1. Use an apostrophe
   a. To form the possessive singular. Add an apostrophe and an *s*:

      man, man's
      firm, firm's
      worker, worker's

   b. To form the possessive plural. Add an apostrophe after the *s*:

      drivers, drivers'
      players, players'
      dealers, dealers'

   c. To form the possessive of a proper noun in which the last letter is not an *s*. Add an apostrophe and an *s*:

      Mr. Wilson's boss
      Mr. Bostrom's interview

   d. To form the possessive singular when the last letter in a proper noun is an *s*. Determine the placement of the apostrophe by the number of syllables in the noun.

When the singular form of a one-syllable noun ends in *s*, form the possessive by adding '*s*:

Jones, Jones's
Ross, Ross's

When the singular form contains more than one syllable and ends in *s* or in an *s* sound, form the possessive by adding an apostrophe only:

Ms. Richards, Ms. Richards'
Mr. Gonzalez, Mr. Gonzalez'

   e. In expressions that indicate ownership. The apostrophe shows omission of a preposition:

      Last year's reports. . . .   Reports of last year. . . .

   f. When the noun presents time or distance in a possessive manner.

      an hour's visit
      three weeks' vacation
      a mile's journey

   g. When a noun precedes a gerund:

Ms. <u>Bowen's</u> receiving the promotion caused . . . .

Mr. <u>Green's</u> taking the gavel indicated . . . .

h. To show whether ownership is joint or separate:

To indicate joint ownership, add an *'s* to the last name only.

<u>Olsen</u> and <u>Howard's</u> accounting firm.

To indicate separate ownership, add an *'s* to each name.

<u>Olsen's</u> and <u>Howard's</u> accounting firms.

2. Do not use an apostrophe

a. In the titles of some organizations. Use the name as the organization uses its name:

National Business <u>Teachers</u> Association

National Sales <u>Executives</u> Association

b. To form the possessive of a pronoun (most pronouns become possessive through a change in spelling; therefore, an apostrophe is not used):

<u>Yours</u>	Not *your's*
<u>Ours</u>	Not *our's*

(*Punctuation* continues after Exercise 13.)

Exercise 13

Which, (a) or (b), uses the apostrophe correctly?

1. **a.** Three week's wages were paid.
   b. Three weeks' wages were paid.
2. **a.** Two service stations were cited: West's and Johnson's.
   b. Two service stations were cited: West and Johnson's.
3. **a.** The responsibility is our's.
   b. The responsibility is ours.
4. **a.** I will appreciate Mary's calling before the 15th.
   b. I will appreciate Mary calling before the 15th.
5. **a.** This company's mission-and-scope statement is excellent.
   b. This companys' mission-and-scope statement is excellent.
6. **a.** October's market decline was severe.
   b. Octobers' market decline was severe.
7. **a.** Mr. Morris's letter of acceptance had been received.
   b. Mr. Morris' letter of acceptance had been received.
8. **a.** Mr. Ross' report was late.
   b. Mr. Ross's report was late.
9. **a.** Ms. Ward's status was uncertain.
   b. Ms. Wards' status was uncertain.
10. **a.** These workers' concerns are warranted.
    b. These worker's concerns are warranted.

PUNCTUATION (continued)

3. Use brackets

   a. To enclose words that are inserted between words or sentences of quoted material:

     "How long will the delay be? No longer than this: [At this point, the speaker tapped the podium three times.] That means no delay at all."

   b. As required in certain mathematical formulas.

   c. To enclose parenthetical material that contains parentheses:

     The motion passed. [The vote (17 for and 4 against) was not taken until midnight.]

   d. To explain, clarify, or correct words of the writer you quote:

     "To [accounting] professionals, the ability to express themselves well is more than a hallmark of educated persons," was quoted from a study conducted by the American Institute of Certified Public Accountants.

4. Use a colon

   a. To suggest that a list will follow a statement that appears in complete-sentence form:

     For three reasons, we have decided to move to a new location: (1) We need an expanded market. (2) We need an inexpensive source of raw materials. (3) We need a ready source of labor.

     Three factors influenced our decision: an expanded market, an inexpensive source of raw materials, and a ready source of labor.

     We need to (1) expand our market, (2) locate an inexpensive source of materials, and (3) find a ready source of labor.

(A colon does not follow *to* because the words preceding the list do not constitute what could be a complete sentence.)

   b. When the verb that would complete a sentence is sufficiently understood and thus omitted:

     The proposal was rejected. The reasons: (1) no money, (2) no technicians, and (3) no work space.

     Verbs such as *are presented, are given,* and *are stated* could be used after "reasons," but they are not essential. Because the thought is complete without them, a colon is used.

   c. To stress an appositive (a noun that renames the preceding noun) at the end of a sentence:

     His heart was set on one thing: promotion.

     Our progress is due to the efforts of one person: Mr. Keating.

   d. After the salutation of a letter (when mixed punctuation is used):

     Dear Dr. Gorga:

     Dear Ms. Campbell:

   e. After a word or phrase followed by additional material in ads or signs:

     No Parking: Reserved for executives

     For Rent: Two-bedroom apartment

   f. Between hours and minutes to express time in figures:

     5:45 p.m.

     11:05 a.m.

(*Punctuation* continues after Exercise 14.)

Exercise 14

Read the following sentences. If a sentence is correct, write "correct." If a sentence is incorrect, rewrite it, correcting the error.

1. The program has one shortcoming: flexibility.
2. Our meetings are scheduled for: Monday, Tuesday, and Friday.
3. We liked this car because of its: price, durability, and appearance.
4. We liked three features of Ms. Cole's resume: her experience, her education, and her attitude.
5. We are enthusiastic about the plan because: (1) it is least expensive, (2) its legality is unquestioned, and (3) it can be implemented quickly.

PUNCTUATION (continued)

5. Use a comma

   a. Between coordinate clauses joined by *and, but, for,* and other coordinate conjunctions:

   > He wanted to pay his bills on time, but he did not have the money.

   b. After participial phrases or dependent clauses:

   > Believing that her earnings would continue to increase, she sought to borrow more money.

   Sentences that begin with prepositions or such words as *if, as,* and *when* almost always need a comma.

   > Under the circumstances, we think you are justified.

   > To get the full benefit of our insurance plan, just fill out and return the enclosed card.

   > Whatever you do, please explain it to your supervisor.

   > As you may know, Mr. Smith has been ill for three weeks.

   > If you can meet us at the plane, please plan to be there by six o'clock.

   > When I left the building, doors were being closed.

   c. To separate words in a series:

   > You have a choice of gray, green, purple, and white.

   Without the comma after "purple," no one can tell for sure whether four choices are available, the last of which is "white," or whether three choices are available, the last of which is "purple and white."

   > You have a choice of purple and white, gray, and green.

   Choice is restricted to three, the first of which is "purple and white."

   d. Between coordinate adjectives (two separate adjectives that modify the same noun):

   > New employees are given a long, difficult examination.

   "Long" and "difficult" both modify "examination."

   > We want quick, factual news.

   "Quick" and "factual" separately modify "news" and are separated by a comma.

The supervisor is an excellent public speaker.

> Do not place a comma between two adjectives when the second adjective may be considered as part of the noun that follows. Technically, "excellent" and "public" are both adjectives. In this sentence, however, "excellent" modifies the noun "public speaker."

e. To separate a nonrestrictive clause (a clause that is not essential to the basic meaning of the sentence) from the rest of the sentence:

Mr. MacMurray, who is head of the collection department, is leaving for a vacation.

> The parenthetical remark is not essential to the meaning of the sentence.

The man who is head of the collection department is leaving for a vacation.

> Commas should not be used because "who is head of the collection department" is essential to the meaning of the sentence.

f. To separate parenthetical expressions from the rest of the sentence:

Ms. Watson, speaking in behalf of the entire department, accepted the proposal.

g. Before and after the year in month-day-year format:

On July 2, 1977, Mr. Kababik made the final payment.

h. Before and after the name of a state when the name of a city precedes:

I saw him in Kansas City, Missouri, on the 12th of October.

i. After a direct address:

John, I believe you have earned a vacation.

j. After the words *No* and *Yes* when they introduce a statement:

Yes, you can count on me.

No, I will have to decline.

k. To set off appositives:

The group heard a speech from Mr. Matthew Welch, a recruit.

Mr. Herbert Jackson, former president of the Jackson Institute, spoke to the group.

A comma before and after an appositive is used for neutral emphasis; a dash (instead of a comma) is used for heavy emphasis.

l. Between contrasted elements:

We need more money, not less.

The job requires experience, not formal education.

m. To show the omission of words that are understood:

Ms. Reno scored 96 percent on the employment examination; Mr. Mehrmann, 84 percent.

n. Before a question that solicits a confirmatory answer:

It's a reasonable price, isn't it?

Our bills have been paid, haven't they?

o. Between the printed name and the title on the same line beneath a signature:

Roy Murr, President

No comma is used if the title is on a separate line:

Cathryn W. Edwards
President of Academic Affairs

p. After an adverbial conjunction:

The check was for the right amount; however, it was not signed.

q. Do not place a comma between compound predicates:

We just ate and ran.

The insurance agent inspected the car and recommended total reimbursement.

The group discussed the proposal and referred it to the finance committee.

(*Punctuation* continues after Exercise 15.)

Exercise 15

Insert needed commas; delete unneeded commas. Some sentences may need more than one comma; others, none.

1. The man who came in late, has not been interviewed, but all other applicants have been interviewed.
2. Margie Harrison a new member of the board, remained silent.
3. Ammonium sulfate which is available at almost all home-supply stores is ideal fertilizer for citrus.
4. This carpet is available in three colors: brown, tan and blue.
5. We had a long bitter discussion.
6. Costs have doubled in the last two years, as the following graph illustrates:
7. By the time I arrived at the meeting the issue had been discussed thoroughly and put aside.
8. If you approve of the changes in paragraph three please place your initials in the margin.
9. We surveyed the entire population but three of the responses were unusable.
10. Because only 21 percent of the members were present, the motion could not be considered.
11. John was awarded $25; Bill $40.
12. We have lost our place in the production line haven't we?
13. We should be spending less money, not more.
14. On November 20 1992 all related documents were submitted.
15. Yes, I agree that the meeting in Oxford, Tennessee should be scheduled in April.

PUNCTUATION (continued)

In typewritten material, the dash is constructed by striking the hyphen key twice with no space before or after. The dash is thus twice as long as the hyphen and has a slight break in the middle. In typeset material, it is longer than a hyphen but has no break.

6. Use a dash.
   a. To place emphasis on appositives:

   His answer--the correct answer--was based on years of experience.

   Compare the price--$125--with the cost of a single repair job.

   She was concerned with one thing--promotion.

   b. When appositives contain commas:

   Their scores--Mary, 21; Sally, 20; and Jo, 19--were the highest in a group of 300.

   c. When a parenthetical remark consists of an abrupt change in thought:

   The committee decided--you may think it's a joke, but it isn't--that the resolution should be adopted.

7. Use an ellipsis to indicate that some words have been omitted from a quotation:

Mr. Thomas said, "We believe . . . our objectives will be accomplished."	Insert a space between the periods.
Mr. Thomas reported, "The time has come when we must provide our employees with inservice training. . . ."	Ellipses at the end of a quotation use four periods, one of which indicates the end of the sentence.

8. Use a hyphen
   a. In such compound words as *self-analysis* and *father-in-law*.
   b. Between the words in a compound adjective. (A *compound adjective* is a group of words joined together and used as a single word to describe a noun that follows.)

   An attention-getting device

   A page-by-page description

An up-to-date record

A technical, hard-to-follow lecture

Observe that each of the hyphenated expressions precedes a noun. Hyphens are not required when a compound adjective follows a noun:

A record that is up to date

A lecture that was hard to follow

An expression made up of an adverb that ends in *ly* and an adjective is not a compound adjective and does not require a hyphen:

commonly accepted principle

widely quoted authority

rapidly advancing leader

   c. To prevent misinterpretation:

A small-business executive	An executive who operates a small business
A small business executive	An executive who is small
Guaranteed used tires	Used tires that are guaranteed
Guaranteed-used tires	Tires that are guaranteed to have been used
Twelve foot-soldiers	Twelve soldiers who travel by walking
Twelve-foot soldiers	Soldiers twelve feet tall
Eight inch blades	Eight blades, each of which is an inch long
Eight-inch blades	Blades eight inches long
Recover a chair	To obtain possession of a chair once more
Re-cover a chair	To cover a chair again

   d. To join the numerator and denominator of fractions:

A <u>two-thirds</u> interest

<u>Three-fourths</u> of the respondents agreed.

Figures are acceptable for expressing fractions: "a $\frac{2}{3}$ interest."

e. In spelling out compound numbers;

<u>Thirty-one</u>

<u>Ninety-seven</u>

f. To avoid repetition of a word:

<u>First-</u> , <u>second-</u> , and <u>third-class</u> mail

<u>Short-</u> , <u>medium-</u> , and <u>long-range</u> missiles

"Short-range, medium-range, and long-range missiles" have the same meaning; but repetition of "range" is not necessary. The hyphens after "short" and "medium" show that these words are connected to another word that will appear at the end of the series.

g. To divide words at the end of a line. (See the discussion of word division in Appendix A.)

h. In a nine-digit ZIP code:

83475-1247

9. Use parentheses
a. For explanatory material that could be left out:

Three of our employees (Mr. Bachman, Mr. Russo, and Mr. Wilds) took their vacations in August.	Dashes may be used instead of parentheses to precede and follow parenthetical material. Dashes have the effect of emphasizing; parentheses, de-emphasizing.
All our employees (believe it or not) have perfect attendance records.	Sentences within sentences neither begin with a capital letter nor end with a period.

b. For accuracy in writing figures:

For the sum of three thousand five hundred dollars ($3,500) . . . .

c. Both before and after that which is parenthetical:

Incorrect: . . . authority to 1) issue passes, 2) collect fees.

Correct: . . . authority to (1) issue passes, (2) collect fees.

d. *After* a period when an entire sentence is parenthetical; *before* a period when only the last part of a sentence is parenthetical:

The board met for three hours. (The usual time is one hour.)

Success can be attributed to one person (Earl Knott).

10. Use a period
a. After imperative and declarative sentences:

Complete this report.

We will attend.

b. After a courteous request:

Will you please complete the report today.

May I have your answer this week.

Technically, the sentences are questions; but they do not suggest a verbal answer. They do suggest an *action* answer.

c. After an abbreviation:

Dr.

M.D.

Mrs.

Ms.

Miss does not take a period because it is not an abbreviation.

d. To end a sentence in which the last word is abbreviated:

Incorrect: **Send to John Cook, Jr..**

Correct: **Send to John Cook, Jr.**

Use only one period; two periods look too much like an ellipsis.

11. Use quotation marks

a. To enclose direct quotations:

The supervisor said, "We will make progress."

"We will make progress," the supervisor said, "even though we have to work overtime."
> Note that the period and comma are keyed within the quotation marks. All other punctuation is keyed outside—unless it is part of the quotation.

b. Before the first word and after the last word of a multiple-sentence quotation:

The president said, "Have a seat, gentlemen. I'm dictating a letter. I should be through in about five minutes. Please wait."

c. To enclose titles of songs, magazine and newspaper articles, and themes within text:

"Home on the Range"

"Progress in Cancer Research"

(Underscore or italicize the titles of books, magazines, and newspapers within text.) Refer to documentation style manuals for correct treatment of these titles in footnotes and bibliographic references.)

d. To define terms:

As used in this report, <u>syntax</u> means "the branch of grammar that has to do with sentence structure."

e. To enclose slang expressions:

We can describe the attacks against our policies with one word--"hogwash."

f. To enclose nicknames:

And now for some comments by Ray "Skinny" Johnson.

g. To imply that a different word may be more appropriate:

Our "football" team. . . .	Hints that the team appears to be playing something other than football.
Our football "team"	Hints that "collection of individual players" would be more descriptive than "team."
. . . out for "lunch."	Hints that the reason for being out is something other than lunch.

h. To enclose quoted material that contains other quoted material:

The budget director said, "Believe me when I say 'A penny saved is a penny earned' is the best advice I ever had."

Note: A quotation that appears within another quotation is enclosed in *single* quotation marks.

i. In their proper position within a sentence. Place periods and commas *inside* quotation marks:

"Take your time," she said, "and the work will be easier."

Place semicolons *outside* quotation marks:

The manager said, "That's fine"; his facial expression conveyed an entirely different message.

Place question marks *inside* quotation marks when the question is within the quotation:

The contractor asked, "When will we begin?"

Place question marks *outside* quotation marks when the question is not within the quotation:

Did the contractor say, "We will begin today"?

(*Punctuation* continues after Exercise 16.)

Exercise 16

Pay special attention to use of the dash, ellipsis, hyphen, parentheses, period, and quotation marks. For each pair of sentences, what is the difference in meaning?

1. **a.** The first speaker will be Red Gaddis.
   b. The first speaker will be "Red" Gaddis.
2. **a.** Have you read *The Power of Ethical Management*?
   b. Have you read "The Power of Ethical Management"?
3. **a.** His accomplishments are summarized on the attached page.
   b. His "accomplishments" are summarized on the attached page.
4. **a.** Tim said the firm plans to establish a sinking fund.
   b. Tim said, "The firm plans to establish a sinking fund."
5. **a.** Only one attorney (Helen Johnson) is working on the case.
   b. Only one attorney—Helen Johnson—is working on the case.
6. **a.** Three day passes will be issued this afternoon.
   b. Three-day passes will be issued this afternoon.
7. **a.** A party is being planned for the ten-game winners.
   b. A party is being planned for the ten game winners.
8. **a.** Check to see whether the sofa can be recovered.
   b. Check to see whether the sofa can be re-covered.
9. **a.** Our accountant said, "Such expenses . . . are not justified."
   b. Our accountant said, "Such expenses are not justified."

PUNCTUATION (continued)

12. Use a semicolon
    a. When a conjunction is omitted:

    Our workers have been extraordinarily efficient this year, and they are expecting a bonus.

    Our workers have been extraordinarily efficient this year; they are expecting a bonus.

    b. In a compound-complex sentence:

    We prefer delivery on Saturday morning at four o'clock, but Friday night at ten o'clock will be satisfactory.

    As indicated earlier, we prefer delivery on Saturday morning at four o'clock; but Friday night at ten o'clock will be satisfactory.

We prefer delivery on Saturday morning at four o'clock; but, if the arrangement is more convenient for you, Friday night at ten o'clock will be satisfactory.

c. Before an adverbial conjunction:

The shipment arrived too late for our weekend sale; therefore, we are returning the shipment to you.

Other frequently used adverbial conjunctions are *however, otherwise, consequently,* and *nevertheless.*

d. In a series that contains commas:

Some of our workers have worked overtime this week: Smith, 6 hours; Hardin, 3; Cantrell, 10; and McGowan, 11.

e. Before illustrative words, as in the following sentences:

We have plans for improvement; for example, we intend to . . . .

The engine has been "knocking"; that is, the gas in the cylinders explodes before the pistons complete their upward strokes.

(*Punctuation* continues after Exercise 17.)

Exercise 17

In each sentence, place a semicolon where it is needed.

1. Expense tickets were not included, otherwise, the request would have been honored.
2. The following agents received a bonus this month: Barnes, $400, Shelley, $450, and Jackson, $600.
3. The bid was not considered, it arrived two days late.
4. This paint does have some disadvantages, for example, its drying time is too long.
5. Soon after the figures have been received, they will be processed, but a formal report cannot be prepared before May 1.

PUNCTUATION (continued)

13. Use symbols
    a. For convenience in filling out forms such as invoices and statements, but not in letters and reports. The dollar sign ($), in contrast with such symbols as %, ¢, @, and #, should be used in letters and reports.

    b. In sentences of letters and reports, spell out terms rather than use symbols:

31 <u>percent</u>	not "31%"
80 <u>cents</u> a foot	not "80¢ a foot"
21 cases <u>at</u> $4 a case	not "21 cases @ $4 a case"
to policy <u>No.</u> 468571	not "to policy # 468571"

14. Use an underscore or italics
    a. To indicate words, letters, numbers, and phrases used as words:

The word <u>effective</u> was used in describing his presentation.

In this sentence, <u>effective</u> is used as an adjective.

He had difficulty learning to spell <u>recommendation</u>.

b. To emphasize a word that is not sufficiently emphasized by other means.

c. To indicate the titles of books, magazines, and newspapers:

<u>Gone with the Wind</u>

<u>The Reader's Digest</u>

<u>The Evening Star</u>

SPELLING

A helpful technique for improving your spelling accuracy is becoming familiar with words that are difficult to spell. Study the following list of the most frequently misspelled words in business communication:*

absence	beneficial	convenience	foreclosure
accessory	beneficiary	correspondence	foreign
accidentally	benefited	council	fulfill
accommodate	biennial	courteous	
achievement	bureau	criticism	grammar
acknowledgment			grateful
affidavit	calendar	dependent	guarantee
alignment	cancellation	develop	hindrance
analyze	casualty	differential	
apologize	category	dissatisfied	illegible
apparent	chauffeur		immigrant
appearance	clientele	eligible	incidentally
approximately	collateral	embarrass	indictment
argument	commission	emigrant	itinerary
arraign	commitment	endeavor	
ascertain	comparative	environment	judgment
assessment	connoisseur	equipped	laboratory
assistance	conscientious	existence	lacquer
attendance	conscious	extension	leisure
auxiliary	consensus	extraordinary	liaison
	controlled	familiar	license
		forbearance	maintenance

*The 132 most frequently misspelled words used in business communication were identified in research conducted by M. J. Casady and D. Moses, as reported in Casady, M. J., & Moses, D. (1992, March). Hi-tech communication demands accuracy. *The Secretary*, pp. 19–20.

maneuver
miniature
miscellaneous
mischievous

necessary
nickel
ninety
noticeable

occasion
occasionally
occurred
occurrence
omission
omitted

opportunity
pamphlet
parallel
paralyze
penicillin
perforated
permissible
perseverance
personnel
persuasion
physician
possession
precede
prejudice

privilege
procedure
proceed
psychology
pursue

questionnaire

recommend
referee
regrettable
repetition
restaurant

separate
similar

simultaneous
statistician
succeed
supersede
susceptible

transferred
truly

undoubtedly
unnecessary

vacuum

wholly

yield

Complete Self-Check Exercises 18-20 and the Review Quiz to test your understanding of grammar, spelling, and punctuation principles.

SELF-CHECK

Exercises 18–20 are designed to reinforce between 20 and 40 of the principles presented in Appendix B. To be certain that you master these principles, complete Exercises 18–20 several times throughout the semester.

Follow these steps to complete Review Exercises 18–20:

a. Place a covered sheet over the right-hand column.
b. Examine the numbered sentence on the left for errors in word usage, spelling, punctuation, abbreviations, number usage, and other principles discussed in Appendix B.
c. Make the needed corrections on a separate page. Do not attempt to revise a sentence and state its idea in an entirely different way. Do not divide a sentence into two sentences.
d. Move the cover sheet down and check your answers against the corrected sentence(s). Making an unnecessary change is a mistake; failing to make a necessary change is a mistake. If a sentence can be corrected in more than one way, two corrected sentences appear on the right.
e. Refer to the pages listed in parentheses to review the reasons for each correction. The first number is a page number in Appendix B; the second number or letter identifies a certain place on the page.
e. Record the number of mistakes in the spaces provided.

Exercise 18

____ **1.** I will appreciate you sending next months report too my home address.

I will appreciate your sending next month's report to my home address. (19, e) (35, b, f) (15, 84)

____ **2.** If I were him, I would include second and third-degree headings in my report.

If I were he, I would include second- and third-degree headings in my report. (22, a) (19, d) (38, 56) (41, 8b) (42, f)

____ **3.** When Miss. Forrest became an aid to the governor her salary was $35,000, but she is now earning $51,000.

When Miss Forrest became an aide to the governor, her salary was $35,000; but she is now earning $51,000. (42, 10c) (4, 6) (38, 5b) (53, 12b) (33, 1c)

____ **4.** Each of the following words were used several times in the report: greatfull, 7, occassion, 7, seperate, 8; recommend, 10, priviledge, 10, recieve, 10, and accomodate, 10.

Each of the following words was used several times in the report: grateful, 7; occasion, 7; separate, 8; recommend, 10; privilege, 10; receive, 10; and accommodate, 10. (23, e) (37, 4a) (45, d) (46) (47)

____ **5.** Our stockbroker has written an article on physical policy, the article will appear in the March 21st issue of "Newsweek".

Our stockbroker has written an article on fiscal policy; the article will appear in the March 21 issue of Newsweek. (8, 40) (44, 12a)(33, b) (43, c)

----- **6.** Only one of the participant's were willing to ask "what do you think"?

Only one of the participants <u>was</u> willing to ask, "What do you think?" (35, a) (23, e) (31, 1b) (43, a, i)

----- **7.** John Hargus's figures are different than mine, therefore I have offered to hire an auditor.

John <u>Hargus'</u> figures are different <u>from</u> mine; therefore, I have offered to hire an auditor. (35, d) (8, 32) (45, c)

----- **8.** If you can complete the survey before July 1, 1990 please procede; otherwise ask the superintendent for a new set of questionaires.

If you can complete the survey before July 1, 1990, please <u>proceed</u>; otherwise, ask the super-intendent for a new set of <u>questionnaires</u>. (38, b) (33, b) (39, g) (44, b) (45, c) (47)

----- **9.** If your martial status is single; you may not be elligible for this $600.00 deductible.

If your <u>marital</u> status is single, you may not be <u>eligible</u> for this <u>$600</u> deductible. (38, b) (10, 57) (46) (33, c)

----- **10.** The balance sheet does not correspond to the work sheet, please check the figures at your convenence.

The balance sheet does not correspond to the work sheet; please check the figures at your <u>con-venience</u>. (6, 24) (44, a) (46)

----- **11.** The contracts, which have an escape clause, have been submitted to our at-torneys; but all others are being pre-pared for signatures.

The contracts <u>that</u> have an escape clause have been submitted to our attorneys, but all others are being prepared for signatures. (39, e) (38, a) (14, 82)

----- **12.** On March 1st, 1990, we moved to a five room suite, it was formally occu-pied by Woodson Travel Agency.

On March <u>1</u>, 1990, we moved to a five-room suite; it was <u>formerly</u> occupied by Woodson Travel Agency.

On March <u>1</u>, 1990 we moved to a five-room suite, which was <u>formerly</u> occupied by Woodson Travel Agency. (33, a, b) (39, g) (38, b) (44, a) (41, 8b) (9, 42) (31, 1a)

----- **13.** Irregardless of recent commentary this book is very unique.

<u>Regardless</u> of recent commentary, this book is unique.

<u>Regardless</u> of recent commentary, this book is very unusual. (9, 48) (38, b)

____ **14.** Neither Joe or Phil have planned to attend the three day conference, however, the superintendent has issued instructions to do so.

Neither Joe <u>nor</u> Phil <u>has</u> planned to attend the <u>three-day</u> conference<u>;</u> however, the superintendent has issued instructions to do so. (12, 62) (23, d) (41, 86) (45, c)

____ **15.** The box which was in Room C has been prepared for mailing all other boxes are to be wrapped with heavy paper, and returned to Room D.

The box <u>that</u> was in Room C has been prepared for mailing<u>;</u> all other boxes are to be wrapped with heavy paper and returned to Room D.

The box <u>that</u> was in Room C has been prepared for mailing<u>, but</u> all other boxes are to be wrapped with heavy paper and returned to Room D. (39, e) (31, a) (44, a) (38, a) (40, q)

____ **16.** Did the principle really use the words "get out of my office?"

Did the <u>principal</u> really use the words<u>,</u> "Get out of my office"<u>?</u> (13, 68) (31, 1b) (11, a) (43, i)

____ **17.** While Jan's request for promotion had been denied three times, her moral was high.

<u>Although</u> Jan's request for promotion had been denied three times, her <u>morale</u> was high.

Jan's <u>request</u> for promotion had been denied three times<u>, but</u> her <u>morale</u> was high. (15, 89) (35, a) (38, a, b) (10, 6)

____ **18.** We need sometime to evaluate procedures, therefore a decision will not be made until November 3.

We need <u>some time</u> to evaluate <u>procedures;</u> therefore<u>,</u> a decision will not be made until November 3. (14, 76) (47) (45, c) (35, b)

____ **19.** Each of the following words are to be added to your list of hard to spell words: cancellation, judgement, convenience, maintenance, similiar, occassion, occured, precede, and neccessary.

Each of the following words <u>is</u> to be added to your list of <u>hard-to-spell</u> words: cancellation, <u>judgment</u>, convenience, maintenance, <u>similar</u>, <u>occasion</u>, <u>occurred</u>, precede, and <u>necessary</u>. (23, e) (41, 8b) (37, 4a) (38, c) (46) (47)

____ **20.** If I filled out this long complicated questionnaire my time would be wasted.

If I filled out this long<u>,</u> complicated questionnaire<u>,</u> my time would be wasted. (38, b, d) (47)

____ **21.** After you have completed your term please write to me, we have some highly-important matters to discuss.

After you have completed your term<u>,</u> please write to me<u>;</u> we have some highly important matters to discuss. (38, b) (44, a, b) (41, 8b)

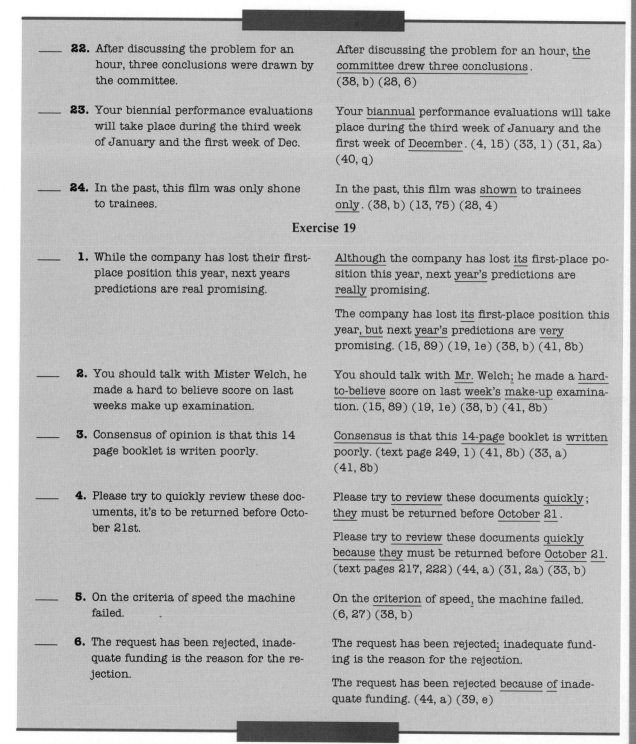

22. After discussing the problem for an hour, three conclusions were drawn by the committee.

After discussing the problem for an hour, <u>the committee drew three conclusions</u>. (38, b) (28, 6)

23. Your biennial performance evaluations will take place during the third week of January and the first week of Dec.

Your <u>biannual</u> performance evaluations will take place during the third week of January and the first week of <u>December</u>. (4, 15) (33, 1) (31, 2a) (40, q)

24. In the past, this film was only shone to trainees.

In the past, this film was <u>shown</u> to trainees <u>only</u>. (38, b) (13, 75) (28, 4)

Exercise 19

1. While the company has lost their first-place position this year, next years predictions are real promising.

<u>Although</u> the company has lost <u>its</u> first-place position this year, next <u>year's</u> predictions are <u>really</u> promising.

The company has lost <u>its</u> first-place position this year<u>, but</u> next <u>year's</u> predictions are <u>very</u> promising. (15, 89) (19, 1e) (38, b) (41, 8b)

2. You should talk with Mister Welch, he made a hard to believe score on last weeks make up examination.

You should talk with <u>Mr.</u> Welch<u>;</u> he made a <u>hard-to-believe</u> score on last <u>week's</u> <u>make-up</u> examination. (15, 89) (19, 1e) (38, b) (41, 8b)

3. Consensus of opinion is that this 14 page booklet is writen poorly.

<u>Consensus</u> is that this <u>14-page</u> booklet is <u>written</u> poorly. (text page 249, 1) (41, 8b) (33, a) (41, 8b)

4. Please try to quickly review these documents, it's to be returned before October 21st.

Please try <u>to review</u> these documents <u>quickly</u>; <u>they</u> must be returned before <u>October 21</u>.

Please try <u>to review</u> these documents <u>quickly</u> <u>because</u> <u>they</u> must be returned before <u>October 21</u>. (text pages 217, 222) (44, a) (31, 2a) (33, b)

5. On the criteria of speed the machine failed.

On the <u>criterion</u> of speed<u>,</u> the machine failed. (6, 27) (38, b)

6. The request has been rejected, inadequate funding is the reason for the rejection.

The request has been rejected<u>;</u> inadequate funding is the reason for the rejection.

The request has been rejected <u>because</u> <u>of</u> inadequate funding. (44, a) (39, e)

7. While the committee agreed with Ms. Sims' conclusions; serious questions were raised as to the questionnaire, which was used as an information gathering instrument.

<u>Although</u> the committee agreed with <u>Ms. Sims's</u> conclusions, serious questions were raised about the questionnaire <u>that</u> was used as an <u>information-gathering</u> instrument.

The committee agreed with <u>Ms. Sims's</u> conclusions, <u>but</u> serious questions were raised about the questionnaire <u>that</u> was used as <u>an</u> <u>information-gathering</u> instrument. (15, 89) (30, a) (35, d) (38, b) (4, 12) (47) (14, 82) (41, 8b)

8. If I was her I would exchange that typewriter for a personal computer, but she thinks computers are too difficult to use.

If I <u>were she</u>, I would exchange that typewriter for a personal computer<u>;</u> but she thinks computers are too difficult to use. (22, 1a) (19, 2d) (38, b) (44, b) (47) (15, 84)

9. The president was not enthused about the new stationary; but, he signed the order form.

The president was not <u>enthusiastic</u> about the new <u>stationery</u>, but <u>he</u> signed the order form. (8, 35) (14, 77) (38, a)

10. We ordered 4 16 pound hammers, but only one was shipped.

We ordered <u>four</u> 16-<u>pound</u> hammers<u>,</u> but only one was shipped.

We ordered <u>four</u> 16-<u>pound</u> hammers<u>;</u> only one was shipped. (34, 2d) (41, 8b) (38, a) (44, a)

11. Because the gravel was to course to meet specifications the inspection engineer halted construction.

Because the gravel was <u>too coarse</u> to meet specifications<u>,</u> the inspection engineer halted construction. (5, 19) (15, 84) (38, b)

12. The committee has been charged with responsibility for a practical equable plan.

The committee has been charged with responsibility for a practical<u>,</u> <u>equitable</u> plan. (13, 67) (8, 37) (38, d)

13. Two thirds of the members thinks the statue should be revised because of its ambiguity.

<u>Two-thirds</u> of the members <u>think</u> the <u>statute</u> should be revised because of its ambiguity. (41, d) (text pages 220, 221, 265) (14, 78)

14. For you and I that price seems very low, however for a recently-hired assistant, it probably seems very high.

For you and <u>me</u>, that price seems very low<u>;</u> however<u>,</u> for a recently hired assistant, it probably seems very high. (38, b) (19, c) (45, c) (41, 8b)

_____ **15.** Only one of the applicant's were well qualified, she was interviewed immediately.

Only one of the applicants was well qualified; she was interviewed immediately.

Only one of the applicants was well qualified, and she was interviewed immediately. (22, 2b) (35, a) (44, a) (38, a)

_____ **16.** The spellchecker was not able to detect all errors, for example, derive was keyed incorrectly as drive.

The spellchecker was not able to detect all errors; for example, _derive_ was keyed incorrectly as _drive_. (45, e) (43, 11d)

_____ **17.** Their research techniques were different than our's, however, their conclusions were similar.

Their research techniques were different from ours; however, their conclusions were similar. (8, 32) (36, b) (45, c) (47)

_____ **18.** 13 respondents thought the company was loosing site of it's objectives.

Thirteen respondents thought the company was losing sight of its objectives. (34, a) (10, 55) (5, 18) (36, b)

_____ **19.** The following have worked a few hours of overtime this week; Welch, 4, Redford, 6, and Woods, 11.

The following employees have worked a few hours of overtime this week: Welch, 4; Redford, 6; and Woods, 11. (9, 41) (37, 4a) (39, m) (45, d)

_____ **20.** If I was able to borrow $150,000.00, I would start a business of my own, but I could never borrow that much.

If I were able to borrow $150,000, I would start a business of my own; but I could never borrow that much. (22, 1ab) (38, b) (33, c) (44, b)

_____ **21.** One news media is planning to present 10 2-hour programs on that subject in February.

One news medium is planning to present 10 two-hour programs on that subject in February. (10, 58) (34, 2d) (41, 8b) (31, 2a)

_____ **22.** Helen made a higher score than any one in her work unit but her promotion was denied because of habitual tardiness.

Helen made a higher score than anyone else in her work unit, but her promotion was denied because of habitual tardiness. (4, 11) (38, a) (39, e) (26, d)

_____ **23.** Because of our highly advertised expansion program; the need for additional capital is becoming acute.

Because of our highly advertised expansion program, the need for additional capital is becoming acute. (41, 8b) (38, b)

_____ **24.** Weather conditions should permit construction to begin in the later part of Febuary.

Weather conditions should permit construction to begin in the latter part of February. (15, 88) (31, 2a)

Exercise 20

___ **1.** I suspect Mistress Russpo is faster than me; but, our performances have not been timed officially.

I suspect <u>Mrs.</u> Russpo is faster than <u>I</u>, but our performances have not been timed officially.

I suspect that <u>Mrs.</u> Russpo is faster than <u>I</u>; <u>how-ever</u>, our performances have not been timed officially. (30, d) (text pages 219, 200) (38, a) (45, c)

___ **2.** Your payments have been arriving ap-proximately 10 days after their due dates; this is causing us some concern.

Your payments have been arriving approxi-mately <u>ten</u> days after their due dates; this <u>tardiness</u> is causing us some concern.

Your payments have been arriving approxi-mately <u>ten</u> days after their due dates; these <u>delays</u> are causing us some concern. (33, a) (15, 83) (21, q)

___ **3.** If you will send your rough drafts to Miss Graff and myself we will edit it throughly.

If you will send your rough drafts to Miss Graff and <u>me</u>, we will edit <u>them</u> <u>thoroughly.</u>

If you will send your rough <u>draft</u> to Miss Graff and <u>me</u>, we will edit <u>it</u> <u>thoroughly</u>. (42, 10c) (19, c) (text pages 217, 220)

___ **4.** Each of our assistants are required to take a short intensive training course.

Each of our assistants <u>is</u> required to take a short<u>,</u> intensive training course.

<u>All</u> our assistants <u>are</u> required to take a short<u>,</u> intensive training course. (23, e) (38, d)

___ **5.** After Mr. Childress's draft has been ed-ited, it will be forwarded to this office for printing.

After Mr. <u>Childress'</u> draft has been edited, it will be <u>sent</u> to this office for printing. (30, b) (35, d) (38, b) (9, 43)

___ **6.** Of the attorneys interviewed one fifth thought the revised statute would have no affect on employee theft.

Of the attorneys interviewed<u>,</u> <u>one-fifth</u> thought the revised statute would have no <u>effect</u> on em-ployee theft. (30, b) (41, d) (14, 78) (4, 5)

___ **7.** The amount of purchases returned have been decreasing, however sales in that district has been increasing.

The <u>number</u> of purchases returned <u>has</u> been de-creasing<u>;</u> however<u>,</u> sales in that district <u>have</u> been increasing. (4, 9) (23, e) (45, c) (40, p)

____ **8.** Among the contestants who made superior scores in word usage, grammar, and punctuation were: Wilson, Brosque, and Martinez respectfully.

Among the contestants who made superior scores in word usage, grammar, and punctuation were Wilson, Brosque, and Martinez, respectively. (38, c) (37, 4a) (13, 73)

____ **9.** In a speech to sophomores the imminent physician inferred that experimental treatment had been totally effective.

In a speech to sophomores, the eminent physician implied that experimental treatment had been totally effective. (38, b) (8, 34) (9, 45)

____ **10.** I except your invitation to participate in the program, it promises to be real beneficial.

I accept your invitation to participate in the program; it promises to be very beneficial.

I accept your invitation to participate in the program because it promises to be really beneficial. (3, 2) (44, a) (15, 85)

____ **11.** One of the major issues was whether or not the concrete should be reinforced with steal.

One of the major issues was whether the concrete should be reinforced with steel. (23, e) (15, 88) (text page 250) (14, 79)

____ **12.** The research techniques are acceptable; however, one of the conclusions seem questionable.

The research techniques are acceptable; however, one of the conclusions seems questionable. (3, 2) (45, c) (40, p) (23, e)

____ **13.** When I compared my results with yours', I found few similiarities.

When I compared my results to yours, I found few similarities. (5, 20) (36, b) (38, b) (47)

____ **14.** A short intensive review will be conducted at 10:00 A.M. April 14th.

A short, intensive review will be conducted at 10 a.m. on April 14. (38, d) (34, 1d) (31, e) (33, b)

____ **15.** In rewriting the final draft, please change the word charge to debit.

In rewriting the final draft, please change the word *charge* to *debit*. (38, 5b) (45, 4a)

____ **16.** When the plan was introduced in 1992 it was well received; but, management discovered several noticable weaknesses.

When the plan was introduced in 1992, it was well received; but management discovered several noticeable weaknesses. (38, b) (44, b) (46)

____ **17.** Prices began their descent in February, and hit their lowest point in Sept..

Prices began their descent in February and hit their lowest point in September. (15, 83) (6, 30) (31, 2a) (40, q)

____ **18.** The commission is too be divided equally between Ray, Coleen, and Edith.

The commission is <u>to</u> be divided equally <u>among</u> Ray, Coleen, and Edith. (15, 84) (4, 8) (38, c)

____ **19.** While the majority of the precedure has been completed the supervisor has asked for a three week extension of the contract.

<u>Although</u> the <u>major</u> <u>portion</u> of the <u>procedure</u> <u>has</u> been completed<u>,</u> the supervisor has asked for a <u>three-week</u> extension of the contract.

<u>Most</u> of the <u>procedure</u> has been completed<u>, but</u> the supervisor has asked for a <u>three-week</u> extension of the contract. (15, 89) (10, 56) (47) (38, b) (41, 8b) (38, a)

____ **20.** In reviewing Ms. Chambliss's application, the director found errors in: 1) spelling, 2) application of the rules of grammar, and 3) punctuation.

In reviewing Ms. <u>Chambliss'</u> application, the director found errors in <u>(1)</u> spelling<u>, (2)</u> <u>grammar</u>, and <u>(3)</u> punctuation. (38, b) (30, a) (35, d) (37, 4a) (38, c) (42, 9c) (text 200)

____ **21.** Only one of the proposals was discussed; but it was placed on the table for farther discussion.

Only one of the proposals was discussed<u>,</u> but it was placed on the table for <u>further</u> discussion. (23, e) (38, a) (8, 38)

____ **22.** Almost 85 percent of the questionairs has been returned, it is now being tabulated.

Almost 85 percent of the <u>questionnaires</u> <u>have</u> been returned<u>; they</u> are now being tabulated. (33, 1a) (47) (text pages 217, 221) (44, a)

____ **23.** The company has changed it's policy, three week vacations are no longer permited.

The company has changed <u>its</u> policy<u>;</u> <u>three-week</u> vacations are no longer <u>permitted</u>. (19, 1e) (36, b) (44, a) (41, 8b) (33, a)

____ **24.** Neither the manager or his assistants are being invited to attend the two day workshop.

Neither the manager <u>nor</u> his assistants are being invited to attend the <u>two-day</u> workshop. (12, 62) (23, d) (41, 8b) (33, a)

REVIEW QUIZ

To test your understanding of the grammar, spelling, and punctuation principles presented in Appendix B, follow these steps for sentences 1–12.

a. Examine the numbered sentences for errors in word usage, spelling, punctuation, and manner of expressing numbers.

b. Make the needed corrections on a separate page. Do not attempt to revise a sentence and state its idea in an entirely different way. Do not divide a sentence into two sentences.

1. Will you please find out weather first and second-year students are eligable too receive that scholarship.

2. George was formerly in charge of security at the capital building, he is not enthused about our firms security system.

3. The questionaires which were mailed on June 1 have been returned; but only a few of those mailed latter in the month have been returned.

4. This years biennial evaluations will take place during the second week of July, and the first week of December.

5. In the passed, only one news media has been invited to attend the meetings.

6. John has submitted more suggestions than anyone in his department but he has yet to receive an award.

7. While the procedure has been highly successful it is not popular in our department.

8. The man, who came late to the meeting, was the only one to leave early.

9. The 3 applicants were waiting to interview for the same job, therefore they had little to say to each other.

10. Only one of my recommendations were considered, this was very disappointing to the superintendant and I.

11. The majority of the discussion was devoted to physical policy, but, as I discovered later, that topic has not been listed on the agenda.

12. Because of the obvious conflict of interest, the accounting firm was suspected of over-stating the companies financial condition.

GRADING SYMBOLS

APPENDIX C

Organization and Development

Word Choice and Style

Punctuation

Mechanics

Format

Your instructor may use the following grading symbols to mark corrections on your writing assignments. The instructor may write the abbreviation (highlighted to the right of the numbers) to identify the major area needing improvement. To provide additional feedback on all or selected errors, the instructor may write the number and letter designating the *specific* principle violated. To review the principles marked on your paper, refer to the pages indicated within the parentheses.

ORGANIZATION AND DEVELOPMENT

1. **seq** Organizational Sequence
   a. Deductive approach to convey good news *(Chapter 9, 303–304)*
   b. Inductive approach to convey bad news *(Chapter 10, 363)*
   c. Persuasive approach if reader must be persuaded *(Chapter 11, 412)*
   d. Special letters *(Chapter 12, refer to specific document)*

2. **ss** Sentences
   a. Normal subject-verb-complement sequence *(253; B-28, #2)*
   b. Related ideas in sentence *(B-28, #3)*
   c. Avoid expletive beginnings *(258–259; B-28, #2)*

   d. Avoid clumsy split infinitives *(222, B-30, #10)*

3. **¶** Paragraphs
   a. Topic sentence presents central idea *(267–268)*
   b. Coherence; ideas connect logically *(268)*
   c. Unity; has beginning, middle (systematic sequence), and ending *(273)*

4. **trans** Transition
   Transition between sentences and paragraphs so that ideas connect; avoid choppy sentences *(274–275)*

WORD CHOICE AND STYLE

5. **read** Readability
   a. Use plain, simple words; use jargon only if reader will understand *(197–198; 268–269)*
   b. Use short sentences *(268–269)*
   c. Avoid long, complicated paragraphs *(271)*

6. **clear** Clarity
   a. Include relevant ideas; develop logically *(295–296; 318–325)*
   b. Specific vs. general word choice *(197; B-17 #1)*

   c. Concrete vs. abstract nouns—word choice *(212; B17, #2)*
   d. Active voice for vivid writing *(259–260; B-24, #5)*
   e. Plain, simple language *(197–198; 259–260)*
   f. Action-oriented ending paragraph *(see example of specific document)*
   g. Cite reference for source *(652, 654; 754–756)*
   h. Verify accuracy of names, places, dates, amounts, etc. *(see case problem)*

WORD CHOICE AND STYLE

7. **concise**   Conciseness
   a. Redundancies *(249–250)*
   b. Clichés *(243–248)*
   c. Brevity (unnecessary words and ideas) *(249–252)*

8. **tone**   Tone
   a. Reader's viewpoint; overuse of first person—I *(214–216; B-24, #3d)*
   b. Emphasize positive ideas: use active voice *(222–223)* second person *(215)*, and positive words *(201–202)*
   c. De-emphasize negative ideas: use passive voice *(222–223)*; *B24, #5b)* and avoid second person *(215)*, positive words *(201–203)*, and subjunctive mood *(260–261; B-22, #1b)*
   d. Use bias-free language *(207–211)*
   e. Condescending *(203)* and demeaning tone *(205–206)*
   f. Misuse of euphemistic tone *(203–204)* and connotative tone *(206–207)*
   g. Expressions of surprise, doubt, and judgment *(252–253)*

9. **agr**   Agreement
   a. Number: subject and verb *(220–221; B-22, #2)*
   b. Person: subject and verb *(221; B-22, #3a–b)*
   c. Tense *(221–222; B-24, #4)*
   d. Mood *(260–261; 271; B-22, 1B)*
   e. Pronoun and antecedent *(217; B18, #1a–c)*

10. **case**   Case
   a. Subjects *(217–218; B-19, #2a)*
   b. Objects *(218–220; B-19, #2b–c)*
   c. With linking verbs *(B-19, #2d)*
   d. Before a gerund *(212–213; B-19, #2e)*
   e. Relative pronouns—who, whom *(B-20, #3a–d)*
   f. Possessives

11. **adj or adv**   Adjectives and Adverbs
   a. Adjectives; use correct degree, avoid superlatives and overly strong adjectives *(224–225, 227; B-26, #1)*
   b. Adverbs; use correct degree, avoid superlatives, and overly strong adverbs *(227–228; B-26 #2)*
   c. Double negatives

12. **frag**   Sentence Fragments *(254; B28-#1)*

13. **ro**   Run-on Sentences
   Review the punctuation of sentence types *(253–255)*

14. **ref**   Pronoun Reference
   a. Ambiguous pronoun reference *(214; B-20, #3f)*
   b. Misuse: using a pronoun to refer to phrase, clause, sentence or paragraph *(B-21, #3g)*
   c. Use of *you* when the meaning is not clear *(215–216)*

15. **Shifts**   Shifts
   a. Person and number *(See agreement)*
   b. Tense and mood *(See agreement)*

16. **mm/dm**   Misplaced and Dangling Modifiers
   a. Misplaced and dangling modifiers *(255–258; B-28-29, #6)*
   b. Relative pronouns *(B-20, #3a; B-28, #4)*
   c. Do not separate subject and verb unnecessarily *(B-28, #5)*

17. **//**   Parallelism *(200–291; B-29, #7)*

18. **emph**   Emphasis
   a. Sentence structure *(261–262)*
   b. Position: first and last positions for emphasis *(262–263)*
   c. Numbers or tabulated enumerations *(263–264; 272)*
   d. Include positive idea in sentence *(263)*

19. **var**   Variety
   a. Sentence length *(271)*
   b. Sentence structure *(271)*
   c. Paragraph length *(271)*

PUNCTUATION

20. . ? ! Terminal Punctuation
Period *(B-42-3, #9)*

21. , Comma
a. Coordinate conjunction—*and, but,* and *for*
(228–229; 265; B-38, #5a)
b. Introductory clause or phrase *(B-38, #5b)*
c. Items in a series *(B-38, #5c)*
d. Coordinate adjectives *(226–227; B-38, 5d)*
e. Nonrestrictive clauses and parenthetical expressions *(B-38, #5e)*
f. Date, city and state *(B-38, #5g–h)*
g. Appositive *(B-38, #5k)*
h. Adverbial conjunction *(B-38, #5p)*
i. Other rules *(B39–40, #5)*

22. ; Semicolon
a. Omitted conjunction *(266; B-44, #12a)*
b. Compound-complex sentence *(266; B-44, #12b)*

c. Adverbial conjunctive *(228–229; 266; B-45, #12c)*
d. Within series that contains a comma *(B-45, #12d)*
e. Other rules *(B-45, #12d–e)*

23. ' Apostrophe
a. Rules for using apostrophes *(B-35, #1)*
b. Rules for not using apostrophes *(B-35, #2)*

24. [ ] : — . . . - ( ) " " Other Marks
a. Brackets *(B-37, #3)*
b. Colon *(B-37, #4)*
c. Dash *(B-41, #6)*
d. Ellipses *(B41, #7)*
e. Hyphen *(B-41, #8)*; compound adjective *(225–227, 266–267; B-41, #8b)*
f. Parentheses *(B-42, #9)*
g. Quotation Marks *(B-43–4, #11)*

MECHANICS

25. **caps** Capitals
a. Capitalize *(B-31, #1)*
b. Do not capitalize *(B-31–2, #2)*
c. Envelope address: all caps and no punctuation *(A-22, A25–6)*

26. **ital** Italics (Underline if software does not support italics.)
a. Words named as words *(B-45–6, #14a)*
b. Emphasis *(B-46, #14b)*
c. Titles of books *(B-46, #14c)*

27. **ab** Abbreviations
a. Abbreviate *(B-30, #1)*
b. Do not abbreviate *(B-30, #2)*
c. Two-letter ZIP code abbreviation *(A-27)*

28. **num** Numbers
a. Use figures *(B-33–41, #1)*
b. Spell out *(B-34, #2)*

29. **div** Word Division
Review rules *(A-6, #1–7)*

30. **sp** Spelling
a. Use spellchecker or proofread carefully for omitted or repeated words
b. Frequently misused word. Locate the correct usage from text pages or a dictionary. *(B-3–15)*
c. Frequently misspelled words *(B46–47)*
d. Verify names, places, dates, amounts, etc. *(see case problem)*

31. **# or ##** Spacing
a. Twice after terminal punctuation and colon *(A-5, #1)*
b. Once after a comma and semicolon *(A-5, #2)*
c. Proper vertical spacing in letters *(A-3–4)*

FORMAT

32. App   Appearance
   a. Poor print quality
   b. Not balanced attractively on page
   c. Unprofessional (submitted with perforated edges; crumpled, etc.)

33. fmt   Format
Letters and Memos
   a. Letter style: block *(A-7–8)*, modified block *(A-8–9)*, simplified block *(A-10)*
   b. Punctuation style: open *(A-7)*, mixed *(A-7)*
   c. Include return address on letter if plain paper is used *(A-11)*
   d. Appropriate salutation *(A12–13)*
   e. Acceptable memo style: traditional *(A-23)*, simplified *(A-24)*
   f. Second-page heading for letters/memos *(A-16–17)*
   g. Appropriate special parts—enclosure, copy, etc. *(A-15–20)*

   h. Envelope format *(A-25)*
   i. Letters signed and memos initialed legibly

Reports
   j. Report title page *(see sample report)*
   j. Contents and list of figures *(see sample report)*
   k. Executive summary *(see sample report)*
   l. Report text *(see sample report)*
   m. Citations: In-text parenthetical APA *(757–758)*; Bottom-of-page or end-of-page, MLA *(759–760)*
   n. Bibliography or references page: MLA *(765–766)*; APA *(767-768)*

Other Documents
   o. Resume *(547–548; 550–554)*
   p. References Page—employment credentials *(549)*
   q. News release *(483)*

INDEX

Abbreviations, 569, A26, A27, B30–B31
Abstract, 712
Abstract nouns, 212, B17
Achievements, Summary of, 533–534
Acknowledgment letters, 318–320
Acronyms, 569
Active voice, 222–224, 250, 259–260, 411, B24–B25
Addenda
  in proposals, 734
  in reports, 713–714
Address
  on envelope, 427–431, A22–A27
  inside letter, A11–A13
Adjectives, 224–227, 232–233
  comparative, B26–B27
  compound, 225–226
  coordinate, 226–227
  overly strong, 224–225
  superlative, 227, B26
Adjustment request
  favorable response to, 306–311
  refusal of, 366–369
Adobe Illustrator, 133, 135
Advancement, and ethics, 163–164
Adverb(s), 227–228, 232–233, B27
Adverbial conjunctions, 229
Advertising
  ethics in, 183
  help-wanted, 555
Age bias, 210, 232
Agreement
  pronoun-antecedent, 217, B18–B19
  subject-verb, 220–221, B22–B23
Analysis
  career, 520–523
  of ethical dilemmas, 167–178
  job, 523–524, 525
  self-analysis, 520, 521, 596
  of style, 239–240
  transactional, 35

of writing, software for, 120, 239–240, 269
Analytical reports, 642, 713
Anecdotes, in speeches, 65, 66, 67
APA style manual, 754, 756, 757–758, 763, 764, 767–769, 770
Apologies, 495–502
Apostrophe, B35–B36
Appeal, letters of, 449–451
Appearance
  in employment interview, 597
  of letters, A1–A6
Appendix, 713–714, 775
Application forms, 611–613
Application letters, 557–573
  boasting in, 563
  checklist for, 576
  with chronological resume, 570–571
  content of, 559–564
  examples of, 569–573
  follow–up letters and, 609, 610
  format of, 571, 572
  with functional resume, 571–573
  length of, 560–561
  mechanics of, 568–569
  organization of, 564
  style of, 564–568
Appositive, 264
Appraisal. *See* Performance appraisals
Appraisal report, 720, 727
Area charts, 688–689
Articulation, 60
Assumptions, avoiding, 752
Asterisks, 757
Attention, faking, 43
Attention getters, 412–416, 427
Attention line, of letter, A15–A16
Audience
  intercultural, 104–110
  of speeches, 61–62, 68, 69–70
Audiotapes, 80
Authorization for reports, 710

Bad news. *See* Unpleasant messages
Bar charts, 684–687, 689
Barriers
  to communication, 30–31, 44, 45
  to cross–cultural communication, 98–103
  to electronic communication, 144–149
Behavior, unethical, 156, 157, 160, 162–167
Behavioral factors in communication, 31–37
Beresford, Dennis R., xxxiv, xl, 248
Bias
  age, 210, 232
  gender, 207–210, 231–232
  against people with disabilities, 210–211, 232
  racial or ethnic, 210, 232
  religious, 210, 232
Bibliography, 713, 762–769
  link to citations, 762–763
  preparing, 763–769
Block feature in word processing, 120
Block format of letters, A7–A8
  modified, A8–A9
  simplified, A10
Body language, 39–41, 101–102. *See also* Nonverbal communication
Boldface type, 119, 130
Bolles, R. N., 521
Brackets, B37
Broken-bar chart, 685
Bruner, K. F., 754
Budget, in proposals, 733–734
Bullet, 264
Bulletin board, electronic, 137
Bureaucracy, 15
Bureau of Employment Security, 522
Bureau of Labor Statistics, 522
Business letters. *See* Letters

Capitalization, B31–B33
Card system, 652–654
Career
    books about, 521–522
    job analysis and, 523–524, 525
    job market and, 626
    planning, 518–520
    research for, 520–530
    setting goals for, 519
    See also Job search
Career analysis, 520–523
Career notebook, 520, 525–530, 543, 549–551, 596, 601–602, 606
Career objectives, 533
Career opportunities, 521
Career person, interview with, 524, 525
Career planning today (Powell), 522
Career services centers, 521, 540, 552–555
Carnegie, Dale, 293
Casady, M. J., B46
Case of pronouns, 217–220, B19–B20
Casual listening, 47
Cause-and-effect connectors, 754
Cellular telephones, 140–141
Central selling point
    in claim letter, 432–433
    in sales letter, 411–412, 414–415, 418, 419
Central tendency, measures of, 676–678
Chalkboards, 78
Channels of communication, 27–28
Charts. *See* Graphics
Chronological resumes, 542, 544–545, 547–548, 550–551, 553–554, 570–571
Citations
    bottom-of-the-page, 758–760, 761
    end-of-report, 760–762
    link to bibliography, 762–763
    parenthetical, 757–758
    preparing, 756–760
    reasons for, 754–755
Civil Rights Act of 1964, 538
Claim letters
    persuasive, 305, 431–434
    routine, 305–311
Clauses, 253–254, 261–262
Clichés, 243–248
Clipart, 133
Closing
    complimentary, A14
    of employment interview, 607–608
    of unpleasant letter, 364, 389–391
Closure principle, 450
Codes of ethics, 170–173
Cody, Sherwin, 412
Coherence, 268, 753–754

Cohesiveness, of sales letters, 416–417
Collection series, 446–453
    appeal, 449–450
    checklist for, 456
    form letters in, 449
    inquiry, 449
    reminder, 447–449
    stages in, 448
    strong appeal, 451
    ultimatum, 451–453
Colons, 264, 266, B37
Commas, 264, 265–266, B38–B40
Commendation, letters of, 486–489, 490, 491
Common language, 675–676
Common nouns, B17
Communication
    barriers to, 30–31, 44, 45, 98–103, 144–149
    behavioral factors in, 31–37
    cross-cultural. *See* Cross-cultural communication
    ethical, 178–184. *See also* Ethics
    fundamental skills in, 194–195
    group, 7–10
    informal, 15–17
    interpersonal, 6–7, 600
    intrapersonal, 6, 38
    kinesic, 39–41, 101–102
    levels of, 6–7
    metacommunication, 38–41
    needs and, 33–34
    nonverbal, 33, 38–41, 44, 101–102, 108–110
    one-to-one, 35–36
    organizational, 7, 14–21
    process of, 25–31, 32
    purposes of, 6
    theory of, 31–33
Communication channels, 27–28
Communication flow, 17–21
    downward, 17–19, 20
    horizontal, 20–21
    lateral, 20–21
    upward, 19
Company profile, 525–530
Comparatives, B26–B27
Complement, 253
Complex sentences, 254, 261
Compliment, 205, 231, 388
Complimentary close of letters, A14
Component bar chart, 685–687
Compositions, 273–275, 283
    emphasis in, 275
    headings in, 275
    sequence in, 273–274
    transitions in, 274–275, 753
    unity in, 273
Compound adjectives, 225–226
Compound-complex sentences, 255

Compound sentences, 254, 261
Computer(s), types of, 139–140. *See also* Electronic communication technology
Computer-assisted interviews, 588–589
Computer-assisted research, 651
Computer-generated reports, 721–722
Computer presentations, 79–80
Conciseness of style, 249–252
Conclusions, in report, 713
Concrete language, in sales letters, 411, 419–420
Concrete nouns, 212, 411, 753, B17
Condescension, 203, 231
Condolence letters, 477–478
Congratulation, letters of, 475–477
Conjunctions, 228–229, 233
Connotation, 206–207, 231
Content outline of reports, 716–717
Contrast connectors, 753
Conviction, writing with, 752
Coordinate adjectives, 226–227
Coordinate conjunctions, 228, 229
Copy notation, in letters, A18–A19, A21
CorelDRAW, 133
Corporate loyalty, 163
Costs, in proposals, 733–734
Credit
    refusal of, 369–371
    request for, 313–315, 316, 317, 369–371
    request for information about, 311–312, 314–315
    routine letters about, 311–315, 316, 317
Cross-cultural communication, 88–110
    barriers to, 98–103
    opportunities for, 88–95
    oral, 106–110
    principles of, 103–110
    written, 104–105
Cross-hatchings, 684, 685
Cue notes, 652
Culture, 95–98
    defined, 95–96
    elements of, 96–97
    manifestations of, 97–98
    space and, 101
    subculture, 97
    time and, 100–101, 108
    See also Cross–cultural communication; Multiculturalism
Cumulative line charts, 688–689

Dangling phrases and modifiers, 256–258, B28–B29
Dash, 264, B40–B41
Data
    collecting, 659–665, 667

demographic, 93–94, 661–662, 663
interpreting, 667–669
organizing, 665–667
quantitative, 674–678
reliability of, 655, 656
security of, 127
validity of, 655
Databases, 125–128
advantages of, 125–127
barriers to communication with,
147
external, 127
internal, 127
searching, 128
software for, 125
Data integrity, 127
Data manipulation technology,
118–128
databases, 125–128, 147
spreadsheets, 124–125, 146–147
word processing, 119–124, 144–146.
See also Word processing
Data presentation technology, 119,
128–135
desktop publishing, 130–133, 134,
147–148
graphics programs for, 133–135, 147
printing, 128–130
Data sharing technology, 119, 135–142
electronic mail, 135–141, 148–149
teleconferencing, 141–142
Decisions, ethical communication of,
178–184
Decoding of messages, 28–29, 38
Dedicated word processor, 119
Deductive paragraphs, 267
Deductive sequence of ideas, 273,
303–304
De-emphasis, 622
Definitions, 753
Delivery of speeches, 68
Demeaning tone, 205–206, 231
Demographic data, 93–94, 661–662,
663
Denotation, 206–207, 231
Dependent clause, 254, 261–262
Desktop publishing, 130–133, 134,
147–148
Dictionary of occupational titles, 522
Disabilities, bias against people with,
210–211, 232
Documentation, 713
bibliography, 713, 762–769
card system and, 652–654
citations, 754–763
of formal reports, 752, 754–769, 775
reasons for, 754–755
Document comments in word process-
ing, 122
Dot matrix printers, 128–129
Doubt, expressions of, 252–253

Downward communication, 17–19, 20
Draft, final, 280–281
Dress code, 597
Duties, theory of, 176–178
Dysphemism, 205

Editing, 275–281, 283
Education
in employment interviews, 600
on resumes, 535
EEOC (Equal Employment Opportunity Commission), 593
Electronic bulletin board, 137
Electronic communication technology,
117–150
barriers to communication with,
144–149
for data manipulation, 118–128
for data presentation, 119, 128–135,
147–148
for data sharing, 119, 135–142,
148–149
executive workstations, 142–144
Electronic mail, 135–141, 148–149
Electronic spreadsheets, 124–125,
146–147
E-mail, 135–141, 148–149
Emotional terms, 752
Empathy
listening with, 47–50
in sales letters, 416
sequence of ideas and, 361–364
style and, 364–366
in unpleasant messages, 361–366
in writing, 292–299
Emphasis
in compositions, 275
de-emphasis, 622
graphics for, 275
in paragraphs, 272
in sentences, 261–264
Employee guidelines, 625–627
Employers, prospective, 549–557
Employment agencies and contractors,
555
Employment interviews, 587, 588–609
beginning, 598–599
closing, 607–608
evaluating, 592
fairness in, 593–594
guidelines for, 592–593, 599–605
humility in, 600–601
job interviewee's role in, 595–609
job interviewer's role in, 590–595
practicing for, 608–609
preparing for, 590, 595–598
questioning in, 591–592, 601–602,
605–606, 608
salary discussion in, 606–607
strengths and weaknesses in,
603–604

thank-you letters following, 610–611,
612
tone in, 592–593
types of, 588–589
Employment messages, 609–624
application forms, 611–613
follow-up letters, 609, 610
job-acceptance letters, 614–615
job-refusal letters, 615, 616
recommendation letters, 618–624
resignation letters, 615–617
thank-you letters, 610–611, 612
See also Application letters; Resumes
Enclosure notation, in letter, 424, A18,
A21
Encoding of messages, 26–27
Endnotes, 760–762, 764
Envelopes, 427–431, A22–A27
Equal Employment Opportunity Commission (EEOC), 593
Espy, Mike, xl, 63, 139, 200
Ethics, 156–185
causes of unethical behavior,
162–167
codes of conduct and, 170–173
communicating decisions and,
178–184
defined, 157–158
examples of unethical behavior, 156,
157, 160
foundation for, 157–161
framework for analyzing ethical
dilemmas, 167–178
legal considerations and, 160,
167–170
moral development and, 159
Pagano Model for, 173–174
preventive defense in, 178
theories of, 174–178
workplace dilemmas with, 161,
162–167
Ethnic bias, 210, 232
Euphemisms, 181, 203–204, 231
Evaluation
of employment interviews, 592
as follow-up to proposals, 733
of job performance. See Performance
appraisals
negative, 360, 383–384, 489–495
positive, 486–489, 490, 491
Evidence, in sales letters, 419–424
Executive summary, 711, 712, 773
Executive workstations, 142–144
Experimental research, 659
Explanatory notes, 756–757
Expletives, 258–259, B28
Extemporaneous speech, 68
External databases, 127
External reports, 643
External system, 14
Eye contact, 69

Facsimile (fax) transmission, 138–139
Fair Employment Practice Guidelines, 593
Fairness, in employment interviews, 593–594
Farewell letters, 485–486
FASB (Financial Accounting Standards Board), 248
Favors
  refusal of, 379–380
  requests for, 379–380, 434–445
Fax transmission, 138–139
Feedback
  in communication process, 29
  in cross-cultural communication, 107
  in electronic mail, 136, 137
  listening and, 42, 43, 50, 52–53
  in performance appraisals, 624–629
Figures, list of, 711–712. *See also* Graphics
Films and filmstrips, 80
Final draft, 280–281
Financial Accounting Standards Board (FASB), 248
First person, 214–215, 752, B23–B24
Flattery, 205, 231
Flip charts, 66, 78
Floor plans, 695, 696
Flowcharts, 692–695
Fog Index, 269–270
Follow-up letters, 609, 610
Footnotes, 758–760, 761, 764
Foreign business firms, 92–93
Formal language, 197–199, 230
Formal memorandum format, A22, A23
Formal organization. *See* Organizations
Formal reports, 641, 642, 749–775
  appendixes of, 713–714, 775
  checklist for, 773–775
  conviction in, 752
  documentation of, 752, 754–769, 775
  executive summary of, 711, 712, 773
  graphics in, 774
  headings in, 719, 769–770, 771
  layout of, 774
  parts of, 706–709, 770–771
  procedures for writing, 750–752
  style of, 752–754
  table of contents in, 710–711, 773
  title page of, 709–710, 773
  transmittal letter or memorandum for, 773
Formats
  block, A7–A10
  of letters, 277–279, 571, 572, A7–A10
  of memorandums, A20–A22, A23, A24
Form letters
  in collections, 449

for refusal of orders, 372, 375, 376
requests for credit information, 312
response to requests, 328, 329
response to requests for credit, 314–315
Form reports, 718–722
Fragments, sentence, 254
Freelance Plus, 134
Functional reports, 644
Functional resumes, 542–545, 552, 553–554, 571–573
Fundamental skills in communication, 194–195

Gender bias, 207–210, 231–232
Gerunds, 212–213, B19–B20
Goals
  career, 519
  of formal organizations, 10
  maintenance, 7
  performance appraisal and, 627, 628
Golden Rule, 158, 173, 175
Good-news letters, 303, 340
Good-news memorandums, 332–333, 340
Goodwill
  ethical communication and, 180–183
  special letters and, 474
Graham, H. Devon, Jr., xl, 59, 91, 158, 295, 607, 731
Grammar, 193–233, B1–B51
  active vs. passive voice, 222–224, 250, 259–260, 411, B24–B25
  adjectives, 224–227, 232–233, B26–B27
  adverbs, 227–228, 232–233, B27
  capitalization, B31–B33
  conjunctions, 228–229, 233
  nouns, 212–213, 232, B17–B18
  numbers, B33–B35
  parallelism, 200–201, 231, B29
  prepositions, 229–230, 233, B29–B30
  pronoun-antecedent agreement, 217, B18–B19
  pronouns, 213–220, 232, B18–B21
  proofreading for, 277
  punctuation, 265–267, B35–B46
  self-checks of, B1–B3, B48–B51
  sentence structure, 253–255, B28–B30
  spelling, 194, 195, B46–B47
  subject-verb agreement, 220–221, B22–B23
  tense, 221–222, 753, B24
  verbs, 220–224, 232, B22–B26
Grammatik, 120, 239–240, 269
Grapevine, 15–17
Graphics, 679–698
  area charts, 688–689
  bar charts, 684–687, 689

for emphasis, 275
ethics in, 183–184
floor plans, 695, 696
flowcharts, 692–695
introducing in text, 695, 698
in letters and memorandums, 330
line charts, 687–689
list of, in report, 711–712
maps, 692, 693
for oral reports, 74, 75, 76, 77
photographs, 695, 697
pictograms, 691–692
pie charts, 690–691
programs for, 133–135, 147
tables, 681–683, 695, 698
See also Visual displays
Grooming, 597
Group communication, 7–10
  defined, 7
  factors in, 8–10
  group norms in, 10
  purposes of, 7–8
Group norms, 10
Guarantees, 424

Half-title page of report, 709
Handouts, 76, 77
Harvard Graphics, 134
Headings
  in compositions, 275
  in letters, A11, A16–A17, A21
  in reports, 719, 769–770, 771
  talking, 275
Help-wanted ads, 555
Hess, Jere W., Jr., xli, 59, 103, 175, 270
Hierarchy
  of needs, 33–34
  organizational, 11–12
Horizontal communication, 20–21
Human needs, 33–34
Humor, 65–66, 69
Hurley, James F., xli, 40, 76, 162, 166, 178, 331, 386, 441, 588, 604, 680
Hyphens, 226, 266–267, B41–B42
Hypothesis, in problem solving, 646–647

Ideas. *See* Sequence of ideas
Imperative mood, B22, B28
Impromptu speech, 68
Independent clause, 254, 261–262
Index
  of readability, 269–271
  of report, 714
Indicative mood, B22
Inductive approach
  in persuasive letters, 436–438, 446
  in unpleasant messages, 363, 385–386, 622
Inductive outline, 385–386, 412

Inductive paragraphs, 267
Inductive sequence of ideas, 273, 363, 385–386
Infinitives, 222
Informal communication, 15–17
Informal language, 197–199, 230
Informal reports, 641, 642, 706
Information
  listening for, 50–51
  personal, on resumes, 538–539
  requests for, 311–312, 314–315, 438–443
Informational interviews, 587
Informational reports, 642
Initials, reference, A15, A21
Inquiry letter, 449
Instructions, 33
Integrated software, 143
Intensive listening, 46
Interdependence, in formal organizations, 11
Internal databases, 127
Internal reports, 643
Internal system, 14, 15–17
International business, 89–93
Interpersonal communication, 6–7
Interpersonal skills, 600
Interquartile range, 678
Interrogative pronouns, B20
Interviews
  with career person, 524, 525
  computer-assisted, 588–589
  for data collection, 660
  employment. See Employment interviews
  guidelines for, 592–593, 599–605
  informational, 587
  interviewee's role in, 595–609
  interviewer's role in, 590–595
  persuasive, 587
  sales, 587
  stress, 589
  structured, 588–589
  telephone, 660
  types of, 586–589
  unstructured, 589
Intrapersonal communication, 6, 38
Intrinsic motivation, 35
Introduction
  of graphics in text, 695, 698
  of oral report, 72–73
  of product in sales letter, 414, 416–418
  of report, 712
  of sales letter, 412–416
  of unpleasant letter, 363, 386–388
Invitations, 478–481
Italic type, 119, 130, B45–B46
Itinerary memorandum, 333, 335

Jacks, Hugh B., xxxiv, xli, 20, 46, 62, 194, 278
Jargon, 104, 106, 278, 330
Job-acceptance letters, 614–615
Job analysis, 523–524, 525
Job market, 626
Job objectives, 533
Job performance appraisals. See Performance appraisals
Job profile, 525–530
Job-refusal letters, 615, 616
Job search
  application letters for, 557–573, 576, 609, 610
  employment messages in, 609–624
  finding prospective employers, 549–557
  interviews during, 588–609
  job market and, 626
  research in, 555–556, 595
  resume for, 518, 530–549, 575
Johari Window, 36–37
Jokes, in speeches, 65–66, 69
Judgments, 253
Justification of margins, A4–A5

Kinesic communication, 39–41, 101–102
Kissinger, Henry, 489
Knowledge
  cultural, 96
  of message receiver, 296–299
Kuehn, Beverly R., xlii, 299, 361, 415, 474, 629

Lair, Jess, 293
Language
  body, 39–41, 101–102. See also Nonverbal communication
  common, 675–676
  concrete, 212, 411, 419–420, 753, B17
  cross-cultural communication and, 96, 97
  jargon, 104, 106, 278, 330
  sexist, 207–210, 231–232
  simplicity vs. formality of, 197–199, 230
  slang, 104, 106
  translation problems of, 102–103
  See also Word(s)
Laptop computers, 139–140
Laser printers, 129–130
Lateral communication, 20–21
Lateral reports, 642
Laws. See Legal considerations
Layout, 277–279
  of formal reports, 774
  of resumes, 545–548
  of tables, 682, 683
Legal considerations

in ethical dilemmas, 160, 167–170
in hiring, 538
in writing recommendations, 622
Letters
  acknowledgment, 318–320
  adjustment, 306–311, 366–369
  appearance of, A1–A6
  application, 557–573, 576, 609, 610
  attention line of, A15–A16
  claim, 305–311, 431–434
  collection, 446–453, 456
  of commendation, 486–489, 490, 491
  complimentary close of, A14
  of condolence, 477–478
  of congratulation, 475–477
  copy notation in, A18–A19, A21
  enclosure notation in, 424, A18, A21
  farewell, 485–486
  follow-up, 609, 610
  form. See Form letters
  formats of, 277–279, 571, 572, A7–A10
  good-news, 303, 340
  headings in, A11, A16–A17, A21
  inside address in, A11–A13
  of invitation, 478–481
  job-acceptance, 614–615
  job-refusal, 615, 616
  mailing notation in, A15
  organization of, 301–303
  parts of, A11–A20, A21
  persuasive, 305, 408–456
  postscript in, A19–A20, A21
  of recommendation, 618–624
  reference initials in, A15, A21
  reference line of, A16
  of regret, 495–502
  of request, 431–445, 455. See also Requests
  of resignation, 615–617
  routine, 303–328, 340
  salutation in, A12–A13, A14
  seasonal, 484, 485
  signature block of, A14–A15, A17–A18
  special, 474–503
  subject line of, A16
  thank-you, 474, 481–482, 610–611, 612
  transmittal, 710, 773
  welcome, 484–485
Libraries
  in job search, 555–556
  in preparing for employment interview, 595
  as research method, 649–655
Line charts, 687–689
Linking verbs, B19, B26
Listening, 42–53
  advantages of, 42

Listening, *continued*
  bad habits in, 43–44
  casual, 47
  effective, 52–53
  with empathy, 47–50
  feedback and, 42, 43, 50, 52–53
  for information, 50–51
  intensive, 46
  overlistening, 44
  for problem solving, 51–52
Long reports, 641–642
Lotus 1-2-3, 125
Loyalty, corporate, 163

McGregor, Douglas, 34
McSweeney, Terence E., xliii, 9, 41,
    194, 215, 303, 365, 559, 608, 611
Mail
  electronic, 135–141, 148–149
  voice, 137–138, 148–149
Mailing, of sales letters, 427–431
Mailing notation, in letter, A15
Mail merge feature in word process-
    ing, 122–124, 146
Maintenance goals, 7
Management, and ethics, 164–165
Management information system
    (MIS), 144
Management styles, 34–35
Maps, 692, 693
Margins, justification of, A4–A5
Martin, David, xlii, 645, 646, 661, 668,
    719, 755
Martin, Lynn, xlii, 3, 626
Martin, Thomas G., xxxiv, xliii, 175,
    495
Maslow, Abraham, 33
Mean, 677
Measures of central tendency, 676–678
Median, 677–678
Memorandums, 328–338
  bad-news, 381–384
  to file, 336, 338
  format of, A20–A22, A23, A24
  good-news, 332–333, 340
  graphics in, 330
  itinerary, 333, 335
  organization of, 301–303, 330, 340
  about personnel changes, 336, 337
  persuasive, 441, 443–445
  policies and procedures, 334–335,
    336
  recommendation, 623, 624
  resignation, 615
  routine, 333, 334–338, 340
  subject line of, 330–331
  transmittal, 710, 773
  unnecessary, 331
Memorized speech, 68
Message
  decoding of, 28–29, 38

  encoding of, 26–27
  feedback and, 29
  transmission of, 27–28
Metacommunication, 38–41
Microsoft Chart, 134
Microsoft Excel, 125
Microsoft Word, 119
Minority groups, 95, 210–211. *See also*
    Culture; Multiculturalism
MIS (management information sys-
    tem), 144
Misplaced elements of sentences,
    255–256
Misspellings, 194, 195. *See also* Spelling
Mixed punctuation style, A7
*MLA Handbook for Writers of Research
    Papers*, 756, 757, 758, 759–760, 763,
    764, 765–766
Mode, 678
Models, 80
Modified block format of letters,
    A8–A9
Modifiers, dangling, 256–258, B28–B29
Mood
  imperative, B22, B28
  indicative, B22
  subjunctive, 260–261, 366, B22
Moral development, 159. *See also*
    Ethics
Moses, D., B46
Motivation, intrinsic, 35
Multiculturalism, 93–95. *See also*
    Cross–cultural communication;
    Culture
Multiple-range bar chart, 685, 686

Needs, hierarchy of, 33–34
Negative evaluations, 360, 383–384,
    489–495
Negative recommendations, 618–623
Negative tone, 201–203, 231, 260–261,
    263. *See also* Unpleasant messages
News releases, 482–483
Nominative case, 217–218, 219–220,
    B19
Nonverbal communication, 33, 38–41,
    44, 101–102, 108–110
Norm
  cultural, 96
  group, 10
Normative survey research, 655–658
Note(s)
  cue, 652
  endnotes, 760–762, 764
  explanatory, 756–757
  footnotes, 758–760, 761, 764
  source, 756
  suggestive, 652
Notebook, career, 520, 525–530, 543,
    549–551, 596, 601–602, 606
Notebook computers, 139–140

Nouns, 212–213, 232, B17–B18
  abstract, 212, B17
  common, B17
  concrete, 212, 411, 753, B17
  possessive, 212–213, B35–B36
  proper, B17
Numbers, B33–B35
Nunan, James, 594

Objective(s), career and job, 533. *See
    also* Goals
Objective case, 218–220, B19
Objectivity
  of reports, 641
  subjectivity vs., 420–421
Observational research, 658–659
Occupational outlook handbook, 522
OD (organizational development), 37
100 percent bar chart, 685–687
One-to-one communication, 35–36
Open punctuation style, A7
Opinions, 658, 752
Oral communication, for intercultural
    audiences, 106–110
Oral reports, 70–81
  body of, 73
  graphics in, 74, 75, 76, 77
  importance of, 81
  introduction to, 72–73
  outlining, 72
  planning, 71–73
  speeches vs., 71
  summary of, 73
  time limits on, 80–81
  visual aids in, 72, 73–80
Orders
  favorable response to, 318–321, 322
  letters containing, 316–318, 319
  refusal of, 372–379
  routine letters about, 315–321, 322
Organization, 299–303, 340
  of application letters, 564
  benefits of, 300–301
  of letters, 301–303, 340
  of memorandums, 301–303, 330, 340
  proofreading for, 277
  of reports, 665–667, 714–718
  of resumes, 541–545
  of speeches, 64
Organizational charts, 12–13, 694–695
Organizational communication, 7,
    14–21
Organizational development (OD), 37
Organizations
  characteristics of, 10–12
  communication flow in, 17–21
  communication systems in, 14–17
  company profile of, 525–530
  foreign, 92–93
  formalized hierarchy of, 11–12
  goal orientation in, 10

interdependence in, 11
international, 89–93
loyalty in, 163
specialization in, 11
structure of, 12–14
Outlining
benefits of, 300–301
content, 716–717
inductive, 385–386, 412
oral reports, 72
sales letters, 412
speeches, 65–68
Overlistening, 44

Pacific Bell Directory, 116
Pagano Model for ethical actions,
173–174
PageMaker, 131
Paper, quality of, A1–A3
Paragraphs, 267–272, 282–283
closing, 364, 389–391
coherence of, 268
deductive, 267
emphasis in, 272
inductive, 267
introductory, 363, 386–388, 412–416
length of, 281
readability and, 268–271
style of, 267–272, 282–283
topic sentence in, 267–268
variety of, 281
Parallelism, 200–201, 231, B29
Paraphrasing, 75–76, 652
Parentheses, 264
Parenthetical citations, 757–758
Parker, Dorothy, 238–239
Participant observation for data collec-
tion, 660
Passive voice, 222–224, 250, 259–260,
411, B24–B25
Performance appraisals, 624–629
employee guidelines for, 625–627
negative, 360, 383–384
supervisor guidelines for, 627–629
Period, B42–B43
Periodic reports, 644
Perkins, Carroll M., xliii, 17, 165, 677
Perrella, James E., 158–159, 173
Personal information, on resumes,
538–539
Personal information manager, 143
Personal interviews for data collection,
660
Personal space, 101
Personnel changes, memorandum
about, 336, 337
Persuasion, 408–456
in collections, 446–453, 456
inductive approach in, 436–438, 446
in memorandums, 441, 443–445
in requests, 431–445, 455

in sales letters, 408–431, 454
Persuasive claims, 305, 431–434
Persuasive interviews, 587
Persuasive speeches, 64
Pharr, Cynthia, xxxiv–xxxv, xliv, 59,
133, 198, 472, 542, 597, 598, 682,
711, 751
Phonation, 58–60
Photographs, 695, 697
Phrases, 242–253, 282, B28–B29
Pictograms, 691–692
Pie charts, 690–691
Plagiarism, 652, 754, 755
Planning
career, 518–520
oral reports, 71–73
resumes, 530–541
sales letters, 409–412
speeches, 64–68
Platitudes, 259
Pleasant messages
good-news letters, 303, 340
good-news memorandums, 332–333,
340
See also Routine letters
Policies and procedures memoran-
dums, 334–335, 336
Portable computers, 139–140
Positive evaluations, 486–489, 490, 491
Positive recommendations, 623–624
Positive tone, 201–203, 231, 260–261,
263, 365–366
Possessive nouns, 212–213, B35–B36
Possessive pronouns, B19–B20, B36
Posters, 78
Postscript, A19–A20, A21
Powell, C. R., 522
Prepositions, 229–230, 233, B29–B30
Price, in sales letters, 422–423
Printers, 128–130
dot matrix, 128–129
laser, 129–130
Printing, of sales letters, 427
Problem solving
defining terms in, 648
hypothesis in, 646–647
limiting problem in, 648
listening for, 51–52
research methods in, 649–659
statement of purpose in, 647–648
steps in, 645
Product
introduction of, 414, 416–418
knowledge of, 410
Professional organizations, 556–557
Professional standards of ethical conduct, 170–173
Profits, emphasis on, 162–163
Projected visual displays, 77, 78
Pronouns, 213–220, 232, B18–B21
agreement of, 217, B18–B19

case of, 217–220,
first-person, 214–215,
interrogative, B20
possessive, B19–B20, B36
reflexive, 220
relative, B20
second-person, 215–216
third-person, 216–217
Pronunciation, 61
Proofreaders' marks, A1, A2
Proofreading, 75, 276–280
Proper nouns, B17
Proposals, 726–734
addenda items in, 734
budget in, 733–734
parts of, 728–734
purpose of, 730–731
recommendations in, 732–733
requests for, 644, 726–728
sample, 734, 735–736
scope of, 731–732
short, 734, 735–736
as special reports, 644
*Publication Manual of the American Psy-
chological Association*, 754, 756,
757–758, 763, 764, 767–769, 770
Public opinion polls, 658
Public speaking, 58–81
eye contact in, 69
oral reports, 70–81
speeches, 61–70
speech qualities in, 58–61
Punctuation, 265–267, B35–B46
apostrophe, B35–B36
brackets, B37
colon, 264, 266, B37
comma, 264, 265–266, B38–B40
dash, 264, B40–B41
ellipsis, B41
for emphasis, 264
hyphen, 226, 266–267, B41–B42
italics, 119, 130, B45–B46
mixed vs. open style of, A7
period, B42–B43
quotation marks, B43–B44
run-on sentences and, 255
semicolon, 266, B44–B45
symbols, 96, B45
underscore, 119, B45–B46
Purpose statement, 647–648

Qualifications, on resumes,
535–538
Quality circles, 35
Quantitative data, 674–678
Quattro Pro, 125
Question(s)
in employment interview, 591–592,
601–602, 605–606, 608
in questionnaires, 662–663
Questionnaires, 659–663

I-7

Rau...
Readab...
Readability
Reader
  reactions of, 30̣
  of reports, 641
  of sales letter, 410, 411, 415–416
Receiver of message
  decoding by, 28–29
  feedback from, 29
  knowledge of, 296–299
Recommendation(s)
  based on research, 669
  in proposals, 732–733
  in reports, 713
Recommendation letters, 618–624
  negative, 618–623
  positive, 623–624
  request for, 618, 619, 620
Redlining feature in word processing,
  121–122
Redundancy, 230, 249–252
Reference initials, A15, A21
Reference line, of letter, A16
References
  in reports, 713
  on resumes, 539–541, 549
  See also Documentation
Reflexive pronouns, 220
Refusal
  of adjustment request, 366–369
  of credit request, 369–371
  of order for merchandise, 372–379
  of request for favor, 379–380
  statement of, 364
Regret, letters of, 495–502
Relative pronouns, B20
Reliability of data, 655, 656
Religious bias, 210, 232
Reminder notice, 447–449
Reports, 640–669, 706–737
  addenda of, 713–714
  analytical, 642, 713
  appendixes in, 713–714, 775
  appraisal, 720, 727
  authorization for, 710
  basis for, 645
  body of, 712
  characteristics of, 640–641
  classifications of, 641–644

computer-generated, 721–722
conclusions in, 713
content outline of, 716–717
data collection for, 659–665, 667
documentation of, 752, 754–769, 775
executive summary of, 711, 712, 773
external, 643
form, 718–722
formal. See Formal reports
functional, 644
graphics in, 711–712, 774
headings in, 719, 769–770, 771
index of, 714
informal, 641, 642, 706
informational, 642
internal, 643
interpreting data in, 667–669
introduction to, 712
lateral, 642
layout of, 774
list of figures in, 711–712
long, 641–642
oral. See Oral reports
organizing data in, 665–667
organizing findings in, 714–718
parts of, 706–714, 770–771
periodic, 644
preliminary parts of, 709–712
procedures for writing, 750–752
proposals, 644, 726–734, 735–736
purpose of, 641
readability of, 755
recommendations in, 713
references in, 713
research methods for, 649–669
short, 641–642, 722–726, 727
size of, 706, 708
style of, 752–754
summary in, 712–713
table of contents in, 710–711, 773
title page of, 709–710, 773
transmittal of, 710, 773
vertical, 642, 643
writing with conviction, 752
Requests
  for credit, 313–315, 316, 317, 369–371
  for favors, 379–380, 434–445
  for information, 438–443
  for information about credit,
    311–312, 314–315
  persuasive, 431–445, 455
  for recommendation, 618, 619, 620
  refusal of, 366–380
  routine, 321–328, 329
Requests for proposals (RFPs), 644,
  726–728
Requests for quotations (RFQs), 728
Resale material, 306
Research, 645, 646, 649–669
  card system in, 652–654

for career information, 520–530
computer-assisted, 651
cue notes in, 652
data collection in, 659–665, 667
data interpretation in, 667–669
data organization in, 665–667
errors in, 667–668
experimental methods in, 659
in job search, 555–556, 595
library methods in, 649–655
observational methods in, 658–659
suggestive notes in, 652
survey methods in, 655–665
Resignation letters, 615–617
Resumes, 518, 530–549
  checklist for, 575
  chronological, 542, 544–545, 547–548,
    550–551, 553–554, 570–571
  construction of, 541–548
  employment interview and, 599
  examples of, 548–549, 550–551, 552,
    553–554
  functional, 542–545, 552, 553–554,
    571–573
  identification on, 532–533
  job and career objectives on, 533
  layout of, 545–548
  organization of, 541–545
  personal information on, 538–539
  planning, 530–541
  qualifications on, 535–538
  references on, 539–541, 549
  standard parts of, 530–531
  Summary of Achievements on,
    533–534
Rewriting, 275–281, 283
RFPs (requests for proposals), 644,
  726–728
RFQs (requests for quotations), 728
RightWriter, 120, 269
Role
  of job interviewee, 595–609
  of job interviewer, 590–595
  in social situation, 33
Routine letters, 303–328
  about claims, 305–311
  about credit, 311–315, 316, 317
  about orders, 315–321, 322
  organization of, 303–305, 340
  about requests, 321–328, 329
Routine memorandums, 333, 334–338,
  340
Rules, 33
Run-on sentences, 255

Salary, discussed in employment inter-
  views, 606–607
Sales Development Associates, 236
Sales interviews, 587
Sales letters, 408–431

central selling point in, 411–412, 414–415, 418, 419
checklist for, 454
cohesiveness of, 416–417
complete, 427, 428, 429–430
concrete language in, 411, 419–420
enclosures with, 424
evidence in, 419–424
first paragraph of, 412–416
introduction of product in, 414, 416–418
last paragraph of, 424–427
outlining, 412
planning, 409–412
price in, 422–423
printing and mailing of, 427–431
readers of, 410, 411, 415–416
unsolicited vs. solicited, 412, 427
writing principles for, 411–412
Sales-promotional material, 306–307
Salsbury Communications, Inc., 84
Salutation, A12–A13, A14
Sampling, 656–658
Search-and-replace feature in word processing, 120, 121, 145–146
Seasonal messages, 484, 485
Second person, 215–216, B23–B24
Segmented bar chart, 685–687
Self-analysis, 520, 521, 596
Self-concept, 9
Selling point. *See* Central selling point
Semicolons, 266, B44–B45
Sender of message, 26–28
Sentence, 253–267, 282
    bad-news, 388–389
    emphasis in, 261–264
    misplaced elements in, 255–256
    run-on, 255
    structure of, 253–255, B28–B30
    topic, 267–268
    transition, 274–275, 753
    types of, 254–255, 261
Sentence fragments, 254
Sequence of ideas, 273–274
    deductive, 273, 303–304
    inductive, 273, 363, 385–386
    in unpleasant messages, 361–364
Sexist language, 207–210, 231–232
Sexual harassment, 166
Shannon, Claude, 25
Short proposal, sample of, 734, 735–736
Short reports, 641–642, 722–726, 727
Sick leave, 165
Signature block, of letter, A14–A15, A17–A18
Similarity connectors, 754
Simple sentences, 254, 261
Simplicity vs. formality of language, 197–199, 230

Simplified block format of letters, A10
Simplified memorandum format, A22, A24
Single-range bar chart, 684–685
Slang, 104, 106
Slides, 66, 73, 77, 79
Social situation, 33
Software
    for databases, 125
    for graphics, 133–135, 147
    integrated, 143
    writing-analysis, 120, 239–240, 269
Solicited sales letters, 412, 427
Source notes, 756
Space, and culture, 101
Spacing, A5–A6
Specialization, 11
Special letters, 474–503
Specific words vs. general words, 197, 230, 411, B17
Speeches, 61–70
    applause for, 68
    audience for, 61–62, 68, 69–70
    delivering, 68
    extemporaneous, 68
    impromptu, 68
    major points in, 67
    memorized, 68
    oral reports vs., 71
    organization of, 64
    outlining, 65–68
    persuasive, 64
    planning, 64–68
    purposes of, 64
    style in, 69–70
    topic selection for, 62–63
    visual displays in, 66
    written-and-read, 68
Speech qualities, 58–61
    articulation, 60
    phonation, 58–60
    pronunciation, 61
Spellchecking, 120, 145, 276
Spelling, 194, 195, B46–B47
Split infinitives, 222
Spreadsheets, 124–125, 146–147
SQL (Structured Query Language), 128
Stacked-bar chart, 685–687
Standards of ethical conduct, 170–173
State abbreviations, A26, A27
Statistics, 65, 66, 67
Status, 9, 33
Stereotypes
    as barrier in cross-cultural communication, 99–100, 106
    as barrier in listening, 44
Strategy, for speeches, 64–65
Stratified random sampling, 657
Stress interviews, 589
Stroking, 35

Strong-appeal letter, 451
Structure
    organizational, 12–14
    of sentences, 253–255, B28–B30
Structured interviews, 588–589
Structured Query Language (SQL), 128
Style, 237–283
    active vs. passive voice, 222–224, 250, 259–260, 411, B24–B25
    analyzing, 239–240
    of application letters, 564–568
    clichés, 243–248
    coherence, 268, 753–754
    compositions, 273–275, 283
    conciseness, 249–252
    dangling modifiers, 256–258, B28–B29
    editing and rewriting, 275–281, 283
    empathy and, 364–366
    emphasis, 261–264, 272
    expletives, 258–259, B28
    of formal report, 752–754
    paragraphs, 267–272, 282–283
    phrases, 242–253, 282, B28–B29
    platitudes, 259
    proofreading for, 277
    punctuation, 265–267, B35–B46
    readability, 268–271, 755
    sentences, 253–267, 282, B28–B30
    in speeches, 69–70
    subjunctive mood, 260–261, 366, B22
    topic sentence, 267–268
    in unpleasant messages, 364–366
    variety, 271, 754
Style manuals, 755
    APA style manual, 754, 756, 757–758, 763, 764, 767–769, 770
    MLA handbook, 756, 757, 758, 759–760, 763, 764, 765–766
Subcultures, 97
Subjectivity vs. objectivity, 420–421
Subject line
    of letter, A16
    of memorandum, 330–331
Subject-verb agreement, 220–221, B22–B23
Subjunctive mood, 260–261, 366, B22
Subordinate conjunctions, 228–229
Suggestive notes, 652
Summary
    of Achievements, 533–534
    executive, 711, 712, 773
    in oral report, 73
    in report, 712–713
Superlatives, 227, B26
Supervisor guidelines, 627–629
Surprise, expressions of, 252–253
Surveys, 655–665
    data collection through, 659–665
    reliability of, 655, 656

Surveys, *continued*
sampling for, 656–658
validity of, 655
Symbols, 96, B45
Sygnis, 672
Synergy, 7
Synopsis, 712. *See also* Summary
Systematic random sampling, 657

Table, 681–683, 695, 698
Table of contents, 710–711, 773
Tabulation, 264, 330, 753
Tact
in application letters, 566–568
in ethical communication, 181–182
positive tone and, 261
Talking headings, 275
Technology. *See* Electronic communication technology
Telecommuting, 139
Teleconferencing, 141–142
Telephone, cellular, 140–141
Telephone interviews for data collection, 660
Tense, 221–222, 753, B24
Testimonials, 424
Text
introducing graphics in, 695, 698
placement on page, A3–A4
Thank-you letters, 474, 481–482, 610–611, 612
Theory
of communication, 31–33
of duties, 176–178
X and Y, 34
Thesaurus feature in word processing, 120
Third person, 216–217, B23–B24
Time, cultural differences in, 100–101, 108
Time connectors, 753
Time limits, on oral reports, 80–81
Title fly, 709
Title page of report, 709–710, 773
Tone, 201–207, 230
condescending, 203, 231
connotative, 206–207, 231
demeaning, 205–206, 231
in employment interviews, 592–593
euphemistic, 181, 203–204, 231
flattering, 205, 231
negative, 201–203, 231, 260–261, 263
positive, 201–203, 231, 260–261, 263, 365–366
Topic selection, for speeches, 62–63
Topic sentence, 267–268
Tracy-Locke/Pharr Public Relations, 472
Transactional analysis, 35

Transition sentences, 274–275, 753
Transmittal of reports, 710, 773
Transparencies, 73, 77, 78
Trust, 36, 37, 42

Ultimatum, in collections, 451–453
Underlining, 119, B45–B46
Unethical behavior
causes of, 162–167
examples of, 156, 157, 160
See also Ethics
United States Sentencing Commission, 173
Unity, 273
Unpleasant messages, 359–393
checklist for, 393
closing paragraph of, 364, 389–391
empathy and, 361–366
initiating, 381–384
introductory paragraph of, 363, 386–388
in memorandums, 381–384
organization and, 302, 303, 361–364
positive tone in, 365–366
refusal of adjustment request, 366–369
refusal of credit request, 369–371
refusal of order for merchandise, 372–379
refusal of request for favor, 379–380
resignation letters, 615–617
special problems of, 385–391
style of, 364–366
Unsolicited sales letters, 412, 427
Unstructured interviews, 589
Upward communication, 19
Utilitarianism, 174–175, 176

Validity of data, 655
Values
cross-cultural communication and, 96
ethics and, 159–160
Variety
of paragraphs, 281
of style, 271, 754
Ventura Publisher, 131
Venture Stores, 636
Verbs, 220–224, 232, B22–B26
active vs. passive voice, 222–224, 250, 259–260, 411, B24–B25
agreement with subject, 220–221, B22–B23
gerunds, 212–213, B19–B20
infinitives, 222
linking, B19, B26
person and, B23–B24
tense of, 221–222, 753, B24

Vertical reports, 642, 643
Videotapes, 80
Visual displays
audiotapes, 80
chalkboards and whiteboards, 78
computer presentations, 79–80
filmstrips and films, 80
flip charts, 66, 78
guidelines for using, 74–76
handouts, 76, 77
models, 80
in oral reports, 72, 73–80
physical objects, 66, 80
posters, 78
projected, 77, 78
slides, 66, 73, 77, 79
in speeches, 66
transparencies, 73, 77, 78
videotapes, 80
See also Graphics
Vocabulary building, 199–200. *See also* Word(s)
Voice, active vs. passive, 222–224, 250, 259–260, 411, B24–B25
Voice mail, 137–138, 148–149
Voice qualities, 58–60

Welcome, letters of, 484–485
What color is your parachute? (Bolles), 521
Whistle-blowing, 156
Whiteboards, 78
Women, and gender bias, 207–210, 231–232
Word(s), 193–233
bias-free, 207–211, 231–232
choice of, 197–211, 230–232
communication without, 33, 38–41, 44, 101–102, 108–110
condescending, 203, 231
connotative, 206–207, 231
denotative, 206–207, 231
division of, A6
euphemistic, 181, 203–204, 231
frequently misused, B3–B17
parallelism of, 200–201, 231, B29
preciseness of, 197, 230
simple vs. formal, 197–199, 230
specific vs. general, 197, 230, 411, B17
spelling of, 194, 195, B46–B47
that describe (adjectives and adverbs), 224–228, 232–233, B26–B27
that join (conjunctions), 228–229, 233
that label (nouns), 212–213, 232, B17–B18
that replace (pronouns), 213–220, 232, B18–B21
that show action (verbs), 220–224, 232

that show relationships (prepositions), 229–230, 233, B29–B30
tone of, 201–207, 230, 231, 260–261, 263, 365–366, 592–593
Wordiness, 249–252
WordPerfect, 119
Word processing
  addresses in, A24, A26
  endnotes in, 762

footnotes in, 758, 761
headings in, 770
special features in, 119–124, 144–146
spellchecking in, 120, 145, 276
Wordstar, 119
Work experience, on resumes, 536–538
Works cited, 713, 765–766. *See also* Bibliography
Workstations, 142–144

Writing-analysis software, 120, 239–240, 269
Writing guidelines, 342–343
Writing style. *See* Style
Written-and-read speech, 68
Written communication, for intercultural audiences, 104–105

ZIP codes, A26